Accounting and Financial Reporting in Life and Health Insurance Companies

LOMA (Life Office Management Association, Inc.) is an international association founded in 1924. LOMA's mission is to help member companies in the insurance and financial services industry improve their management and operations through quality employee development, research, information sharing, and related products and services. Among LOMA's activities is the sponsorship of the FLMI Insurance Education Program—an educational program intended primarily for home office and branch office employees.

The **FLMI Insurance Education Program** consists of two levels—Level I, "Fundamentals of Life and Health Insurance," and Level II, "Functional Aspects of Life and Health Insurance." Level I is designed to help students achieve a working knowledge of the life and health insurance business. Level II is designed to further the student's career development by providing a more detailed understanding of life and health insurance and related business and management subjects. Upon the completion of both levels, the student is designated a Fellow of the Life Management Institute (FLMI) and is awarded a diploma.

Accounting and Financial Reporting in Life and Health Insurance Companies

Elizabeth A. Mulligan, FLMI, ACS, AIAA, ALHC
Gene Stone, FLMI, ACS

FLMI Insurance Education Program
Life Management Institute LOMA
Atlanta, Georgia

LOMA®

Authors:	Elizabeth A. Mulligan, FLMI, ACS, AIAA, ALHC Gene Stone, FLMI, ACS
Project manager:	Dennis W. Goodwin, FLMI, ACS, HIA
Editors:	Ruth D. Handley, J.D. Cynthia Mathis Henry, FLMI, ACS, ALHC Kenneth Huggins, FLMI/M
Copyeditor:	Robert D. Land, FLMI, ACS
Permissions editor:	Laura D. Cook, ACS, AIAA
Production coordinator:	Sally Miller Farnham
Printing coordinator:	Elizabeth A. Pedley
Administrative support:	Cheryl Brightly, Debra Bailey Helwig, Marion Markus, Linda Rybicki, and Cara Taylor
Typography:	Puffin Typography: BJ Nemeth and Heather King
Printing:	RR Donnelley & Sons Company
Cover design:	Zoila Harmouche and Robert McClurkan

ISBN 0-939921-85-5

Library of Congress Catalog Card Number 96-77388

Printed in the United States of America

Contents

Preface xv

Acknowledgments xvii
Textbook Development Panel xvii
Additional Expert Reviewers xviii
LOMA Staff/Consultants xix

Chapter 1: The Accounting Function 2

The Purpose of Accounting 4
Who Uses Accounting Information and How Do They Use It? 6
Internal Users 6
External Users 7
Fields of Accounting and Accounting Principles 9
Financial Accounting 11
Management Accounting 13
Who Performs the Accounting Function? 15
Private Accounting 16
Public Accounting 19
How Accounting is Regulated 19
Insurance Accounting Regulation in the United States 19
Insurance Accounting Regulation in Canada 25
The Accounting Profession 28
Certified Public Accountant 28
Chartered Accountant 29
Certified Management Accountant 29
Certified General Accountant 30
Other Designations 30
Textbook Overview 30

Chapter 2: Accounts and the Double-Entry System 32

Classification of Accounts 33
Balance Sheet 37
Statement of Operations 42
Double-Entry Accounting 46
The Basic Accounting Equation 47
Debits and Credits 50
Account Balances 51
Simple and Compound Accounting Entries 56

Chapter 3: The Accounting Cycle 58

Accounting Records 59
Journals 60
Ledgers 62
Trial Balance 65
Adjusting Entries 67
Closing Entries 68

Financial Statements 70
Annual Report 70
The U.S. Annual Statement 73
The Canadian Annual Return 75

Chapter 4: The Conceptual Framework of Financial Accounting 78

Financial Statement Concepts 79
Entity Concept 79
Going-Concern Concept 81
The Quality of Accounting Information 82
Reliability 82
Relevance 82
Consistency 83
Comparability 85
Materiality 86
Conservatism 89
Principles for Maintaining Accounts 90
Cost Concept 91
Measuring-Unit Concept 92
Full-Disclosure Concept 94
Time-Period Concept 94
Recognition of Revenues and Expenses 95
Accounting Basis 100
Accrual-Basis Accounting 101
Cash-Basis Accounting 102

Chapter 5: The Annual Report 106

The Annual Report 107
Letter to Stockholders and Financial Highlights 108
Financial Statements 109
Balance Sheet 110
Statement of Operations 114
Statement of Cash Flows 119
Statement of Owners' Equity 125
Summary of Financial Statements 131
Notes and Supplementary Information 131
Auditor's Report 134
Financial Statement Integration 135

Chapter 6: An Overview of the Annual Statement 140

Balance Sheet 142
Assets 143
Liabilities, Surplus and Other Funds 150
Summary of Operations 158
Capital and Surplus Account 162
Statutory to GAAP Reconciliation 167

Other Statements and Schedules . . . 170
Cash Flow . . . 170
Analysis of Operations by Lines of Business . . . 173
Five-Year Historical Data . . . 174
Other Exhibits . . . 174

Chapter 7: Accounting for Invested Assets . . . 180

Asset Classification and Valuation . . . 183
Bonds . . . 188
Accounting for the Purchase and Sale of Bonds . . . 192
Accrued Bond Interest Income . . . 193
Bond Discounts and Bond Premiums . . . 194
Bonds and the Annual Statement/Annual Return . . . 200
Stocks . . . 201
Accounting for the Purchase and Sale of Stocks . . . 205
Accounting for Cash Dividends . . . 206
Accounting for Stock Dividends . . . 207
Stocks and the Annual Statement/Annual Return . . . 208
Mortgage Loans . . . 211
Accounting for Mortgage Loans . . . 212
Foreclosure . . . 216
Mortgage Loans and the Annual Statement/Annual Return . . . 218

Chapter 8: Accounting for Other Assets . . . 222

Real Estate . . . 223
Accounting for the Purchase and Sale of Real Estate . . . 223
Property Taxes and Foreclosure . . . 227
Rental Income and Rental Expense . . . 229
Real Estate on the Annual Statement/Annual Return . . . 229
Derivatives . . . 232
Policy Loans . . . 236
Accounting for Policy Loans . . . 238
Policy Loan Interest . . . 239
Policy Loans and the Annual Statement/Annual Return . . . 240
Accounting for Cash and Short-Term Investments . . . 241
Cash . . . 242
Bank Reconciliation . . . 243
Accounting for Other Short-Term Assets . . . 247
Investment Income Due and Accrued . . . 248
Premiums Due . . . 248
Prepaid Expenses . . . 249
Accounting for Other Assets . . . 250
Reinsurance Ceded . . . 250
Deferred Policy Acquisition Costs . . . 254
Electronic Data Processing Equipment . . . 255
Separate Accounts (Segregated Funds) . . . 256

Chapter 9: Accounting for Liabilities: Reserves 262

Reserves for Different Accounting Requirements 268
The Effects of Reserve Strength on Solvency and Profitability 270
Actuarial Assumptions and Reserves 271
Voluntary Strengthening and Destrengthening of Reserves 274
Policy Reserves for Life Insurance. 275
Calculating Life Insurance Policy Reserves in the United States 275
Calculating Life Insurance Policy Reserves in Canada 280
Policy Reserves for Annuities 281
Statutory Reserves during the Accumulation and Payout Periods 282
GAAP Annuity Reserves in the United States and Canada. 283
Reserves for Accident and Health Insurance 283
Active Life Reserves. 284
Claim Reserves. 286
Surplus Strain 288
Using Reinsurance to Reduce Surplus Strain 289
Reserving Methods that Limit Statutory Surplus Strain 291
Limiting Surplus Strain under GAAP 292
Policy Reserves Calculated for Tax Purposes 294
Other Types of Reserves. 295
Claim Fluctuation Reserves 295
Premium Deficiency Reserves. 295
Contingency Reserves 296
Asset Fluctuation Reserves 297

Chapter 10: Accounting for Policy Benefits and Other Liabilities 304

Policy Dividends. 305
Policy Dividend Liabilities 309
Policy Dividend Payment Options 312
Nonforfeiture Options 316
Cash Surrender. 316
Reduced Paid-Up or Extended Term Insurance 319
Claim Settlements 321
Life Insurance Claims 321
Accident and Health Insurance Claims 328
Annuity and Supplementary Contract Payments. 332
Annuity Benefits 333
Supplementary Contract Payments 334
Other Liabilities 335
Premiums Paid in Advance 335
Premium Deposits 336
Short-Term and Long-Term Debt Obligations 337

General Expenses Due or Accrued 338
Agents' Commissions Due or Accrued 339
Taxes, Licenses, and Fees Due or Accrued 339
Amounts Retained by the Company as Agent or Trustee 339
Premium Suspense Accounts 340
Dividends to Stockholders Declared and Unpaid 341
Financial Reporting Requirements 341
Annual Statement 341
Annual Return 342

Chapter 11: Accounting for Capital and Surplus 344

Essential Concepts of Capital and Surplus 346
Internal Sources 349
External Sources 354
Capital and Surplus Accounts 363
Common Stock and Additional Paid-In Capital 366
Retained Earnings 368
Treasury Stock 368
Unrealized Gains and Losses 369
Special Surplus 371
Unassigned Surplus 372
Financial Reporting Requirements 373
United States 375
Canada 376

Chapter 12: Accounting for Revenues 380

Income Classifications 382
Premium Income 386
Premium Accounting Systems 387
Accounting for Premiums 389
Accounting for Policy Loan Interest and Policy Dividends 397
Investment Income 399
Accounting for Investment Income 400
Other Sources of Revenues 401
Financial Reporting of Revenues 401
Premium Income 402
Investment Income 403

Chapter 13: Accounting for Expenses 408

Agent Commissions and Salaries 410
Objectives of Commission Accounting 412
Factors that Affect Commission Accounting 412
Accounting for Agent Commissions 414
Accounting for Agent Salaries 416

Operating Expenses 418
Taxes, Licenses, and Fees 420
Federal Income Taxes 420
Premium Taxes 428
Guaranty-Fund Assessments 430
CompCorp 431
Financial Reporting of Expenses 432

Chapter 14: The Time Value of Money 436

The Time Value of Money 437
Interest 438
Interest Rates 439
Simple Interest 440
Compound Interest 440
Risk and Inflation 441
Calculating Future Value 443
Future Value of a Single Amount 443
Future Value Interest Factors 447
Future Value of an Annuity 450
Future Value of an Annuity Interest Factors 451
Future Value of an Uneven Stream of Payments 454
Calculating Present Value 454
Present Value of a Single Amount 455
Present Value Interest Factors 456
Present Value of an Annuity 457
Present Value of an Annuity Interest Factors 458
Present Value of an Uneven Stream of Payments 460
A Note about Interest Factors 460
Insurance Operations and the Time Value of Money 460
Establishing Premium Rates 461
Investing Premium Income 462
Investing Cash 463
Meeting Future Obligations 463

Chapter 15: Management Accounting 466

Functions of Management and Management Accounting 468
Four Functions of Management 468
The Role of Management Accounting 470
Financial Accounting vs. Management Accounting 476
Intended Audience 476
Time Focus 477
Statutory and GAAP Requirements 479
Level of Precision 479
Use of Non-Monetary Information 480
Elective Nature 480

Chapter 16: Cost Accounting 482

Uses of Cost Accounting 484
Basics of an Effective Cost Accounting System 484
Cost Classifications 485
Costs Classified by Description 485
Costs Classified by Behavior 487
Costs Classified by Measurement 489
Cost Perspectives 493
Cost Accumulation and Cost Allocation 493
Cost Accumulation 494
Cost Allocation 496
Analyzing Costs 505
Change Analysis 505
Functional Costing 506
Activity-Based Costing 509
Cost and the Pricing of Products 513
Cost-Volume-Profit Analysis 514

Chapter 17: Budgeting 520

Why Budget? 521
The Master Budget 524
The Budgeting Process 526
Approaches to Budgeting 526
Who Prepares Budgets? 528
Types of Budgets 529
Classifications of Budgets 532
Operational Budgeting 535
Revenue Budgets 535
Expense Budgets 537
Pro Forma Statement of Operations 539
Cash Budgeting 540
Elements of Cash Flows 541
The Cash Budget 543
Pro Forma Statements 545
Capital Budgeting 548
Capital Budgeting Process 548
Selecting the Appropriate Discount Rate 551
Capital Budgeting Methods 552
Factors Affecting Capital Budgeting Decisions 556

Chapter 18: Responsibility Accounting 560

Goal Congruence 562
Management by Objectives 563
Effectiveness vs. Efficiency 563
Responsibility Centers 564
Cost Centers 564
Profit Centers 565

Investment Centers 565
Performance Measurement and Evaluation 565
Performance Evaluation Issues 581
Problems with Evaluation Criteria 582
Cost Allocation 585
Revenue Allocation 586
Transfer Pricing 587

Chapter 19: Financial Statement Analysis 590

External and Internal Analysis 591
External Analysis 592
Internal Analysis 592
Horizontal and Vertical Analysis 593
Horizontal Analysis 593
Vertical Analysis 598
Benchmarking. 601
Analysis of the Statement of Cash Flows 602
Ratio Analysis. 604
GAAP Ratios 606
Statutory Ratios 616
Regulatory Analysis of Financial Statements 620
IRIS Ratios 620
Financial Analysis and Solvency Tracking System 622
Monitoring Capital and Surplus Requirements 624
Health Insurance Financial Analysis. 628

Chapter 20: Internal Control and Auditing 632

Internal Control 633
Preventive Controls and Detective Controls 636
Managing the Limitations of Internal Controls 636
Compliance and Monitoring 637
Key Participants in the Internal Control System 638
Elements of Effective Control 643
Examples of Internal Controls. 648
Auditing 649
Internal Auditing 652
External Auditing. 655
Types of Internal and External Audits 660

Appendix 667

Glossary 673

Index 697

Preface

The purpose of *Accounting and Financial Reporting in Life and Health Insurance Companies* is to provide a broad overview of the concepts of financial accounting, management accounting, and financial reporting requirements for life and health insurance companies in the United States and Canada. The text is divided into 20 chapters. The first six chapters provide an overview of financial accounting principles and practices, including financial reporting requirements. Chapters 7 through 13 describe accounting for various account classifications under generally accepted accounting principles and statutory accounting practices. Chapter 14 discusses the time value of money. Chapters 15 through 18 provide an overview of management accounting practices. Chapter 19 discusses financial statement analysis, and Chapter 20 discusses the concepts of internal control and auditing.

This book has been designed for students who are preparing for LOMA's FLMI 361 examination. Several features have been included in each chapter to help you organize your studies, reinforce your understanding of the materials, and prepare for the examination. As we describe each of these features, we offer suggestions for studying the material.

- **Learning Objectives:** The first page of each chapter contains a list of learning objectives to help you focus your studies. Before reading each chapter, review these learning objectives. Then, as you read the chapter, look for material that will help you meet the learning objectives.

- **Chapter Outline:** The first page of each chapter also provides an outline of the chapter. Review this outline to get an overview of the material that will be covered and scan the chapter to familiarize yourself with how the information is presented. By looking at the headings and figures, you will get an idea of how various subjects relate to each other.

- **Key Terms and Concepts:** This text assumes that you have a basic knowledge of the key terms and concepts associated with insurance principles and products. In some cases, these basic terms and concepts are also reviewed and explained in this text. All "new" insurance and accounting terminology introduced in this text is defined or explained when it is first used. Important insurance and accounting terminology is highlighted in italic, boldface type when the term is first used or defined and is included in a list of key terms and concepts at the end of each chapter. All key terms are also included in a comprehensive glossary at the end of the book. As you read each chapter, pay special attention to these key terms.

- **Insights:** Excerpts from industry publications and other sources appear throughout the text and are designed to amplify the text's descriptions of certain topics. These Insights should help you get a better feel for accounting in life and health insurance companies.

- **Prep Pak assignment:** Besides this book, LOMA's *Prep Pak for FLMI 361* (Ruth D. Handley, J.D., Cynthia Mathis Henry, FLMI, ACS, ALHC, Robert MacGrogan, FLMI, Martha Parker, FLMI, ACS, ALHC, and Stephan E. Wolter, J.D., ISBN 0-939921-88-X, ©1997) is assigned reading for students preparing for the FLMI Program examination. Used along with this textbook, the *Prep Pak* will help you master the course material. Included in the *Prep Pak* are chapter review exercises, practice exam questions, a full-scale sample examination in both paper form and on a 3½-inch diskette, and appendices with answers to every question in the *Prep Pak*.

LOMA recommends that you use all the study aids available for this course. **Studies indicate that students who use LOMA study aids consistently perform significantly better on FLMI Program examinations than other students.**

Acknowledgments

No matter how much work the authors put into developing a book, many other individuals provide valuable expertise and assistance that make the book possible. Developing *Accounting and Financial Reporting in Life and Health Insurance Companies* required the combined efforts of many highly qualified experts in insurance accounting and financial reporting. On behalf of LOMA and its membership, we would like to express appreciation to those individuals who generously gave their time and energy and shared their considerable expertise for the development of this textbook.

Textbook Development Panel

Our foremost thanks go to the members of the textbook development panel who reviewed the outline of the entire book and each chapter as it was written. These individuals have overseen the entire project from beginning to end and have made many valuable contributions. Their critical judgment, diligence, patience, and technical expertise were essential to the book's accuracy and completeness. The members of the textbook development panel include

- Thomas Allen, CPA, FLMI, Corporate Accounting Administrator, The Union Central Life Insurance Company

- Alan E. Close, CPA, FLMI, Associate Controller, Northwestern Mutual Life Insurance Company

- Larry J. Esposito, CPA, FLMI, Corporate Vice President, New York Life Insurance Company

- Susan I. Flynn, CGA, FLMI, ACS, AIAA, Senior Vice President and Chief Financial Officer, Financial Life Assurance Company of Canada

- Jerry Hogya, FLMI, Manager, Comptroller Systems Management, Mutual of Omaha

- Laurie Kitchen, CA, FLMI, Investment Financial Reporting Officer, Mutual Life of Canada

- Patricia K. London, CPA, FLMI, Assistant Vice President and Controller, Greater Georgia Life Insurance Company

- Roberta McClellan, FLMI, Associate Manager, Financial Reporting, Great-West Life Assurance Company

- Martha A. Meyer, CPA, FLMI, Executive Director, Insurance Compliance, GenMark

- Steven D. Morris, CPA, FLMI, Manager, Finance and Claims, Advance Insurance Company

Additional Expert Reviewers

Besides the members of the textbook development review panel, many other individuals contributed their considerable expertise to ensuring the accuracy and reliability of various specialized aspects of the book. The following industry experts read one or more chapters or provided their expertise in specific subject areas: Dan Boyd, CMA, CCM, FIIC, Vice President, Corporate Finance, ING North America; Connie Caycedo, FLMI, Accountant of Subsidiaries, Cotton States Life Insurance Company; Joseph F. Clark, CPA, FLMI, Senior Manager, Arthur Andersen LLP; David W. Kirkwood, CPA, ARM, FLMI, Technical Accounting Supervisor, Woodmen of the World Life Insurance Society/Omaha Woodmen Life Insurance Society; C. L. (Cliff) Oliver, FSA, FCIA, Senior Vice President and Chief Actuary, Colonial Life Insurance Company; Elliot A. Seligman, CPA, Financial Management and Planning, MetLife; and William C. Weller, FSA, MAAA,

Senior Actuary, Policy Development and Research, Health Insurance Association of America (HIAA).

The following accounting professionals reviewed specific chapters of the text through the coordination of Kris Bryant, Director of Sales and Marketing, MCS Insurance Industry Services, Price Waterhouse LLC: Bill Fuessler, CPA, Principal Consultant; Bill Goldstein, Principal Consultant; Doug Levy, CPA, Manager; Steve Lowry, FLMI, Principal Consultant; Chris Oliver, Principal Consultant; Rosemarie Sansone, Principal Consultant; and Michael Wicke, CPA, Principal Consultant.

LOMA Staff/Consultants

All textbooks developed by LOMA are team projects. The following individuals deserve special mention for the work they performed on this text: Cynthia Mathis Henry, FLMI, ACS, ALHC, Senior Associate, Examinations Department, and Patricia Smith, CPA, ACS, Associate, Financial Management Products and Services, reviewed the entire manuscript and made many helpful suggestions. Patti E. Palmich, CPA, ACS, former Associate, Financial Management Products and Services, reviewed several chapters and helped to recruit reviewers with specific expertise. Gregory P. Storey, FLMI, ACS, CIA, Senior Associate, Financial Management Products and Services, reviewed the auditing chapter and provided materials on financial reporting topics.

Kenneth Huggins, FLMI/M, served as manuscript editor of the entire text. Ruth D. Handley, J.D., Assistant, Curriculum Department, developed many of the text's figures, drafted the glossary, and selected articles for chapter insights. Robert D. Land, FLMI, ACS, drafted the index and copyedited the entire manuscript.

Patricia A. Brown, FLMI, ACS, AIAA, Training Coordinator, Training and Management Development Division, and Mary Anne Cole, Administrative Assistant II, Marketing Division, reviewed several chapters of the text for clarity and readability. Olivia Blakemore, Technical Assistant, Information Center, assisted with the extensive research required for the project. Laura D. Cook, ACS, AIAA, Editorial/Research Assistant, Curriculum Department, obtained permissions for the use of copyrighted material. Elizabeth A. Pedley, Business Coordinator, Curriculum Department, made arrangements for printing the text. Robert McClurkan, Graphic Artist, Marketing Division, and Zoila Harmouche, Graphics Manager, prepared the cover design and artwork. Paul M. Stephens, FLMI System Coordinator, Curriculum Department, assisted with the development of line diagrams for the text. Debra Bailey Helwig, now Associate Editor, Publications Department, Linda Rybicki, Cheryl Brightly, Marion Markus, Administrative Assistant II, Examinations Department, and Cara Taylor,

Administrative Assistant II, Curriculum Department, provided administrative support at various stages of text development. Cara Taylor also assisted in proofing the text during production. Sally Miller Farnham, Editorial/Desktop Publishing Coordinator, Curriculum Department, designed the inside of the text and coordinated the entire production process.

We would also like to thank William H. Rabel, Ph.D., FLMI, CLU, Senior Vice President, Education Division, Ernest L. Martin, Ph.D., FLMI, Assistant Vice President, Curriculum Department, and Dennis W. Goodwin, FLMI, ACS, HIA, Assistant Vice President, Curriculum Department for their encouragement and support throughout the text's development.

Elizabeth A. Mulligan, FLMI, ACS, AIAA, ALHC

Gene Stone, FLMI, ACS

CHAPTER 1

The Accounting Function

Learning Objectives

After studying this chapter, you should be able to

- Define the term *accounting*
- Explain the purpose of accounting and why it is important to all individuals and businesses, including life and health insurance companies
- Explain who uses financial information and how they use it
- Distinguish between generally accepted accounting principles and statutory accounting practices
- Describe the characteristics of financial accounting and management accounting
- Identify who performs the accounting function
- List the typical activities performed as part of the accounting function
- Distinguish between private accounting and public accounting
- Describe the role of governmental entities and various professional organizations in regulating accounting and financial reporting

Chapter Outline

The Purpose of Accounting

Who Uses Accounting Information and How Do They Use It?

Internal Users

External Users

Fields of Accounting and Accounting Principles

Financial Accounting

Management Accounting

Who Performs the Accounting Function?

Private Accounting

Public Accounting

How Accounting Is Regulated

Insurance Accounting Regulation in the United States

Insurance Accounting Regulation in Canada

The Accounting Profession

Certified Public Accountant

Chartered Accountant

Certified Management Accountant

Certified General Accountant

Other Designations

As individual employees, we often think of success in terms of having met certain goals: whether we provided the best customer service, made the right underwriting decision, handled a particular claim fairly and to a customer's satisfaction, or whether we spent enough time learning a new software package so that we can use it effectively on the job. Rarely, however, do we think of these work-related goals and the decisions we make in terms of their financial impact on our company. Keeping track of and helping to forecast that financial impact is the business of accounting. ***Accounting*** is a system or a set of rules and methods for collecting, recording, summarizing, reporting, and analyzing a company's financial operations. Accounting provides us with an established system for categorizing, measuring, and monitoring a company's financial condition, including what the company owns, what it owes, what it earns, what it spends, and what it retains.

Today's life and health insurance companies are organizationally too complex for a company's managers simply to sit down at the end of each month and count how much money the company has left after paying its bills. The sheer volume of business in the life and health insurance industry, which in 1994 included $1.94 trillion in assets and $326 billion in premium income for U.S. insurers, requires an effective and efficient accounting system.[1] Accounting for these assets alone is an enormous task. Because insurers provide financial protection for millions of policyowners and annuity contract holders, the accounting function must help an insurance company to meet all its contractual obligations.

To successfully manage a complex, dynamic insurance company, the company's managers must have ready access to all sorts of financial transaction records and reports. Accounting provides a structured way of summarizing and reporting the information contained in a company's financial records so that a company's managers can stay abreast of the company's financial condition and profitability. In so doing, accounting enables a company's managers to make informed decisions about managing the company's resources. One of the major benefits gained from a knowledge of accounting is that it improves our ability to make the types of important economic decisions required in today's business environment. The more we know about the potential impact a particular decision may have—on a company's financial position, its cash flow streams, or employee morale, for example—the better prepared we are to weigh the alternatives and make the best decision possible.

Given its importance in the business environment and its necessity for effective decision making, accounting is an activity you will almost certainly encounter in your work. No matter what position you hold today, you probably are involved in some aspect of generating accounting information, gathering it, or interpreting it. Therefore, understanding accounting methods and practices will help enhance your own work performance. To use accounting information effectively, you must understand accounting terminology and the major accounting principles and concepts that an insurer uses to prepare its accounting records and reports. Moreover, knowing how to read and interpret financial statements can also help you when you need to make personal investment choices and other household financial decisions.

Another important reason to familiarize yourself with accounting is that all companies, including life and health insurers, are required by law to maintain accounting records of their financial transactions. Even if an insurance company contracts with a payroll or recordkeeping service, the accounting function remains responsible for the accuracy of these accounting records. For these and other reasons we discuss in the next section, it is important that you have a solid understanding of what accounting is, how it works, and how it can help you to interpret a company's financial information.

The Purpose of Accounting

Accounting is often referred to as *the language of business.* As such, one of its primary functions is to provide a company with financial information about itself and its operations. Accounting helps company employees and managers answer questions such as:

- What is our current financial condition?
- Which products are earning a profit and which are not?
- Given our claims experience, what is the appropriate level of spending for underwriting?
- Should we consolidate all field offices with our regional offices in the United States and Canada?
- Are we over budget on travel expenses?
- How can our accounting system enable managers to make informed business decisions at the operational level?

To provide answers to these and many other questions, the accounting function monitors and measures a company's financial transactions. Virtually all business transactions in an insurance company, or any other corporation, are financial transactions because most business transactions typically involve a transfer of funds, or the promise of a transfer of funds or another resource that has monetary value.

In this context, accounting is a *service activity* designed to translate data about a company's financial transactions into information useful to decision makers. The need for financial information in the decision making process is the primary reason for preparing accounting records and reports. In this text, *financial information* refers to all financial data compiled for and from accounting records. Examples of financial information include financial statements, annual reports, budgets, invoices, bank statements, sales forecasts, and payroll records. As shown in Figure 1-1, a company's accounting system of people and processes collects and records data about all the company's transactions that involve money or other items of value and stores the data for current or future use. Then, either as needed or according to some predetermined schedule, the accounting system processes the data by categorizing and summarizing it into financial information that various decision makers can use. Employees in the accounting function and in other functional areas analyze, convert,

Figure 1-1. How an accounting system works.

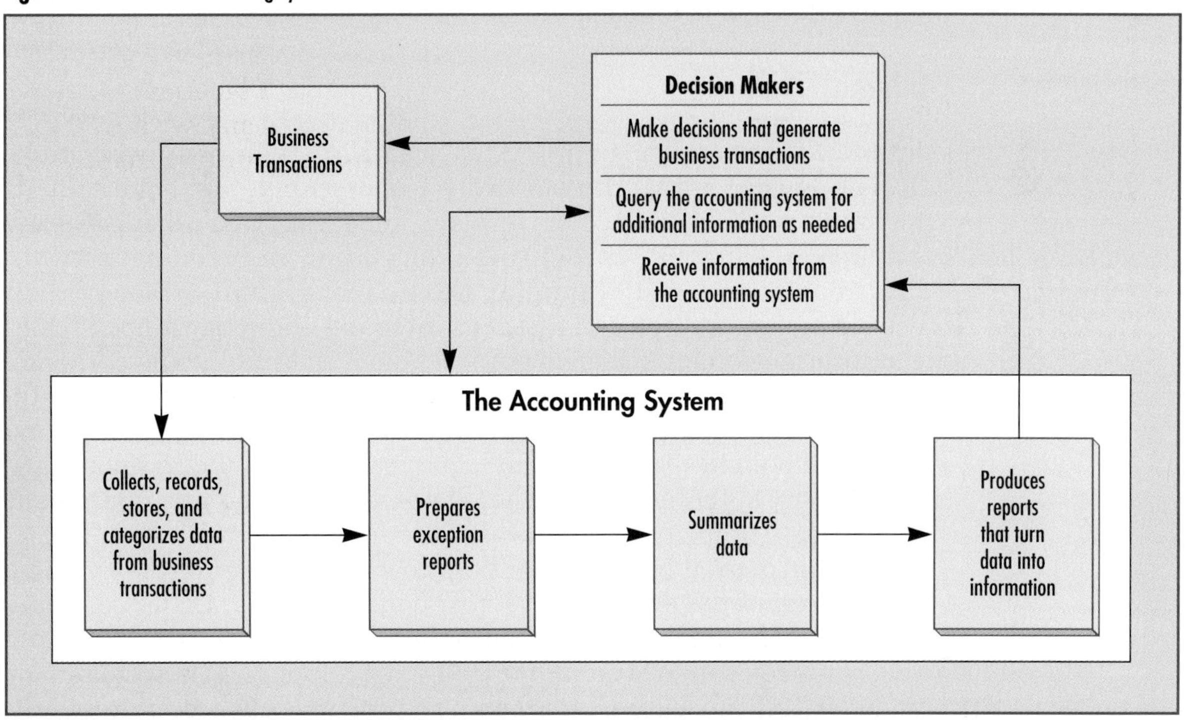

and communicate this information to interested decision makers through various mechanisms.

The accounting system should enable a company to maintain accurate, timely, and complete financial information concerning all its business transactions. Using this financial information, the company's managers can make sound business decisions and satisfy financial reporting requirements. By studying a company's accounts and financial statements, we can learn about the company's financial activities and can make informed projections about the company's financial prospects. A company's financial reports show whether a company is financially sound and whether it is making a profit. By analyzing these reports, a company's managers can identify trends, opportunities, and problem areas for the company and then develop appropriate strategies to take advantage of the opportunities or to improve the company's financial performance.

Who Uses Accounting Information and How Do They Use It?

Many people and organizations rely on the financial information contained in a company's accounting records and reports. These interested parties consist of two groups: internal users and external users of financial information. The types of financial decisions each group makes influence the structure and content of the financial reports developed for each group.

Internal Users

Internal users are those individuals within a company who make decisions that affect the company's operations. Such individuals include a company's directors, officers, managers, and other company employees. They use accounting information in planning, controlling, monitoring, and evaluating the financial implications of their decisions. For example, an insurer's directors and officers need financial information for strategic purposes such as establishing corporate goals and policies and monitoring financial performance. The insurer's managers use financial information to establish departmental goals and policies, to prepare and analyze budgets, and to make various decisions, including whether the insurer should buy equipment or lease it. Company managers also use financial information to prepare departmental budgets that help to control costs and to evaluate the success of the department's cost control efforts. Other company employees use financial information in their job activities: managing the company's investment portfolio, developing a new claim or underwriting procedure, establishing a product's gross premium, billing policyowners, paying for company purchases, or preparing paychecks, claim payments, and agent commission payments. As a company manager or employee, you may have other needs for financial information in order to perform your particular job responsibilities.

Many life and health insurance companies are decentralized, meaning that parts of the accounting function have been incorporated into each functional area or line of business. Employees in each line of business maintain the accounting records and other activities, such as advertising and marketing, associated with that particular line of business. Other insurers operate in a centralized environment, in which functional areas like marketing and accounting are consolidated in the home office. Regardless of company structure, most insurers have one centralized accounting system that consolidates all records and reports of company transactions. In a decentralized company, employees in functional areas feed the accounting system data regarding the various business transactions, which concern premiums, investment purchases and sales, agent commissions, payroll, invoices, and so on. Feeder systems, which house the transaction data from the various lines of business or functional areas, then connect with the company's central accounting system.

However, in a centralized company, employees who work in the accounting function serve the financial information needs of all other functional areas. The accounting system generates reports on each function's financial performance or budget activity. Each line of business then reconciles the reports provided by the accounting function with its own records. Typical accounting reports that are useful to an insurer's internal users include reports on paid premiums, departmental expenses, sales or income by line of business, and company profitability.

External Users

External users include individuals and organizations outside a company who need financial information about the company in order to make personal, corporate, investment, or regulatory decisions about the company. Typically, only regulatory authorities have direct access to the company's accounting records. Other external parties must rely on financial reports provided by the company's accounting function. External users typically have either (1) a *direct financial interest* or (2) an *indirect financial interest* in the company.

Direct Financial Interest

An individual or organization has a ***direct financial interest*** when that individual or organization can gain or lose money as a result of a company's financial performance. Those directly affected by the financial performance of stock, mutual, and fraternal insurers include individual and group policyowners, insureds and their beneficiaries, agents, brokers, creditors, stockholders, and potential investors. An insurer's policyowners are primarily concerned with the premiums an insurer charges and its ability to survive and meet its future obligations. Agents and brokers focus on the insurer's ability to meet their clients' needs and to make commission payments. Creditors, such as banks and product or service suppliers, generally analyze an insurer's financial strength before deciding whether and under what terms to extend credit to the insurer.

In a stock insurance company, stockholders are the owners of the company, and they could lose some or all of their investment in the company if it were to fail. For this reason, they are interested in examining an insurer's financial reports to determine whether the insurer is financially secure. They are also interested in the insurer's current and projected financial performance. If the insurer's financial performance is not good, then the return on investment for the stockholder may be inadequate. In this case, stockholders may sell their stock and invest elsewhere for a higher return on their investment. The policyowners of a mutual or fraternal insurance company are its owners. Their concerns are similar to those of a stock company's owners. They are concerned about a company's financial strength and the amount and frequency of an insurer's policy dividends.

Indirect Financial Interest

An ***indirect financial interest*** means that the individual or organization seeking financial information is doing so on behalf of others. External parties who have an indirect financial interest in a company include regulatory authorities, tax authorities, external auditors, independent financial analysts, and rating agencies. Regulatory authorities need financial information to analyze the company's financial condition and to determine its compliance with federal and state or provincial regulations. These regulatory authorities include the National Association of Insurance Commissioners (NAIC), state insurance departments, and the Securities and Exchange Commission (SEC) in the United States and the Office of the Superintendent of Financial Institutions (OSFI) in Canada. Other organizations—the American Institute of Certified Public Accountants (AICPA) and the Financial Accounting Standards Board (FASB) in the United States and the Canadian Institute of Chartered Accountants (CICA)—also have an indirect financial interest in insurers. Various stock exchanges, and organizations that assess life and health insurance companies to minimize their risk of financial failure, such as state guaranty funds in the United States and CompCorp in Canada, too have an interest in the financial condition of insurers. Tax authorities, including the U.S. Internal Revenue Service (IRS) and Revenue Canada at the federal level, use a company's financial information to assess its tax burden for federal, state or provincial, and local taxes.

Figure 1-2. Internal and external users of financial information.

Financial Information		
Internal Users	**External Users**	
Direct Financial Interest	**Direct Financial Interest**	**Indirect Financial Interest**
Board of Directors	Policyowners	Securities and Exchange Commission
Company Officers	Beneficiaries	Office of the Superintendent of Financial Institutions
Division/Department Heads	Insureds	National Association of Insurance Commissioners
Managers and Supervisors	Outside Agents	American Institute of Certified Public Accountants
Other Employees	Brokers	Canadian Institute of Chartered Accountants
Company Agents	Creditors	Financial Accounting Standards Board
	Stockholders	Rating Agencies
	Potential Investors	Stock Exchanges
		State Guaranty Funds
		CompCorp
		Taxation Authorities (Federal, State or Provincial, and Local)

External auditors include public accounting firms that an insurer's board of directors hires to provide an independent auditor's report on the insurer's financial reports and statements. Independent financial analysts use a company's financial information to make recommendations to potential investors concerning the purchase of company stock. Rating agencies use an insurer's financial information to rate the insurer's ability to fulfill contractual obligations on its life and health insurance policies and other contracts. Rating agencies that publish ratings on the financial condition of life and health insurance companies include A.M. Best, Moody's, and Standard & Poor's. Rating agencies emphasize an insurer's overall financial condition in their ratings, so many policyowners rely on these ratings in deciding whether to buy an insurance policy from a particular company. Because rating agencies also rate an insurance company's debt obligations, a potential investor can consider these ratings in determining whether to invest in the company's stock or debt. Other parties with an indirect financial interest include attorneys, economists, consumer groups, business publications, the financial press, and a company's competitors. Figure 1-2 summarizes an insurer's primary internal and external users of financial information.

Fields of Accounting and Accounting Principles

All accounting involves recording and reporting financial information about business transactions. However, there are different ways of summarizing and looking at the effects of these transactions. As noted, various interested parties use a company's financial information for different purposes. As a result, different fields of accounting have developed to accommodate these diverse needs.

The two major fields of accounting that we discuss in this text are *financial accounting* and *management accounting.* Financial accounting is performed according to generally accepted accounting principles (GAAP) and statutory accounting practices. All U.S. life and health insurance companies follow statutory accounting practices in preparing the financial reports that they file with state insurance departments. All public companies follow GAAP in recording accounting entries and presenting financial information. A complexity of accounting for insurance companies is that different types of insurers follow different guidelines in recording and reporting for different users of accounting information. U.S. stock insurers comply with statutory accounting requirements in completing reports filed with state insurance departments, and they comply with GAAP in preparing financial statements for stockholders and the general public. Canadian insurers use Canadian GAAP for all financial reporting purposes. Insurers in the United States and Canada use financial accounting for tax reporting purposes. In addition, many U.S. mutual and fraternal insurers prepare GAAP-based financial statements in order to compare their financial condition and performance with that of stock insurers. Figure 1-3 lists the typical financial statements and reports prepared under financial accounting and management accounting. We discuss financial accounting and management

Figure 1-3. Typical financial reports prepared under financial accounting and management accounting.

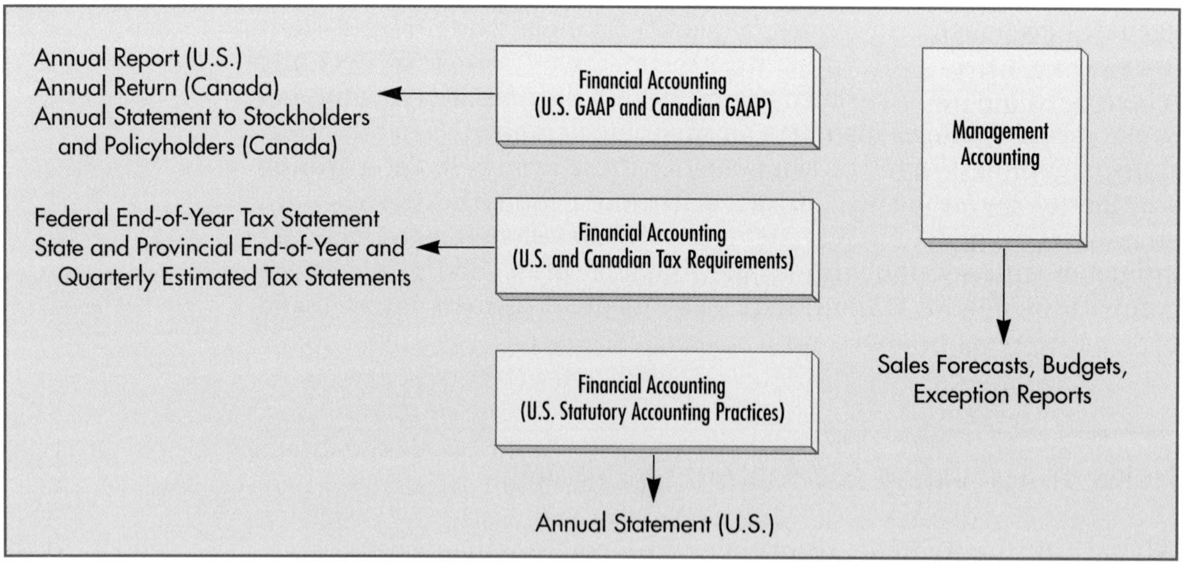

accounting in the following sections and review this discussion in Chapter 15.

Financial Accounting

Financial accounting focuses primarily on reporting a company's financial information to meet the needs of the company's external users. Using financial accounting, a company communicates the summarized results of numerous transactions primarily through its financial statements. ***Financial statements*** include the *balance sheet,* the *statement of operations* (commonly known as the *income statement*), the *statement of cash flows,* and the *statement of stockholders' equity* or *policyowners' equity.* Companies typically include their financial statements and accompanying notes and other disclosures in an annual report that presents their financial condition and the results of normal business operations to interested parties. Insurance companies include these financial statements, prepared under specified requirements, in the U.S. Annual Statement or Canadian Annual Return that they file with insurance regulators. Financial statements report major financial events and transactions that have already occurred. As such, financial statements report almost exclusively on a company's historical financial information. Companies must prepare and present their financial statements according to applicable laws, regulations, and accounting principles and practices. We discuss financial statements throughout the text.

Generally Accepted Accounting Principles

Generally accepted accounting principles (GAAP) are a set of financial accounting standards that all U.S. stock companies and all Canadian companies follow when preparing financial statements. In the United States, the Securities and Exchange Commission (SEC) has delegated its responsibility for establishing U.S. GAAP to the Financial Accounting Standards Board (FASB). In Canada, the Canadian Institute of Chartered Accountants (CICA) establishes Canadian GAAP for companies to follow in recording and presenting their financial information. Under current financial reporting requirements, all publicly traded U.S. companies, including wholly owned subsidiaries, must file most of their financial statements according to U.S. GAAP. Thus, insurance companies prepare GAAP-based financial statements if they or their parent company is a publicly held company. Under certain circumstances, U.S. mutual and fraternal insurers also must comply with GAAP. For example, U.S. mutual and fraternal insurance companies that offer equity-based insurance products or that issue debt must also comply with GAAP in preparing financial reports other than the Annual Statement. However, even if a U.S. insurer complies with GAAP reporting requirements for its general purpose financial statements, the insurer must also comply with statutory accounting practices in preparing the Annual Statement. On the other hand, Canadian insurers follow Canadian GAAP in completing financial statements for regulators, stockholders, and the general public, and they adapt GAAP information for tax reporting purposes. Thus, Canadian insurers generally comply with only one set of financial reporting requirements.

The term *generally accepted* means that GAAP is well known by the accounting profession. Therefore, financial statements prepared according to GAAP provide interested users with financial information that is based on common definitions, valuation methods, and formats. Because all public companies in the United States and all Canadian companies prepare certain financial statements according to GAAP, interested parties such as investors and creditors are better able to evaluate one company's financial performance from year to year or compare the financial performance of several companies across a variety of industries in a given year. Without GAAP, these comparisons would not be meaningful. However, while U.S. GAAP and Canadian GAAP are quite similar, they do differ in some ways. We point out these differences where applicable.

Because of the formal approach of establishing GAAP and its broad acceptance in the accounting profession, GAAP forms a solid foundation for accumulating, organizing, interpreting, and presenting financial information. Further, there is a presumption that readers of a company's financial statements have a basic understanding of GAAP. Otherwise, it would be difficult to interpret the information in these financial statements. These accounting principles, which evolve over time as a result of changes in the economy, technology, and the financial services industry, define the accepted principles and practices associated with financial accounting. Some accounting concepts and principles were adopted through their wide use and acceptance by business. Other GAAP standards are the result of official pronouncements issued by the appropriate accounting organizations, such as the FASB or the CICA. In this text, we cover only the key principles and practices that apply to accounting and financial reporting for life and health insurance companies. We discuss specific GAAP pronouncements when we reach the particular area of accounting to which they apply.

Statutory Accounting Practices

Insurers in the United States have historically and by law followed statutory accounting practices, a type of financial accounting that specifically focuses on the requirements of insurance regulators and policyowner interests. ***Statutory accounting practices,*** sometimes called *statutory accounting principles,* are the accounting bases that all U.S. life and health insurers must follow when preparing the

Annual Statement and certain other financial reports. The purpose of statutory accounting is to provide state insurance regulators with information about an insurer's financial condition, particularly its ability to meet its obligations to policyowners. Like GAAP, statutory accounting has evolved over time. However, statutory accounting practices change through state legislation or regulations imposed by the state insurance department or commission. On the other hand, GAAP evolves on a nationwide basis as a result of a formalized process through the FASB and other organizations.

Sometimes statutory accounting does not address how to record or report a particular type of business transaction. In such cases, accountants may refer to the GAAP-statutory accounting hierarchy (described later in this chapter) or seek guidance from the insurance commissioner of its state of domicile. Because GAAP and statutory accounting sometimes follow different rules, U.S. life and health insurance companies often must prepare two different sets of financial statements: one to satisfy U.S. GAAP requirements and one to satisfy statutory requirements. In addition, statutory reporting requirements can vary between states, meaning insurance companies that do business in several states must satisfy different requirements for different states. Insight 1-1 explains how insurance companies and regulators in the United States are working to develop one set of comprehensive statutory guidelines for all states to follow.

Management Accounting

Management accounting, also called *managerial accounting,* is the process of identifying, measuring, analyzing, and communicating financial information. With management accounting information, internal managers can make more informed decisions regarding the acquisition and use of a company's resources. Although a company's internal decision makers rely heavily on reports and statements that are generated from financial accounting, management accounting reports supply much of the information managers use in planning and controlling day-to-day business operations. Management accounting, which includes such activities as analyzing operating costs, overseeing the company's budgeting process, and analyzing the profitability of each line of business, also helps managers direct the company toward fulfilling its strategic objectives.

Considering the valuable financial and non-financial information that management accounting reports provide, it would be difficult for a manager to perform his or her role successfully without them. The management accounting function in most companies has changed with the development of automated accounting systems, which can generate information for both financial accounting and management accounting requirements. An insurer can compile and present finan-

Insight 1-1 Q&A on Codification

At the time this textbook was written, the statutory accounting practices required of U.S. insurance companies were under review. This review process is called the Project to Codify Statutory Accounting Principles. Deeply involved in codification is Mark Parkin of the public accounting firm, Deloitte & Touche LLP. Mr. Parkin is D&T's Associate National Audit partner for Insurance Industry Services. The following question and answer session with him should provide you with an overview of codification: what it is, how it works, and what its potential impact will be.

Briefly, what is the codification of statutory accounting?
Codification is a project to comprehensively enumerate the statutory principles into a single source. The codified principles will become the standard for determining whether a company's financial statements comply with statutory accounting. The codification is more than simply accumulating existing rules. It includes a challenge of existing rules that often leads to proposed changes.

What led to the need for codification?
Under current statutory accounting practices there are many inconsistencies in the way insurance companies prepare financial statements. Some of the reasons for these inconsistencies are that certain principles allow for many options in applying rules, some of the areas are not covered or it is unclear as to what the accounting should be, certain states set their own rules, and regulators can "permit" different rules for different companies, making the application of the rules difficult.

When rules are generally prescribed or permitted by regulators, then any state regulator can allow a company in its state to use rules that differ from those prescribed by the NAIC or even in state guidelines. If it wanted to, a state could allow certain assets to be admitted at their discretion. State regulators have had the authority to do so, and this has made it difficult to know what rules each state's regulators permit or do not permit. As a result of these inconsistencies, companies have had difficulty knowing all the rules, and auditors had difficulty determining the standards.

What steps are involved in the process of codification?
For each accounting topic there is a need to *identify* current statutory and GAAP guidelines, *propose* the statutory rules, *expose* the proposal to industry and others for comment, *consider* the comments and revise them (if appropriate), *accumulate* the comments into a combined manual, *expose* the combined manual for comment, and *finalize* the manual, based on comments.

What is your role in codification?
Our role is that of consultants to NAIC staff and the Codification Working Group. We also draft issue papers with initial proposed guidance, interpret statutory and GAAP to assist the Working Group in assessing alternatives, and revise papers based on the Working Group's decisions.

Who decides what changes will become effective?
The Working Group makes all decisions in the selection of principles. Ultimately, however, the final product will be subject to the full NAIC committee review process.

What are "issue papers"?
Issue papers are documents that contain the proposed accounting principle for each accounting topic. Each paper contains a *Summary of Issue*, a *Summary Conclusion* (the proposed principles), a *Discussion* (identification of current statutory rules, identification of current GAAP and discussions of the differences between current statutory, GAAP, and proposed statutory), and any *Relevant Literature* (excerpts of the relevant current statutory and GAAP literature).

What are some of the key issue papers? In other words, where will the effects of codification probably be felt most?
Of the papers released to date, and for which comments have been received, the papers that appear to have the greatest impact are those that focus on asset admission or valuation. For example, electronic data processing (EDP) equipment would become nonadmitted. Currently many states allow admission of EDP equipment. Many assets would need to be written down for other than temporary impairments or collectability problems, even when other statutory rules exist.

When did codification begin, and when is it expected to be complete?
This codification project began in the Fall of 1994. It is expected to be completed at the end of 1997, effective for 1998.

(continued)

Insight 1-1 Q&A on Codification, continued

Generally speaking, how will statutory accounting be different once codification is complete?
There will be a single, comprehensive guide that will document the accounting principles. This guide will provide a basis for companies, regulators, and auditors to measure compliance with principles. Some states may maintain requirements that differ. Companies filing an Annual Statement in those states will be required to identify the extent to which their financial statements differ from codified statutory principles, and auditors will be required to report such differences in their independent auditors' reports.

It would be wonderful if all the states agreed to follow one set of rules. But some states have said they will continue to write a few of their own rules. Whether or not that causes a problem depends on how extensive it is. The NAIC hopes it will be minimal, and that the items specific to one state will show up as "disclosed exceptions" to the codification rules. That way, someone reviewing the Annual Statement will be able to understand why this company's results are different from other companies.

Why is codification such a sensitive issue among insurance companies, regulators, etc.?
Codification requests change. The concern voiced by insurance companies arises from their cost to implement this change. Also, many issue papers propose rules that are more conservative than existing rules. The Working Group has agreed to look at overall impacts to industry surplus, but it is not clear what the outcome will be. Initially, there was concern as to the closed nature of the codification process. However, the Working Group meetings that discuss comments have been opened to the public, and have facilitated better communication. Some state regulators believe that codification will take away their ability to set their own rules. Regulators will be able to set their own rules. However, the effects of those unique rules will become much more visible to anyone looking at financial statements of companies in those states.

cial information faster, more easily, and in a wider variety of formats than was possible under a manual accounting system. As a result, the insurer can quickly develop custom reports to meet the needs of a manager who requests specific financial information. For example, a claim department manager may need a weekly list of medical claim expenses by diagnosis. Rather than sending a written request to the accounting department, as might have been done in the past, the manager can now obtain needed operational information simply by entering a few commands into his or her personal computer. The effective use of management accounting information is critical to life and health insurance companies because of the increased competitiveness of the financial services environment, the need to develop new insurance products and services quickly, and the increased emphasis on total quality management, reengineering, and customer service.

Who Performs the Accounting Function?

When it comes to performing the accounting function, the accounting profession generally recognizes two main areas of accounting:

Figure 1-4. Relationship between private and public accounting and the fields of accounting.

Accounting Activities	Private Accountants	Public Accountants
Financial Accounting	• Accounting Transactions • Financial Statement Preparation • Tax Preparation • Financial Analysis • Internal Auditing*	• Management Advisory Services • Tax Service • Financial Analysis • Regulatory Reviews • External Auditing
Management Accounting	• Budgeting • Cost Accounting • Financial Analysis • Internal Auditing*	• Management Advisory Services

* Although internal auditors perform activities associated with the accounting function, they typically report their findings directly to a company's chief financial officer or the audit committee of the company's board of directors.

private accounting and public accounting. Accountants who work in *private accounting* are company employees who prepare financial accounting reports and statements for the company's external users as well as management accounting reports for the company's internal users. Those engaged in *public accounting* are not employees of the company for which they are providing accounting services. Instead, they are employees of an outside firm that the company hires to examine the company's accounting records and reports for financial reporting requirements or to provide related, specified services.

Historically, public accounting almost exclusively focused on financial accounting. With the growth and development of management advisory services by public accounting firms in recent years, many public accounting firms are also engaged in aspects of management accounting. Figure 1-4 is a list of various accounting duties under public accounting and private accounting and their relationship to financial and management accounting.

Private Accounting

Many accounting duties are generally centralized in a company's accounting department. The head of the accounting function typically is the ***controller (comptroller),*** a title which reflects the fact that a primary function of a company's accounting activities is to control the company's operations and protect its resources and wealth. Reporting relationships among the controller and other company officers and employees vary from insurer to insurer. For example, the controller may report to the chief financial officer, the vice president of corporate finance, or the president of the company. Reporting to the controller may be an assistant controller, an accounting manager, or a chief accountant. Other employees in the accounting department include senior accountants, cost accountants, accounting analysts, assistant accountants, and accounting clerks. A large insurer might employ several hundred accountants; most companies have fewer. Figure 1-5 is an example of an organization chart of a life and health insurance company's accounting function.

In a life and health insurance company, activities conducted by the accounting staff typically include

- Establishing the system of accounts
- Maintaining the company's accounting records
- Recording cash receipts and cash disbursements
- Preparing and analyzing accounting records, statutory financial statements, and other financial reports
- Preparing tax returns
- Assisting line-of-business managers with interpreting financial results
- Analyzing operating costs and allocating costs and expenses to areas throughout the company
- Compiling budgets and preparing budget variance reports

From this list, you can see that the accounting function provides some of the most essential financial information used in managing a company successfully. Accounting personnel provide the company's managers with the information needed to plan and implement business strategies. These activities are keys to helping a company's managers in planning and controlling their operations. Conducting internal audits of accounting records, procedures, and reports is also an integral part of the accounting function, but because internal audit activities monitor the accounting function, they are separate from other accounting activities. Large companies may even have a separate internal audit department.

Because every department or functional area performs activities that involve business transactions, there is a great deal of interaction between the accounting department and all other departments within a company. For example, the insurer's accounting function interacts often with its actuarial function. In many companies, the accounting department completes reports, such as the Annual Statement, that a

Figure 1-5. The accounting function in a life and health insurance company.

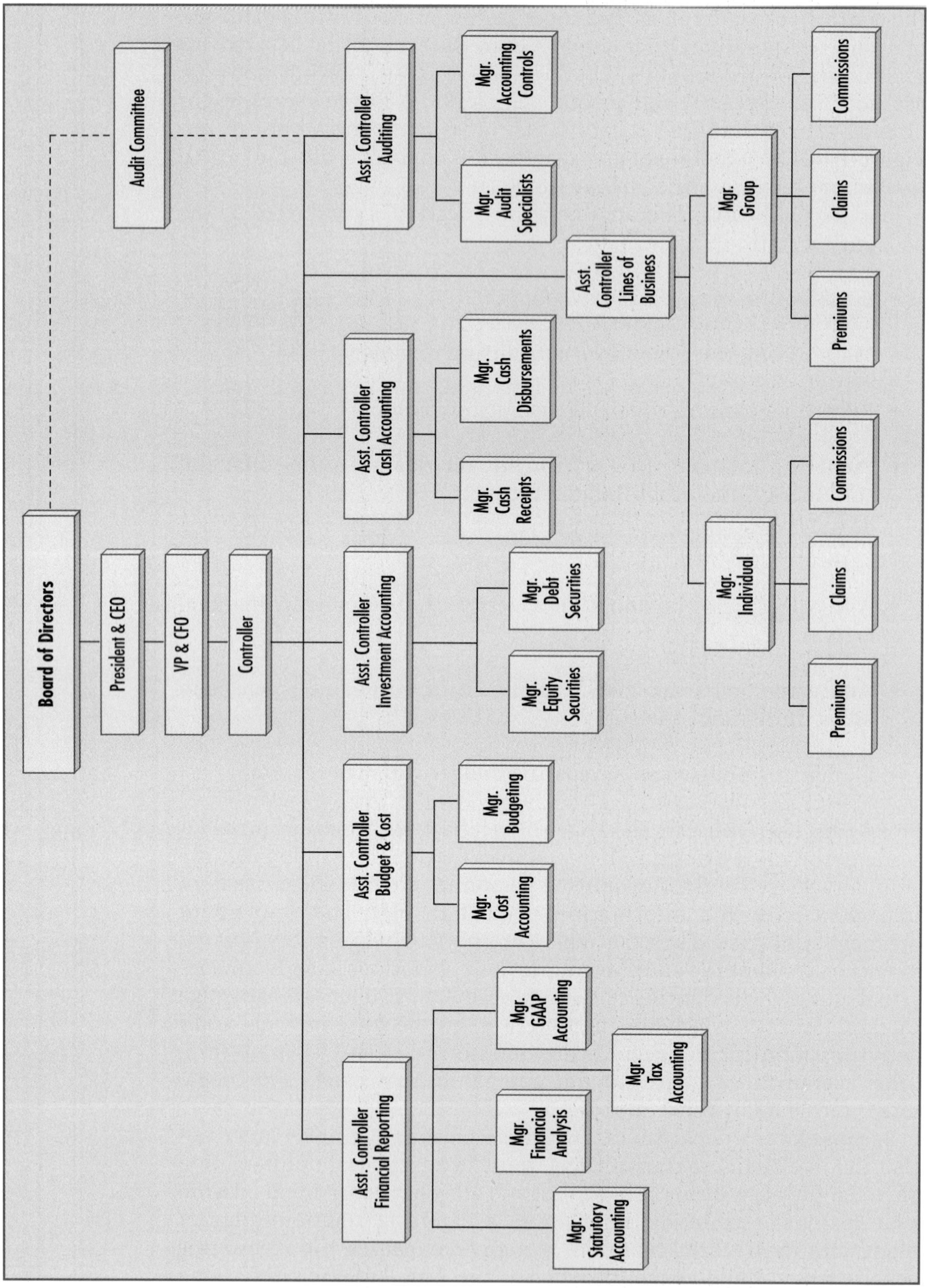

company files with regulatory authorities. But to complete various sections of the Annual Statement, the accounting function needs the actuarial function to calculate certain amounts. Thus, cooperation between a company's actuarial and accounting units is essential. Other functional areas with which the accounting function interacts frequently include claim administration, human resources, and agency administration.

Public Accounting

The primary focus of public accounting is to provide an external audit or independent review and to render an opinion on a company's financial statements for the benefit of external parties. Because the accountant performing the external audit is not an employee of the company being audited, this independence helps ensure that external audits are objective. Public accountants also offer tax services and management advisory services to their clients. Public accounting includes the accountants responsible for overseeing the financial services industry. These accountants are usually employees of, or affiliated with, a government agency or regulatory authority.

How Accounting Is Regulated

Because the insurance industry controls vast sums of funds, and because many people rely on insurance companies for financial protection in the event of a loss, the public can be injured if insurers do not adhere to prudent standards in their business transactions. The financial health of the insurance industry is in the public's best interest. Because an insurance contract is a promise to pay benefits at some future date if certain events occur, the public must be able to trust an insurer to honor its promise. Regulation helps ensure that each insurer makes provisions for the eventual payment of policyowner benefits. In both the United States and Canada, a variety of organizations regulate financial accounting practices. These groups work to control many actions of the accounting function, from how often financial reports need to be filed to what information should appear in each report.

Insurance Accounting Regulation in the United States

Five organizations have a significant impact on accounting in life and health insurance companies in the United States: the National Association of Insurance Commissioners, the Internal Revenue Service, the American Institute of Certified Public Accountants, the Securities and Exchange Commission, and the Financial Accounting Standards Board.

National Association of Insurance Commissioners

The ***National Association of Insurance Commissioners (NAIC)*** is an association of state insurance commissioners designed to promote consistent insurance regulation. Although the NAIC has no legal power, its recommendations and actions carry great weight with the individual state insurance commissioners, the state legislatures, and the insurance industry. The NAIC's influence on life and health insurance accounting is strongest with regard to the preparation of the Annual Statement and the quarterly financial statements submitted to the NAIC. The *Annual Statement,* also called the *Convention Blank* or the *Blue Book,* contains detailed accounting and statistical data.

The NAIC uses information in an insurer's Annual Statement to evaluate the company's financial condition as well as its compliance with insurance laws and regulatory requirements. The purpose of the Annual Statement is to demonstrate a company's ability to meet its future financial obligations. The NAIC specifies the format and content of the Annual Statement, and nearly every insurer must file a copy of its Annual Statement with the NAIC and in each state or territory in which it is licensed to do business. To examine insurance companies, the NAIC uses a zone system, under which each insurer typically is examined every three to five years. After this examination, insurance examiners prepare a report of their findings for the state insurance commissioner. Upon adoption by the state insurance commission, the report becomes a matter of public record.

Other statutory reports that insurers file with state insurance departments include quarterly financial statements, independent auditor's reports, and internal control letters. Canadian and other international life and health insurance companies also comply with NAIC requirements for their business that is conducted in the United States.

Internal Revenue Service

Life and health insurers operating in the United States adhere to the rules and regulations of the *Internal Revenue Code (IRC),* commonly called the tax code, as administered by the ***Internal Revenue Service (IRS)*** of the Department of the Treasury. Although the IRS has no legislative power over insurance companies, the IRS significantly influences the way in which insurance companies do business. The tax code affects not only the taxes that an insurer must pay, but also which products can be considered *life insurance products* for the tax purposes of both the insurer and its policyowners. For complex legal and financial reasons, whether the tax code defines a product as a life insurance product affects the way the product's benefits will be taxed and the way the product can and should be marketed. For example, in selling tax-sheltered annuities, insurers can emphasize the tax-deferred earnings that annuities can provide to contract holders.

Insurers can use this marketing strategy because the tax code states that the earnings on annuities accumulate on a tax-deferred basis.

The IRS also identifies, for tax assessment purposes, the components of an insurer's income and deductions, as well as the value of those items. Complying with the numerous changes in the tax code is a critical and complex part of accounting. A further complication is that the tax code does not necessarily follow GAAP or statutory accounting practices, so insurers often must maintain separate accounting records, and, in some cases, a separate tax accounting department, just for tax purposes.

American Institute of Certified Public Accountants

The ***American Institute of Certified Public Accountants (AICPA)*** is a professional association of Certified Public Accountants (CPAs) in the United States. Although the AICPA has no regulatory powers, its influence is widespread. The AICPA also administers the CPA examination and, through its Auditing Standards Board, develops generally accepted auditing standards (GAAS). These auditing standards are followed by CPAs who conduct external audits on an insurer's GAAP-based or statutory-based financial statements. The AICPA also played an active role in the development of GAAP, although it yielded this role to the Financial Accounting Standards Board in 1973. Nevertheless, the AICPA still influences accounting practice through its (1) technical advisory committees, (2) publications, such as *Statements of Position (SOPs)* and *Technical Bulletins,* that clarify accounting principles, and (3) development of a code of professional conduct for accounting professionals.

Securities and Exchange Commission

The ***Securities and Exchange Commission (SEC)*** is a U.S. federal government agency that regulates the investment industry. Its main purpose is to protect investors. The SEC has jurisdiction over all corporations whose stocks or bonds are *publicly traded,* that is, offered for sale to the general public. With this jurisdiction comes the legal authority to prescribe the accounting methods such companies use. Although individual states of domicile regulate life and health insurers, many insurers are also subject to SEC regulations. For a life and health insurer, the two main tests for whether SEC regulations apply are as follows:

- *Is the company a stock company?* All stock companies, including life and health insurance companies that have publicly traded shares of stock, are subject to SEC regulation.

- *Does the company sell equity-based insurance products such as variable annuities or variable life insurance?* **Equity-based**

insurance products are those in which the cash value and the benefit level fluctuate according to the performance of a portfolio of equity investments, such as stocks. Equity-based products are subject to SEC regulation because they are as much investment products as they are insurance products, and the SEC regulates investment products.

A company that operates under SEC regulation must meet the SEC's registration and financial reporting requirements, which, for the most part, adhere to GAAP. Thus, virtually all stock insurance companies must file with the SEC a set of audited GAAP-prepared financial statements. Currently, mutual and fraternal insurance companies that market equity-based products can submit statutory financial statements to the SEC. The purpose of these and other SEC requirements is to ensure uniform reporting of financial information so that an investor can compare one insurer's financial position with that of other insurers or with companies in different industries. As noted earlier, the SEC has delegated some of its regulatory power to the FASB.

Financial Accounting Standards Board

The ***Financial Accounting Standards Board (FASB),*** commonly referred to as the FASB (pronounced "faz-bee") is a private organization funded by the accounting profession and companies with an interest in accounting. The FASB's primary role is to establish and promote GAAP. The FASB consists of seven leading accountants who give up their other affiliations while working for the FASB. Members of the FASB, along with their staff, work with other interested parties to develop or modify accounting principles for all companies. A function of the FASB is to issue *pronouncements,* which are statements of financial accounting standards and interpretations of standards. The FASB's pronouncements apply to the U.S. business of Canadian and other international insurance companies that operate in the United States.

The FASB pronouncements establish the standards for U.S. GAAP. Most of these pronouncements are *Statements of Financial Accounting Standards,* and are referred to as *SFAS X, FASB Statement X,* or *FAS X,* where *X* refers to the pronouncement number. Figure 1-6 includes brief descriptions of one FASB Interpretation and several FASB Statements that have significantly affected life and health insurance company accounting.

A company must identify and report all material departures in its financial reports from FASB statements or other generally accepted accounting principles. Because of the potential confusion that could result from the numerous publications and pronouncements that deal with GAAP, the AICPA established a GAAP hierarchy for entries that describes the order of authority of sources of GAAP:

- **Level 1:** FASB Statements and Interpretations, Accounting Practice Board (APB) Opinions, and AICPA Accounting Research Bulletins
- **Level 2:** FASB Technical Bulletins, AICPA Industry Audit and Accounting Guides, and AICPA Statements of Position
- **Level 3:** Consensus Positions of the FASB Emerging Issues Task Force and AICPA Practice Bulletins
- **Level 4:** AICPA Accounting Interpretations, "Qs and As" published by the FASB staff, as well as *Industry Practices Widely Recognized and Prevalent*[2]

In other words, these are the resources to which accountants refer, with Level 1 sources being most important, when they are unsure as to the appropriate GAAP standards that apply to particular business transactions.

Similarly, accountants can refer to the statutory accounting hierarchy presented in Figure 1-7 to help resolve conflicts. If statutory accounting practices do not address a particular accounting issue, then an insurer's accountants reference material below Level 3 in the GAAP hierarchy. In practice, however, most insurance companies seek guidance from the insurance commissioner in their state of domicile whenever statutory accounting does not address a particular accounting matter.

Figure 1-6. Significant FASB pronouncements in life and health insurance accounting.

FASB Interpretation 40: "Applicability of GAAP to Mutual Life Insurance and Other Entities," requires insurers, including mutual companies, to follow all applicable authoritative accounting pronouncements when issuing financial statements that are in accordance with GAAP.

FASB Statement 60: "Accounting and Reporting by Insurance Enterprises," prescribes the generally accepted accounting principles that stock life insurance companies should follow. (This FASB statement complements the AICPA publication, *Audits of Stock Life Companies,* an important source of information.)

FASB Statement 97: "Accounting and Reporting by Insurance Enterprises for Certain Long-Duration Insurance Contracts and for Realized Gains and Losses from the Sale of Investments," addresses GAAP for investment-based products such as universal life insurance and participating annuities, which were not covered in FASB 60.

FASB Statement 113: "Reporting for Reinsurance of Short-Duration and Long-Duration Contracts," sets out GAAP for reinsurance contracts.

FASB Statement 115: "Accounting for Certain Investments in Debt and Equity Securities," requires that insurers use GAAP to value securities that are categorized as readily available for sale, trading, or being held to maturity.

Figure 1-7. Statutory accounting practices hierarchy.

Level 1		
NAIC Accounting Practices and Procedures Manuals including GAAP Reference Material (Levels 1, 2, and 3 from the GAAP Hierarchy) to the extent it has been adopted by the NAIC and in the order of hierarchy specified by the AICPA		
FASB Bulletins and Interpretations, APB Opinions, and AICPA Accounting Research Bulletins (GAAP Level 1)	FASB Technical Bulletins, AICPA Industry Audit and Accounting Guides, and AICPA Statements of Position (GAAP Level 2)	Consensus positions of the FASB Emerging Issues Task Force and AICPA Practice Bulletins (GAAP Level 3)

Level 2				
Official NAIC Proceedings	NAIC *Annual Statement Instructions: Life, Accident, and Health*	*Purposes and Procedures of the Securities Valuation Office of the NAIC*	Consensus positions of the Emerging Accounting Issues Working Group (adopted by the NAIC)	NAIC Model Laws and Regulations

Level 3
GAAP reference material below Level 3 in the GAAP Hierarchy

Source: NAIC and FASB.

As you can see from the above presentation, accounting professionals in life and health insurance companies monitor and closely follow all FASB pronouncements with respect to their possible effects on an insurer's financial statements. If neither the FASB nor the NAIC has yet commented on a particular issue in accounting, then accountants should use a fair, legal, and ethical method of recording and reporting the financial information involved and disclose the method used in an accompanying note to the financial statements.

The FASB derives its authority from a number of sources including state boards of accountancy, professional accounting associations, and the SEC. Each of the state boards that licenses CPAs has endorsed the FASB's pronouncements. As a result, any CPA who independently audits a company's financial records and determines that those records do not comply with GAAP must note such an exception in the auditor's report. Failure to do so is a violation of the AICPA Code of Professional Conduct and can result in the loss of the accountant's CPA license, thus effectively putting him or her out of the business of public accounting.

Besides the AICPA, several other professional accounting organizations also provide information and support for the FASB's activities. These groups include the American Accounting Association, the Institute of Management Accountants, the Financial Executives Institute, the Association for Investment Management and Research, and the Insurance Accounting and Systems Association. Figure 1-8 briefly describes each organization.

Finally, the SEC has designated the FASB as the only organization with authority for establishing GAAP. However, the SEC still retains the right to overrule the FASB if the SEC determines that any of the FASB's pronouncements are not in the public interest. Since 1973, the SEC has overruled the FASB only once.

Insurance Accounting Regulation in Canada

In Canada, the organizations that have a significant impact on accounting in life and health insurance companies are the *Office of the Superintendent of Financial Institutions*, the *Canadian Institute of Chartered Accountants*, and *Revenue Canada*.

Office of the Superintendent of Financial Institutions

The agency primarily responsible for overseeing Canadian insurance companies and ensuring compliance with federal laws is the ***Office of the Superintendent of Financial Institutions (OSFI).*** With respect to insurance companies, the most important federal law is the *Insurance Companies Act* of 1992. The Act specifically stipulates how federally

Figure 1-8. Additional professional organizations addressing accounting issues in the United States.

American Accounting Association (AAA): Promotes accounting research and education and influences the development and promotion of generally accepted accounting principles.

Institute of Management Accountants (IMA): Conducts research on management accounting methods and procedures, and, through the Institute of Certified Management Accountants (ICMA), administers the CMA program.

Financial Executives Institute (FEI): Sponsors research in both management accounting and generally accepted accounting principles.

Association for Investment Management and Research (AIMR): Includes the Financial Analysts Federation and the Institute of Chartered Financial Analysts (ICFA), administers the Chartered Financial Analyst (CFA) designation, and fosters and maintains a body of knowledge in financial accounting and portfolio analysis.

Insurance Accounting and Systems Association (IASA): Provides a forum for the exchange of information between accountants and other technical and professional employees in the insurance industry.

registered life and health insurance companies must operate in Canada. For example, the Act mandates that

- A company's audit committee consist of at least three directors.
- A life insurance company's actuary be a member of the Fellow of the Canadian Institute of Actuaries.
- The OSFI conduct an examination of each federally registered or provincially registered company at least once every three years. The examination is similar to that conducted according to the NAIC's zone system in the United States.
- A company file its financial statements according to Canadian GAAP, unless otherwise specified by the OSFI.
- A company register each year with OSFI and submit to OSFI an Annual Return, which presents the company's financial condition as of year's end.

The OSFI issues the *Annual Return,* also known as form number *OSFI-54,* which is similar to the Annual Statement in the United States. The OSFI also establishes financial reporting requirements for Canadian insurers and for international insurers doing business in Canada. In addition, OSFI monitors the financial stability of both federally registered and provincially registered insurers. Although not required to do so, most mutual and fraternal insurers make available to the public financial statements that present in summary form the financial information contained in the Annual Return.

Canadian Institute of Chartered Accountants

The ***Canadian Institute of Chartered Accountants (CICA)*** is a professional accounting association that parallels the AICPA and the FASB in the development of GAAP pronouncements. An Act of Parliament established the CICA, which regularly contributes to governmental legislative deliberations in the areas of accounting and finance. In addition, the CICA has a consultative relationship with Revenue Canada, the Department of Finance, the Department of Consumer and Corporate Affairs, and other related agencies at both the federal and provincial levels. The CICA is the only accounting organization that sets national auditing and accounting standards for financial reporting in Canada. Through its Accounting Standards Committee (AcSC), the CICA is responsible for the *Handbook of the Canadian Institute of Chartered Accountants,* commonly called the *CICA Handbook.* Under the *Insurance Companies Act,* insurers must follow this handbook except when OSFI specifies an alternate accounting method. To date, OSFI has not exercised its option to specify an alternate accounting method or procedure for Canadian GAAP. Thus, all Canadian insurers file the Annual Return according to GAAP, as described in the *CICA Handbook.*

The CICA also prepares and grades the Uniform Final Examination (UFE), which the provincial Institutes of Chartered Accountants administer to prospective chartered accountants (CAs). In addition, the CICA offers continuing education and professional development programs for chartered accountants and conducts and publishes research on issues of concern in financial accounting and auditing.

Revenue Canada

Revenue Canada is the governmental agency that is responsible for enforcing the provisions of the *Canadian Income Tax Act.* The Act includes modifications designed to address the unique nature of the insurance business. In addition to describing corporate taxation, the Act describes the taxable portion of cash value insurance products. Tax accounting differs from Canadian GAAP, so insurers must convert accounting income to taxable income in preparing federal income tax returns. Because the Act contains strict definitions of *life insurance products,* some products widely marketed in the United States are not as popular in Canada because of their tax status. Each year, Canadian insurers must provide policyowners and Revenue Canada with statements indicating the portion of the benefits of a taxable life or disability income insurance policy that represents taxable income to the policyowner.

Besides the organizations described above, several other professional accounting organizations serve the continuing education and research needs of accountants in Canada. Figure 1-9 briefly describes the activities of these organizations.

Figure 1-9. Additional professional organizations addressing accounting issues in Canada.

Society of Management Accountants (SMA): Publishes the *Management Accounting Practices Handbook and the Management Accounting Guideline* and administers the CMA program in Canada.

Certified General Accountants Association Canada (CGA-Canada): Develops educational programs to prepare accountants for leadership positions in accounting and financial management and administers the CGA program.

Canadian Life and Health Insurance Association (CLHIA): Provides information on accounting changes and represents the insurance industry in an advisory capacity.

Life Insurance Institute of Canada (LIIC): Provides educational and training programs, including accounting programs, to serve the needs of life and health insurance companies.

The Accounting Profession

Accounting professionals bring a significant combination of education and experience to their jobs. In the United States and Canada, those responsible for the accounting function typically have a college or university education in addition to professional certifications and years of on-the-job experience. Many company controllers, accounting professionals in insurers' accounting departments, and most public accountants are Certified Public Accountants (CPAs) in the United States or Chartered Accountants (CAs) in Canada. Although individuals engaged in private accounting do not have to obtain any special license to practice, many have earned the CPA or CA designation. In the following section we discuss these and other common designations for U.S. and Canadian accountants.

Certified Public Accountant

The major professional accounting designation in the United States is the ***Certified Public Accountant (CPA)*** designation, which all accountants who work in public accounting must earn. Each U.S. state and territory has a board of accountancy that licenses CPAs to practice accounting in that jurisdiction. The licensing procedure protects the public by helping to ensure that only qualified individuals engage in public accounting. Although specific CPA licensing requirements vary from state to state, they have many common characteristics. Individ-

If you don't mind, it's 'legume comptroller' rather than 'bean counter.'

From *The Wall Street Journal*—Permission, Cartoon Features Syndicate

uals who have passed a rigorous uniform national examination and have complied with specified state or territory requirements for educational achievement and job experience can become licensed CPAs.

The American Institute of Certified Public Accountants (AICPA) develops, administers, and grades the national qualifying examinations for the CPA designation. The examination, which the AICPA administers twice a year, tests individual knowledge of accounting theory and practice, auditing, and business law. The AICPA and some jurisdictions also may require additional examinations in areas such as economics and professional ethics for accountants to be eligible for licensing. After becoming licensed, CPAs must also meet annual requirements for continuing education in the appropriate jurisdiction.

Chartered Accountant

The major professional accounting designation in Canada is the ***Chartered Accountant (CA)*** designation. A licensed CA can perform independent audits in all provinces. All CAs must have a university degree, though specific course requirements vary among the provinces. Once a student completes the appropriate courses, he or she may take the Uniform Final Examination (UFE), a rigorous, comprehensive examination, similar to the CPA exam in the United States. The provincial Institutes of Chartered Accountants award the CA designation to those accountants who pass the UFE and who have met provincial education and work experience requirements. Most CAs attend continuing education courses after having obtained the designation, as recommended by professional codes of conduct.

Certified Management Accountant

Many U.S. and Canadian accountants have also earned the ***Certified Management Accountant (CMA)*** designation, which indicates that an accountant has met certain educational and experience requirements, is competent in financial accounting and management accounting practices, has passed a uniform national examination on management accounting practices, and has fulfilled certain practical experience requirements. The CMA examination typically covers broad areas of business knowledge. The Institute of Management Accountants (IMA) in the United States and the Society of Management Accountants (SMA) in Canada sponsor the CMA designation and help establish management accounting standards by issuing *Management Accounting Practice (MAP) Statements* and providing continuing education programs for management accountants.

Certified General Accountant

Another designation that Canadian accountants pursue is the ***Certified General Accountant (CGA)*** designation, which has a required university-level course of study as well as a practical experience component. The CGA program is administered by each provincial Certified General Accountants Association. Required courses include economics, accounting, computer applications, and finance. Upon satisfying provincial education and work experience requirements and passing a certifying examination, an accountant earns the CGA designation. As with other professional designations, after obtaining the CGA designation, an accountant continues to upgrade his or her skills on a regular basis.

Other Designations

Besides the professional designations described above, accountants also can pursue a number of other designations. For example, internal auditors can earn the *Certified Internal Auditor (CIA)* designation sponsored by the Institute of Internal Auditors (IIA). This designation also involves meeting certain educational and experience requirements plus passing a national examination geared toward internal auditing. Accountants who work in the U.S. life and health insurance industry can also pursue the *Associate, Insurance Accounting and Finance (AIAF)* designation. Jointly sponsored by LOMA and the Insurance Institute of America (IIA), this designation is designed for employees who work in accounting and financial areas, especially those who work with financial data to evaluate insurer performance. Candidates for this designation can pursue either the life/health track or the property/liability track. Each track covers areas such as company operations, information systems, financial management, and statutory accounting.

Textbook Overview

The purpose of this textbook is to give you an understanding of what goes on in the accounting function in life and health insurance companies. Our goal is give you an overview of the different accounting activities and how they influence company operations and affect the various segments of an insurance company. After reading this text, you will be better able to understand and interpret the numbers presented in an insurer's accounting records and other financial statements. The first part of this text explains the general activities associated with financial accounting: what is done, who does it, why it is done, when it is done, and how it is done. Subsequent sections of the text delve deeper into the ways life and health insurance companies apply key financial accounting principles and practices in accounting and financial reporting.

We first discuss financial accounting, including transaction processing, accounting principles and practices, and financial reporting requirements. We then focus on how an insurer accounts for and reports its key account classifications: assets, liabilities, capital and surplus, revenues, and expenses. Next we discuss how an insurance company's managers use management accounting to apply the information contained in its accounting records to improve current business operations and to plan strategically for an increasingly competitive environment. The last two chapters discuss topics that are useful in both financial accounting and management accounting: financial statement analysis and internal control and auditing. By the end of this text, you should be able to see more readily why the accounting function is so important to life and health insurance companies.

Key Terms and Concepts

accounting
direct financial interest
indirect financial interest
financial accounting
financial statements
generally accepted accounting principles (GAAP)
statutory accounting practices
management accounting
controller (comptroller)
National Association of Insurance Commissioners (NAIC)
Internal Revenue Service (IRS)
American Institute of Certified Public Accountants (AICPA)
Securities and Exchange Commission (SEC)
equity-based insurance products
Financial Accounting Standards Board (FASB)
Office of the Superintendent of Financial Institutions (OSFI)
Canadian Institute of Chartered Accountants (CICA)
Revenue Canada
Certified Public Accountant (CPA)
Chartered Accountant (CA)
Certified Management Accountant (CMA)
Certified General Accountant (CGA)

References

1. ACLI *1995 Life Insurance Fact Book Update*, p. 4.

2. Statement of Auditing Standards No. 69. The Meaning of *Present Fairly in Conformity with Generally Accepted Accounting Principles* in the Independent Auditor's Report. *Journal of Accountancy* (March 1992), p. 110.

CHAPTER 2

ACCOUNTS AND THE DOUBLE-ENTRY SYSTEM

LEARNING OBJECTIVES

After studying this chapter, you should be able to

- Describe the concept of accounts
- Describe the balance sheet
- Identify and describe the account classifications that appear on the balance sheet
- Describe the statement of operations
- Identify and describe the major accounts that appear on the statement of operations
- Identify the basic accounting equation
- Define *debit* and *credit*
- List the rules for increasing and decreasing accounts on the balance sheet and the statement of operations
- Summarize the rules of double-entry accounting
- Distinguish between simple and compound accounting entries

CHAPTER OUTLINE

Classification of Accounts

Balance Sheet

Statement of Operations

Double-Entry Accounting

The Basic Accounting Equation

Debits and Credits

Account Balances

Simple and Compound Accounting Entries

In Chapter 1 we introduced you to the accounting function, the people inside and outside a company who use the information provided by accounting, the people in a company who perform the accounting function, and the organizations that oversee the accounting profession and regulate accounting and financial reporting in the United States and Canada. Beginning with this chapter, we move away from the big picture and look inward toward the basics of accounting. We introduce you to the fundamental accounting concepts, which provide you with a foundation for understanding the other aspects of accounting discussed throughout this book.

In Chapter 2, we explain what an accounting entry is, and we present and explain the five account classifications. We also provide an introduction to two primary financial statements: the balance sheet and the statement of operations. Next, we discuss double-entry accounting, the dual concept, and the basic accounting equation. We provide illustrative examples, and we repeat crucial information when necessary, because understanding these concepts is essential not only for you to gain a solid grasp of information that is introduced in later chapters, but also to help make your study of accounting easier and even enjoyable.

Classification of Accounts

As noted in Chapter 1, accounting is a set of rules and methods for collecting, recording, summarizing, reporting, and analyzing a company's financial operations. Accounting is an activity designed to translate data about a company's business transactions into useful information for decision makers. To be recorded in the company's accounting system, a ***business transaction,*** also called a *financial transaction,* must have a financial impact on the company. Whether the financial impact is large or small, or actual or contingent, the company must assign an objective monetary value to the transaction. In accounting terminology, to ***record*** a business transaction is to enter or input the appropriate accounting entries for the transaction into the company's accounting system. An ***accounting entry,*** also called a *journal entry,* consists of at least two parts that are journalized (recorded) in a company's journal for each business transaction. To record the effects of a company's business transactions, an accountant must have a source from which to compile this information.

At the heart of all accounting operations are the documents and records companies create and use as the basis for compiling financial statements and reports. ***Source documents*** for accounting records are the various business papers and electronic forms that contain original information about a company's daily business transactions. Source documents verify that a business transaction occurred, by providing details of the transaction, such as the date and conditions of the transaction, and who approved the transaction. Examples of source documents include

- Checks
- Receipts
- Invoices
- Purchase orders
- Confirmations of investment purchases and sales
- Premium notices
- Employee time sheets or time cards
- Policy surrender forms
- Claim forms
- Bank statements
- Approved policy applications

Although source documents have historically been in paper form, computer technologies, such as *electronic data interchange (EDI),* are enabling insurers to create, use, and store some source documents exclusively in electronic form. Generally, an insurer provides source documents in paper form if those documents, such as audited financial statements, contain authorized signatures. In many cases, source documents stored through microfiche, advanced imaging, or laser optic technology are acceptable substitutes for paper forms. A summary page of a computer output bearing an authorized signature is sufficient to enable an insurer to trace a particular business transaction from beginning to end.

The recordkeeping aspect of the accounting function is known as ***transaction processing,*** or *bookkeeping.* Accurate, complete, and timely transaction processing is an essential building block of any

DILBERT reprinted by permission of United Feature Syndicate, Inc.

accounting system, whether manual or automated. Transaction processing generates the records to create an audit trail, which enables interested users, including internal and external auditors, to trace business transactions from source documents to their impact on an insurer's financial statements.

The business transactions recorded from a company's source documents typically involve the five basic account classifications: assets, liabilities, owners' equity, revenues, and expenses. We describe each of these account classifications later in the chapter. Account classifications form the basis of a company's ***chart of accounts,*** also called the *system of accounts,* which is a numbered or alphabetical list of all the company's account names. Each insurer devises its own chart of accounts that is most suitable to the company's financial transactions. Also, statutory regulations require insurers to include a few specific accounts in the chart of accounts. Figure 2-1 depicts a portion of an insurer's chart of accounts.

Figure 2-1. Sample portion of an insurer's chart of accounts.

Chart of Accounts

Account Group	Account Description
11100000	Assets
12100000	Liabilities
13100000	Surplus
14100000	Premiums
15100000	Claims
16100000	Expenses
17100000	Investments
18100000	Miscellaneous
19100000	Clearing Accounts used with Feeder System

Developing and maintaining the chart of accounts is typically the responsibility of a company's controller and his or her staff. An ***account*** is the basic storage unit used to record, group, and summarize similar types of business transactions. In this text we use the common convention of presenting specific account titles, such as Cash and Premium Income, with initial capital letters. To help your understanding of how an account is used to record, group, and summarize similar types of business transactions, let's look at an example.

Every insurance company has access to its cash to pay the expenses associated with its daily business transactions. To keep track of the amount of cash that it has on any given date, the company establishes an account called Cash. An account's ***balance*** is the amount in the account as of a specified date. For example, if there is $1,000 in the Cash account, it is common to say that the Cash account has a balance of $1,000. To ***balance*** an account means to compare and reconcile the total amount in the account as shown in a company's accounting records with independent data. For example, an insurer balances Cash by reconciling the total in its Cash account with the ending cash balance on its bank statement. We discuss this type of balancing in the section on double-entry accounting and again in Chapter 8.

The balances in some accounts may remain relatively stable during an accounting period, but a company's Cash balance typically changes continuously throughout the month as the company receives and pays out cash. Suppose a company's Cash balance is $50,000 at the beginning of January. During January, the company receives—that is, has *cash receipts* of—$75,000. Also during January, the company spends—that is, has *cash disbursements* of—$80,000. The company's Cash balance as of January 31 is calculated as follows:

January 1 Cash balance	$ 50,000
During January, *add* cash receipts of	$ 75,000
	$125,000
During January, *subtract* cash disbursements of	$ (80,000)
January 31 Cash balance	$ 45,000

The company then compares its $45,000 balance (account total) in Cash with its bank statement to balance (reconcile with independent data) the Cash account. Because of the activity in the account during the month, the Cash balance fell to $45,000. The $45,000 becomes the new Cash balance as of February 1, and so on. Note that this example shows only summary amounts rather than the amounts resulting from each cash receipt or disbursement. The insurer records the transactions that led up to these summary amounts in its journals and ledgers. Before we discuss an insurer's journals and ledgers, let's first discuss the basic account classifications contained in two of an insurer's primary financial statements.

Balance Sheet

The ***balance sheet,*** also known as a *statement of financial position* or *statement of financial condition,* shows a company's financial status as of a particular date. A balance sheet summarizes what a company owns (assets), what it owes (liabilities), and its owners' investment in the company (owners' equity) on a specified date. As we discuss later, what the company owns must equal what it owes plus the owners' investment. The balance sheet is a primary financial statement for determining an insurer's financial strength. Figure 2-2 presents a simplified balance sheet for life and health insurers.

A balance sheet is a snapshot of a company's financial condition. The amounts listed on the balance sheet represent the company's summarized account balances on the date shown at the top of the balance sheet. In this context, a balance sheet is a *static measure* of a company's financial position.

Assets

Assets, the first account classification presented on the balance sheet, are all items of readily determinable value owned by a company. Assets can be tangible (physical), such as buildings and office equipment, or intangible (not physical), such as stocks and bonds. Amounts that are *receivable,* or promised to be paid, are also assets. Assets represent a company's resources for generating cash, which in turn the

Figure 2-2. A simplified balance sheet for a life and health insurance company.

Industry Life and Health Insurance Company
Balance Sheet
December 31, XXXX

Assets		**Liabilities**
Investments		Policy and claim reserves
Cash		Accounts payable
Accounts receivable		Other liabilities
Property		
Equipment		**Owners' Equity**
		Stock
		Retained earnings
Total Assets	=	**Total Liabilities and Owners' Equity**

insurer can use to fulfill its obligations. For example, insurance companies typically invest in bonds, an asset. Whenever the bonds pay interest, mature, or are sold by the insurer, the insurer receives cash, which it can use to settle policyowner claims. Examples of assets for a life and health insurance company include

- Cash and cash equivalents
- Bonds (issued by governmental agencies or other companies)
- Stocks (issued by other companies)
- Mortgage loans
- Real estate

Many non-insurance companies list their assets on the balance sheet in order of ***liquidity,*** which represents the ease with which an asset can be converted into cash. Liquid assets are ***short-term assets*** in that they are expected to be converted into cash or consumed within the current accounting period, generally one year. Examples of short-term assets are cash and cash equivalents, such as certificates of deposit (CDs), Treasury bills, commercial paper, and receivables, such as premiums due and reinsurance ceded. ***Long-term assets,*** on the other hand, are those that are less liquid and thus are not directly or easily converted into cash. Long-term assets are those that a company plans to retain for a long time to generate income. Long-term assets include real estate, property, equipment, furniture, and other assets that a company intends to hold indefinitely or until maturity.

Under GAAP or statutory accounting, life and health insurance companies seldom divide their assets between short-term and long-term. Instead, insurers divide their assets between cash and invested assets and other assets. Insurers typically list their investments first, including stocks, bonds, and real estate, followed by cash and cash equivalents, other short-term assets, then long-term assets. Figure 2-3 depicts the assets section of an insurer's balance sheet. We discuss assets in Chapters 7 and 8.

Liabilities

Liabilities, which comprise the second major account classification on the balance sheet, are a company's monetary values for its current and future obligations. Liabilities represent demands against a company's assets resulting from a monetary commitment management has made on behalf of the company. An amount that is *payable,* or a promise of payment by the company to another party, is a liability. Typical liabilities for life and health insurance companies include

- Policy reserves
- Claim reserves
- Advance premiums
- Unpaid policy claims
- Accounts payable
- Notes payable
- Agent commissions payable
- Income taxes payable

A life and health insurance company must have more than enough assets to cover its liabilities, most of which consist of the actual and expected claims of its policyowners, annuitants, and beneficiaries.

As with assets, the order of presentation of liabilities also typically differs between non-insurance companies and life and health insurers.

Figure 2-3. Assets section of an insurer's balance sheet.

ABC Life and Health Insurance Company
Balance Sheet
(in thousands)
December 31

	2000	1999
Assets		
Investments:		
Fixed securities	$13,182,326	$12,962,194
Equity securities	620,026	1,351,455
Mortgage loans on real estate	1,136,750	285,265
Other long-term investments	201,726	204,657
Short-term investments	566,689	471,053
Total Investments	$15,707,517	$15,274,624
Cash	$ 223,413	$ 136,138
Premiums receivable	331,977	279,528
Property and equipment	461,246	323,230
Other assets	328,823	257,306
Total Assets	$17,052,976	$16,270,826

Non-insurance companies typically list their liabilities according to maturity, which means in the order in which a company must pay them. Debts that must be paid in one year or less are known as ***short-term liabilities.*** Examples of short-term liabilities include Accounts Payable and Salaries Payable. On the other hand, liabilities such as Notes Payable, which do not have to be paid in full during the current accounting period, are known as ***long-term liabilities.*** Sometimes a liability may be considered both short-term and long-term. For example, if a company has a five-year note payable, the interest and principal portion payable within one year or less is a short-term liability, because the company normally makes installment payments on the note throughout the year. Because the company will not pay off the remaining principal on the note for up to an additional four years, it lists the rest of the note as a long-term liability. Chapter 10 presents an example of a business transaction that includes both a short-term and a long-term liability.

An insurance company typically lists its liabilities on the balance sheet according to their financial impact on the company. Thus, liabilities for future policy benefits, which represent the largest dollar amount of an insurer's liabilities, appear first. Figure 2-4 depicts the liabilities section of the balance sheet for a life and health insurance company. We discuss the primary liabilities for life and health insurance companies in Chapters 9 and 10.

Figure 2-4. Liabilities section of an insurer's balance sheet.

ABC Life and Health Insurance Company
Balance Sheet
(in thousands)
December 31

	2000	1999
Liabilities		
Future policy benefits:		
Life insurance	$ 7,032,225	$ 6,537,829
Annuities	3,627,905	3,613,819
Accident and health	2,780,114	2,905,129
Advance premiums	402,846	363,493
Unpaid policy claims	812,066	661,686
Total Policy Liabilities	$14,655,156	$14,081,956
Notes payable	$ 222,062	$ 225,800
Commissions payable	918,133	908,715
Total Liabilities	$15,795,351	$15,216,471

Owners' Equity

The third major account classification on a balance sheet is owners' equity. ***Owners' equity,*** also called *stockholders' equity,* represents the owners' investment in the company. In this text, we use the term *stockholders' equity* when we discuss financial reporting requirements for stock insurers under generally accepted accounting principles (GAAP). Typical owners' equity accounts include

- Common Stock
- Preferred Stock
- Additional Paid-in Capital
- Treasury Stock
- Unassigned Surplus (statutory accounting) or Retained Earnings (GAAP)

The components of owners' equity represent a residual claim against a company's assets. In other words, if a company goes out of business, the company's owners—that is, the stockholders of a stock insurer or the policyowners of a mutual insurer—are entitled to whatever remains of the company's assets after all creditor and policyowner claims have been paid. In this sense, owners' equity is the difference between a company's assets and its liabilities:

Owners' Equity = Assets – Liabilities

For certain purposes, insurance companies replace the term *owners' equity* with *capital and surplus.* ***Capital*** represents the money that a company's owners have invested in a stock insurance company. ***Surplus*** is the amount that remains when an insurer subtracts its liabilities and capital from its assets. Because mutual and fraternal insurers do not have stockholders, they rarely have capital accounts. As a result, their capital and surplus accounts typically consist entirely of surplus. Regardless of corporate form, however, all insurers report their surplus on the Annual Statement or Annual Return.

Figure 2-5 is an example of the owners' equity section of a stock insurer's balance sheet. Note that because this is a stock insurance company using a GAAP-based financial statement, we use the term *stockholders' equity* rather than owners' equity. We discuss capital and surplus accounts in Chapter 11.

Figure 2-6 shows the complete balance sheet after assembling the components from Figures 2-3 through 2-5. Note that the total assets equal total liabilities plus stockholders' equity. In other words, the two sides *balance,* which gives this statement its name.

Figure 2-5. Stockholders' equity section of an insurer's balance sheet.

ABC Life and Health Insurance Company
Balance Sheet
(in thousands)
December 31

	2000	1999
Stockholders' Equity		
Common stock of $10 par value. Authorized and issued 8,500 shares	$ 85,000	$ 85,000
Additional paid-in capital	40,000	40,000
Retained earnings	1,144,625	929,355
Treasury stock	(12,000)	0
Total Stockholders' Equity	$1,257,625	$1,054,355

Statement of Operations

During its normal business activities, a company generates revenues and incurs expenses. The company's net income or net loss depends on the relationship between revenues and expenses. If revenues exceed expenses, the result is *net income* or *profit.* If expenses exceed revenues, the result is a *net loss:*

Revenues – Expenses = Net Income (Loss)

A ***statement of operations*** reports on this profit or loss for a given period by summarizing the company's revenue and expense accounts for that period. The statement of operations is also called a *summary of operations* under statutory accounting, or an *income statement,* a *profit and loss statement,* and an *income and expense statement* under GAAP. Figure 2-7 shows a simplified example of a statement of operations.

Unlike the balance sheet, which presents a company's financial position as of a single date, the statement of operations presents the company's revenues earned and expenses incurred during an accounting period, usually a year, quarter, or month. The balance sheet is a ***static measure,*** that is, a snapshot of a company on a specified date. The statement of operations, however, is a ***dynamic measure,*** which means that it measures the movement or flow of business transactions over a specified accounting period. The statement of operations can be thought of as a motion picture, in that it covers the period from the date of the previous statement of operations up to, and including, the date of the current statement of operations. Thus, the date indicated

Figure 2-6. Complete insurance company balance sheet.

ABC Life and Health Insurance Company
Balance Sheet
(in thousands)
December 31

	2000	1999
Assets		
Investments:		
Fixed securities	$13,182,326	$12,962,194
Equity securities	620,026	1,351,455
Mortgage loans on real estate	1,136,750	285,265
Other long-term investments	201,726	204,657
Short-term investments	566,689	471,053
Total Investments	$15,707,517	$15,274,624
Cash	$ 223,413	$ 136,138
Premiums receivable	331,977	279,528
Property and equipment	461,246	323,230
Other assets	328,823	257,306
Total Assets	$17,052,976	$16,270,826

	2000	1999
Liabilities and Stockholders' Equity		
Liabilities:		
Future policy benefits:		
Life insurance	$ 7,032,225	$ 6,537,829
Annuities	3,627,905	3,613,819
Accident and health	2,780,114	2,905,129
Advance premiums	402,846	363,493
Unpaid policy claims	812,066	661,686
Total Policy Liabilities	$14,655,156	$14,081,956
Notes payable	$ 222,062	$ 225,800
Commissions payable	918,133	908,715
Total Liabilities	$15,795,351	$15,216,471
Stockholders' Equity:		
Common stock, $10 par value. Authorized and issued 8,500 shares	$ 85,000	$ 85,000
Additional paid-in capital	40,000	40,000
Retained earnings	1,144,625	929,355
Treasury stock	(12,000)	0
Total Stockholders' Equity	$ 1,257,625	$ 1,054,355
Total Liabilities and Stockholders' Equity	$17,052,976	$16,270,826

Figure 2-7. A simplified statement of operations for a life and health insurance company.

Industry Life and Health Insurance Company
Statement of Operations
For the year ended December 31, XXXX

Revenues
Premium income
Annuity considerations
Net investment income

Expenses
Policy benefits
Agent commissions
Operating expenses
Income taxes
Net Income (Loss)

on the balance sheet is a specific date, such as "December 31, 1998," whereas the date listed on the statement of operations is for a specific accounting period, such as "for the year ended December 31, 1998."

Revenues

Revenues, the first group of accounts on the statement of operations, represent the amounts earned from a company's sales of products and services to its customers. The company may also earn other revenues from leasing or renting its assets and providing services outside its normal business operations. Typical revenues for life and health insurers include

- Premium income
- Investment income
- Fee income

Revenue generated from policy sales, or premium income, is a major source of revenue for life and health insurance companies. An insurer obtains investment income from interest and dividends on the bonds, stocks, and other investments it owns. An insurer's investments are assets, but the investment income earned on those assets is revenue. Fee income results from providing services such as third party administration services.

An increase in revenues generally increases assets. For example, when a policyowner pays a policy premium, this transaction not only increases an insurer's revenues, but also its cash, which is an

Figure 2-8. Revenues section of an insurer's statement of operations.

ABC Life and Health Insurance Company Statement of Operations (in thousands) For the years ended December 31		
	2000	**1999**
Revenues		
Premiums	$5,123,674	$4,963,012
Net investment income	799,723	683,166
Fee income	80,255	79,576
Total Revenues	$6,003,652	$5,725,754

asset. Figure 2-8 depicts a sample revenues section from an insurer's statement of operations. We discuss an insurer's revenue accounts in Chapter 12.

Expenses

The second major account classification on the statement of operations is expenses. ***Expenses*** are the amount of one or more assets a company uses to receive a certain benefit or service. Expenses are a necessary part of doing business because a company cannot generate revenues without also incurring expenses. Unlike revenues, expenses decrease a company's assets. For example, when a company pays its monthly utility bill (an expense), the company's cash (an asset) decreases. Typical expenses for life and health insurance companies include

- Policy benefits
- Selling expenses
- Operating expenses
- Taxes, licenses, and fees

Insurers classify expenses according to the reason for their incurrence. For example, policy benefits include annuity and policy surrenders, and claim payments for life, health, and disability insurance, all of which an insurer records in different accounts. ***Selling expenses*** include agent commissions, advertising, agent training, and rent and utilities on field and branch offices related to marketing a company's products and services. Agent commissions are such a significant selling expense for many insurers which use the agency distribution system that insurers itemize agent commissions separately on the statement of operations. Although policy benefits and agent commissions are unique to insurance companies, all companies have accounts for reporting operating expenses on the statement of operations. ***Operating expenses*** occur as a result of undertaking certain activities in the course of normal business operations to generate sales revenues. Companies usually establish individual accounts for each type of operating expense so they can monitor expenses in detail. Operating expenses include the salaries of home office employees, rent and utilities on the home office building, and home office supplies used to indirectly support the generation of revenues. Besides these general expenses, life and health insurance companies also must pay taxes, licenses, fees, and other expenses. Figure 2-9 provides a sample of the expenses section of an insurer's statement of operations. We discuss an insurer's expenses in Chapter 13.

Figure 2-10 shows the complete statement of operations after assembling the components from Figures 2-8 and 2-9. As you can see, because the company's revenues exceeded its expenses, it earned net income in both years.

Double-Entry Accounting

All accounting principles and accounting systems are based on a principle called the ***dual concept,*** which states that every business

Figure 2-9. Expenses section of an insurer's statement of operations.

ABC Life and Health Insurance Company
Statement of Operations
(in thousands)
For the years ended December 31

	2000	1999
Expenses		
Benefits and claims	$4,332,003	$4,024,533
Operating expenses:		
Agent commissions	651,786	544,895
Insurance expenses	558,813	400,337
Other operating expenses	101,547	104,663
Total Operating Expenses	$1,312,146	$1,049,895
Total Benefits and Expenses	$5,644,149	$5,074,428

Figure 2-10. Complete insurance company statement of operations.

ABC Life and Health Insurance Company
Statement of Operations
(in thousands)
For the years ended December 31

	2000	1999
Revenues		
Premiums	$5,123,674	$4,963,012
Net investment income	799,723	683,166
Fee income	80,255	79,576
Total Revenues	$6,003,652	$5,725,754
Expenses		
Benefits and claims	$4,332,003	$4,024,533
Operating expenses:		
Agent commissions	651,786	544,895
Insurance expenses	558,813	400,337
Other operating expenses	101,547	104,663
Total Operating Expenses	$1,312,146	$1,049,895
Total Benefits and Expenses	$5,644,149	$5,074,428
Income before income taxes	$ 359,503	$ 651,326
Income tax expense (40 percent)	143,801	260,530
Net Income	$ 215,702	$ 390,796

(Arrows in the figure indicate: Total Revenues minus Total Benefits and Expenses = Income before income taxes.)

transaction has two aspects that always offset and balance each other. The dual concept, also called the *dual-aspect concept* and the *principle of duality,* is the cornerstone of *double-entry accounting.* In ***double-entry accounting,*** the foundation of modern accounting, every business transaction affects at least two accounts. There must be at least one debit and one credit for each transaction, and the sum of the debits must equal the sum of the credits for each transaction. We can illustrate the dual concept and double-entry accounting by showing how they are used to maintain the basic accounting equation. Insight 2-1 discusses the origins of double-entry accounting.

The Basic Accounting Equation

The ***basic accounting equation*** is a mathematical expression of the dual concept and is fundamental to the accounting function. The

Insight 2-1 Father of Accounting Is a Bit of a Stranger to His Own Progeny

Doctors have Hippocrates and philosophers have Plato. But who is the father of accounting? Knowing that accountants have long had inferiority complexes, two Seattle University professors decided that the profession should have a father and that he should be Luca Pacioli.

Accounting Profs. William Wels and David Tinius planned a big celebration in Sansepoicro, Italy, the birthplace of Pacioli. The occasion: the 500th anniversary of the publication of his seminal work on double-entry bookkeeping.

Messrs. Wels and Tinius dreamed up the Pacioli quincentennial in 1986 on a ski trip to Austria. "Things were sort of dull and we were goofing around, so we decided to zip over to Italy." There, they decided that a Pacioli fete "could be fun and get some prestige for the profession," which Prof. Tinius said has "a terrible image."

The pair persuaded four of the six biggest accounting firms, among others, to cough up $125,000 to make a 27-minute video. They were also going to commission a formal portrait of Pacioli, in hopes of promoting it onto a U.S. commemorative stamp. But the Postal Service turned them down, Prof. Tinius says, because a commemorative stamp celebrating the 100th anniversary of accounting in the U.S. that was issued in 1987 "didn't sell very well." The anniversary stamp, picturing a quill pen and ledger, "wasn't very exciting."

Five centuries ago, Pacioli published *"Summa de Arithmetica, Geometria, Proportioni et Proportionalita."* It contained a slender tract for merchants on double-entry bookkeeping, which had been in wide use in Venice for years. Because of that, some accounting historians including Profs. Wels and Tinius credit Pacioli with codifying accounting principles for the first time. That would seem to establish paternity.

But others are skeptical, and even go so far as to question Pacioli's links to luminaries of his day. "It's hard to believe that Pacioli knew all the famous people attributed to his circle," says Richard Vangermeersch, an accounting professor at the University of Rhode Island and former president of the Academy of Accounting Historians. "Since his life has been re-created from scanty references of that day, some historians like myself feel that some tales about his acquaintances are apocryphal."

Prof. Vangermeersch says the origins of double-entry bookkeeping are open to question. "If you're crediting people of past centuries for contributions to accounting, you should include Leonardo of Pisa, who brought Arabic numerals to the West; James Peele, who initiated journal-entry systems; and Emille Garcke and J.M. Fells, who applied accounting to factory use," he says. All these men have another thing in common, he adds: They are just as obscure as Luca Pacioli.

Prof. Tinius insists that the tribute to Pacioli is deserved because his "Summa" contained the first complete textbook on accounting.

Although Profs. Wels and Tinius desperately tried to spur interest in the quincentennial, their efforts were unsuccessful. Only a dozen accountants signed up, so it was canceled. Apparently, unfamiliarity with Pacioli was the impetus of the lack of response from accountants. Even Eugene Flegm, general auditor of General Motors Corp. and a member of the quincentennial committee, conceded the general state of ignorance. "I showed the Pacioli video to about 30 accountants at my company and only two or three had ever heard of him," he said.

Even in literature, said Prof. Vangermeersch, the only famous accountant was Daniel Defoe, who wrote *Robinson Crusoe.* Unfortunately, Defoe was a terrible businessman and failed in a series of ventures, the professor observes. "Even as a dissenter and pamphleteer he was tarred and feathered by the public."

Source: Adapted from Lee Berton, "Father of Accounting Is a Bit of a Stranger to His Own Progeny," *The Wall Street Journal* (January 29, 1993), p. A1. Reprinted by permission of *The Wall Street Journal,* © 1993 Dow Jones & Company, Inc. All Rights Reserved Worldwide.

basic accounting equation presents the relationship among the three account classifications on the balance sheet: assets, liabilities, and owners' equity. For this reason, the basic accounting equation is sometimes called the *balance sheet equation.* The relationship is expressed as

Assets = Liabilities + Owners' Equity

When insurance companies replace owners' equity with capital and surplus, the basic accounting equation is rewritten as Assets = Liabilities + Capital and Surplus.

We can expand the basic accounting equation to include all five account classifications:

Assets = Liabilities + Owners' Equity + Revenues – Expenses

Later in the text, we demonstrate the relationship between revenues, expenses, and owners' equity accounts.

To maintain an accurate balance sheet, a company must keep both sides of the basic accounting equation in balance. Accomplishing this task requires double-entry accounting. Every business transaction that changes the total of one side of the basic accounting equation must be offset by at least one change to the other side of the equation. We demonstrate this process and provide the accounting entries that accompany the business transactions in the following example.

1. Jack Crane and James Good form a business by investing a total of $1,000 of their own money. The investment of $1,000 provides the company with $1,000 worth of assets in the form of cash. The sum is attributable solely to the owners. Therefore, the balance of the owners' equity account is $1,000. The liabilities amount remains at zero because it was unaffected by this business transaction. If the company were to go out of business at this time, the entire amount of its capital would be returned to the owners, Jack Crane and James Good. At the time of the initial investment, the basic accounting equation is

Assets = Liabilities + Owners' Equity
$1,000 = 0 + $1,000

2. The company buys $400 worth of furniture on account. Because the company purchases the furniture without paying cash, in essence, the company has borrowed $400 to make the purchase. The assets of the company now include $400 worth of furniture, plus the original $1,000 in cash. However, the company has incurred a debt of $400, which it records as a liability in an account such as Accounts Payable. Note that this transaction does not affect the company's owners' equity. If the company went out of business at this time, $400 would be paid first to the creditor who financed the purchase of the furniture. When the creditor is paid, the assets and liabilities would be reduced by $400, and the owners would receive only their original investment of $1,000 ($600 in cash and $400 in furniture). After the purchase of the furniture, the basic accounting equation is

Assets = Liabilities + Owners' Equity
$1,400 = $400 + $1,000

3. The company sells the furniture for $700 cash. The sale of the furniture has two effects on assets. First, the asset total decreases by $400 because the company no longer owns the furniture asset. Second, the company increases its asset total by the $700 in cash received from the sale. The effect is a net increase of $300 in assets. No creditor is involved in this transaction, so the company's liabilities do not change. The additional $300 in owners' equity represents an increase in the owners' wealth due to a profit made on the sale of the furniture. If the company went out of business at this point, the furniture creditor would be paid the debt of $400, leaving $1,300 in assets to be distributed to the company's owners. The basic accounting equation after the sale of the furniture is

Assets	=	Liabilities	+	Owners' Equity
$1,700	=	$400	+	$1,300

4. The company pays its creditor the $400 owed. Because the company pays the creditor in cash, assets are reduced by $400. In addition, the liabilities are reduced by $400 (to $0). The company no longer has any liabilities because it does not owe money to anyone. The owners are entitled to all the company's assets. The amount of owners' equity has risen from the original investment of $1,000. This increase is directly attributable to the $300 profit made on the sale of the furniture. The basic accounting equation is now

Assets	=	Liabilities	+	Owners' Equity
$1,300	=	0	+	$1,300

Note that each transaction in the example has two effects on the basic accounting equation. Specifically, the purchase of furniture on account increases assets and liabilities, and the sale of furniture increases assets and owners' equity. Because the basic accounting equation must always remain in balance, we cannot increase or decrease the total on one side of the equation without having a corresponding increase or decrease in one or more accounts on the other side of the equation.

Debits and Credits

One of the best ways to learn about double-entry accounting and to comprehend the activity taking place in an account is with a graphical tool known as a T-account. The use of T-accounts is also helpful in analyzing complex business transactions that affect many accounts. A ***T-account,*** named because its shape resembles the letter "T," records the activity in a particular account during a given accounting period. As you can see from the T-account for Cash depicted in Figure 2-11, a T-account consists of three parts: (1) the account's

Figure 2-11. T-account for Cash.

Cash	
Debit Side	Credit Side

title, which is centered over the top of the "T," (2) the left side, called the *debit* side, and (3) the right side, called the *credit* side.

Changes to an account are referred to as *debits* and *credits.* A ***debit*** is a change made to the *left* side of an account. A ***credit*** is a change made to the *right* side of an account. You may sometimes see debit and credit abbreviated as "dr." and "cr.," respectively. Students new to accounting often get confused about the meaning of the terms *debit* and *credit.* However, all you have to remember is that debit means left side and credit means right side.

Although we use T-accounts to help visualize the effects of business transactions on particular accounts, you should be aware that T-accounts are used primarily for illustration purposes and are not generally used in a company's accounting system. Instead of a T-account, most accounting systems use a variation of the accounting entry depicted below, in which debits appear first, followed by credits. We indent credits for illustrative purposes. A brief explanation or description of the business transaction associated with the accounting entry follows the entry to provide for easier analysis and review of a company's business transactions long after they have occurred. In our example, Equipment is the debited account, Cash is the credited account, and *xxx* represents a dollar amount.

Equipment	xxx	
Cash		xxx

To record the purchase of equipment for cash.

Insurers typically name their accounts for components of business transactions. Account titles and account numbering schemes vary from insurer to insurer because each insurer has a unique chart of accounts. Although the account titles in our text examples may not be the same as the ones that each insurer uses, we use simple, descriptive titles so you can see more easily how business transactions affect an insurer's accounts.

Account Balances

We use T-accounts to learn about account balances. An account's balance is the difference between the account's debits and its credits. When an account's debits exceed its credits, the account has a *debit balance;* when an account's credits exceed its debits, the account has a *credit balance.* The ***normal balance*** is the side of the account in which *increases* to the account are recorded. Accounts that are increased by debits typically have a debit balance at the end of each accounting period. A debit balance means that the account's balance is on the left side of the T-account. When you balance the account, typically the account's balance will also be a debit amount. These accounts are commonly referred to as ***debit-balance accounts,*** because their normal balance appears in the debit column. For example, when a transaction increases the balance in an asset account or an expense account, these increases are recorded on the left side of the "T." Thus, asset and expense accounts are debit-balance accounts. ***Credit-balance accounts*** are accounts that increase by credits. For example, when transactions increase liability, owners' equity, and revenue accounts, the amount of the increase is shown on the right side of the "T." Therefore, liability, owners' equity, and revenue accounts are credit-balance accounts.

Certain rules determine whether a debit or a credit increases or decreases the total in a particular account. If you visualize the balance sheet in Figure 2-2, these rules should be easier to remember. What accounts appear on the *left side* of (or are listed first on) the balance sheet? Assets. Therefore, *debits* increase the totals in asset accounts. Now, what accounts appear on the *right side* of (or are listed second on) the balance sheet? Liabilities and Owners' Equity. Therefore, *credits* increase the totals in liability and owners' equity accounts. On the other hand, *credits* decrease the totals on the left side of the balance sheet (asset accounts), and *debits* decrease the totals on the right side of the balance sheet (liability and owners' equity accounts). Again, in accounting, *debit* means the left side and *credit* means the right side. Figure 2-12 summarizes these relationships.

For accounts listed on the statement of operations, the debit and credit rules are as follows: *debits* increase expense accounts and decrease revenue accounts. Conversely, *credits* increase revenue accounts and decrease expense accounts. Figure 2-13 summarizes the rules for debits and credits as they apply to accounts that appear on the statement of operations.

An easy way to remember the debit and credit rules for statement of operations accounts is to remember the general equation:

Figure 2-12. The rules for increases and decreases in balance sheet accounts.

Assets		=	Liabilities		+	Owners' Equity	
Debit for Increase	Credit for Decrease		Debit for Decrease	Credit for Increase		Debit for Decrease	Credit for Increase

Figure 2-13. The rules for increases and decreases in statement of operations accounts.

Expenses	
Debit for Increase	Credit for Decrease

Revenues	
Debit for Decrease	Credit for Increase

Revenues – Expenses = Net Income. Because revenues represent an increase in cash and expenses represent a decrease in cash, then what is true for revenues will not be true for expenses. In other words, if credits increase revenue accounts, then credits must decrease expense accounts. Similarly, if debits decrease revenue accounts, then debits must increase expense accounts.

Figure 2-14 combines the information contained in Figures 2-12 and 2-13 to show the overall effects of debits and credits on the basic accounting equation, which is expanded to include statement of operations accounts:

Assets = Liabilities + Owners' Equity + Revenues – Expenses

To sum up the rules for debit and credit increases and decreases:

- *Debits increase assets and expenses*
- *Debits decrease liabilities, owners' equity, and revenues*
- *Credits increase liabilities, owners' equity, and revenues*
- *Credits decrease assets and expenses*

Throughout this text, we discuss how to make accounting entries to record the business transactions that take place each day in an

Figure 2-14. The rules for increases and decreases in five major account classifications.

Debits Increase Assets Expenses	**Credits Increase** Liabilities Revenues Owners' Equity
Debits Decrease Liabilities Revenues Owners' Equity	**Credits Decrease** Assets Expenses

insurance company. To lay the groundwork for those discussions, let's look at a few sample journal entries in an insurer's accounting system. Remember the basic rules of double-entry accounting: (1) each accounting entry must have at least one debit and one credit, (2) the total dollar amount of debits must equal the total dollar amount of credits, and (3) each accounting entry must maintain the basic accounting equation:

Assets = Liabilities + Owners' Equity

Recording transactions is essentially a three-step process:

1. Identify the applicable accounts that reflect the transaction to be recorded.

2. Analyze how the transaction affects each account (that is, does the account balance increase or decrease).

3. Determine the appropriate debit and credit entries and apply the appropriate amounts.

Assume that an insurer uses $10,000 of cash to purchase real estate. Step 1 is to determine what accounts this transaction affects. For the purpose of this simple example, two accounts are affected: Cash and Real Estate. Step 2 is to determine how the transaction affects each account. The $10,000 cash purchase decreases Cash by $10,000 because the insurer spends $10,000 to purchase real estate. In turn, Real Estate increases by $10,000 because the insurer now has $10,000 worth of additional real estate as a result of this transaction. Step 3 is to determine the appropriate debit and credit entries. A debit increases an asset account and a credit decreases an asset account. Thus, the insurer *debits* Real Estate for $10,000 (that is, the insurer records $10,000 on the left side of the Real Estate T-account) to indicate the increase in the Real Estate account. The insurer *credits* Cash for $10,000 (that is, the insurer records $10,000 on the right side of the Cash T-account) to indicate the decrease of $10,000 in Cash. The following T-accounts represent this business transaction:

Real Estate	
10,000	

Cash	
	10,000

The accounting entry for this transaction is

Real Estate 10,000
Cash 10,000
To record the purchase of real estate for cash.

The debit appears on the left side of the entry and the credit appears on the right side of the entry. Again, debit means left, and credit means right. Therefore, when we say "debit Real Estate for $10,000," we are saying "record $10,000 on the left side of the account," or in this case, "increase Real Estate by $10,000," because a debit to an asset account increases the total amount of that asset. Because this accounting convention is universally recognized, a person familiar with double-entry accounting can tell from the above accounting entry, even without reading the accompanying description, that a company used $10,000 cash to purchase $10,000 worth of real estate. Another accounting convention is the elimination of dollar signs from accounting entries. Recall that companies record accounting entries only for those business transactions that have a monetary value, so the numbers debited and credited are assumed to be dollar amounts.

The above example reinforces the characteristics of double-entry accounting. First, as you can see, there is at least one debited account and one credited account. Second, the total debits equal the total credits. Finally, the basic accounting equation stays in balance because the only accounts that are affected are two asset accounts, which the insurer has debited and credited for the same amount. Every other accounting entry you see in this text will follow the same rules of double-entry accounting. If an asset account is increased, either another asset account must be decreased or a liability or owners' equity account must be increased to keep the basic accounting equation in balance. On the other hand, if an asset account is decreased, either another asset account must be increased or a liability or owners' equity account must be decreased to keep the basic accounting equation in balance.

For our second example, let's use a transaction that affects both sides of the basic accounting equation. Assume that the insurer purchases the real estate by obtaining a mortgage loan for $10,000 instead of paying cash for the real estate. Again, the insurer debits Real Estate for $10,000, but in this case, credits Mortgage Loans Payable, a liability account, for $10,000. The T-accounts for this business transaction are

Real Estate	
10,000	

Mortgage Loans Payable	
	10,000

The accounting entry for this transaction is

Real Estate 10,000
    Mortgage Loans Payable 10,000
To record the purchase of real estate with a mortgage loan.

From this entry, you can see that the insurer debited Real Estate and credited Mortgage Loans Payable for $10,000. Because debits increase assets and credits increase liabilities, both Real Estate and Mortgage Loans Payable increased by $10,000 as a result of this business transaction. Again, note how this accounting entry demonstrates the facts we mentioned earlier. First, there is at least one debit and one credit in this accounting entry. Second, the total debits and credits are equal in dollar amount. Finally, the basic accounting equation stays in balance after this transaction. In the second example, the insurer's total assets and total liabilities and owners' equity each increase by $10,000.

Simple and Compound Accounting Entries

So far, each of our examples of double-entry accounting has involved a ***simple accounting entry,*** which is an accounting entry that affects only two accounts. Many entries, however, affect more than two accounts. For example, suppose the insurer in the above example purchases real estate for $10,000, by paying $2,000 in cash and obtaining a mortgage loan for the remaining $8,000. The accounting entry that the insurer uses to record this transaction is called a ***compound accounting entry,*** because it involves more than two accounts. In our example, Cash, Real Estate, and Mortgage Loans Payable are the three accounts affected by this business transaction. The transaction decreases Cash by $2,000, increases Real Estate by $10,000, and increases Mortgage Loans Payable by $8,000. Below are the T-accounts for this business transaction:

Cash		Real Estate		Mortgage Loans Payable	
	2,000	10,000			8,000

The accounting entry for this transaction is

Real Estate	10,000	
Cash		2,000
Mortgage Loans Payable		8,000

To record the purchase of real estate with $2,000 in cash and an $8,000 mortgage.

As is the case with simple accounting entries, total debits must equal total credits in compound accounting entries. In our example, $10,000 (debit) = $2,000 + $8,000 (credits). Remember, the *dollar* amount of the total debits and total credits must be equal.

Conclusion

In this chapter, we introduced you to account classifications, the balance sheet, the statement of operations, and double-entry accounting. Chapter 3 builds on this foundation by focusing on (1) the accounting cycle, (2) the annual report, which contains the balance sheet and the statement of operations, as well as additional financial statements and accompanying notes and supplementary information, and (3) the Annual Statement, which insurers submit in each state or province in which they do business.

Key Terms and Concepts

business transaction
record
accounting entry
source documents
transaction processing
chart of accounts
account
balance
balance sheet
assets
liquidity
short-term assets
long-term assets
liabilities
short-term liabilities
long-term liabilities
owners' equity
capital
surplus
statement of operations
static measure
dynamic measure
revenues
expenses
selling expenses
operating expenses
dual concept
double-entry accounting
basic accounting equation
T-account
debit
credit
normal balance
debit-balance accounts
credit-balance accounts
simple accounting entry
compound accounting entry

CHAPTER 3

THE ACCOUNTING CYCLE

LEARNING OBJECTIVES

After studying this chapter, you should be able to

- Identify the steps in the accounting cycle
- Compare the information contained in a journal with that contained in a ledger for the same business transaction
- Distinguish between adjusting entries and closing entries
- Discuss the general types of information contained in a company's annual report
- Discuss the general types of information contained in an insurer's Annual Statement or Annual Return

CHAPTER OUTLINE

Accounting Records

Journals
Ledgers
Trial Balance
Adjusting Entries
Closing Entries

Financial Statements

Annual Report
The U.S. Annual Statement
The Canadian Annual Return

In Chapter 2, we noted what characteristics are necessary for a company to record its business transactions in the accounting system, and we listed some common source documents that support the audit trail for business transactions. We continue that discussion in Chapter 3 with an explanation of the typical steps involved in the ***accounting cycle,*** which is the sequence of steps that occur during one accounting period, usually a calendar year or a fiscal year. During the accounting cycle, a company transfers information about its business transactions from source documents to accounting entries in the company's journals and ledgers. Next, the company prepares a trial balance and records adjusting entries for the appropriate accounts. Then, the company creates financial statements from these trial balances. Finally, the company records closing entries for specified accounts to establish correct account balances for the end of the current year and the beginning of the next year. Figure 3-1 depicts this cycle.

Accounting Records

All companies, especially companies such as life and health insurers that operate under intense regulatory scrutiny, must maintain timely, detailed information about their business transactions. A company uses accounting entries to record the specifics of its business transactions. Thus far, we have illustrated the recording of transactions by using T-accounts and simple and compound accounting entries. Recall that a T-account separates the portions of an accounting entry by account name, whereas an accounting entry combines in one place all the accounts affected by a business transaction.

Because there are many types and variations of accounting systems, the exact process and precise format of an insurer's accounting entries may differ from the examples that we provide here. A purely manual accounting system consists of a set of physical "books," a general journal and specialized journals, and a general ledger and one or more subsidiary ledgers. On the other hand, an automated accounting system maintains the insurer's journals and ledgers electronically. In each case, the format of an insurance company's journals and ledgers may vary significantly. However, the accounting function, the types of accounting entries, and the purpose of recording and posting transactions remain the same regardless of the specific format.

Figure 3-1. The accounting cycle.

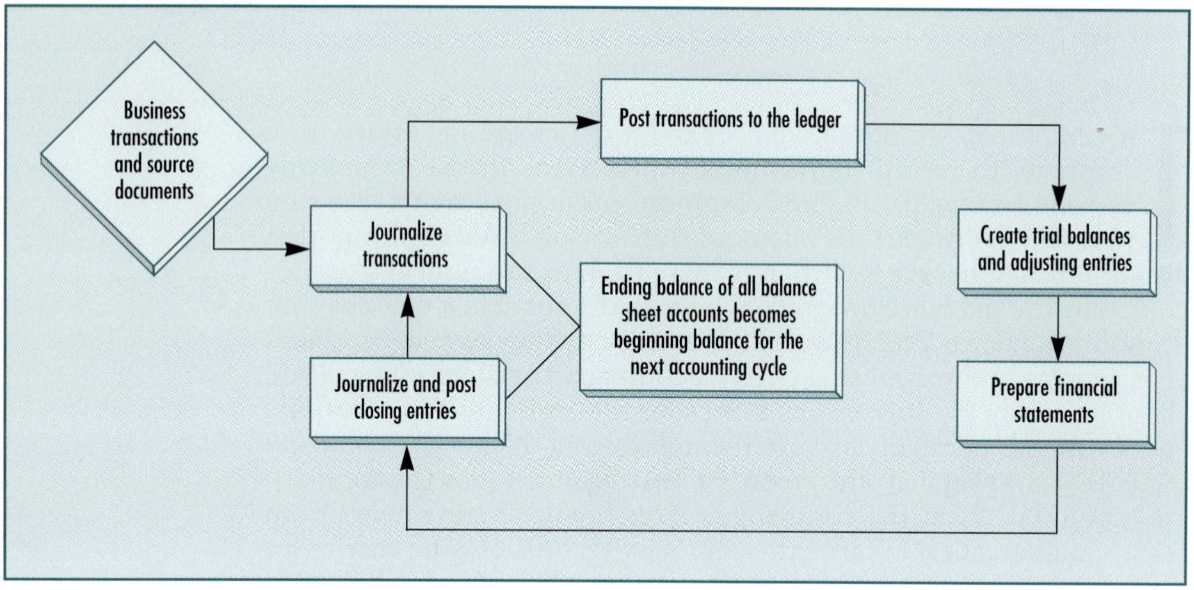

Journals

A ***journal*** contains all the original, chronological records of a company's financial transactions. As such, a journal provides in one place a complete historical record of a company's business transactions, in the order in which they occurred. In this respect, an accounting journal is similar to a personal journal, which contains a daily record of a person's activities, or to a daily newspaper, which reports on the day's activities and events. In many companies, each functional area, such as investments and new business, maintains a journal for the business transactions that occur in that area and feeds this information in summary form to the accounting function according to a specified schedule. In the past, the journal was actually a bound book. Today, however, most companies have automated journals, sometimes called *transaction registers.* Regardless of format, the journal is the sole source for recording accounting entries that represent a company's transactions. For this reason, only accounting entries recorded in the journal can change an account's balance. The conventional format for recording a journal entry is similar to the accounting entries that we presented in Chapter 2.

Recall that *accounting entries* are journalized (recorded) in a company's journal. As shown in Figure 3-2, a company's journal typically contains the name of the journal and columns for recording the following information about each business transaction:

- Transaction date
- Account name
- Account number
- Transaction description
- Posting reference
- Debits
- Credits

A ***posting reference,*** sometimes called a *journal reference,* is a code that links an accounting entry in a journal to one or more source documents associated with a business transaction. Later in this chapter we demonstrate how posting references can link a company's

Figure 3-2. Sample pages from a journal.

Bond Investments Journal				Page 16
Date	**Accounts and Explanation**	**Posting Reference**	**Debit**	**Credit**
June 8, 1999				
	Bonds (001-010)	L.27	1,000	
	Cash (000-001)	L.25		1,000
	Purchased bonds for cash			

Bond Investments Journal				Page 21
Date	**Accounts and Explanation**	**Posting Reference**	**Debit**	**Credit**
June 23, 1999				
	Cash (000-001)	L.25	6,000	
	Bonds (001-010)	L.27		6,000
	Sold bonds for cash			

ledger entries with their corresponding journal entries. An automated accounting system typically assigns the posting reference number.

The accounting entry for the journalized transaction (Figure 3-2) on June 8, 1999, is

Bonds	1,000	
Cash		1,000

To record the purchase of bonds with cash.

The accounting entry for the June 23, 1999, journalized transaction is

Cash	6,000	
Bonds		6,000

To record the sale of bonds for cash.

To provide managers with ready access to the effects of specified business transactions, most companies maintain both a general journal and several specialized journals, such as journals for Cash Receipts, Cash Disbursements, Premium Income, Stock Investments, and Bond Investments. After recording its accounting entries in a journal, an insurer then *posts* (transfers) this information, either in total or in summary form, from its journals to its ledgers.

Ledgers

As you have learned, a journal presents accounting entries in chronological format. Insurers generally create and maintain additional records that focus on the non-chronological aspects of its financial transactions. The purpose of these additional records, which include ledgers, is to help managers and accountants focus their attention on financial transactions in a way that a journal does not. A ***ledger*** is a set of account books (manual system) or a set of electronic records (automated system) that provides detailed information on the dollar amounts in each of a company's accounts.

Each section in the ledger has an account name and account number. A company typically establishes a general ledger and one or more subsidiary ledgers in its accounting system. A ***general ledger*** is a summary of all accounts with their current balances. ***Subsidiary ledgers*** contain more detailed sub-accounts within the account categories listed in the general ledger. Assume that an insurer's general ledger has an account called Real Estate. Subsidiary ledgers provide details of each parcel of real estate that the insurer owns, including the name and location of each property, its purchase price, property taxes, and any business transactions that apply to that particular property. At the end of each accounting period, the sum of the account totals for each real estate property in the insurer's subsidiary ledger must equal the Real Estate account total in the insurer's general ledger. Subsidiary ledgers make accounting information more accessible by dividing it into more convenient segments. Automated accounting systems maintain accounting records in a database that allows users to call up any needed accounting information in a variety of required formats, including the level of detail, if not the traditional format, provided by subsidiary ledgers.

Whereas a journal is arranged chronologically, a ledger typically follows the order of a company's accounts as listed on the chart of accounts. Thus, the balance sheet accounts (Assets, Liabilities, and Owners' Equity) usually come first, followed by the statement of operations accounts (Revenues and Expenses). The company obtains information for the ledger from the journal's accounting entries. ***Posting*** is the process of transferring the amounts listed in a journal to the appropriate accounts in a ledger. For example, the accounting system posts all journalized transactions affecting money owed by a company to its employees to the Salaries Payable ledger account and posts all journalized transactions involving the company's investments to the Investments ledger account, and so on. Most automated accounting systems are programmed to post journalized entries to ledger accounts on an overnight basis. In other cases, a posting command may be necessary for on-line postings to ledger accounts. Regardless of how often the system posts journalized entries to the ledger, there must be an exact match between the account name, transaction date, and amount recorded in both the journal and the ledger. The journalized accounting entry for the June 8, 1999, purchase of $1,000 of Bonds with cash is posted to a ledger in two separate places, rather than with one entry, as in the journal. For the ledger entries, the insurer debits $1,000 to the Bonds ledger account and credits $1,000 to the Cash ledger account, as illustrated in the following simplified T-accounts:

Bonds	
1,000	

Cash	
	1,000

Most automated accounting systems do not duplicate the information already contained in an insurer's journals or subsidiary ledgers, but simply accumulate the debits and credits and summarize the insurer's activities for the accounting period. The accounting system can produce a detailed ledger, however, by merging the insurer's journal entries with its ledger balances. The result typically contains columns listing

- The account name and number
- The date of the transaction

- A posting reference
- An indication that the transaction is a debit or a credit transaction
- An indication that the account has a debit or credit balance

A column called *Item,* or *Description,* is used by insurers if an explanation of a particular transaction is necessary.

Figure 3-3 shows two detailed ledger accounts as they might appear in a company's accounting system. Note that each ledger account includes postings from the journal entries presented earlier in Figure 3-2. Each ledger account also has a posting reference that links the amounts in the ledger accounts to the exact accounting entries they refer to in the company's journal. The practice of using posting references to link accounting entries provides the added benefit of creating an audit trail for the company's accounting entries.

Also note the following additional points about the Cash ledger account in Figure 3-3. The account's beginning balance of $50,000 is

Figure 3-3. Sample monthly ledger accounts.

Ledger Accounts

Cash					Account No. 25	
					Balance	
Date	Item	Post Ref.	Debit	Credit	Debit	Credit
1999					50,000	
1-Jun		J.11	5,000		55,000	
3-Jun		J.14	7,500		62,500	
4-Jun		J.14		3,000	59,500	
7-Jun		J.15	4,500		64,000	
8-Jun	Bond purchase	J.16		1,000	63,000	
15-Jun		J.18		3,000	60,000	
23-Jun	Bond sale	J.21	6,000		66,000	
30-Jun		J.25		4,500	61,500	

Bonds					Account No. 27	
Date	Item	Post Ref.	Debit	Credit	Debit	Credit
1999					90,000	
8-Jun	Bond purchase	J.16	1,000		91,000	
23-Jun	Bond sale	J.21		6,000	85,000	

in the debit column of the balance section of the ledger. This balance changes as debits and credits to Cash occur with various business transactions. Recall that debits increase Cash, whereas credits decrease Cash, so Cash is a debit-balance account. The account's ending balance of $61,500 occurs on June 30, the end of the accounting period.

In other words, the insurer's Cash account had a beginning balance of $50,000. Through various business transactions, the insurer debited $23,000 to Cash and credited $11,500 to Cash during the month of June. The closing balance, shown on the last line of the Debit Balance column, is $61,500. The process of calculating an account's ending balance as of a particular date is known as ***footing*** the account. In this example, the $61,500 balance at the end of the accounting period is the result of footing the Cash account by adding $23,000 to, and subtracting $11,500 from, the beginning period's $50,000 balance. Just as you would carry forward the balance in your checking account from one month to the next, the insurer will begin July 1 with a $61,500 balance in the Cash ledger account.

An insurer can use the information in its ledger accounts to produce routine financial reports that enable the insurer to monitor its accounts. For example, by reviewing the Salaries Expense ledger account and comparing it to the insurer's monthly budget for salaries, a human resources manager can ascertain whether the insurer is over or under budget for personnel salaries for the current accounting period. Because the ledger format provides a running total of an account, the account's current balance is readily available.

Trial Balance

Accounts in the general ledger summarize the individual entries in all the subsidiary ledgers. For this reason, the ending balances in the general ledger must agree with those in each subsidiary ledger. Before transferring the account totals from the general ledger to their financial statements, companies can conduct an interim step to help ensure that the ledger accounts are in balance. This interim step is the ***trial balance,*** a listing of all ledger accounts with their debit or credit balances. A company uses a trial balance to determine whether total debits equal total credits. Many automated accounting systems update the balances in all accounts with each accounting entry and immediately identify accounting entries or other items that are out of balance. As a result, the risk of an insurer's accounts being out of balance is small. Nonetheless, trial balances are available on demand, overnight, or at pre-established intervals such as weekly or monthly, depending on the insurer's accounting system. Figure 3-4 is an example of a simple trial balance for a fictional company that operates with only three asset accounts (Cash, Bonds, and Buildings), one

Figure 3-4. A simple trial balance.

Account Name	Debit Balance	Credit Balance
Cash	$ 61,500	
Bonds	85,000	
Buildings	450,000	
Accounts Payable		$ 50,000
Stockholders' Equity		546,500
	$596,500	$596,500

liability account (Accounts Payable), and one owners' equity account (Stockholders' Equity).

Although a trial balance can show that an error has occurred, the source of the error may require some investigation. In the example above, suppose the Buildings balance were incorrectly listed as a credit balance. An observer would quickly note that the debits did not equal credits because of the credit balance in Buildings, and would correct the error. Typical errors that might cause a trial balance to be out of balance are

- Reversed or unbalanced debits and credits
- Posting to the wrong accounts
- Arithmetic errors
- The omission of certain amounts or accounts
- Errors that involve *transpositions* or *slides*

The error described above could have resulted from crediting, rather than debiting, the Buildings account. Arithmetic errors can cause a trial balance to be out of balance because of incorrect addition or subtraction. Other potential errors include *transpositions,* which result from the incorrect arrangement of a number, such as posting $546 to an account instead of $456, or *slides,* which result from the improper placement of a decimal point or comma, such as posting $45.60 or $4,560 instead of $456 to an account.

While a trial balance that is out of balance indicates an error, a trial balance that shows total debits equal to total credits does not necessarily demonstrate that the accounts are correct. In the sample trial balance provided, Buildings could have been incorrectly listed as having a balance of $400,000, and Accounts Payable could have had a zero balance. In this case, the \$546,500 in debits would equal the \$546,500 in credits, but there would be two errors, each one canceling out the other in the trial balance. Duplicate entries, entirely omitted entries, entries that are posted in the wrong amounts or to the wrong accounts or both, and two or more errors that exactly offset each other are examples of accounting errors that cannot be discovered through preparing a trial balance. In Chapter 20, we discuss internal control methods that a company uses to detect or prevent such accounting errors.

Adjusting Entries

Adjusting entries may be necessary for a company to determine the appropriate amounts that the company should include in its financial statements for a particular accounting period. Besides being used to correct errors, ***adjusting entries*** account for transactions that apply to more than one accounting period. Such transactions include insurance premiums paid in advance by a policyowner. Because adjusting entries typically apply to ongoing activities, not all adjusting entry transactions are likely to have a specific source document, but they usually are supported by a worksheet or similar form. For example, salaries that have been earned by a company's employees during this year, but which the company will not pay until next year, may not yet have a time sheet or the equivalent source document available. Nonetheless, at the end of the year, the company makes an adjusting entry, using the following liability accounts:

Accrued Salaries. xxx
    Salaries Payable xxx
To adjust for salaries that have been earned but not yet paid.

Another example of an adjusting entry involves depreciation on equipment. Suppose that, on January 1, 2001, a company purchases equipment for \$100,000. The company expects the equipment to have a useful life of 10 years, after which it will have no salvage value. The company chooses to depreciate the equipment's cost evenly over the 10-year period. In this case, annual depreciation expense equals \$10,000 (\$100,000 ÷ 10). On December 31, 2001, the company records the following adjusting entry to reflect the amount of depreciation on the equipment, that is, the amount of the equipment's value that was "spent" or "used up" during the year 2001:

Depreciation Expense 10,000
    Accumulated Depreciation—Equipment 10,000
To adjust for the amount of accumulated depreciation on equipment.

An insurer records adjusting entries to account for incurred but not yet paid expenses and to account for earned but not yet received revenues. Insurers also use adjusting entries to record changes in other accounts, including reserves. After making the appropriate adjusting entries at the end of an annual accounting period, a company prepares a post-closing trial balance and its financial statements, then posts the applicable *closing entries.* In this way, the company's journals and ledgers are ready for the start of the next year.

Closing Entries

Earlier we noted that companies accumulate and carry forward the Cash balance at the end of an accounting period from one accounting period to the next. All balance sheet accounts, including assets, liabilities, and owners' equity, are handled in this manner. In contrast, if the account is a statement of operations account, including revenues or expenses, a company does not accumulate and carry forward the account's year-end balance to the next year. Recall that the balance sheet provides information about the accounts at a point in time, whereas the statement of operations measures performance for the accounting period. A company closes out or *zeroes out* its statement of operations accounts through the use of ***closing entries,*** which are accounting entries that a company makes at the end of the year to start the next annual accounting period with a zero balance. Revenues and expenses must be closed out at the end of each annual accounting period because an expense incurred or revenue earned in one year pertains to that year only. For accounting purposes, it cannot also be an expense or revenue in another year.

Another way to understand this difference in handling balance sheet accounts and statement of operations accounts is to use the analogy of static and dynamic measures, which we discussed in Chapter 2. Balance sheet accounts, which are static measures, are like pools in which money is held as of a specified date. The money in each pool varies from accounting period to accounting period, but at the beginning and end of each period, there is a definite amount of money in each pool. Statement of operations accounts, which are dynamic measures, are like hoses through which money flows. Their purpose is not to hold money but to direct it to some other account, ultimately to a balance sheet account, in this case, one of the pools. Because statement of operations accounts record the movement of funds rather than the location of funds, they do not carry balances from one year to another.

Balance sheet accounts, including Cash, are not closed out at the end of the accounting period because they are ***permanent accounts.*** Permanent accounts are the only accounts in the basic accounting equation, *Assets = Liabilities + Owners' Equity.* ***Temporary accounts,*** also called *nominal accounts,* include accounts listed on the statement of operations. Revenues and expenses are therefore temporary accounts, which means that they do not have a cumulative balance from one year to the next. Temporary accounts are closed out to permanent accounts at the end of each annual accounting period. In other words, all statement of operations accounts are closed out to balance sheet accounts, specifically to Owners' Equity. A simple example of closing out a revenue or expense account follows. Review this example with the T-accounts depicted below.

Suppose a fictional company operates with only one expense account and one revenue account. The balance in each account at the beginning of the year is -0-. Therefore, all amounts posted to revenue or expense apply only to the current year. The company incurs expenses in the following amounts—$2,000, $100, and $500—on three separate dates. Because incurred expenses *increase* the Expense account, they are debits (that is, recorded on the left side of the "T"). By *footing* the Expense account, we obtain a total of $2,600 in Expense during the year. The company also earns revenues on four separate dates in the following amounts: $1,000, $800, $500, and $900. Because earned revenues *increase* the Revenue account, these amounts are credits (that is, recorded on the right side of the "T").

Expense	
2,000	
100	
500	
2,600	

Revenue	
	1,000
	800
	500
	900
	3,200

At the end of the year, the company *credits* the Expense account for $2,600 in order to make the balance -0-. Similarly, the company *debits* the Revenue account for $3,200 in order to zero it out. The difference between these two figures is $600, the amount of net income (*Revenue – Expense = Net Income*). Net income is the amount the company adds to an owners' equity account such as Retained Earnings or Surplus. A net loss would be subtracted from the appropriate owners' equity account. For example, under GAAP, a net loss becomes a debit to Retained Earnings, which decreases Retained Earnings. In contrast, net income becomes a credit to Retained Earnings, which increases Retained Earnings. Although companies may differ in their specific procedures in closing revenue and expense accounts, all companies close these accounts at the end of the year. In this context, you can think of all revenue and expense accounts, which are temporary accounts, as subsidiary accounts to Owners' Equity, because this is the account classification to which a company closes all revenue and expense accounts at the end of the year. In other words, the company adds net income earned during the year to its Owners' Equity at the beginning of the year to obtain a new amount for Owners' Equity at the end of the year. For this reason, we can also express the basic accounting equation as

Assets = Liabilities + Owners' Equity (beginning of year) + Net Income

The accounting cycle begins anew with the next accounting year.

Financial Statements

The financial statements and reports produced by the accounting staff provide an essential source of information for an insurance company's managers, owners, policyowners, customers, regulators, competitors, and stockholders, in the case of public companies. A company prepares financial reports for both internal and external uses. The company prepares certain reports, including operating budgets, financial forecasts, expense analyses, and analyses of the profitability of product lines, individual products, or sales territories, primarily for the company's management. One required financial report that a life and health insurance company prepares for external parties is the statutory Annual Statement in the United States and the Annual Return in Canada. State governmental authorities in the United States and federal governmental authorities in Canada prescribe the exact form of the Annual Statement or Annual Return, which includes the primary financial statements as well as detailed schedules and exhibits of investments and insurance activities. In addition, many companies also publish an *annual report* to their stockholders (stock insurers), policyowners (mutual insurers), or members (fraternal benefit societies).

Annual Report

Any company that is publicly traded, that is, a company that sells shares of its own stock on a public stock exchange, must prepare an annual report for its stockholders. An ***annual report*** is the report that a company's management sends to its stockholders and other interested parties to report on the company's performance during the past year. Virtually all publicly traded companies in the United States, including stock insurers, must prepare for their stockholders an audited annual report in accordance with GAAP to comply with the requirements of the Securities and Exchange Commission (SEC). Currently under debate is the issue of whether mutual insurers and fraternal benefit societies should be required to prepare an annual report for their policyowners or members. Many of them already do so in order to offer a simpler, condensed version of much of the information contained in the Annual Statement. In accordance with *FASB Statement No. 120* and the AICPA *Statement of Position 95-1,* mutual and fraternal insurers should also adopt GAAP reporting for their annual reports for fiscal years after December 1995. In Canada, securities laws require that publicly traded companies prepare an annual report for their stockholders. The stock exchange on which a publicly traded company is registered may have additional reporting requirements.

The primary financial statements for an insurer are the (1) balance sheet, (2) statement of operations, (3) statement of cash flows, and (4) statement of stockholders' equity (for stock insurers) or statement of policyowners' equity (for mutual and fraternal insurers). We introduced the balance sheet and the statement of operations in Chapter 2. The ***statement of cash flows,*** also known as a *cash flow statement,* provides information about a company's cash receipts (inflows) and cash disbursements (outflows) during a given accounting period. The ***statement of stockholders' equity,*** also called the *statement of owners' equity* or *statement of shareholders' equity,* shows the changes that occurred in the Stockholders' Equity balance sheet account during the accounting period covered. All publicly traded life and health insurance companies must provide this statement in their annual report to stockholders. Insight 3-1 discusses the complexity of financial statement analysis and interpretation.

In addition to a company's financial statements, an annual report contains other required material such as

- Notes to the financial statements
- A letter from the company's president to its stockholders/policyowners
- A description of the company and its business activities
- A multi-year summary of selected financial highlights
- A management report on the company's operating results and its financial condition
- An analysis of the financial data
- An independent auditor's report
- A list of the company's officers and directors

Insight 3-1 Reading Financial Statements Isn't for the Inexpert

The Financial Accounting Standards Board (affectionately known as Fasbee) has flatly said the reader of financial statements is expected to have a reasonable knowledge of the subject. It's a puzzle that so many investors stubbornly assume otherwise.

When reading financial statements, take special care not to overlook the footnotes. To be sure, the very word suggests something marginal that can be read or ignored at the user's option. Not so. [Companies are free to choose from among accounting policies having a wide range of effects.] Without the footnotes, it is impossible to know whether the earnings have, so to speak, been calculated on a Celsius or Fahrenheit scale. Why pay for a company that is a hot 50 degrees Celsius when all you're getting is one that is 50 degrees Fahrenheit and merely tepid?

The consolidated financial statements that are required by Fasbee often resemble a compost heap. None of the components can be identified; it's impossible to see whether one good business is masking losses elsewhere.

Investors do not have access to the detailed financials that are available to management. But they should not overlook the required footnote that provides operating data for each of the major business segments, which makes it more difficult for management to gloss over its failures.

Most folks calculate their income in terms of cash-in, cash-out. Accountants are not like most folks. The financial statements of a business are almost invariably prepared on something called the accrual basis. The rub is that accrual-basis accounting is more art than science. When all is said and done, the income statement that emerges is very useful, but no one should think that there is anything precise about it.

Financial statements are prepared, not by the independent auditors who merely review them, but by management. Even when the performance is poor, corporate executives try to give themselves good grades.

A constructive and realistic view is that, in analyzing a business, the financial statements are a wonderful place to begin—but no more than that. Certainly, Fasbee has never claimed more than that.

What with cyclical and other factors, the earnings of any one year are often meaningless. Worse yet, the prospect of a bad year, or even a disappointing one, encourages a weedy crop of bad accounting practices. For investors, the remedy is to look beyond any one number and any one year. By examining the results for a 5- to 10-year period, the cyclical factors can be averaged out and the so-called "nonrecurring" items and other financial sleights-of-hand can be averaged in.

By the enlightened mandate of the Securities and Exchange Commission, a Management Discussion and Analysis (MD&A) appears in the annual report of every public company. In it the company must tell us such things as why this year's earnings are not indicative of the next, in short whether it has papered over this year's problems. The MD&A is not always as forthcoming as it should be, but it is a big help.

Consider, too, the statement of cash flows. Starting where the income statement leaves off, the statement of cash flows explains the adjustments necessary to translate net income into the cash balance at the end of the year. Each of the two statements compensates for the limitations of the other, and taken together they are more informative than either alone.

Because all this can be intimidating, investors may be tempted to rely on those experts, the security analysts, who are supposedly doing the work for us. But analysts are paid, and often handsomely, primarily to generate trading commissions and to attract as clients the very corporations they are evaluating. The results are often disappointing.

Source: Excerpted from Louis Lowenstein, "Like Courting a Princess . . . Reading Financial Statements Isn't for the Inexpert," *Barron's Business and Financial Weekly* (December 28, 1992), p.18. Reprinted by permission of *Barron's Business and Financial Weekly*,

In the United States, the SEC requires that a company's annual report include the current and previous year's balance sheet and the current and previous two years' statements of operations, statements of cash flows, and statements of stockholders' equity, so stockholders and other interested parties can evaluate the company's performance over time. In preparing the annual report, Canadian insurers follow the guidelines established under the *Insurance Companies Act* and by the Office of the Superintendent of Financial Institutions (OSFI) as well as from the *CICA Handbook* and securities regulations. Most of the contents outlined above for U.S. annual reports are also applicable to Canadian annual reports.

Publicly traded companies in the United States are required to file an annual Form 10-K report and a quarterly Form 10-Q report with the SEC. Form 10-K contains audited financial statements; Form 10-Q contains *un*audited financial statements. Form 10-K and Form 10-Q reports are similar to the annual report, but they contain more detailed financial information. Through its *Integrated Disclosure System,* the SEC further requires that all annual reports and Form 10-K reports contain a common body of information. This common body of information includes the

- Audited financial statements and their accompanying notes
- Independent auditor's report
- Five-year historical summary of revenues, expenses, earnings per share, and total assets and liabilities
- Two-year summary of quarterly market price information on the company's common stock, including high and low prices during that time period
- Management Discussion and Analysis of Financial Condition and Results of Operations (MD&A)

Publicly traded Canadian insurers must file an Annual Information Form (AIF) with each province in which they conduct business. The information contained in the AIF is similar to the Form 10-K for U.S. public companies.

The U.S. Annual Statement

Regulatory requirements often determine the accounting and financial reporting practices of life and health insurance companies. These requirements are reflected in the U.S. Annual Statement, which companies prepare for state regulatory authorities and the National Association of Insurance Commissioners (NAIC). The Annual Statement contains detailed accounting and statistical data that authorities need to evaluate a company's statutory solvency and compliance with insurance regulations. An insurer has ***statutory solvency*** if it maintains at least the minimum amount of capital and surplus specified by insurance regulators. In the United States, the Annual Statement's format and content are specified by the NAIC and state insurance commissioners. The Annual Statement differs from a company's annual report in that the Annual Statement is compiled according to statutory accounting practices, and the annual report is typically prepared according to generally accepted accounting principles (GAAP).

The Annual Statement form used in the United States includes the following reports and other information:

- A balance sheet in the format of separate pages for *Assets* and for *Liabilities, Surplus, and Other Funds*
- A statement of operations in the format of the *Summary of Operations*
- A *Capital and Surplus Account*
- A *Cash Flow* statement
- Notes to the financial statements
- Exhibits, schedules, and supplemental reports

The Annual Statement's exhibits and schedules support the totals shown in the insurer's primary financial statements, such as the balance sheet. Examples of information that can be found in the Annual Statement's exhibits and schedules are

- Analyses of operations by lines of business
- Five-year historical data
- Policy claims and reserves
- Premiums and annuity considerations
- Dividends applied, reinsurance ceded, and commissions incurred
- Listings of investments and investment income
- Dividends to policyowners
- Nonadmitted assets
- Expenses and taxes

A company must file its Annual Statement with the NAIC and in each state, and in the District of Columbia and U.S. territories, if applicable, in which it is licensed to do business.

The Canadian Annual Return

Canadian companies registered under the *Insurance Companies Act* are required to file an Annual Return with the OSFI and the applicable provincial governments. The Canadian Annual Return has the same general form as the U.S. Annual Statement in that it consists of the basic financial statements supported by exhibits and schedules as listed below:

- A balance sheet in the format of a *Statement of Assets* and a *Statement of Liabilities, Policyholders' and Shareholders' Equity*
- *Income Statement*
- *Reconciliation of Surplus*
- Exhibits, schedules, and supplemental reports

Canadian companies file information about their total business. Non-Canadian companies report only their Canadian business on the specified form, but this form must be supplemented by the total business statement that is submitted in their home jurisdiction. Life and health insurance companies in Canada must also file the Annual Return in each province where the company is licensed to do business. A provincial company that is not federally registered must complete a prescribed form, which is modeled closely after the federal form.

Conclusion

This chapter introduced you to the accounting cycle and the key financial reporting requirements with which life and health insurers must comply. In the next chapter, we discuss the accounting principles and practices that apply to preparing and reporting the required financial statements. Chapters 5 and 6 discuss further the annual report, the Annual Statement, and the Annual Return.

Key Terms and Concepts

- accounting cycle
- journal
- posting reference
- ledger
- general ledger
- subsidiary ledgers
- posting
- footing
- trial balance
- adjusting entries
- closing entries
- permanent accounts
- temporary accounts
- annual report
- statement of cash flows
- statement of stockholders' equity
- statutory solvency

CHAPTER 4

The Conceptual Framework of Financial Accounting

Learning Objectives

After studying this chapter, you should be able to

- Outline the main points of the entity concept and the going-concern concept, with respect to financial reporting
- Explain the key qualitative factors that affect accounting information
- Discuss the main points in the cost concept, the measuring-unit concept, the full-disclosure concept, and the time-period concept with respect to financial reporting
- Discuss the realization principle and the matching principle with respect to revenue and expense recognition under generally accepted accounting principles
- Distinguish between accrual-basis accounting and cash-basis accounting

Chapter Outline

Financial Statement Concepts

Entity Concept

Going-Concern Concept

The Quality of Accounting Information

Reliability

Relevance

Consistency

Comparability

Materiality

Conservatism

Principles for Maintaining Accounts

Cost Concept

Measuring-Unit Concept

Full-Disclosure Concept

Time-Period Concept

Recognition of Revenues and Expenses

Accounting Basis

Accrual-Basis Accounting

Cash-Basis Accounting

As we noted in Chapter 1, financial accounting is based on a number of principles and concepts that have evolved over the years. Usually, these accounting principles and concepts apply to both generally accepted accounting principles (GAAP) and statutory accounting practices; we note where the two differ. These principles and concepts have *predictive quality* and serve as blueprints for recording and reporting a company's business activities. By ***predictive quality,*** we mean that financial information based on accounting principles and concepts should enable interested users to develop a reasonably accurate estimate of a company's financial strength or earnings potential if the users analyze the company's financial statements.

We begin our discussion with two concepts that underlie financial statements: the entity concept and the going-concern concept. Next, we discuss the qualitative characteristics of accounting information: reliability, relevance, consistency, comparability, materiality, and conservatism. Finally, we discuss the accounting principles and concepts that relate to the maintenance of accounts: the cost concept, the measuring-unit concept, the full-disclosure concept, the time-period concept, the realization principle, the matching principle, and accounting basis. Figure 4-1 summarizes the key accounting concepts, characteristics, and principles that influence financial reporting.

Financial Statement Concepts

In accounting, the *entity concept* and the *going-concern concept* underlie all financial statements. We discuss each in the following sections.

Entity Concept

An ***entity*** is the basic economic unit for which a company maintains distinct accounting records and reports. An entity may be a person or an organization. It may be a business or a portion of a business, such as the subsidiary of a corporation. The ***entity concept,*** also known as the *accounting-entity concept* or the *business-entity concept,* states that a company must account separately for the business activities of each economic unit. Thus, to help avoid confusion, an individual who owns a business should separate personal accounting records from business accounting records. With the entity concept, anyone

Figure 4-1. Key accounting concepts, characteristics, and principles.

Overall Framework	Information Quality	Account Principles
Entity Concept	Reliability	Cost Concept
Going-Concern Concept	Relevance	Measuring-Unit Concept
	Consistency	Full-Disclosure Concept
	Comparability	Time-Period Concept
	Materiality	Realization Principle
	Conservatism	Matching Principle
		Accounting Basis

looking at a collection of accounting records should know to whom or to what organization the records refer.

Under the entity concept, a company can define its own accounting entities. For example, a corporation is an entity for accounting purposes. Within the entity of the corporation, however, there can be many additional entities. If a corporation owns subsidiary companies, and each subsidiary prepares its own financial statements, then each subsidiary is an accounting entity. Further, accounting entities within a company can be smaller portions of the company itself, such as divisions, departments, lines of business, profit centers, and so on. Typically, entities at lower levels maintain detailed records of accounting transactions; these records in turn are summarized and consolidated into a higher-level entity's financial reports.

To understand and interpret a company's financial information, and to compare this information with information about one or more other companies, you must first be able to identify which entity the company's financial statements represent: Is it the parent company alone? An individual subsidiary? Or a consolidation of the parent company and one or more subsidiaries? Accounting principles provide two methods for identifying the correct entity. First, a company must clearly label each entity's financial statements with the entity's name. If the statements are for the Keystone Company only, then the headings should read "Keystone Company." If the statements are consolidated financial statements for Keystone and its subsidiaries, then the headings should read "Consolidated Financial Statements of Keystone Company." Second, the Financial Accounting Standards Board (FASB) in the United States and the *CICA Handbook* in Canada require that the activities of a parent company's various business operations be disclosed in the annual report in the notes and supplementary information to the company's consolidated financial statements. These notes describe in detail the source of the amounts represented on the consolidated statements.

Going-Concern Concept

The ***going-concern concept*** means that accounting processes are typically based on the assumption that a company will continue to operate for an indefinite period of time. Thus, unless there is evidence to the contrary, accounting does *not* assume that a company is about to be liquidated. ***Liquidation*** is the process of converting a company's assets to cash, usually to pay off the company's liabilities. The going-concern concept is an underlying premise of GAAP. It is not, however, entirely presumed under statutory accounting. Financial statements prepared according to statutory accounting follow a *modified* going-concern concept because the primary objective is to ensure that an insurer can meet its current and future obligations. The primary focus of statutory accounting is on an insurer's solvency. Generally, the statutory approach is perceived as a more conservative accounting stance than that of the going-concern concept under GAAP.

The going-concern concept primarily affects financial reporting in the following ways. First, this concept allows a company to defer (postpone) certain costs because they contribute to future earnings. For example, a manufacturing company that purchases new machinery expects the machinery to help generate earnings for several years, not just during the accounting period in which the company purchases the machinery. Because of the going-concern concept, the company can defer some of the cost of the machinery to future years. We discuss this process, known as *capitalization,* later in this chapter. Second, the going-concern concept assumes that a company will pay its liabilities over time as scheduled, not immediately or in full during the current accounting period. Thus, a company will pay its current liabilities in the short-term accounting period and its long-term liabilities out of earnings the company generates in future accounting periods. Figure 4-2 summarizes the entity concept and the going-concern concept.

Figure 4-2. Financial statement concepts.

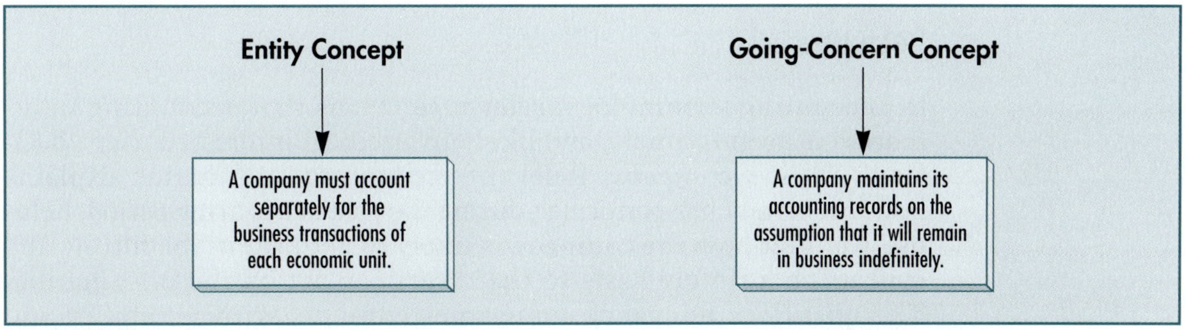

The Quality of Accounting Information

Because quality information in a company's financial statements is critical for the sound operation of the company, the FASB and the *CICA Handbook* mandate that accounting information must exhibit certain qualitative characteristics. It must be *reliable, relevant, consistent, comparable, material,* and *conservative.* These qualities help ensure that a sophisticated analysis of a company's financial statements will provide an accurate and useful understanding of the company's financial condition.

Reliability

Accounting information has the quality of ***reliability*** if it is accurate, objective, and free from bias and misrepresentation. Reliability, which encompasses the quality of *objectivity,* applies to all information contained in a company's financial statements and their accompanying notes and supplementary information. Reliable information is objective and neutral. It faithfully and fairly represents a company's financial position or profitability and does not mislead an interested party. A company must record and report accounting information in such a manner that outside experts, such as external auditors, can verify that the information is truthful and based on objective measurements. For example, when the total dollar amount of claim payments to policyowners equals the amount in an insurer's accounting records and source documents, then the information is reliable. For information to be reliable, the company must record a given transaction in a consistent manner each time a similar transaction occurs. An independent third party must be able to evaluate and interpret specific amounts on a financial statement easily and through standard techniques. Note, however, that objectivity in accounting is sometimes difficult. In some cases, for example, a company's managers must use their own judgment to determine a particular dollar amount of a business transaction.

Relevance

In accounting terminology, ***relevance*** means that accounting information is useful, timely, and likely to affect an interested user's decisions about a company. Relevant accounting information explains how a company has performed during the past accounting period, helps users project how the company is likely to perform in the future, and appears on a timely basis so that users can act on the information. The quality of relevance sometimes conflicts with reliability and objectivity. For example, information that an insurance company is planning to market a new product is relevant because it could affect an investor's decision to purchase the company's stock. This information is also relevant because it could affect the marketing strategies of the company's competitors. However, if the company has not yet developed the product, there is no *certainty* that the insurer will market the product. Further, there is no apparent financial data available about the relevant information. Therefore, the information, though relevant, lacks reliability and objectivity, so the company would probably not report it as accounting information. For accounting purposes, reliability and objectivity typically outweigh relevance because accuracy and independent verification are key components of a company's accounting records and financial statements.

On the other hand, the conflict of relevance with reliability and objectivity does not always lead to a simple choice between one quality and the others. Sometimes relevant accounting information is reliable and objective to some extent, but not entirely. This may lead to a compromise in the way a company presents the information. For example, information that an insurer has developed but not yet started to sell a new product is relevant, but the company will not include the potential revenues of this product's sales in its financial statements. Why? Because there is no *objective* revenue figure for the product because the new product has not yet been sold. The company, however, would have objective figures regarding any expenses or liabilities already incurred because of new product development. The company would include these expenses in the financial statements and explain them in its notes to the financial statements. The company may also include a discussion of its prospects for success with the new product in its Management Discussion and Analysis of Financial Condition and Results of Operations (MD&A) or in a separate Message to Stockholders or Policyowners. Interested users could then combine this objective information with revenue estimates to forecast the potential impact of the new product on the insurer's future financial performance.

Consistency

In accounting terminology, ***consistency*** means that a company uses the same accounting policies and procedures in its financial statements from one accounting period to the next, unless there is a sound reason for changing a policy or procedure. A company violates the concept of consistency if it changes an accounting policy without disclosing the financial effects of the change. Meaningful and *comparable* financial statements are a direct result of accounting consistency. Consistency enables interested parties to compare a company's financial performance over time if the company consistently uses the same accounting policies and methods.

Both GAAP and statutory accounting may offer more than one acceptable method for calculating or valuing a particular account disclosed in the financial statements. A company's management therefore should choose the methodology appropriate to the nature of the company's operations, then apply that methodology consistently across accounting periods. However, a company does not have to use the same methodology for every account. For example, the company may use one valuation method for the Bonds account and another valuation method for the Real Estate account, as long as the company applies each valuation method consistently across accounting periods.

Sometimes, however, a company may change its accounting policies and procedures entirely. For example, an insurer might legitimately make such a change because

- Changes in statutory accounting practices or GAAP require it
- Changes made by other regulatory bodies such as the Internal Revenue Service or Revenue Canada require it
- Changes in the insurer's structure, goals, or procedures make the old accounting policies ineffective
- Changes in the business environment make the old accounting policies obsolete
- The insurer discovers that using different accounting policies and methods will more accurately and fairly present the information in its financial statements

Under GAAP, a company must fully disclose the impact of any change in accounting policies in the financial statements for the affected accounting periods. Interested parties can then consider the impact of these changes in their financial analysis of the company. Accounting changes that a company should explain in a note to the financial statements include

- Any and all changes in accounting policies or principles (for example, a change in the method used to value invested assets)
- Changes that affect the specific entity being reported (for example, a change to the consolidated financial statements of a parent company instead of individual financial statements for the parent company and each subsidiary)

Figure 4-3 is an excerpt from a hypothetical U.S. insurer's notes to the financial statements regarding changes in accounting policies.

Figure 4-3. Summary of significant accounting policies.

Accounting Pronouncements Adopted in 199X:

The accompanying consolidated financial statements have been prepared in conformity with generally accepted accounting principles (GAAP), which vary in certain respects from reporting practices prescribed or permitted by the Insurance Department of State A, and include the following significant accounting policies:

Deferred Policy Acquisition Costs: The costs of acquiring most new individual life business are deferred and amortized with interest over the premium-paying period of the related policies. For traditional life policies, such amounts are amortized in proportion to the ratio of the annual premium income to the total anticipated premium income. Such anticipated premium income is estimated using the same assumptions. . . .

Investments: Fixed maturities held for investment are stated at amortized cost. Fixed maturities available for sale are stated at fair value in 199X and at the lower of the aggregate cost or market in 199X. The cost of securities sold is determined by . . .

Income Taxes: The Company and XYZ Brokerage Services, Inc., filed a consolidated federal income tax return. ABC Marketing Resources, Inc., filed a separate federal income tax return. . . .

Earnings per Share: Earnings per share of common stock are based on the weighted average number of common shares outstanding. The effect of unexercised stock options is not significant. . . .

The effect of an accounting change can be documented on a

- *Retroactive basis* (for example, an adjustment to correct a material error in a previous accounting period)
- *Current basis* (for example, an adjustment to the previous year's net income to determine the current year's net income)
- *Prospective basis* (for example, spreading the effects on income over the current and future accounting periods)

Mathematical errors or incorrect account classifications do not qualify as accounting changes. Therefore, a company treats an adjustment made on a retroactive basis to disclose the effects of an accounting change separately from an adjustment made to correct Retained Earnings because of an accounting error. Because accounting changes affect a company's financial statements, an independent auditor must note in its opinion whether the company has consistently applied the same accounting policies and procedures over time. The auditor must also comment on the validity of the accounting change.

Comparability

Comparability means that a company's financial statements enable an interested party to identify similarities and differences in financial information across accounting periods and among different companies.

For this reason, U.S. GAAP requires that every annual report must include five years of historical data and comparative financial statements for three accounting periods (two accounting periods for balance sheets). Similarly, Canadian GAAP requires comparative financial statements for two accounting periods for the statement of operations and for the balance sheet in the annual report. Also, the provincial securities commissions require five years of comparative financial information for publicly traded companies. To encourage comparability, accounting principles also define and specify the basic format of standard financial statements. Comparability and consistency are interrelated because they both require a company to use the same accounting policies and procedures from one accounting period to the next, unless there is a valid reason to make a change. As with consistency, comparability requires a company to disclose the nature and impact of any changes to its accounting policies or procedures.

The effectiveness of comparability also depends on the use of uniform accounting principles and concepts among different companies. Although publicly traded insurance companies, mutual and fraternal insurers, and non-insurance companies may follow GAAP, they may not necessarily apply the same acceptable methods of valuing assets and liabilities, recognizing revenues and expenses, and calculating net income. Unfortunately, diversity in the use of GAAP and statutory accounting can reduce the effectiveness of comparing financial statements between two different companies. In the United States, state laws and regulations govern the implementation of statutory accounting, with which all insurers comply. Although most states have adopted the NAIC model laws and accounting regulations, many states have variations of the definition or calculation of a particular account value, and these variations can affect comparability. Since 1992, mutual insurers in Canada have complied with Canadian GAAP in preparing the Annual Return, so there are fewer comparability problems between the financial statements of Canadian stock insurers and mutual insurers. Insight 4-1 discusses accounting standards among different countries and the need for international accounting standards.

Materiality

The accounting concept of ***materiality*** requires that companies disclose all significant information in their financial statements. Significant or *material* information is information that, if a company omitted it or presented it in a misleading manner, could substantially affect an interested user's opinion of the company. Materiality has two related aspects. First, materiality requires a company to include in its financial statements all significant accounting information. This aspect relates to the concept of *full disclosure,* which

Insight 4-1 Bean Counters, Unite!

Not so many years ago, enthusiasts for international accounting standards seemed doomed to eternal frustration. Differences in the ways in which companies in different countries presented their financial results appeared so profound that no amount of compromise would result in meaningful international standards. Suddenly these differences appear smaller.

Helped by globalisation of capital markets, the International Accounting Standards Committee (IASC) has won wide support for its efforts to harmonise accounting rules. If it can clear a few remaining hurdles, the IASC should be able to produce a workable framework by the end of the decade. The greater ease with which companies' disclosures could then be compared would benefit investors and issuers alike.

The IASC's task will not be easy, however. Political arguments about obscure accounting rules are surprisingly passionate. The most palpable tensions have been between America and Germany, two countries that epitomise very different approaches to financial reporting. America, led by its Securities and Exchange Commission (SEC) and Financial Accounting Standards Board (FASB), believes that the guiding principle should be for companies to give a "true and fair" view to shareholders. Germany, in contrast, prefers that companies exercise "prudence" on behalf of stakeholders—which, in practice, thanks to Germany's weak equity culture, means on behalf of creditors and employees rather than shareholders. German accounts are largely driven by tax considerations.

All this came to a head in 1993 when Daimler-Benz, a top German car maker, broke ranks with other big German companies that were thinking of listing in America, and accepted some American accounting rules as a requirement for listing its shares. The American authorities took the view that the other German firms were trying to wriggle out of proper disclosure; the Germans accused the FASB and the SEC of trying needlessly to foist American standards on respectable international companies. The bitter quarrel suggested that accounting differences were too rooted in national corporate cultures to be overcome.

This impression was, however, misleading. For one thing, after nearly two decades of well-intentioned muddle, the IASC had begun to be more effective towards the end of the 1980s. A project to promote international harmonisation was beginning to yield tighter and more coherent standards.

At the same time, the continuing globalisation of capital markets has given firms a powerful incentive to abandon their resistance to change. Unless they can present their results in ways that foreign investors understand, companies may be unable to tap new sources of capital. They could, like Daimler-Benz, adopt the standards of the foreign market. But it would be much more convenient to agree on a single set of international rules that could be incorporated into, or sit alongside, the local ones. The greater the degree of incorporation, the closer firms would be to a single set of global accounts.

Momentum in this direction has never been so strong. The IASC has never been so strong. The IASC has been working closely with the International Organisation of Securities Commissions (IOSCO), a club of securities-market regulators which includes America's SEC, in an effort to ensure that its standards are accepted by financial markets. When IOSCO holds its annual get-together next month, it is expected to announce a three-year programme with the IASC, to push standard-making along.

The two bodies' efforts have already yielded fruit. In April 1994 the SEC allowed foreign companies that wish to raise capital in America to use an international standard on cash-flow statements. Recently, two further international standards were given the nod. More approvals are expected. "Our desire is for high-quality standards," says Linda Quinn, head of the SEC's corporate-finance division. "That does not mean that they have to be identical with existing American standards."

Softening

Compromise is in the air on the other side of the Atlantic too. Last year Bayer and Schering, two big German companies, adopted international standards for their 1994 accounts. Johannes Maret of Arthur Andersen, an accounting firm, thinks many more German firms will follow suit. Dozens of Swiss companies have already beaten them to it.

Perhaps most remarkably, German officialdom has recently indicated that it is prepared to make concessions. Last month Herbert Biener, a Justice Ministry official who represents Germany on an IOSCO accounting-standards working party, proposed that Germany should "tolerate" the use of international standards for consolidated accounts by companies seeking listings abroad. This would ease the reporting burden on Daimler-Benz and others that may choose to follow its lead. Instead of publishing

(continued)

Insight 4-1 Bean Counters, Unite!, continued

two sets of group accounts to satisfy both German and American authorities, such firms could publish a single, internationally accepted set.

Even so, plenty could still go wrong. One potential interferer is the European Commission. European accounting laws are badly out of date and interpreted inconsistently. Officials of Brussels resent European firms' drift towards American standards. Although they have given up the dream of a set of European standards, the commission is still responsible for seeing that IASC standards conform with European law.

The prospect of any meddling appals nearly everyone, particularly if it becomes, in effect, a further layer of standards. Sir Bryan Carsberg, the IASC's recently appointed secretary-general, and a former head of Britain's Office of Fair Trading, would prefer to strengthen the commission's involvement with the IASC. Mr. Biener is blunter. He describes the commission's interest as "superfluous."

A second danger comes from the slow pace of standard setting. The IASC must fill the remaining gaps in its armoury before it can claim to have a comprehensive set of standards. Sir Bryan accepts that the IASC is a "handful of years away from a complete set of standards." But he is optimistic that he can keep the body on course.

There are plenty of rocks on which it might founder. The body's attempt to introduce a comprehensive standard for the way firms should account for their use of hedging instruments such as derivatives was almost derailed last month by political infighting. As a result, America's FASB, which is expected to come out with such standards later this year, could beat Sir Bryan to it, thereby reopening tensions between the two camps. A proposed IASC standard on segment reporting (results by business or geography) will also highlight differences.

More generally, European firms remain suspicious about extending standards too far. They view American standards as excessively burdensome, pointing to over-zealous litigation as the cause of bloated and inflexible rulebooks. Europeans complain that in its recent tightening up of standards, the IASC has tilted too far towards America's rule-bound approach. The IASC will have to negotiate a fine line.

Still, for the moment, the winds are blowing in the IASC's favour. Next year the German government will start selling Deutsche Telekom, its telecoms monopoly, in a huge share offering that is bound to exceed the meager appetite of local investors. The firm and its myriad advisers are already negotiating with the SEC on how it must report if it is to obtain a listing in America. Both sides are keen for a deal, which would in turn set a powerful precedent for other companies wishing to tap the American market. A happy outcome should make the IASC's task a little easier.

Source: "Bean Counters, Unite!" *The Economist* (June 10, 1995), pp. 67–68.

we discuss later in this chapter. Second, materiality relieves a company from having to report all items as if each item carried the same financial significance. For example, under materiality, a company does not have to treat a pencil with the same significance as its automated accounting system. Both are assets, but the automated accounting system has greater materiality than a pencil.

Whether accounting information is material or not relies heavily on the judgment of a company's accountants and management. In practice, materiality may vary from company to company. What is material to one company may not be material to another. For example, a large life and health insurer may consider office supply purchases of less than $5,000 to be immaterial, whereas a much smaller insurer may establish a lower minimum requirement, perhaps $100, for materiality purposes. The subject of the information also helps determine its materiality. For example, an insurer may decide that a $2,000 difference in the way it calculates depreciation expense is immaterial, whereas a $2,000 difference in cash *is* material. Most companies establish an arbitrary percentage of net income or current assets below which the monetary amount is immaterial. A company may decide, for example, that only monetary amounts that are greater than 5 percent of the company's net income are material to its statement of operations and that a balance sheet item is material only if the amount is greater than 4 percent of short-term assets. The company would include items that are below either threshold, although it would not separately list them on its financial statements.

However, the combined effect of many individually immaterial items may produce an aggregate result that is material to the company's financial information. For this reason, the magnitude of a transaction or the dollar amount or percentage relationship to an account classification is only one clue as to the transaction's materiality. The effects that an item may have on a company's solvency and profitability can also determine its materiality. Ultimately, though, the rule for applying the concept of materiality is as follows: If the disclosure, the lack of disclosure, or the misrepresentation of an item of information could lead interested users to change their opinions about the company's financial strength or profitability, then the item is material in nature.

Conservatism

By its nature, accounting is conservative. This quality helps to offset the tendency of many businesses (and many people) to overstate their successes and understate their failures. The intent of accounting conservatism is to protect customers, investors, the general public, and the companies themselves from unforeseen occurrences and from problems that can arise from an imprudently optimistic point of view. The phrases "anticipate no profits and provide for all losses" and "list the lowest values for assets and the highest values for liabilities" illustrate accounting conservatism. According to the principle of conservatism, a company (1) records revenues only when they are certain, (2) records expenses when they are expected, not necessarily certain, (3) reports losses immediately, and (4) reports gains only after they actually occur. In precise accounting terminology, ***conservatism*** is the choice of a financial reporting method that results in the projection of lower values for a company's assets, higher values for its liabilities and expenses, and a lower level of net income than would be the case if a company used a more optimistic reporting method.

The definition of conservatism may differ in the fields of accounting. For example, a statutory balance sheet is generally more conservative than a GAAP-based balance sheet. On the other hand, a

GAAP-based statement of operations may sometimes be more conservative than one prepared on a statutory basis. So, which type of financial accounting is more conservative: statutory accounting or GAAP? The answer depends on the purpose and the actual financial statement under consideration. Generally, conservatism is more fundamental to statutory accounting than to GAAP because GAAP reporting is oriented toward potential investors. However, both types of financial accounting are conservative in nature.

In the life and health insurance industry, conservative accounting methods result in policy reserves and surplus that are adequate to protect an insurer's policyowners and beneficiaries from adverse financial conditions. For example, an insurer calculates its statutory policy reserve liabilities without regard to policy lapses or cash surrenders, thus assuming that all policies will remain in force until they mature. Conservatism also determines the assumptions an insurer makes concerning mortality and morbidity rates, policy expenses, and interest rates on investment earnings. Under conservatism, an insurer's actuaries tend to project higher mortality and morbidity rates and policy expenses, but lower expected investment earnings for life and health insurance policy reserves. For annuity products, the insurer's actuaries generally project *lower* mortality rates because of the effects of adverse selection associated with purchases of annuity contracts.

Insurers, however, must keep accounting conservatism in perspective, because when misapplied, conservatism can lead to inaccurate or misrepresented financial statements. For example, an overly conservative stance in one accounting period can result in skewed financial information in the next accounting period. Assume that a company owns a building and places an excessively low or conservative value on the building. For each subsequent accounting period, the company's net income will be overstated because the depreciation expense for the building the company will deduct from revenues will be unrealistically low. (We discuss *depreciation* later in this chapter.)

Because of the possibility of bias, conservatism must remain secondary to the qualitative characteristics of reliability, consistency, and materiality. A company should apply accounting conservatism to its financial statements only if such conservatism does not violate more important financial reporting concepts. Figure 4-4 summarizes the qualitative characteristics of accounting information.

Principles for Maintaining Accounts

To ensure that a company maintains its accounts according to the qualitative characteristics just discussed, the accounting profession

Figure 4-4. Accounting information qualities.

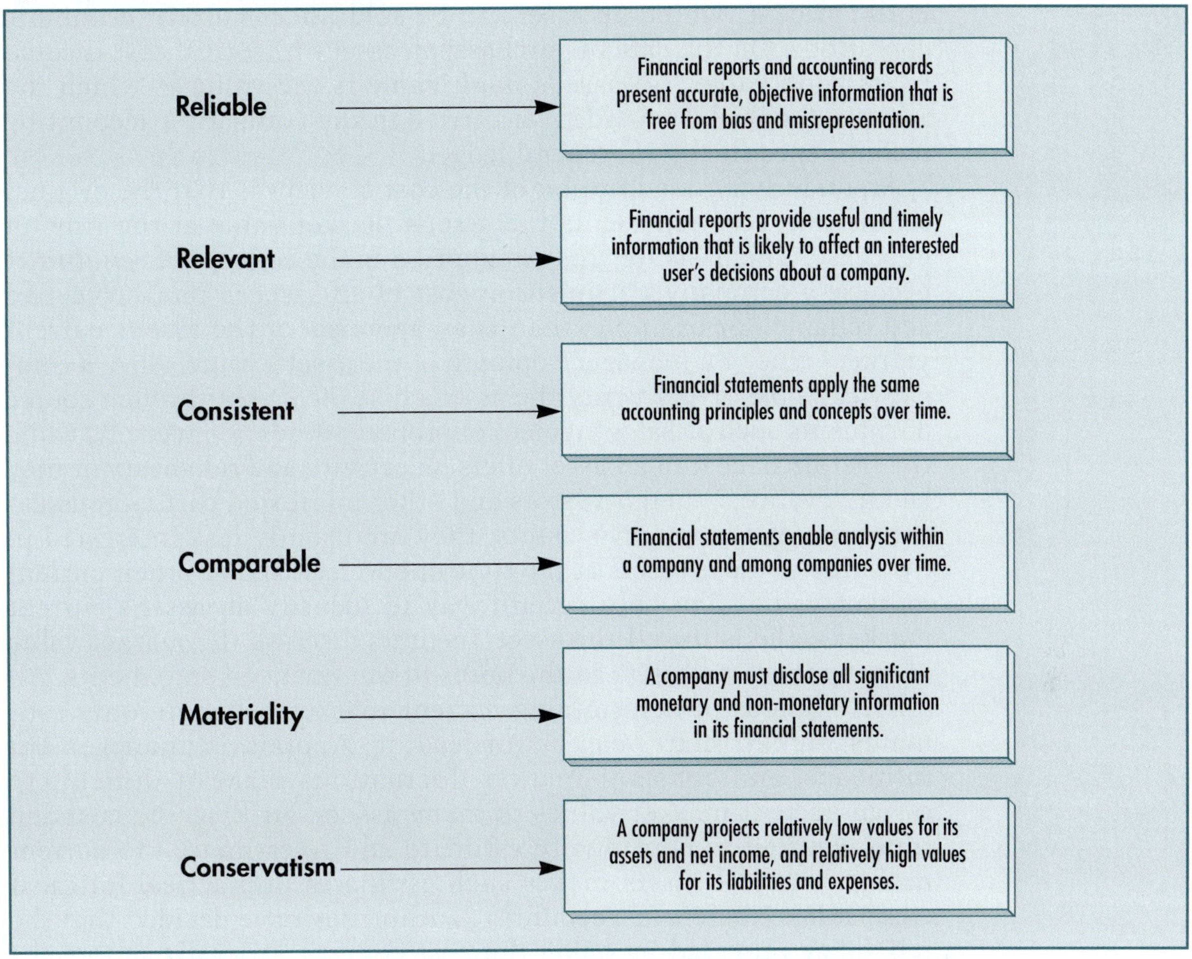

has developed specified concepts, principles, and guidelines that all companies should follow. Among these ideas are the cost concept, the measuring-unit concept, the full-disclosure concept, the time-period concept, the realization principle, the matching principle, and the various accounting bases. We discuss each of these in the following sections.

Cost Concept

An extension of the going-concern concept is the ***cost concept,*** also called the *historical-cost concept, initial-recording concept,* or the *acquisition-cost concept.* The cost concept states that companies should post items on the balance sheet and the statement of operations according to their actual cost at the time of purchase. For example, a company will record the actual amount paid for an asset, its ***historical cost,*** not the asset's current market value. The ***current***

market value, also called *fair market value* or simply *market value,* is the price at which an asset can be sold under current economic conditions. On the date of purchase, an asset's historical cost is equal to its book value. An asset's ***book value*** is the value at which the asset is "booked," recorded, or carried in the company's accounting records, specifically its general ledger.

An underlying assumption of the cost concept is that the original acquisition cost represents the asset's market value at the time of purchase. The basis for this assumption is the concept of *reliability,* because a company's acquisition cost of an asset is more objective and reliable, for example, than is an appraisal of the asset's current market value or a manager's opinion of the asset's value. Also, a company can objectively verify the asset's historical cost through source documents such as sales invoices or property deeds. Conversely, while the historical cost of an asset offers objectivity and reliability, it may lack relevance. When investors and other interested parties consider the value of a company's assets, they are usually less interested in the value of those assets at the time of purchase than in their current market value. The only certain way to identify an asset's current market value is to sell the asset. Insurers disclose the market value of many invested assets in the notes to the financial statements. All other methods of determining current market value are only estimates, and estimates can be misleading. Appraisals, management influence, and constant market fluctuations make it difficult to assign current market values to many assets. Further, the cost and time required to continually estimate and re-estimate the current market value of assets makes such estimates impractical for most companies. Therefore, accounting authorities have decided that the reliability provided by using the cost concept generally outweighs the loss of relevance it may cause.

Measuring-Unit Concept

The ***measuring-unit concept,*** also called the *stable-monetary-unit concept,* the *unit-of-measurement concept,* or the *stable-dollar concept,* states that a company should record the amounts associated with its business transactions in monetary terms, such as U.S. or Canadian dollars. There are two assumptions regarding the measuring-unit concept: (1) that the appropriate unit of measure for business transactions is money and (2) that the measuring unit's value is stable over time. Recall that a company includes in its financial statements only those transactions that it can represent in monetary terms. In the United States and Canada, companies report virtually all account classifications in dollar amounts. Some exceptions occur on financial statements. For example, the number of outstanding shares of a company's common stock is not a dollar amount. Similarly, verbal descriptions of a company's accounts as well as supplementary information and notes to the financial statements provide valuable accounting information that is not given solely in dollar amounts. Ultimately, though, the bulk of accounting information consists of monetary values.

The measuring-unit concept has two major limitations. First, significant items or facts that do not have a precise, measurable monetary value are not quantified or included in a company's financial statements. These items include, for example, the company's effectiveness in providing customer service, the morale of the company's employees, the company's intellectual capital, and the condition of the company's property, plant, and equipment. These factors, while significant, are not easily measurable in monetary terms. Second, unlike other measuring units, money is not stable over time. From one year to the next, for example, an acre of land includes the same amount of land. However, the value of a dollar changes over time. The amount of food that a dollar will buy this year may not be the same amount it will buy next year. Therefore, if the purchasing power of a measuring unit changes significantly, then the measuring-unit concept can limit our ability to analyze and compare a company's financial statements over time.

Suppose a company purchases a piece of real estate for $50,000. Ten years later, it sells the real estate for $100,000. The company then reports a $50,000 *capital gain* (the excess of sale price over purchase price) on the sale of the real estate. However, if the purchasing power of the dollar has declined by half during the 10-year period, the company is no better off in terms of purchasing power than it was 10 years before. That is, because $50,000 10 years ago could buy the same amount as $100,000 today, the company has made no real "gain" in purchasing power because of the changing value of the dollar, which is the measuring unit.

Despite these limitations, accounting authorities still consider the measuring-unit concept to be a valuable tool. Like the cost concept, the measuring-unit concept provides objectivity and reliability, even though its relevance may fluctuate as the value of the measuring unit itself fluctuates. Accounting authorities prefer that companies avoid the subjectivity involved in continually estimating the changing value of a measuring unit. They do, however, recognize that when significant changes occur in a measuring unit's value, users of accounting information should become aware of the fact. For example, during periods of high *inflation,* which is a general increase in the price level, the FASB has required U.S. companies to disclose in their annual reports the potential impact that high inflation has on the values listed in the financial statements.

Full-Disclosure Concept

The ***full-disclosure concept,*** also called the *adequate-disclosure concept,* states that financial statements must contain all material information about a company and that the company must disclose any additional information or fact that, by its omission, could mislead an interested user of the accounting information. The full disclosure concept implies the inclusion of every item that is *material, relevant, reliable,* and *comparable,* as well as *understandable,* to provide to an interested user a fair presentation of a company's financial statements. This concept points to the critical role of notes, schedules, and supplementary information that accompany financial statements. The full-disclosure concept does not require the inclusion of excessive details, however. For example, an independent financial analyst is no better informed about a company's financial strength if the company clutters its balance sheet with detailed descriptions of every government security that the company owns. In this case, summary information is more useful.

Typical disclosures are notes and supplementary information regarding the nature and substance of contingent liabilities, commitments, potential losses, and the accounting methods and policies used in preparing financial statements. Beyond these points, other information requiring disclosure is open to professional judgment. Decisions rendered in recent U.S. court cases have broadened the definition of the types of information that need disclosure, so company management has tended to disclose supplementary information as a matter of course. The SEC, the FASB, the *CICA Handbook,* and other sources of accounting standards have also reinforced the importance of fair, accurate, and complete financial statements.

Time-Period Concept

The ***time-period concept,*** also called the *concept of periodicity,* states that a company's financial statements should report the company's business operations during a specified time period. This time period, called an ***accounting period,*** is a specified length of time during which a company's business transactions are recorded, summarized, and reported. Typical accounting periods are one month, one quarter, and one year. Any specific accounting period is in itself arbitrary, given the assumed indefinite life associated with the *going-concern concept.* However, the alternative to artificially imposed accounting periods is to postpone a company's financial statements until the end of the company's life, when all debts are paid and all investor claims are settled. Because many individuals need financial information during the life of the company, the time-period concept has evolved. The time-period concept assumes that a company can identify an accounting period, reach a suitable cut-off date, and provide summary financial information as of that date. All companies must file certain financial statements at the end of each one-year period. Most companies also produce financial statements or reports more frequently. These statements, such as monthly budgets and quarterly statements, are known as *interim financial statements* or *interim reports* to distinguish them from annual accounting period statements and reports.

Nearly two-thirds of all companies use the *calendar year*—that is, from January through December—as a standard accounting period. Most insurers select an accounting period based on the calendar year because this is the accounting period required for tax reporting and Annual Statement purposes. Other companies choose to operate on a *fiscal-year basis.* A ***fiscal year*** is simply a 12-month accounting period chosen by a company. A fiscal year may or may not coincide with the calendar year. North American retailers, for example, often choose to end their fiscal year on January 31 or February 28 in order to avoid having to compile financial statements during the busy holiday season in November and December. Thus, a retailer's fiscal year may run from February through January or from March through February. Many other companies also close their accounting year during a slow period in their natural business cycle. In such cases, a company's fiscal year is known as its *natural business year.* In the United States and Canada, though, insurance companies typically use a December 31 year-end for financial reporting purposes.

The drawback to the time-period concept is that a company does not complete all of its transactions within one accounting period. A company continues doing business and making transactions without regard to the artificial constraints of periodicity. Because not all transactions are easily identified with a single accounting period, a company's management must ask the question, "When should we record each revenue and each expense?" To help companies answer this question, accountants have developed two principles, the *realization principle* and the *matching principle,* to match revenues and expenses to each other and to the appropriate accounting period.

Recognition of Revenues and Expenses

The process of determining the amount of a company's net income for financial reporting purposes entails both *revenue recognition* and *expense recognition.* In accounting terminology, ***recognition*** refers to the process of classifying an item in a financial statement as an asset, liability, owners' equity, revenue, or expense. Generally, a company recognizes revenue when a product is sold, when a service is completed or when cash changes hand as part of a business transaction. In order for an item to be *recognized,* the item must be

- One of the *accounting elements,* which include the account classifications for assets, liabilities, owners' equity, revenues, and expenses

- *Measurable,* which means that the item is quantifiable in some manner

- *Relevant,* which means that the information is useful, timely, and may affect the decisions of interested parties

- *Reliable,* which means that the information provided represents the company's transactions in an objective and fair manner, and that the information is generally free from error and bias

Although revenue recognition (the *realization principle*) and expense recognition (the *matching principle*) are interrelated, we describe them separately. However, before we go any further into a discussion of revenue and expense recognition, we need to discuss some of the intricacies of two terms that we use here frequently and throughout the rest of the book: *costs* and *expenses.*

A ***cost*** is the amount of a company's resources (assets) consumed or used for any purpose. As we discuss in the next few pages, a cost may be classified either as an expense or an asset. If a cost represents resources that are consumed during the current accounting period, then the cost is considered an expense. Recall that an expense is a reduction in a company's assets that applies to the current accounting period. As a very simple example, if you buy office supplies today and use them all today, the cost of the supplies is an expense. Because expenses represent resources consumed during the current period, they are sometimes referred to as *expired costs.* Employee salaries, office rent, and agent commissions are all expenses because they are costs paid in exchange for resources consumed during the current accounting period. If, however, a cost represents a resource that can provide benefits for future periods, then that cost may be considered an asset. Suppose a company buys a computer system that the company assumes will provide it with benefits for the next five years. Because the cost of the computer system will provide benefits in future accounting periods, this cost is considered an asset. In this case, depreciation is the expense that is spread out over the useful life of the company's computer system. Now, let's continue with the discussion of revenue recognition.

Revenue Recognition and the Realization Principle

An insurer does not necessarily receive all of its revenues in the same accounting period in which it earns them. As a result, the insurer follows certain guidelines to match the revenue with its proper accounting period, that is, the period in which the company has earned the revenue. Under GAAP, the ***realization principle,*** also known as the *revenue principle* or *revenue recognition principle,* states that a company should recognize revenue when it is earned. Generally, revenue is earned at the time a service is rendered or when a good passes from the legal ownership of a company to the legal ownership of the customer. For example, a clothing store earns revenue when it sells a sweater, an auto repair shop earns revenue when it repairs a car, and a life insurance company earns revenue when it provides insurance coverage. The realization principle requires a company to recognize revenues during the accounting period in which they have been earned, regardless of when cash changes hands. If the company does not receive immediate payment in cash, a legal and reasonable expectation should exist that the client or customer will remit payment in full.

In accounting for life and health insurance, revenue recognition applies primarily to the receipt of premiums. Under both GAAP and statutory accounting, insurers recognize insurance premiums as they are earned over the premium-paying period of the policy. For example, assume that the Big Corporation signs a contract with the Friendly Life and Health Insurance Company for a group life insurance policy that will provide coverage to Big's employees from January 1, 1999, to December 31, 1999. The annual premiums for this policy are $36,000, payable in quarterly installments of $9,000. Big decides to pre-pay the entire $36,000 on January 1. On March 31, 1999, Friendly will have *earned* premium income for only one quarter, even though it will have received payment for four quarters. Although the company expects it will eventually earn the entire annual premium income, it has not yet provided the necessary coverage. Therefore, on its March 31 financial statements, Friendly recognizes only the first $9,000 of premium revenues. Figure 4-5 shows the amount of premium income that Friendly recognizes each quarter from its contract with the Big Corporation.

Figure 4-5. Quarterly revenue recognition: The Friendly Life and Health Insurance Company.

Statement of Operations	Revenue Recognition	Amount
For the quarter ended March 31, 1999	Revenue for Jan. 1 – March 31	$ 9,000
For the quarter ended June 30, 1999	Revenue for April 1 – June 30	9,000
For the quarter ended September 30, 1999	Revenue for July 1 – Sept. 30	9,000
For the quarter ended December 31, 1999	Revenue for Oct. 1 – Dec. 31	9,000
	Total	$36,000

Expense Recognition and the Matching Principle

While the realization principle governs the recognition of revenues, the matching principle governs the recognition of expenses. The ***matching principle*** states that a company should recognize expenses when the company earns the revenues related to those expenses, regardless of when the company receives cash for the revenues earned.

The company also matches losses with revenues during the appropriate accounting period. The realization and matching principles work in tandem. First, a company reports revenues according to the *realization principle.* Next, the company identifies, quantifies, and matches the expenses required to earn those revenues. Then the company records the expenses according to the matching principle. The match between revenues and related expenses does not mean that the amounts for revenues and expenses must be equal, nor is *matching* the same as balancing an accounting entry. For example, a company may match Agent Commissions (an expense account) of $100 with Premium Income (a revenue account) of $200, even though there is no specific journal entry to note this specific match. By following the guidelines set forth in the matching principle, a company can prepare its statement of operations with an accurate net income or net loss amount for the accounting period. Under GAAP, three approaches to expense recognition are generally allowed: (1) associating cause and effect, (2) systematic and rational allocation, and (3) immediate recognition.

Associating Cause and Effect. Some costs have a direct association with specific revenues. This direct relationship is known in accounting as ***associating cause and effect.*** Using this approach, costs that can be recognized as having a direct relationship to certain future earnings or specific elements of revenue are charged to earnings of future accounting periods instead of being charged to the current accounting period.

For example, Agent Commissions is a typical expense account in most life and health insurance companies. The commissions that insurers pay to their agents are often called ***policy acquisition costs,*** which are *directly* attributable to the production of new business. Under GAAP, a company recognizes an expense during the same accounting period in which the company recognizes the revenue arising from that expense. Thus, an insurer typically matches the expenses for an agent's commissions against the premium income from the new business that the agent writes. For example, an insurer typically pays the largest portion of an agent's commission when a policy is sold. On the other hand, premium income from that policy is often spread evenly over many accounting periods. Typically, U.S. GAAP calls for the insurer to spread the recognition of its commission expenses over the same period in which it receives the premium income generated by those commission expenses. This process of deferring the recognition of expenses until future accounting periods is known as ***capitalization.*** Statutory accounting and Canadian GAAP do not allow insurers to capitalize policy acquisition costs, so insurers recognize all incurred expenses in the current accounting period. In Chapter 8, we discuss how U.S. GAAP enables insurers to defer policy acquisition costs.

To further illustrate the association of cause and effect, assume that a company incurs $1,000,000 in policy acquisition costs in one year. The company's experience indicates that most of the business put on the books will continue in force for years into the future. If the company follows statutory accounting or Canadian GAAP, the entire $1,000,000 is recorded as an expense for the year, thereby recognizing all incurred expenses in the current accounting period, because the funds that have been spent are no longer available to pay future policy benefits. In contrast, under U.S. GAAP, the company records as an expense during the current period only a small part of the $1,000,000, capitalizes the remainder of the cost as an asset (typically Deferred Policy Acquisition Costs), and turns this asset into an expense over future accounting periods. The company calculates the amount to treat as an expense each year according to the relationship of current year's premium income to estimated future years' premium income.

Systematic and Rational Allocation. Sometimes a direct association of cause and effect between expenses and revenues is not clearly recognizable or measurable. In such cases, a company uses another method to match revenues and expenses. This method, known as ***systematic and rational allocation,*** expenses an asset's cost over its estimated useful life, regardless of when the company realizes revenues from using the asset. One example of such systematic allocation is asset depreciation. ***Depreciation*** is the process of spreading (allocating) the cost of an asset over the asset's estimated useful life. As with the method of associating cause and effect, a company capitalizes costs under systematic and rational allocation. Assume that a company spends $1,000,000 one year to buy and install a new computer system. Management cannot know for certain how long the system will provide financial benefits or what its financial benefits will be. Without a recognizable and measurable association between cause and effect, management uses the expense recognition approach to capitalize the cost in the present accounting period, recognize the cost as an asset, and begin systematic and rational allocation. If the company estimates that the useful life of the system is eight years, anticipates no salvage value for the system, and uses the *straight-line method of depreciation,* then the company records $125,000 ($1,000,000 ÷ 8) as a full year's expense during each year of the system's estimated life. After eight years, the company will have expensed (allocated) the entire $1,000,000.

Immediate Recognition. Sometimes a company cannot match expenses incurred during an accounting period with revenues earned for that period, nor can it match the expenses with revenues it expects to generate in the future. Under GAAP, sometimes expenses cannot be matched with revenues, and incurred costs provide no objectively recognizable future benefits. Neither associating cause and effect nor systematic and rational allocation is an applicable approach for expense recognition. In such cases, the company uses the immediate recognition approach.

Under ***immediate recognition,*** a company recognizes all costs as expenses during the current accounting period. Immediate expense recognition is common under statutory reporting requirements. The fees that a company pays to lawyers and consultants are typically reported as expenses under the immediate recognition approach under both GAAP and statutory accounting. Similarly, a company recognizes training costs as current period expenses. Expenditures such as training costs certainly provide future revenues for a company, but their potential effect cannot be measured in a quantifiable, objective manner. Thus, the company treats training costs as an expense in the current accounting period. Some expenses, such as employee salaries and utility bills, cannot be attributed to one particular type of revenue earned. In such cases, a company reports these expenses in the accounting period in which they occur, whether or not the company can match these costs directly with revenues earned.

A company can change its approach for recognizing expenses if the nature of a cost changes over time. For example, suppose an insurer capitalizes the cost of computer equipment. The company recognizes the cost associated with the equipment over several accounting periods. But before the end of its estimated useful life (and before its total cost has been recognized and expensed), the equipment becomes obsolete and is discarded. At this point, the company can use the immediate recognition approach to recognize the remainder of the cost as an expense and write this amount off as a lump sum in the current accounting period.

Figure 4-6 summarizes the principles, concepts, and guidelines that all companies should follow for maintaining accounts.

Accounting Basis

The realization principle and the matching principle are both central concepts for a manner of accounting called *accrual-basis accounting.*

Figure 4-6. Principles for maintaining accounts.

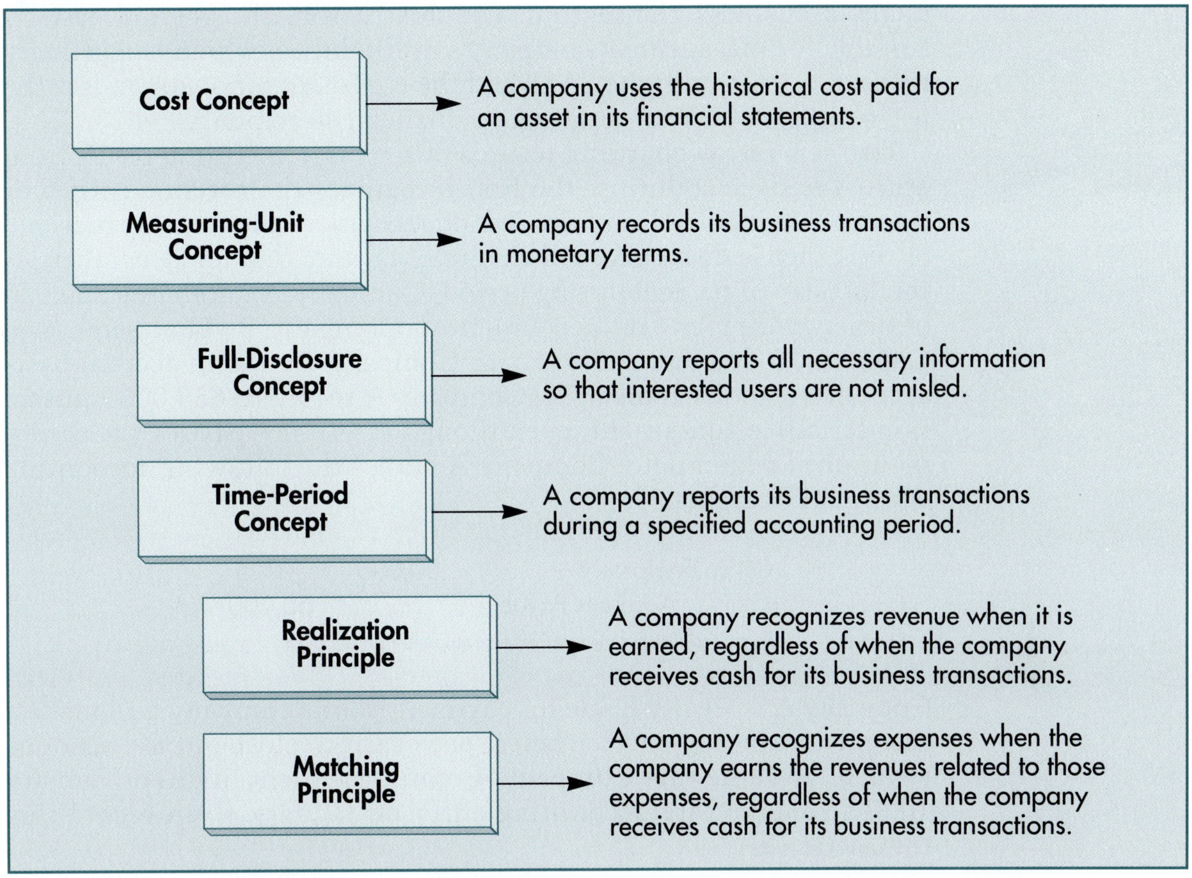

Both GAAP and statutory accounting require companies to record their financial transactions on an accrual basis. A few companies, such as sole proprietorships, may use *cash-basis accounting* to record transactions. In addition, insurance companies must report some items on a cash basis for statutory reporting purposes. In the remainder of this chapter, we discuss accrual-basis accounting and cash-basis accounting.

Accrual-Basis Accounting

Under ***accrual-basis accounting,*** a company records revenues when they are earned and expenses when they are incurred, even if cash has not actually changed hands. Accrual-basis accounting records revenue according to the *realization principle* and expenses according to the *matching principle.* The purpose of the accrual basis of accounting is to record a transaction when the company incurs a financial obligation either as the payer or payee. Thus, accrual-basis accounting enables an interested party to view the consequences of obligations incurred by a company whether or not the company ultimately completes a business transaction. For this reason, the accrual basis is suitable for measuring a company's profitability, which is a primary focus of GAAP. Both the FASB and the *CICA Handbook* mandate the use of accrual-basis accounting in financial statements.

Two separate accounting records of a transaction often result from accrual-basis accounting: the first recognizes the revenue earned or the expense incurred, and the second recognizes the revenue received or the expense disbursed. For example, assume that on December 31, the last day of its accounting period, Company A purchases $50,000 of office equipment on account from Company B. That same day, Company B delivers the order to Company A. Using accrual-basis accounting, on December 31, Company A records a $50,000 transaction for office equipment, even though it will not pay for the equipment until a later date. Company A makes the following accounting entry on December 31:

Office Equipment	50,000	
Accounts Payable		50,000

To record the purchase of office equipment on account.

Company A is legally liable for payment, so the company will make a second accounting entry when it pays cash to close out the account payable. Assume that Company A remits payment in full on January 10. The appropriate accounting entry on January 10 to record this transaction is

Accounts Payable	50,000	
Cash		50,000

To record payment in full for office equipment.

Accrual-basis accounting provides information on the consequences of transactions, including a company's earnings potential and financial performance. Companies that use accrual-basis accounting must make adjusting entries to their accounting records at the end of each accounting year to match revenues and expenses in their financial statements for that accounting period.

Cash-Basis Accounting

Cash-basis accounting is a system in which a company recognizes revenues or expenses only when it receives or disburses cash. Thus, neither the realization principle nor the matching principle applies under cash-basis accounting. Instead, cash receipts and cash disbursements are two of the most important components of cash-basis accounting. A ***cash receipt*** is a check, money order, electronic funds transfer (EFT), or other cash transaction that is remitted to a company as some form of payment. A company records a cash receipt in the same accounting period in which it receives the cash. A ***cash disbursement*** is the payment of cash by a company to a recipient such as a policy beneficiary. Under cash-basis accounting, a company records a cash disbursement in the same accounting period in which it remits payment. In a pure cash-basis system, a company makes no entries to record unpaid bills or pending income. Also, the company calculates net income by subtracting paid expenses from revenues received. For example, if Company A from our earlier example uses cash-basis accounting rather than accrual-basis accounting, no accounting entry would be made for the receipt of the equipment on December 31. Instead, Company A makes only one accounting entry, when it disburses the $50,000 cash on January 10:

Office Equipment	50,000	
Cash		50,000

To record the payment in full for office equipment.

Figure 4-7 compares the accounting entries for January 10 under cash-basis accounting with those for December 31 and January 10 under accrual-basis accounting.

Accrual-basis accounting helps to match expenses with revenues, a process that typically enables companies to develop more relevant, reliable, and comparable financial statements. Because cash-basis

Figure 4-7. Cash-basis and accrual-basis accounting entries.

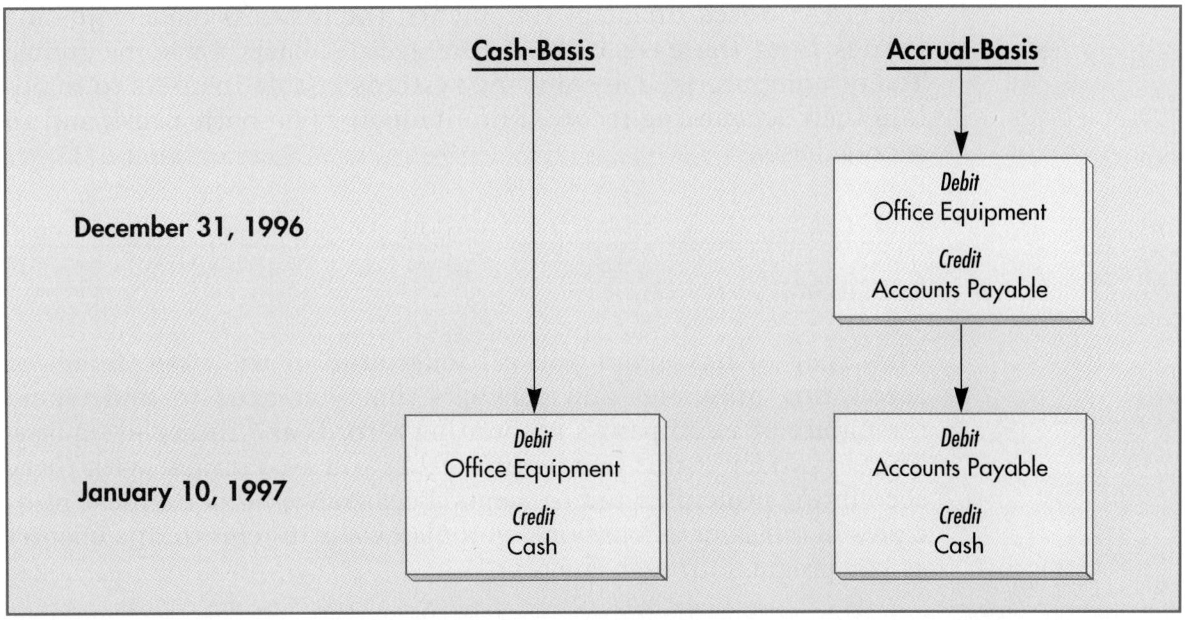

accounting does not apply the realization principle or the matching principle, misleading financial statements can result. For example, under a cash-basis system, Company A's December 31 balance sheet would not show that the balance of the Office Equipment account has increased by $50,000, nor that the company owes $50,000 for the new equipment. This information could be critical for a potential investor in Company A. For this reason, few companies use a pure cash-basis accounting system. Further, under GAAP, financial statements must report the results of *noncash* transactions, such as depreciation, as well as cash transactions that occur during an accounting period.

Most cash-basis accounting is actually a combination of cash-basis and accrual-basis accounting, known as ***modified cash-basis accounting.*** The nature of life and health insurance lends itself to modified cash-basis accounting. That is, for a policyowner's insurance coverage to remain in force, the policyowner must pay the premium. However, because an insurance policy is a unilateral contract, the policyowner has no legal obligation to pay the premium. Therefore, insurers have no legal assurance that they will receive premium income until it is actually remitted by the policyowner. As a result, an insurer may record premium income for some policies only when money is received. On the other hand, investment income is legally collectible and earned by the due date. An insurer therefore typically recognizes investment income when it comes due rather than waiting until the income is received.

In the past, insurance companies in the United States accounted for transactions under both statutory and GAAP by using cash-basis accounting for most initial accounting. Then, to prepare statutory and GAAP-based financial statements, the insurers made adjusting entries from the cash basis to the accrual basis for some items. Today, computerized accounting systems enable insurers to maintain their accounting records simultaneously on both a cash and an accrual basis.

Conclusion

This chapter has given you a background of the basic financial accounting principles and concepts that you need to understand the nature of a company's accounting records and financial reports. The remainder of this text assumes that you are familiar with these accounting principles and concepts. Because we build on these principles in our later discussions, you may want to refer to this chapter as you progress through the text.

Key Terms and Concepts

predictive quality
entity
entity concept
going-concern concept
liquidation
reliability
relevance
consistency
comparability
materiality
conservatism
cost concept
historical cost
current market value
book value
measuring-unit concept
full-disclosure concept
time-period concept
accounting period
fiscal year
recognition
cost
realization principle
matching principle
associating cause and effect
policy acquisition costs
capitalization
systematic and rational allocation
depreciation
immediate recognition
accrual-basis accounting
cash-basis accounting
cash receipt
cash disbursement
modified cash-basis accounting

CHAPTER 5

THE ANNUAL REPORT

LEARNING OBJECTIVES

After studying this chapter, you should be able to

- List the major components of an insurer's annual report to stockholders or policyowners
- Distinguish between the static measures and dynamic measures used to develop financial statements
- Describe the components and purposes of the statement of cash flows
- Describe the components and purposes of the statement of owners' equity
- Explain the importance of notes and supplementary information
- Provide an example of the relationships among the various financial statements

CHAPTER OUTLINE

The Annual Report

Letter to Stockholders and Financial Highlights

Financial Statements

Balance Sheet

Statement of Operations

Statement of Cash Flows

Statement of Owners' Equity

Summary of Financial Statements

Notes and Supplementary Information

Auditor's Report

Financial Statement Integration

Accounting provides a company with a structured way to maintain accurate, timely, and complete financial information about its business transactions. Accounting also provides the company with the information it needs to make sound business decisions and to satisfy financial reporting requirements. Managers use a company's financial statements to identify general business trends so that they can develop appropriate strategies for improving performance in problem areas. Similarly, by studying a company's financial statements, investors and regulators learn about its financial activities. They gain insight into its financial soundness and its profitability. As a result, they are better able to make informed decisions about the company's financial prospects.

In this chapter and the next, we introduce you to the primary financial statements and reports used to communicate accounting information to external users. General-purpose financial statements prepared according to generally accepted accounting principles (GAAP) comprise an insurer's *annual report.* Financial statements prepared in conformity with statutory accounting practices comprise an insurer's *Annual Statement.* This chapter focuses on GAAP and the annual report. Chapter 6 describes the Annual Statement.

The Annual Report

As noted in Chapter 3, an *annual report* is the yearly report that a company's management sends to its stockholders, policyowners, and other interested parties to describe the company's performance during the previous year. All publicly owned companies, including stock insurers, must provide an annual report to stockholders and must prepare the financial statements according to generally accepted accounting principles (GAAP). Mutual insurers may voluntarily provide an annual report to policyowners and the public. However, the Financial Accounting Standards Board (FASB) requires mutuals to prepare financial statements according to GAAP in order to receive an *unqualified,* or favorable, opinion from an independent auditor of the annual report. The SEC has recently decided to let stand the current language in the auditor's report that enables mutual and fraternal insurers to include statutory financial statements in the annual report. We discuss auditors' opinions in Chapter 20.

Most companies regard the annual report as an important document, not only from an accounting point of view, but also from a promotional point of view. An annual report is an opportunity for a company to promote itself to its current owners and to potential investors and customers. Generally, companies print their annual reports on high-quality paper and include numerous illustrations and graphs.

A company's typical annual report consists of: (1) a letter from the president to stockholders or policyowners, (2) a description of financial highlights, (3) four financial statements: balance sheet, statement of operations, statement of cash flows, and statement of owners' equity, (4) notes to the financial statements and supplementary information, and (5) an independent auditor's report. Annual reports for Canadian insurers also contain a report from an Appointed Actuary, and a summary of the dividend policy for companies with participating policies. The heart of the annual report consists of the four financial statements and their accompanying notes and supplementary information. These financial statements contain the information that accounting specialists believe is essential for an external user to gain a general understanding of the financial condition, activities, and prospects of the company providing the report. For this reason, we spend the majority of this chapter discussing the four financial statements.

Letter to Stockholders and Financial Highlights

Most annual reports begin with a letter from one or more top officers of the company, usually the president or chief executive officer (CEO), to the company's stockholders or policyowners. In this letter, the executive describes the company's performance during the past year. Typically, the letter emphasizes the company's successes, such as the development of new products or increases in revenues or company size. However, the letter also discusses company problems or unfavorable economic conditions, though usually in an optimistic tone, and indicates the remedies that the company has developed to overcome the problems. After discussing the past year and the company's current situation, the letter typically concludes with an overview of the company's plans for the coming year. This discussion might include goals for increasing income, improving productivity, reducing expenses, entering new markets, creating new products, and continuing employee development.

Following the letter to stockholders or policyowners, the company sometimes includes a table of financial highlights that presents summaries of the company's financial achievements during the previous 5 or 10 years. Typically, graphs, charts, and diagrams augment the financial data in the highlights table. These graphic elements present trends in the company's performance, often emphasizing the positive aspects of the trends. Critics say that because the company presents only selected financial information, these highlights are neither complete nor objective and, therefore, are of little value to external interested parties. Others, however, find valuable information in the financial highlights and see no harm in including them in the annual report.

Financial Statements

In this section, we present the four primary financial statements contained in a company's annual report—balance sheet, statement of operations, statement of cash flows, and statement of owners' equity. Although we present these statements as parts of a company's annual report, a company can develop these financial statements at any time and for many purposes. Whether presented in an annual report or elsewhere, these financial statements provide information for

- Investors, who are deciding whether to purchase a company's stock or bonds or to make some other sort of investment in a company
- Rating agencies, who incorporate financial statement information into the ratings that they assign to insurance companies
- Company managers, who base certain decisions in part on information contained in financial statements
- The board of directors, which seeks to determine the company's overall condition and profitability
- Policyowners and company employees, who seek a general status report about the company
- Taxation authorities, who usually require that a company attach its financial statements to tax returns
- Potential creditors, who are deciding whether to make a loan or extend some other form of credit to a company
- Independent insurance brokers, investment analysts, and financial advisors, when they are deciding whether to recommend a particular company's products to clients

The preparation of financial statements is the end product of financial accounting. The monetary amounts on insurers' financial statements represent thousands, millions, and even billions of dollars. Companies usually round these amounts off to the nearest thousand or million. The heading of every financial statement generally includes three pieces of information: (1) the name of the company to which the financial statement applies, (2) the name of the statement, and (3) the date of the statement or the accounting period covered by the statement. The date that appears on a company's financial statements is generally the last day of the company's fiscal year or accounting period.

A company that owns more than 50 percent of the stock of a subsidiary company will usually compile its financial statements for the annual report on a *consolidated* basis. ***Consolidated financial statements*** combine the assets, liabilities, owners' equity, revenues, and expenses of the subsidiary company with those of the parent company. Because the parent company controls the subsidiary company, the parent and its subsidiary are considered a single operation, despite being separate legal entities. Parent companies usually provide separate financial information for each subsidiary or line of business in the annual report. Maintaining separate financial information is particularly useful in management decision making. Separate financial information on subsidiaries and lines of business is also useful for external parties in situations in which a parent company is considering the sale of a particular subsidiary. For example, in 1993, potential investors benefited from segmented financial information for Allstate Insurance, which—until its stock became available to the public—was a 100 percent subsidiary of Sears, its parent company. Merely reviewing Sears' consolidated financial statements would not have provided enough information about Allstate's financial strength, because Sears' consolidated financial statements represented the performance of Sears, as well as that of Coldwell Banker and Dean Witter, which were also Sears' subsidiaries during part of that time. Having segmented financial information on Allstate allowed investors to analyze Allstate's performance separately from that of its parent company.

Balance Sheet

As we noted in Chapter 2, the *balance sheet* is a snapshot of a company's financial position as of a specified date. The essential components of the balance sheet are the three account classifications: Assets, Liabilities, and Owners' Equity. Figure 5-1 illustrates the basic components of the balance sheet for a typical insurance company. Figure 5-2 presents the GAAP-prepared consolidated balance sheets for Industry Life and Health, a U.S. stock insurer.

"This is Wylie Watson, Controller and Vice President of Balance Sheet Special Effects."

From *The Wall Street Journal*—Permission, Cartoon Features Syndicate

Not every company or even every insurer has exactly the same account titles as on the balance sheets depicted here. For example, within the three balance sheet account categories, some balance sheet accounts are unique to life and health insurers, such as the liability account Future Policy Benefits. Later in the text, we review the major accounts associated with a typical insurance company's balance

Figure 5-1. A simplified example of an insurer's balance sheet.

Balance Sheet			
Assets		**Liabilities**	
Invested assets	$3,000	Short-term liabilities	$2,100
Cash	650	Long-term liabilities	1,000
Other assets	1,000		
		Owners' Equity	
		Capital	$ 550
		Retained earnings	1,000
Total Assets	$4,650	**= Total Liabilities and Owners' Equity**	$4,650

Figure 5-2. Consolidated, GAAP-prepared balance sheets for Industry Life and Health Insurance Company.

December 31 $000 omitted	2000	1999
Assets		
Investments:		
Bonds and other debt securities	$12,204,000	$11,225,000
Equity securities (stocks)	50,380	66,800
Policy loans	1,392,580	824,995
Mortgage loans	1,225,000	1,404,500
Total Investments	$14,871,960	$13,521,295
Cash	$ 634,696	$ 718,200
Short-term investments	225,500	257,680
Premiums receivable	743,665	554,880
Investment income due and accrued	133,455	368,945
Deferred policy acquisition costs	91,045	373,375
Property and equipment	93,404	66,283
Total Assets	$16,793,725	$15,860,658
Liabilities and Stockholders' Equity		
Policy liabilities:		
Future policy benefits:		
Life	$ 7,118,245	$ 7,083,486
Annuity	3,198,254	3,120,002
Health	2,117,168	1,855,780
Claims payable	211,559	184,180
Total Policy Liabilities	$12,645,226	$12,243,448
Accounts payable	$ 193,732	$ 94,380
Expenses due and accrued	124,730	120,019
Cash dividends payable to stockholders	272,511	243,100
Long-term liabilities	23,558	69,543
Total Liabilities	$13,259,757	$12,770,490
Stockholders' equity:		
Common stock, $0.50 par value; 40,000,000 shares authorized; 40,000,000 shares outstanding	$ 20,000	$ 20,000
Additional paid-in capital	341,356	341,356
Unrealized gain (loss)	112,230	100,950
Retained earnings	3,060,382	2,627,862
Total Stockholders' Equity	$ 3,533,968	$ 3,090,168
Total Liabilities and Stockholders' Equity	$16,793,725	$15,860,658

sheet and the procedures for recording transactions for each account.

Balance sheets appear in one of two forms: the *account form* or the *report form.* Under the ***account form*** of presentation, asset items appear on the left and liabilities and owners' equity appear on the right. The simplified balance sheet presented in Figure 5-1 illustrates the account form of presentation. In contrast, the ***report form*** lists asset, liability, and owners' equity accounts in order vertically, as depicted in Figure 5-2. The balance sheet in a company's annual report typically appears in report form.

A balance sheet is fundamental to accounting because it demonstrates a company's fulfillment of the *basic accounting equation:*

Assets = Liabilities + Owners' Equity

Consider the basic accounting equation as follows: the left side of the equation—Assets—represents what the company *owns,* and the right side of the equation—Liabilities and Owners' Equity—represents what the company *owes* to its creditors and stockholders or policyowners. Similarly, on the account form of the simplified balance sheet, the left side reports on the company's assets, and the right side reports on the company's liabilities and owners' equity. The total of the left side of the balance sheet must equal the right side—they must balance—just as in the basic accounting equation.

Every business compiles a balance sheet. The main purpose of the balance sheet is to measure the owners' wealth—that is, at a given time, what remains after subtracting what a company owes from what it owns. Remember, the annual report presents GAAP-prepared financial statements that focus on the company as a *going concern.* Thus, a balance sheet answers the following general question: As of a certain date, what and how much does a company own, what and how much does it owe, and what remains for the company's owners? For an insurer, a large portion of what it owns (assets) consists of various investments, such as bonds and other debt securities, mortgage loans, stocks, and real estate. Most of the insurer's obligations (liabilities) are future benefits to policyowners. When you review a list of a company's assets, you see, in summary form, what the company's managers purchased with the funds provided by the company's creditors, policyowners, and stockholders.

Under GAAP, a company uses a variety of methods to value its assets depending on the type of asset and its purpose. For example, a company generally lists its holdings of common stock at their current market value as of the balance sheet date. Besides current market value, other balance sheet accounts may be valued according to

- Historical cost
- Amortized cost
- Historical cost or current market value, whichever is lower (this is known informally as the *lower of cost or market rule*)

The rules for valuing each balance sheet account classification differ between GAAP and statutory accounting and may differ between U.S. and Canadian requirements. We discuss specific differences in Chapter 6. For now, you should be aware that the GAAP-prepared balance sheet that an insurer presents in its annual report will differ from the statutory balance sheet it presents in the Annual Statement.

Although a balance sheet contains much valuable information about a company's financial position, it does not reveal how or why the company obtained particular assets or liabilities. By comparing several years of the company's balance sheets, it is possible to form some conclusions about the amounts listed for each account classification and to discern certain company performance trends, such as whether the company is increasing its assets or its liabilities over time. Finally, to fully understand the balance sheet in the annual report, you must study any accompanying notes that apply specifically to the balance sheet. These notes, which may appear on the same page as the balance sheet or in a separate section of the annual report, are an integral part of the balance sheet. We discuss these notes later in the chapter.

Statement of Operations

Earlier we compared the balance sheet to a snapshot of a company's financial position as of a specific date. In contrast, the *statement of operations* is a moving picture of a company's financial performance over a specific accounting period. This financial statement shows how much money a company has realized from its operations during an accounting period and, ultimately, to what extent the company's general operations resulted in an increase or decrease in its assets. A company's statement of operations answers the question: Do revenues exceed expenses? If so, the company earns net income. ***Net income*** refers to the excess of total revenues over total expenses. When total expenses exceed total revenues, the result is a ***net loss.*** Thus, the basic formula for the statement of operations is

Revenues – Expenses = Net Income (Loss)

Figure 5-3 shows the general form of an insurer's statement of operations. Figure 5-4 shows the consolidated statements of operations

Figure 5-3. A simplified example of an insurer's statement of operations.

Revenues	
Premium income	$1,000
Annuity considerations	300
Investment income	800
Total Revenues	$2,100
Expenses	
Policy benefits	$ 800
Annuity payments	200
Operating expenses	100
Other expenses	50
Total Expenses	$1,150
Earnings before Income Taxes	$ 950
Income taxes	(380)
Net Income (Loss)	$ 570

(Total Revenues minus Total Expenses)

for Constitution Life and Health Insurance Company. Both of these figures highlight revenues and expenses. Later in this section, we discuss two other account classifications, gains and losses, which are also essential for understanding the statement of operations.

As you can see in Figures 5-3 and 5-4, the company first lists its sources of revenues. Then the company subtracts its expenses from its revenues to obtain its earnings before income taxes, after which it subtracts income taxes to obtain the net income or net loss for the accounting period. The statements of operations in Figures 5-3 and 5-4 are examples of the ***single-step statement of operations,*** which depict one step in subtracting total operating expenses from total revenues. This condensed version of the statement of operations often appears in the annual report. A more detailed format is the ***multiple-step statement of operations,*** which draws out subtotals for each category of revenues or expenses. Manufacturing firms are more likely to use the multiple-step format than insurance companies. Either format results in the same net income or net loss, however.

While the balance sheet measures a company's financial condition, the statement of operations measures profitability, which is one key to survival for all insurers, including mutual insurance companies and fraternal benefit societies. ***Profit*** is the extra income not needed to pay for the cost of providing insurance, and this profit contributes to the insurer's surplus, an owners' equity account. Profit, however, cannot simply be equated with net income. For example, if a publicly traded company pays cash dividends to stockholders, the amount of "profit" left for the company after paying these dividends will be less

Figure 5-4. Consolidated, GAAP-prepared statements of operations for Constitution Life and Health Insurance Company.

Years Ended December 31: $000 omitted	2000	1999
Revenues		
Premium income:		
Life	$3,056,220	$2,867,302
Annuity considerations	1,256,012	904,616
Health	853,446	611,356
Total Premium Income	$5,165,678	$4,383,274
Net investment income	$1,758,592	$1,499,764
Other revenues	24,906	8,582
Total Revenues	$6,949,176	$5,891,620
Benefits and Expenses		
Life benefits	$2,451,479	$2,085,486
Annuity benefits	1,006,972	871,951
Health benefits	798,660	587,500
Increase in liability for future benefits	55,402	189,362
Total Benefits	$4,312,513	$3,734,299
Operating expenses:		
Agent commissions	$ 189,074	$ 205,888
Salaries	922,811	854,138
General expenses	1,392,314	996,200
Total Operating Expenses	$2,504,199	$2,056,226
Total Benefits and Expenses	$6,816,712	$5,790,525
Earnings before income tax expense	$ 132,464	$ 101,095
Income tax expense (40%)	52,986	40,438
Net Income	$ 79,478	$ 60,657
Earnings per share of common stock (40,000,000 shares):	$ 1.99	$ 1.52

(Total Revenues minus Total Benefits and Expenses, for each year.)

than the net income figure on the statement of operations. Profit is not a precise accounting term, and accountants are cautious in their use of the word.

Recall that the Securities and Exchange Commission (SEC) requires that U.S. companies present three years of statements of operations in an annual report. The *CICA Handbook* requires that Canadian companies provide two years of financial statements, including the statement of operations, in the annual report. Also, the provincial securities commissions in Canada require five years of comparative financial statement information. These requirements allow external users to see whether a company has experienced increasing revenues or expenses during the most recent accounting periods.

A company must disclose in its GAAP statement of operations any gains or losses that result from transactions involving (1) the disposition of a business segment (called *discontinued operations*) or (2) any extraordinary items that are not likely to occur in the future. In addition, the company must disclose the impact of any changes in accounting policies on statement of operations accounts.

Gains and Losses

Figures 5-3 and 5-4 depict the statement of operations based primarily on a company's normal business activities. However, an insurance company sometimes conducts activities that are independent of the company's core business functions of (1) selling insurance policies and annuities and (2) investing premium income. In this context, a ***gain*** is income obtained by a transaction other than a core business function. A gain ultimately increases a company's net income. Similarly, a ***loss*** occurs when a company loses money on an activity that does not arise from normal business operations. A loss ultimately decreases a company's net income. Because they occur independent of a company's normal business, gains and losses appear separately on the statement of operations. For example, an insurer classifies proceeds that it receives from the sale of its home office furniture as a gain rather than as revenue because the insurer's primary business involves the sale of insurance products, not furniture. A retail furniture store, however, includes the proceeds from the sale of furniture in a revenue account because selling furniture is part of its primary business operations. Thus, the account classification of a company's gains and losses depends on the company's core business functions.

A gain or loss can result from ***discontinued operations,*** which are one-time transactions that result from ending operations, through their sale or other disposition, in a business segment. An insurer's sale of its health insurance division to another insurer is an example of a discontinued operation. To report the discontinued operation on its statement of operations, the insurer reports two amounts: (1) the year-to-date net income or loss of the segment that is disposed of and (2) the net gain or loss associated with the sale or disposal of the segment. It is necessary to break out these two amounts because, in many cases, a company sells a segment after operating it for part of the year. Thus, there is net income or a net loss from the segment's operations for that part of the year, and a gain or loss from the sale or disposal itself.

Sometimes a company reports an *extraordinary item*—either an extraordinary gain or an extraordinary loss—on the statement of operations. An ***extraordinary item*** is a non-core business transaction that is (1) unusual, (2) rare in occurrence, and (3) not based primarily on management decisions. Extraordinary items include, for example, losses from natural disasters, losses from the enactment of a new law, and gains from the expropriation of a company's land and buildings for a highway. Gains or losses resulting from the following are *not* considered extraordinary:

- Disposal of a business segment
- Changes in the value of a foreign currency
- Sale or disposal of a fixed asset
- Effects of a labor strike

A company reports the amount of the extraordinary gain or loss, plus or minus any tax consequences caused by extraordinary events.

Discontinued operations and extraordinary items—because of their size, dollar value, and/or uniqueness—appear separately from typical revenues and expenses that result from a company's normal (or continuing) operations so as not to distort the income from continuing operations. For example, suppose a company generates $2,000,000 in revenues from continuing operations, and pays $1,250,000 in expenses. The company's net income for the period is $750,000, as follows:

Revenues	$ 2,000,000
Expenses	(1,250,000)
Net Income (Loss)	$ 750,000

Suppose the company also suffers a net $1,000,000 extraordinary loss due to a fire at its home office facility. If the company includes the extraordinary loss along with normal business expenses, it would report a net loss of $250,000 for the period, as follows:

Revenues	$ 2,000,000
Expenses	(2,250,000)
Net Income (Loss)	$ (250,000)

To avoid misrepresenting net income from continuing operations in this way, the company should report the extraordinary loss separately, as follows:

Revenues	$ 2,000,000
Expenses	(1,250,000)
Income from continuing operations	$ 750,000
Extraordinary loss	(1,000,000)
Net Income (Loss)	$ (250,000)

By separating this $1,000,000 extraordinary loss from income from continuing operations, the company's revenue and expense accounts can be compared over time to discern trends about the company's ***operating efficiency,*** which is the company's ability to manage the relationship between revenues and expenses. Including in revenues and expenses such one-time, unusual gains or losses that do not affect the company's operating efficiency would mislead interested users of financial information.

Earlier we stated the basic formula for the statement of operations as

Revenues – Expenses = Net Income (Loss)

We can now expand this basic formula to include gains and losses:

Revenues – Expenses + Gains – Losses = Net Income (Loss)

Net income ultimately determines, among other things, whether owners' equity will increase and whether a stock insurer will be able to pay cash dividends to stockholders. Net income increases owners' equity while a net loss decreases owners' equity. Generally, this "bottom line" figure—so called because net income is usually found on the last line of the statement of operations—indicates whether the company is profitable and is likely to remain in business.

Statement of Cash Flows

The third major financial statement presented in an annual report is the *statement of cash flows,* commonly referred to as the *cash flow statement.* The statement of cash flows provides information about a company's cash receipts (inflows) and cash disbursements (outflows) during a given accounting period. Figure 5-5 shows the major components of

Figure 5-5. A simplified example of an insurer's statement of cash flows.

Statement of Cash Flows	
Net cash provided by operating activities	$ 700
Net cash provided by investing activities	500
Net cash used by financing activities	(300)
Net Change in Cash	$ 900
Cash at beginning of year	800
Cash at End of Year	$1,700

Figure 5-6. Consolidated, GAAP-prepared statement of cash flows for Allgood Life and Health Insurance Company.

December 31, 2000		
Cash Flows from Operating Activities		
Cash receipts:		
Premium income	$ 353,047	
Investment income	23,658	
Total Cash Receipts		$ 376,705
Cash disbursements:		
Policy benefits	$ (178,445)	
Policy dividends	(26,779)	
Operating expenses	(100,458)	
Income taxes	(27,549)	
Total Cash Disbursements		(333,231)
Net Cash Flows from Operating Activities		$ 43,474
Cash Flows from Investing Activities		
Sales of securities	$ 902,345	
Purchase of securities	(894,400)	
Purchase of equipment	(4,300)	
Net Cash Flows from Investing Activities		3,645
Cash Flows from Financing Activities		
Cash payment for stockholder dividends	$ (22,709)	
Net Cash Flows Used for Financing Activities		(22,709)
Net increase (decrease) in cash		$ 24,410
Beginning period cash balance		35,750
Ending Cash Balance		$ 60,160

a typical statement of cash flows. Figure 5-6 depicts the consolidated statements of cash flows for the Allgood Life and Health Insurance Company. *FASB Statement No. 95* mandates that all U.S. companies include a statement of cash flows as part of the annual report. In Canada, the *CICA Handbook* stipulates that companies provide a *statement of change in financial position (SCFP)*, which is similar to the statement of cash flows required for U.S. companies.

The statement of cash flows reconciles the cash the company has on hand at the beginning and at the end of the accounting period. In providing information about a company's cash flows, this statement also provides insight into a company's operating, investing, and financing activities. It answers the following questions:

- How did the company raise cash during the accounting period?
- How did the company spend cash during the accounting period?
- Did the company have to sell assets or borrow funds to generate cash?
- What are the company's likely prospects for generating cash in the future?
- What is the relationship between the company's cash flows and its net income?
- Is new product development being financed with debt (borrowing money) or equity (offering company stock for sale)?

Like the statement of operations, the statement of cash flows is a *dynamic* measure that shows a change over time. In essence, the statement of cash flows is a rearrangement of the changes that occurred between the current and previous balance sheet, which as we noted earlier, is a *static* measure of a company's financial position. The importance of a positive cash flow cannot be overemphasized. A company may have billions of dollars worth of assets, but if it does not have enough cash on hand to cover current expenses, then it may be unable to pay bills and obligations as they come due. This situation is similar to the expression "house rich, cash poor," which refers to a person who has nearly all of his or her money tied up in a residence, but no cash available to pay household bills. An insurance company that is cash poor may not be in quite as dire a position as a cash-poor homeowner, because a company can sell its bond and stock investments in a matter of days, whereas real estate is much less liquid and generally takes much longer to sell. However, an insurer that is forced to sell assets to support ongoing operations may take a loss on the sale, which, in most cases, is undesirable. On the other hand, having too much available cash may cause investors, policyholders, and creditors to be concerned that idle cash is not being put to more productive uses. As you might expect, managing cash effectively is one of management's most important tasks.

A company prepares the statement of cash flows from information obtained in the balance sheet and statement of operations. The statement of cash flows is similar to a check register in that both show the amount and the source of any increases or decreases in receipts (cash inflows) and disbursements (cash outflows). In accounting terminology, a ***cash inflow*** is a *source* of funds. The cash received by an insurer when it sells an asset becomes a source of funds. A ***cash outflow*** is a *use* of funds. A cash payment to purchase a bond is a use of funds.

With respect to balance sheet and statement of operations accounts, a company's cash inflows—its sources of cash—*increase* as a result of

- A decrease in an asset account (selling an asset for cash)
- An increase in a liability account (taking out a loan)
- An increase in stockholders' equity (issuing common stock)
- A receipt of revenue (selling policies)
- Net income

Cash outflows have the opposite effect on an insurer's balance sheet and statement of operations accounts. A company's cash outflows—its uses of funds—*increase* as a result of

- An increase in an asset account (purchasing an asset)
- A decrease in a liability account (paying off a loan)
- A decrease in stockholders' equity (retiring or repurchasing a company's own common stock)
- A payment of expenses
- A net loss

You can calculate a company's net cash flow for an accounting period by using the following formula:

Cash Inflows – Cash Outflows = Net Cash Inflow (Outflow)

or

Sources of Funds – Uses of Funds = Net Change in Cash

The net cash inflow or outflow represents the net increase or decrease in cash for the accounting period. Net increase or decrease is also known as the *net change in cash.* Theoretically, the net change in cash equals the difference between the cash balance (as shown on the balance sheet) at the beginning of the period and the cash balance at the end of the period. For example, a statement of cash flows dated "for the year ended December 31, 2000," accounts for the difference in the cash balance between the company's December 31, 1999, balance sheet and its December 31, 2000, balance sheet.

Changes in a company's cash flow occur as a result of three activities: operating activities, investing activities, and financing activities.

1. ***Operating activities*** are those activities associated with a company's major lines of business and involve transactions that directly determine a company's net income. An insurer's operating activities are generally associated with the sale and maintenance of insurance products and services. These activities include (1) selling insurance and annuity products, (2) paying claims, (3) receiving investment income (such as bond interest and dividend income on stocks), (4) increasing or decreasing the liability for future policy benefits, and (5) paying expenses.

2. ***Investing activities*** are transactions that involve the purchase or sale of long-term assets and the lending of funds to another entity. An insurer's investing activities include (1) purchasing and selling bonds, mortgage loans, stocks, real estate, equipment, and other long-term assets, and (2) making loans and collecting the principal and interest on those loans.

3. ***Financing activities*** are transactions involving borrowed funds and cash payments to or from owners of the company. Financing activities include transactions associated with (1) issuing, repurchasing, or retiring common stock, (2) paying cash dividends to stockholders, and (3) borrowing and repaying funds loaned by creditors.

If for any of the three activities the cash inflows exceed the cash outflows, the result is a net cash flow *from* or *provided by* that activity. If the reverse is true, then the result is a net cash flow *used in* or *used by* that activity. For example, under operating activities, if the company receives $10,000 in revenue and pays $8,000 in expenses, the statement of cash flows shows *$2,000 net cash provided by operating activities.* Further, under investing activities, if the company sells $150,000 worth of bonds and purchases $160,000 in mortgage loans, the statement of cash flows would show *$10,000 net cash used by investing activities.* Figure 5-7 classifies the common transactions that fall under each type of activity.

The distinction among the cash flows from operating, investing, and financing activities is important when a company prepares its statement of cash flows. Companies use one of two methods—the *direct method* or the *indirect method*—to prepare this statement.

Figure 5-7. Cash flow transactions classified by type of activity.

Type of Activity	Transactions Resulting in Cash Inflows	Transactions Resulting in Cash Outflows
Operating Activities	• Cash sales to customers • Receipt of securities interest and dividends • Increases in current liabilities	• Payments to employees and suppliers • Interest payments to bondholders • Decreases in current liabilities
Investing Activities	• Sales of bonds, mortgage loans, stocks, property, buildings, and other long-term assets • Receipt of principal and interest on loan repayments	• Purchase of bonds, mortgage loans, stocks, property, buildings, and other long-term assets • Making loans to others
Financing Activities	• Issuance of common stock • Issuance of bonds and notes • Loans from creditors	• Dividend payments to stockholders • Payment of principal and interest on bonds, loans, notes, and other debt

The only difference between the two methods is in the computation of cash flows from operating activities. Cash flows from investing and financing activities are calculated the same under either method.

Calculating Cash Flows from Operating Activities

When using the ***direct method*** to prepare the statement of cash flows, a company determines net cash flow from operating activities by taking its major types of operating cash receipts and then subtracting each major type of cash disbursement. The difference between the cash receipts and the disbursements is the net cash for the period. The statement of cash flows for the Allgood Life and Health Insurance Company, depicted in Figure 5-6, uses the direct method. Although this method seems straightforward, it can be quite expensive and time consuming to track every cash transaction, particularly in a large company. Therefore, many companies use the ***indirect method,*** also called the *reconciliation method,* which begins with the net income figure as reported on the statement of operations, then reconciles this amount to operating cash flows through a series of additions and subtractions, as shown in Figure 5-8. The actual preparation of a statement of cash flows using the indirect method is outside the scope of this text. Many companies prefer the indirect method because it focuses on the differences between net income and cash flows from operations, and it is usually easier and less expensive to gather the data required for the indirect method than for the direct method.

Figure 5-8 compares the direct method and indirect method of determining net cash from operating activities. The top half of the figure shows the direct method. Note that this company lists operating cash receipts and then subtracts operating cash disbursements to

Figure 5-8. Insurance company cash flows from operating activities: direct method and indirect method.

December 31, 2000		
DIRECT METHOD		
Cash Flows from Operating Activities		
Cash receipts:		
Premiums received	$ 513,807	
Investment income received	65,292	
Total Cash Receipts		$579,099
Cash disbursements:		
Policy benefits	$(271,876)	
Policy dividends	(11,230)	
Operating expenses	(208,683)	
Income taxes	(39,168)	
Total Payments		(530,957)
Net Cash Flows from Operating Activities		$ 48,142
INDIRECT METHOD		
Cash Flows from Operating Activities		
Net Income		$ 58,753
Adjustments to reconcile net income to net cash from operating activities:		
Add: Increase in benefits payable	$ 53,047	
Subtract: Increase in accrued investment income	(51,220)	
Subtract: Increase in deferred policy acquisition costs	(12,438)	
Total Adjustments		(10,611)
Net Cash Flows from Operating Activities		$ 48,142

arrive at an amount of $48,142 in net cash from operating activities. The bottom half of Figure 5-8 shows the indirect method, which begins with the net income amount reported on the statement of operations. To this amount, the company makes adjustments to "indirectly" arrive at $48,142 of net cash from operating activities.

Statement of Owners' Equity

The final financial statement we discuss is the *statement of owners' equity,* which publicly traded life and health insurance companies also provide in their annual reports to stockholders. Stock insurers often call this the *statement of stockholders' equity.* Mutual insurers may voluntarily include in their GAAP-based annual report a similar

Figure 5-9. A simplified example of a U.S. insurer's statement of stockholders' equity.

Statement of Stockholders' Equity	
Stock	$ 500
Additional paid-in capital	100
Retained earnings	250
Treasury stock	(100)
Unrealized gain (loss)	(50)
Total Stockholders' Equity	$ 700

statement called the *statement of policyowners' equity.* Most of the items in this statement are the same for stock and mutual companies. We note the items that apply only to one or the other. Figure 5-9 shows the basic components of the statement of stockholders' equity for a U.S. insurer. Figure 5-10 provides an example of Granite Life and Health Insurance Company's consolidated statements of stockholders' equity.

A company uses the statement of owners' equity to reconcile, or explain, any changes in equity accounts that occur from one balance sheet to the next. This reconciliation is similar to the reconciliation of changes in cash on the statement of cash flows. Events that cause owners' equity accounts to change include the (1) issuance of stock, (2) purchase of treasury stock, (3) retention of net income, and (4) payment of cash dividends on stock. The next section briefly describes some of the typical accounts that appear on a U.S. statement of stockholders' equity, including Common Stock and Preferred Stock, Additional Paid-In Capital (these accounts are called a company's *contributed capital accounts*), Treasury Stock, Unrealized Gains (Losses), and Retained Earnings.

Stock

Investors who wish to own a portion of a company buy shares of that company's stock. A share of ***stock*** represents an ownership interest in a company. A company sells shares of its own stock to raise money to help the company continue or expand its operations. A company that wants to sell stock must *authorize* in its corporate charter a specific number of shares that are available for sale. When a share of stock sells, it is considered to have been *issued.* Stock that has been issued is called ***outstanding stock*** or *stock outstanding.* Outstanding stock does not include a company's treasury stock. A company is under no obligation to issue all of the shares that its charter authorizes, but the company cannot issue more shares than it authorizes.

Investors buy stock because they expect to profit from their investment, either by reselling their shares at a higher price or by receiving

Figure 5-10. Consolidated, GAAP-prepared statements of stockholders' equity for Granite Life and Health Insurance Company.

For the Years Ended December 31 $000 omitted			
		2000	1999
Stock	Balance at beginning of year	$ 20,000	$ 20,000
	Capital stock issued during year	0	0
	Balance at end of year	$ 20,000	$ 20,000
Additional Paid-In Capital	Balance at beginning of year	$ 435,000	$ 435,000
	Change during year	0	0
	Balance at end of year	$ 435,000	$ 435,000
Treasury Stock	Balance at beginning of year	$ 0	$ 0
	Purchases during year	(10,000)	0
	Balance at end of year	$ (10,000)	$ 0
Net Unrealized Gains (Losses)	Balance at beginning of year	$ (126,290)	$ 87,445
	Change during year	334,628	(213,735)
	Balance at end of year	$ 208,338	$ (126,290)
Retained Earnings	Balance at beginning of year	$2,774,350	$2,700,885
	Net income (loss)	201,865	198,445
	Dividends paid	(165,750)	(124,980)
	Balance at end of year	$2,810,465	$2,774,350
Total Stockholders' Equity at End of Year		$3,463,803	$3,103,060

dividends, which are distributions of earnings that the company pays to stockholders. A dividend that a company pays in the form of cash is known as a ***cash dividend.*** For example, a company that declares a 20 cents per share dividend pays stockholders 20 cents for each share of stock they own. Most dividends are cash dividends, but occasionally a company pays dividends in the form of additional shares of the company's stock. This type of dividend is known as a ***stock dividend.*** Stock is usually synonymous with *common stock,* but stock can also be sold as *preferred stock.* These two types of stock differ primarily in the rights and benefits each one offers to investors. ***Common stock*** is a unit of ownership that typically entitles the owner to vote on the selection of directors and on other important company matters and entitles the owner to receive dividends. However, the company is not *required* to pay dividends to common stockholders, and the amount of the dividends paid can vary over time. ***Preferred stock*** is a unit of ownership that does not ordinarily carry the voting rights of common stock, but it does carry a stated dividend rate or amount that has a priority over common stock. In other words, companies that issue both common and preferred stock must pay dividends in the stated amount to all preferred stockholders before they can pay any dividends to common stockholders. In addition, if a company liquidates its assets, a preferred stockholder's claims to the company's assets precede the claims of common stockholders.

The stock account on the U.S. Annual Statement is called *Capital Stock* or *Paid-In Capital.* On the Canadian Annual Return, the account is known as *Capital Stock Issued and Paid* or *Capital Stock Paid.* Alternatively, a company may use the account names Common Stock and Preferred Stock to distinguish between the two types of stock issues. In the United States, Capital Stock consists of the number of outstanding shares of a company's stock multiplied by its par value per share. ***Par value*** is the designated legal value assigned to each outstanding share of stock. For example, if a U.S. company authorizes 1,000,000 shares of $2 par value common stock and issues 500,000 shares, the balance in the Common Stock account is $1,000,000 (500,000 × $2). A stock's par value is an arbitrary amount chosen at the time of issuance and is printed on each stock certificate. Companies use par value primarily for accounting purposes and normally set it well below the stock's expected market value.

Additional Paid-In Capital

When a U.S. company issues a share of stock for a price above its par value, the company records the difference per share between the issue price and the par value in an account called ***Additional Paid-In Capital,*** also known as *Paid-In Capital in Excess of Par* or *Premium on Common Stock.* For example, assume that the company from the previous example issues the 500,000 shares of common stock at $7 per share instead of the $2 par value per share. The balance of the Common Stock account remains $1,000,000, and the balance of the Additional Paid-In Capital account is $2,500,000 ($5 × 500,000 shares). The appropriate accounting entry to record this transaction is

	Debit	Credit
Cash	3,500,000	
Common Stock		1,000,000
Additional Paid-In Capital		2,500,000

To record the issue of 500,000 shares of $2 par value common stock at $7 per share.

The Additional Paid-In Capital account also includes the contributions of stockholders to accounts other than Common Stock.

Canadian life and health insurance companies do not refer to the par value of stock. Therefore, a Canadian company's balance sheet does not have an Additional Paid-In Capital line. If the company in the previous example is a Canadian company, the appropriate accounting entry to record the same transaction is

Cash 3,500,000
Common Stock 3,500,000
To record the issue of 500,000 shares of common stock at $7 per share.

Treasury Stock

The ***Treasury Stock*** account represents an insurer's purchase of its own outstanding stock. Treasury stock is issued stock that is no longer outstanding. A company may have a number of reasons for repurchasing its stock, such as the following:

- To have stock available for its employees' stock option program
- To prevent or reduce the possibility of a hostile takeover by another company
- To maintain a favorable market for its stock by creating an apparent demand and buoying the price per share
- To improve its *earnings per share,* a key financial ratio often used by potential investors

A treasury stock purchase reduces the balance of assets (Cash) and owners' equity. The company records the total cost of the repurchase in a Treasury Stock account without regard to the stock's par value. In addition, the original Common Stock account remains unchanged. For example, if the U.S. company from the previous example repurchases 100,000 shares of its stock at $9 per share, the appropriate accounting entry to record the transaction is

Treasury Stock. 900,000
Cash. 900,000
To record the purchase of 100,000 shares of treasury stock at $9 per share.

On the statement of owners' equity, the Treasury Stock line is usually listed as a negative amount, as in Figures 5-9 and 5-10. Because owners' equity normally carries a credit balance, and a debit to treasury stock reduces owners' equity, many accountants refer to treasury stock as a *contra owners' equity account.* Note that treasury stock is not an asset as is the company's investment in the stock of another company. Why? Because a company cannot have a claim of ownership (called a *residual claim*) against its own assets. A residual claim is one of the typical advantages for a stock investor. Moreover, one reason that a company purchases an asset is to generate current and future operating income, but a company does not receive dividends on any of its treasury stock nor does it typically purchase treasury stock with the intent to sell it again.

Unrealized Gains and Losses

The market price of many invested assets changes during an accounting period. For example, at the end of a period, the price of a bond owned by an insurer may be either higher or lower than the value as shown on the company's books. For invested assets such as stocks, certain bonds, and certain mortgages, the difference between the asset's book value and its admitted value (statutory accounting) or its current market value (GAAP) as of the financial statement date is an ***unrealized gain (loss)*** that the company must acknowledge. If the security's market price as of the statement date is higher than its book value, the result is an unrealized gain. If the security's market price as of the statement date is lower than the book value, the result is an unrealized loss. Stock and mutual insurers in the United States are required to report the aggregate (total) unrealized gain or loss of most securities on the GAAP statement of owners' equity. These gains and losses are *unrealized* because the company has not yet sold the security. Once the company sells the assets, the gains and losses are *realized.*

Retained Earnings

Under GAAP, retained earnings increases or decreases as a result of the net change in owners' equity resulting from revenues, expenses, and realized gains and losses in the company's operations, including any cash dividends paid to stockholders. The amount shown on the Retained Earnings line of the statement of owners' equity is often difficult to understand because it does not represent the amount of cash or earnings available to a company. Rather, ***retained earnings*** is the cumulative amount of a company's earnings that has been kept (retained) in the company over time in order to finance its continuing operations. Retained earnings are an important source of company financing and are of interest to the company's investors and creditors. Most retained earnings come from income generated by core business functions: the sale of the company's products and services. We compute the change in retained earnings from one period to the next by adding net income (or a net loss) to the beginning Retained Earnings balance, then subtracting any cash dividends paid to stockholders. For mutual insurers, the change in Retained Earnings equals the amount of net income or net loss for the period. Refer to Figure 5-10 to see the change in retained earnings for Granite Life and Health Insurance Company. Generally, Retained Earnings increases when the company realizes net income, and Retained Earnings decreases when the company suffers a net loss.

Certain requirements, including a state or provincial law or a loan agreement with a creditor, may prohibit a company from paying dividends on its common stock. For example, a company may have to set aside a certain amount of retained earnings known as *restricted retained earnings,* to comply with the law or the loan agreement. These restrictions are intended to ensure that a company uses its earnings wisely. A company may also voluntarily restrict retained

Figure 5-11. Financial statement dates: static measures and dynamic measures.

	December 31, 1999	For the year ended December 31, 2000	December 31, 2000
Static Measures	Balance Sheet		Balance Sheet
Dynamic Measures		Statement of Operations Statement of Cash Flows Statement of Stockholders' Equity	

earnings through an *appropriation of retained earnings.* An appropriation of retained earnings, which has no direct effect on a company's financial statements, is normally disclosed in the letter to stockholders in the annual report. The letter explains why the company has chosen not to declare a dividend on its common stock or, if the company has declared a dividend, why it is lower or higher than stockholders had expected.

In addition, under GAAP, companies exclude from net income corrections or adjustments related to previous accounting periods, called ***prior period adjustments.*** These adjustments include (1) mathematical errors that cause net income to be significantly higher or lower than originally reported, (2) the omission or misapplication of an important accounting principle or significant business transaction, and (3) income tax settlements that result from an error. The company corrects errors and omissions and reports the corrections as adjustments, with accompanying explanations, to the *beginning* Retained Earnings balance on the statement of owners' equity.

Summary of Financial Statements

In Chapter 2, we identified the balance sheet as a static measure and the statement of operations as a dynamic measure. Figure 5-11 expands this concept for the primary GAAP-based financial statements that an insurer includes in the annual report. Note that the balance sheet is the only static measure and that the statement of operations, the statement of cash flows, and the statement of owners' equity reconcile the differences between two consecutive balance sheets.

Notes and Supplementary Information

Although not considered separate financial statements, notes and supplementary disclosures to financial statements are an integral part of a company's annual report. Therefore, you should not review a company's annual report without reading the accompanying notes and supplementary information. Insight 5-1 discusses a proposal by

Insight 5-1 Investors Will Fish for Footnotes in 'Abbreviated' Annual Reports

There are investors for whom the sight of an annual report is like a still-wrapped present on Christmas morning—replete with the promise of unknown treasure and hours of pleasurable diversion. Now, the Securities and Exchange Commission wants to ruin the fun.

With little fanfare, the agency has asked for comment on a proposal to permit corporations to omit numerous (and often juicy) footnotes from their annual reports. Say, for instance, you want to know what a company earned on foreign-currency swings. Or you are anxious about its exposure to derivatives. Or maybe, before investing, you want to know more about the business that is the company's breadwinner, or whether it has been more profitable in Tanzania or Tuscaloosa. The annual report mailed to investors may soon be barren of such chestnuts, as well as numerous others—such as the cost of executive options, and restrictions on the company's cash.

Under the SEC proposal, a company could distribute an "abbreviated" report, devoid of many now-required footnotes. Companies would still have to file all footnotes with the SEC, and they would have to provide them to investors brazen enough to ask.

The proposal stems from the SEC's (and Chairman Arthur Levitt's) desire to streamline regulations. Though the agency is asking for public comment, its favorable tilt seems obvious. An SEC questionnaire for small investors lists the footnotes that would still be included in the abbreviated report and coyly asks respondents to name any others they can think of that they would miss. Good luck, folks. (More than 25 types of notes would be omitted.)

An abbreviated report, the SEC goes on, might save companies "substantial" money. This is unlikely. As the information must be compiled in any case, the only savings would be that of printing and mailing a tome slightly more svelte. The typical report costs $300,000 to $500,000 to produce, according to New York-based Pentagram Design. But companies cough up much of that unnecessarily, on six-color glossy photos. At Capital Cities/ABC Inc., which eschews pictures (the numbers have usually looked good enough), reports cost only about $150,000, plus a like amount for distribution. Ronald Doerfler, chief financial officer, says the savings would be "inconsequential."

What's driving the SEC proposal is the fear, shared by accountants who have lobbied for the change, that readers of financial statements are suffering from overload. Meredith Cross, the agency's deputy director of corporate finance, argues that a more concise annual report might be more effective. "Some people claim that these documents are so daunting that people don't read them at all," she says.

Many companies' activities are quite complex, however, and will remain so even if their reports are pureed of "confusing" details. According to Stephen Farley, managing partner of New York-based Farley Capital, an annual report without footnotes would be next to useless as a guide for intelligent investing—presumably the kind the SEC wants to encourage.

What's worse, many investors would assume the opposite—that if the SEC doesn't require dissemination of notes, the notes must be a waste of time.

Of course, many people don't read footnotes now. "If it isn't a dividend check, many individual shareholders will pitch into the trashcan anything that a company sends them," writes Jack Ciesielski, in the Baltimore-based *Analyst's Accounting Observer.* But plenty do read them, including some who wouldn't take the trouble if they had to ask.

People who find notes confusing, Mr. Ciesielski adds, hopefully will realize they are in over their heads and turn to a professional, where they belong. To banish the notes for fear they will turn off readers would be like eliminating fractions from math books on the theory that the average student prefers to work with whole numbers. Such a dumbing-down wouldn't lead to better mathematicians.

Annual reports aren't that dense, anyway (the notes are tucked unobtrusively behind the financial statements). After a couple of hours' study, most yield a vivid picture of the business at hand.

But the SEC proposal may merely be the first, and mildest, effort to skinny down the reports. Bradley Belt, of the Center for Strategic & International Studies, a Washington think tank, wishes the agency would do away with the requirement that companies disseminate annual reports at all. People who wanted one could dial up the Internet, or call the company. The SEC also is seeking comment on that radical (and embryonic) notion, and on a proposal to permit companies to distribute only a simplified annual "summary." It seems that dumbing-down is not only bliss, it is catching.

Source: Adapted from Roger Lowenstein, "Investors Will Fish for Footnotes in 'Abbreviated' Annual Reports," *The Wall Street Journal* (September 14, 1995), p. C1. Reprinted by permission of *The Wall Street Journal,*

the SEC that would allow companies to omit notes from their annual reports.

Notes to the financial statements, which are factual in nature and disclose the details behind some of the amounts presented in the financial statements, usually accompany or immediately follow the financial statements in a company's annual report. These notes enable users to understand some of the more complex items in the published financial statements. Notes also appear on the financial statement pages themselves, either in footnote form or as parenthetical comments beside a particular line on the financial statement. *Supplementary information* usually follows the notes in an annual report. An explanatory note for a company's fixed assets, such as company-occupied real estate, is one example of the additional information that you may obtain from notes to the financial statements. The balance sheet generally lists one total for Property, Plant, and Equipment. An accompanying note will disclose the depreciation method and itemize each component of this particular asset.

The notes to the financial statements often take up a significant amount of space in a company's annual report. This point illustrates the importance accorded to the information contained in the notes. The name, order, and placement of the notes may vary, but the annual reports of most life and health insurance companies contain some or all of the typical notes summarized in Figure 5-12.

Figure 5-12. Typical notes to the financial statements.

Accounting Policies Note: Explains the significant accounting policies that a company followed in preparing its financial statements. This note also identifies how the company classified and calculated the value of each account.

Note on Income Taxes: Explains the impact of taxes on insurance operations.

Segment Information Note: Summarizes segmented financial statements for specific subsidiaries or major lines of business.

Contingency Note: Describes liabilities that a company may or may not incur, such as a pending lawsuit.

Commitments: Identifies long-term leases on real estate, outstanding contracts for the purchase or lease of major equipment, and contracts underway for the construction or major renovation of any facility.

Subsequent Events Note: Discloses significant events that occur between the end of the accounting period and the annual report publication date.

Quarterly Data Note: Itemizes the revenues, expenses, net income, and earnings per share for each quarter of the accounting period.

Related Party Transactions: Identifies transactions that occur between the parent company and one or more of its subsidiaries.

Prior Period Adjustments: Describes corrections or adjustments from previous accounting periods.

Publicly traded companies in both the United States and Canada must include in the annual report a ***Management Discussion and Analysis of Financial Condition and Results of Operations (MD&A),*** sometimes called the *Financial Review.* The MD&A presents the analysis and interpretation of a company's financial statements and company performance from management's point of view. More technical than the letter to stockholders, this section includes management's comments on the company's liquidity, the effects of certain economic conditions on the company's operations, commitments to capital expenditures, unusual transactions, and expected changes in the debt-equity mix of the company's financial operations. Generally, the MD&A delivers management's comments on the company's future prospects and a qualitative, as well as quantitative, analysis of the company's fundamentals from the perspective of a corporate insider.

Another example of supplementary information includes a 5- or 10-year historical comparison of major balance sheet and statement of operations items, as well as a historical comparison of dividends, earnings per share, and working capital from previous accounting periods. In addition, the FASB encourages companies to disclose the effects of inflation on the company's financial statement amounts. Supplying this information is not as important during periods of low inflation, but the FASB has required such information during periods of high inflation, which significantly affects purchasing power. The FASB also requires large, publicly traded companies to disclose inflationary effects on replacement costs for significant equipment purchases.

Auditor's Report

An annual report includes an ***auditor's report,*** also called the *accountant's report,* which is a statement by independent public accountants who have audited the annual report. The purpose of the auditor's report is for an objective third party to attest that the information contained in the annual report fairly represents the operations of the company. The auditor's report is a short statement, typically consisting of only three paragraphs. The first paragraph identifies the financial statements that are subject to the auditor's report and identifies the responsibilities of the company and the independent auditors regarding the annual report. The second paragraph states that the auditor's examination was performed according to generally accepted auditing standards (GAAS). In the final paragraph, the independent auditors state whether or not the financial statements appear to have been prepared according to GAAP. The auditor's opinion does not guarantee the accuracy of the financial statements. It simply indicates whether the annual report appears to offer a fair representation of the company's financial position and operations in accordance with GAAP.

Financial Statement Integration

A company's financial statements are *integrative*—that is, they relate to, explain, and complement each other. Figure 5-13 illustrates the interrelationship among the balance sheet, statement of operations, statement of cash flows, and statement of stockholders' equity for the Embassy Life and Health Insurance Company, a stock insurer.

The statement of operations and the statement of cash flows are dynamic measures and provide the critical links between the changes in two consecutive balance sheets, which are static measures. Recall that net income in the statement of cash flows minus cash dividends paid to stockholders equals the change in retained earnings on the balance sheet between two accounting periods. Another relationship between the balance sheet and the statement of operations is that an increase in various expenses (statement of operations accounts) decreases cash or increases short-term or long-term liabilities (balance sheet accounts), depending on the nature of the expense. Review Figure 5-13 to see how net income connects the financial statements in the following ways:

1. The $1,000,009 of net income on the statement of operations appears in the statement of stockholders' equity and helps explain the change in owners' equity.

2. The net income figure of $1,000,009 is also a cash flow provided by operating activities on the statement of cash flows.

3. The stockholders' equity section of the balance sheet is a summary of the figures obtained from the statement of stockholders' equity, which includes the amount of net income.

A net loss in the statement of operations results in a decrease in retained earnings in the statement of stockholders' equity. A net loss is also a cash flow *used* in operating activities on the statement of cash flows. Net income is thus the balancing figure between retained earnings on the statement of stockholders' equity and retained earnings on the balance sheet.

The indirect method of preparing the statement of cash flows demonstrates the interrelationship between the statement of operations,

Figure 5-13. Interrelationships among Embassy Life and Health Insurance Company's primary financial statements.

Embassy Life and Health Insurance Company
GAAP-Basis Consolidated Statements of Operations

For the years ended December 31,	2000	1999
Revenues		
Premiums:		
Life	x,xxx,xxx	x,xxx,xxx
Accident and health	x,xxx,xxx	x,xxx,xxx
Investment income	xxx,xxx	xxx,xxx
Other	xx,xxx	xx,xxx
Total Revenues	x,xxx,xxx	x,xxx,xxx
Benefits and Expenses		
Life and other benefits	x,xxx,xxx	x,xxx,xxx
Accident and health benefits	x,xxx,xxx	xx,xxx
Increase in liability for future policy benefits	xx,xxx	xx,xxx
Commissions and fees	xxx,xxx	xxx,xxx
Salaries	xxx,xxx	xxx,xxx
Other operating expenses	x,xxx,xxx	xx,xxx
Income Before Income Tax Expense	x,xxx,xxx	x,xxx,xxx
Income Tax Expense (Benefit)	xx,xxx	xx,xxx
Net Income (Loss)	1,000,009	x,xxx,xxx

Embassy Life and Health Insurance Company
GAAP-Basis Consolidated Statements of Stockholders' Equity

For the years ended December 31, 1999 and 2000	Capital Stock	Additional Paid-In Capital	Net Realized Gain (Loss) on Securities Available for Sale	Retained Earnings
Balance, January 1, 1999			x,xxx	x,xxx
Net income				x,xxx,xxx
Issuance of common stock, 1,500,000 shares	x,xxx,xxx	x,xxx,xxx		
Change in net unrealized gain on securities available for sale				
Balance, December 31, 1999	x,xxx,xxx	x,xxx,xxx	x,xxx	x,xxx,xxx
Net income				x,xxx,xxx
Change in unrealized gain (loss) on securities available for sale			(xxx,xxx)	1,000,009
Balance, December 31, 2000	x,xxx,xxx	x,xxx,xxx	(xxx,xxx)	5,446,766

Figure 5-13. Interrelationships among Embassy Life and Health Insurance Company's primary financial statements (continued).

Embassy Life and Health Insurance Company
GAAP-Basis Consolidated Statements of Cash Flows

For the years ended December 31,	2000	1999
Cash Flows from Operating Activities		
Net income	1,000,009	x,xxx,xxx
Adjustments to reconcile net income to net cash from operating activities:		
Depreciation and amortization	xxx,xxx	xxx,xxx
Gain (loss) on sale of securities available for sale	xxx	(xxx)
Loss on disposition of property and equipment	xxx	xxx
Changes in assets and liabilities:		
Policy liabilities	xxx,xxx	xxx,xxx
Expenses due and accrued	(xx,xxx)	(xx,xxx)
Cash dividends payable to stockholders	xxx,xxx	xxx,xxx
Net Cash from Operating Activities	x,xxx,xxx	x,xxx,xxx
Cash Flows from Investing Activities		
Additions to property and equipment	(xx,xxx)	(xx,xxx)
Proceeds from sale of equipment	x,xxx	xxx
Purchases of securities available for sale	(x,xxx,xxx)	(x,xxx,xxx)
Proceeds from sales of securities available for sale	x,xxx,xxx	x,xxx,xxx
Proceeds from maturities of securities available for sale	x,xxx,xxx	x,xxx,xxx
Net Cash Used in Investing Activities	(x,xxx,xxx)	(x,xxx,xxx)
Cash Flows from Financing Activities		
Proceeds from issuance of capital stock	x,xxx,xxx	x,xxx,xxx
Net Increase (Decrease) in Cash and Cash Equivalents	(xxx,xxx)	xxx,xxx
Cash and Cash Equivalents		
Beginning of year	xxx,xxx	xxx,xxx
End of year	xxx,xxx	xxx,xxx

Net Income

Embassy Life and Health Insurance Company
GAAP-Basis Consolidated Balance Sheets

December 31,	2000	1999
Assets		
Securities available for sale:		
Debt securities	xx,xxx	xx,xxx
Equity securities	xxx,xxx	xxx,xxx
Cash and cash equivalents	xxx,xxx	xxx,xxx
Total Securities Available for Sale	xx,xxx,xxx	xx,xxx,xxx
Premiums Receivable		
Investment income due and accrued	x,xxx,xxx	x,xxx,xxx
Deferred policy acquisition costs	xx,xxx	xx,xxx
Total Receivables and Other Assets	x,xxx,xxx	x,xxx,xxx
Property and equipment, net	xx,xxx	xx,xxx
Total Assets	xx,xxx,xxx	xx,xxx,xxx
Liabilities and Stockholders' Equity		
Policy liabilities:		
Future policy benefits:		
Life	x,xxx,xxx	x,xxx,xxx
Accident and health	xxx,xxx	xxx,xxx
Unpaid claims	xxx,xxx	xxx,xxx
Other	xxx,xxx	xxx,xxx
Total Policy Liabilities	x,xxx,xxx	x,xxx,xxx
Expenses due and accrued	xx,xxx	xx,xxx
Cash dividends payable to stockholders	x,xxx,xxx	x,xxx,xxx
Total Liabilities	x,xxx,xxx	x,xxx,xxx
Stockholders' Equity		
Common stock, $2.00 par value;	x,xxx,xxx	x,xxx,xxx
authorized—5,000,000 shares;	x,xxx,xxx	x,xxx,xxx
issued and outstanding—1,500,000	x,xxx,xxx	x,xxx,xxx
Additional paid-in capital	xxx,xxx	xxx,xxx
Unrealized gain (loss)	(xx,xxx)	(xx,xxx)
Retained earnings	5,446,766	x,xxx,xxx
Total Stockholders' Equity	x,xxx,xxx	x,xxx,xxx

Retained Earnings

the balance sheet, and the statement of cash flows. Recall that, under the indirect method, the statement of cash flows begins with net income, which is taken directly from the statement of operations. This figure is then adjusted up or down according to changes on the balance sheet, such as increases or decreases to policy liabilities, expenses due and accrued, and cash dividends payable to stockholders.

Conclusion

In this chapter, we introduced you to the GAAP-based financial statements found in the annual reports of most stock and mutual insurance companies. Throughout the text, we discuss in more detail the major financial items and concepts introduced here. The next chapter discusses the main components of the U.S. Annual Statement and the Canadian Annual Return. In later chapters, we discuss how managers can apply and adapt the information contained in the company's financial statements in order to make decisions that will enable the company to achieve its goals.

Key Terms and Concepts

consolidated financial statements
account form
report form
net income
net loss
single-step statement of operations
multiple-step statement of operations
profit
gain
loss
discontinued operations
extraordinary item
operating efficiency
cash inflow
cash outflow
operating activities
investing activities
financing activities
direct method
indirect method
stock
outstanding stock
dividends
cash dividend
stock dividend
common stock
preferred stock
par value
additional paid-in capital
treasury stock
unrealized gain (loss)
retained earnings
prior period adjustments
notes to the financial statements
Management Discussion and Analysis of Financial Condition and Results of Operations (MD&A)
auditor's report

CHAPTER 6

An Overview of the Annual Statement

Learning Objectives

After studying this chapter, you should be able to

- Identify the components and explain the purpose of the U.S. Annual Statement and Canadian Annual Return
- Provide examples of admitted assets and nonadmitted assets
- Distinguish among deferred premiums, uncollected premiums, advance premiums, and unearned premiums
- Describe an insurer's policy and contract claims
- Explain the key differences between GAAP-based financial statements and the statutory Annual Statement
- Explain the purposes of the interest maintenance reserve and the asset valuation reserve for U.S. life and health insurance companies

Chapter Outline

Balance Sheet

Assets

Liabilities, Surplus and Other Funds

Summary of Operations

Capital and Surplus Account

Statutory to GAAP Reconciliation

Other Statements and Schedules

Cash Flow

Analysis of Operations by Lines of Business

Five-Year Historical Data

Other Exhibits

Insurance companies have an obligation to keep many different individuals informed of their operating performance and financial condition. As we saw in the previous chapter, all stock insurers and many mutual companies use the annual report as a vehicle to provide financial information to stockholders, policyowners, investors, and other members of the general public.

An arguably even more important financial document for U.S. life and health insurance companies is the Annual Statement. Recall from Chapter 1 that the ***Annual Statement*** is a financial report that every U.S. insurer must file annually, as well as on a quarterly basis, with the National Association of Insurance Commissioners (NAIC) and with the insurance commissioner or department of all states in which the insurer conducts business. The Canadian equivalent of the Annual Statement is the ***Annual Return,*** which must be filed with the Office of the Superintendent of Financial Institutions (OSFI) and in all provinces in which an insurer does business. The purpose of the Annual Statement and Annual Return is the same: to show the status of an insurer's assets, liabilities, capital and surplus (the specific owners' equity accounts for life and health insurance companies), revenues, and expenses, with an emphasis on demonstrating the insurer's solvency. However, the preparation of these two statements differs. Insurers with U.S. business prepare the Annual Statement according to statutory accounting practices. Insurers with Canadian business prepare the Annual Return according to Canadian generally accepted accounting principles (GAAP), which is similar to U.S. GAAP.

The Annual Statement is known as a *statutory financial statement* because government statute prescribes its format. Specifically, the NAIC establishes a standardized format for the Annual Statement. The insurance department of each state specifies which Annual Statement schedules and exhibits that insurers doing business in the state must file. For example, all insurers with business in State A file the Annual Statement schedules required by State A's insurance commissioner. Insurers also file a copy of the Annual Statement with the NAIC. In Canada, the OSFI prescribes the Annual Return for use by companies registered under the *Insurance Companies Act.* Because the accounting, insurance, regulatory, investment, and economic environments are always changing, the respective countries' regulatory bodies usually update the Annual Statement and Annual Return forms each year. The financial reporting date of the Annual Statement is December 31, but the financial reporting date of the Annual Return can be either October 31 or December 31.

Unlike the annual report, which contains general-purpose financial statements for public use, only regulators and rating agencies normally review the Annual Statement. Because the Annual Statement is a public document, other interested parties may obtain a copy of an insurer's Annual Statement by contacting the state insurance department. A company's Annual Statement contains considerable data extracted from the company's accounting, actuarial, and statistical records. The Annual Statement includes a balance sheet in the form of separate pages for (1) assets, (2) liabilities, surplus, and other funds, (3) a summary of operations, and (4) a statement of cash flows. The Annual Statement also contains numerous supporting exhibits and schedules that provide details to support the summary information found in the primary financial statements. To give you an idea of its size, the 1995 U.S. Annual Statement consisted of 112 pages of financial data, including 22 schedules and 18 exhibits.

A word of encouragement: Do not be intimidated by the extent of information you encounter in this chapter. The goal is not for you to memorize every line item of every schedule and exhibit in the Annual Statement. Instead, our aim is to introduce you to the major statutory statements so you can understand their importance and the characteristics that distinguish them from the GAAP-based financial statements found in annual reports. As with our discussion of the annual report, we begin with the balance sheet.

Balance Sheet

When you look at an insurer's Annual Statement, you will not see the term "balance sheet" on any of the exhibits or schedules. Instead, the Annual Statement presents an *Assets* page and a *Liabilities, Surplus and Other Funds* page. These pages face each other and together comprise a complete balance sheet. The corresponding pages on the Annual Return are (1) an *Assets* page and (2) a *Liabilities, Policyholders' and Shareholders' Equity* page. The Annual Statement *Assets* page format differs from the assets portion of the balance sheet in the annual report. The purpose of this format is to demonstrate the insurer's degree of *statutory solvency:* the minimum amount of capital and surplus specified by insurance regulators. Statutory solvency is not equivalent to ***economic solvency,*** also called *technical solvency,* which is the ability of a company to meet its financial obligations as they come due. Economic solvency is a concern for all companies. Insurance companies, because of the nature of their business, are also subject to statutory solvency. Most references to solvency in this text refer to statutory solvency.

Despite its usefulness as a financial statement, the balance sheet is not a guarantee of an insurer's solvency. First, a balance sheet is a snapshot of a company's financial strength as of a specified date. Therefore, the amounts reported in the insurer's asset, liability, and capital or surplus accounts are likely to differ from one date to another. During periods of rapidly changing economic conditions, the differences between one balance sheet "snapshot" and another could be large and could occur quickly. Thus, a company that appeared solvent on one balance sheet may appear borderline or even insolvent in another. Second, the value of an insurer's assets can vary depending on the valuation method used for the balance sheet. For example, real estate is normally shown on the balance sheet at book value less encumbrances (valid claims on the property, such as a mortgage), even though this amount may not reflect the current market value (the actual price at which the property could be sold today).

Because an insurer's obligations span many economic cycles, it is important for regulators to monitor the financial condition with an emphasis on solvency. For this reason, the main focus of the Annual Statement balance sheet is on whether an insurer has sufficient assets, conservatively measured, to provide for the settlement of policy claims immediately due or due in the future. These limitations that are inherent in the balance sheet exemplify the importance of reviewing all of a company's financial statements together, not just one of them in isolation.

Assets

Assets on the Annual Statement, as on the GAAP-based annual report, represent things of value owned by an insurance company. Figures 6-1 and 6-2 show the *Assets* pages from the Annual Statement and the Annual Return, respectively. In this chapter, we use the Annual Statement pages for the Industry Life Insurance Company for illustrative purposes. As you can see, these pages show many of the same categories of assets—bonds, stock, real estate, and cash—that an insurance company lists on its GAAP-based balance sheet in the annual report. However, the asset amounts in the annual report seldom, if ever, equal the asset amounts on the *Assets* page of the U.S. Annual Statement. Statutory accounting differentiates between two basic types of assets: *admitted assets* and *nonadmitted assets.*

Admitted assets are those assets that state insurance law permits to be included on the *Assets* page of the Annual Statement. ***Nonadmitted assets*** are those assets that state insurance law prohibits from being included on the *Assets* page. In other words, an annual report balance sheet shows *all* an insurer's assets, while the Annual Statement *Assets* page shows only the total of *admitted* assets. The reason for

Figure 6-1. *Assets*—U.S. Annual Statement.

ASSETS			
		1 December 31, 1995	2 December 31, 1994
1.	Bonds (less .... $0 liability for asset transfers with put options)	316,689,427	312,135,670
2.	Stocks:		
	2.1 Preferred stocks		
	2.2 Common stocks	2,000	
3.	Mortgage loans on real estate	71,428,839	64,547,665
4.	Real estate:		
	4.1 Properties occupied by the company (less .... $0 encumbrances)		
	4.2 Properties acquired in satisfaction of debt (less .... $0 encumbrances)	5,816,146	7,534,676
	4.3 Investment real estate (less .... $0 encumbrances)		
5.	Policy loans	51,740,233	50,719,951
6.	Premium notes, including .... $0 for first year premiums		
7.	Collateral loans		
	8.1 Cash on hand and on deposit	2,460,584	2,544,758
	8.2 Short-term investments		
9.	Other invested assets		
10.	Aggregate write-ins for invested assets	654,485	
10A.	Subtotals, cash and invested assets (Lines 1 to 10)	448,791,714	437,482,720
11.	Reinsurance ceded:		
	11.1 Amounts recoverable from reinsurers	1,708,484	182,664
	11.2 Commissions and expense allowances due	143,958	2,122
	11.3 Experience rating and other refunds due	50	1,597
12.	Electronic data processing equipment	205,714	182,229
13.	Federal income tax recoverable	485,562	1,349,091
14.	Life insurance premiums and annuity considerations deferred and uncollected	6,170,771	6,322,794
15.	Accident and health premiums due and unpaid		
16.	Investment income due and accrued	6,498,487	6,637,745
17.	Net adjustment in assets and liabilities due to foreign exchange rates		
18.	Receivable from parent, subsidiaries and affiliates		
19.	Amounts receivable relating to uninsured accident and health plans		
21.	Aggregate write-ins for other than invested assets	268,811	219,296
22.	Total assets excluding Separate Accounts business (Lines 10A to 21)	464,273,551	452,380,258
23.	From Separate Accounts Statement		
24.	Totals (Lines 22 and 23)	464,273,551	452,380,258
	DETAILS OF WRITE-INS		
1001.	Accounts receivable — sale of securities	654,485	
1002.			
1003.			
1098.	Summary of remaining write-ins for Line 10 from overflow page		
1099.	Totals (Lines 1001 thru 1003 plus 1098) (Line 10 above)	654,485	
2101.	State guarantee fund	260,902	214,907
2102.	Other miscellaneous assets	7,909	
2103.	Leasehold improvements		4,389
2198.	Summary of remaining write-ins for Line 21 from overflow page		
2199.	Totals (Lines 2101 thru 2103 plus 2198) (Line 21 above)	268,811	219,296

Figure 6-2. *Assets*—Canadian Annual Return.

Non-Consolidated Financial Statements
ASSETS
($'000)

Reference Page		Line	Current Year (01)	Prior Year (02)
	Cash	02		
40.60	Accrued Investment Income	07		
70.60	Accounts Receivable	10		
	Investments and Loans:			
	Fixed Term Investments:			
	Short Term Investments	15		
	Policy Loans	20		
	Other Loans	21		
	Bonds and Debentures:			
	Fixed Term	23		
	Convertible	24		
	Other	28		
70.21	Mortgage Loans	30		
	Preferred Shares—Fixed Term	31		
	Total Fixed Term Investments	39		
	Equity Investments:			
	Preferred Shares	42		
	Common Shares	45		
70.29	Real Estate	51		
	Other Equity Investments	59		
	Total Equity Investments	60		
70.14	Other Invested Assets	62		
	Total Investments and Loans	70		
70.14	Interests in Joint Ventures	78		
70.11–12	Investments in Subsidiaries	79		
	Deferred Income Taxes	80		
70.60	Goodwill and Other Assets	81		
	TOTAL ASSETS	89		
	Total Assets in Segregated Funds	99		

the distinction is accounting conservatism. One way that state regulators ensure accounting conservatism among insurance companies is by assigning limited value or no value to certain assets, that is, nonadmitted assets. In the following sections, we discuss specific types of assets that regulators classify as admitted and nonadmitted.

Admitted Assets

Admitted assets fall into three general classifications under statutory accounting: (1) invested assets, (2) other admitted assets, and (3) deferred, due, and accrued income. *Invested assets* are assets that produce income in the form of interest, rent, dividends, and capital gains. The major portion of an insurer's investment holdings consists of debt instruments, such as bonds, mortgage loans, and other investments that promise payment of fixed amounts on specified dates. Insurers invest a smaller percentage of funds in assets that are subject to wider market fluctuations, such as stocks and real estate. Invested assets also include cash, short-term investments, policy loans, and other investments not specifically categorized, such as joint ventures and partnership interests. Detailed information regarding invested assets appears in supporting schedules and exhibits in the Annual Statement, not on the *Assets* page itself. Supporting schedules and exhibits list the values of invested assets as of the statement date, including changes in value and the income received from each type of investment during the year. The schedule for mortgage loans, for example, lists mortgages by type of security, type of mortgage, and by state.

An insurer's *other admitted assets* may include reinsurance ceded, federal income tax recoverable, receivables from parent, subsidiary, or affiliate companies, and other items. ***Reinsurance*** is a transaction between two insurance companies in which one company—the ceding company—transfers part or all of its insurance risk to another company—the reinsurer. For a ceding company, the account Reinsurance Ceded includes (1) amounts recoverable from reinsurers, (2) commissions and expense allowances due from reinsurers, and (3) experience ratings and other refunds due. Federal income tax recoverable represents the amount of federal income taxes the insurer overpaid and expects to receive as a refund.

Deferred, due, and accrued income consists of (1) deferred and uncollected life insurance premiums and annuity considerations, (2) accident and health insurance premiums due and unpaid, and (3) investment income due and accrued. ***Deferred premiums,*** which are specific to U.S. insurers, are those life insurance premiums due after the date of the Annual Statement but before the next policy anniversary date and the next Annual Statement date. The deferred premium classification applies to premium payments made more frequently than annually. In other words, a deferred premium is a *modal* (for example, monthly, quarterly, semiannually) premium payment with a due date that falls between the Annual Statement date and the policy's next anniversary date. Because Canadian insurers use different methods of calculating policy reserves than those used by U.S. insurers, establishing an asset for deferred premiums is unnecessary for Canadian insurers.

Uncollected premiums (***premiums outstanding*** in Canada) are individual life insurance premiums and annuity considerations that are due on or before the Annual Statement date but that the insurer has not received by that date. Uncollected premiums for accident and health insurance and group life insurance premiums are typically called ***premiums due*** or *due premiums.* An *accident and health insurance premium due and unpaid* is one that is due before the Annual Statement date but that has not been paid by the policyowner as of the statement date. The terms *uncollected premiums* and *premiums due* are essentially equivalent. The difference is that, on the Annual Statement, the former refers primarily to life insurance and annuities, while the latter refers primarily to accident and health insurance. In short, deferred premiums are due after the statement date, whereas uncollected premiums are due before the statement date. On an Annual Statement dated December 31, one example of a *deferred* premium is the second installment of a semiannual premium that is due on January 15, before the policy anniversary date. An example of an *uncollected* premium is one that is due December 15 but is not paid until January 15. These two types of premiums are combined on the Annual Statement for statutory reporting purposes.

Accrued investment income is dividend income or interest income that, as of the statement date, the insurer has earned but not yet received. Assume that a company in which the insurer owns stock declares a cash dividend on December 29, and it intends to pay the dividend on January 10. As of December 31, the insurer considers that dividend to be accrued investment income.

Deferred and uncollected premiums are sometimes called *premium assets.* However, not all of a premium asset is admitted on the Annual Statement *Assets* page. Insurers can admit only the value of the *net premium*—that is, the gross premium minus the loading. The ***gross premium*** is the amount that policyowners must pay for their insurance coverage. The ***loading,*** also called *expense loading,* is a charge added to the net premium to (1) cover the insurer's operating expenses, (2) compensate for the loss of income when policies lapse, (3) provide contingency funds in the event of unexpected events like natural disasters, and (4) provide margins for profits and contributions to the insurer's surplus. The ***net premium*** is the amount of money needed to provide life insurance benefits for a policy. Insurers calculate the net premium by using an assumed interest rate and a tabular mortality rate, independent of the loading. Under statutory accounting, the net premium funds the policy's reserve.

Let's look at a numerical example that illustrates the relationship of gross premiums, net premiums, and loading. Assume that a policy's gross premium is $1,000, and the loading is 20 percent (or $200) of the gross premium. Given that we know

Net Premium = Gross Premium – Loading

then the net premium equals $800. The insurer includes this $800 premium asset on the *Assets* page and the $200 is reported elsewhere in the Annual Statement.

Nonadmitted Assets

Recall from our earlier definition that nonadmitted assets are assets to which U.S. insurance regulators assign no value or limited value in statutory reporting. Examples of nonadmitted assets include uncollected premiums that are more than 90 days overdue and furniture. Again, the purpose of restricting the presentation of certain assets is to ensure that an insurance company values its assets conservatively. The effect of not admitting certain assets is to reduce an insurer's reported surplus. In other words, if you reduce the total on the assets side of the basic accounting equation, you must reduce the total on the liabilities and surplus side by the same amount to keep the equation in balance.

Nonadmitted assets, most of which appear in a separate exhibit in the Annual Statement, include (1) *partially admitted assets* and (2) *entirely nonadmitted assets.* A *partially admitted asset* is an asset for which a portion of the value is admitted and the remainder is nonadmitted. Partially admitted assets include (1) investments that have a lower market value than their current book value and (2) investments that are below investment grade. *Investment-grade* assets are those assets that receive the NAIC Securities Valuation Office (SVO) Manual's top two ratings designations, which are equivalent to the top four categories of ratings provided by Moody's, Standard and Poor's, and other rating agencies. Because investments usually fluctuate in value, statutory accounting limits the value of the investment that an insurance company can admit. If an investment's current market value is lower than its book value, the difference is considered a nonadmitted asset. Suppose an insurer owns a non-investment-grade bond with a book value of $1,000 and a current market value of $750. For the Annual Statement, the insurer *writes down* the value of the asset to $750. Writing down the value of the bond in this way is an example of accounting conservatism. As we discuss later, the company then charges the remaining $250 to surplus as an unrealized loss.

As its name implies, no portion of an *entirely nonadmitted asset* can appear on the *Assets* page. Most entirely nonadmitted assets are those acquired in carrying out the normal process of doing business:

furniture, automobiles, most computer software, office supplies, most equipment, and amounts advanced to agents against future commissions. Ownership of nonadmitted assets is not necessarily a sign of financial weakness. Some of these assets, such as amounts advanced to agents, may be fully collectible. However, for the purposes of solvency and consistency with the conservatism of statutory accounting, this second category of nonadmitted assets is accorded no value on the *Assets* page.

The Canadian Annual Return does not distinguish between admitted and nonadmitted assets. Assets that are classified as nonadmitted on the U.S. Annual Statement are included on the *Assets* page of the Annual Return under Goodwill and Other Assets.

Separate Accounts

Separate accounts (called ***segregated funds*** in Canada) are accounts maintained outside a life insurance company's general account to help manage funds placed in nonguaranteed insurance products, such as equity-based or variable products. Unlike separate accounts, segregated funds also include policy proceeds payable on the death of the insured or upon surrender or maturity of the policy. A ***general account*** is an undivided account in which a life and health insurer maintains funds from guaranteed insurance products such as ordinary life insurance. An insurer typically maintains only one general account, but it may have more than one separate account. On the *Assets* page of both the Annual Statement and the Annual Return, insurance companies list assets in their separate accounts apart from assets in their general account. Insurers typically use separate accounts to fund

- Group and individual variable life insurance
- Group and individual universal life insurance
- Group and individual variable annuities
- Group pension contracts and other employee benefit plans

By maintaining separate accounts, insurers are able to modify some of their investment strategies without affecting the funds in the general accounts. The policyowner assumes most of the risks and rewards on investments in an insurer's separate accounts, whereas insurers guarantee minimum investment returns on the general account. Each separate account shows the assets and investment returns for that account and the flow of separate account funds to and from the general account. The insurer typically values the assets in its separate accounts at current market value as of the Annual Statement date. Besides including separate accounts on the *Assets* and *Liabilities* pages of the Annual Statement, U.S. insurers also file a Separate Accounts Annual Statement along with the Annual Statement. For Canadian insurers, the Segregated Funds (OSFI-85) is the equivalent document.

Liabilities, Surplus and Other Funds

Insurance companies identify all of their liabilities and sources of capital and surplus on the *Liabilities, Surplus and Other Funds* page of the Annual Statement. As on a GAAP balance sheet, most of an insurer's Annual Statement liabilities apply to (1) policies currently in force and (2) policies that have terminated with a remaining liability. The major item under the former category is policy reserves. The latter category includes death claims incurred but unpaid and settlement amounts left on deposit with the insurer. A smaller percentage of an insurer's liabilities represents unpaid administrative, maintenance, and corporate costs.

Liabilities on the Canadian Annual Return include net actuarial liabilities (reserves), other policy and contract liabilities, net deferred gains (losses) on the disposal of investments, and deferred income taxes. Figures 6-3 and 6-4 depict the *Liabilities, Surplus and Other Funds* page of the Annual Statement and the *Liabilities, Policyholders' and Shareholders' Equity* page of the Annual Return. In the following sections, we describe some of the liability and capital and surplus items commonly found on the Annual Statement and Annual Return.

Policy Reserves

The liability that shows the amount of money that, together with an insurer's future expected premiums and investment income earned from in-force policies, the insurer expects will be sufficient to pay future benefits on its in-force policies is known as ***policy reserves.*** To fund the proceeds of an insurance policy, insurers must maintain a reserve on the policy until the death claim is paid (for a whole life policy) or for the period of coverage specified in the policy (for term insurance and endowment contracts). Insurance companies show the aggregate of all policy reserves on the *Liabilities* page of the Annual Statement, which separates policy reserves into reserves for (1) life policies and contracts and (2) accident and health (A&H) policies. Individual state laws determine how insurers doing business in each state must calculate policy reserves for the Annual Statement. The Canadian Annual Return describes policy reserves as *net actuarial liabilities,* and Canadian insurers use the policy premium method (PPM) to calculate reserves. Policy reserves are often called *actuarial reserves* or *actuarial liabilities* because calculating these reserves is typically the responsibility of a company's actuaries. The Annual Statement also shows changes in the valuation bases of a company's

Figure 6-3. *Liabilities, Surplus and Other Funds*—U.S. Annual Statement.

LIABILITIES, SURPLUS AND OTHER FUNDS		1 December 31, 1995	2 December 31, 1994
1.	Aggregate reserve for life policies and contracts .... $359,410,607 (Exh. 8, Line H) less .... $0 included in Line 7.3 (including .... $33,233 Modco Reserve)	359,410,607	353,310,073
2.	Aggregate reserve for accident and health policies (Exhibit 9, Line 17, Col. 1) (including .... $0 Modco Reserve)		
3.	Supplementary contracts without life contingencies (Exhibit 10, Line 11, Col. 1) (including .... $0 Modco Reserve)	2,485,520	2,715,088
4.	Policy and contract claims:		
	4.1 Life (Exhibit 11, Part 1, Line 4d, Column 1 less sum of Columns 9, 10 and 11)	6,597,034	4,522,038
	4.2 Accident and health (Exhibit 11, Part 1, Line 4d, sum of Columns 9, 10 and 11)		
5.	Policyholders' dividend and coupon accumulations (Exhibit 10, Line 16, col. 1)	11,711,422	12,041,237
6.	Policyholders' dividends .... $126,012 and coupons .... $0 due and unpaid (Exhibit 7, Line 10)	126,012	116,809
7.	Provision for policyholders' dividends and coupons payable in following calendar year — estimate amounts:		
	7.1 Dividends apportioned for payment to .... April 30, 1996	1,370,721	1,425,894
	7.2 Dividends not yet apportioned	2,877,502	3,214,400
	7.3 Coupons and similar benefits		
8.	Amount provisionally held for deferred dividend policies not included in Line 7		
9.	Premiums and annuity considerations received in advance less .... $0 discount; including .... $0 accident and health premiums (Exhibit 1, Part 1, Col. 1, sum of Lines 4 and 14)	86,019	151,919
10.	Liability for premium and other deposit funds:		
	10.1 Policyholder premiums, including .... $0 deferred annuity liability	96,413	126,503
	10.2 Guaranteed interest contracts, including .... $16,735,681 deferred annuity liability	16,735,681	18,149,937
	10.3 Other contract deposit funds, including .... $1,477,990 deferred annuity liability	11,858,087	9,488,495
11.	Policy and contract liabilities not included elsewhere:		
	11.1 Surrender values on cancelled policies		
	11.2 Provision for experience rating refunds, including .... $0 A&H experience rating refunds		
	11.3 Other amounts payable on reinsurance assumed		
	11.4 Interest maintenance reserve (Page 48, Line 6)	3,422,631	2,749,515
12.	Commissions to agents due or accrued — life and annuity .... $0 accident and health $0		
12A.	Commissions and expense allowances payable on reinsurance assumed	219	(181)
13.	General expenses due or accrued (Exhibit 5, Line 12, Col. 5)	2,334,481	1,896,544
13A.	Transfers to Separate Accounts due or accrued (net)		
14.	Taxes, licenses and fees due or accrued, excluding federal income taxes (Exhibit 6, Line 9, Col. 5)	205,879	365,975
14A.	Federal income taxes due or accrued, including .... $391,037 on capital gains (excluding deferred taxes)		
15.	"Cost of collection" on premiums and annuity considerations deferred and uncollected in excess of total loading thereon	859,042	1,132,601
16.	Unearned investment income (Exhibit 2, Line 10, Col. 2)	56,478	36,762
17.	Amounts withheld or retained by company as agent or trustee	632,428	842,957
18.	Amounts held for agents' account, including .... $0 agents' credit balances	94,390	165,591
19.	Remittances and items not allocated	393,553	145,827
20.	Net adjustment in assets and liabilities due to foreign exchange rates		
21.	Liability for benefits for employees and agents if not included above	1,517,240	1,395,083
22.	Borrowed money .... $0 and interest thereon .... $0.		
23.	Dividends to stockholders declared and unpaid		
24.	Miscellaneous liabilities:		
	24.1 Asset Valuation Reserve (Page 49, Line 12, Col. 7)	5,071,383	4,462,724
	24.2 Reinsurance in unauthorized companies		29,192
	24.3 Funds held under reinsurance treaties with unauthorized reinsurers		
	24.4 Payable to parent, subsidiaries and affiliates	297,427	
	24.5 Drafts outstanding		
	24.6 Liability for amounts held under uninsured accident and health plans		
	24.7 Funds held under coinsurance		
25.	Aggregate write-ins for liabilities	1,513,481	1,224,034
26.	Total liabilities excluding Separate Accounts business (Lines 1 to 25)	429,753,650	419,709,017
27.	From Separate Accounts Statement		
28.	Total Liabilities (Lines 26 and 27)	429,753,650	419,709,017
29.	Common capital stock	6,600,000	6,600,000
30.	Preferred capital stock		
31.	Aggregate write-ins for other than special purpose funds		
32.	Surplus Notes		
33.	Gross paid in and contributed surplus (Page 3, Line 33, Col. 2 plus Page 4, Line 44a, Col.1)	13,835,804	12,085,872
34.	Aggregate write-ins for special purpose funds	400,000	400,000
35.	Unassigned funds (surplus)	13,684,097	13,585,369
36.	Less treasury stock, at cost:		
	(1) .... 0 shares common (value included in Line 29 .... $0)		
	(2) .... 0 shares preferred (value included in Line 30 .... $0)		
37.	Surplus (Total Lines 31 + 32 + 33 + 34 + 35 − 36)	27,919,901	26,071,241
38.	Totals of Lines 29, 30 and 37 (Page 4, Line 48)	34,519,901	32,671,241
39.	Totals of Lines 28 and 38 (Page 2, Line 24)	464,273,551	452,380,258
	DETAILS OF WRITE-INS		
2501.	Post retirement benefit	747,611	536,711
2502.	Due to reinsuring company	160,000	206,000
2503.	Miscellaneous liabilities	605,870	481,323
2598.	Summary of remaining write-ins for Line 25 from overflow page		
2599.	Totals (Lines 2501 thru 2503 plus 2598) (Line 25 above)	1,513,481	1,224,034
3101.			
3102.			
3103.			
3198.	Summary of remaining write-ins for Line 31 from overflow page		
3199.	Totals (Lines 3101 thru 3103 plus 3198) (Line 31 above)		
3401.	Reserve for state guaranty funds	400,000	400,000
3402.			
3403.			
3498.	Summary of remaining write-ins for Line 34 from overflow page		
3499.	Totals (Lines 3401 thru 3403 plus 3498) (Line 34 above)	400,000	400,000

Figure 6-4. *Liabilities, Policyholders' and Shareholders' Equity*—Canadian Annual Return.

Non-Consolidated Financial Statements
LIABILITIES, POLICYHOLDERS' AND SHAREHOLDERS' EQUITY
($'000)

Reference Page			Current Year (01)	Prior Year (02)
	Liabilities			
	Net Actuarial Liabilities			
50.70	Under Insurance Policies	02		
50.70	Under Annuity Contracts	03		
	Provision for Policyholder Dividends and Experience Rating Refunds	11		
	Outstanding Claims and Adjustment Expenses	12		
	Policyholder Amounts on Deposit	13		
60.11	Other Insurance Policy & Contract Liabilities	14		
60.11	Accounts Payable	31		
	Income Taxes Payable	32		
	Mortgage Loans and Other Real Estate Encumbrances	33		
60.11	Other Liabilities	39		
	Net Deferred Gains (Losses) on Disposal of Portfolio Investments	40		
	Deferred Income Taxes	49		
20.94	Subordinated Debt	50		
20.95	Other Debt	52		
	Total Liabilities	69		
	Policyholders' and Shareholders' Equity			
	Policyholders' Equity			
30.40	Participating Account	70		
30.40	Non-Participating Account (Mutual Companies Only)	72		
	Currency Translation Account	73		
	Shareholders' Equity			
10.60	Capital Stock	75		
10.60	Contributed Surplus	76		
30.40	Retained Earnings	77		
	Currency Translation Account	78		
	Total Policyholders' and Shareholders' Equity	79		
	TOTAL LIABILITIES AND EQUITY	89		
	Total Liabilities in Segregated Funds	99		

reserves. Changes occur because of adjustments in the mortality rate, morbidity rate, and interest rate assumptions the insurer's actuaries originally used to calculate policy reserves.

Policy and Contract Claims

Life insurance contracts obligate an insurance company to provide a benefit when a loss occurs, such as the death of an insured individual. Following the loss, the company is presented with a claim, and in most cases, the company knows the amount of its obligation to each policyowner. In the Annual Statement, the company must acknowledge any claims it has received but not yet paid. ***Policy and contract claims,*** also called *claim liabilities,* are liabilities for all types of insurance policy and annuity contract claims that must be settled. These claims include (1) due and unpaid claims, (2) resisted (contested) claims, (3) claims in the course of settlement, and (4) incurred but not reported (IBNR) claims.

- ***Due and unpaid claims*** are claims that have been approved by an insurer but have not yet been paid to the policy beneficiary.

- ***Resisted claims,*** also called *disputed claims,* are claims that an insurer has refused to pay but that it may pay in the future.

- ***Claims in the course of settlement*** are claims that have been reported to an insurer and that are being investigated.

- ***Incurred but not reported (IBNR) claims*** are claims that were incurred during an accounting period but have not been reported to the insurer as of the Annual Statement date. An insurer estimates its liability for IBNR claims based on its past claim experience. Then, the insurer categorizes these claims as either life claims or accident and health claims and reports the full amount of the benefits claimed—even if the amount is in dispute—on the *Liabilities* page.

Policy Dividend Liabilities

Liabilities for all policy dividends that have been declared by a company's board of directors, but which have not yet been paid, are known as ***policy dividend liabilities,*** or, for U.S. fraternal insurers, *refund accumulations* or *refunds due and unpaid.* A ***policy dividend,*** also called a *policyowner dividend* or *policyholder dividend,* is a policyowner's share of an insurer's divisible surplus. The ***divisible surplus*** is the amount of an insurer's surplus that is available for distribution to owners of participating policies. In essence, a policy dividend is a refund of premiums as a result of better-than-expected claim experience for a particular block of policies. Policy dividends also may include a distribution of ownership from the insurer to its policyowners.

Under a participating insurance policy or annuity contract, a policyowner typically is eligible to receive policy dividends if two conditions are met: (1) the policy must be in force on its anniversary date and (2) the policy's premiums must be current as of a specified date. Some policy dividends may never become payable because these conditions will not have been met. Under statutory accounting, an insurer estimates its policy dividend liability on the basis of its estimates for the next year's dividend payments. In contrast, under GAAP, the insurer estimates as a component of its policy reserves the present value of *all* future policy dividends, not just next year's dividend payments. The *present value* of future policy dividends is the amount that must be invested on a specified date in order to accumulate to the required amount on the date the dividends are to be paid. We discuss present value in Chapter 14.

Liability for Premium and Other Deposit Funds

Occasionally, policyowners pay premiums more than one year before their due date. A company that receives this premium deposit must record it as a liability and must credit interest to it annually. The Annual Statement lists amounts left with an insurer to accumulate interest under ***liability for premium and other deposit funds.*** In addition to premiums received by the company more than one year before their due date, this liability category includes guaranteed interest contracts and other contract deposit funds. A ***guaranteed interest contract (GIC),*** also called a *guaranteed income contract* or a *guaranteed investment contract,* is a funding vehicle in which an insurer accepts a deposit from a pension plan sponsor for a specified period of time, such as five years, and holds the deposit at a specified rate of interest. At the end of the period, the insurer returns the deposited funds, including accumulated interest, to the pension plan sponsor, who in turn can reinvest the plan assets with the same insurer or with another financial institution.

Unearned Income

Unearned income includes (1) advance premiums and (2) investment income received in advance and any portion of investment income that has already been received but which may be allocable to the following calendar year. ***Advance premiums,*** also called *premiums paid in advance,* is the total of life insurance premiums received by the company before the statement date but which are due after the statement date and on or after the next policy anniversary date. Some life insurance companies include in this category premiums paid several years in advance, but these amounts are usually considered amounts held on deposit, as described in the preceding section. ***Unearned premiums,*** also called *unearned premium reserves,* is that portion of an insurance premium received by the statement date, applicable to the insurance coverage to be provided in the following period but before the next policy anniversary date. Unearned premiums are not included with advance premiums. Instead, the unearned portion of the premium is reported with the policy reserves and labeled *unearned premium reserve* on the Annual Statement. Unearned premiums are typically associated with accident and health insurance policies. However, they may also apply to life insurance policies under certain reserve methods. We discuss unearned premium reserves in more detail in Chapter 9. The important distinction between unearned and advance premiums is that advance premiums are amounts received by the statement date but due *on or after* the next policy anniversary date, while unearned premiums are amounts received by the statement date but due *before* the next policy anniversary date and the next statement date. To illustrate this difference, assume that, on December 1, 1999, the Mainstream Life and Health Insurance Company receives a premium payment of $288 from policyowner George McCleary. The annual premium on the policy is $144, and the policy anniversary date is December 1. On its December 31, 1999, Annual Statement, Mainstream reports the following amounts from Mr. McCleary's remittance:

Premium income	$ 12	(for Dec. 1, 1999, through Dec. 31, 1999)
Unearned premium	132	(for Jan. 1, 2000, through Nov. 30, 2000)
Advance premium	144	(for Dec. 1, 2000, through Nov. 30, 2001)
	$288	

Below is a timeline that differentiates among *advance premiums, unearned premiums,* and earned, collected premiums (*premium income*) for Mr. McCleary's policy:

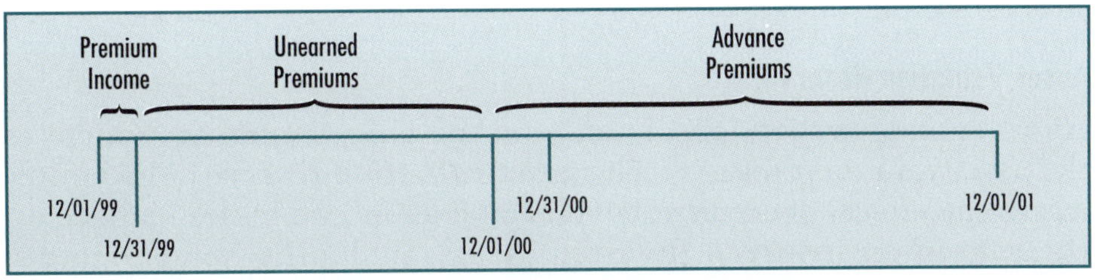

Amounts Temporarily Held for Disposition

Amounts temporarily held for disposition covers only a few items on the *Liabilities* page of the Annual Statement but represents most of the company's liabilities associated with cash transactions. These transactions include (1) deposits by mortgagors to escrow accounts that will be used to pay future taxes and property/casualty or hazard insurance premiums on real estate, (2) amounts withheld from wages and salary payments, such as income tax withholdings, social security taxes, and employee contributions to pension plans, and (3) amounts, other than commissions, held for agents (such as bonuses and expense reimbursements).

Interest Maintenance Reserve

The ***interest maintenance reserve (IMR)*** is a reserve that absorbs the realized net gains and losses, caused by changes in the economy, from the sale of fixed-income securities by U.S. life and health insurance companies. Canadian insurers use a different method for recognizing these realized gains and losses. For the IMR to absorb these realized gains and losses, they must be related to changes in interest rates, rather than to changes in a particular investment's rating or some other reason. The IMR is a liability that amortizes (spreads) into investment income over the remaining life of an investment the gain (loss) from the sale of the investment. As a result, the insurer is able to report only a portion of one investment's realized gain or loss on the statement of operations in a given year. The IMR prevents companies from showing an inflated net income from the sale of a security for a relatively high price, or from being unduly hurt by the sale of a security for a relatively low price.

The IMR helps to protect an insurer's net gain from operations and its surplus from the effects of interest rate risk. ***Interest rate risk*** refers to the potential problems caused by unpredictable fluctuations in interest rates. In addition to calculating IMR for its general account, under certain conditions, the insurer must also calculate the IMR for each of its separate accounts that maintains assets at values other than current market values. An insurer does not need to calculate the IMR for a separate account that contains only variable annuities, however.

Asset Valuation Reserve

Another reserve that appears only on the U.S. Annual Statement is the asset valuation reserve. The ***asset valuation reserve (AVR)*** minimizes the effects of credit-related capital gains and losses realized on the sale of an insurer's invested assets, including bonds, stocks, mortgages, and real estate. There is no equivalent reserve for Canadian insurers. The AVR excludes cash, policy loans, and similar assets that typically do not have substantial exposure to ***credit risk,*** which is the financial risk that an obligation will not be paid, resulting in a loss. Below are examples of credit risk that can change the value of an invested asset:

- A bond issuer fails to pay interest or principal on the bond.
- A mortgage borrower fails to make mortgage payments.
- A stock issuer suffers financial hardship and files for bankruptcy.
- Real estate owned to generate rental income remains unoccupied.

The AVR thus focuses on the quality of assets in an insurer's investment ***portfolio,*** which is a collection of financial assets such as stocks and bonds. In contrast, the IMR focuses on how changes in interest rates affect the value of the insurer's investments.

To illustrate the difference between the IMR and the AVR, assume that the Formidable Life and Health Insurance Company purchases two different bonds for $1,000 each. One year later, it sells the bonds for $900 each. The value of Bond A declined during the year because of a rise in interest rates. The value of Bond B declined because, during the year, several bond rating agencies lowered the bond's quality rating to below investment grade. Formidable includes the $100 realized loss on Bond A in its IMR calculation, because the realized loss resulted from a change in interest rates. On the other hand, the realized loss on Bond B was credit-related. Therefore, Formidable includes the realized loss on Bond B in the AVR.

Capital Stock and Surplus

In the United States, capital and surplus items appear on the *Liabilities, Surplus and Other Funds* page of the Annual Statement. The statement subdivides capital stock into common capital stock and preferred capital stock, each of which represents the number of outstanding shares of a company's stock multiplied by its par value per share. Recall that Canadian companies make no reference to a stock's par value. Therefore, stock on the Annual Return is calculated by multiplying the number of outstanding shares by the actual price paid for the shares at issue.

Surplus on the U.S. Annual Statement consists of the sum of the following categories, minus any treasury stock (repurchases of the insurer's own outstanding stock):

- *Surplus notes,* also called *surplus debentures* or *contribution certificates,* which are a form of long-term, unsecured debt obligation that provide for the payment of (1) semiannual interest and (2) principal on or before a set maturity date. Surplus notes have characteristics of both debt and equity, though companies include them among surplus for statutory reporting purposes. Under GAAP, surplus notes must be reported as liabilities. Insurers issue surplus notes to raise money for normal business operations, for expansion, or for other purposes. Principal and interest payments must be approved by the state insurance department.

- *Gross paid-in and contributed surplus,* which is the aggregate amount paid above the par value for shares of the insurer's stock. This item is similar to Additional Paid-in Capital on a GAAP-based balance sheet.

- *Unassigned funds (surplus),* which is the total amount of undistributed and unapportioned surplus remaining in the company since it began operations. To determine the change in unassigned surplus from one statement to the next, the company deducts liabilities, capital, and special surplus funds from admitted assets. Dividends paid to stockholders are withdrawn from unassigned funds. This item is similar to Retained Earnings on a GAAP-based balance sheet.

We discuss these surplus accounts in Chapter 11.

The *Liabilities* page of the Canadian Annual Return separates owners' equity accounts into policyholders' equity and shareholders' equity. Policyholders' equity includes three items: (1) a participating account (for participating life insurance policies), (2) a nonparticipating account (mutual companies only), and (3) a currency translation account. The shareholders' equity section contains four items (the first two have equivalent items on the U.S. Annual Statement): (1) capital stock, (2) contributed surplus (gross paid-in and contributed surplus on the U.S. Annual Statement), (3) retained earnings, and (4) currency translation account. Keep in mind that the Annual Statement and Annual Return are similar to the GAAP-based balance sheet in that total assets must equal total liabilities and capital and surplus. You can verify this fact by comparing the total amounts, above the Details of Write-Ins, of Figure 6-1 with Figure 6-3.

Summary of Operations

The *Summary of Operations* page on the U.S. Annual Statement and the *Income Statement* on the Canadian Annual Return show a company's net income for the year. To compute a net gain (loss) from operations, the company totals its premium and investment income, then deducts benefit payments and expenses. Next, to determine its net income for the year, the company deducts dividends to policyholders and federal income taxes paid and adds *net* realized gains, which equal realized gains minus realized losses. Note that this is essentially the same format as the GAAP statement of operations. Figures 6-5 and 6-6 present the *Summary of Operations* page from the Annual Statement and the *Income Statement* page from the Annual Return, respectively. Compare these figures with the statement of operations in Figure 5-4.

The *Summary of Operations* page includes several broad categories. This page cross-references other Annual Statement exhibits that provide considerable detail regarding an insurer's specific revenue and expense items. A brief listing of some significant items on the *Summary of Operations* follows:

- *Premiums and annuity considerations* consists primarily of insurance premiums, annuity considerations, and considerations for supplementary contracts with and without life contingencies.

- *Net investment income* consists of the total of interest, dividends, and rent derived from invested assets, less depreciation on real estate and all costs of service and accounting for investments and investment income. Net investment income also includes amortization of discounts and premiums on securities. However, net investment income does not include gains or losses from the sale of equity investments (stocks and real estate) and gains and losses caused by changes in credit risk.

- *Policy benefits* consists of all types of contractual policy payments. These payments include death benefits, matured endowments, annuity benefits, disability benefits, benefits under accident and health insurance policies, surrender benefits, and payments on supplementary contracts, with and without life contingencies.

- *Increase in policy reserves* includes increases in reserves for policies with and without life contingencies.

- Other classifications included in the *Summary of Operations* are agent commissions, operating expenses, taxes, policy dividends, and increases in loading.

Compare these *Summary of Operations* items with those on the *Income Statement* page of the Canadian Annual Return:

- *Revenue* includes premiums from insurance and annuities, net investment income, fee income, and other revenue.

Figure 6-5. *Summary of Operations*—U.S. Annual Statement.

SUMMARY OF OPERATIONS
(Excluding Unrealized Capital Gains and Losses)

		1 1995	2 1994
1.	Premiums and annuity considerations (Exhibit 1, Part 1, Line 20d, Col. 1, less Col. 11)	49,074,909	44,511,322
1A.	Deposit-type funds		
2.	Considerations for supplementary contracts with life contingencies (Exhibit 12, Line 3, Col. 1)	38,990	150,766
3.	Considerations for supplementary contracts without life contingencies and dividend accumulations (Exhibit 12, Lines 4 and 5, Col. 1)	1,003,043	1,157,571
3A.	Coupons left to accumulate at interest (Exhibit 12, Line 5A, Col. 1)		
4.	Net investment income (includes .... \$0 equity in undistributed income or loss of subsidiaries) (Exhibit 2, Line 16)	35,401,410	32,957,027
4A.	Amortization of interest maintenance reserve (IMR) (Page 48, Line 5)	330,465	265,754
5.	Commissions and expense allowances on reinsurance ceded (Exhibit 1, Part 2, Line 26a, Col. 1)	199,785	76,877
5A.	Reserve adjustments on reinsurance ceded (Exhibit 12, Line 9A, Col. 1)	(20, 957)	1,478
6.	Aggregate write-ins for miscellaneous income	17,642	47,949
7.	Total (Lines 1 to 6)	86,045,287	79,168,744
8.	Death benefits	25,833,750	22,144,478
9.	Matured endowments (excluding guaranteed annual pure endowments)	462,995	353,189
10.	Annuity benefits (Exhibit 11, Part 2, Line 6d, Cols. 4 + 8)	12,564,960	13,158,250
11.	Disability benefits and benefits under accident and health policies	110,920	(25,195)
11A.	Coupons, guaranteed annual pure endowments and similar benefits (Exhibit 7, Line 15, Cols. 3 + 4)		
12.	Surrender benefits and other fund withdrawals	10,930,405	13,434,160
13.	Group conversions		
14.	Interest on policy or contract funds	1,570,828	1,932,810
15.	Payments on supplementary contracts with life contingencies (Exhibit 12, Line 20.1, Col. 1)	456,525	470,183
16.	Payments on supplementary contracts without life contingencies and of dividend accumulations (Exhibit 12, Lines 20.2 and 21, Col. 1)	1,829,911	1,790,878
16A.	Accumulated coupon payments (Exhibit 12, Line 21A, Col. 1)		
17.	Increase in aggregate reserves for life and accident and health policies and contracts	4,700,534	(2,089,691)
17A.	Increase in liability for premium and other deposit funds		
18.	Increase in reserve for supplementary contracts without life contingencies and for dividend and coupon accumulations	(559,383)	(276,543)
19.	Totals (Lines 8 to 18)	57,901,445	50,892,519
20.	Commissions on premiums and annuity considerations (direct business only) (Exhibit 1, Part 2, Line 30, Col. 1)	5,648, 170	4,975,978
21.	Commissions and expense allowances on reinsurance assumed (Exhibit 1, Part 2, Line 26b, Col. 1, less Col. 11)	14,281	22,167
22.	General insurance expenses (Exhibit 5, Line 10, Cols. 1 + 2 + 3)	14,019,241	13,412,068
23.	Insurance taxes, licenses and fees, excluding federal income taxes (Exhibit 6, Line 7, Cols. 1 + 2 + 3)	1,454, 103	1,377,158
24.	Increase in loading on and cost of collection in excess of loading on deferred and uncollected premiums	(163,900)	81,658
24A.	Net transfers to or (from) Separate Accounts		
25.	Aggregate write-ins for deductions	62,931	57,024
26.	Totals (Lines 19 to 25)	78,936,271	70,818,572
27.	Net gain from operations before dividends to policyholders and federal income taxes (Line 7 minus Line 26)	7,109,016	8,350,172
28.	Dividends to policyholders (Exhibit 7, Line 15, Cols. 1 and 2)	4,875,971	4,356,970
29.	Net gain from operations after dividends to policyholders and before federal income taxes (Line 27 minus Line 28)	2,233,045	3,993,202
30.	Federal income taxes incurred (excluding tax on capital gains)	172,492	188,921
31.	Net gain from operations after dividends to policyholders and federal income taxes and before realized capital gains or (losses) (Line 29 minus Line 30)	2,060,553	3,804,281
32.	Net realized capital gains or (losses) less capital gains tax and transferred to the IMR (Exhibit 3, Footnote (a), Line 3C)	(162,185)	(2,448,382)
33.	Net income (Line 31 plus Line 32)	1,898,368	1,355,899

Figure 6-6. *Income Statement*—Canadian Annual Return.

Non-Consolidated Financial Statements
INCOME STATEMENT
($'000)

Reference Page			Current Year (01)	Prior Year (02)
	Revenue			
	Premiums			
40.10/30	Insurance	01		
40.10	Annuities	03		
40.60	Net Investment Income	10		
40.70	Other Revenue	23		
	Total Revenue	29		
	Policy Benefits and Expenses			
	Policyholder Benefits			
40.20/30	Claims	30		
40.20	Annuity Payments	31		
	Other	32		
	Net Changes to Policy Liabilities			
	Insurance	33		
	Annuities	34		
	Policyholder Dividends and Experience Rating Refund	35		
	Commissions	40		
	Interest on Policyholder Amounts on Deposit	51		
	Interest on Subordinate Debt	52		
	Other Interest Expense	53		
40.70	General Expenses and Taxes (excl. Income Taxes)	60		
	Total Benefits and Expenses	68		
	Net Income Before Income Tax and Extraordinary Items	69		
	Provision for Income Taxes			
	Current	71		
	Deferred	72		
	Net Income (Loss) from Subsidiaries	73		
	Net Operating Income Before Extraordinary Items	80		
	Extraordinary Items (net of income taxes of $	85		
	Net Income	99		

Net Income is Attributable to:			
Participating Policyholders	101		
Non-Participating Account (Mutual Cos. Only)	103		
Shareholders	105		
Total	109		

- *Policy benefits and expenses* includes claims, annuity payments, changes in policy liabilities, policyholder dividends and experience rating refunds, commissions, and expenses other than income taxes.

- *Net income before income tax and extraordinary items* is the difference between total revenues and total benefits and expenses.

- *Net operating income before extraordinary items* is net income less income taxes.

- *Net operating income* is net income less extraordinary items.

- *Net income.*

Recall from Chapter 5 the relationships among an insurer's primary financial statements. Similarly, there are many inherent connections among the financial statements, exhibits, and schedules presented in the Annual Statement. The treatment of policy dividends on the *Summary of Operations* page and on the *Liabilities, Surplus and Other Funds* page illustrates one connection. For example, at the end of each year, the board of directors of a company that sells participating policies determines what, if any, dividends to pay to policyholders in the coming year. In making the decision to pay policy dividends, the company creates a liability: Policy Dividends Due and Unpaid. This liability recognizes that a certain amount is to be paid in the future. The actual payment of the first dividend (usually on or about the policy's anniversary date) reduces the liability but creates an expense such as Policy Dividends Paid. As the company pays more dividends, the liability decreases and the expense increases. The *Summary of Operations* includes the amount of policy dividends the insurer paid during the past year (an expense), while the *Liabilities* page shows the amount of policy dividends that are still due and payable from the past year (a liability).

Capital and Surplus Account

As you know, insurance companies record every business transaction in dollars received or receivable and spent or incurred. An insurer's managers can then summarize and analyze these transactions to determine their effect on the company's surplus during the year. The bottom section of the *Summary of Operations* page highlights the

"And this one is real scary ... he accidentally files a T-81 without completing Section 3."

Farcus ® comics by David Waisglass and Gordon Coulthart were reprinted with the permission of Laughingstock Licensing Inc.

changes in the capital and surplus account. Capital on the Annual Statement is similar to stock on the GAAP balance sheet. Surplus on the Annual Statement is what remains when liabilities and capital are subtracted from assets. The main capital and surplus categories on the Annual Statement are common capital stock, surplus notes, gross paid-in and contributed surplus, unassigned funds, and treasury stock. Figure 6-7 shows the *Capital and Surplus Account* section of the Annual Statement, while Figure 6-8 shows the *Capital Stock* and *Contributions to Surplus* sections of the Annual Return. Compare the GAAP-based statement of owners' equity (Figure 5-10) with the Annual Statement's *Capital and Surplus Account* section.

Net income (loss) from the *Summary of Operations* is one cause of the change in a life insurance company's surplus, which is why the *Summary of Operations* and the *Capital and Surplus Account* appear on the same page of the Annual Statement. But net income (loss) is not the only cause. We refer to several other sources of surplus changes as *direct changes in surplus.* The principal sources of surplus changes, as illustrated in the *Capital and Surplus Account* section, include the following:

Figure 6-7. *Capital and Surplus Account*—U.S. Annual Statement.

CAPITAL AND SURPLUS ACCOUNT		
34. Capital and surplus, December 31, previous year (Page 3, Line 38, Col. 2)	32,671,241	29,744,684
35. Net income (Line 33)	1,898,368	1,355,899
36. Change in net unrealized capital gains or (losses)	152,000	(82,500)
37. Change in non-admitted assets and related items (Exhibit 14, Line 13, Col. 3)	223,324	(872,573)
38. Change in liability for reinsurance in unauthorized companies (Page 3, Line 24.2, Col. 2 minus Col. 1)	29,192	27,231
39. Change in reserve on account of change in valuation basis, (increase) or decrease (Exh. 8A, Line D, Col. 4)		
40. Change in asset valuation reserve (Page 49, Col. 7, Line 2 thru Line 3a plus Line 11, Col. 7)	(608,659)	(175,779)
41. Change in treasury stock (Page 3, Lines 36 (1) & (2), Col. 2 minus Col. 1)		
42. Change in surplus in Separate Accounts Statement		
43. Capital changes:		
a. Paid in		
b. Transferred from surplus (Stock Dividend)		
c. Transferred to surplus (Exhibit 12, Line 24, Col. 1, capital portion)		
44. Surplus adjustments:		
a. Paid in	1,749,932	896,776
b. Transferred to capital (Stock Dividend) (Exhibit 12, Line 25, inside amount for stock $)		
c. Transferred from capital (Exhibit 12, Line 24, Col. 1, surplus portion)		
d. Change in surplus as a result of reinsurance		
45. Dividends to stockholders		
46. Aggregate write-ins for gains and losses in surplus	(1,595,497)	1,777,503)
47. Net change in capital and surplus for the year (Lines 35 through 46)	1,848,660	2,926,557
48. Capital and surplus, December 31, current year (Lines 34 + 47) (Page 3, Line 38)	34,519,901	32,671,241
DETAILS OF WRITE-INS		
0601. Miscellaneous profit on sundries	17,642	47,949
0602.		
0603.		
0698. Summary of remaining write-ins for Line 6 from overflow page		
0699. TOTALS (Lines 0601 thru 0603 plus 0698) (Line 6 above)	17,642	47,949
2501. Miscellaneous interest paid	62,931	57,024
2502.		
2503.		
2598. Summary of remaining write-ins for Line 25 from overflow page		
2599. TOTALS (Lines 2501 thru 2503 plus 2598) (Line 25 above)	62,931	57,024
4601. Additional Actuarial Reserves-asset/liability analysis	(1,595,497)	
4602. Change in mortgage loan valuation reserve		1,777,503
4603.		
4698. Summary of remaining write-ins for Line 46 from overflow page		
4699. TOTALS (Lines 4601 thru 4603 plus 4698) (Line 46 above)	(1,595,497)	1,777,503

Figure 6-8. *Capital Stock and Contributions to Surplus*—Canadian Annual Return.

CAPITAL STOCK
($'000)

		Description of Class of Shares			
		Common (01)	(02)	(03)	(04)
Authorized					
Number of shares	01				
Amount ($'000)	02				
Issued					
Beginning of Year					
Number of shares	10				
Amount ($'000)	11				
Calls Received					
Number of shares	20				
Amount ($'000)	21				
Shares issued					
Number of shares	30				
Amount ($'000)	31				
....	32				
....	33				
Forfeitures or Cancellations					
Number of shares	40				
Amount ($'000)	41				
End of Year					
Number of shares	50				
Amount ($'000)	51				
Balance Counted as MCCSR Capital*	55				
Dividends Declared During Year	60				

* If remaining period to redemption is 5 years or less, the balance (if qualifying) should be amortized in accordance with the MCCSR rules.

CONTRIBUTIONS TO SURPLUS
($'000)

Balance at Beginning of Year	70				
Change during Year**	71				
Balance at End of Year	72				

1. Have any shares been paid for in consideration other than Cash?

   75 (01) Yes ____ (02) No ____

   If yes, specify the type of consideration given, the market value of that consideration, the amount recorded in the books of the company and the number of shares issued.

   Type of consideration ______________________

Market Value of Consideration	80	
Amount Recorded in the Books of the Company	81	
Number of Shares Issued	82	

** Please provide details of changes to surplus.

- *Change in net unrealized capital gains or (losses),* which is similar to the unrealized gains and losses described in Chapter 5.

- *Changes in nonadmitted assets and related items,* which refer primarily to increases and decreases in the book values of assets such as furniture and equipment used in insurance operations. A separate exhibit specifies nonadmitted assets. This surplus change item is not found in the Canadian Annual Return because nonadmitted assets is a U.S.-specific term.

- *Change in reserve on account of change in valuation basis* represents a change in policy reserves that is treated as a direct change in surplus. For example, such a change may occur when a company decides to value policy reserves for an existing block of business on a more conservative basis than the law requires. The process of revaluing and increasing policy reserves, called ***reserve strengthening,*** results in a decrease in surplus. An insurer may also reduce policy reserves, which in turn increases surplus. This reduction in reserves is called ***reserve destrengthening.***

- *Change in asset valuation reserve* is the increase or decrease in the AVR for the year.

- *Capital changes* represent the changes made to the *Paid-In Capital* account and to and from the *Surplus* account.

- *Surplus adjustments* represent the changes made to the *Paid-In Capital* account and transfers to and from the *Capital* account. A separate line on the *Capital and Surplus Account* section reports changes in surplus that occur as a result of any changes in surplus between the insurer's separate accounts and its general account.

- *Dividends to stockholders* are direct distributions of surplus, much the same as dividends are paid out from retained earnings on a GAAP statement. On the other hand, dividends to policyowners are an operating expense and, as such, appear as a component of net income under the *Summary of Operations.*

Because an adequate level of capital and surplus is essential for insurers to remain solvent, regulators establish the minimum required amount of capital and surplus that every insurer must maintain. These requirements are called *Risk-Based Capital (RBC)* requirements in the United States and *Minimum Continuing Capital and Surplus Requirements (MCCSR)* in Canada. We discuss these requirements in Chapter 19.

Statutory to GAAP Reconciliation

So far, we have described some of the statutory accounting practices required to prepare the Annual Statement. We have refrained from presenting too many direct comparisons between statutory accounting and U.S. GAAP accounting. In this section, however, we present some basic ways that statutory accounting differs from GAAP. Figures 6-9 and 6-10 show an insurer's generic balance sheet and a statement of operations, each containing three columns of numbers. The first column shows the amount of each line item as if the company had prepared the financial statement according to statutory accounting. The third column shows the amount of the same item as if the company had prepared the statement according to U.S. GAAP. The middle column shows the amount of the adjustment, if any, from statutory accounting to GAAP. The actual calculations of these adjustments are outside the scope of this text. The important point is for you to note what types of items are likely to differ between the two accounting methods.

For example, total assets on the GAAP balance sheet is higher than total assets on the statutory statement, primarily because statutory accounting does not allow companies to defer policy acquisition costs and amortize (spread) them over several accounting periods, nor does statutory accounting allow nonadmitted assets, such as furniture and equipment, to appear on the *Assets* page. Generally, GAAP emphasizes measuring the company's ability to match revenues to expenses, while statutory accounting stresses measuring the company's ability to pay current and future claims and obligations. From the statutory viewpoint, once policy acquisition costs (such as agent commissions) are paid, the funds used to pay those costs are no longer available to cover future liabilities. For this reason, statutory accounting does not permit the deferral of policy acquisition costs. Instead, under statutory accounting practices, U.S. insurers must expense policy acquisition costs as they are incurred.

Let us look at an example involving admitted and nonadmitted assets to review the difference between the preparation of statements under statutory accounting practices and GAAP. The example we use assumes that a U.S. insurer's basic accounting equation as of a certain statutory statement date is

Assets = Liabilities + Capital and Surplus
$20,000 = $13,000 + $7,000

Immediately after preparation of this statement, the insurer undertakes two transactions. First, the insurer pays $1,000 cash to purchase

Figure 6-9. Statutory to GAAP reconciliation on the balance sheet.

December 31, 2000

	Statutory	Adjustment	GAAP
Assets			
Investments:			
Bonds and other debt securities	$11,204,000	$ 229,975	$11,433,975
Mortgage loans	940,476		940,476
Policy loans	787,104		787,104
Total Investments	$12,931,580	$ 229,975	$13,161,555
Cash	$ 104,696		$ 104,696
Deferred and uncollected premiums	10,975	$ 2,647	13,622
Deferred policy acquisition costs		1,373,375	1,373,375
Furniture and equipment		89,283	89,283
Total Assets	$13,047,251	$1,695,280	$14,742,531
Liabilities and Stockholders' Equity			
Policy Liabilities:			
Reserves for future policy benefits	$ 7,618,245	$ (206,775)	$ 7,411,470
Claims payable	1,472,472		1,472,472
Policy dividends payable in following year	656,698	(656,698)	
Total Policy Liabilities	$ 9,747,415	$ (863,473)	$ 8,883,942
Accounts payable	$ 113,002		$ 113,002
Expenses due and accrued	124,730		124,730
Cash dividends payable to stockholders	172,511		172,511
Interest maintenance reserve	101,477	(101,477)	
Asset valuation reserve	178,490	(178,490)	
Federal income tax:			
Current	97,752		97,752
Deferred		246,263	246,263
Total Liabilities	$10,535,377	$ (897,177)	$ 9,638,200
Stockholders' equity:			
Capital stock	$ 40,000		$ 40,000
Additional paid-in capital	341,356		341,356
Unrealized gain (loss)	112,230	$ 185,455	297,685
Retained earnings		4,425,290	4,425,290
Surplus	2,018,288	(2,018,288)	
Total Stockholders' Equity	$ 2,511,874	$2,592,457	$ 5,104,331
Total Liabilities and Stockholders' Equity	$13,047,251	$1,695,280	$14,742,531

Figure 6-10. Statutory to GAAP reconciliation on the statement of operations.

Years Ended December 31:	Statutory	Adjustment	GAAP
Revenues			
Premium income	$6,225,934		$6,225,934
Net investment income	2,668,257		2,668,257
Total Revenues	$8,894,191	$ 0	$8,894,191
Benefits and Expenses			
Policy Benefits	$4,051,479		$4,051,479
Change in reserves for future benefits	1,035,780	$ (78,435)	957,345
Total Benefits	$5,087,259	$ (78,435)	$5,008,824
Operating expenses:			
Agent commissions	$ 746,222		$ 746,222
Salaries	1,437,984		1,437,984
Change in Deferred Policy Acquisition Costs		$ (34,344)	(34,344)
General expenses	1,392,314		1,392,314
Total Operating Expenses	$3,576,520	$ (34,344)	$3,542,176
Total Benefits and Expenses	$8,663,779	$(112,779)	$8,551,000
Earnings before income tax expense	$ 230,412	$ 112,779	$ 343,191
Income tax expense:			
Current	43,778		43,778
Deferred		59,907	59,907
Total Income Taxes	$ 43,778	$ 59,907	$ 103,685
Net Income	$ 186,634	$ 52,872	$ 239,506

an investment-grade bond, an admitted asset. Next, the insurer pays $2,000 cash to purchase furniture, a nonadmitted asset. As a result of the first transaction, total assets remain the same under both GAAP and statutory accounting. The $1,000 increase in Bonds offsets the $1,000 decrease in Cash:

Assets = Liabilities + Capital and Surplus
$20,000 = $13,000 + $7,000

However, the two types of accounting differ in the way they report the second transaction. Under GAAP, the first and second transactions have the same impact on the balance sheet. The Furniture account increases by $2,000, and the Cash account decreases by $2,000. Because both accounts are asset accounts and because a GAAP-based annual report makes no distinction between admitted assets and nonadmitted assets, the insurer's basic accounting equation remains unchanged. In contrast, a U.S. Annual Statement, which is prepared in accordance with statutory accounting practices, cannot admit the $2,000 furniture asset, so the asset balance decreases by the $2,000 decrease in Cash. Because both sides of the equation must balance, and because the furniture purchase transaction does not affect any liability item, the insurer must reduce its surplus by $2,000. Therefore, under statutory accounting, the insurer's basic accounting equation after this furniture purchase is

Assets = Liabilities + Capital and Surplus
$18,000 = $13,000 + $5,000

Other Statements and Schedules

As we stated earlier in this chapter, the Annual Statement contains numerous statements and schedules, many of which support the primary statements we have discussed already. In this section, we describe a few other important exhibits, including the *Cash Flow, Analysis of Operations by Lines of Business, Five-Year Historical Data,* and other exhibits that detail investments, reserves, premiums, expenses, and claims.

Cash Flow

Insurance companies must identify in the Annual Statement the movement of cash during the year. Each company includes this information on the *Cash Flow* page of the U.S. Annual Statement or the *Statement of Change in Financial Position* of the Canadian Annual Return. These statements, depicted in Figures 6-11 and 6-12, show where the company's cash came from, what cash was used for, and changes in the company's Cash balance during the year. The cash flow statement separates cash flows from different types of activities. In this way, it generally parallels the GAAP-based cash flow statement depicted in Figure 5-6. The *Cash Flow* page on the Annual Statement contains three sections: (1) net cash from operations, (2) net cash from investments, and (3) net cash from financing and miscellaneous sources.

Increases in cash from operations include policy premiums, annuity considerations, premium deposits, and investment income received

Figure 6-11. *Cash Flow*—U.S. Annual Statement.

CASH FLOW	1 1995	2 1994
1. Premiums and annuity considerations	49,051,442	44,264,542
2. Deposit-type funds		
3. Other premiums, considerations and deposits	1,042,033	1,308,337
4. Allowances and reserve adjustments received on reinsurance ceded	59,427	43,536
5. Investment income received (excluding realized gains/losses and net of investment expenses)	35,109,392	32,402,974
6. Other income received	17,642	47,949
7. Total (Lines 1 to 6)	85,279,936	78,067,338
8. Life and accident and health claims paid	25,889,321	21,468,435
9. Surrender benefits and other fund withdrawals paid	10,930,405	13,429,557
10. Other benefits to policyholders paid	16,638,392	17,157,831
11. Total (Lines 8 to 10)	53,458,118	52,055,823
12. Commissions, other expenses and taxes paid (excluding FIT)	20,789,754	20,018,208
13. Net transfers to or (from) Separate Accounts (operational lines only)		
14. Total (Lines 12 to 13)	20,789,754	20,018,208
15. Dividends to policyholders paid	5,258,839	5,339,064
16. Federal income taxes paid (excluding tax on capital gains)	(238,550)	(995,269)
17. Net increase or (decrease) in policy loans and premium notes	1,020,282	(4,294,523)
18. Other operating expenses paid	62,931	57,024
19. Total (Lines 15 to 18)	6,103,502	106,296
20. Net cash from operations (Line 7 minus Line 11 minus Line 14 minus Line 19)	4,928,562	5,887,011
21. Proceeds from investments sold, matured or repaid:		
21.1 Bonds	128,899,705	172,462,891
21.2 Stocks	242,317	
21.3 Mortgage loans	11,959,692	17,710,211
21.4 Real estate	1,522,000	
21.5 Collateral loans		
21.6 Other invested assets		
21.7 Net gains or (losses) on cash and short-term investments	8	(314)
21.8 Miscellaneous proceeds		768,023
21.9 Total investment proceeds (Lines 21.1 to 21.8)	142,623,722	190,940,811
22. Tax on capital gains	(61,450)	1,739,534
23. Total (Line 21.9 minus Line 22)	142,685,172	189,201,277
24. Other cash provided:		
24.1 Capital and surplus paid in	1,749,932	896,776
24.2 Borrowed money .... $0 less amounts repaid $0		
24.3 Other sources	2,195,948	418,861
24.4 Total other cash provided (Lines 24.1 to 24.3)	3,945,880	1,315,637
25. Total (Line 20 plus Line 23 plus Line 24.4)	151,559,614	196,403,925
26. Cost of investments acquired (long-term only):		
26.1 Bonds	131,711,950	193,156,216
26.2 Stocks	102,029	2,500
26.3 Mortgage loans	18,708,081	3,087,688
26.4 Real estate		
26.5 Collateral loans		
26.6 Other invested assets		
26.7 Miscellaneous applications	654,485	
26.8 Total investments acquired (Lines 26.1 to 26.7)	151,176,545	196,246,404
27. Other cash applied:		
27.1 Dividends to stockholders paid		
27.2 Other applications (net)	467,243	2,897,502
27.3 Total other cash applied (Lines 27.1 and 27.2)	467,243	2,897,502
28. Total (Lines 26.8 and 27.3)	151,643,788	199,143,906
29. Net change in cash and short-term investments (Line 25 minus Line 28)	(84,174)	(2,739,981)
RECONCILIATION		
30. Cash and short-term investments:		
30.1 Beginning of year	2,544,758	5,284,739
30.2 End of year (Line 29 plus Line 30.1)	2,460,584	2,544,758

Figure 6-12. *Statement of Change in Financial Position*—Canadian Annual Return.

STATEMENT OF CHANGE IN FINANCIAL POSITION*
($'000)

		Current Year (01)	Prior Year (02)
OPERATIONS			
Net Income	01		
Adjustments to convert income to a cash basis:			
Increase (decrease) in policy benefit liabilities	04		
Increase (decrease) in policyholders' funds	07		
Increase (decrease) in deferred income taxes	10		
Other Adjustments	13		
	16		
	19		
Cash provided by (applied to) operations	**29**		
INVESTMENT ACTIVITIES			
Sale of Investments	33		
	36		
	39		
Purchase of Investments	42		
	45		
	48		
Cash provided by (applied to) Investments	**59**		
FINANCING ACTIVITIES			
Issue of Shares	62		
Issue of Debentures	65		
Increase (Decrease) in Long Term Debt	68		
	72		
Redemption of Shares	75		
Redemption of Debentures	78		
Shareholders Dividends	81		
	84		
Cash provided by (applied to) Financing Activities	**89**		
Cash and Short Term Investments at beginning of year	**90**		
Cash and Short Term Investments at end of year	**99**		

* This Statement is provided as a guide only. Companies may complete this page or attach a Statement of Change in Financial Position as prepared for the company's financial statements.

by the insurer. The insurer reduces these total increases by items such as payments of claims, surrender benefits, other policy benefits, federal income taxes, commissions, and other operating expenses. Next, the statement notes changes in the insurer's cash caused by investments sold, matured, and repaid, and other cash transactions. The final section of the *Cash Flow* page shows the beginning-of-year and end-of-year totals for the insurer's cash and short-term investments. Note that the *Cash Flow* page follows the direct method, and the *Statement of Change in Financial Position* follows the indirect method of reporting cash from operations.

Analysis of Operations by Lines of Business

The *Analysis of Operations by Lines of Business,* called the *Analysis of Income by Line of Business* in Canada, reports a company's net gain (loss) from operations for each line of business. From an accounting standpoint, a ***line of business (LOB)*** is a segment of the insurance market that is distinctively different from other segments, often because of sales approaches or policyowner service functions. Examples of an insurer's lines of business include group life insurance, group health insurance, debit insurance, individual life insurance, individual health insurance, employee benefit plans, and individual annuities.

The items presented in the U.S. and Canadian analysis pages are similar, but some line of business differences exist. For example, the U.S. Annual Statement instructions define the major and secondary lines of business for the allocation of receipts and expenses. The Annual Statement groups lines of business into the following categories:

- Industrial Life
- Ordinary—Life Insurance, Individual Annuities, and Supplementary Contracts
- Credit Life—Group and Individual
- Group—Life Insurance and Annuities
- Accident and Health—Group, Credit (Group and Individual), and Other
- Aggregate of All Other Lines of Business

The Canadian *Analysis* page uses broader categories for grouping lines of business: life (participating and nonparticipating), which is then subdivided into individual and group insurance and annuities, and accident and sickness (individual and group). Figure 6-13 shows the *Analysis of Operations by Lines of Business* and Figure 6-14 shows the *Analysis of Income by Line of Business*.

The *Analysis of Operations* is useful to management for determining realized gains or losses from insurance operations. The net gain (loss) for each line indicates the amount that each line contributes to an insurer's total operations. For insurers operating under similar circumstances, comparisons based on figures shown for each line of business can be helpful in locating relative weaknesses or unprofitability in operations. As do the figures contained in the *Summary of Operations*, the *Analysis of Operations* cross-references other Annual Statement exhibits that provide considerable detail on the sources of income and expense items. This interrelationship also exists between the *Income Statement* and the *Analysis of Income* in the Canadian Annual Return.

Five-Year Historical Data

As its name implies, the statement of *Five-Year Historical Data* is a schedule of an insurer's financial data for the past five years. This schedule can be quite useful in identifying trends in an insurer's performance. Some of the information available in the U.S. *Five-Year Historical Data* is

- Life insurance in force
- New business issued
- Premium income—lines of business
- Total nonadmitted and admitted assets
- Benefits and reserve increases

Although the Canadian Annual Return had an equivalent page in the past, five-year historical data is no longer included in the Annual Return for domestic or foreign insurers.

Other Exhibits

Both the Annual Statement and the Annual Return include accompanying exhibits and schedules with detailed supplementary data. Many of these exhibits and schedules pertain to investments, reserves, premiums, claims, and expenses. Other information includes reinsurance amounts, resisted claims, policy dividend information, listings of depositories for company cash, reconciliation of assets between years, and general interrogatories and footnotes, which serve a purpose similar to the notes to the financial statements in the annual

Figure 6-13. *Analysis of Operations by Lines of Business* (Gain and Loss Exhibit) (Excluding Capital Gains and Losses)—U.S. Annual Statement.

	1	2	Ordinary			6	Group		Accident and Health			12
			3	4	5		7	8	9	10	11	
	Total	Industrial Life	Life Insurance	Individual Annuities	Supplementary Contracts	Credit Life (Group and Individual)	Life (a) Insurance	Annuities	Group	Credit (Group & Individual)	Other	Aggregate of All Other Lines of Business
1. Premiums and annuity considerations	49,074,909		45,058,341	4,016,568	X X X							X X X
1A. Deposit-type funds					X X X							
2. Considerations for supplementary contracts with life contingencies	38,990		X X X	X X X	38,990				X X X	X X X	X X X	
3. Considerations for supplementary contracts without life contingencies and dividend accumulations	1,003,043		761,886		241,157							
3A. Coupons left to accumulate at interest												
4. Net investment income	35,401,410		24,476,130	6,588,515,	466,188			3,870,577				
4A. Amortization of Interest Maintenance Reserve (IMR)	330,465		264,636	22,670	1,619			41,540				
5. Commissions and expense allowances on reinsurance ceded	199,785		199,785									
5A. Reserve adjustments on reinsurance ceded	(20,957)		(20,957)									
6. Aggregate write-ins for miscellaneous income	17,642		10,985	3,942				2,715				
7. Totals (Lines 1 to 6)	85,045,287		70,750,806	10,631,695	747,954			3,914,832				
8. Death benefits	25,833,750		25,833,750	X X X				X X X	X X X	X X X	X X X	
9. Matured endowments (excluding guaranteed annual pure endowments)	462,995		462,995						X X X	X X X	X X X	
10. Annuity benefits	12,564,960		X X X	10,600,649		X X X	X X X	1,964,311	X X X	X X X	X X X	
11. Disability benefits and benefits under accident and health policies	110,920		110,920									
11A. Coupons, guaranteed annual pure endowments and similar benefits												
12. Surrender benefits and other fund withdrawals	10,930,405		10,930,405						X X X	X X X	X X X	
13. Group conversions				X X X				X X X				
13A. Transfers on account of group package policies and contracts	X X X	X X X	X X X	X X X	X X X						X X X	
14. Interest on policy or contract funds	1,570,828		459,868	706	(3,628)			1,113,882				
15. Payments on supplementary contracts with life contingencies	456,525		X X X	X X X	456,525				X X X	X X X	X X X	
16. Payments on supplementary contracts without life contingencies and dividend accumulations	1,829,911		1,372,441		457,470							
16A. Accumulated coupon payments												
17. Increase in aggregate reserves for life and accident and health policies and contracts	4,700,534		4,030,691	1,453,205	(237,117)			(546,245)				
17A. Increase in liability for premium and other deposit funds												
18. Increase in reserve for scwolc and for dividend and coupon accumulations	(559,383)		(331,151)	1,336	(229,568)							
19. Totals (Lines 8 to 18)	57,901,445		42,869,919	12,055,896	443,682			2,531,948				
20. Commissions on premiums and annuity considerations (direct business only)	5,648,170		5,469,181	178,989								
21. Commissions and expense allowances on reinsurance assumed	14,281		14,281									
22. General insurance expenses	14,019,241		13,687,800	193,201	21,880			116,360				
23. Insurance taxes, licenses and fees, excluding federal income taxes	1,454,103		1,440,184	8,107	918			4,894				
24. Increase in loading and cost of collection in excess of loading on deferred and uncollected premiums	(163,900)		(163,899)	(1)								
24A. Net transfers to or (from) Separate Accounts												
25. Aggregate write-ins for deductions	62,931		62,931									
26. Totals (Lines 19 to 25)	78,936,271		63,380,397	12,436,192	466,480			2,653,202				
27. Net gain from operations before dividends to policyholders and federal income taxes (7–26)	7,109,016		7,370,409	(1,804,497)	281,474			1,261,630				
28. Dividends to policyholders	4,875,971		4,795,595	625	66,690			13,061				
29. Net gain from operations after dividends to policyholders and before federal income taxes (27–28)	2,233,045		2,574,814	(1,805,122)	214,784			1,248,569				
30. Federal income taxes incurred (excluding tax on capital gains)	172,492		332,475	(382,561)	33,335			189,243				
31. Net gain after dividends FIT and before realized capital gains or (losses) (Line 29 – Line 30)	2,060,553		2,242,339	(1,422,561)	181,449			1,059,326				
DETAILS OF WRITE-INS												
0601. Miscellaneous profit on sundries	17,642		10,985	3,942				2,715				
0602.												
0603.												
0698. Summary of remaining write-ins for Line 6 from overflow page												
0699. Totals (Lines 0601 thru 0603 plus 0698) (Line 6 above)	17,642		10,985	3,942				2,715				
2501. Miscellaneous interest paid	62,931		62,931									
2502.												
2503.												
2598. Summary of remaining write-ins for Line 25 from overflow page												
2599. Totals (Lines 2501 thru 2503 plus 2598) (Line 25 above)	62,931		62,931									

(a) Includes the following amounts for FEGLI/SGLI: Line 1 $0 , Line 8 $0 , Line 13 $0 , Line 22 $0 , Line 23 $0 ,

Figure 6-14. *Analysis of Income by Line of Business*—Canadian Annual Return.

NON-CONSOLIDATED FINANCIAL STATEMENTS
ANALYSIS OF INCOME BY LINE OF BUSINESS
($'000)

	Life - Participating				Life - Non-Participating				Accident & Sickness		Other	Total
	Individual		Group		Individual		Group		Individual	Group		
	Insurance (01)	Annuity (02)	Insurance (03)	Annuity (04)	Insurance (05)	Annuity (06)	Insurance (07)	Annuity (08)	(09)	(10)	(11)	(12)
Revenue												
Premiums												
Insurance.......01												
Annuities.......03												
Net Investment Income.......10												
Other Revenue.......23												
Total Revenue.......29												
Policy Benefits and Expenses												
Policyholder Benefits												
Claims.......30												
Annuity Payments.......31												
Other (Includes Surrenders).......32												
Net Changes to Policy Liabilities												
Insurance.......33												
Annuities.......34												
Policyholder Dividends and Experience Rating Refunds.......35												

report. Although the U.S. and Canadian supplementary exhibits and schedules are generally similar, the following discussion notes any major differences. The purpose of these exhibits and schedules is to provide insurance regulators with sufficient detail to aid in their analysis of a life and health insurance company and their measurement of the company's solvency.

- **Investments:** Both the U.S. and Canadian statements include supplementary information about an insurer's investments. Investments are classified by type: stocks and bonds, mortgage loans, real estate, and other investments. The schedule showing capital stock owned, for example, lists the name of each stock, number of shares owned, the book value, and the market value, as of the statutory statement date.

- **Reserves:** The Annual Statement presents the reserve amount by valuation basis, that is, by interest and mortality table, then subdivides the amounts by lines of business. Other information includes changes in the valuation basis, if that basis changes from year to year. In addition to this information, the Canadian Annual Return shows the amount of insurance in force and whether reserves are for participating or nonparticipating policies.

- **Premiums:** On the U.S. Annual Statement, premium exhibits show premium income in three categories: (1) direct premiums received, (2) premiums due and uncollected, and (3) premiums assumed and ceded on reinsurance. Premium exhibits also show premiums and annuity considerations by line of business and by first-year business, single premium business, and renewal business. The Canadian Annual Return presents premium information in a similar manner.

- **Expenses:** The Annual Statement schedule of expenses shows a company's expenses by type. Included among these expenses are policy claim investigation and settlement expenses, rent, salaries and wages, legal fees and expenses, postage, travel expenses, and advertising costs. Expense information is allocated between insurance operations and investments. A separate schedule itemizes taxes, licenses, and fees. The Canadian Annual Return has similar expense schedules.

- **Claims:** Information presented for claims includes both claims incurred and settled during the year and the liability for unpaid claims at the end of the year. The Annual Statement and Annual Return present claim information by line of business.

Conclusion

This chapter provided you with an introduction to the U.S. Annual Statement and the Canadian Annual Return. The next seven chapters expand on the concepts introduced in this chapter. In order, we describe accounting for assets, reserves, policy benefits and other liabilities, capital and surplus, revenues, and expenses.

Key Terms and Concepts

Annual Statement
Annual Return
economic solvency
admitted assets
nonadmitted assets
reinsurance
deferred premiums
uncollected premiums (premiums outstanding)
premiums due
gross premium
loading
net premium
separate accounts (segregated funds)
general account
policy reserves
policy and contract claims
due and unpaid claims
resisted claims
claims in the course of settlement
incurred but not reported (IBNR) claims
policy dividend liabilities
policy dividend
divisible surplus
liability for premium and other deposit funds
guaranteed interest contract (GIC)
unearned income
advance premiums
unearned premiums
amounts temporarily held for disposition
interest maintenance reserve (IMR)
interest rate risk
asset valuation reserve (AVR)
credit risk
portfolio
reserve strengthening
reserve destrengthening
line of business (LOB)

CHAPTER 7

Accounting for Invested Assets

Learning Objectives

After studying this chapter, you should be able to

- Identify and describe an insurance company's typical short-term and long-term investments
- Describe the characteristics of investment-grade bonds
- Make the appropriate accounting entries for the purchase and sale of bonds, stocks, and mortgage loans
- Calculate a realized gain or loss on the sale of invested assets
- Explain how an insurer records the purchase of a bond at a discount or premium
- Discuss how an insurance company accounts for cash dividends and stock dividends
- Describe the purpose of an escrow account for a mortgage loan
- Make the appropriate accounting entries to record a foreclosed mortgage on real estate
- Discuss how an insurer presents its bond, stock, and mortgage loan investments in the Annual Statement and the Annual Return

Chapter Outline

Asset Classification and Valuation

Bonds

Accounting for the Purchase and Sale of Bonds

Accrued Bond Interest Income

Bond Discounts and Bond Premiums

Bonds and the Annual Statement/ Annual Return

Stocks

Accounting for the Purchase and Sale of Stocks

Accounting for Cash Dividends

Accounting for Stock Dividends

Stocks and the Annual Statement/ Annual Return

Mortgage Loans

Accounting for Mortgage Loans

Foreclosure

Mortgage Loans and the Annual Statement/ Annual Return

Assets, which are all things of value that a company owns, are critical to any business, in part because they represent a potential source of current and future income. Thus, assets play an integral role in the financial operations of life and health insurance companies. In calculating both the premium rates that an insurer should charge for its products and the amount of reserves it should maintain for future policy benefits, an insurer's actuaries assume that the insurer will earn a certain rate of return on its assets. If the actual rate of return falls short of the assumed rate, the insurer may experience a loss and a reduction in its surplus that could prove harmful to the insurer's policyowners and stockholders.

The ***investment accounting*** function typically is responsible for recording all accounting entries related to the assets in an insurer's investment portfolios. Recall from Chapter 6 that *invested assets* produce income in the form of interest, dividends, and capital gains. Be aware that invested assets are often referred to as *securities* or *investments.* An insurer uses the income generated by its invested assets to support its reserves for future policy benefits. The investment accounting function includes asset/liability management as well as maintaining compliance with routine statutory and GAAP reporting requirements. ***Asset/liability management (ALM)*** is an activity that coordinates the administration of an insurer's investment portfolios with the administration of its policy liabilities to achieve the best possible financial effects. The investment accounting function also identifies the cash inflows and cash outflows associated with an insurer's investments, so those who perform the cash accounting function can be made aware of the insurer's flow of funds.

In Chapters 7 and 8 we discuss accounting for assets. Chapter 7 begins our discussion of an insurer's invested assets. Figure 7-1 shows where an insurer typically lists its invested assets on the balance sheet. The investment department in a life and health insurance company examines the financial marketplace, recommends investment strategies to the company's finance committee of the board of directors, and manages the company's invested assets according to the policies approved by the board of directors. Because of (1) the number of investment alternatives available, (2) the number of investment transactions made by insurers, and (3) the legal restrictions placed on investing, a thorough understanding of investment accounting is important to the study of accounting in life and health insurance companies. The rest of this chapter discusses three types of invested assets: bonds, stocks, and mortgage loans. Chapter 8 completes our

Figure 7-1. Highlight of the invested assets section of a typical insurance company balance sheet.

December 31, 19XX

Assets	
Invested assets:	
Bonds	xxx
Mortgage loans	xxx
Stocks	xxx
Total Invested Assets	xxx
Real estate	xxx
Policy loans	xxx
Investment income due and accrued	xxx
Cash and cash equivalents	xxx
Premiums due	xxx
Deferred policy acquisition costs (GAAP only)	xxx
Reinsurance ceded	xxx
Other assets	xxx
Total Assets	5,000,000

Liabilities and Capital and Surplus	
Liabilities:	
Policy reserves:	
Life insurance	xxx
Annuities	xxx
Accident and health	xxx
Total Policy Reserves	xxx
Claim reserves:	xxx
Life insurance	xxx
Accident and health	xxx
Total Claim Reserves	xxx
Policy dividends due and unpaid	xxx
Unpaid policy claims	xxx
Premium deposits	xxx
Advance premiums	xxx
Interest maintenance reserve	xxx
Asset valuation reserve	xxx
Other liabilities	xxx
Total Liabilities	4,300,000
Capital and Surplus:	
Stock	xxx
Additional paid-in capital	xxx
Special surplus	xxx
Unassigned surplus	xxx
Net unrealized gains (losses)	(xxx)
Treasury stock	(xxx)
Total Capital and Surplus	700,000
Total Liabilities and Capital and Surplus	5,000,000

discussion of invested assets, then focuses on an insurer's cash and other assets.

Asset Classification and Valuation

To help organize all the different kinds of assets into a meaningful order, accounting and financial experts have, over a number of years, assigned assets to various classifications. These classifications are an organizational tool. They are not perfect. For example, some assets fit into more than one classification, while others do not fit comfortably into any classification. However, the classifications do help us understand some of the relationships among the different kinds of assets. They help companies and accounting professionals organize assets into a reasonable order.

Assets generally are classified as *short-term* or *long-term.* Recall from Chapter 2 that a short-term asset, also called a *current asset,* is one that a company expects to convert to cash within the current accounting period, usually 12 months. A long-term asset, sometimes referred to as a *noncurrent asset,* is one that has a long time to maturity or that a company expects to retain for more than one year. Although an insurer's annual report and Annual Statement do not differentiate between short-term and long-term assets, we generally use these terms because short-term and long-term indicate the insurer's intended holding period for an investment.

Short-term assets include cash and short-term investments. ***Cash*** is the amount of currency on hand or on deposit at an insurer's bank. ***Short-term investments,*** including *money market funds* and *Treasury bills,* are investments that a company expects to turn into cash within one year. ***Cash equivalents,*** a type of short-term investment, can typically be converted to cash within 90 days with little or no risk of losing value. Short-term investments serve two basic purposes: (1) they provide a company with the means of earning interest on cash that might otherwise lie idle, and (2) they are a readily available source of cash that a company can use in its normal business operations. Because short-term assets are very liquid, they are also sometimes referred to as *liquid assets.* Recall that liquidity indicates the ease with which an asset can be converted to cash. Generally, long-term assets are less liquid than short-term assets. Because insurers match their long-term assets with long-term liabilities to provide returns over long periods of time, they typically do not use long-term assets as a source of ready cash.

Assets can be tangible or intangible. A ***tangible asset*** has physical substance. An insurer's home office building and computer equipment are two examples of tangible assets. Under GAAP, buildings and equipment are often referred to as *plant assets.* An ***intangible asset*** does not have physical substance. Intangible assets include bonds, stocks, and other securities. Insight 7-1 illustrates how tangible and intangible assets relate to profits. Figure 7-2 identifies several typical insurance company assets and possible ways to classify each one.

Government and corporate bonds, stocks, real estate, and mortgage loans make up the majority of an insurer's long-term invested assets. In recent years, these assets have accounted for the majority of the life and health insurance industry's assets in the United States and Canada. Figures 7-3 and 7-4 illustrate these proportions in dramatic fashion, based on 1994 numbers.

To comply with statutory reporting requirements, U.S. life and health insurers also classify their assets as admitted assets or nonadmitted assets in the Annual Statement. As we discussed in Chapter 6, admitted assets are those assets whose values U.S. insurers may report on the *Assets* page of the Annual Statement. The purpose of differentiating between admitted assets and nonadmitted assets is to enable state insurance regulators to readily determine which assets can be most easily converted to cash.

Each year, the NAIC, through its Securities Valuation Office (SVO), publishes a *Valuation of Securities* manual that U.S. insurers use when preparing the Annual Statement. This manual prescribes the procedures for valuing bond and stock assets. The values of the securities listed on a U.S. insurer's Annual Statement are their values as of December 31. Insurers report the values of their investments in several sections of the Annual Statement. For example, an insurer reports its long-term bond and stock investments on one schedule

Figure 7-2. Typical classifications of insurance company assets.

Types of Assets	Investment Classifications				
	Short-Term	Long-Term	Invested Asset	Tangible	Intangible
Stocks		X	X		X
Bonds		X	X		X
Real estate		X	X	X	
Mortgage loans		X	X		X
Land		X		X	
Buildings		X	X	X	
Money market funds	X				X
Certificates of deposit	X				X
Treasury bills	X				X
Computer equipment		X		X	

Insight 7-1 Why Profits Don't Matter

New technologies have fundamentally changed the way we do business. Any executive could point to dozens of ways business is conducted differently from just a decade ago. But while so much else has undergone a seismic shift, the way business continues to account for profits remains as outmoded as the clipper ship.

To put it bluntly, reported profits have become increasingly meaningless. You won't get very far explaining this to your banker or to your shareholders, but it's undeniably true. Basically, profits measure the rate of change in a company's assets. Increase assets by $10 million and you report a $10 million profit. Write down $15 million in inventory and profits go down by the same amount.

Double-entry bookkeeping, developed by Luca Pacioli in 1494, lets businesses keep track of changes in their asset base. But this system, still in use today, deals primarily with tangible assets such as cash, inventory, accounts receivable, factory plants and equipment. It ignores intangible assets: goodwill, employee knowledge, quality of management, customer relationships, information infrastructure, trade secrets, patents, etc. What companies report today are really "old profits" based on changes in tangible assets. But any meaningful measure of profits would have to include the rate of change in the total asset base—both tangible and intangible.

When Henry Ford developed his mass-production system, this distinction was largely meaningless. The skill of his workers was not an important concern for him. In fact, Ford envisioned that his system would permit him to make workers as interchangeable as the parts that flowed along the assembly line. Ford minimized the need for a skilled work force so successfully that during one year he hired 50,000 workers to keep 15,000 production-line jobs filled—an annual turnover rate of more than 300 percent. Clearly, intellectual capital was not an issue. And because these "tangible assets" were not of significant value, it made little sense to include them in the calculation of profits.

Why is this old way of measuring profits now so misleading? If we suppose that, in the industrial age, 80 percent of the assets important to a business were tangible, today this ratio is probably reversed. Information-age companies generate a great deal of revenue using fewer physical assets but many more intangible ones. For example, they have far less invested in plants, equipment and finished-goods inventory than in talent. Conventional accounting might show a company making large "old profits" while its intangible assets are actually losing value (e.g., top programmers are defecting). By the time those losses begin to show, a company may already be noncompetitive. Some of America's most important companies were suffering from rapidly declining intangible assets long before the problems showed up in their profit-and-loss statements. IBM, General Motors and Digital Equipment all reported substantial "old profits" while their businesses were in fact falling apart. If they had been forced to take writeoffs as the decline in intangible assets occurred, the problems would have been visible much sooner.

It has long been said that managements get what they measure. If the measurement systems are wrong, management is certain to devote its energies to producing wrong results. The problem is that accountants don't know how to value most intangible assets. The stock market, however, has a fair idea of their worth. Companies like Microsoft, loaded with valuable intangibles, have market capitalizations greatly exceeding their book value. But those with poor market positions, bad relationships with customers and suppliers, poor business infrastructures and demoralized employees often trade in the market at below book value.

Accountants should admit that their measurement tools are flawed and take a first step toward valuing those intangible assets that can be measured. Credit-card and mail-order companies know the cost of acquiring a customer. Also, training investments can be accurately determined. Therefore those costs could be capitalized and depreciated.

Assigning value to intangible assets does let management play new games. If a company has to announce that sales are down, it might also announce a breakthrough in the laboratory expected to generate millions in revenue. Writing up intellectual capital would allow the reporting of record "new profits."

Obviously, information-age accountants are faced with a difficult challenge: live with the old systems and distort the truth, or develop a new system fraught with the dangers of measuring intangibles. "Old profits" don't matter, but we can't yet accurately compute "new profits." What we need, it seems, is a totally different system for measuring business. Now try explaining that to your banker.

Source: William Davidow, "Why Profits Don't Matter," *Forbes* (April 8, 1996), p. 24. Reprinted By Permission of *FORBES ASAP* Magazine,

Figure 7-3. U.S. insurance industry assets, 1994.

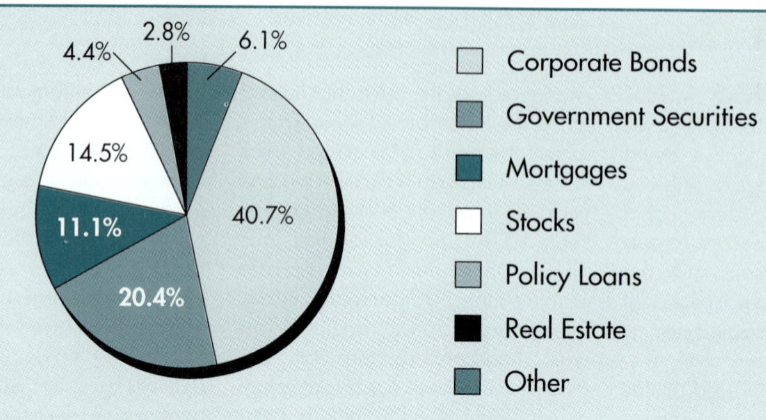

Source: *Spectator Year Book* and ACLI *1995 Life Insurance Fact Book Update*, p. 4.

and its short-term securities on a separate schedule. From the information reported in the Annual Statement, an insurer constructs various exhibits that detail many aspects of the status and performance of its invested assets.

Various methods exist for calculating the dollar value of an insurer's assets. State legislation or insurance department rulings specify the methods of valuing different types of investments for U.S. insurers. For example, insurers use the current market values of their common stock and preferred stock as of the reporting date. On the other hand, statutory accounting defines the values of bonds according to the NAIC Bond Classifications, which we discuss later in this chapter. An asset's current market value fluctuates over time and may vary

Figure 7-4. Canadian insurance industry assets, 1994.

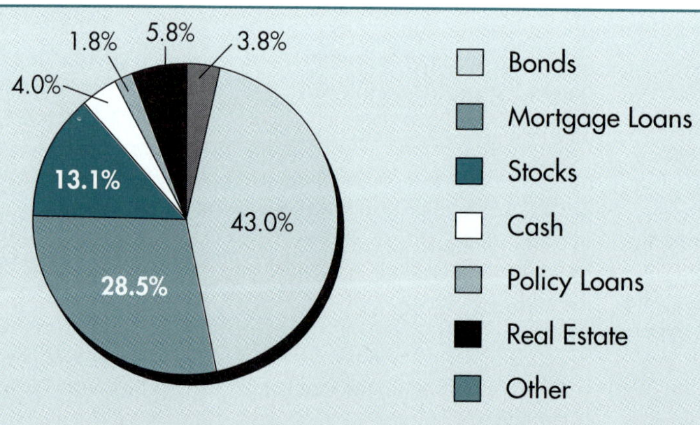

Source: *Reports of the Superintendent of Financial Institutions*, Ottawa, and CLHIA *1995 Facts*, p. 21.

considerably from its historical cost and ***amortized cost,*** which is an asset's historical cost net of any adjustment to the asset's book value. Recall that the book value of an asset is the value at which the asset is carried on the insurer's balance sheet. Only on the date of purchase does the historical cost equal the book value for every asset.

Under statutory accounting, U.S. insurers report some bond values according to the ***lower of cost or market (LCM) rule,*** meaning that the bond's value is either its historical cost, amortized cost, or current market value, whichever is lowest. The difference between the bond's historical cost and its current market value is nonadmitted for statutory reporting purposes. Suppose a particular bond must be reported at the lower of cost or market. The bond has a historical cost of $350 and a market value of $300. For statutory purposes, the bond's admitted value is its market value, and its nonadmitted value is $50 ($350 – $300). In this case, a U.S. insurer reports the bond on the Annual Statement's *Assets* page with a value of $300. In contrast, under GAAP, the insurer would report the same bond at $300 or $350, depending upon whether the insurer expects to hold the bond until maturity.

The process of recording a permanent decrease in the value of an asset is called ***writing down*** its value. If the book value of bonds is higher than the current market value, then an insurer debits an account such as Realized Loss—Bonds and credits an asset account, such as Bonds, for the amount of the difference between book value and current market value. To write down a bond's book value from $1,500 to $1,200, an insurer debits Realized Loss—Bonds and credits Bonds for $300. If a U.S. insurer needs to write down the value of the bonds permanently, it uses the Asset Valuation Reserve (AVR) or the Interest Maintenance Reserve (IMR), which offset most realized and unrealized capital losses. Without the AVR or IMR, the permanent write-down of an asset would decrease an insurer's surplus because assets are decreased and liabilities are unaffected by the transaction. Canadian insurers report the book value of their assets on the Annual Return according to historical cost, amortized cost, or current market value. For example, an insurer values its bonds at amortized cost and values its stock investments according to the moving average market method, discussed later in this chapter.

In the United States, stock insurers, and mutual insurers that wish to obtain an unqualified GAAP audit opinion on their financial statements, follow GAAP in their financial reporting, except in preparing the Annual Statement. The differences between GAAP and statutory accounting lead insurers to assign different values to their assets, depending on the guidelines they are following. The difference between asset valuation under statutory accounting practices and under GAAP can be illustrated by considering the treatment of certain assets. Under GAAP, furniture and equipment are reported in an insurance company's financial statements at their ***net book value,*** which is an asset's historical cost less accumulated depreciation. The net book value of these assets may be much higher than their market value if the insurer had sold them to a used equipment dealer. However, under statutory accounting practices, furniture and equipment are typically nonadmitted assets, so no value appears for them on the *Assets* page of the Annual Statement.

Bonds

Corporations and governments need money to accomplish their goals. Corporations receive most of their money by selling their goods and services. Governments collect most of their money from taxes. Frequently, however, these sources of funds are not enough to meet the needs of a business or a government. Therefore, businesses and governments must find other ways to raise funds. One way to raise money is through the issuance of *bonds.* A ***bond*** is a certificate of indebtedness issued by a corporation, government, or other legal entity. It is a contractual arrangement in which (1) the bond's purchaser agrees to lend the bond's issuer a certain sum of money, (2) the bond's issuer agrees to pay a specified rate of interest on the borrowed amount as long as the indebtedness is outstanding, and (3) the bond's issuer agrees to pay on a specified future maturity date the amount of money borrowed from the bond purchaser. The bond issuer is legally obligated to the bond purchaser (bondholder) for both interest payments and principal payments. The ***principal*** is the amount of money originally borrowed, deposited, or invested. Principal is also known as *par value, face value,* or *maturity value.* The date on which the bond issuer must pay the principal to the bondholder is the ***maturity date.*** A bond has a fixed maturity, generally from 2 to 30 years or longer.

A bond is a type of ***debt security,*** or *debt instrument,* which is an investment in the debt of one or more entities. For example, an investor who purchases a $1,000 bond with 8 percent interest for 10 years is lending the issuer $1,000 for 10 years. Bonds can be either secured or unsecured. A ***secured bond*** is one in which the issuer pledges collateral to guarantee the safety of the bondholder's investment. ***Collateral*** is something of value, usually a portion of the bond issuer's assets, which the bondholder will receive if the bond issuer fails to make the contracted interest and principal payments on the bond. An unsecured bond is called a ***debenture,*** which is backed simply by the bond issuer's creditworthiness.

An issuer may offer its bonds through public offerings or private placements. A ***public offering*** is the sale of bonds to the general public. The issuer of public bonds first registers them with the appropriate securities commission(s) in the United States and Canada. Then, the bonds are available for sale to the public through an exchange that handles the purchase and sale of bonds. ***Private placements*** include bonds offered by the bond issuer directly to specific financial institutions such as insurance companies. A bond issuer does not need to register private-placement bonds with a government agency because the issuer and the purchaser negotiate the terms of privately placed bonds.

Insurance companies are among the most important purchasers of bonds in the United States and Canada. In 1994, U.S. insurance companies invested 61 percent of their assets in government and corporate bonds and Canadian insurers invested 43 percent of their assets in government and corporate bonds. By purchasing bonds, insurers provide businesses and governments with the funds they need to grow, thus having a major impact on local, regional, and national economies. Insurers, of course, have other reasons for investing in bonds. As mentioned earlier, insurers must be reasonably certain that their investments provide the return necessary to meet future obligations, such as the payment of death claims, medical benefits, annuities, and matured endowments. Because bonds offer a predictable amount of income in the form of interest, as well as the eventual return of principal, insurers can be reasonably certain that their bond investments will provide the returns needed to meet their obligations.

Most bonds are originally issued at par value, which generally is in increments of $1,000. Although it may seem logical that a bond's purchase price should remain at $1,000, a bond's price fluctuates whenever its stated rate of interest differs from the prevailing market rate of interest. When market interest rates increase, bond prices decrease. Conversely, when interest rates decrease, bond prices increase. This inverse relationship between bond prices and interest rates results from the competitive market for bonds. Because of the inverse relationship between interest rates and bond prices, a bond's purchase price often differs from its par value. When the bond is first issued, an insurer would most likely purchase the bond at par value, typically $1,000. If the insurer pays more than the par value for the bond, then the insurer buys the bond at a ***premium.*** On the other hand, if the insurer pays less than par value for the bond, then the insurer buys the bond at a ***discount.*** In either case, the insurer amortizes the bond's premium or discount over the time it holds the bond.

Suppose you buy a $1,000 bond for $1,000. That is, you pay *par value* for the bond. The bond pays 8 percent interest annually. After owning the bond for three months, you decide to sell it. Unfortunately, market interest rates have risen since you bought your bond, and today a similar bond now offers 10 percent annual interest. Therefore, no one is willing to buy your bond at par value, because bonds now entering the market at the same par value as your bond are offering a higher rate of interest. The only way you can sell your bond is to offer it at a discount to its par value. That way, the buyer of your bond receives (1) regular interest payments and (2) the difference between the bond's par value and discounted value. Together, the interest and bond discount equates to the 10 percent rate of return currently offered by other bonds. On the other hand, if interest rates had dropped to 6 percent after you had purchased the 8 percent bond, investors would be willing to buy your bond at a premium, because your bond provides a more attractive interest payment than similar bonds currently being offered. In sum, your 8 percent bond will sell at a *discount* if market interest rates increase to 10 percent and at a *premium* if market interest rates decrease to 6 percent.

Besides the relationship between interest rates and bond prices, the relationship between risk and return also affects the buying and selling of bonds. As with all investments, an insurance company that is buying a bond must weigh the return it expects to receive from the bond against the risk it incurs by investing in the bond. For example, if an insurer buys a bond, even a secured bond, the insurer cannot be certain that the issuer won't ***default*** on the bond, that is, fail to pay the contractual interest and principal amounts. The issuer of a bond with a higher risk of default must offer a higher rate of return on the bond to offset the risk that the purchaser is taking.

The level of risk varies from bond to bond, depending on the soundness of the entity that issues the bond. For example, bonds issued by the U.S. and Canadian federal governments are backed by the full faith and credit of those governments. Because these two federal governments are strong and reliable, their bonds are considered virtually free from default risk. Bonds issued by less stable governments carry a higher default risk and, therefore, must offer a higher rate of return to attract investors. As risk goes up, return must also go up. As risk goes down, return goes down. This relationship between risk and return is called the ***risk-return tradeoff,*** and it applies to all types of investments and to all types of risk. To help purchasers make well-informed risk-return decisions, several independent rating agencies, including Moody's and Standard and Poor's (S&P), publish bond ratings that indicate the relative safety and soundness of corporate bonds. Similarly, other rating agencies specialize in rating government bonds.

In the United States, the *Purposes and Procedures* manual of the Securities Valuation Office (SVO) includes a section that describes the NAIC's interpretation of classifying bonds by the bond ratings that are widely available through Moody's, S&P, and other rating agencies. This manual provides insurers with NAIC values for specific investments for Annual Statement purposes. Figure 7-5 presents a synopsis of the NAIC's six bond classifications and the equivalent bond ratings published by Moody's and S&P. What is important to

Figure 7-5. NAIC bond classifications.

NAIC Classification	Published Ratings	
	Moody's	S&P
1 Highest quality	Aaa to A3	AAA to A–
2 High quality	Baa	BBB
3 Medium quality	Ba	BB
4 Low quality	B	B
5 Lower quality	Caa to C	CCC to C
6 In or near default	Caa to C	C1, D

Source: Adapted from *Purposes and Procedures of the Securities Valuation Office of the National Association of Insurance Commissioners,* (New York, New York: NAIC Securities Valuation Office, 1995), p. 3.

remember from this classification is that most insurers invest primarily in the top two classifications of bonds (highest quality and high quality). For investment purposes, these two classifications are investment-grade bonds and the remaining classifications are non-investment-grade bonds. ***Investment-grade*** bonds are typically those that are in the NAIC's Classifications 1 and 2. The values of bonds with classifications 1 through 5 are admitted, that is, appear on the *Assets* page of the Annual Statement. If a life insurer owns a bond with a rating of Classification 6, then its admitted value for Annual Statement purposes usually follows the LCM rule. In other words, the bond's admitted value is listed on the *Assets* page and its non-admitted value is listed elsewhere in the Annual Statement.

An insurer's general ledger summarizes the activity involving all of its bond holdings. For each bond that it owns, the insurer typically establishes a subsidiary ledger account that contains more detailed information than that contained in the general ledger. This detailed information includes the principal amount, interest rate, interest payment dates, premium or discount, issuer, issue date, and maturity date of each bond, as well as any debit and credit transactions for that bond which affect the general ledger balance. An insurer creates a subsidiary ledger for each type of investment and maintains a control account in the general ledger to record the totals for each investment category, such as short-term bonds and long-term bonds. The total of the subsidiary ledger account balances for a specific investment category must always be equal to the control account balance in the general ledger for that investment category.

Certain information about a bond appears on the face of the bond certificate. This information includes the bond's principal (hence the term "face value"), interest rate, and maturity date. Bond interest is typically payable semiannually. Thus, the owner of a $1,000 par value bond that pays an annual interest rate of 10 percent will receive a $50 interest payment twice each year ($1,000 par value × 10 percent rate of interest ÷ 2 payments each year). The rate of interest specified on the bond certificate is known as the ***stated rate,*** *coupon rate,* or *nominal rate.* The interest rate payments are sometimes referred to as *coupon payments* because, before the development of automated investment systems, bondholders clipped coupons from their bonds to redeem for semiannual interest payments. In this section, we examine accounting for bonds with the insurer as the purchaser, rather than the issuer, of bonds.

Accounting for the Purchase and Sale of Bonds

When an insurer purchases a bond, the insurer records the bond at *cost,* which is the price that the insurer pays for the bond, whether or not that amount matches the par value of the bond. If an insurer buys a $1,000 bond at par value, then the insurer debits an asset account, such as Bonds, and credits Cash for the par value of the purchased bond. Thus, a typical entry to record the purchase of a $1,000 bond at par is

Bonds.	1,000	
Cash		1,000

To record the purchase of a bond at par value.

Likewise, if the insurer purchases a $1,000 bond for $950, the insurer debits Bonds for $950 and credits Cash for $950.

Bond investments may result in capital gains or losses for an insurer. For accounting purposes, these gains and losses are categorized in the United States as either realized or unrealized. In the United States, a realized capital gain or loss would generally result only from the sale of a bond or other asset. The ***realized gain (loss)*** from the sale of an asset is the difference between that asset's net sales proceeds and its book value. In this context, book value is the value of an asset according to an insurer's accounting records. If the asset's sale price is greater than its book value, the sale results in a gain that appears on the Annual Statement as *profit on sale.* Similarly, if the asset's sale price is less than its book value, the sale results in a loss that appears on the Annual Statement as *loss on sale.* Canadian insurers report the value of fixed-term investments, such as bonds, at amortized cost on the *Assets* page and report all realized gains or losses as deferred gains on the *Liabilities* page of the Annual Return.

Unlike a realized gain (loss), an *unrealized gain (loss)* does not result from the actual sale of an asset. Recall from Chapter 5 that an *unrealized gain (loss)* is the difference between an asset's book value and its admitted value (statutory accounting) or its current market value (GAAP). Unrealized gains or losses are recorded directly to surplus for statutory reporting purposes.

To determine whether a gain or loss has resulted from the sale of an asset, an accountant must know the value of the asset being sold. In accounting for the sale of a bond, an insurer records the bond's sale price and its purchase price on a ***net basis,*** which means that both the sale price and the purchase price reflect adjustments for expenses incurred in the purchase and sale of bonds. Most of these expenses consist of commissions paid to securities brokers. An insurer adds the expenses incurred in purchasing a bond to the bond's purchase price and subtracts the expenses incurred in selling a bond from the bond's sale price. This is an example of capitalizing asset costs, a concept we first introduced in Chapter 4. To *capitalize* means to record a cost as an asset and then amortize (expense) this asset over time. To illustrate, if the purchase price of a bond is $1,000 and the commission paid to a broker on this purchase is $50, then an insurer records the bond's historical cost as $1,050 ($1,000 purchase price + $50 commission). Thus, an appropriate journal entry to record such a bond purchase is

Bonds	1,050	
Cash		1,050

To record the purchase of a bond at par value plus commission.

Suppose the insurer subsequently sells this bond for $1,200, incurring brokerage commissions of $50. After deducting the brokerage commissions, the sale results in a $100 realized capital gain for the insurer ($1,200 sales price – $50 commission – $1,050 purchase price). An appropriate journal entry to record this transaction is

Cash	1,150	
Bonds		1,050
Gain on Sale of Bonds		100

To record the sale of bonds at a gain.

Accrued Bond Interest Income

Accrued bond interest income for a particular bond is the amount of interest that has been earned but is not yet payable as of the Annual Statement date. Accrued Bond Interest Income is an account receivable that typically is reported with other accrued income under Investment Income Due and Accrued, an asset on the balance sheet. If an insurer buys a bond between interest payments, the insurer receives accrued bond interest income as part of the next interest payment, even though the bond's seller earned this interest. To compensate the seller for this lost interest, the bond's purchase price must include an amount equal to the interest income that has accrued up to the purchase date. For example, if an insurer purchases a $1,000 bond at par with a 10 percent interest rate and semiannual interest (meaning two payments per year of $50 each) with $20 interest accrued as of the purchase date, the insurer records the following journal entry:

Bonds	1,000	
Accrued Bond Interest Income	20	
Cash		1,020

To record the purchase of bonds with accrued interest income.

Note that the insurer includes the amount of accrued interest in the cash paid to the seller of the bond. The debit to Accrued Bond Interest Income demonstrates that the additional $20 the insurer paid to the seller of the bond is attributable to the amount of bond interest income that the seller would have earned during the interest payment period in which the seller sold the bond. The insurer records the accrued interest as an account receivable because the insurer expects to receive the full amount of the bond interest income, $50 in our example, when the next semiannual interest payment is made. Upon receipt of this interest payment, the insurer debits Cash for $50, the full amount of the semiannual interest payment, credits Accrued Bond Interest Income for $20 (which zeroes out the accrual), and credits Bond Interest Income for $30. The $30 is the portion of the $50 semiannual interest that the insurer earned and received. In this case, the journal entry to record receipt of the semiannual interest payment is

Cash	50	
Accrued Bond Interest Income		20
Bond Interest Income		30

To record the receipt of bond interest income.

Note that Accrued Bond Interest Income, like all accrued revenues, is an asset account, whereas Bond Interest Income is a revenue account. Thus, insurers report accrued revenues on the balance sheet and revenues on the statement of operations. Most insurance companies debit accrued interest on bond purchases to an account created specifically for payment of such interest. By creating such an account, an insurer can easily obtain a total of its accruals. Insurers disclose the amount of accrued investment income in the Annual Statement or Annual Return.

Bond Discounts and Bond Premiums

As mentioned earlier, the annual amount of interest paid on a bond is a stated amount, obtained by multiplying the par value of the bond by the bond's stated rate of interest. This amount is payable to the bond owner regardless of the actual price paid for the bond. If a price other than par is paid, the actual rate of return, known as the ***effective interest rate,*** also called the *effective rate of return* or the *true interest rate,* on the amount paid for the bond will differ from the stated rate of return because interest on bonds and most other investments is compounded more often than annually. For example, if a company pays $900 for a $1,000 bond that earns a 10 percent annual interest rate, its *effective interest rate* will be greater than 10 percent because the annual interest payments the company receives will be 10 percent of $1,000 (or $100) rather than 10 percent of $900 (or $90). To find the effective interest rate, divide the interest payments by the amount paid for the bond. In this case, the effective interest rate is 11.1 percent ($100 interest ÷ $900 purchase price of bond).

Earlier we defined the difference between the price paid for a bond (disregarding any accrued interest) and the bond's par value as a bond *discount* if the price paid for the bond is less than par, and as a bond *premium* if the price paid for the bond is greater than par. As a rule, when a bond is purchased at a discount, the effective interest rate will be higher than the bond's stated rate of return, as the above example demonstrates. Conversely, when a bond is purchased at a premium, the effective interest rate will be lower than the bond's stated rate of return. Suppose a company purchases a $1,000 bond for $1,100. In this case, the effective interest rate is 9.1 percent ($100 interest ÷ $1,100 purchase price of the bond).

An insurer purchases a bond at a discount or premium to achieve a desired rate of return on a particular investment. Assume that the current interest rate available on newly issued bonds is 12 percent. On any of its bond investments, the insurer generally wants to receive at least the 12 percent rate of return that could be realized in the current bond market. To realize this rate of return, the insurer could buy a bond with a stated rate of 12 percent. However, 12 percent bonds may not be available for purchase at that time. In such a case, the insurer could purchase, at a discount, a bond with a lower stated rate of return. Alternatively, the insurer could pay a premium for a bond with a stated rate of return higher than 12 percent. In either case, the insurer's investment could yield the rate of return currently available on similar investments.

To illustrate, assume that the Cornerstone Life and Health Insurance Company purchases a $1,000 par value 8 percent bond that matures in one year. However, Cornerstone hopes to realize a 10 percent effective interest rate on this bond. To achieve this 10 percent rate of return, Cornerstone pays $982 to the bond seller. By buying the bond for $982, Cornerstone has purchased the bond at an $18 discount. At maturity (in this case, one year) the insurer will have collected $1,080 ($1,000 principal + $80 interest income). This will yield a 10 percent return on the $982 investment ($1,080 – $982 = $98, which is approximately 10 percent of $982).

Assume, on the other hand, that when the market interest rate on bonds is 10 percent, the only bonds available for purchase are previously issued $1,000 par value bonds that mature in one year with a 12 percent stated rate of interest. Because the owner of these bonds is presently earning 2 percent more interest than is available in the current market, an insurer would have to pay an amount greater than the $1,000 par value to make the sale of the 12 percent bonds worthwhile to the current owner. By paying a premium for the bonds, the insurer will realize an effective interest rate lower than the stated rate of return.

For example, the Wellspring Life and Health Insurance Company wants to purchase a $1,000 par value 12 percent bond that matures in one year to realize a 10 percent rate of return. While Wellspring might want to earn 12 percent on the investment, in a market dominated by 10 percent interest rates, a bond owner would not be likely to give up an investment that is currently yielding 12 percent. The bond owner could reinvest the money received from such a sale only at the current 10 percent rate, assuming a similar investment vehicle. In exchanging a 12 percent rate of return for a 10 percent rate of return, the bond owner making the exchange would be accepting a loss of potential income. To achieve the desired 10 percent rate of return, Wellspring has to pay the bond owner $1,018 for the $1,000 par value bond. Upon maturity of the bond, Wellspring will have collected $1,120 for its investment ($1,000 maturity value + $120 interest income), a 10 percent effective interest rate on its $1,018 investment ($1,120 – $1,018 = $102, which is approximately 10 percent of $1,018).

The price that an investor is willing to pay for a bond is the bond's market value. A bond's market value is equal to the *present value,* at the effective rate of interest, of (1) the principal amount due at maturity and (2) the periodic interest payments. For example, assume that an insurer purchases a $1,000 par value bond with an interest rate of 8 percent and a 10-year maturity one year after the issue date to yield a 10 percent effective interest rate. If the insurer holds the bond until maturity, it will earn $720 interest income ($1,000 × 8 percent × 9 years). The present values at the 10 percent effective interest rate of the $1,000 maturity value and the $720 interest income result in a market value for that bond of $885. (Knowledge of the exact method of calculating present values, which we discuss in Chapter 14, is not necessary for this discussion.) The entry to record the purchase of a $1,000 par value bond at a $115 discount ($1,000 – $885), net of brokerage commissions or other expenses, consists of an $885 debit to Bonds and an $885 credit to Cash.

An insurer records a journal entry each accounting period to account for the amortization of a bond premium or the accrual of a bond discount for bonds purchased at a premium or discount. ***Amortization*** is an accounting process by which an insurer periodically and systematically adjusts the book value of an investment so that, on the maturity date, the book value equals that investment's par value. Amortization can be calculated using several methods. For example, most state insurance commissioners and GAAP require that U.S. insurers use the *interest method of amortization.* Regardless of the method used to calculate amortized values, however, the purpose of amortization is to recognize the difference between historical cost and par value as income from the purchase date until the bond's maturity. Amortization, which applies to bonds and certain other assets, is necessary because it enables an insurer to allocate the amount of discount or premium to each accounting period that the insurer owns the bond. This allocation matches the correct amount of interest income to the period in which the income will be earned. We demonstrate the amortization process in the following example. However, the methods for calculating amortization are outside the scope of this text.

Suppose the Able Life and Health Insurance Company purchases a $10,000 par value bond for $9,421. The bond has a stated interest rate of 8 percent and a maturity date 3.5 years from today. Able purchases this bond to obtain a 10 percent effective interest rate and intends to hold the bond until it matures. The accounting entry for the bond purchase is

Bonds.	9,421	
Cash		9,421

To record the purchase of a bond at a discount.

Upon receipt of a semiannual interest payment of $400 ($10,000 par value × 8 percent interest rate × ½ year), Able records the receipt of the interest payment by debiting Cash and crediting Bond Interest Income:

Cash.	400	
Bond Interest Income.		400

To record the receipt of bond interest income.

In our example, Able uses the interest method to record the amortization of interest income. Able multiplies $9,421, the cost of the bond, by the bond's effective interest rate for one-half year to obtain $471 ($9,421 × 10 percent × ½ year). Subtracting the $400 semiannual interest from $471 results in $71 of additional income. Able debits Bonds for $71 to adjust (increase) the bond's book value, and Able credits Bond Interest Income for $71 to reflect the additional investment income. This entry increases the interest income on the insurer's books to $471 for the six months and increases the book value of the bonds to $9,492 ($9,421 + $71). To determine the amortization

Figure 7-6. Amortization of bond discount.

1 Period	2 Beginning Book Value	3 Interest at Stated Rate	4 Interest at Effective Rate (2) × .10 × .5	5 Amortization Amount (4) – (3)	6 Adjusted Book Value (2) + (5)
1	$9,421	$400	$471	$71	$ 9,492
2	$9,492	$400	$475	$75	$ 9,567
3	$9,567	$400	$478	$78	$ 9,645
4	$9,645	$400	$482	$82	$ 9,727
5	$9,727	$400	$486	$86	$ 9,813
6	$9,813	$400	$491	$91	$ 9,904
7	$9,904	$400	$496	$96	$10,000

entry for the next six-month period, Able multiplies $9,492 by ½ of 10 percent. The result of this calculation is $475. Assume that Able amortizes the discount every six months until the bond's maturity. At maturity, the bond's book value will equal its par value: $10,000. Figure 7-6 shows the amortization process over the life of this bond.

If an insurer purchases a bond at a premium, the amortization entry is the reverse of that described for bonds purchased at a discount. For bonds purchased at a premium, the effective rate of interest is lower than the stated rate. As a result, the insurer debits the income account to decrease earned income and credits the asset account to reduce the book value of the bonds.

For example, assume that the Bountiful Life and Health Insurance Company purchases a five-year $10,000 bond with an 8 percent stated rate of interest. If, because of current market rates, Bountiful can obtain only a 6 percent effective interest rate, Bountiful would pay approximately $10,853 for this bond, a premium of $853. Assume that Bountiful amortizes the bond premium every six months to systematically reduce the value of the bond from the book value to the par value.* The stated semiannual interest payment is $400 ($10,000 × 8 percent × ½ year), and the effective interest payment is approximately $326 ($10,853 × 6 percent × ½ year). Therefore, the amortization amount for the first six months is approximately $74 ($400 – $326). The accounting entry to record the amortization of the bond premium is

Bond Interest Income 74
  Bonds 74
To record the amortization of bond interest income.

* In reality, insurers amortize every reporting period, whether monthly, quarterly, semiannually, or annually.

Figure 7-7. Amortization of bond premium.

1 Period	2 Beginning Book Value	3 Interest at Stated Rate	4 Interest at Effective Rate (2) × .06 × .5	5 Amortization Amount (4) – (3)	6 Adjusted Book Value (2) + (5)
1	$10,853	$400	$326	$(74)	$10,779
2	$10,779	$400	$323	$(77)	$10,702
3	$10,702	$400	$321	$(79)	$10,623
4	$10,623	$400	$319	$(81)	$10,542
5	$10,542	$400	$316	$(84)	$10,458
6	$10,458	$400	$314	$(86)	$10,372
7	$10,372	$400	$311	$(89)	$10,283
8	$10,283	$400	$308	$(92)	$10,191
9	$10,191	$400	$306	$(94)	$10,097
10	$10,097	$400	$303	$(97)	$10,000

Upon recording this entry, the adjusted book value of the bond is approximately $10,779 ($10,853 – $74). Bountiful uses this amount to determine the amortization entry for the next interest period, so the amortized premium for the next six-month accounting period is approximately $77. As in the above example with bonds purchased at a discount, the insurer continues the amortization process every six months until the bond's maturity date, when the book value of the bond is equal to its par value. Figure 7-7 shows the complete amortization process for a bond purchased at a premium. Again, the book value and the par value of the bond are equal on the maturity date.

In an alternate method of accounting for bonds purchased at a discount or premium, an insurer establishes a separate account for the bond discount or premium, and carries the bond at par value. For Annual Statement valuation, the statement value of a bond recorded on the books in this manner is still the par value adjusted for (*net of*) the premium or discount as applicable. With the alternate method of bond accounting, the entry for a $1,000 bond purchased for $950 on the first day of an interest period is

Bonds.	1,000	
Accrued Discount on Bonds.		50
Cash		950

To record a bond purchase on the first day of an interest period.

When the insurer receives each interest installment, the insurer records the amortization entry, as illustrated in the following journal entry:

Accrued Discount on Bonds xxx
Bond Interest Income xxx
To record the amortization of bond interest income.

The dollar amounts for these amortization entries depend on the effective interest rate and the stated interest rate on the bond in question. If the insurer sells this bond before its maturity date, the insurer debits Accrued Discount on Bonds with an amount that brings that account's balance to zero. Under this alternate method of accounting for the purchase of bonds, if the insurer has paid a premium for the bond, then the insurer debits the purchase amount in excess of par value to Unamortized Premium on Bonds on the purchase date. Then the insurer credits Unamortized Premium on Bonds and debits Bond Interest Income for the purchase amount. If the insurer sells the bond before maturity, it records any difference between the selling price and the book value as either a gain (if the selling price is greater than the book value) or a loss (if the selling price is less than the book value).

Bonds and the Annual Statement/Annual Return

On the U.S. Annual Statement, an insurer reports bonds at their *admitted value,* or *statement value,* which is generally the bonds' amortized cost. Recall that the amortized cost of a bond is the amount originally paid for the bond, adjusted for amortization of the bond premium or discount as applicable. The NAIC, however, considers some bonds to be unamortizable or values them at less than their cost because they are in default, for example. For the purposes of the U.S. Annual Statement, unamortizable bonds are valued at their market values, usually a lower amount than their amortized cost. As shown in Figure 7-8, the Annual Statement requires that an insurer group its bond investments by the type of issuer, investment quality, and maturity.

The *CICA Handbook* classifies a Canadian insurer's assets as either equity or fixed-term. Fixed-term assets include money market funds, bonds, mortgages, and preferred stock that has a fixed redemption date. Canadian insurers carry bonds at amortized cost. They also amortize bond premiums, bond discounts, and gains or losses that arise from the sale of bonds to income over the term to maturity. No adjustment is made to the bond's market value for bonds and other fixed-term investments, because the amortization of a bond premium or discount results in a reasonable and systematic adjustment to the bond's par value, which is in essence its market value at maturity. However, Canadian insurers disclose a bond's market value, as well as the difference between the bond's market value and its amortized cost, in the Annual Return.

The account used to amortize the gain or loss is *Deferred Realized Gains (Losses),* also called *Deferred Net Capital Gains (Losses),* which operates similarly to an unearned revenue account, as both accounts are amortized through the statement of operations. Suppose a Canadian insurer sells a bond with an amortized cost of $900 for $1,000. The accounting entry is

Cash	1,000	
Bonds		900
Deferred Realized Gains (Losses)		100

To record the sale of a bond at a gain.

If the insurer sells this bond two years before its maturity date, the insurer recognizes half the gain this year and half next year. In this case, the accounting entry for each year is

Deferred Realized Gains (Losses)	50	
Amortization of Realized Gains (Losses)—Bonds		50

To recognize the amortization of deferred realized gains on the sale of a bond.

If the insurer sells the bond for a loss, then the accounting entry is a debit to Cash, a debit to Deferred Realized Gains (Losses), and a credit to Bonds. In this case, if the insurer sells the bond at a loss two years before its maturity, then the accounting entry to recognize the amortization of deferred realized gains (losses) is a debit to Amortization of Realized Gains (Losses)—Bonds and a credit to Deferred Realized Gains (Losses). Suppose that, instead of selling the bond, the insurer *writes down* the value of the bond because of poor credit quality (for example, the bond issuer has missed one or more interest payments and the bond is in default). In this case, the insurer reports the difference between the bond's book value and its written-down value as a loss on the current year's statement of operations. The insurer cannot defer and amortize the loss until the bond's maturity because the loss in value is a result of credit quality. Canadian life and health companies itemize the amortization of gains and losses on bonds in the Annual Return.

Stocks

As with bonds, the sale of stock is a means for businesses to raise money. However, while bonds are debt securities, stocks are *equity securities,* which means that stock represents not a loan but ownership in a business. Stock is sold in shares, and anyone who owns shares of stock in a company is a ***stockholder*** or a *shareholder.* The

Figure 7-8. Schedule D—Part 1A—Section 1—U.S. Annual Statement.

Quality and Maturity Distribution of All Bonds Owned December 31, At Statement Values by Major Types of Issues and NAIC Designations											
1 Quality Rating Per the NAIC Designation	2 1 Year or Less	3 Over 1 Year Through 5 Years	4 Over 5 Years Through 10 Years	5 Over 10 Years Through 20 Years	6 Over 20 Years	7 Total Current Year	8 Col. 7 as a % of Line 7.7	9 Total From Column 7 Prior Year	10 % From Column 8 Prior Year	11 Total Publicly Traded	12 Total Privately Placed (a)
1A. U.S. Governments, Schedules D & DA (Group 1 in part)											
1A.1 Class 1						0	0.0		0.0		
1A.2 Class 2						0	0.0		0.0		
1A.3 Class 3						0	0.0		0.0		
1A.4 Class 4						0	0.0		0.0		
1A.5 Class 5						0	0.0		0.0		
1A.6 Class 6						0	0.0		0.0		
1A.7 TOTALS	0	0	0	0	0	0	0.0	0	0.0	0	0
1B. Other Governments, Schedules D & DA (Group 1 in part)											
1B.1 Class 1						0	0.0		0.0		
1B.2 Class 2						0	0.0		0.0		
1B.3 Class 3						0	0.0		0.0		
1B.4 Class 4						0	0.0		0.0		
1B.5 Class 5						0	0.0		0.0		
1B.6 Class 6						0	0.0		0.0		
1B.7 TOTALS	0	0	0	0	0	0	0.0	0	0.0	0	0
2. States, Territories and Possessions and Political Subdivisions of States, Territories and Possessions (Direct and Guaranteed), Schedules D & DA (Groups 2 & 3)											
2.1 Class 1						0	0.0		0.0		
2.2 Class 2						0	0.0		0.0		
2.3 Class 3						0	0.0		0.0		
2.4 Class 4						0	0.0		0.0		
2.5 Class 5						0	0.0		0.0		
2.6 Class 6						0	0.0		0.0		
2.7 TOTALS	0	0	0	0	0	0	0.0	0	0.0	0	0
3. Special Revenue & Special Assessment Obligations and all Non-Guaranteed obligations of agencies and authorities of governments and their political subdivisions, Schedules D & DA (Group 4)											
3.1 Class 1						0	0.0		0.0		
3.2 Class 2						0	0.0		0.0		
3.3 Class 3						0	0.0		0.0		
3.4 Class 4						0	0.0		0.0		
3.5 Class 5						0	0.0		0.0		
3.6 Class 6						0	0.0		0.0		
3.7 TOTALS	0	0	0	0	0	0	0.0	0	0.0	0	0
4. Public Utilities (Unaffiliated), Schedules D & DA (Group 5)											
4.1 Class 1						0	0.0		0.0		
4.2 Class 2						0	0.0		0.0		
4.3 Class 3						0	0.0		0.0		
4.4 Class 4						0	0.0		0.0		
4.5 Class 5						0	0.0		0.0		
4.6 Class 6						0	0.0		0.0		
4.7 TOTALS	0	0	0	0	0	0	0.0	0	0.0	0	0
5. Industrial & Miscellaneous and Credit Tenant Loans (Unaffiliated), Schedules D & DA (Groups 6 and 7)											
5.1 Class 1						0	0.0		0.0		
5.2 Class 2						0	0.0		0.0		
5.3 Class 3						0	0.0		0.0		
5.4 Class 4						0	0.0		0.0		
5.5 Class 5						0	0.0		0.0		
5.6 Class 6						0	0.0		0.0		
5.7 TOTALS	0	0	0	0	0	0	0.0	0	0.0	0	0

Figure 7-8. Schedule D—Part 1A—Section 1—U.S. Annual Statement (continued).

Quality and Maturity Distribution of All Bonds Owned December 31, At Statement Values by Major Types of Issues and NAIC Designations.

1 Quality Rating Per the NAIC Designation	2 1 Year or Less	3 Over 1 Year Through 5 Years	4 Over 5 Years Through 10 Years	5 Over 10 Years Through 20 Years	6 Over 20 Years	7 Total Current Year	8 Col. 7 as a % of Line 7.7	9 Total From Column 7 Prior Year	10 % From Column 8 Prior Year	11 Total Publicly Traded	12 Total Privately Placed (a)
6. Parent, Subsidiaries and Affiliates, Schedules D & DA (Group 8)											
6.1 Class 1						0	0.0		0.0		
6.2 Class 2						0	0.0		0.0		
6.3 Class 3						0	0.0		0.0		
6.4 Class 4						0	0.0		0.0		
6.5 Class 5						0	0.0		0.0		
6.6 Class 6						0	0.0		0.0		
6.7 TOTALS	0	0	0	0	0	0	0.0	0	0.0	0	0
7. Total Bonds Current Year											
7.1 Class 1	0	0	0	0	0	0	0.0	XXX	XXX	0	0
7.2 Class 2	0	0	0	0	0	0	0.0	XXX	XXX	0	0
7.3 Class 3	0	0	0	0	0	0	0.0	XXX	XXX	0	0
7.4 Class 4	0	0	0	0	0	0	0.0	XXX	XXX	0	0
7.5 Class 5	0	0	0	0	0	0	0.0	XXX	XXX	0	0
7.6 Class 6	0	0	0	0	0	0	0.0	XXX	XXX	0	0
7.7 TOTALS	0	0	0	0	0	(b) 0	0.0	XXX	XXX	0	0
7.8 Line 7.7 as a % of Col. 7	0.0	0.0	0.0	0.0	0.0	0.0	XXX	XXX	XXX	0.0	0.0
8. Total Bonds Prior Year											
8.1 Class 1						XXX	XXX	0	0.0		
8.2 Class 2						XXX	XXX	0	0.0		
8.3 Class 3						XXX	XXX	0	0.0		
8.4 Class 4						XXX	XXX	0	0.0		
8.5 Class 5						XXX	XXX	0	0.0		
8.6 Class 6						XXX	XXX	0	0.0		
8.7 TOTALS	0	0	0	0	0	XXX	XXX	(b) 0	0.0	0	0
8.8 Line 8.7 as a % of Col. 9	0.0	0.0	0.0	0.0	0.0	XXX	XXX	0.0	XXX	0.0	0.0
9. Total Publicly Traded Bonds											
9.1 Class 1						0	0.0		0.0	0	XXX
9.2 Class 2						0	0.0		0.0	0	XXX
9.3 Class 3						0	0.0		0.0	0	XXX
9.4 Class 4						0	0.0		0.0	0	XXX
9.5 Class 5						0	0.0		0.0	0	XXX
9.6 Class 6						0	0.0		0.0	0	XXX
9.7 TOTALS	0	0	0	0	0	0	0.0	0	0.0	0	XXX
9.8 Line 9.7 as a % of Col. 7	0.0	0.0	0.0	0.0	0.0	0.0	XXX	XXX	XXX	0.0	XXX
9.9 Line 9.7 as a % of Line 7.7, Col. 7, Section 7	0.0	0.0	0.0	0.0	0.0	0.0	XXX	XXX	XXX	0.0	XXX
10. Total Privately Placed Bonds											
10.1 Class 1						0	0.0		0.0	XXX	0
10.2 Class 2						0	0.0		0.0	XXX	0
10.3 Class 3						0	0.0		0.0	XXX	0
10.4 Class 4						0	0.0		0.0	XXX	0
10.5 Class 5						0	0.0		0.0	XXX	0
10.6 Class 6						0	0.0		0.0	XXX	0
10.7 TOTALS	0	0	0	0	0	0	0.0	0	0.0	XXX	0
10.8 Line 10.7 as a % of Col. 7	0.0	0.0	0.0	0.0	0.0	0.0	XXX	XXX	XXX	XXX	0.0
10.9 Line 10.7 as a % of Line 7.7, Col. 7, Section 7	0.0	0.0	0.0	0.0	0.0	0.0	XXX	XXX	XXX	XXX	0.0

(a) Includes $0 freely tradeable under SEC Rule 144 or qualified for resale under SEC Rule 144A.

(b) Includes $0 current year $0 prior year of bonds with Z designations. The letter "Z" indicates an obligation whose NAIC designation was not approved by the Securities Valuation Office at the date of the statement.

two major classes of stock are common stock and preferred stock. Of these two classes, common stock comprises the majority of all stock issued.

When a U.S. company issues stock, it typically assigns the new stock a par value that appears on each stock certificate—for example, $3 per share. The stock issuer uses the par value to determine the amount of its journal entry upon receiving cash from the sale of its stock. Unlike the par value of a bond, the par value of a stock has no effect on an insurer's accounting for the purchase or sale of the stock, nor does the par value have a direct impact on the subsequent market value of the stock. Recall that Canadian insurers are no longer required to list a stock's par value.

Investment income resulting from stock ownership generally is in the form of *cash dividends,* which typically are made in quarterly payments by a company to owners of its preferred and common stock. Cash dividends are a means of sharing a company's earnings with its owners. Most preferred stock has a provision for cash dividends. Common stock may or may not have a provision for cash dividends, as many companies that issue common stock prefer to reinvest earnings in core business operations rather than pay it to common stockholders.

Usually, cash dividends on common stock are expressed as an annual dollar amount per share. Cash dividends on preferred stock typically are expressed as a percentage of par value per share. For example, a common stock with a current market value of $25 per share may have an annual cash dividend of $1 per share. An insurer that owns 1,000 shares of common stock will receive a cash dividend of $250 each quarter on this stock (1,000 shares × $1 ÷ 4). A preferred stock that has a cash dividend expressed as 10 percent of its par value of $10 results in an annual dividend of $1 per share. The journal entry to record the receipt of cash dividends is Dividend Income—Common Stock or Dividend Income—Preferred Stock, both of which are revenue accounts. Recall that cash dividends that have been earned but not yet received as of the Annual Statement date are reported under Investment Income Due and Accrued, an asset account.

Common stock comprises a much smaller portion of an insurer's investment portfolio than bonds. The primary reason for this smaller proportion is risk. Common stocks carry a greater investment risk than do bonds. Unlike bonds, the rate of return on common stocks is rarely guaranteed and is more strongly influenced by market and economic conditions. Because life and health insurers must meet or exceed the rate of return that their actuaries assume when calculating premium rates and policy reserves, insurers limit their investments in the unpredictable stock market. Because of their responsibilities to policyowners, which call for them to maintain a predictable flow of income, insurance companies tend to be *risk-averse* (non-risk-taking) organizations. Insurance regulators are even more risk averse. Most states limit an insurer's common stock holdings to a percentage of the insurer's total assets or surplus.

Nevertheless, stock is still an important part of most insurers' investment strategies. Although the rates of return on common stock are unpredictable, they can often be much higher than the rates provided by bonds. Moreover, common stock investments help to diversify an investment portfolio. For example, an insurer can use common stocks to counterbalance changes in bond valuations. In the securities markets, when bond values go down, stock values tend to go up, and vice versa. Thus, an insurer can use a diversified investment portfolio to protect its invested assets from large fluctuations in overall value.

As in our discussion of bonds, this chapter examines accounting for stocks from the stockholder's point of view, with the assumption that an insurance company is the stockholder. In Chapter 11, we discuss accounting for stocks from the point of view of the insurer as issuer.

Accounting for the Purchase and Sale of Stocks

Accounting principles for the purchase and sale of stock are similar to the accounting principles for the purchase and sale of bonds. The stockholder records stock purchases at cost. The Stocks account referred to throughout the following examples is a general ledger asset account. The insurer maintains a subsidiary ledger for each specific stock owned. The subsidiary ledger for a particular stock typically includes the date and amount of the transaction, the number of shares owned, and a description of the issuing company. In addition, the insurer notes the market value per share of each stock owned on December 31 to facilitate the preparation of the Annual Statement and to determine the amount of an unrealized gain (loss) on that stock.

Suppose the Stalwart Life and Health Insurance Company purchases 100 shares of XYZ Corporation stock for $89 per share with a brokerage commission of $600. Stalwart records the transaction by debiting the cost of the stock to the Stocks account and crediting Cash for the same amount. The accounting entry is

Stocks	9,500	
Cash		9,500

To record the purchase of XYZ stock.

When Stalwart sells the stock, the accounting entry is a debit to Cash for the amount of cash received, which is typically the number of shares sold times the market price per share at the time of sale. If Stalwart sells the stock for $8,000, after deducting brokerage commissions, then the accounting entry is

Cash	8,000	
Loss on Sale of Stock	1,500	
Stocks		9,500

To record the sale of XYZ stock at a loss.

Suppose Stalwart instead sells the XYZ stock for $12,000, after paying a brokerage commission. The journal entry to record the stock sale is

Cash	12,000	
Stocks		9,500
Gain on Sale of Stock		2,500

To record the sale of XYZ stock at a gain.

Accounting for Cash Dividends

If a company's board of directors declares a cash dividend before a reporting date, but the dividend is payable after that date, then an insurer that owns shares of this company's stock records the amount of the dividend on the Annual Statement as part of investment income due and accrued, provided the insurer held the stock as of the ex-dividend date. The ***ex-dividend date,*** or *ex-date,* which is the date that the dividend is effective, determines whether the stockholder is eligible to receive a declared dividend. Suppose a company declares a $1 per share cash dividend on its common stock on December 1 for stockholders of record on December 15, the ex-dividend date. The company will pay the dividend January 15. In this example, the declaration date is December 1, the ex-dividend date is December 15, and the payment date is January 15. Cash dividends are accrued investment income on the declaration date. If the insurer owns 200 shares of the stock, when the dividend is declared, the insurer makes the following journal entry to record the cash dividend income due and accrued:

Investment Income Due and Accrued	200	
Dividend Income—Common Stock		200

To record cash dividend income due and accrued.

The insurer makes the following journal entry upon receiving the cash dividend:

Cash	200	
Investment Income Due and Accrued		200

To record a cash dividend on common stock.

Accounting for Stock Dividends

Typically, a stock dividend is declared as a percentage of outstanding stock. The dollar value used to record the transaction is either the par value of the stock or, in the case of stock with no par value, an amount determined by the company's board of directors. Under U.S. GAAP, rules for determining the stock dividend's value depend in part on the size of the stock dividend. For example, U.S. GAAP defines a *small stock dividend* as less than one-quarter of the issuing company's issued stock. If the dividend is more than one-quarter of the company's issued stock, then it is called a *stock split* or a *large stock dividend.* Canadian GAAP does not distinguish between small and large stock dividends.

The amount of stock received is based on the amount of stock owned by the stockholder at the time. If an insurer owns stock in a company that declares a stock dividend, the insurer does not need to post a journal entry to record the dividend. The stock issuer has not transferred assets to the insurer and other stockholders, as it would have in the case of a cash dividend. The insurer instead notes the number of shares received in a stock dividend in the subsidiary ledger for that stock so that the insurer can correctly calculate the cost per share of stock in determining realized or unrealized gains (losses) on the stock.

Suppose the Infinity Life and Health Insurance Company owns 100 shares of Acme Corporation stock that Infinity originally purchased for $9,000. If Acme declares a 50 percent stock dividend (a large stock dividend), holders of Acme stock are entitled to a 50 percent increase in the number of shares owned. Hence, the number of shares of Acme stock that Infinity owns increases to 150. In Infinity's general ledger, the $9,000 cost of the stock remains unaffected, but Infinity lowers the stock's book value per share in the subsidiary account from $90 ($9,000 cost ÷ 100 shares) to $60 ($9,000 cost ÷ 150 shares). Note that the total value of Acme's stock owned by Infinity remains the same before and after the stock dividend: $9,000 (100 shares × $90) or (150 shares × $60).

If Infinity sells any of this stock, Infinity calculates the gain or loss on the sale by taking the difference between the sale price and the adjusted cost of $60 per share. Thus, if Infinity sells 50 shares of the Acme stock for $65 per share (after expenses of sale), the gain on that sale is $250 [($65 selling price – $60 cost per share) × 50 shares]. The entry to record the sale is a debit to Cash for $3,250 ($65 × 50 shares), a credit to Stocks for $3,000 ($60 cost per share × 50 shares), and a credit to a capital gain account for the realized gain of $250:

	Debit	Credit
Cash	3,250	
Stocks		3,000
Gain on Sale of Stock		250

To record the sale of Acme common stock at a gain.

As another example, if Infinity sells the entire 150 shares at $70 per share, the accounting entry is

Cash	10,500	
Stocks		9,000
Gain on Sale of Stock		1,500

To record the sale of Acme common stock at a gain.

Canadian insurers credit Deferred Realized Gains (Losses) instead of Gain on Sale of Stock in the above accounting entries, then amortize a percentage of the gain on the statement of operations. Although the *CICA Handbook* does not specify the exact percentage, a 15 percent per year amortization rate on stock is understood for Annual Return reporting purposes.

Stock sold can also result in a capital loss. If Infinity sells the stock for $55 per share, then Infinity has a realized a capital loss of $750 [($60 – $55) × 150 shares]. The amount received on the sale is $8,250 ($55 × 150 shares), and a capital loss account, Loss on the Sale of Stock, is debited for the difference between the cost and the sale price of the stock. The journal entry is

Cash	8,250	
Loss on Sale of Stock	750	
Stocks		9,000

To record the sale of Acme common stock at a loss.

Canadian insurers debit Deferred Realized Gains (Losses) instead of Loss on Sale of Stock in the above accounting entries, then amortize a designated percentage of the Deferred Realized Gain (Loss) into income on the statement of operations, as stipulated in the *CICA Handbook.*

Stocks and the Annual Statement/Annual Return

Most insurers list their common stock investments on the U.S. Annual Statement at their market value as of the statement date with two notable exceptions. The NAIC determines the statement values of common stocks that are not publicly traded, that is, those stocks that are not sold through a stock exchange. Also, the common stock of an insurer's subsidiary or affiliated companies and other companies controlled by the insurer are usually valued by the *equity method,* which is prescribed by the NAIC. Regardless of the method used, insurers make sure that the valuation basis used and the resulting values are appropriate to the circumstances. Most preferred stock in good standing is valued at its cost. In this context, "good standing" means that the stock is investment-grade and currently trading at an amount higher than its original cost. Under statutory accounting practices, an insurer reports preferred stock that is not in good standing at market value on the Annual Statement. The insurer also reports an unrealized loss for the difference between the stock's original cost and its current market value, if the current market value is less than the original cost. Figure 7-9 depicts the schedule showing all common stocks owned by the insurer as of the Annual Statement date.

Earlier we noted that the *CICA Handbook* categorizes a Canadian insurer's investments as either fixed-term or equity. An insurer's equity investments include common stock, preferred stock without a fixed redemption date, and real estate. Canadian insurers use the ***moving average market method (MAMM)*** to systematically adjust unrealized gains (losses) that result from changes in current market value of equity investments over a period of years. Canadian insurers report both the book value and the market value of a stock in the Annual Return. The difference between the asset's book value and its current market value is amortized into income on the statement of operations over time. The moving average market method is an attempt to better measure long-term investment performance while minimizing the effects of volatile market values for invested assets in the short-term. Suppose a stock that a Canadian insurer purchases on January 1 for $100 per share has a market value of $110 per share on December 31. Using MAMM, the insurer reports the value of the stock at $101.50 per share ($100 + [($110 – $100) (.15)]) in the Annual Return. The accounting entry to recognize the $1.50 per share difference between market value and book value is

Stocks	1.50	
Amortization of Unrealized Gains/Losses . . .		1.50

To recognize the amortization of an unrealized gain on stock.

Suppose the insurer can sell the stock for $120 under the MAMM. The insurer then recognizes a gain of $18.50 per share ($120 – $101.50). Instead of reporting the $18.50 gain on the statement of operations, the insurer reports this amount under Deferred Realized Gains (Losses) and amortizes this amount into income at 15 percent per year until the total amount is amortized. The purpose of Deferred Realized Gains (Losses) is to minimize the financial effect of realized gains (losses) on an insurer's net income. The annual amortization amount of this gain is $2.78 ($18.50 × .15). The accounting entries are

Cash	120	
Stocks		101.50
Deferred Realized Gains (Losses).		18.50

To record the amount of a realized gain on the sale of stock.

Figure 7-9. Schedule D—Part 2—Section 2—U.S. Annual Statement.

Showing all COMMON STOCKS owned December 31 of Current Year												
	1	2	3	4	5	6	Dividends		8	9	10	11
CUSIP Identification	Description	Number of Shares	Book Value	Rate per Share Used to Obtain Market Value	Market Value	Actual Cost	7.1 Declared but Unpaid	7.2 Amount Received During Year	Increase by Adustment in Book Value During Year	Decrease by Adjustment in Book Value During Year	NAIC Designation (a)	Year Acquired
0599999 TOTAL — COMMON STOCKS			0	XXX	0	0	0	0	0	0	XXX	XXX
9999999 TOTAL — PREFERRED AND COMMON STOCKS			0	XXX	0	0	0	0	0	0	XXX	XXX

(a) For all common stocks bearing the NAIC designation "U" provide: the number of such issues 0, the total S value (included in Column 5) of all such issues $0.

Deferred Realized Gains (Losses). 2.78
Amortization of Realized Gains/Losses on Stocks 2.78
To record the amortization of a capital gain as income.

If the insurer does not sell the stock, at the end of the next accounting year, the insurer compares the stock's market value with its book value and calculates the amount to amortize to income. Separate exhibits in the Annual Return itemize the amortized unrealized gains (losses) and the deferred realized gains (losses) associated with an insurer's stock.

Mortgage Loans

In 1994, mortgage loans comprised approximately 11 percent of the U.S. life and health insurance industry's total assets. In Canada, mortgages represented about 28 percent of the industry's total assets in 1994. Under the terms of a ***mortgage loan,*** a person, business, or other entity borrows money from a lender and offers some specific piece of real estate, such as a house, farm, or office building, to the lender as *collateral.* If the borrower fails to (1) make the required periodic payments of interest and principal, (2) pay taxes on the property promptly, or (3) maintain and insure the property adequately, the lender may foreclose the mortgage. In other words, the lender (typically the insurer in our examples) may seize the mortgage loan's collateral, usually the property named in the mortgage. ***Foreclosure*** is a legal procedure by which a lender recovers the unpaid loan balance by gaining title to the real estate offered as collateral if the borrower defaults in the obligation to meet the terms of the loan. We discuss the effects of foreclosure on an insurer's mortgage loan investments and accounting records later in this section. Instead of taking legal title in a foreclosure, Canadian insurers have the option of a ***power of sale,*** which allows the lender to settle the mortgage debt by selling the property on behalf of the owner of the property's legal title. Any money remaining from the sale of a property and payment of all associated expenses is paid to the property titleholder. Accounting entries are similar to those for an outright foreclosure.

The same piece of property can be used as collateral for more than one mortgage loan. The original mortgage secured by a piece of real estate is called the ***first mortgage.*** The difference between the current market value of the property and the amount of mortgage loan and other claims outstanding is the property owner's *equity.* Equity in this context is similar to *owners' equity* in the basic accounting equation in that equity is what remains after the property owner sells the property and settles all claims against the property. If the property owner's equity is large enough, the property owner may be able to take out a ***second mortgage*** against the owner's equity. Most jurisdictions limit insurance companies from investing too heavily in second mortgages because second mortgages pose a greater risk for the lender. The holders of first mortgages have a prior claim against the borrower's assets in case of default. The holders of second mortgages stand in line behind those who hold first mortgages. If the holder of a second mortgage must foreclose because the borrower has not made the agreed-upon payments, the holder of the second mortgage *must* assume the first mortgage to foreclose on the property.

Some mortgage loans in the United States and Canada are guaranteed by government agencies such as the U.S. Federal Housing Authority (FHA), the Veterans Administration (VA), and the Canadian Mortgage Housing Corporation (CMHC). Mortgage loans not insured or guaranteed by a government agency are called ***conventional mortgage loans.*** The maximum term of most conventional residential mortgages in the United States ranges from 15 to 30 years. In Canada, mortgage terms range from 6 months to 10 years with amortization of payment to a maximum of 30 years. On a government-backed loan, the term is usually a multiple of 5 years up to a maximum of 35 years. On conventional commercial mortgages, the lock-in term is generally 15 to 30 years in the United States and 1 to 20 years, with amortization up to 30 or 35 years, in Canada.

Most insurers today invest primarily in ***collateralized mortgage obligations (CMOs),*** which are mortgage-backed bonds secured by a pool of residential mortgage loans. CMOs are highly rated debt securities for statutory accounting purposes. Life and health insurance companies invest in mortgage loans and CMOs for several reasons. A borrower typically repays a mortgage loan to the lender on a monthly basis. Because of this frequent payment system, mortgage loans offer an insurer a predictable flow of funds. Even most variable rate mortgages, in which the rate of interest payable on the loan principal varies according to market conditions, have a minimum rate of return, usually referred to as a ***floor rate.*** Further, CMOs provide a high degree of safety for an insurer's investment in residential mortgages. Commercial mortgage loans can provide not only for a fixed rate of interest, but also for other potential income. For example, a mortgage loan can include provisions that grant the mortgagor a percentage of the gross revenues or net income earned by the borrower during use of the property.

Accounting for Mortgage Loans

When a life and health insurance company issues a mortgage loan, the insurer usually establishes a subsidiary ledger account that includes the following specific characteristics of each mortgage loan:

- Monthly payment
- Due date
- Amount due
- Interest rate
- Location of property
- Principal value
- Maturity date
- Borrower identification name, address, etc.
- Property's appraisal value
- Type of loan, such as farm, non-farm, commercial, conventional, FHA, VA, and CMHC

To account for a mortgage loan, the insurance company debits Mortgage Loans, an asset account, and credits Cash for the amount of the loan. Generally, the borrower pays ***closing costs,*** which are the expenses incurred in transferring property from seller to buyer, including legal fees and title search fees. The lender may require the borrower to pay additional amounts to an escrow account or trust account, at mortgage issue or during each year that the mortgage continues. The lender, in turn, creates an ***escrow account*** to record these payments and uses the money to pay property taxes, insurance premiums, and other expenses related to the mortgaged property. Not all mortgage agreements require an escrow account. After all, paying for such expenses as property taxes and insurance is the responsibility of the borrower. However, by establishing an escrow account, the lender assures itself that certain required expenses are paid and the mortgaged property is maintained at some minimum level. Therefore, many lenders require their borrowers to place money in escrow.

The lender credits the amount held in escrow to a liability account. If the borrower pays $900 in escrow funds, the lender records the borrower's remittance of these funds as follows:

Cash	900	
Escrow Funds—Mortgages		900

To record borrower's remittance of escrow funds.

Because escrow accounting entries do not affect mortgage loan balances in the general ledger, some insurers prefer to keep escrow entries in a separate subsidiary ledger account. Subsidiary ledger accounts for escrow balances typically include

- Payee name
- Escrow identification
- Type of escrow fund
- Loan identification
- Amount due
- Due date

The escrow accounts are monitored by a general ledger control account established specifically for escrow deposits. Escrow accounts typically apply to residential mortgages, not to commercial mortgages.

As mentioned earlier, most mortgage loans are repayable in monthly installments. Although insurers have no legal obligation to notify borrowers of the due dates of mortgage payments, many insurers send a monthly statement or payment due notice shortly before the due date. Some insurers provide the borrower with a book of dated coupons that are to be detached and submitted to the insurer along with a loan payment when payment is due. Other insurers use a preauthorized check (PAC) or other electronic funds transfer (EFT) system. If a borrower is late in making a mortgage payment, the borrower usually is assessed a penalty. The lender credits penalty charges for late payment to Interest Income—Mortgages or to a miscellaneous investment income account.

The monthly payment made by the borrower includes elements of principal, interest, and, in many cases, an escrow amount. Typically, the borrower pays the same total amount each month to cover interest and principal. The portion of each monthly mortgage payment applicable to interest, however, is slightly smaller each month because each monthly principal repayment reduces the amount of the loan on which interest is payable. In other words, the mortgage loan is *amortized* over the payment period. As the interest portion decreases, the percentage of each mortgage payment applicable to corresponding principal increases. The amount to be placed in escrow remains the same each month until a change in taxes, insurance premiums, or other expenses necessitates a change.

To illustrate, a $10,000, 20-year mortgage loan at 12 percent interest requires a monthly repayment from the borrower (exclusive of escrow items) of $110.11. The interest income for the first month is $100 ($10,000 × 12 percent ÷ 12), which the lender credits to an income account. The remaining $10.11 reduces the loan balance. If the total monthly payment including property taxes is $145.11, the amount the lender credits to the escrow account is $35 ($145.11 – $110.11). A journal entry made for the first monthly payment is

Cash	145.11	
Mortgage Loans		10.11
Interest Income—Mortgages		100.00
Escrow Funds—Mortgages		35.00

To record the first monthly mortgage payment with escrow funds.

When the lender pays taxes or insurance premiums on the borrower's property, the lender debits the escrow account and credits Cash for the exact amount paid.

A borrower may pay off a mortgage loan before the end of its term. For example, assume a mortgage loan has a debit balance of $6,500, and the borrower sells the mortgaged property to pay off the loan. If this $6,500 loan has $32 in accrued interest and an escrow account with a $61 credit balance, the borrower must remit $6,471 ($6,500 loan + $32 accrued interest – $61 escrow) to pay off the outstanding mortgage loan. The entry to record the payoff of the mortgage is

Cash	6,471	
Escrow Funds—Mortgages	61	
Mortgage Loans		6,500
Interest Income—Mortgages		32

To record the payoff of a mortgage with escrow funds.

The credit to the interest income account and the debit to the escrow account serve to clear these account balances with regard to this particular loan. Sometimes a mortgage loan requires that the borrower pay additional charges if the loan is paid off before maturity. In such cases, the lender debits Cash and credits Mortgage Prepayment Income for the prepayment penalty.

If a mortgaged property is sold to a third party before the mortgage is paid off, and if the new owner assumes the mortgage (that is, takes responsibility for its payments), the lender does not need to post a journal entry. However, the insurer changes its subsidiary ledger account to indicate the new owner of the property.

Many mortgage loans made by insurance companies are made through real estate firms or mortgage brokers that service such loans for a fee, usually a percentage of the unpaid loan balance. These servicing firms are called ***mortgage correspondents.*** To account for fees paid to mortgage correspondents, the insurer debits Mortgage Service Fees Paid, an expense account.

Besides directly approving mortgage loans to borrowers and purchasing CMOs, insurance companies can invest in mortgages by purchasing them from other lenders, through brokers or joint ventures, for example. Depending on the circumstances, an insurance company may purchase a mortgage loan for an amount equal to the balance of the loan, or at a premium or discount depending on the market interest rate. (Mortgage loans, like bonds, are *debt securities,* so there is an inverse relationship between their current market value and market interest rates.) The borrower may be unaware of the sale, because the seller of the mortgage often continues to service the loan and receive the regular monthly payments. In turn, the mortgage seller remits the regular mortgage payments to the buyer of the mortgage loan. An insurer purchases a mortgage loan at a discount or premium for the same reasons that an insurer purchases a bond at a discount or premium: to achieve a desired rate of return on a particular investment or to help manage the relationship between the cash inflows (income streams) of its assets and the cash outflows (payment streams) of its liabilities.

An insurer periodically determines the amortization amount of the premium or discount on a mortgage loan. If a U.S. insurer purchases a mortgage loan at a discount, the insurer then debits the additional amount of interest earned to Unamortized Discount on Mortgages and credits this amount to Interest Income—Mortgages. The entry made to amortize $20 of mortgage discount is

Unamortized Discount on Mortgages	20	
Interest Income—Mortgages.		20

To record the amortization of a mortgage discount.

If the U.S. insurer purchases the mortgage loan at a premium, the insurer's amortization entry serves to reduce the amount of interest earned. Thus, to record the amortization of a mortgage loan purchased at a premium, the insurer debits Interest Income—Mortgages and credits Unamortized Premium on Mortgages for the amortization amount. Some companies prefer to record the adjustment to income resulting from the amortization of a discount or premium in a subdivision of the Interest Income—Mortgages account. Recording these transactions directly to an interest income account facilitates preparation of the Annual Statement because an insurer must report separately the annual amortization relating to mortgage loans.

Foreclosure

Occasionally, an insurance company must foreclose a mortgage loan on real estate. On the date the insurer forecloses the mortgage, the unpaid balance of the loan plus any accrued interest, foreclosure costs, and unpaid property taxes are recorded in the insurer's books as the value of a real estate asset acquired, as long as this value does not exceed the fair market value at foreclosure. The essence of this transaction is the conversion of a *mortgage loan* asset into a *real estate foreclosed* asset. The following example illustrates some elements of a foreclosure.

Assume that an insurer forecloses a mortgage to which the following dollar amounts apply:

Fair market value	$10,000
Unpaid loan balance	$ 7,290
Accrued interest	$ 710
Legal fees for foreclosure	$ 300

Upon foreclosure, the insurer debits Real Estate Foreclosed for the property's book value ($8,300), which is the total of the loan balance ($7,290), accrued interest ($710), and legal fees for foreclosure ($300). The fair market value of the property has no impact on the insurer's journal entry if the fair market value is higher than the book value. However, the book value of the property should not exceed its fair market value. If it does, then the insurer must write down the value of the property, thus incurring a capital loss. An insurer credits a revenue account, such as Interest Income—Mortgages, when it records the accrued interest. The insurer also credits Mortgage Fees Payable, a liability account, to record the foreclosure expenses owed by the borrower. A typical journal entry for a transaction where the insurer has sufficient information is

Real Estate Foreclosed	8,300	
Mortgage Loans		7,290
Interest Income—Mortgages		710
Mortgage Fees Payable		300

To record a foreclosed mortgage on real estate.

The above accounting entry assumes that the insurer pays the legal expenses. When the insurer issues a check for payment of the legal expenses, the insurer debits the Mortgage Fees Payable account to result in a zero balance for this account, as demonstrated in the following entry:

Mortgage Fees Payable	300	
Cash		300

To record the payment of legal expenses on foreclosed real estate.

If the borrower pays the legal expenses, the insurer debits Real Estate Foreclosed for $8,000 and an account receivable for $300 for the legal expenses in the above accounting entry.

Mortgage Loans and the Annual Statement/Annual Return

For Annual Statement purposes, insurers typically record mortgage loans at the amount of the unpaid principal balance or net book value when acquired. If, however, a loan in default declines in value to less than the unpaid principal balance, the insurer records an appropriate valuation allowance, a type of *contra asset account,* which is a subsidiary ledger account used to deduct specified amounts from a company's accompanying asset account. We discuss contra accounts in Chapter 8.

As shown in Figure 7-10, mortgage loans appear in the Annual Statement according to type: farm, commercial, and residential, which include purchase money mortgages. A ***purchase money mortgage*** is a mortgage in which the seller of the property grants credit to the purchaser, and the purchaser uses the real estate being purchased as collateral for the mortgage loan. Large mortgages—that is, those that (1) exceed one million dollars or (2) comprise at least ½ of 1 percent of an insurer's admitted assets—appear separately in the Annual Statement.

Canadian insurers disclose both the book value and the market value of their mortgage loans on an exhibit in the Annual Return. If a mortgage loan is in default, then an insurer writes down its value and reports a loss on this asset in the current accounting year. Again, the insurer cannot defer and amortize the decreased asset value over time.

Conclusion

With this chapter, we shifted our focus from accounting principles and processes to a closer look at the major account classifications that appear on an insurer's balance sheet and statement of operations. Chapter 7 introduced you to some of the typical invested assets that U.S. and Canadian life and health insurance companies include on the balance sheet. In Chapter 8, we conclude our discussion of an insurer's invested assets and then discuss an insurer's other assets, including cash.

Key Terms and Concepts

investment accounting
asset/liability management (ALM)
cash
short-term investments
cash equivalents
tangible asset
intangible asset
amortized cost
lower of cost or market (LCM) rule
writing down

Figure 7-10. Schedule B—Part 1—Section 1—U.S. Annual Statement.

Summary of Long-Term Mortgage Loans (including foreclosed liens subject to redemption) Owned at December 31 of Current Year and changes therein during the year

	Farm Mortgages		Residential Mortgages (1 to 4 Families)			Commercial Mortgages			9
	1 Purchase Money	2 Other than Purchase Money	3 Insured or Guaranteed	4 Purchase Money	5 All Other	6 Insured or Guaranteed	7 Purchase Money	8 All Other	Total
1. Book value of mortgages owned, December 31st of previous year			371,910		5,167			64,170,588	64,547,665
2. Loans in cash or granted on disposal of real estate								18,706,464	18,706,464
3. Cost of mortgages, insured and other, purchased									
4. Additional cash loaned on .... $0 of refunded mortgages			1,617						1,617
5. Interest covered by increase in, or refunding of, mortgages									
6. Taxes covered by increase in, or refunding of, mortgages									
7. Other items covered by increase in, or refunding of, mortgages									
8. Accrual of discount on mortgages purchased								97,785	97,785
9. Transfers									
10. Aggregate write-ins for increases									
11. Totals			373,527		5,167			82,974,837	83,353,531
12. Payments on principal including cash on mortgages refunded			116,890		1,343			11,806,459	11,924,692
13. Mortgages foreclosed and transferred to real estate									
14. Mortgages on properties acquired by deed, in lieu of foreclosure, and transferred to real estate									
15. Decrease in book value of mortgages refunded or by adjustment in book value of mortgages									
16. Amortization of premium on mortgages purchased									
17. Transfers									
18. Aggregate write-ins for decreases									
19. Total Deductions			116,890		1,343			11,806,459	11,924,692
20. Book value of mortgages owned, end of year, per Exhibit 13, Line 3, Col. 1			256,637		3,824			71,168,378	71,428,839
DETAILS OF WRITE-INS									
1001.									
1002.									
1003.									
1098. Summary of remaining write-ins for Line 10 from overflow page									
1099. Totals (Lines 1001 thru 1003 plus 1098) (Line 10 above)									
1801.									
1802.									
1803.									
1898. Summary of remaining write-ins for Line 18 from overflow page									
1899. Totals (Lines 1801 thru 1803 plus 1898) (Line 18 above)									

GENERAL INTERROGATORY

1. Are any investments other than mortgage loans, such as ground rents, included in Schedule B? Yes [ ] No [X]

Key Terms and Concepts (continued)

net book value
bond
principal
maturity date
debt security
secured bond
collateral
debenture
public offering
private placements
premium
discount
default
risk-return tradeoff
investment-grade
stated rate
realized gain (loss)
net basis
effective interest rate
amortization
stockholder
ex-dividend date
moving average market method (MAMM)
mortgage loan
foreclosure
power of sale
first mortgage
second mortgage
conventional mortgage loans
collateralized mortgage obligations (CMOs)
floor rate
closing costs
escrow account
mortgage correspondents
purchase money mortgage

CHAPTER 8

Accounting for Other Assets

Learning Objectives

After studying this chapter, you should be able to

- Record the appropriate journal entries pertaining to real estate, policy loans, and reinsurance ceded
- Define and provide examples of an insurer's typical derivative assets
- Outline the bank reconciliation process
- Identify and describe an insurer's short-term assets
- Explain how deferred policy acquisition costs are treated under GAAP
- Explain the purpose of separate accounts

Chapter Outline

Real Estate

Accounting for the Purchase and Sale of Real Estate
Property Taxes and Foreclosure
Rental Income and Rental Expense
Real Estate on the Annual Statement/Annual Return

Derivatives

Policy Loans

Accounting for Policy Loans
Policy Loan Interest
Policy Loans and the Annual Statement/
Annual Return

Accounting for Cash and Short-Term Investments

Cash
Bank Reconciliation

Accounting for Other Short-Term Assets

Investment Income Due and Accrued
Premiums Due
Prepaid Expenses

Accounting for Other Assets

Reinsurance Ceded
Deferred Policy Acquisition Costs
Electronic Data Processing Equipment
Separate Accounts (Segregated Funds)

In the last chapter, we introduced you to investment accounting and to an insurer's primary invested assets: bonds, stocks, and mortgage loans. Chapter 8 continues our discussion of the invested assets of life and health insurance companies. Other topics in this chapter include cash, short-term investments, and other assets. Figure 8-1 shows the location on a typical insurance company balance sheet of the assets we discuss in this chapter.

Real Estate

Real estate includes buildings, undeveloped land, or both. Most insurers own three types of real estate: (1) properties occupied by the insurer, such as home office and regional office buildings, (2) properties held for sale, and (3) properties held for the production of income, such as investment properties. Real estate investments generally constitute a relatively small but growing percentage of the investments of most life insurance companies. In 1994, real estate investments comprised approximately 3 percent of the assets of U.S. life companies and 6 percent of the assets of Canadian life companies. Accounting for real estate is a specialized topic. This section is an overview of accounting for real estate investments in life and health insurance companies.

Accounting for the Purchase and Sale of Real Estate

Insurers record the cost of real estate as an asset. The cost of a piece of real estate equals the purchase price of that real estate plus any acquisition costs, such as title insurance premiums and legal fees, incurred during the purchase. Thus, if an insurer purchases real estate for $50,000, *plus* $8,000 in acquisition costs, the insurer makes the following journal entry:

Real Estate	58,000	
Cash		58,000

To record the purchase of real estate.

When a U.S. insurer owns real estate, the insurer *depreciates* the cost of that real estate over the useful economic life of the property. What amortization is to stocks and bonds, depreciation is to real

Figure 8-1. Highlight of the other assets section of a typical insurance company balance sheet.

December 31, 19XX			
Assets		**Liabilities and Capital Surplus**	
Invested assets:		**Liabilities:**	
Bonds	xxx	Policy reserves:	
Mortgage loans	xxx	Life insurance	xxx
Stocks	xxx	Annuities	xxx
Total Invested assets	xxx	Accident and health	xxx
		Total Policy Reserves	xxx
Real estate	xxx	Claim reserves:	
Policy loans	xxx	Life insurance	xxx
Investment income due and accrued	xxx	Accident and health	xxx
Cash and cash equivalents	xxx	**Total Claim Reserves**	xxx
Premiums due	xxx		
Deferred policy acquisition costs (GAAP only)	xxx	Policy dividends due and unpaid	xxx
Reinsurance ceded	xxx	Unpaid policy claims	xxx
Other assets	xxx	Premium deposits	xxx
		Advance premiums	xxx
Total Assets	5,000,000	Interest maintenance reserve	xxx
		Asset valuation reserve	xxx
		Other liabilities	xxx
		Total Liabilities	4,300,000
		Capital and Surplus:	
		Stock	xxx
		Additional paid-in capital	xxx
		Special surplus	xxx
		Unassigned surplus	xxx
		Net unrealized gains (losses)	(xxx)
		Treasury stock	(xxx)
		Total Capital and Surplus	700,000
		Total Liabilities and Capital and Surplus	5,000,000

estate, in that both amortization and depreciation spread or allocate a cost or gain (loss) over time. Canadian insurers generally do not depreciate real estate. Typically, they carry real estate at historical cost less write-downs and they include a moving average market method (MAMM) adjustment. However, Canadian insurers can depreciate the cost of improvements to real estate. It is important to remember that land is never depreciated under U.S. or Canadian accounting standards. Instead, the insurer values land at its original cost until disposing of it. The accounting entry to record depreciation of an insurer's real estate is a debit to Depreciation on Real Estate (an expense account) and a credit to Accumulated Depreciation on Real Estate (a contra asset account).

A ***contra account*** always accompanies a specified account and has a normal balance that is the opposite of the companion account. The purpose of a contra account is to provide additional information on the activity that occurs in its companion account. The amounts in a contra account decrease the balance in its companion account. Typically, contra accounts are associated with assets such as property, plant, and equipment. A ***contra asset account,*** sometimes called a *negative-asset account* or an *asset offset account,* is a ledger account used to deduct specified amounts from a company's asset account. In Chapter 7, we briefly discussed the use of contra asset accounts in accounting for mortgage loans. By using contra asset accounts for real estate, an insurer can record Accumulated Depreciation (a contra asset account) separately from Real Estate (an asset account), thus maintaining the original cost of the real estate in its accounting records. Maintaining separate contra asset accounts for real estate depreciation also facilitates preparation of Annual Statement exhibits and schedules associated with an insurer's real estate assets.

Suppose the Mainstay Life and Health Insurance Company, a U.S. insurer, purchases a building called Property A for $100,000, independent of the price of the land. Assume that depreciation expense on Property A is $3,000 per year. In this case, Mainstay makes the following accounting entry each year to acknowledge the property's depreciation:

Depreciation Expense—Property A	3,000	
Accumulated Depreciation—Property A. . . .		3,000

To record depreciation expense of $3,000 on Property A.

Note that because Accumulated Depreciation—Property A is a contra asset account, a credit increases its total. Because a contra asset account is opposite (contra) to its companion asset account, you increase it with a credit entry and decrease it with a debit entry—the *opposite* of increasing and decreasing an asset account. At the end of the first accounting period, Mainstay's balance sheet includes the following:

Property A	100,000
Less Accumulated Depreciation	3,000
Book Value of Property A	97,000

The accumulated depreciation entry does not affect the Property A control account in Mainstay's general ledger because deductions from the value of Property A are handled through the contra asset account (Accumulated Depreciation—Property A), instead of the real estate account. Mainstay reports Property A on its balance sheet at its book value, which is its historical cost net of accumulated depreciation. In this example, Property A's book value is $97,000 ($100,000 historical cost – $3,000 accumulated depreciation). After three years, assuming depreciation expense of $3,000 per year, Mainstay's balance sheet shows Property A with a book value of $91,000 [$100,000 historical cost – ($3,000 depreciation expense × 3 years = $9,000 accumulated depreciation)].

When a U.S. insurer sells a piece of real estate, the insurer closes both the asset account and the appropriate accumulated depreciation account in the subsidiary ledger for that property. For example, assume that Mainstay sells for $105,000 real estate that cost $100,000 (exclusive of the land cost). Accumulated depreciation to date totals $9,000. The entry to record the sale of this property is

Cash	105,000	
Accumulated Depreciation on Real Estate	9,000	
Real Estate		100,000
Gain on Sale of Real Estate		14,000

To record the sale of real estate at a gain.

The debit to Accumulated Depreciation on Real Estate and the credit to Real Estate serve to close out those accounts for this particular property. Mainstay calculates the capital gain or loss on the sale by subtracting from the sale price the property's cost minus any accumulated depreciation. In equation form

Capital Gain (Loss) = Sale Price – (Cost – Accumulated Depreciation)

or

Capital Gain (Loss) = Sale Price – Book Value

Thus, in the example above

Capital Gain (Loss) = 105,000 – (100,000 – 9,000)
= 105,000 – 91,000
= 14,000

Because the amount is positive, Mainstay has a realized capital gain of $14,000, which the company credits to Gain on Sale of Real Estate. Mainstay subtracts costs incurred during the sale from the sale price when determining the capital gain or loss on the sale. The types of costs typically incurred in the sale of real estate include brokerage commissions and closing costs.

If Mainstay instead sells the property for $80,000, the insurer realizes an $11,000 capital loss [$80,000 sale price – ($100,000 historical cost – $9,000 accumulated depreciation)]. While the debit to Cash in this case is for $80,000 and the debit to Loss on the Sale of Real Estate is for $11,000, the entries to Accumulated Depreciation on Real Estate and Real Estate remain the same to close out those accounts for the particular piece of property sold. The accounting entry is

Cash	80,000	
Accumulated Depreciation on Real Estate	9,000	
Loss on Sale of Real Estate	11,000	
Real Estate		100,000

To record the sale of real estate at a loss.

Canadian insurers use Deferred Realized Gains instead of Gain (Loss) on Sale of Real Estate and amortize the gain (loss) into income similar to the method used in the sale of stocks.

Property Taxes and Foreclosure

When a company purchases real estate, it pays a pro rata share of the property taxes already collected on the real estate. A U.S. insurer does not include these taxes in the asset account balance for real estate that it owns. Instead, the insurer records property taxes as an investment expense, unless the insurer acquires the property through foreclosure. Taxes are generally payable in advance at specified times during the year. For example, property taxes on real estate are due on a specified annual date or are divided into quarterly payments. When real estate is bought or sold, taxes *accrue* (accumulate) between tax payment dates. If an insurer purchases property after the seller has paid the taxes for the current tax period, the insurer must return to the seller the amount of tax applicable to the remainder of the tax period. This concept is similar to that described in the example in Chapter 7 in which both the bond seller and purchaser each earn bond interest income during the same interest period. For example, assume that an insurer is purchasing a piece of real estate to which the following dollar amounts apply:

Purchase price	$100,000
Title insurance premium	1,000
Legal fees of purchase	1,500
Taxes paid by seller at outset of tax period	1,200

If two-thirds of the tax period has passed when the insurer purchases this property, then the insurer must return $400 (one-third of $1,200) to the seller. This $400 represents the amount of tax applicable to the time that the insurer will own the property during that tax period. To record this real estate purchase, the insurer (1) debits Real Estate for $102,500 for the cost of the purchase ($100,000 purchase price + $1,000 title insurance premium + $1,500 legal fees), (2) debits Real Estate Taxes for $400 (the amount paid to the seller), and (3) credits Cash for the total of the debits. The journal entry is

Real Estate	102,500	
Real Estate Taxes	400	
Cash		102,900

To record the purchase of real estate.

Sometimes an insurer purchases real estate for which the taxes have not been paid in advance. In this case, the seller of the real estate either (1) pays to the insurer the amount of any accrued and unpaid taxes or (2) reduces the purchase price by that amount. Using the dollar amounts from the previous example but assuming that no taxes had been paid on the property, if $800 in taxes have accrued at the time of purchase, the insurer credits the $800 to Real Estate Taxes, an expense account. The journal entry is

Real Estate	102,500	
Real Estate Taxes		800
Cash		101,700

To record the purchase of real estate.

When the insurer pays the property tax of $1,200 on the tax payment date, the insurer debits Real Estate Taxes for $1,200. The $1,200 debit gives that account (assuming a zero balance at the outset of the transaction) a debit balance of $400, the amount of tax applicable to the part of the tax period during which the insurer owned the property.

An insurer has two options when it obtains property through foreclosure: (1) put the property up for resale or (2) rent the property to produce investment income. When real estate obtained through foreclosure is offered for resale, an insurer usually capitalizes the property taxes on the real estate. Recall that to capitalize means to record a cost as an asset. In this case, the insurer adds the amount of property taxes to the cost of the property. Thus, if the Herald Life and Health Insurance Company has foreclosed on property and is carrying that property on its books at $60,000, the payment of a $500 property tax assessment on that property would increase Herald's cost of the property to $60,500.

An insurer treats property taxes differently if the insurer obtains property through foreclosure, has completed the foreclosure proceedings, and is renting the property to produce additional income. After completing the foreclosure proceedings, the insurer treats any property taxes it has paid as an operating expense. Consider the example above. During foreclosure proceedings Herald debits $500 of property taxes to Real Estate Foreclosed, an asset account. After foreclosure proceedings are finished, however, Herald will debit any future property taxes to Real Estate Taxes. When an insurer sells a foreclosed property, the insurer *adds* the amount it received for prepaid taxes to, and *subtracts* the amount of accrued taxes or expenses from, the sale price before calculating the capital gain or loss on the property. The insurer debits the amounts paid for accrued taxes to the Real Estate Taxes account.

Rental Income and Rental Expense

To show the proper amount of investment income and expense in the Annual Statement, statutory accounting typically requires that the insurer charge itself rent for occupancy of its home office building. The journal entry for this transaction consists of a debit to Rental Expense and a credit to Rental Income for the rent amount. The amount of rent that a company charges to itself can be based either on (1) an estimate of the current market rental value of the property or (2) a figure determined by the amount of expenses, taxes, and depreciation on the property plus an amount representing interest on the investment in the home office building. Typically, the expense and the income offset each other, so there is no effect on an insurer's net income or surplus associated with rental income and rental expense on the insurer's home office building. When an insurer rents property to another entity, the entry to record rental income received consists of a debit to Cash and a credit to Rental Income. Expense transactions regarding rental properties appear in the journal as a debit to Real Estate Expense and a credit to Cash.

Real Estate on the Annual Statement/Annual Return

A U.S. insurer reports the value of its real estate on the Annual Statement at the book value or appraised value, whichever is lower. Under statutory accounting, the value of a piece of real estate equals its book value (historical cost less accumulated depreciation) less *encumbrances* (for example, mortgages payable to others that may exist on the property). If the book value of the real estate is greater than its appraised value, then the insurer must either report this excess as a nonadmitted asset or write down (reduce) the real estate book value so that it equals the appraised value. Figure 8-2 shows the summary of real estate in the Annual Statement. Canadian insurers value real estate using MAMM, as discussed in Chapter 7. They also must obtain appraisals on their real estate holdings at least every three years.

Figure 8-2. Schedule A—Part 1—U.S. Annual Statement.

Showing all Real Estate OWNED December 31 of Current Year

Number	1 Location and Description of Property	2 Date Acquired	3 Year of Last Appraisal	4 Name of Vendor	5 Amount of Encumbrances	6 Cost to Company	7 Book Value Less Encumbrances	8 Market Value Less Encumbrances (a)	9 Statement Value	10 Increase or (Decrease) by Adjustment in Book Value During Year (b)	11 Expended for Additions and Permanent Improvements During Year	12 Amounts Received During Year for Sales of Rights or Privileges	13 Gross Income Earned Less Interest Incurred on Encumbrances (c)	14 Taxes, Repairs and Expenses Incurred	15 Net Income	16 Amount of Mortgage at The Time of Acquisition as Real Estate	17 Amt of Taxes, Foreclosure Costs & Other Exp Capitalized in B.V. of Real Estate	18 Amt of Past Due & Accrued Interest Capitalized in B.V. of Real Estate
	A. Acquired prior to current year and owned at end of current year (but not then under contract of sale)																	
0199996	Summary—Items of less than $25,000 (No)		XXX	XXX	0	0	0	0	0	0	0	0	0	0	0	XXX	XXX	XXX
0199997	Items from $25,000 to $49,999 (No)		XXX	XXX	0	0	0	0	0	0	0	0	0	0	0	XXX	XXX	XXX
0199998	Items from $50,000 to $99,999 (No)		XXX	XXX	0	0	0	0	0	0	0	0	0	0	0	XXX	XXX	XXX
0199999	Part 1 A				0	0	0	0	0	0	0	0	0	0	0	XXX	XXX	XXX
	B. Acquired during current year and owned at end of current year (but not then under contract of sale)																	
0299999	Part 1 B				0	0	0	0	0	0	0	0	0	0	0	0	0	0
0399999	TOTALS — Part 1 A and B				0	0	0	0	0	0	0	0	0	0	0	XXX	XXX	XXX

Figure 8-2. Schedule A—Part 1—U.S. Annual Statement (continued).

Showing all Real Estate OWNED December 31 of Current Year

C. Acquired prior to current year and owned under contract of sale at end of current year

Number	1 Location and Description of Property	2 Date Acquired	3 Year of Last Appraisal	4 Name of Vendor	5 Amount of Encumbrances	6 Cost to Company	7 Book Value Less Encumbrances	8 Market Value Less Encumbrances (a)	9 Statement Value	10 Increase or (Decrease) By Adjustment in Book Value During Year (b)	11 Expended for Additions and Permanent Improvements During Year	12 Amounts Received During Year for Sales of Rights or Privileges	13 Gross Income Earned Less Interest Incurred on Encumbrances (c)	14 Taxes, Repairs and Expenses Incurred	15 Net Income	Contract Sale Price: 16 Total	17 Due to Date under Contract	18 Actually Paid to Date	19 Due Current Year and Unpaid
0499996	Summary—Items of less than $25,000	( )	XXX	XXX	0	0	0	0	0	0	0	0	0	0	0	0	0	0	0
0499997	Items from $25,000 to $49,999	( )	XXX	XXX	0	0	0	0	0	0	0	0	0	0	0	0	0	0	0
0499998	Items from $50,000 to $99,999	( )	XXX	XXX	0	0	0	0	0	0	0	0	0	0	0	0	0	0	0
0499999	PART 1 C				0	0	0	0	0	0	0	0	0	0	0	0	0	0	0

(a) State basis on which market value was determined
(b) State grand total increases $0, decreases $0.
(c) State rent received for space occupied by company (give items and amounts)

Showing all Real Estate OWNED December 31 of Current Year

D. Acquired during current year and owned under contract of sale at end of current year

Number	1 Location and Description of Property	2 Date Acquired	3 Year of Last Appraisal	4 Name of Vendor	5 Amount of Encumbrances	6 Cost to Company	7 Book Value Less Encumbrances	8 Market Value Less Encumbrances (a)	9 Statement Value	10 Increase or (Decrease) By Adjustment in Book Value During Year (b)	11 Expended for Additions and Permanent Improvements During Year	12 Amounts Received During Year for Sales of Rights or Privileges	13 Gross Income Earned Less Interest Incurred on Encumbrances (c)	14 Taxes, Repairs and Expenses Incurred	15 Net Income	16 Amount of Mortgage at the Time of Acquisition as Real Estate	17 Amt of Taxes, Foreclosure Costs & other Exp Capitalized in B.V. Real Estate	18 Amt of Past Due & Accrued Interest Capitalized in B.V. of Real Estate	
0599999	PART 1 D				0	0	0	0	0	0	0	0	0	0	0	0	0	0	0
0699999	TOTALS — PART 1 C and D				0	0	0	0	0	0	0	0	0	0	0	XXX	XXX	XXX	XXX
0799999	TOTALS — PART 1				0	0	0	0	0	0	0	0	0	0	0	XXX	XXX	XXX	XXX

(a) State basis on which market value was determined
(b) State grand total increases $0, decreases $0.
(c) State rent received for space occupied by company (give items and amounts)

CLASSIFICATION — Showing the total amount of Real Estate owned in each State and Foreign Country

1 State	Statement Value 2 Farm Properties	3 Other than Farm Property	1 State	Statement Value 2 Farm Properties	3 Other than Farm Property	1 State	Statement Value 2 Farm Properties	3 Other than Farm Property	1 State	Statement Value 2 Farm Properties	3 Other than Farm Property	1 State	Statement Value 2 Farm Properties	3 Other than Farm Property	1 State	Statement Value 2 Farm Properties	3 Other than Farm Property	4 Foreign Country	Statement Value 5 Farm Properties	6 Other than Farm Property
01 AL			11 GA			21 MD			31 NJ			41 SC			51 WY					
02 AK			12 HI			22 MA			32 NM			42 SD			52 AS					
03 AZ			13 ID			23 MI			33 NY			43 TN			53 GU					
04 AR			14 IL			24 MN			34 NC			44 TX			54 PR					
05 CA			15 IN			25 MS			35 ND			45 UT			55 VI					
06 CO			16 IA			26 MO			36 OH			46 VT			56 CN					
07 CT			17 KS			27 MT			37 OK			47 VA								
08 DE			18 KY			28 NE			38 OR			48 WA								
09 DC			19 LA			29 NV			39 PA			49 WV								
10 FL			20 ME			30 NH			40 RI			50 WI								
															8999999 TOTAL	0	0		0	0

Depreciation on real estate is an investment expense item for Annual Statement purposes because an insurer deducts depreciation from gross investment income to determine its net investment income. The insurer describes each item of real estate it owns in a separate schedule of the Annual Statement. Both the Annual Statement and the Annual Return contain additional schedules that itemize an insurer's real estate holdings. For example, the Annual Statement includes schedules that show real estate sold during the year, verification between years, and an analysis of real estate the insurer acquired in satisfaction of mortgage indebtedness. The Annual Return includes the appraised values of real estate and the amortization of unrealized gains and losses on the insurer's real estate holdings.

Derivatives

In this section, we introduce you briefly to derivatives, a small but growing part of an insurer's invested assets. Life and health insurers invest in derivatives, and the impact of derivatives on an insurer's assets is critical to the insurer's success. By definition, a ***derivative*** is a financial instrument that obtains (*derives*) its value from the underlying security on which it is based. The contractual terms of the derivative can cause the value to be a modified form of the underlying security. In Chapter 7, we introduced you to one type of derivative: collateralized mortgage obligations (CMOs), which are derived from residential mortgage loans. Insurers report derivatives on the balance sheet or disclose them in the notes to the financial statements. Although a thorough discussion of derivatives is outside the scope of this text, it is important for you to have a general understanding of the topic. Insight 8-1 discusses derivatives and their usefulness in limiting risk.

Life and health insurance companies use derivatives as a protective *hedge.* A ***hedge*** is an investment strategy undertaken to protect a future (unrealized) gain, to minimize a potential loss on invested assets, or to reduce costs or increase current investment income. Insurers also use derivatives as a protective hedge to manage the relationship of the maturity dates, rates of return, and cash inflows and outflows between their assets and their liabilities. Most insurers also use derivatives to hedge their exposure to interest rate risk and to foreign exchange risk. Recall that interest rate risk is the potential risk of loss on the value of assets caused by changes in market interest rates. ***Foreign exchange risk*** is the risk exposure to changes in the exchange rate between two currencies, such as the U.S. dollar and the Japanese yen. Two types of derivatives are interest rate swaps

Insight 8-1 Safe When Used Properly

Procter and Gamble shamefacedly told shareholders that it had lost $157 million pretax speculating in derivatives. We can understand P&G's embarrassment, but we can't buy the alibi that this $30 billion globe-spanning outfit was a naive victim. More likely the treasurer's office thought to impress the board by skinning a few bucks speculating in interest rates or currencies—and lost.

There have been a slew of announcements about losses from derivative trading by corporations (and mutual funds), accompanied by the customary noises from politicians looking to get their names in the newspapers. The fact is that derivatives serve useful purposes in business.

For every P&G or Gibson Greetings that has lost money speculating, many others have used derivatives in businesslike ways to limit risk and make their finances more orderly and predictable, less subject to the vagaries of the currency and money markets.

Derivatives are financial instruments derived from an underlying asset. The interest on a bond is, for example, a derivative and in a long-term bond more valuable than the promise to pay itself. The stream of interest can be and often is separated from the bond and sold as a derivative. The most common is an interest rate swap, which involves swapping one stream of bond interest for another.

Esoteric? Not really. Intelligently used, these swaps can enable a company to obtain long-term funding while paying no more than short-term interest rates—plus what amounts to a small fee for the swapping service.

Or let's suppose you're going to build a factory in Italy that will take three years to build. You haven't a clue what the dollar/lira exchange rate will be three years from now, but you need to tell your board precisely what the plant will cost. So you buy a derivative—either lira forwards or a call on lira at a set rate for as far as you need into the future.

It can and does get much more complicated (*Forbes, Mar. 29, 1993*), and fortunes can be and are won or lost. Which is why it's a field best left to those who understand the game and can afford to lose.

Many business objectives served by derivatives could be achieved without them—at much higher cost. Explains Mark Brickell, head of the Derivatives Strategies Group at J.P. Morgan: "With the derivatives, the corporate treasurer calls the swaps dealer and converts his fixed-interest payment for a floating-rate. One phone call and very low transaction costs."

Some derivatives are a form of insurance that simply expire, like other forms of insurance. For example, a firm buys the right to buy a foreign currency at a predetermined price to pay a foreign supplier in the future, capping its cost. When the supplier bill comes in, the exchange rate might be more favorable, and the right to buy the currency expires, unused.

For banks and financial institutions, derivatives are especially useful tools. In one year in particular, Banc One made almost $450 million from interest rate swaps. Many of its swaps involved swapping interest payments so that it received (higher) fixed rates and paid (lower) floating rates. However, profits or losses made from derivatives by nonfinancial corporations are much harder to spot.

It's not possible to draw a precise line between the business use of derivatives and the speculative use. But if a soapmaker speculates on a scale out of proportion to its business needs, shareholders should be told. People buy P&G stock because they want to invest in a soapmaker; if they want a business that plays derivatives full time, they will buy Salomon Inc.

Problem is, it's not easy to know whether a company is using derivatives on a large scale. For example, derivative contracts opened and closed within the yearly reporting period are not required by the Financial Accounting Standards Board to be disclosed, and unless the auditor thinks the losses are material, no line item on the income statement need appear. So you're never quite sure whether the company made its money selling shoes or speculating on currencies. In this regard, a bit more disclosure might be in order.

Profits or losses in swaps contracts are usually booked over the life of the contract.

When we talk of "making money" in derivatives we often simply mean that the company avoided a hit or performed better than planned. Gokul Hemmady of US West "made" $20 million last year by hedging an exposure in British pounds. US West needed £100 million for its cellular phone operation. One pound cost $1.90. Believing the pound would fall, Hemmady bought sterling options at $1.90 even if exchange rates rose, while leaving US West open to fund its investment at a lower

(continued)

Insight 8-1 Safe When Used Properly, continued

rate. DuPont, as well, improved its pretax earnings by $15 million by using derivatives.

Companies like P&G that lost heavily when interest rates turned suddenly upward had simply guessed wrong. Other companies might have done well with derivatives if they had used them as a hedge against a rise in rates rather than as a bet on low rates.

"We have used derivatives to improve our yields on our portfolio," explains Arvind Sodhani, treasurer of Intel. "That's our definition of profit center—a return over a benchmark." Intel's goal is to shave at least 2 percent off its borrowing costs or to increase the yields on its cash or liquid investments by 2 percent. It does this by skillfully transforming long-term obligations into short-term assets. You could call it gambling, but Intel isn't trying to act like an investment house; it's simply trying to keep its interest costs low and return on cash high. With a portfolio of $5 billion, Intel probably "makes" around $100 million a year—or 24 cents a share pretax.

Mobil Corp. is another smart and experienced user. "We have made $65 million more on $4 billion of our U.S. dollar debt than we could have done without derivatives," says Elizabeth Glaeser, who manages interest rate risk for Mobil. "With the type of portfolio Mobil or other large companies have, the risks exist anyway. Being a large, sophisticated user of derivatives just manages them better."

What about the gamblers? George Soros and other hedge fund players use derivatives to gamble on the currencies, bonds and stocks. But what they do is best left to them. Individuals and most corporate treasurers should use them with care.

Derivatives mysterious? To anyone who has ever hedged a bet or laid off part of a bet, there should be nothing esoteric about derivatives.

Source: Adapted from Rita Koselka, "Safe When Used Properly," *Forbes* (August 15, 1994), pp. 47–48. Reprinted By Permission of *Forbes* Magazine, © Forbes Inc., 1994.

and forward contracts. *Interest rate swaps* enable an insurer to minimize interest rate risk associated with unfavorable fluctuations in market interest rates on its fixed-rate investments such as bonds and mortgage loans. Such an investment also enables insurers to match cash flows of assets and liabilities. An insurer uses specific types of *forward contracts* to offset its exposure to unfavorable changes in foreign currency exchange rates that could affect its invested assets.

Suppose an insurer owns common stock in its investment portfolio, and that this stock has an unrealized gain, which means that the stock's current market value is higher than its original cost paid by the insurer. The insurer does not want to sell these stocks to realize this gain until it needs the funds to pay specified claims. On the other hand, the insurer does not want to lose the unrealized gain on the stock. To protect the unrealized gain, the insurer may purchase put options on the stock. A *put option* on common stock provides its owner with the right to sell the specific stock at a specified price within a specified time period to the investor who sold the put option.

For example, the Alright Life and Health Insurance Company buys 100 shares of stock for $50 a share. Two months later the stock increases in value to $60 a share, giving Alright an unrealized gain of $10 a share. Alright does not want to lose this gain, but it also wants to hold on to its 100 shares for another month, so it can obtain the best possible match of cash inflows to cash outflows. Therefore, Alright buys a put option that states that the seller of the put option will buy the 100 shares from Alright for $60 a share any time during the next month, no matter what the market value of the shares. Alright does not have to sell the shares during the next 30 days; it simply has the *option* to sell if it chooses. If the value of its optioned stock drops below $60 a share, Alright is very likely to exercise its option. However, if the value of the stock rises above $60 a share (say, to $63 a share), Alright will probably let the option expire and sell the stock on the open market at its new high value of $63. As you can see, Alright's put option is a financial instrument that derives its value from the stock, the investment on which it is based.

Derivatives that insurers use as a protective hedge, either to protect an unrealized gain or to minimize interest rate risk, include *caps, futures, rights, puts, calls, warrants, and floors.* Figure 8-3 briefly describes each of these derivatives. Key internal controls, including ongoing management review and segregation of accounting

Figure 8-3. Common derivatives used by insurance companies.

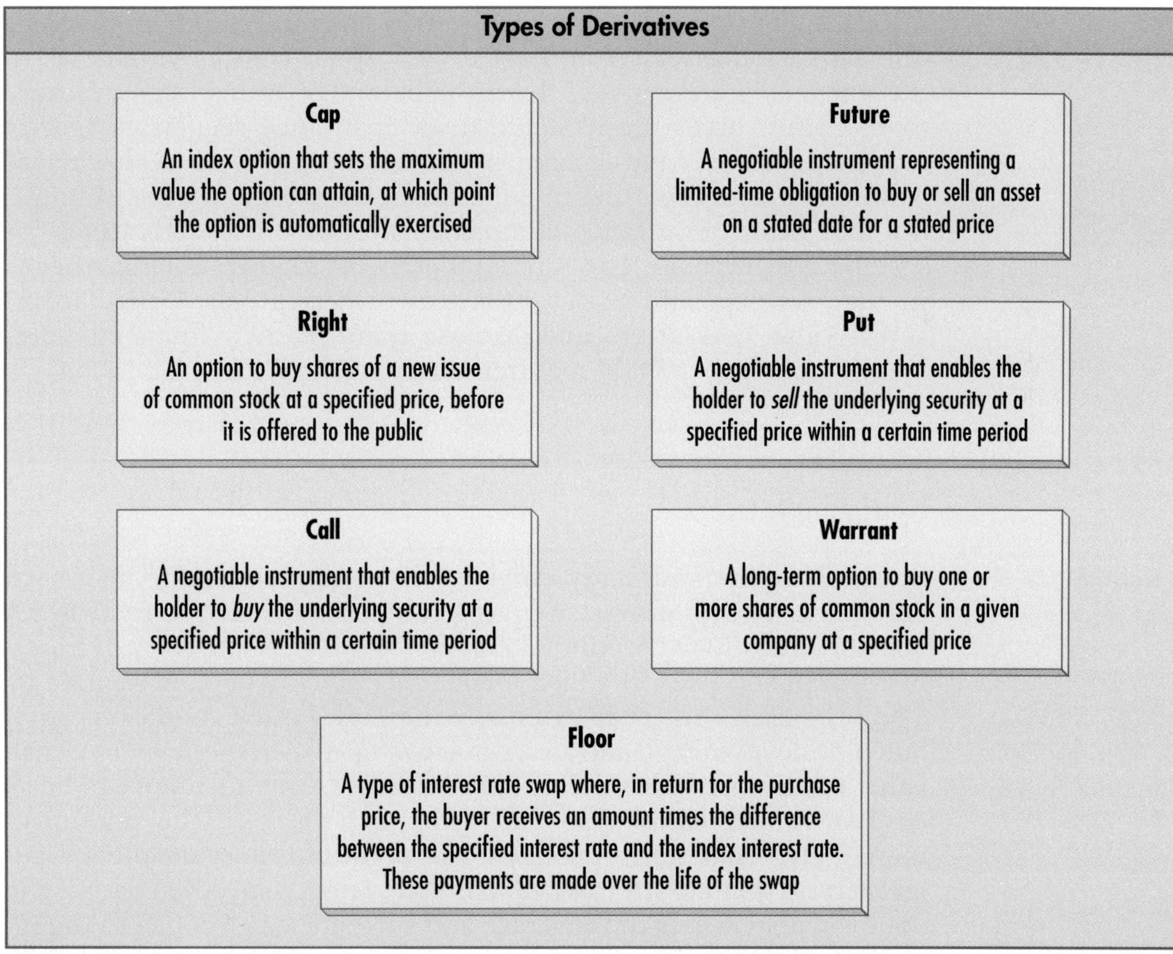

duties, are critical in managing the risk associated with an insurer's derivative investments. We discuss these controls in Chapter 20.

Under GAAP, an insurer typically accounts for its derivative investments, purchased for hedging strategies, in the same way that it accounts for the derivatives' underlying securities. Suppose an insurer purchases put options that have common stocks as their underlying security. The insurer values these derivatives at current market value because this is the valuation method for common stocks. The insurer recognizes and reports unrealized gains or losses in the current accounting period, as the insurer cannot defer them.

Insurance companies in the United States follow *FASB Statement No. 119: Disclosure about Derivative Financial Instruments and Fair Value of Financial Instruments* in determining the values of derivatives. This accounting standard requires each insurer to identify and describe its derivatives and disclose the credit risk and the accounting procedures associated with the derivatives. The insurer discloses its exposure to risk from derivatives and itemizes its investment strategy and individual investments in the accompanying notes to the financial statements.

Remember that derivatives are valued separately from an insurer's other invested assets. You must review the accompanying notes to the financial statements to learn the details of an insurer's exposure to risk from investing in derivatives. Insurance regulators specify requirements on investments in derivatives as well as disclosure requirements for reporting them in financial statements. For example, life and health insurance companies may not use derivatives for speculative purposes. The Annual Statement requires each insurer to itemize its exposure to several types of derivatives. Canadian insurers value derivatives and disclose them in their financial statements according to OSFI requirements and the *CICA Handbook*.

Policy Loans

Most whole life and many universal life and variable life insurance policies contain a provision giving the policyowner the right to request a policy loan. A ***policy loan,*** called a *certificate loan* in fraternal benefit societies, is a loan made to a policyowner and secured by a policy's cash surrender value as collateral. Policy conditions vary, but a policyowner usually can borrow up to the policy's net cash value minus one year's policy loan interest. A life insurance policy's ***cash surrender value,*** also called *net cash value,* is the amount of money, after adjusting for policy loans, premiums due, and other similar factors, that a policyowner will receive on a specified date if the policyowner cancels the coverage and surrenders the policy to the insurance company. If there is an outstanding policy loan, either upon policy surrender or upon payment of other policy benefits, the insurer deducts the amount of any outstanding policy loan and interest from the policy's cash value or death benefit, respectively. An insurer makes a policy loan from funds that it would otherwise invest to provide for future policy benefits. Because premium rates are based in part on an anticipated investment return, and funds lent to policyowners are not available for an insurer to invest, the insurer charges interest on the loans. Policy loans were approximately 4 percent of U.S. life insurance company assets and 2 percent of Canadian life and health insurance company assets in 1994.

Under statutory accounting, policy loans are considered an admitted asset, as long as the loan amount plus interest does not exceed the policy's cash value plus paid-up additions. However, an insurer's investment department typically does not handle or manage policy loans, even though policy loans are investments and the insurer treats policy loan interest as investment income. The reasons that policy loans differ from an insurer's other invested assets are listed in Figure 8-4.

An insurer usually calculates policy loan interest so that it is payable on the policy anniversary date. Some companies charge interest on policy loans at the end of the policy year, and some charge interest in advance. Two types of policy loans are *conventional policy loans* and

Figure 8-4. How policy loans differ from other invested assets.

- The decision to obtain a policy loan comes from the policyowner, not the insurer, because taking out a policy loan is a contractual right of the policyowner.
- Policy loans historically were not the best investment for an insurer because interest rates on policy loans were typically lower than what the insurer could obtain through investing in bonds, for example. More recently issued policies, however, have policy loan interest rates that are tied to market interest rates.
- In contrast to other loans, policy loans do not have contractual maturity dates or principal payments, although insurers typically provide policyowners with a predetermined monthly payback schedule, including policy loan interest.
- A policyowner need not pay policy loan interest as long as his or her policy has sufficient cash surrender value plus paid-up additions, if applicable, to secure the loan plus any accrued policy loan interest.
- Policy loans do not require systematic repayment plans, as do other loans. An insurer adds unpaid policy loan interest to the amount of the policy loan. If the total of an outstanding loan and its accrued interest exceeds the policy's cash surrender value, however, the policy will terminate without further value, and the insurance contract will no longer be in force. To prevent this from happening, many insurance companies encourage systematic repayment of the principal, and most companies bill for interest annually.

automatic premium loans. A ***conventional policy loan*** is made to a policyowner when he or she uses the policy as security for the loan. Some insurers require the policyowner to submit the policy to the insurer for an endorsement showing that a policy loan has been obtained against the cash surrender value of the policy. This endorsement protects banks and other loan sources if the policyowner tries to assign the policy as security for another loan. An ***automatic premium loan (APL)*** is a nonforfeiture option that allows the insurer to pay overdue premiums on a policy by establishing a loan against the policy's cash value. An APL does not require a special loan agreement.

Accounting for Policy Loans

The basic journal entry to record that a policyowner has taken out a policy loan is a debit to an asset account—Policy Loans—and a credit to Cash:

Policy Loans	xxx	
Cash		xxx

To record a policy loan.

Policy loans sometimes require compound accounting entries. Assume that a policy loan is made (1) to provide $100 cash for the policyowner and (2) to pay a premium due of $25. The journal entry for this policy loan is

Policy Loans	125	
Renewal Premiums		25
Cash		100

To record a renewal premium and a policy loan.

Three months later, this policyowner borrows another $100, so the insurer makes the following accounting entry in a subsidiary ledger for that policyowner:

Policy Loans	100	
Cash		100

To record a policy loan.

Policy Loans is a general ledger control account that summarizes the activity of all of an insurer's loans to policyowners. Insurers often maintain subsidiary ledger accounts that show the policy loan activity for each policyowner. If a policyowner takes out more than one loan, the insurer typically combines the two loans in the subsidiary ledger.

If an APL is used to pay for a delinquent premium payment, the insurer can debit the amount to a special loan account, such as Automatic Premium Loans. Although some insurance companies maintain separate subsidiary ledger accounts for an APL and a conventional policy loan made to the same policyowner, many companies consolidate the two loans into one account. This consolidation is often preferable if the insurer sends the policyowner a single bill for policy loan interest on both loans. Policy loan consolidation is also preferable for maintaining subsidiary ledger accounts and for calculating net cash value amounts. However, other insurers maintain APL loans separately from conventional policy loans because the interest rates are different on each type of loan.

Accounting for policy loans involves keeping records of both the principal and interest on each policy loan. The principal amount of the policy loan plus the interest due or accrued cannot be greater than the policy's cash surrender value, as noted above. If the policyowner requests a loan for more than the cash surrender value, most companies process a loan for the highest possible amount and notify the policyowner of the reason for not granting the full amount of the request. The amount of interest due is shown on the premium notice. If an insurer charges interest in advance and the policyowner repays all or part of the principal during the year, then the insurer makes a partial refund of the interest already paid by the policyowner or records policy loan interest paid in advance.

Policy Loan Interest

On policies that have a policy loan outstanding, a bill for policy loan interest usually accompanies the policy's premium notice or appears on the premium notice itself. An exception to this billing procedure occurs (1) when the premiums on a policy are paid on a date other than the policy anniversary date, (2) when a policy is paid up, or (3) when premiums are paid through electronic funds transfer (EFT) or a similar arrangement. Although a policyowner may obtain a policy loan at any time during the policy year, the insurer usually calculates interest on the policy's anniversary date.

The entry on an insurer's books when an insurer receives $100 in policy loan interest is

Cash	100	
Policy Loan Interest		100

To record the receipt of policy loan interest.

An insurer reports accrued policy loan interest along with other investment income due and accrued on the balance sheet. If payment for the interest has not been received and the policy's cash surrender value is sufficient to cover the interest due, then the insurer adds the interest to the loan on the policy anniversary date. Again, whenever the amount of a loan plus any accrued policy loan interest becomes equal to or greater than the cash surrender value of the policy, the policyowner must pay some or all of the interest due to avoid cancellation of his or her insurance policy.

As mentioned earlier, a policyowner is generally entitled to a refund or credit of prepaid interest if interest on a policy loan has been paid in advance and a loan payment is made before the next interest date. A prepaid interest refund can reduce the amount required to pay off the loan. For example, assume that a policyowner has paid one year's worth of policy loan interest in advance at a discounted interest rate of 6 percent on a $200 loan. Assume also that the policyowner pays back the loan three months before the next interest due date. In such a case, the entry on the insurer's books to reflect the $200 loan repayment is

Cash	197	
Policy Loan Interest	3	
Policy Loans		200

To record repayment of a policy loan.

The $3 debit to Policy Loan Interest reduces the interest income for the insurer from the $12 collected in advance to the correct amount of interest, $9, for the period during which this policy loan was outstanding.

If a policyowner has not paid any interest in advance, he or she pays the accrued interest when repaying the loan principal. For example, when a policyowner pays in full a $200, 6 percent policy loan three months before the policy's next anniversary date, the insurer collects nine months' worth of accrued interest in addition to the loan principal. Assume the insurer had not been recording accruing interest in its accounting records. In this case, the accounting entry to record the repayment of the $200 loan and payment of $9 ($\frac{9}{12} \times 6$ percent $\times$ $200) in accrued interest is

Cash	209	
Policy Loan Interest		9
Policy Loans		200

To record the repayment of policy loan and policy loan interest.

Policy Loans and the Annual Statement/Annual Return

As noted earlier, policy loans are admitted assets under statutory accounting. However, if a policy loan exceeds the cash surrender value of the policy because an insurer made an administrative error in granting a policy loan, the excess of the loan over the policy's cash surrender value is a nonadmitted asset. On both the Annual Statement and the Annual Return, an insurer reports policy loans at book value, which means the original loan amount plus accrued interest minus principal repayments. Policy loans (assets) are reported separately from policy loan interest (revenues). Policy loan interest that is due and accrued is reported as part of Investment Income Due and Accrued, an asset account. Both these accounts are on the *Assets* page. Policy loan interest that has been earned and received is reported as income under Investment Income on the *Summary of Operations.* Neither the Annual Statement nor the Annual Return includes a separate schedule for policy loans.

Accounting for Cash and Short-Term Investments

Besides holding idle cash on hand and on deposit, including certificates of deposit that mature within 90 days, insurers also keep funds ready for rapid use in short-term investments. As we discussed in Chapter 7, short-term investments include cash equivalents. On the Annual Statement or Annual Return, insurers report one total for all short-term investments. Because time to maturity defines the difference between cash equivalents and short-term investments, an insurer can purchase either a cash equivalent or another short-term investment, depending on the insurer's expectations about the timing of its policy benefit payments and other obligations. For example, a 90-day certificate of deposit is classified as cash on deposit, while commercial paper with a 6-month maturity is classified as a short-term investment. *Certificates of deposit (CDs)* represent funds placed on deposit with a financial institution, such as a bank. Other typical short-term investments that insurers purchase include

- *Money market investments,* which have no maturity date and can be redeemed for cash at any time without penalty
- *Commercial paper,* which is issued by large corporations and which offers maturities that range from 30 days to nine months
- *Banker's acceptances,* which are letters of credit issued by a bank to finance international trade
- *U.S., Government of Canada, or Canadian provincial treasury bills,* which are issued by U.S. or Canadian governments

In this section we discuss how an insurer accounts for its cash.

Cash

Cash is an asset account that includes the funds, both paper currency or coin, that are on hand or on deposit in a bank account, and, therefore readily available for disbursement. To determine its cash balance as of a specified date, the insurer counts the total amount of cash in its Cash account. Obtaining this total is relatively easy for most cash amounts, except for the insurer's checking account, which may have many outstanding checks and deposits as of the reporting date. However, the Annual Statement total is the amount in the insurer's general ledger account for Cash.

Most insurers maintain one or more checking accounts with a bank. For example, an insurer may have separate checking accounts for premium collection, claim payments, and agent commissions. Checking accounts may be interest bearing or non-interest bearing. Interest-bearing checking accounts generally pay a lower rate of interest than is available on short-term investments, such as treasury bills. Therefore, insurers try to keep the minimum cash balance required to pay their current obligations. To establish a checking account at a bank, an insurer must designate one or more authorized employees who can sign checks against the insurer's checking account. The insurer provides the bank with a signature card that contains the legal signatures of all persons authorized to sign checks. Generally, the insurer's treasurer is authorized to sign company checks. For internal control purposes, checks for large sums often require two authorized signatures. We discuss the primary internal controls associated with a company's cash in Chapter 20.

Investment accounting may also include accounting for an insurer's cash. However, most life and health insurance companies distinguish between investment accounting and cash accounting. ***Cash accounting*** relates to the management and maintenance of records for all cash transactions, namely funds deposited or withdrawn from an insurer's bank accounts. Cash accounting may also include the investment and management of short-term investments (or cash equivalents) other than cash. In some insurance companies, cash accounting is considered to be an aspect of *treasury operations* or *cash management,* which also includes the forecasting of cash flows and the reconciliation of an insurer's records against its bank statements. An insurer that administers its cash accounting separately from its investment accounting must be careful to coordinate the activities of the two accounting systems. For example, an insurer may own a bond on which interest is paid semiannually. Under investment accounting guidelines, the insurer records a monthly accrual that represents the portion of the total interest earned in each month. Alternatively, under cash accounting or cash management, the earned interest is not reported in the cash balances until the interest payment is physically collected at the end of the six-month period. For this reason, open communication channels between the cash accounting and investment accounting functions is critical to ensure that information on an insurer's cash flow statement is correct and current.

Bank Reconciliation

An insurer reports its cash balance in both the annual report and the Annual Statement. ***Bank reconciliation,*** which ensures that the reported amount accurately reflects the insurer's cash balance, is the process of identifying and explaining the difference between (1) the balance presented on the bank statement and (2) the balance in the insurer's general ledger, sometimes referred to as the *book balance.*

If you have a checking account and you balance it regularly, then you are already familiar with the bank reconciliation process. Balancing your checkbook is a means of bringing your account balance into agreement with what your bank statement states is your account balance. Bank statements differ among banks, but all of them include

- The insurer's checking account balance at the beginning of the month
- Deposits and other additions to the account balance during the month
- Cashed checks, fees, and other subtractions from the account balance during the month
- The insurer's checking account balance at the end of the month

Figure 8-5 depicts a sample bank statement.

At any given time, a company's checking account book balance (general ledger balance) rarely matches the balance on its bank statement because of timing differences and errors. Also, insurers incur a high volume of transactions through their checking accounts, so bank reconciliation is especially important. Timing differences occur because the bank has already recorded certain transactions for which the insurer is not yet aware, and vice versa. Most timing differences are a result of specific transactions —outstanding checks or deposits, nonsufficient funds (NSF) checks, service charges, and interest income, for example—that have cleared either the insurer's records or the bank's records, but not both. Further, the bank or the insurer may have committed an error in recording one or more transactions. To balance these differences, the insurer undertakes bank reconciliation,

Figure 8-5. A sample bank statement.

Account Number: 12345678-9
Statement Period: 4/1/97 – 4/30/97
Number of Transactions: 11

Beginning Balance: $43,946.48

Add 3 items:

Deposit Amount	Date
$ 8,715.40	4/5/97
$12,733.96	4/16/97
$ 5,066.14	4/28/97
$26,515.50	

Additions: $26,515.50
$70,461.98

Subtract 8 items:

Check	Amount	Check	Amount
9870	$ 4,050.08	9874	$ 1,992.01
9871	$ 2,139.75	9875	$ 7,469.86
9872	$ 1,699.12	9876	$ 3,578.94
9873	$ 5,364.97	9877	$ 2,454.90
	$13,253.92		$15,495.71

Subtractions: $28,749.63
Ending Balance: $41,712.35

generally upon receipt of the monthly bank statement. We describe the major factors, either caused by timing differences or errors, that contribute to the difference in account balances:

- **Outstanding checks:** ***Outstanding checks*** are those that the insurer has written, deducted from its book balance, and sent to payees, but which have not yet cleared the bank. As a result, the bank has not yet deducted them from its account balance.

- **Unrecorded deposits:** ***Unrecorded deposits,*** also called *deposits in transit,* are those deposits that the insurer added to its book balance after the closing date on the bank statement. Therefore, the bank has not yet added them to its account balance.

- **Service charges:** Most banks assess service charges on checking accounts. These include charges for monthly account service, check processing, and stop payment orders. Usually, the insurer learns the amount of its service charges when it reviews its monthly bank statement.

- **Interest income:** If the checking account is interest bearing, the amount of interest income earned will appear on the monthly bank statement. The bank has already added this amount to its balance, but the insurer may not know the exact amount of the interest income until the bank statement arrives.

- **Nonsufficient funds (NSF) checks:** A ***nonsufficient funds (NSF) check*** is a check that has "bounced." That is, the payor did not have enough money in its checking account to pay the amount of the check. Although insurance companies rarely write NSF checks, they sometimes receive NSF checks from their policyowners. When an insurer receives a check, it assumes that the check is good, adds the amount of the check to its book balance, and sends the check as a deposit to its bank. The insurer's bank also assumes the check is good and adds the amount of the check to the insurer's account, then sends the check to the payor's bank for payment. If the balance in the payor's checking account is not sufficient to pay the check, the payor's bank refuses to pay the check and sends an NSF notice, along with the check, to the insurer's bank, which then subtracts the amount of the check from the insurer's account balance and attempts to collect the amount of the check from the payor. The bank statement discloses to the insurer that the check did not clear the payor's account. The insurer must then deduct the amount from its book balance to reconcile its own book balance with the bank statement.

- **Errors:** Either the bank or the insurer may make an error in the process of journalizing the checking account balance. Typically, an insurer finds errors by investigating the reasons for differences between the bank statement balance and the insurer's book balance. Often this involves tracing each transaction from the date that the checking account last balanced with the bank through the closing date indicated on the latest bank statement. If the bank made the error, the insurer notifies the bank, which in turn corrects its records. If the insurer made the error, then the insurer makes the appropriate accounting entries to correct the error.

The procedure for bank reconciliation is fairly straightforward. The insurer first determines that it has accounted for all the canceled (cashed) checks that the bank statement listed as having cleared the account and that the amount of each check corresponds with the bank's records. The insurer also verifies that all deposits have been included in the account balance. In most cases, an insurer can use the format for balancing the checking account that accompanies most bank statements.

The totals for both the bank statement balance and the insurer's book balance should agree after adding and subtracting the appropriate amounts to each beginning balance. If they do not agree, the insurer must investigate and resolve the discrepancy. Once the balances agree, the insurer posts the appropriate accounting entries to adjust the balance in its ledger, if necessary, to correct errors or to record NSF checks and bank charges. For example, the Highlight Life and Health Insurance Company reconciled its book balance with the bank statement balance as follows:

Bank Statement Balance:	**$4,600**	**Highlight's Book Balance:**	**$4,500**
Outstanding Deposits	50	Interest Income	10
Outstanding Checks	(190)	Service Charges	(20)
		NSF Check	(30)
Reconciled Accounts:	$4,460		$4,460

To reconcile the two balances, Highlight first adds the $50 of outstanding deposits to the bank statement balance and subtracts $190 of outstanding checks from the bank statement balance. The bank statement balance then becomes $4,460. Then the insurer adds the $10 of interest income to its book balance and subtracts the $20 service charge and the $30 NSF check from its book balance. (In this example, we assume that the bank includes the charge for NSF checks in its service charge to Highlight.) Highlight's book balance becomes $4,460, and the two balances now agree. Highlight then prepares the appropriate adjusting entries for the current checking account balance and increases NSF Checks, an account receivable, by the amount of the NSF check, because the premium is due but has not yet been paid.

Although insurers have different methods of adjusting for this balance, an adjusting entry that Highlight could make, given the above circumstances, is

Service Charge Expense	20	
NSF Checks	30	
Interest Income		10
Cash		40

To adjust for bank reconciliation.

In the above accounting entry, Highlight debits Service Charge Expense, an expense account, and credits Interest Income, a revenue account, to increase those account balances. Highlight debits NSF Checks, an asset account, for $30 to record the NSF check. Some insurers use Premium Suspense as the account debited for NSF checks. In either case, Highlight assumes that it will be able to collect the $30 premium payment from the policyowner soon.* To balance this accounting entry, Highlight credits Cash for $40, which is the differ-

* Highlight theoretically would have a subsidiary account, such as NSF Checks—John Doe, for the policyowner whose premium check was returned to the bank. However, for the sake of the example, we use the general account NSF Checks as the account to which Highlight posts the NSF check.

ence between Highlight's checking account balance and its reconciled balance ($4,500 – $4,460). This credit reflects the fact that during this particular month Highlight paid $20 in service charges and received $30 less cash than it had thought, but it has earned $10 in interest. The net difference is a $40 decrease in Cash.

Alternatively, Highlight could have obtained the same result by making three separate accounting entries to record each adjustment. Compare the effect of the three accounting entries below with the single adjusting entry above so you can understand that the ultimate effect on Highlight's book balance is the same in either case:

(1)	Cash	10	
	Interest Income		10
	To record interest earned on the insurer's checking account.		
(2)	NSF Checks	30	
	Cash		30
	To charge a policyowner's account for the NSF check.		
(3)	Service Charge Expense	20	
	Cash		20
	To record the bank's monthly service charges on the insurer's checking account.		

Accounting for Other Short-Term Assets

Accounting terminology generally divides assets into short-term assets and long-term assets. The element of time distinguishes the two. Short-term (current) assets are those assets that a company expects to use up or convert to cash during the current operating period, which for most companies is one year. Long-term assets have more than one year to maturity, or the insurer expects to retain them for more than one year. Regulators, lenders, and other external parties are particularly interested in the amount and composition of an insurer's short-term assets because these assets must be sufficient to pay for the company's current obligations to policyowners and creditors. An insurer's short-term assets include

- Cash and short-term investments
- Investment income due and accrued
- Premiums due
- Prepaid expenses

Although a U.S. insurer reports all these short-term assets on a balance sheet prepared according to generally accepted accounting principles (GAAP), the insurer typically reports them as admitted assets, with the exception of prepaid expenses, which is a nonadmitted asset on the statutory Annual Statement. In this section we discuss three of an insurer's other short-term assets: investment income due and accrued, premiums due, and prepaid expenses.

Investment Income Due and Accrued

Due income is income that was expected by the insurer before the reporting date but that has not yet been received. A rent payment due on December 15, but which the insurer has not received by December 31, is an example of due income. ***Accrued income*** consists of income that the insurer has already earned, but which is not receivable until a specified date in the next accounting period—that is, income that is due *after* the insurer's financial reporting date. Accrued income is thus earned during one accounting period, but not receivable until a later accounting period. For example, an insurer reports interest earned on its bond investment portfolio in December but not receivable until the following January as accrued investment income. Both *due income* and *accrued income* are assets because the income is called for in a contractual arrangement, so the insurer can legally expect to receive the income. Investment Income Due and Accrued is the account used to report both due income and accrued income on the Annual Statement. Accrued Investment Income is the equivalent account on the Annual Return. A typical accounting entry to report earned but not received income is

Investment Income Due and Accrued	xxx	
Investment Income		xxx

To record investment income that has been earned but not yet received.

When income is earned, then the insurer posts the income to the revenue section of the statement of operations.

Premiums Due

A company expects to receive full payment for its goods and services in the short term. A *receivable* represents money owed to a company. Most non-insurance companies have a variety of receivables, including Accounts Receivable and Notes Receivable. Receivables are not as important in the insurance industry, because most policyowners pay their premiums in cash before the policy issue date or anniversary date. The one receivable that applies specifically to the life and health insurance business is *premiums due,* which is a short-term asset. As we discussed in Chapter 6, premiums due typically consists of two types of receivables: (1) premiums due and (2) deferred and uncollected premiums. These terms are essentially equivalent in that they represent premiums with due dates before the Annual Statement date that have not been received by the insurer as of that date. Premiums due typically apply to accident and health insurance or group life insurance policies, whereas deferred and uncollected premiums typically apply to individual life insurance products. For example, if a monthly accident and health premium is due on December 20, 1998, but the insurer has not received it by the Annual Statement dated December 31, 1998, then the Annual Statement reports the amount of the premium as a premium due.

In determining premium rates and policy reserves, an insurer's actuaries use the *mean reserve method,* which assumes that all premiums are paid on an annual basis at the beginning of the policy year. In practice, however, premiums may be paid in installments more frequently than annually, such as on a monthly or quarterly basis. Because an insurer establishes policy reserves, a liability account, under the assumption that all premiums are paid at the beginning of the policy year, the insurer offsets the additional reserves with an asset account. Deferred premiums exist because of the actuarial assumptions and methods used to calculate an insurer's policy reserves. Again, policies with annual premiums that are paid in full on the policy anniversary date do not generate deferred premiums.

Prepaid Expenses

In accounting, ***prepaid expenses*** are those expenditures that the insurer expects will provide a future value or benefit. Examples of prepaid expenses include rents, subscriptions, service contracts, and any other fees or charges that the insurer has paid before receiving the goods and services associated with those charges. Under GAAP, prepaid expenses are classified as current (short-term) assets, even though it is difficult for a company to convert these assets into cash. Prepaid expenses are short-term assets because a company has used cash or will use cash in the *next* accounting period to obtain these services. Also, prepaid expenses will provide a company with benefits in the short term; hence, prepaid expenses are short-term assets. An insurer typically matches prepaid expenses against the appropriate revenues during the accounting period in which the insurer receives the related revenues. Under statutory accounting, prepaid expenses are nonadmitted assets. As a result, most U.S. insurers have few prepaid expenses.

Accounting for Other Assets

In the United States, state insurance laws identify which assets are admitted and which are nonadmitted for Annual Statement purposes. Certain other assets, while not specifically authorized, are admitted assets because of their relationship to company operations. This section deals with insurance company assets other than invested assets, cash, and short-term investments.

Reinsurance Ceded

Recall from Chapter 6 that reinsurance is a transaction between two insurance companies that involves the transfer of all or part of an insurance risk from one company (the ceding company) to another company (the reinsurer). A ceding company uses an asset account to record amounts that reinsurers owe to the ceding company. The accounting entries for reinsurance ceded depend on the terms of the reinsurance agreement. We use generic accounting entries in our examples to demonstrate the accounting function regarding reinsurance transactions.

The Annual Statement includes itemized reinsurance ceded schedules for (1) life insurance and annuities, (2) accident and health insurance, and (3) a five-year exhibit of reinsurance ceded business. The Annual Return includes exhibits that itemize reinsurance ceded to unregistered life and accident and health companies, with separate schedules for reinsurance transactions that are approved and not approved by OSFI. Let's take a closer look at three subcategories of reinsurance ceded: *amounts recoverable from reinsurers, commissions and expense allowances due,* and *experience rating and other refunds due.* Figure 8-6 shows one of the schedules for reinsurance ceded that U.S. insurers include in the Annual Statement.

Amounts Recoverable from Reinsurers

When an insurer obtains reinsurance on a policy, the ceding company is still responsible for paying the policy benefits when they come due. However, because the reinsurer has assumed all or part of the policy's risk, the reinsurer is obligated to pay its contracted share of the benefits to the ceding company, in keeping with the terms of the reinsurance agreement. The money that the reinsurer is obligated to pay the ceding company is an account receivable. A typical accounting entry for the ceding company to record this receivable is

Amounts Recoverable from Reinsurers	xxx	
Death Claims Paid		xxx

To record the account receivable from reinsurance.

Figure 8-6. Schedule S—Part 1—U.S. Annual Statement.

Showing Names and Locations of Companies and Amounts Recoverable on Paid and Unpaid Losses for all Reinsurance Ceded						
NAIC Company Code	Federal ID Number	Effective Date	1 Name of Company	2 Location	3 Paid Losses	4 Unpaid Losses
			LIFE AND ANNUITY			
			Affiliates:			
0199999 Totals—Affiliates						
			Non-Affiliates:			
0299999 Totals—Non-Affiliates						
0399999 Totals—Life and Annuity						
			ACCIDENT AND HEALTH			
			Affiliates:			
0499999 Totals—Affiliates						
			Non-Affiliates:			
0599999 Totals—Non-Affiliates						
0699999 Totals—Accident and Health						
0799999 Totals—Life, Annuity and Accident and Health						

This entry assumes that a *life* insurance policy has been reinsured. The insurer credits a different account if it purchases reinsurance for a health insurance policy. The insurer credits Death Claims Paid because the amount recoverable represents a reduction in, or reimbursement of, the death claim that the ceding company paid to the policy beneficiary. (Some insurers use a *contra benefit account* such as Reinsurance on Death Claims, so they can track the total amount of death claims paid and reinsurance collected independent of other claim payments. In this case, Reinsurance on Death Claims is a contra benefit or contra expense account because its companion account is Death Claims Paid, an expense account with a normal debit balance. Thus, Reinsurance on Death Claims has a normal credit balance.)

Assume that the Centrist Life and Health Insurance Company issues a life insurance policy with a $250,000 death benefit. If Centrist Life's ***retention limit***—that is, the highest amount of risk that Centrist will assume on a single policy without reinsurance—is $200,000, the company reinsures $50,000 of the policy through Parker Reinsurance. While the policy is in force, the insured dies and Centrist determines that the policy beneficiary is entitled to the full death benefit. To record this transaction, Centrist makes the following accounting entry:

Death Claims Paid	250,000	
Cash		250,000

To record payment of death benefit to beneficiary.

Upon the death of the insured, Parker Reinsurance owes Centrist $50,000. Centrist makes the following journal entry to record the amount of reinsurance receivable:

Amounts Recoverable from Reinsurers	50,000	
Death Claims Paid		50,000

To record the account receivable from reinsurance.

When Parker pays the $50,000, Centrist records the following entry:

Cash	50,000	
Amounts Recoverable from Reinsurers		50,000

To record the amount received from reinsurance.

This entry shows that Parker has satisfied its obligation to Centrist. The claim history for this policy is complete, now that Parker has reimbursed Centrist for $50,000.

Many insurers post accounting entries for reinsurance transactions to facilitate financial disclosure requirements. For example, suppose the Topmost Life and Health Insurance Company posts the following accounting entry for a reinsurance transaction:

Death Claims Paid	35,000	
Amounts Recoverable from Reinsurers	10,000	
Death Claims Reinsured		10,000
Death Claims Payable		35,000

To record a death claim on a policy that has been reinsured.

In this accounting entry, total death claim expenses are $35,000, both reinsurance recoverable and Death Claims Reinsured are $10,000, and the liability for the total amount payable is $35,000. The amount posted to Death Claims Paid, Amounts Recoverable from Reinsurers, and Death Claims Reinsured results in a net expense of $25,000 ($35,000 – $10,000) to Topmost. When Topmost pays this death claim, the accounting entry is a debit to Death Claims Paid and a credit to Cash for $35,000. When Topmost receives the amount recoverable from the reinsurer, it debits Cash and credits Amounts Recoverable from Reinsurers for $10,000.

In the United States, a reinsurer must have a license to write business in the ceding company's state of domicile. When the reinsurer is not licensed in that state, the ceding company obtains some collateral, usually in the form of letters of credit, to qualify the amount of reinsurance ceded. The ceding company establishes on its books a liability account for Reinsurance in Unauthorized Companies when the reinsurer fails, is not licensed in the ceding company's state of domicile, or cannot produce any form of collateral. Canadian insurers disclose their transactions with unregistered companies, which are similar to unauthorized companies for U.S. insurers.

Commissions and Expense Allowances Due

As part of the agreement between companies involved in reinsurance transactions, certain allowances are made for expenses like commissions and policy issue costs incurred by the ceding company in writing the direct business. The reinsurer generally reimburses the ceding company for an appropriate share of these expenses. The ceding company posts the unpaid portion of the reimbursable amount to an asset account such as Commissions and Expense Allowances Due—Reinsurance Ceded.

Experience Rating and Other Refunds Due

When setting reinsurance premium rates, the reinsurer builds an element of profit into the premium assessed the ceding company. The reinsurer bases its profit on an estimate of the claims it expects to pay. Many reinsurers provide for a partial premium refund if the actual claims experience is better than the projected claims experience.

When a ceding company expects a partial premium refund from a reinsurer, the ceding company records the unpaid portion of the reimbursable amount in Experience Rating and Other Refunds Due, an asset account. As in the case of amounts recoverable from reinsurers, the reinsurer must be licensed in the ceding company's state of domicile for the refund to be an admitted asset.

Deferred Policy Acquisition Costs

Deferred policy acquisition costs (DPAC), also called *deferred acquisition costs (DAC),* is an asset account allowed under U.S. GAAP to enable an insurer to capitalize certain costs associated with a block of new products or new business and amortize them over the premium-paying periods of traditional insurance products. The insurer matches those costs associated with certain insurance products with the estimated gross margins (profits) generated by these products. This asset account only appears on a U.S. insurer's GAAP-based balance sheet—not on the statutory Annual Statement. Canadian insurers include deferred policy acquisition costs in their reserve calculations, so there is no need to establish an asset account for these costs.

Under statutory accounting practices in the United States, an insurer expenses, rather than capitalizes, the costs associated with acquiring and retaining insurance business. In other words, an insurer reports most expenses during the accounting period in which they are incurred. However, under U.S. GAAP, insurers *match* the expenses incurred to acquire business with the revenues obtained as a result of those incurred expenses, as long as the revenues exceed the expenses. In this way, the typically large amounts of product development costs associated with new products do not understate an insurer's income in the initial years of a new product or line of business.

In the United States, *FASB Statement No. 60* describes DPAC as costs that relate primarily and directly to acquiring new business and retaining current business. Examples of costs that fall in this category include policy issue costs, product development costs, and agent commissions. Specific policy issue costs include those associated with policy forms, policy delivery, and calculating the premium for a new block of insurance policies. Under *FASB Statement No. 60,* the insurer's estimated premium income determines the amortization of DPAC. According to *FASB Statement No. 97,* DPAC is amortized over the life of the business based on the present value of the gross profits associated with the business. Further, an insurer adjusts the amount of DPAC amortized whenever expectations change regarding the insurer's future gross profits.

When matching DPAC to premium revenues received during an accounting period, an insurer first determines whether an incurred expense qualifies under the definition of DPAC before establishing an asset account for these costs. Although insurers primarily capitalize and amortize those costs directly attributable to the production of new business, they may also include a reasonable allocation for the indirect costs associated with new business. Suppose that, for every additional $10,000 an insurer spends on agent commissions, the insurer receives an additional $50,000 of premium income over the life of a policy. In our simple example, the DPAC amortized is 20 percent ($10,000 ÷ $50,000) of premium income. However, more intricate relationships can and do exist between deferred costs and revenues. Our example shows a direct relationship between expenses and revenues, but few company decisions result in such obvious cause-and-effect relationships between these two variables.

Electronic Data Processing Equipment

As of the publication date of this text, most states classify a U.S. insurer's *electronic data processing (EDP)* equipment as an admitted asset under statutory accounting practices. It is expected that, in the near future, EDP equipment will no longer be an admitted asset. The most recent NAIC accounting guidance concludes that the accounting for EDP equipment should be consistent with that of an insurer's furniture and equipment, which are nonadmitted assets. Early in its development, EDP equipment generally had a higher resale value than most of an insurer's nonadmitted assets. Mainframe computers were expensive and could be relied on for many years of service. Therefore, capitalizing the costs of such equipment seemed appropriate.

By treating EDP equipment as an admitted asset, insurance regulators enabled insurers to capitalize the equipment's high costs and to amortize these costs over a number of years. Otherwise, an insurer would have to expense the EDP equipment's full cost against its surplus in the accounting period in which it purchased the equipment. With such a negative impact on surplus, insurers would have found themselves at a distinct disadvantage to other financial service companies that did not have to comply with statutory requirements. Today, however, personal computers are becoming the dominant EDP equipment used in insurance companies. These computers and their software are much less expensive than mainframes, and their resale value drops quickly after only a year or two of use. From the point of view of cost and resale value, this EDP equipment seems more like a nonadmitted asset, such as office furniture, than do mainframe computers. To stay competitive in the financial services market, however, insurers must maintain up-to-date information management systems, and to maintain these systems, insurers must regularly invest in new EDP equipment. Despite the lower prices of personal computers and personal computer software, EDP equipment can still be a substantial investment.

Separate Accounts (Segregated Funds)

Until the 1960s, statutory accounting required insurers to pool all of their accounts into their *general account,* which is the undivided account in which life and health insurers have recorded all their incoming and outgoing funds for traditional insurance products. As a result, an insurer was unable to designate an asset or group of assets to support a specific liability or group of liabilities. Insurance companies, however, wanted to market products—including variable annuities, variable life insurance, pension funds, and mutual funds—that do not offer the guaranteed investment returns of traditional products. In these *equity-based insurance products,* the cash value and the benefit level fluctuate according to the performance of a portfolio of equity investments such as stocks. The customers who bought these nontraditional products began to assume more investment risk. To attract customers to these higher risk products, which are registered with the SEC in the United States and with OSFI in Canada, insurers needed to offer the opportunity for higher returns. They needed to use investment strategies besides those available for traditional insurance products. Therefore, insurance companies obtained permission from regulators to establish one or more separate accounts.

As we described in Chapter 6, an insurer maintains its *separate accounts,* called *segregated funds* in Canada, apart from the general account. An insurer uses a separate account to manage the funds used for nonguaranteed products. Depending on the policyowner's investment strategy, an insurer can invest separate account assets in higher risk and higher return investments than are available for the insurer's general account. By maintaining one or more separate accounts, an insurer is not restricted to the strategies established for the general account and is in a better position to compete with financial institutions that offer financial instruments other than insurance. In 1994, Canadian insurance companies held approximately \$27.7 billion of assets in segregated funds.[1] During the same year, U.S. insurers held about \$350 billion of assets in separate accounts.[2]

Assets held in a separate account are generally insulated from policyowner and creditor claims against the insurer's general account in case of insurer insolvency. On the other hand, an insurer's general account may be subject to the claims of policyowners whose assets are invested in an insurer's separate account if, for example, adverse claims experience occurs on the insurer's variable insurance products. Typically, the assets in separate accounts support pension funds, which are invested in mutual funds or stocks and bonds. ***Mutual funds*** are diversified, professionally managed portfolios that invest in a variety of debt and/or equity securities. Insurers in the United States report their separate account assets and liabilities at current market value on the *Separate Accounts Annual Statement,* also called the

Green Blank, which insurers file with the NAIC and with each state in which an insurer conducts business. Insurers typically complete this statement concurrently with the Annual Statement. Canadian insurers report separate account assets at current market value on the *Segregated Funds Annual Return,* which is filed with OSFI and with each province in which an insurer conducts business. In addition, Canadian insurers separately summarize segregated funds and variable contracts within each province, as shown in Figure 8-7.

Because an insurer manages its separate accounts apart from the general account, a U.S. insurer prepares a Separate Accounts Annual Statement to record the operations of any or all of its separate accounts that pertain to equity-based (variable) insurance products. An insurance company that offers only guaranteed insurance products does not have to prepare a Separate Accounts Annual Statement. However, an insurance company that offers only variable products or a combination of guaranteed and variable insurance products prepares both the Separate Accounts Annual Statement and the Annual Statement. The number of separate accounts that a company maintains depends on the company's products and its customers, as well as the combination of securities held in the separate accounts. In other words, the nature of an insurer's variable products drives the accounting function concerning separate accounts. Typically, insurance product transactions are reported in the Annual Statement, whereas investment transactions are reported in the Separate Account Annual Statement. For example, an insurer reports premiums on variable products in the Annual Statement but reports how these funds were invested in the Separate Account Annual Statement. Also, although an insurer reports separate account totals on the *Assets* page of the Annual Statement, the insurer presents more detailed information in the Separate Accounts Annual Statement, including the segregation of specified sets of securities and investors.

The *Assets* page of the Separate Accounts Annual Statement resembles a shortened version of the company's Annual Statement *Assets* page, depicted in Figure 6-1. One aspect of the Separate Accounts Annual Statement that differentiates it from the Annual Statement is that the terms *admitted asset* and *nonadmitted asset* do not appear. Separate accounts are valued at current market value. For this reason, an insurer must conduct a daily accounting to determine the unit value per share in each separate account because policyowners can purchase or surrender their variable insurance products at any time.

Conclusion

Chapters 7 and 8 have provided you with an introduction to an insurer's asset accounts. In the next three chapters, we continue our

Figure 8-7. *Segregated Funds Summary* and *Variable Contracts Summary*—Canadian Annual Return.

SEGREGATED FUNDS SUMMARY
($'000)

Segregated Funds		Newfoundland (01)	P.E.I. (02)	Nova Scotia (03)	New Brunswick (04)	Quebec (05)	Ontario (06)	Manitoba (07)
Fund at beginning of year	01							
Net Income of Investment	02							
Premium and Resv. allocation	03							
Other	04							
Transfer from other funds	05							
Withdrawals	06							
Benefits	07							
Transfer to other fund	08							
Subtotal	09							
Balance at end of year	10							

VARIABLE CONTRACTS SUMMARY
($'000)

Variable Contracts		Newfoundland (01)	P.E.I. (02)	Nova Scotia (03)	New Brunswick (04)	Quebec (05)	Ontario (06)	Manitoba (07)
Fund at beginning of year	21							
Net Income of Investment	22							
Premium & Resv. allocation	23							
Other	24							
Transfer from other funds	25							
Withdrawals	26							
Benefits	27							
Transfer to other fund	28							
Subtotal	29							
Balance at end of year	30							

Figure 8-7. *Segregated Funds Summary* and *Variable Contracts Summary*—Canadian Annual Return (continued).

SEGREGATED FUNDS SUMMARY
($'000)

Saskatchewan (08)	Alberta (09)	British Columbia (10)	Yukon (11)	Northwest Territories (12)	Miscellaneous (13)	Out of Canada (18)	Total (20)	
								01
								02
								03
								04
								05
								06
								07
								08
								09
								10

VARIABLE CONTRACTS SUMMARY
($'000)

Saskatchewan (08)	Alberta (09)	British Columbia (10)	Yukon (11)	Northwest Territories (12)	Miscellaneous (13)	Out of Canada (18)	Total (20)	
								21
								22
								23
								24
								25
								26
								27
								28
								29
								30

discussion of an insurance company's typical balance sheet accounts. Chapters 9 and 10 discuss liability accounts, and Chapter 11 discusses capital and surplus. Beginning with Chapter 12, we shift our focus from balance sheet accounts to the statement of operations accounts.

Key Terms and Concepts

real estate
contra account
contra asset account
derivative
hedge
foreign exchange risk
policy loan
cash surrender value
conventional policy loan
automatic premium loan (APL)
cash accounting
bank reconciliation
outstanding checks
unrecorded deposits
nonsufficient funds (NSF) check
due income
accrued income
prepaid expenses
retention limit
deferred policy acquisition costs (DPAC)
general account
mutual funds

References

1. CLHIA *1995 Facts,* p. 24.
2. ACLI *1995 Life Insurance Fact Book Update,* p. 44.

CHAPTER 9

ACCOUNTING FOR LIABILITIES: RESERVES

LEARNING OBJECTIVES

After studying this chapter, you should be able to

- Explain the purpose of reserves in the insurance industry
- Discuss the implications of reserving practices for an insurer's solvency, growth, and profitability
- Describe the prospective and retrospective methods of calculating policy reserves
- Explain the differences between statutory policy reserves, GAAP policy reserves, and policy reserves calculated for tax purposes
- Define reserves in the context of accounting and financial reporting in life insurance, accident and health insurance, and annuity transactions
- Explain surplus strain and how it can be relieved by modified reserve methods
- Identify and describe other typical reserves that insurers maintain

CHAPTER OUTLINE

Reserves for Different Accounting Requirements

The Effects of Reserve Strength on Solvency and Profitability

Policy Reserves for Life Insurance

Policy Reserves for Annuities

Reserves for Accident and Health Insurance

Surplus Strain

Policy Reserves Calculated for Tax Purposes

Other Types of Reserves

Of all the words used in the insurance industry, *reserves* is one of the most important and also one of the most easily misunderstood. Typically, in our day-to-day lives, we use the term *reserves* to mean something extra, something that is available in addition to our usual supply. For example, people who live in a desert may speak of their water reserves, meaning the supply of water that they store during the rainy season so that they can have water during the dry season. Generals refer to their tactical or strategic reserves, meaning the soldiers and weapons they have available besides those currently on the front lines. In a broad financial sense, reserves can also refer to a fund of additional money that a company or a person keeps in case of some special need.

In the insurance industry, however, reserves are *not* typically a source of money. Rather, ***reserves*** are estimates of the amounts of money that an insurer needs to pay future business obligations or to help absorb the financial impact of realized or unrealized gains and losses on the insurer's invested assets. Using mathematical probabilities, actuaries estimate the amount and timing of future claims, future interest rates and expense amounts, and the rate at which policies will lapse or will be surrendered. On the basis of these calculations and the expected amounts of premium income and investment income, actuaries estimate the amounts needed to pay future benefits to policyowners. The actuaries then provide these calculated reserve amounts to the insurer's accountants, who generally record the amounts as liabilities in the insurer's accounting records.

Reserves are a critical component of an insurance company's financial condition. Because reserves are only estimates, *material* differences between reserve estimates and an insurer's actual experience can have a significant impact on the insurer's operations and financial strength. For example, if reserves to pay future policyowner obligations are underestimated, the insurer's surplus initially will be overstated and the insurer may appear financially stronger. When these obligations come due, the insurer will use more of its assets than it anticipated to pay these obligations, which, in turn, reduces surplus. This unexpected reduction in surplus could impair future operations or, if sufficiently significant, threaten the insurer's solvency. On the other hand, if reserves to pay future policyowner obligations are overestimated, then the insurer's surplus initially will be understated, the company will not appear as financially strong, future operations may be impeded or business opportunities missed.

Figure 9-1. Highlight of the reserves section of a typical insurance company balance sheet.

December 31, 19XX			
Assets		**Liabilities and Capital Surplus**	
Invested assets:		**Liabilities:**	
Bonds	xxx	Policy reserves:	
Mortgage loans	xxx	Life insurance	xxx
Stocks	xxx	Annuities	xxx
Total Invested Assets	xxx	Accident and health	xxx
		Total Policy Reserves	xxx
Real estate	xxx	Claim reserves:	
Policy loans	xxx	Life insurance	xxx
Investment income due and accrued	xxx	Accident and health	xxx
Cash and cash equivalents	xxx	**Total Claim Reserves**	xxx
Premiums due	xxx	Policy dividends due and unpaid	xxx
Deferred policy acquisition costs (GAAP only)	xxx	Unpaid policy claims	xxx
Reinsurance ceded	xxx	Premium deposits	xxx
Other assets	xxx	Advance premiums	xxx
Total Assets	5,000,000	Interest maintenance reserve	xxx
		Asset valuation reserve	xxx
		Other liabilities	xxx
		Total Liabilities	4,300,000
		Capital and Surplus:	
		Stock	xxx
		Additional paid-in capital	xxx
		Special surplus	xxx
		Unassigned surplus	xxx
		Net unrealized gains (losses)	(xxx)
		Treasury stock	(xxx)
		Total Capital and Surplus	700,000
		Total Liabilities and Capital and Surplus	5,000,000

Consequently, insurance companies and regulators both place great emphasis on establishing adequate reserves. Figure 9-1 highlights the reserves section of a typical insurance company balance sheet.

The most common types of reserves are *policy reserves* and *claim reserves.* In Chapter 6, we defined *policy reserves* as liabilities that identify the amount that, together with the insurer's future expected premiums and investment income earned from in-force policies, the insurer expects to pay in future benefits on in-force policies. Other terms used for policy reserves are *legal reserves, tabular reserves,* or *statutory reserves* in the United States and *required reserves, provision for future policy benefits,* or *net actuarial liabilities* in Canada. Policy reserves specifically apply to individual life insurance policies and to noncancelable and guaranteed renewable accident and health (A&H) insurance policies.

Claim reserves, also called *disabled life reserves,* are liabilities that identify the amounts that an insurer will pay in the future on claims that have been reported to the insurer before the date of the financial statement but have not yet been paid in full. In other words, the insurer is aware of its obligation to settle specified claims, but has not yet done so. The insurer also provides estimates of *claims incurred but not reported (IBNR)* as part of its *claim liabilities,* which we discuss in Chapter 10. Claim reserves are primarily associated with policies that have ongoing losses such as A&H policies, rather than a single loss, as is the case with most life insurance policies. Insurers do establish claim reserves for their life insurance business such as reserves for pending claims (or claims that have been received but are not yet processed). But because of the frequency and sometimes long-term nature of A&H insurance claims, claim reserves are a more significant factor in A&H policies. Figure 9-2 summarizes the distinguishing characteristics of an insurer's policy reserves and claim reserves.

Because obligations to pay future benefits generally represent significant amounts of money, policy reserves and claim reserves are

Figure 9-2. Policy reserves and claim reserves.

Type of Liability	Product Type	Benefit Payment
Policy Reserves	Life	One-time
Policy Reserves	Accident & Health (unearned premium reserve, active life reserves)	One-time
Claim Reserves	Life (pending claims, claims incurred but not reported, and claims in the course of settlement)	Ongoing
Claim Reserves	Accident & Health (pending claims, claims incurred but not reported, claims in the course of settlement, and the present value of amounts not yet due)	Ongoing

both critical factors in any insurance company's financial position. Figure 9-3 depicts the percentages by line of business, of policy reserves, and other obligations of U.S. and Canadian life insurance companies. Reserves represent the vast majority of an insurer's liabilities, and *policy reserves* and *claim reserves* represent the majority of an insurer's reserves. For simplicity, we discuss policy reserves in the section pertaining to life insurance policies and claim reserves in the section on A&H insurance policies. Keep in mind, however, that policy reserves and claim reserves affect both life and A&H insurance policies to varying degrees.

Another way to understand policy reserves is to compare them to bond debt. When a company issues bonds, it is borrowing money that it can use in the present, but it is also creating an obligation to

Figure 9-3. Shares of policy reserves (by lines of business) and total policy reserves and other obligations of U.S. and Canadian life insurers.

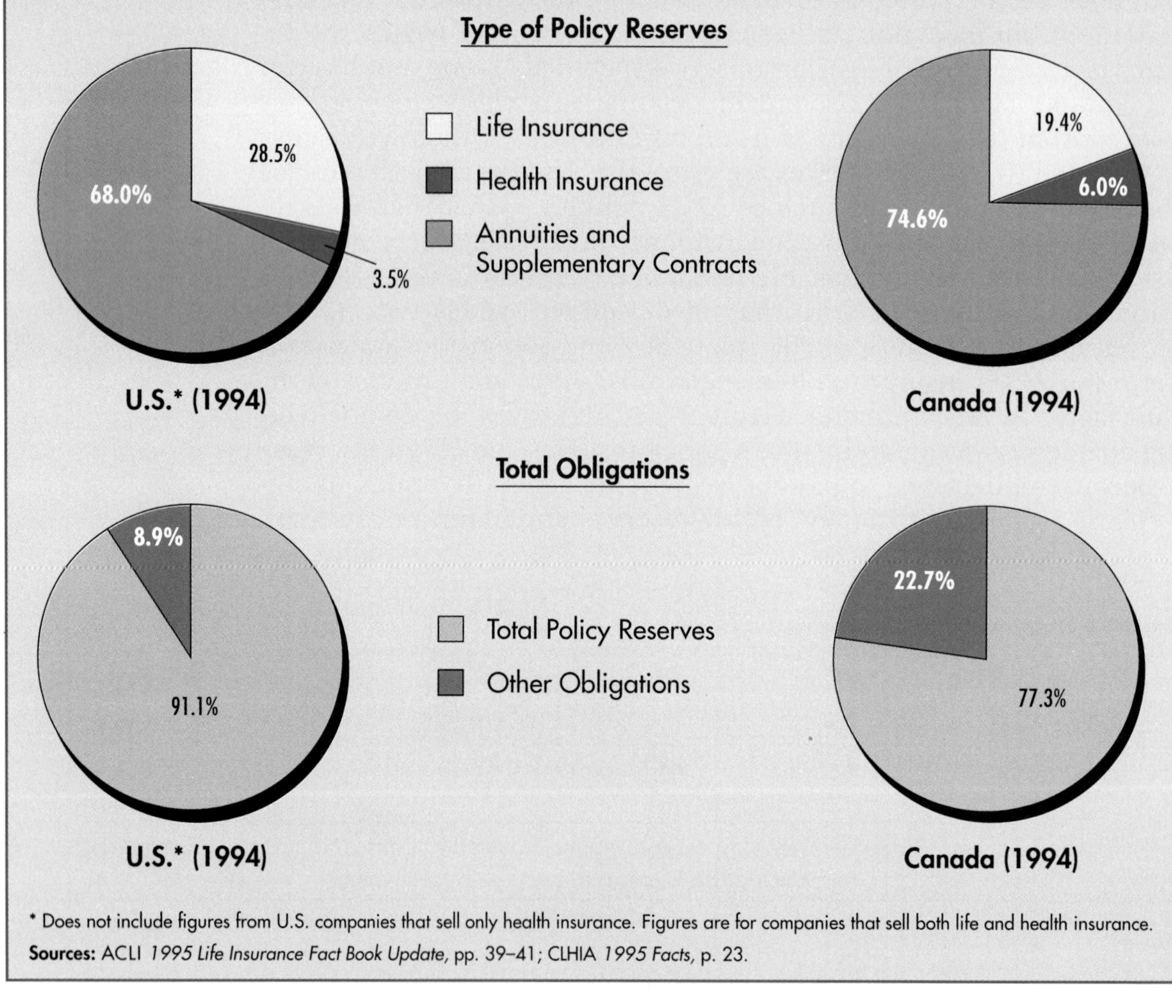

* Does not include figures from U.S. companies that sell only health insurance. Figures are for companies that sell both life and health insurance.

Sources: ACLI *1995 Life Insurance Fact Book Update*, pp. 39–41; CLHIA *1995 Facts*, p. 23.

repay that money in the future. Upon issuing bonds, the company creates liability accounts to record its future obligations to bondholders. Similarly, when an insurer sells a life insurance product, it receives premium income. In exchange for the premiums, the insurer promises to pay benefits in the future. The insurer's policy reserve accounts, which are liability accounts, represent this obligation to pay benefits in the future. The insurer will pay the benefits out of its asset accounts such as Cash. When the insurer pays these amounts from the asset accounts, thereby decreasing assets, it also decreases reserves. Thus, the insurer maintains the balance of the basic accounting equation (Assets = Liabilities + Capital and Surplus).

However, a critical difference between accounting for an insurer's reserves and accounting for its other liabilities is that insurers generally do not reduce reserves immediately for each benefit payment. The concept of reserves is an *aggregate* one. Whenever you see policy reserves on an insurer's balance sheet, you are looking at an aggregate number. Reserve adequacy is measured in the aggregate by computer, so insurers can and do calculate reserves on individual policies. However, policy reserves are recorded at the end of an accounting period for that period's transactions, rather than each time the insurer pays a claim or receives a premium payment.

A typical procedure for the accountant, upon receiving the updated actuarial amounts of policy reserves applicable to each block of policies, is to record the appropriate adjusting entry to ensure that the updated amount of policy reserves is reported on the valuation date. Typically, the valuation date coincides with the last day of the accounting period. The accounting entry for the product type or line of business is usually an adjustment to Change in Reserves or Increases/Decreases in Provision for Future Policy Benefits, which are statement of operations accounts, and an adjustment to Policy Reserves, a balance sheet account. Insurance companies may call the aggregate reserves account something simple, like Policy Reserves—Life or Claim Reserves—Accident and Health, and they report their reserves for each line of business on the *Liabilities* page of the Annual Statement.

For example, assume that an insurer's first-quarter balance sheet lists \$2.5 million in policy reserves for life insurance policies. Suppose that, during the second quarter, the insurer has a higher volume of benefit payments and higher benefit amounts for each claim than the actuaries originally projected. The actuaries review the insurer's accounting records for benefit payments and recalculate the amount of policy reserves, given the insurer's second quarter transactions. If the updated reserve amount should be \$2.7 million, then the actuaries notify the accounting department of that amount. The insurer records an adjusting entry to update its life policy reserves for financial reporting purposes. In our example, the insurer makes the following adjusting entry:

Change in Reserves—Life 200,000
Policy Reserves—Life 200,000
To adjust upward the amount of life policy reserves on the balance sheet.

As a result of this adjusting entry, the insurer reports $2.7 million in life policy reserves on its balance sheet for the second quarter. Had the updated reserve amount been $2.4 million instead of $2.7 million, the adjusting entry is to decrease reserves by $100,000 ($2.5 million – $2.4 million), as follows:

Policy Reserves—Life 100,000
Change in Reserves—Life 100,000
To adjust downward the amount of life policy reserves on the balance sheet.

A reserve is *released* each time a policy benefit is paid or a policy lapses. A ***released reserve*** is a policy reserve that was originally established in connection with an in-force policy but is no longer required. For practical reasons, changes in reserves typically are not posted until the end of each accounting period. Therefore, it may be difficult to see the interrelationship among reserves, premium income, and changes in other account classifications such as assets and surplus. Figure 9-4 presents a simplified flowchart of the accounting entries resulting from the sale and settlement of one policy over time. Again, we show financial transactions associated with a block of insurance policies because reserves are an aggregate policy concept, rather than an individual policy concept.

In this chapter, we discuss the effect that different accounting systems have on an insurer's reserve accounts and the assumptions that actuaries use to calculate reserve liabilities. Then we examine several types of reserves, giving most of our attention to the policy reserves and claim reserves that insurers maintain to support their obligations under life insurance policies, annuities, and A&H insurance policies. We conclude the chapter by discussing other types of reserves, some of which an insurer establishes for purposes other than to cover obligations to policyowners.

Reserves for Different Accounting Requirements

Insurers generally maintain more than one set of accounting records to accommodate several reporting requirements. For every set of accounting records, insurers also maintain a set of reserves, each calcu-

Figure 9-4. Flowchart of the effect of reserves on an insurer's other accounts.

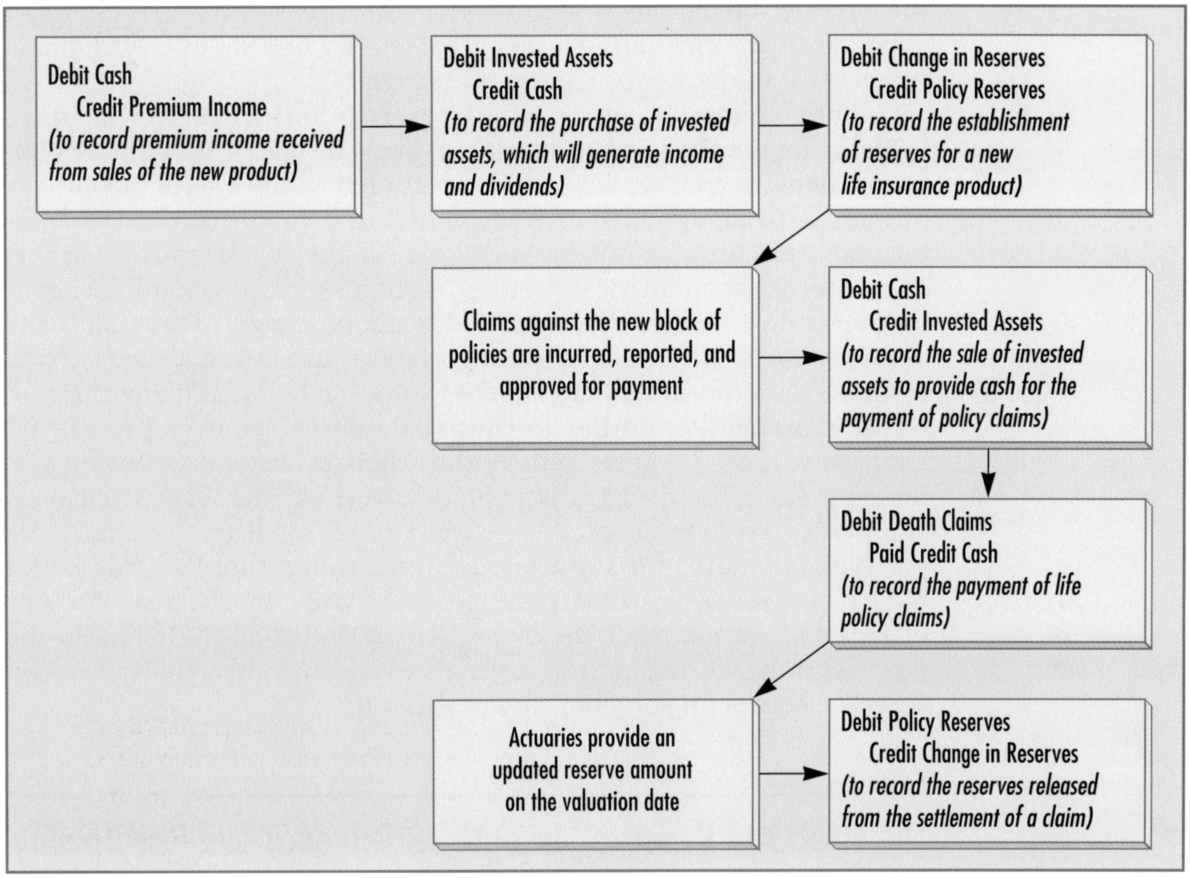

lated according to particular accounting requirements. Most U.S. insurers calculate at least the following sets of reserves:

- Statutory reserves
- GAAP reserves
- Reserves calculated for tax purposes
- Reserves calculated for the insurer's internal accounting system

Statutory reserves are established to satisfy the requirements of state insurance regulators, whereas U.S. GAAP reserves are calculated according to guidelines determined by the Financial Accounting Standards Board (FASB). Compared to statutory accounting, U.S. GAAP generally produces larger asset values and smaller values for reserves and other liabilities. Therefore, because capital and surplus equals assets minus liabilities, U.S. GAAP generally produces larger capital and surplus values than does statutory accounting. In Canada, the distinction between statutory accounting and GAAP does not exist because Canadian insurers prepare only one set of GAAP-based financial statements for regulatory purposes.

In both countries, an insurer's reserves influence the insurer's income tax liability. For example, insurers in the United States typically calculate another set of reserves for federal and state income tax purposes. An insurer also uses the values of its liabilities and reserves for management accounting purposes. Because each insurer uses its own internal accounting system, it is impossible to generalize about reserves calculated for these internal systems, except to say that many insurers use an internal accounting system that is a modified version of GAAP. For these insurers, reserve values calculated using their internal systems are similar to those calculated according to GAAP. Generally, most insurers believe that their internal accounting systems produce the most realistic picture of their financial situation.

In our discussion of reserves, we examine the differences between reserves calculated for statutory accounting and those calculated for GAAP, as well as various practices used only in Canada. We also briefly discuss tax reserves in the United States and Canada. In the next section, we use policy reserves to discuss the effect of an insurer's reserves on solvency and profitability.

The Effects of Reserve Strength on Solvency and Profitability

Recall that an insurer does not adjust its policy reserves until the end of an accounting period. If an insurer establishes a $400,000 reserve for a $1,000,000 block of policies, then the insurer releases $400,000 of reserves upon payment of $1,000,000 of policy benefits. At the end of the accounting period, the insurer's actuaries provide the accounting department with updated reserve figures for this block of policies. Then the insurer posts an adjusting entry to ensure that its balance sheet reports the updated reserve amount for that accounting period. However, the insurer's net income, and ultimately its surplus, do not necessarily reduce by $1,000,000 for this block of policies. Instead, the insurer's net income decreases by $600,000, which is the difference between the amount of the benefit payments and the amount of the reserve released from the financial transactions for this block of policies, all other factors remaining equal. Because the insurer adds net income to its surplus, assuming no policy dividends or stockholder dividends, the impact on surplus is also only $600,000, not $1,000,000. From this simplified example, you can see how reserves serve to ultimately cushion the impact of benefit payments on the insurer's surplus.

Statutory requirements in the United States specify the minimum size of insurers' statutory policy reserves but do not specify any maximum. Further, U.S. GAAP policy reserves, Canadian GAAP policy reserves, and several other types of reserves form the basis for the insurer's projections of future conditions. Insurers have considerable discretion concerning the size of these reserves. For example, if an insurer forecasts investment earnings between 7 percent and 9 percent in its general account, the insurer can base its GAAP reserves on an earnings assumption of 7 percent, 9 percent, or any rate between those two levels. The investment earnings assumption will influence the size of the reserves.

The degree of conservatism used in the calculation of policy reserves is an important business decision. Conservative reserving practices produce relatively large reserves, all other factors remaining equal. The relative conservatism of an insurer's reserving practices has important implications for the insurer's solvency, as well as for its profitability. The more conservative an insurer's reserves, the more assets an insurer has made available to pay off its obligations. Thus, the insurer provides itself with more protection against insolvency. Conservative reserving typically improves an insurer's rating from insurance rating agencies. A strong rating can have a positive impact on the insurer's competitive position, because many consumers prefer the perceived security of doing business with a highly rated insurer.

On the other hand, conservative reserving can damage an insurer's competitive position by forcing up prices for the insurer's products. If an insurer maintains conservative reserves, it may need to charge a relatively high premium to generate sufficient assets to cover its high reserve liability. In addition, conservative reserving can hurt an insurer's competitive position by increasing the insurer's level of *surplus strain,* a condition we discuss later in this chapter. In the following sections, we discuss the business decisions insurers make that determine the strength of their reserves, including the effect that an insurer's actuarial assumptions have on reserves. We then explain how an insurer can strengthen or destrengthen reserves through voluntary increases or decreases in reserve amounts.

Actuarial Assumptions and Reserves

The amounts that insurers record in their reserve accounts are, of necessity, estimates. When an insurer establishes reserves for a block of traditional insurance policies, it knows the total amount of the face value of the block of policies. Therefore, it knows its future obligation to its policyowners. However, the insurer can only estimate the amount of investment income it will earn on the policyowner premiums it invests. Further, the insurer does not know precisely when a policyowner or beneficiary will submit a claim on the policy or if a policy will lapse before benefit payments become due.

Because of such uncertainties, insurers must make conjectures, called ***actuarial assumptions,*** about future events when they calculate the amounts to report in their reserve accounts. In the context of policy reserve valuation, actuarial assumptions include the interest rates, mortality or morbidity rates, withdrawal rates, and reserve methods used to calculate policy reserves for a block of insurance policies. The actuarial assumptions that an insurer chooses to use determines how conservative the insurer's policy reserves will be. Insurers assume the likelihood of future conditions and base their calculations on those assumptions. Over their many years of experience, insurers have learned to make fairly accurate estimates and to adjust those estimates as needed. Therefore, an insurer's financial statements usually provide a clear indication of its financial strength and profitability.

Interest Rates

The higher the rate of interest used to compute reserves, the lower the reserves will be. For example, Figure 9-5 compares the reserve levels for an ordinary life policy using different interest rate assumptions. The reserve calculations assume $1,000 of coverage issued to the same person and use the same mortality rate. The reserve, using a 3.5 percent interest rate, is larger than the reserve using a 5.5 percent interest rate by 52.6 percent at 10 years ($92.98 versus $60.93), by 39.7 percent at 20 years ($215.15 versus $153.98), and by 28.8 percent at 30 years ($362.64 versus $281.64). Ultimately, an insurer must have sufficient funds to pay claims. This table shows that, with higher rates of return on its investments, an insurer can rely more on investment income to fund claim payments rather than the sale of assets and thus reduce its need for asset-backed reserves.

Mortality and Morbidity Rates

The mortality and morbidity assumptions that an insurer selects also affect the amount of its reserves. Recall that *mortality rates* are the rates at which death occurs among a defined group of people and that *morbidity rates* are the rates at which injury or sickness occur among a defined group of people. In most cases, the higher the mortality or morbidity rates used to calculate reserves for life and accident and health insurance policies, the larger the reserves will be.

As long as they adhere to all statutory restrictions, insurers can use different mortality or morbidity tables to produce the desired level of reserve strength if the use of these tables results in the fair presentation of its obligations to policyowners. Figure 9-6 shows the results of calculating reserves using three different mortality tables. All figures are for a $1,000 whole life policy issued to the same person, based on an interest rate of 5.5 percent. However, each mortality table is based on statistics from different eras or gathered in different ways. Thus,

Figure 9-5. The effect of interest rate assumptions on reserve values.

Interest Rate	10th Year Reserve	20th Year Reserve	30th Year Reserve
3.5 percent	$92.98	$215.15	$362.64
4.0 percent	$83.60	$197.84	$340.47
4.5 percent	$75.19	$181.92	$319.58
5.0 percent	$67.65	$167.33	$299.98
5.5 percent	$60.93	$153.98	$281.64
(All reserve figures are based on an insured of the same age and sex, $1,000 of coverage, and identical mortality rates.)			

an older table, such as the *Commissioners' 1941 Standard Ordinary Table* (1941 CSO table), reflects the higher mortality rates of more than half a century ago. Even the differences between the 1958 CSO table and the 1980 CSO table can be significant and can cause significant changes in reserve calculations. In Figure 9-6, using the 1958 CSO table rather than the 1980 CSO table produces a reserve that is 18 percent larger after 10 years ($109.67 versus $92.98), 18.9 percent larger after 20 years ($255.89 versus $215.15), and 17.8 percent larger after 30 years ($427.36 versus $362.64).

Withdrawal Rates

To assure conservative reserve estimates, insurers in the United States do not consider lapses and withdrawals when calculating statutory policy reserves. Therefore, withdrawal rates are an issue only in calculating U.S. GAAP reserves and Canadian GAAP reserves. In some cases, a higher withdrawal rate produces a lower reserve. In other cases, a higher withdrawal rate may produce a higher reserve because of a specified product's design.

Valuation Method

Several valuation methods are used by insurers to calculate (*value*) their statutory policy reserves. These methods include the *net level premium approach* and the *full preliminary term method* for U.S. insurers and the *policy premium method* for Canadian insurers.

Figure 9-6. The effect of mortality assumptions on reserve values.

Mortality Table	10th Reserve	20th Reserve	30th Reserve
1941 CSO Table	$117.63	$269.08	$442.49
1958 CSO Table	$109.67	$255.89	$427.36
1980 CSO Table	$ 92.98	$215.15	$362.64
(All reserve figures are based on an insured of the same age and sex, $1,000 of coverage, and a 5.5 percent interest rate.)			

Voluntary Strengthening and Destrengthening of Reserves

An insurer may determine that its reserves are inadequate for a certain type of policy, block of policies, or product line. In such situations, the insurer may engage in reserve strengthening, which *increases* the amount of its reserves as a result of changes in actuarial assumptions. For example, an insurer could strengthen its reserves by recalculating them with a lower interest rate. Likewise, if an insurer decides that its reserves are too conservative, the insurer may undertake reserve destrengthening, which *decreases* the amount of its reserves as a result of changes in actuarial assumptions.

Note that the periodic adjusting entries made to increase or decrease aggregate policy reserves as a result of business transactions differs from reserve strengthening or reserve destrengthening. In the case of adjusting entries to report updated policy reserve amounts, only the dollar amount of the reserve changes, not the insurer's underlying actuarial assumptions. For instance, refer to the example earlier in this chapter, in which an insurer adjusted its reserves from $2.5 million to $2.7 million. If 4 percent were the actuarially assumed interest rate for a specified block of insurance policies, then the insurer used a 4 percent interest rate assumption to calculate both the $2.5 million and the $2.7 million reserve amounts.

The minimum size of an insurer's statutory reserves is determined by law at the time a product is issued. Thereafter, if the insurer's statutory reserves are equal to the legal minimum, the insurer cannot destrengthen its reserves. However, if an insurer's reserves are larger than the law requires, then the insurer may be able to destrengthen its statutory reserves, as long as the reserves remain at least as large as those required by law and, in the United States, as long as the insurer obtains permission from the insurance commissioner in its state of domicile. The accounting treatment for reserve strengthening and destrengthening involves a direct change to an insurer's balance sheet, whereas a change in reserves goes through the statement of operations.

Suppose an insurer has been calculating statutory policy reserves on a certain block of business using 3.5 percent interest and the 1980 CSO table. However, at the time the block of policies was issued, the law specified that minimum reserves must be based on the 1980 CSO table, at a maximum 5.5 percent interest rate, which is two percentage points higher than the insurer has so far chosen to use. Therefore, the insurer can destrengthen the reserves on this business by recalculating with any interest rate greater than 3.5 percent but not greater than 5.5 percent. Alternatively, the insurer can strengthen these reserves by using an interest rate lower than 3.5 percent.

Under U.S. GAAP, as opposed to statutory requirements, insurers normally *cannot* alter their actuarial assumptions to change the strength of their reserves. Throughout the life of the policy, an insurer must calculate GAAP reserves using the insurer's assumptions at the time of policy issue. In Canada, an insurer may, without receiving regulatory permission, change its reserve assumptions from year to year to reflect its experience. Canadian actuaries review actuarial assumptions annually and change the amount of reserves as necessary. In Canada, changes in the actuarial assumptions for calculating reserves flow through the statement of operations. Of course, a U.S. or Canadian insurer has full discretion over the amount of reserves selected for management accounting purposes. The insurer can strengthen or destrengthen these reserves at will.

Reserve strengthening or destrengthening can serve a number of business purposes. Recall from Chapter 6 that, when an insurer decreases its liabilities by destrengthening its reserves, the insurer increases its capital and surplus. The insurer can then use the increased capital and surplus for other purposes, such as to support new business. On the other hand, an insurer may strengthen its reserves if its experience with a product reveals that the assumptions used to calculate policy reserves were too optimistic. In such a situation, the insurer may decide to strengthen its reserves to protect its rating or its solvency. To do so, however, it decreases its capital and surplus, thus leaving fewer funds available for future growth.

Policy Reserves for Life Insurance

In most years, an insurer typically receives more money in net premiums than it pays out in benefits on a block of policies. The insurer invests the excess of net premiums over benefits. The insurer uses this excess, plus the interest earned from investing it, plus any net premiums it receives in the future, to pay the benefits that become payable later in the life of the block of policies. When calculating the amount of policy reserves it should maintain, an insurer takes into account the excess of the net premiums received over the benefits paid, plus interest earned on premium income, during the life of a block of policies.

Calculating Life Insurance Policy Reserves in the United States

One method U.S. insurers use to calculate life insurance policy reserves is the ***net level premium approach.*** This approach assumes that the amount of a policy's net premiums does not increase or decrease during the life of the policy. Insurers typically use one of two variations of this approach, called the *prospective method* and the *retrospective method.* In the United States, the ***prospective method*** looks ahead at a policy's future premiums and benefits and calculates policy reserves using the following equation:

$$\text{Policy Reserve} = \text{Present Value (PV) of Future Benefits} - \text{Present Value (PV) of Future Net Premiums}$$

The ***present value of future benefits*** equals the net single premium at the insured's attained age for the remaining policy benefits. The ***present value of future net premiums*** is the present value of a life annuity due, assuming whole life policies, rather than limited-pay policies. Figure 9-7 illustrates the process of calculating the policy reserve for a block of policies using the prospective method. We discuss present value in Chapter 14.

The ***retrospective method*** looks back at a policy's past premiums and benefits to determine policy reserves and defines the policy reserve for a block of policies according to the following equation:

$$\text{Policy Reserve} = \text{Accumulated Value of Net Premiums} - \text{Accumulated Cost of Insurance}$$

The ***accumulated value of net premiums*** equals the amount of net premiums received since the beginning of the contract, plus interest.

Figure 9-7. Calculating the policy reserve for a block of policies using the prospective method.

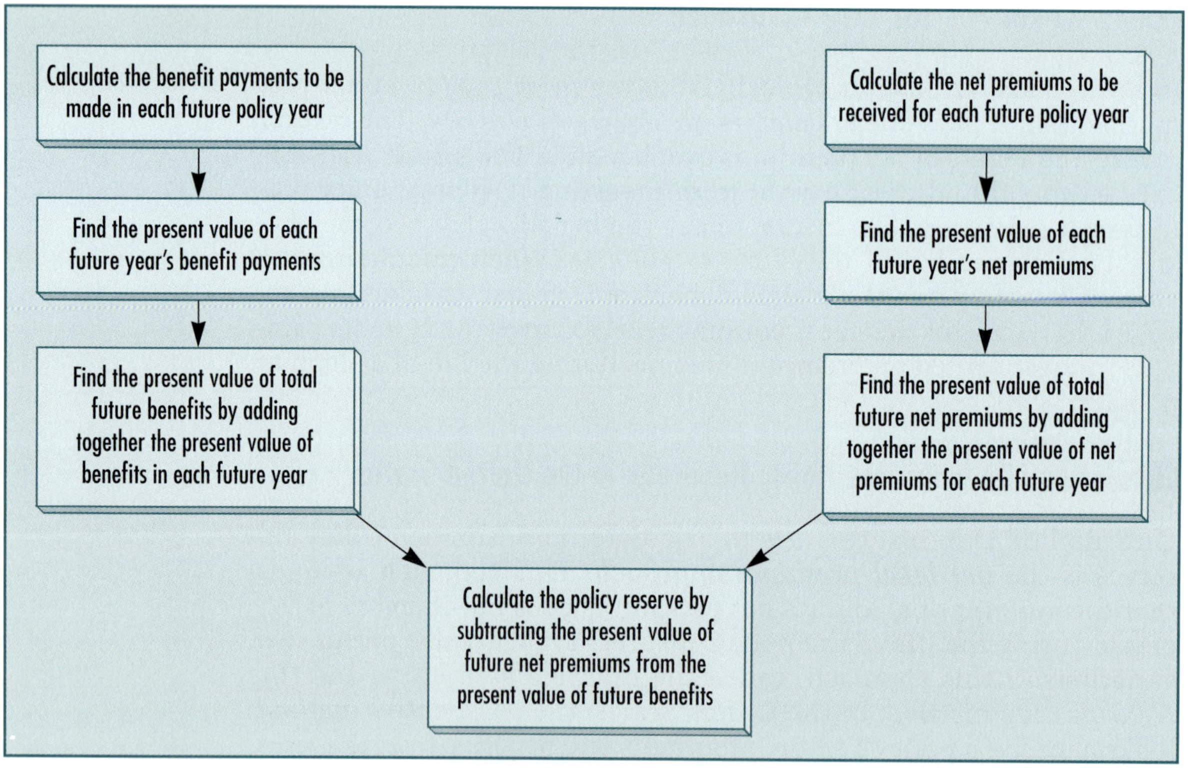

Figure 9-8. Calculating the policy reserve for a block of policies using the retrospective method.

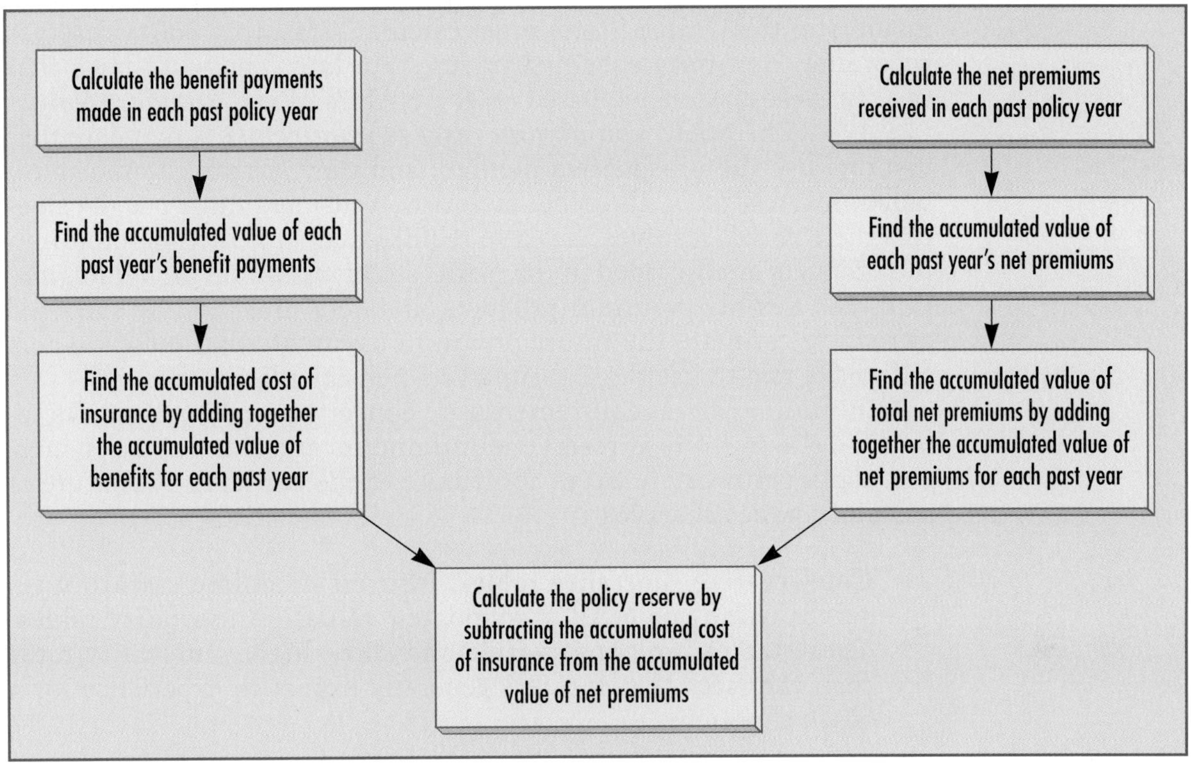

The ***accumulated cost of insurance*** equals the amount that the insurer has paid in benefits since the beginning of the contract, accumulated with interest. Figure 9-8 summarizes the process of calculating policy reserves using the retrospective method. We discuss accumulated future value in Chapter 14.

In the absence of reserve strengthening or destrengthening, an insurer calculates policy reserves using mortality and interest rates specified at policy issue, rather than the insurer's actual mortality and interest experience. The retrospective method and the prospective method, as described above, always yield the same reserve amount, so long as an insurer uses the same actuarial assumptions. The following table summarizes reserve calculation in the United States according to the prospective and retrospective approaches.

Policy Reserves
The prospective policy reserve is equal to the present value of future benefits minus the present value of future net premiums.
The retrospective policy reserve is equal to the accumulated value of net premiums minus the accumulated cost of insurance.

Statutory and GAAP Policy Reserves

Insurers in the United States must calculate statutory policy reserves according to criteria specified under state law. The state laws that specify these criteria are based on the NAIC's *Model Standard Valuation Law.* The NAIC's ***minimum reserve requirements*** mandate that insurers use the prospective method, and they specify the mortality tables, interest rates, and other factors that insurers must use to calculate their policy reserves. Reserve requirements for flexible-premium life products are included in the NAIC's *Universal Life Model Regulation.* For flexible-premium products, insurers must follow specified criteria to estimate the future premium payments that policyowners will make and to use those estimates when calculating reserves.

Minimum reserve requirements are conservative. Three factors related to the minimum reserve requirements and the way an insurer calculates statutory reserves contribute to the conservative nature of statutory policy reserves:

- **Conservative mortality tables:** Insurers calculate statutory reserves using the NAIC's mandated valuation mortality tables. These tables are conservative and show higher mortality rates than the rates that insurers generally expect to experience for a block of policies.

- **Low interest rates:** Insurers calculate statutory reserves using conservative interest rates, which are lower than the rates that most insurers expect to earn on their invested assets.

- **No lapses or withdrawals:** Insurers calculate statutory reserves assuming that no policyowners will withdraw from coverage. This requirement means that the present value of future benefits is often considerably greater than insurers actually expect because some policyowners are almost sure to withdraw from coverage or allow their coverage to lapse.

The minimum reserve requirements defined under state laws are revised frequently. Such revisions do not affect policy contracts that are already in force. The new minimum standards set forth in revised laws apply only to contracts issued after the date that a state adopts the revision. Insurers establish and maintain policy reserves based on the minimum standards in force at policy issue. For this reason, the task of calculating an insurer's overall statutory reserves can be highly complex. For example, a recent Annual Statement for a large insurer listed a total of 129 statutory valuation standards for life insurance alone. The mortality tables used in these standards ranged from the *American Experience Table,* first published in 1868, to the

1980 CSO table, and the standard interest rates ranged from 2.5 percent to 8.16 percent. These standards applied to policies issued from before 1900 to the date of the Annual Statement.

Calculating GAAP policy reserves for U.S. stock insurance companies differs in several ways from calculating statutory policy reserves. For flexible-premium life products, GAAP policy reserves are equal to the policy's account value. For fixed-premium products, GAAP policy reserves are less conservative than statutory policy reserves. The primary factors that account for the less conservative nature of GAAP reserves compared to statutory reserves are as follows:

- **Mortality rate:** Under GAAP, insurers may use mortality rates they feel approximate their mortality expectations. Insurers generally base GAAP reserve mortality rates on basic tables, though they often use a higher percentage of the rates shown in the basic table than they use for pricing products.

- **Interest rate:** Under GAAP, insurers may use interest rates they feel approximate their interest rate expectations.

- **Lapses and withdrawals:** Insurers may recognize that not all life insurance policies will remain in force until maturity. They may use withdrawal rates that approximate their expectations.

An insurer calculates GAAP reserves for fixed-premium products based on its expectations for mortality, interest, and withdrawals at policy issue. The expectations determined at policy issue typically apply for the life of the policy, as GAAP generally does not allow insurers to modify the basis on which they calculate reserves, even if the insurer's expectations at policy issue turn out to be wrong. In contrast, under certain conditions, insurers can strengthen or destrengthen their statutory policy reserves after business has been in force by altering the assumptions used to calculate the reserves.

Another important difference between the calculation of GAAP and statutory reserves is the nature of the present value of future benefits under each system. For statutory reserves, the present value of future benefits includes only one element: the present value of future death benefits. Under GAAP, the present value of future benefits includes four elements: (1) the present value of future death benefits, (2) the present value of future surrender benefits, (3) the present value of all expected policy dividends, and (4) the present value of the insurer's expected maintenance expenses for the business. Of course, the present value of future surrender benefits is a factor only for products that offer a surrender benefit, and the present value of future policy dividends is a factor only for participating policies. In addition, owing to the mathematics of policy reserve calculations, the present value of future maintenance expenses generally influences the size of policy reserves only for limited-payment products, such as a single-premium policy or a 20-premium whole life plan.

Under U.S. GAAP, reserve calculations for fixed-premium products are based primarily on the insurer's expected results for mortality, investment return, and withdrawals. Three models for reserves exist for U.S. GAAP. The one model we focus on in this section is the *provision for adverse deviation,* which is contained in *FASB Statement No. 60.* By definition, the ***provision for adverse deviation*** is a safety margin to allow for unfavorable variations from actuarial assumptions. Adding this safety margin increases the size of GAAP reserves for U.S. stock insurers, although GAAP reserves generally are considerably smaller than statutory reserves. Figure 9-9 summarizes the characteristics of statutory and GAAP policy reserves in the United States.

Calculating Life Insurance Policy Reserves in Canada

The methods used to calculate policy reserves in Canada differ in several ways from the methods used to calculate GAAP policy reserves in the United States. When calculating policy reserves, insurers in Canada must use the *policy premium method.* The ***policy premium method (PPM)*** is a reserve method that uses gross premiums instead of net premiums. Canadian insurers cannot use the retrospective method with the PPM because the calculation of policy reserves using the PPM and the prospective method produces different policy reserves than does the retrospective method, given the same actuarial assumptions.

When following the PPM, insurers calculate policy reserves using the following equation:

$$\text{Policy Reserve} = \begin{array}{c}\text{Present Value (PV)}\\ \text{of Future Benefits}\end{array} - \begin{array}{c}\text{Present Value (PV) of}\\ \text{Future } \textit{Gross} \text{ Premiums}\end{array}$$

As with U.S. GAAP, the value of future benefits under Canadian GAAP includes projected dividends and maintenance expenses.

Another important characteristic of the policy reserve calculation in Canada is that insurers must use scenario analysis for annuity products. ***Scenario analysis*** is the process of altering assumptions to see how changes in assumptions affect results. Guidelines from the Canadian Institute of Actuaries (CIA) help insurers choose which scenarios to use to select the appropriate interest rates, mortality or morbidity rates, and lapse rates for each product type. By analyzing a number of scenarios (possible conditions), insurers can predict a

Figure 9-9. Characteristics of statutory and GAAP policy reserves under *FASB Statement No. 60.*

Statutory Policy Reserves	GAAP Policy Reserves
• Calculated using valuation mortality tables, which contain a safety margin • Calculated using a lower-than-anticipated interest rate • Calculated assuming no withdrawals • Future benefits include death benefits only	• Calculated using basic mortality tables, which contain realistic mortality rates, although they may also include a provision for adverse deviation • Calculated using a realistic interest rate • Calculated assuming a realistic withdrawal rate • Future benefits include death benefits and, where appropriate, surrender benefits, dividends, and maintenance expenses

range within which their future benefits will most likely fall. Using this range, they calculate the reserves needed to safeguard their policyowners' interests. Insurers should be relatively conservative in choosing their reserves. In other words, given a range of possible values for their reserves, insurers generally should select a value near the high end of the range.

Canadian insurers do not have to conduct scenario analysis when developing reserves for participating products. Instead, insurers calculate participating policy reserves based on their expected future experience, including their expected future policy dividend payments. This practice reflects the assumption that dividends will provide a buffer against adverse deviations. Should an insurer experience adverse deviations, it can simply decrease the amount of policy dividends.

Unlike U.S. GAAP, Canadian GAAP does not require insurers to use the actuarial assumptions chosen at policy issue to establish minimum reserves for the entire life of a product. Instead, insurers in Canada can change actuarial assumptions each year, based on their emerging experience and their new expectations for the future. For interest-sensitive products, an insurer predicts future premiums as part of the scenario analysis carried out to calculate policy reserves. The insurer then uses these predicted future premiums and the PPM to calculate policy reserves for these products.

Policy Reserves for Annuities

For most annuities, the policy reserve calculated using the prospective approach is equal to the present value of future benefits, because most annuities sold today are either *flexible-premium deferred annuities*

(FPDAs) or *single-premium annuities,* such as *single-premium deferred annuities (SPDAs)* or *single-premium immediate annuities (SPIAs).* In the case of single-premium annuities, there are no further premiums paid after the initial premium. In the case of flexible-premium deferred annuities, the insurer cannot know for certain what future premium payments the annuity contract holder will make. Therefore, an insurer calculates the policy reserve with the assumption that the annuity contract holder will pay no further premiums. For the purposes of calculating policy reserves, future premiums for single-premium and flexible-premium annuities are equal to zero. Therefore, the equation used to calculate policy reserves

Policy Reserve = PV of Future Benefits – PV of Future Premiums

becomes

Policy Reserve = PV of Future Benefits – 0

which can be reduced to

Policy Reserve = PV of Future Benefits

Generally, benefits can be received under a deferred annuity contract in one of three ways:

1. The annuity contract holder can surrender the contract during the accumulation period and receive the surrender value.

2. The annuity contract holder can keep the contract in force until the annuity matures and receive the periodic annuity income benefit as the annuitant.

3. If the annuitant dies during the accumulation period, and the annuity provides a survivor benefit, the annuitant's beneficiary receives the benefit.

Annuity reserving varies according to whether a contract is in its accumulation period or its payout period.

Statutory Reserves during the Accumulation and Payout Periods

In the United States, the NAIC's *Model Standard Valuation Law* requires that, during a deferred annuity's accumulation period, insurers calculate statutory reserves on a worst-case-scenario basis. In other words, during the accumulation period, the insurer must calculate the present value of future benefits for each of the following circumstances:

1. The annuity contract holder surrenders the contract in any year before the beginning of the benefit period.

2. The annuitant dies in any year before the beginning of the benefit period (for annuities that feature a survivor benefit).

3. The annuity remains in force until it matures.

By law, an insurer must base the policy reserve on whichever of these calculations creates the largest reserve.

Once the accumulation period ends, only one of the three benefit possibilities remains: the annuity income benefit. Therefore, during the payout period, the reserve is equal to the present value of future annuity benefits. For both the accumulation period and the payout period, the *Model Standard Valuation Law* specifies the mortality and interest assumptions that U.S. insurers use to calculate minimum statutory reserves. Insurers must maintain annuity reserves at least as large as those calculated using these conservative minimum reserve requirements.

GAAP Annuity Reserves in the United States and Canada

For GAAP reserves in the United States, an annuity's reserve during the accumulation period is equal to the annuity contract holder's account value. During the payout period, the reserve is equal to the present value of future benefits. Insurers may use mortality and interest assumptions that reflect their future expectations. In Canada, an annuity's reserve during the accumulation period is not necessarily equal to the annuity contract holder's account value, as with U.S. GAAP. Instead, Canadian insurers use scenario analysis to predict the nature and amount of future benefits. Insurers then use the scenario analysis results to determine the level of reserves that will satisfy the obligations under the annuity contract.

Reserves for Accident and Health Insurance

Two important classes of A&H insurance are medical expense insurance and disability income (DI) insurance. Insurers estimate the reserves needed for A&H insurance just as they do for life insurance.

However, claims experience used to determine reserves for A&H is much less predictable than the claims experience used for life reserves. The main reasons are the variety of products and coverages offered by different companies, and the variety of underwriting standards among insurers. Further, industry morbidity tables may be derived from the experience of many companies, which may not reflect the experience of individual companies. Delays in reporting, processing, and paying claims vary widely with the practices of each insurer and the promptness of its policyowners in submitting claims. An insurer sometimes settles a claim many months after receiving the claim form. Reasons for this delay include the following:

- The insurer needs time to investigate and determine whether a claim is eligible for coverage under the policy's provisions. Claim investigation is especially important when the insurer contests a claim or the policy restricts coverage.

- Determining the proper payee or ascertaining the amount payable may be difficult.

- An insured person might not file a claim until some time after the claim is first incurred, particularly in the case of a disability.

The date a claim is incurred determines the beginning of the insurer's liability, regardless of the date the insurer receives the claim. In the case of A&H insurance, unless the policy provides otherwise, a claim may be incurred on the date the sickness or injury first manifests itself if the policy is in force on that date. Many DI insurance policies include a waiting period provision that excludes benefit payments until an insured has been disabled for a specified period. In such cases, two significant dates for establishing the company's liability exist: (1) the date the disability begins and (2) the date the waiting period restriction is satisfied. The insurer creates a liability of an indefinite amount as of the first date. The insurer knows this date only after it receives a claim. On the second date, the insurer records a liability equal to the present value of future benefit payments. The two forms of reserves that are critical to A&H policies are (1) *active life reserves* and (2) *claim reserves,* which are commonly referred to as *disabled life reserves.* We discuss active life reserves next.

Active Life Reserves

Active life reserves can be thought of as policy reserves for A&H insurance. Active life reserves can be divided into two types: *unearned premium reserves* and *additional reserves.*

Unearned Premium Reserves

For individual medical expense insurance, insurers report *unearned premium reserves* on the balance sheet whenever a medical expense policy provides coverage that crosses two or more accounting periods. Recall from Chapter 6 that *unearned premium reserves,* also called *unearned premiums,* is a liability that equals the portion of a premium received by the statement date that applies to coverage to be provided in the following accounting period but before the next policy anniversary date.

Suppose the Groundwork Company has a group A&H insurance contract with the Abacus Life and Health Insurance Company. Groundwork usually pays its annual premium each year on January 31. The annual premium is $3,600 for the next 12 months of coverage, and the premium is paid in advance. Each year, on December 31, Abacus has one month's unearned premium from Groundwork. If Abacus uses the monthly pro rata method on its financial statements prepared as of December 31, then Abacus reports an unearned premium reserve equal to $300, that is, one month's premium or one-twelfth of Groundwork's annual premium.

If a policyowner pays premiums annually and happens to pay the annual premium near the end of the year, the unearned premium reserve might be quite large, representing 10 or 11 months of coverage. If the policyowner pays a monthly premium, the reserve is likely to be small, representing less than a month's premium. If the policyowner pays a monthly premium on the first day of each month, the insurer will not need to create any unearned premium reserve for that policyowner.

Rather than calculate the precise unearned premium for each policy in force, most insurers approximate their total unearned premium reserves. To do this, they make various assumptions. For example, many insurers assume that they receive all annual premiums on July 1, so one-half of all annual premiums are unearned premiums. Such approximations generally provide an adequate representation of an insurer's unearned premium liability. Unearned premium reserves for both individual and group credit A&H insurance policies are similar to those for other A&H lines of business.

Additional Reserves

Additional reserves are reserves that reflect expected future claim costs. Additional reserves are necessary because level premiums are insufficient to cover future claim payments as the policies mature. Additional reserves ensure that level-premium policies are supported as the policies age. The NAIC identifies the morbidity tables and the methods that a U.S. insurer can use to calculate minimum additional reserves. Different tables are used to calculate reserves for different types of products. Insurers disclose in the Annual Statement the valuation method as well as the specific interest rates and morbidity tables they used to calculate additional reserves.

For individual DI products, for example, insurers establish additional reserves similar to the policy reserves established for individual life products. In the United States, insurers use the prospective method to calculate statutory additional reserves for individual DI policies. As with statutory life reserves, an insurer calculates statutory additional DI reserves according to the minimum reserve requirements in force at policy issue. Again, an insurer's additional DI reserves may be larger than the required minimum reserves.

Under U.S. GAAP, an insurer can calculate additional reserves for DI insurance policies using the insurer's realistic expectations for morbidity, mortality, persistency rates, and investment returns. As with life products, insurers use the same assumptions from policy issue throughout the life of the product. Canadian insurers calculate additional DI insurance reserves using the PPM and scenario analysis and make changes in their reserve amount as a result of actual experience.

Insurers in the United States sometimes must establish additional reserves for their group A&H policies that contain conversion privileges to individual A&H policies. Many group A&H insurance plans also are underwritten along with a group life insurance plan. Therefore, establishing additional reserves, unless required by regulatory authorities, is typically unnecessary. More common is the requirement to establish additional ***reserves for future contingent benefits*** for deferred maternity benefits or medical expense policies with high deductibles for which the deductible has nearly been satisfied. Generally, the NAIC requires additional reserves for these and other group A&H policies that provide benefit extensions.

Claim Reserves

A *claim reserve* (disabled life reserve) is the present value of amounts not yet due. Insurers establish this reserve to estimate payment of future A&H claims that are either reported or unreported. Determining the amount of this reserve requires the company's paid claim and investment experience. An insurer establishes claim reserves for all the following types of pending claim payments:

- **Claims that have been incurred but not yet reported:** The category of incurred but not reported claims is also referred to as *IBNR claims.* Insured events have occurred for which the claimants have not yet filed a claim. The claimant may simply not yet have found time to file the claim, or, in the case of a disability claim, the waiting period may not yet have ended. For DI insurance, no benefit is payable until the disability has continued past the end of the waiting period.

- **Claims that have been reported but not yet approved:** Insurers have received a number of claims that they have not yet processed and approved. Time is required to investigate a claim and determine whether the policy covers the claim.

- **Claims that have been approved but not yet paid:** Insurers have approved a number of claims that they have not yet paid. The insurer may have difficulty determining the amount payable or the proper payee.

- **Claims that require ongoing payments over a number of years:** Insurers are obligated for a number of claims requiring an ongoing series of payments. An insurer establishes this reserve for DI claims that require payments that continue for a number of years.

- **Claims that have been reported but denied by the insurer:** The insurer estimates the amount of its liability for denied claims that have been resisted (contested) and provides a contingency reserve in case a court determines that the insurer is liable for the claim payment.

Figure 9-10 summarizes these categories of pending claims. Recall that claim reserves apply to an insurer's individual, group, and credit lines of business, which have continuing benefit payments. Insurers calculate claim reserves using present values, which we discuss in Chapter 14.

Figure 9-10. Categories of pending claims.

Pending Claims	Incurred?	Reported?	Approved?	Paid?
Incurred but not yet reported (IBNR)	Yes	No	No	No
Reported but not yet approved	Yes	Yes	No	No
Approved but not yet paid	Yes	Yes	Yes	No
Approved but not yet paid in full	Yes	Yes	Yes	Ongoing
Reported but denied	Yes	Yes	No	No

Surplus Strain

So far in this chapter, when illustrating the prospective and retrospective methods of calculating policy reserves as practiced in the United States, we have used the net level premium approach to calculate policy reserves. However, using this approach to calculate policy reserves for such products as ordinary life, multi-year term life, and noncancelable and guaranteed renewable DI, can create a condition called *surplus strain*. ***Surplus strain,*** also known as *issue strain* or *new business strain,* is the decrease in an insurer's surplus caused by the high first-year costs and the reserving requirements associated with new products.

An insurer's first-year expenses for many products are substantial. In addition, the insurer must establish reserves for the product in the product's first year. The increase in a U.S. insurer's assets resulting from a product's first-year premium is often smaller than the increase in the insurer's liabilities created by the reserve the insurer must establish for the product. In such situations, the insurer's surplus must be reduced to provide for the increase in reserves. Remember, reserves and surplus are both on the right-hand side of the balance sheet. If assets cannot be increased to match the increase in reserves, and thus balance the basic accounting equation, then surplus must be decreased to create the balance.

For example, suppose the Prominent Life and Health Insurance Company sells a policy with a first-year premium of $150 and first-year expenses of $100. After paying its expenses, Prominent gains $50 in assets from this sale in the policy's first year. However, assume that Prominent, under the net level premium approach, establishes a first-year reserve liability of $100. Let's look at this transaction in reference to the balance sheet:

Balance Sheet	
Assets	**Liabilities**
+$50	+$100
	Capital and Surplus
	–$ 50

Because Prominent's assets increase by less than its liabilities, the insurer's surplus must decrease to keep the equation in balance. Thus, the sale of this policy results in $50 of surplus strain.

Insurers with strong capital and surplus accounts can easily manage surplus strain. However, for insurers that are not as well capitalized, such as small, newly formed companies, the decrease in surplus created by their new business can cause their surplus to fall to an intolerably low level. Even for well-capitalized companies, the decrease in surplus caused by surplus strain can hinder their ability to carry out their business plans. Therefore, surplus strain is an obstacle to new business.

Because of the use of the policy premium method (PPM) to establish reserves, surplus strain is generally less severe in Canada than in the United States. According to the PPM, the policy reserve equals the present value of future benefits minus the present value of future gross premiums. A product's gross premium is equal to the net premium plus a loading charge for expenses. As a result, the present value of future gross premiums is typically larger than the present value of future net premiums. Therefore, the policy reserve calculated using gross premiums is smaller than the policy reserve calculated using net premiums. With this smaller reserve, surplus strain is less severe.

Using Reinsurance to Reduce Surplus Strain

As we discussed in Chapter 8, *reinsurance* is a transaction between two insurance companies in which one company—called the *assuming company* or the *reinsurer*—agrees to take on (assume) some of the insurance risks of another insurance company—called the *ceding company*. The reinsurer agrees to pay claims on a portion of the ceding company's insurance business. A ceding company uses reinsurance primarily to reduce the amount of risk it assumes when it sells an insurance policy. But insurers also use reinsurance to reduce surplus strain.

Suppose the Legacy Life and Health Insurance Company sells $1 million worth of A&H insurance policies and wishes to transfer a portion of the risk to a reinsurer. Legacy's reinsurance agreement stipulates the ***quota share method of reinsurance,*** in which a ceding company reinsures a percentage of the premium amount and the claim dollars incurred on a block of insurance policies, typically A&H or disability income (DI) policies. Assume that Legacy's quota share is 25 percent, the amount of premiums for the block of policies is $400,000, and the amount of claims incurred is $100,000. The premium amount Legacy pays to the reinsurer is $100,000 (25 percent × $400,000) and the claim payments for which Legacy is expecting reimbursement from the reinsurer total $25,000 (25 percent × $100,000). Legacy records the following accounting entries for these transactions:

Reinsurance Premiums Paid	100,000	
Cash..........................		100,000

To record a premium paid to a reinsurer.

Amount Recoverable from Reinsurers. 25,000
A&H Claims—Reinsurers 25,000
To record the account receivable from the reinsurer.

Under the reinsurance agreement, the ceding company is responsible for accumulating sufficient reserves to provide for $750,000 worth of benefits, the amount of its retention limit. The reinsurer is responsible for accumulating reserves on the $250,000 it is reinsuring. By reinsuring 25 percent of the block of policies, the ceding company has reduced its surplus strain by 25 percent. Suppose the reserve for the full $1,000,000 in risk is $700,000, and Legacy maintains its 25 percent quota share. Because of its reinsurance agreement, however, the ceding company maintains a reserve only on the $750,000 that it is *retaining*. The ceding company's actuaries, therefore, can provide the accounting department with the updated reserve estimate of $525,000 (75 percent × $700,000) for this block of policies at the end of the accounting period. Legacy then makes the following accounting entry to record the decrease in reserves resulting from its reinsurance agreement:

Active Life Reserves—A&H 175,000
Change in Reserves 175,000
To adjust downward the amount of A&H claim reserves as a result of reinsurance.

During the next accounting period, assume that the ceding company receives and approves $200,000 in claim payments for this block of policies. In this case, Legacy debits A&H Claims Paid and credits Cash for $200,000 upon payment of these claims. Because the reinsurer is obligated by the reinsurance agreement to pay Legacy one-quarter of all claim payments made for this block of policies, the reinsurer pays Legacy $50,000. Upon receipt of this amount from the reinsurer, Legacy makes the following accounting entry:

Cash. 50,000
Amounts Recoverable from Reinsurers 50,000
To record the amount of A&H claims recovered from the reinsurer.

Legacy can also receive experience rating refunds from the reinsurer. In the context of reinsurance, an ***experience rating refund*** is the portion of a reinsurance premium that is returned to the ceding company when claims experience is better than had been expected at the time the premium was calculated. Experience rating refunds are similar to policy dividends in that they represent a return of premium to the policyowner, in this case, the ceding company. Generally, policy dividends apply to individual policies, whereas experience rating refunds apply to group insurance policies and reinsurance agreements. Suppose the reinsurer had calculated the $100,000 premium on the basis that $250,000 in claims would be paid during the accounting period. The ceding company's actual claims experience was $200,000, as noted above, so the reinsurer may send Legacy an experience rating refund at the end of the accounting period. Assuming the refund is proportionate to the amount of actual versus expected claims, the reinsurer would send Legacy $10,000 ($50,000 × 20 percent), because actual experience was 20 percent lower than expected experience. Upon receipt of this refund, Legacy records the following accounting entry:

Cash.	10,000	
Experience Rating Refund—Reinsurance . .		10,000

To record the receipt of an experience rating refund from the reinsurer.

An insurer also considers its retention limit and the conditions of the reinsurance agreement in calculating active life reserves and claim reserves for reinsured A&H policies. Otherwise, the calculation and reporting of active life reserves and claim reserves for reinsured policies is similar to that for policies that have not been reinsured. In Chapter 11, we continue our discussion of the effects of reinsurance on an insurer's surplus.

Reserving Methods that Limit Statutory Surplus Strain

Another way U.S. insurers can protect against statutory surplus strain is to use a modified reserve method to calculate policy reserves. A ***modified reserve method*** for calculating policy reserves is one that creates smaller first-year statutory reserves than those calculated using the net level premium approach. Using a modified reserve method, the insurer experiences less surplus strain and can issue more new business without compromising its financial situation.

The modified reserving methods that U.S. insurers may use for life products are outlined in the *Commissioners' Reserve Valuation Method (CRVM),* which is part of the *Model Standard Valuation Law.* Most companies use CRVM for calculating reserves on new insurance products. According to the CRVM, insurers can use the full preliminary term method to calculate reserves for most life policies. The ***full preliminary term method*** is a modified reserving method according to which the first-year reserve is equal to the end-of-year reserve of a one-year term policy, which is $0. For certain life products with exceptionally high net level annual premiums, the CRVM requires a different modified reserve method that creates a first-year reserve, which is higher than $0 but lower than that created by the net level premium approach.

Reserving practices for accident and health insurance appear in the NAIC's *Minimum Reserve Standards for Individual and Group Health Insurance Contracts.* For noncancelable and guaranteed renewable

DI products, insurers may use the two-year full preliminary term reserve, which allows the insurer to maintain a $0 reserve for the policy's first two years. Modified reserving methods apply only to life and DI insurance products under statutory accounting for U.S. life and health insurance companies.

Refer again to our previous example concerning the Prominent Life and Health Insurance Company. Suppose that the appropriate modified reserve method permits Prominent to establish a first-year reserve of $0 for the product. Illustrated below are the contrasting changes in capital and surplus produced by the net level premium approach and the modified reserve method:

Net Level Premium Approach	
Assets	**Liabilities**
+$50	+$100
	Capital and Surplus
	–$ 50

Modified Reserve Method	
Assets	**Liabilities**
+$50	+$ 0
	Capital and Surplus
	+$50

In this example, whereas the net level premium approach reduces the insurer's capital and surplus by $50 in the first policy year, the modified reserve method allows capital and surplus to increase by $50 in the first year. After the first year, the modified reserve remains smaller than the net level reserve, but the annual increase in aggregate reserves will be higher under the modified reserve method. However, as the years pass, the difference between the reserves calculated by the two methods grows smaller and the modified reserve approaches the net level reserve.

Limiting Surplus Strain under GAAP

Under U.S. GAAP, insurers cannot use modified reserve methods. Instead, GAAP limits surplus strain by permitting insurers to amortize (spread) first-year expenses over several years. When an insurer amortizes first-year expenses, only a portion of these expenses appears on the insurer's income statement for the year the expenses occur. In the next year, another portion of the amortized expenses appears on the insurer's income statement, and so on in future years until all the expenses in question have been recognized. Note that the insurer must still pay all first-year expenses in the first year. However, the insurer need not recognize all the expenses in its statement of operations for that year.

When amortizing first-year expenses under GAAP, U.S. insurers create an asset account called *deferred policy acquisition costs*

(DPAC). Recall from Chapter 8 that DPAC is a U.S. GAAP accounting tool that enables an insurer to amortize its first-year expenses that are directly related to a product type. The use of a DPAC asset in effect permits an insurer to defer the recognition of costs that the insurer has already paid. In the year that the first-year expenses are incurred and paid, the insurer increases the DPAC account by an amount equal to the portion of the expenses that is being deferred until a later year. In each succeeding year, the insurer decreases the DPAC account by the amount of deferred expenses recognized in that year. The effect of this process is that an insurer's first-year acquisition expenses gradually affect an insurer's capital and surplus, rather than all at once in the policy's first year. In this way, an insurer can reduce or eliminate surplus strain.

When analysts examine an insurer's reserves to evaluate its strength, they generally pay attention not only to the insurer's GAAP reserves, but also to its *net GAAP reserves*. ***Net GAAP reserves*** equal the insurer's GAAP policy reserves minus the insurer's deferred policy acquisition costs, as stated in the following equation:

Net GAAP Reserves = GAAP Policy Reserves – DPAC

Net GAAP reserves are similar to modified statutory reserves in that both types of reserves represent the insurer's policy liabilities modified by an allowance for the high cost of first-year expenses.

To illustrate, let's return to the example of the Prominent Life and Health Insurance Company. Recall that the first-year premium for the insurer's product was $150 and the first-year expenses were $100. Let's also say that the GAAP first-year reserve is $75.

Without the use of a DPAC account, the sale of this policy would cause the following change in the insurer's assets:

Premium	$150
Expenses	– 100
	$ 50

Therefore, the sale with a first-year GAAP reserve of $75 results in surplus strain of $25, as illustrated below:

Basic Accounting Equation	
Assets	**Liabilities**
+$50	+$75
	Capital and Surplus
	–$25

The $50 increase in assets ultimately results from the excess of premium income (a cash inflow) over expenses (a cash outflow).

By establishing an asset account to identify the amount of first-year expenses that can be deferred to later years, insurers can avoid surplus strain. For example, assume that Prominent can defer to later years $70 of its first-year expenses. Prominent therefore establishes a DPAC account of $70. The following table shows the net change in the insurer's assets caused by issuing this policy:

Premium	$150
Expenses	− 100
DPAC	+ 70
	$120

The change in Prominent's assets is found by subtracting the first-year expenses from the first-year premium, then adding back the DPAC. Therefore, in this example, the sale of the policy creates an increase in assets of $120.

The effect on Prominent's balance sheet of issuing this policy is shown in the following table:

Basic Accounting Equation		
Assets		**Liabilities**
Cash	+$50	+$75
DPAC	+$70	**Capital and Surplus**
		+$45

The value for cash is obtained by subtracting $100 in expenses from $150 in premium income. The increase in assets offsets the increase in Prominent's liabilities of $75, to create an increase in capital and surplus of $45. The net GAAP reserve on this policy in its first year equals the GAAP policy reserve ($75) minus DPAC ($70). Therefore, by subtracting $70 from $75, we calculate a net GAAP reserve for this policy of $5.

Policy Reserves Calculated for Tax Purposes

In both the United States and Canada, an increase in an insurer's policy reserves may be treated as a tax-deductible business expense for federal income tax purposes. However, both countries mandate specific methods for calculating reserves for federal income tax purposes that effectively set a ceiling on the insurer's income tax deduction for increases in reserves. Federal tax law in the United States specifies the same mortality rates required to calculate statutory reserves but a higher interest rate. The higher interest rate means that policy reserves calculated for tax purposes are smaller than statutory reserves. Therefore, the insurer's tax liability is larger than if it had used statutory reserves for this purpose. In Canada, federal tax law specifies a set of assumptions that produce the maximum allowable value for policy reserves calculated for tax purposes, but there are legislative changes underway. The insurer may use actual tax reserves that are equal to or less than the maximum allowable reserves.

Other Types of Reserves

Besides policy reserves and claim reserves, insurers maintain a number of other types of reserves to draw a complete picture of their financial obligations. Among these additional types of reserves are *claim fluctuation reserves, premium deficiency reserves, contingency reserves,* and *asset fluctuation reserves.*

Claim Fluctuation Reserves

One reserve that an insurer establishes to protect itself against unfavorable claims experience is the *claim fluctuation reserve.* This reserve typically applies, under both GAAP and statutory accounting, to group medical insurance policies that have experience ratings, especially to small group health experience that tend to be less predictable than the experience of large groups. Typically, a claim fluctuation reserve enables an insurer to offer a small group relatively stable premium rates in future years. By establishing a claim fluctuation reserve, an insurer thus avoids the situation of distributing policy dividends or refunds one year, only to increase premium rates the next year because of fluctuations in claims from one year to the next.

Premium Deficiency Reserves

In the United States, a policy's *gross premium*—the amount that policyowners pay for a policy—is sometimes lower than the net annual premium used to calculate the statutory policy reserve for a block of life insurance policies. In this situation, statutory accounting requires the insurer to hold a separate reserve, known as a *premium deficiency reserve,* in addition to the policy's regular reserve. Insurers typically are not required to hold premium deficiency reserves for their A&H insurance policies because of the nature of claim reserves and claim liabilities established for ongoing A&H insurance claims. Because the PPM uses gross premiums to calculate policy reserves, Canadian insurers do not have to establish premium deficiency reserves.

To understand the necessity of premium deficiency reserves, look again at the prospective formula for policy reserves:

Policy Reserve	=	Present Value (PV) of Future Benefits	–	Present Value (PV) of Future Net Premiums

If the net premium is larger than the gross premium, then the insurer will calculate the policy reserve by substituting the net premium with the gross premium in the above formula. The resulting statutory policy reserve will be larger as a result of this substitution.

In the United States, two highly correlated circumstances commonly lead to the situation where gross premiums are smaller than valuation net premiums:

1. For some highly competitive products, such as term insurance, competition sometimes drives gross premiums so low that they are less than statutory net premiums, because the insurer believes that actual experience will be more favorable than the estimates used to determine statutory net premiums and reserves.

2. Sometimes the legally prescribed mortality table used to determine reserves shows mortality rates considerably higher than those the company expects to experience. When the mortality rates used for setting reserves are higher than those used for pricing, the statutory net premium may be larger than the gross premium.

The second situation occurs when the statutory valuation mortality table has been in use for a considerable number of years and is out of date. Most states periodically update statutory mortality tables to reduce the necessity of establishing premium deficiency reserves, which ultimately result in higher policyowner premiums.

Contingency Reserves

Contingency reserves are reserves created by U.S. insurers as a cushion against various special risks. The purpose of contingency reserves is to supplement the insurer's reserve liabilities. Insurers usually set up some contingency reserves voluntarily, whereas others are mandatory. For example, an insurer can establish a contingency reserve

Figure 9-11. Common types of contingency reserves.

Type of Contingency Reserve	Purpose
Group contingency reserve	Provides a reserve for greater-than-anticipated losses caused by an unusual concentration of risk under a group program. Some states require group contingency reserves.
Group annuity contingency reserve	Absorbs losses in the general account from increased longevity among group annuitants.
Participation in separate accounts	Absorbs increases in future actual expenses, as compared to the expense charge assumed in the guarantees of separate account variable annuities.
Mortality fluctuation reserve	Absorbs unusual deviations in assumed mortality or unusual losses from such causes as war or epidemics, usually for individual policies as opposed to group contracts. These reserves can cover fluctuations in the general account, separate accounts, or both.
Contingency reserve for large risks	Absorbs the effect of paying claims insured under large policies that an insurer has not reinsured.
Special contingency reserve	Provides for paying the costs caused by various unforeseen events.

to pay for any unexpected monetary awards resulting from litigation against the insurer. An important difference between an insurer's other reserves and its contingency reserves is that contingency reserves are surplus accounts, not liabilities. Therefore, they also may be called *special surplus, assigned surplus, appropriated surplus,* or *earmarked surplus.* Contingency reserves occur only in statutory accounting, as GAAP specifically disallows contingency reserves. Moreover, contingency reserves are not deductible from an insurer's taxable income. Figure 9-11 describes several common types of contingency reserves.

Asset Fluctuation Reserves

The reserves we have discussed to this point relate to the insurer's obligations to its policyowners arising from its products in force. In the United States, insurers also must establish two statutory reserves to absorb gains and losses in the insurers' invested assets. These two reserves are the *interest maintenance reserve (IMR)* and the *asset valuation reserve (AVR).* Neither the IMR nor the AVR, which we introduced in Chapter 6, is allowed under U.S. GAAP or Canadian GAAP.

Sometimes an insurer gains or loses money on an asset when the insurer sells the asset and *realizes* a higher or lower price than the asset's book value. When an insurer sells an investment at a price higher than the asset's book value, the difference is a *capital gain*. Selling an asset for less than its purchase price results in a *capital loss*. Capital gains and losses are determined by calculating the difference between an asset's book value and its market value. On an insurer's balance sheet, capital gains and losses either increase or decrease the insurer's assets. The insurer must balance the change in assets with a change in either liabilities or capital and surplus. If capital gains and losses were allowed to affect an insurer's capital and surplus accounts, then, under certain circumstances, the insurer's capital and surplus might be subject to considerable short-term fluctuations, which most likely would not accurately represent the insurer's overall financial condition. Therefore, under U.S. statutory accounting, capital gains and losses are instead reflected in the IMR and the AVR. These two reserves act as a buffer for the insurer's capital and surplus, causing capital and surplus to be affected only gradually by capital gains and losses. Thus, these two reserves help to ensure the stability of an insurer's capital and surplus accounts. Insight 9-1 offers a discussion regarding how reserves are assessed in the AVR.

Interest Maintenance Reserve

As noted in Chapter 6, the *interest maintenance reserve (IMR)*, which is a liability account, helps to absorb realized capital gains and losses caused by changes in interest rates. A capital gain or loss is *realized* when the insurer sells an investment. A capital gain or loss remains *unrealized* as long as the insurer holds the investment. The IMR reflects only those interest rate–related realized gains and losses on bonds, preferred stock, and mortgages, because these asset types are most directly and explicitly influenced by changes in interest rates. When interest rates rise, the value of these asset types generally falls. When interest rates fall, the value of these asset types generally rises. Capital gains caused by interest rate changes increase the IMR, whereas capital losses caused by interest rate changes decrease the IMR.

After an insurer posts to the IMR realized capital gains and losses on an investment, the insurer *amortizes* the gains and losses through income against its capital and surplus for the remaining original term of that investment. The insurer then transfers a portion of each capital gain or loss from the IMR to capital and surplus each year until, at the date the investment would have matured, the insurer has transferred the entire gain or loss to capital. In this way, these types of capital gains and losses affect capital and surplus gradually, as if the insurer had held the investment until maturity. Therefore, the capital and surplus account is more stable than it would be without the IMR.

In Canada, as in the United States, capital gains and losses caused by interest rate changes are amortized into capital and surplus

Insight 9-1 GAO Hits Asset Valuation Reserve

The National Association of Insurance Commissioners' asset valuation reserve (AVR) offers little or no assurance that reserves are sufficient to cover losses on risky and troubled assets, according to a new report by the General Accounting Office.

GAO said both the AVR and the interest maintenance reserve (IMR) are designed to buffer insurance company reported capital from fluctuations in the market value of assets.

"By delaying the impact of credit-related investment losses on capital, the AVR masks the impact of losses for insurers with deteriorating investments," GAO said.

Like the mandatory securities valuation reserve (MSVR), GAO said, AVR and IMR can hinder the assessment of an insurer's capital adequacy. GAO noted that AVR and IMR were designed to replace MSVR.

In a letter to GAO, NAIC Executive Vice President David B. Simmons said the authors of the GAO report "have a distinct bias for market-value accounting." This bias taints the analysis. "As the NAIC has made clear on a number of occasions, both to the GAO and in Congressional testimony, market value accounting for all assets of insurers is not in the best interests of insurance consumers," Mr. Simmons added.

GAO acknowledged that the AVR is broader than was MSVR. Unlike the MSVR method that covered only stocks and corporate and municipal bonds, the AVR method extends coverage to mortgages, real estate, and other investments.

"Increasing statutory asset reserves to cover these additional investments is a significant improvement because these types of investments accounted for nearly 20 percent of the reported value of all assets held by life insurers in 1992," GAO said.

Still, it continued, the AVR method does not assure adequate reserves. Since AVR accumulates gradually, an insurer may not build up sufficient asset reserves to cover its losses, GAO said.

Moreover, according to GAO, the AVR formula is unlikely to reflect an individual insurer's risk of loss. In developing the reserve factors for the AVR formula, GAO said, the NAIC assumed that current and future credit risk could be projected from past market behavior.

This assumption may be reasonable for standardized, publicly-traded assets with long histories, GAO said, but for other assets, NAIC uses ad hoc estimates and subjective judgments to set the AVR factors.

The ability of an insurance regulator to intervene when a company is troubled can be hampered by statutory accounting practices designed to buffer insurer's surplus from market fluctuations, GAO said.

Determining when to take corrective action, GAO added, is difficult because AVR does not realistically reflect an insurer's ability to absorb declining asset prices and investment losses.

GAO said that asset reserves should be more closely linked to market values of an individual insurer's risky and troubled assets and should fully reflect investment losses at the time they occur.

But Mr. Simmons argued that it is immaterial to decide precisely what a life insurer's assets are worth today if, in fact, they will not be demanded for use today and will be kept until maturity.

Moreover, Mr. Simmons said, the GAO report looks at AVR and IMR in a vacuum, and ignores the many other tools designed by NAIC to monitor solvency.

Source: Steven Brostoff, "GAO Hits Asset Valuation Reserve," *National Underwriter Life & Health/Financial Services Edition,* No. 25 (June 20, 1994), p. 17. Reprinted with permission from *National Underwriter,* © 1996, The National Underwriter Company, *Life & Health/Financial Services Edition,* 1994.

through net income rather than directly to the capital and surplus account. For Canadian insurers, the *deferred realized gains and losses* is a similar account to the IMR in that capital gains and losses are reflected in a liability account that is amortized into income over time. However, no formal reserve similar to the IMR exists for Canadian insurers. Under U.S. GAAP, an insurer immediately recognizes, instead of amortizes, capital gains and losses in capital and surplus.

Asset Valuation Reserve

In the United States, the *asset valuation reserve (AVR)* is the liability account that absorbs both realized *and* unrealized credit-related capital gains and losses. In Canada, there is no equivalent to the AVR. Instead, credit-related losses are reported on the statement of operations. Whereas the IMR absorbs capital gains and losses caused by interest rate changes, the AVR absorbs changes in the value of assets caused by credit-related factors. Some common examples of credit-related factors that generally decrease an asset's value are as follows:

- The issuer of a bond experiences financial difficulties and ceases paying interest or principal on the bond.
- A mortgage borrower stops making mortgage payments.
- An insurer cannot find renters for an office building held as a real estate investment.
- A stock issuer experiences unfavorable financial circumstances or goes bankrupt.

Although these are all examples of how an asset can decline in value, the market value of assets may also increase for credit-related reasons.

U.S. statutory requirements mandate that credit-related capital gains and losses be reflected, on the right side of the accounting equation, in the AVR. Capital gains increase the AVR, while capital losses decrease the AVR. The AVR has two components—an *equity component* and a *default component.* The equity component reflects an insurer's capital gains and losses on equity investments, such as stocks and real estate. The default component reflects gains and losses on debt investments, such as bonds and mortgages.

At the end of every accounting year, an insurer may be required to increase its AVR by transferring an amount from its capital and surplus accounts. The amount that the insurer transfers from capital and surplus to the AVR depends on the risks associated with the insurer's investments. The riskier the insurer's investments, the larger the AVR the insurer must maintain. Each reporting period, the insurer performs a calculation, based on the risks of its assets, to determine the amount by which it increases its AVR.

Because the AVR is a liability account, a large AVR may restrict an insurer's ability to support new business, to purchase another company, to make dividend payments to stockholders or to policyowners, or to accomplish any of the other purposes for which capital and surplus can be used. Therefore, some insurers seek to reduce the amount of their required AVR to increase the amount of their capital and surplus, and thus increase their strategic and operational flex-

Figure 9-12. Characteristics of certain reserves.

Claim Fluctuation Reserve (Statutory and GAAP)	• Enables the insurer to absorb unexpected claims experience while offering stable premiums to group medical insurance policyholders
Premium Deficiency Reserve (Statutory only)	• Must be established when the valuation net premium exceeds the gross premium
Contingency Reserves (Statutory only)	• Established voluntarily • Serve as a cushion against future adverse experience • Considered a surplus account on the balance sheet
Interest Maintenance Reserve (IMR) (Statutory only)	• Absorbs capital gains and losses on certain investments caused by interest rate changes • Gains and losses must be realized • Covers bonds, mortgages, and preferred stock only • Allows gains and losses to gradually affect the capital and surplus accounts
Asset Valuation Reserve (AVR) (Statutory only)	• Absorbs credit-related capital gains and losses • Absorbs realized *and* unrealized gains and losses • Each year insurers must perform calculations in order to determine whether they must increase their AVR • Allows gains and losses to gradually affect the capital and surplus accounts

ibility. Because an insurer's maximum AVR depends on the risks of its investments, an insurer might decide to restructure its investment portfolio to reduce its risk level. By reducing risk in its investment portfolio, the insurer also reduces the size of its required contributions to the AVR, thus increasing available capital and surplus.

Although the IMR and AVR are liabilities, some analysts, when they assess an insurer's financial strength, consider an insurer's IMR and, even more often, its AVR, to be part of the insurer's adjusted capital and surplus. In this respect, the AVR and IMR are similar to contingency reserves. Figure 9-12 summarizes some of the major characteristics of the types of reserves we have discussed in this section.

Conclusion

In this chapter, we introduced you to an insurer's primary liabilities: reserves. In the next chapter, we discuss other liabilities that insurers maintain besides reserve accounts. We describe the accounting and financial reporting requirements for these liabilities and the relationship between accounting for reserves and accounting for other liabilities.

Key Terms and Concepts

reserves
claim reserves
released reserve
statutory reserves
actuarial assumptions
net level premium approach
prospective method
present value of future benefits
present value of future net premiums
retrospective method
accumulated value of net premiums
accumulated cost of insurance
minimum reserve requirements
provision for adverse deviation
policy premium method (PPM)
scenario analysis
active life reserves
reserves for future contingent benefits
surplus strain
quota share method of reinsurance
experience rating refund
modified reserve method
full preliminary term method
net GAAP reserves
contingency reserves

CHAPTER 10

Accounting for Policy Benefits and Other Liabilities

Learning Objectives

After studying this chapter, you should be able to

- Describe the objectives of accounting for policy benefits
- List the three classifications of policy dividend liabilities
- Describe the types of information included in the master dividend record
- Record the journal entries required for different policy dividend payment options
- Describe the accounting methods for various nonforfeiture options
- List items that are added to or subtracted from the face amount of a life insurance policy to determine the amount of the claim payment
- Describe the different journal entries used for reporting benefit payments for death claims, matured endowments, accident and health insurance, annuities, and supplementary contracts
- Identify and describe an insurer's other liabilities

Chapter Outline

Policy Dividends

Nonforfeiture Options

Claim Settlements

Annuity and Supplementary Contract Payments

Other Liabilities

Financial Reporting Requirements

Recall that an insurer's liability accounts typically consist of reserves, payables, and other liabilities. In Chapter 9, we discussed how insurers account for their various reserves. In this chapter, we discuss an insurer's other liabilities. Generally, the objectives of accounting for an insurer's policy benefits and other liabilities are to

- Record all policy benefit payments after proper payment authorization
- Maintain a historical record of all policy benefit payments
- Provide an audit trail from the point of disbursement authorization to accounting entry to the relevant account and policyowner master file
- Provide data that can help an insurer calculate its unpaid policy liabilities

An insurer uses most of its income to meet current and future obligations to policyowners. These obligations include the payment of policy benefits and supplementary contract benefits. Policy and contract benefits can be one of four categories:

1. Policy dividends
2. Nonforfeiture options
3. Claim settlements
4. Annuity and supplementary contract payments

Besides these four major categories of benefit liabilities, an insurance company must account for a number of other liabilities, which we discuss at the end of this chapter. Figure 10-1 highlights the other liabilities section of a typical insurer's balance sheet.

Policy Dividends

Recall that an insurer's actuaries determine policy premiums using actuarial assumptions for mortality and morbidity rates, interest rates, and expenses. However, when actual experience is more favorable

Figure 10-1. Highlight of the other liabilities section of a typical insurance company balance sheet.

December 31, 19XX

Assets		**Liabilities and Capital Surplus**	
Invested assets:		**Liabilities:**	
Bonds	xxx	Policy reserves:	
Mortgage loans	xxx	Life insurance	xxx
Stocks	xxx	Annuities	xxx
Total Invested Assets	xxx	Accident and health	xxx
		Total Policy Reserves	xxx
Real estate	xxx	Claim reserves:	
Policy loans	xxx	Life insurance	xxx
Investment income due and accrued	xxx	Accident and health	xxx
Cash and cash equivalents	xxx	**Total Claim Reserves**	xxx
Premiums due	xxx	Policy dividends due and unpaid	xxx
Deferred policy acquisition costs (GAAP only)	xxx	Unpaid policy claims	xxx
Reinsurance ceded	xxx	Premium deposits	xxx
Other assets	xxx	Advance premiums	xxx
		Interest maintenance reserve	xxx
Total Assets	5,000,000	Asset valuation reserve	xxx
		Other liabilities	xxx
		Total Liabilities	4,300,000
		Capital and Surplus:	
		Stock	xxx
		Additional paid-in capital	xxx
		Special surplus	xxx
		Unassigned surplus	xxx
		Net unrealized gains (losses)	(xxx)
		Treasury stock	(xxx)
		Total Capital and Surplus	700,000
		Total Liabilities and Capital and Surplus	5,000,000

than expected experience, an insurer can refund money to participating policyowners in the form of *policy dividends.* For example, an insurer can declare a policy dividend if it experiences (1) lower mortality or morbidity experience, (2) lower expenses, or (3) higher interest rates than expected during the fiscal year. Annual dividends on participating policies are generally payable on policy anniversaries after a policy has been in force for one or more years. Recall that a policy dividend represents in part the excess amount of a participating policyowner's premium that was not needed by an insurer for policy expenses. Although mutual insurers primarily issue participating policies, stock insurers can also issue them. Because policy dividends can vary in amount and frequency among policy types, insurers typically account separately for each block of participating policies. Insight 10-1 offers some interesting statistics regarding policy dividends.

An insurer's board of directors has the authority to declare a policy dividend if the insurer's experience indicates that participating policy earnings are sufficient to maintain the required amount of surplus and have enough funds remaining to distribute policy dividends. The board decides the specified amount of the insurer's surplus and approves the method of calculating policy dividends. The board's resolution authorizing the payment of policy dividends usually applies to policies with anniversaries within a certain calendar period. The total amount of policy dividends payable in each upcoming year is contingent upon the number of policies still in force on their anniversary dates. For this reason, the amount of policy dividends payable that an insurer reports in the Annual Statement or Annual Return is necessarily an estimate provided by the insurer's actuaries. The insurer does not know what its experience will be until after the end of the year, so it cannot determine the exact amount of a policy dividend until after December 31. A policy dividend declared in 1998, for example, typically will not be paid to participating policyowners until sometime in 1999. The policy dividend year (1998) and the calendar year (1999) differ, so policy dividends typically are declared payable at a future date.

Policy dividends are relatively small when compared to premiums, especially in the early years that a policy is in force. In later years, however, the policy dividend may be large enough to pay most or all of the premium. Most insurers use dividend schedules to calculate policy dividends and record accounting entries on an aggregate basis to minimize the costs associated with accounting for policy dividends. The policyowner master file contains a policy dividend record. The insurer reviews this record regularly for policies that have a policy anniversary date falling on a defined future day. Shortly before the date that a dividend becomes payable, an insurer's computerized database generates a dividend notice and a current dividend transaction

Insight 10-1 Every Major Mutual Earned Dividends Again in '94

In 1994, for the third consecutive year, after a five-year drought from 1987 to 1991, every major mutual life insurer earned its policyholder dividend scale, aided by reductions in dividend scales to offset falling interest rates.

All 50 U.S. mutual life insurers with more than $450 million in invested assets had operating earnings (before dividends, income taxes, and interest maintenance reserves), which exceeded their total policy dividends paid in 1994.

Technically, Prudential, the largest mutual life insurer, reported an operating loss including its equity in losses of subsidiaries. Excluding its subsidiary losses, Prudential earned its dividend scale in 1994.

In 1987, the mutual life industry incurred $1.3 billion of operating losses in individual and group health and in individual and group annuity lines. Pretax earnings (after policy dividends) fell to $1.4 billion.

In just six years, pretax earnings quadrupled to $6 billion of earnings in the four business lines, which had large losses in 1987. But, pretax earnings retreated to $3.8 billion in 1994.

Pretax return on mean equity exceeded 12 percent each year from 1990 to 1993, but fell to 7 percent in 1994. After-tax return on mean equity exceeded 7.9 percent from 1990 to 1993, but fell to 2.8 percent in 1994, reflecting increasing tax burdens from DAC (deferred acquisition cost) tax and the equity tax, and Pru's large subsidiary losses.

Earnings before policy dividends and taxes peaked at an industry high of $16.2 billion in 1993, then fell 12 percent in 1994 to $14.8 billion.

Despite lower distributable earnings in 1994, policy dividends rose to $10.5 billion, nearly matching the record high of $10.7 billion in 1989 (when Equitable Life, Mutual Benefit and Fidelity Mutual were existing mutuals).

The ratio of pretax earnings (retained by mutual life insurers) to policy dividends (paid to policyholders) rose from 14.7 percent in 1987 to 57.9 percent in 1993, as mutual life insurers retained earnings to improve their ratings and capital ratios, but fell to 35.9 percent in 1994.

Mutual life insurers increased their capital ratio from 7.2 percent in 1990 to 10 percent in 1993, falling back to 9.6 percent in 1994 when surplus funds rose only $36 million while invested assets rose by $20 billion.

The number of mutual life insurers fell 39 percent, from 171 in 1953 to 105 on December 31, 1994. Since 1994, State Mutual Life Assurance and Guarantee Mutual have both demutualized, and New England Mutual and Connecticut Mutual are due to merge into Metropolitan and MassMutual, respectively.

Demutualizations, mergers, sales of business lines, and joint ventures will continue to occur, not only to survive current conditions, but also to achieve efficient expense ratios and offer competitive products, whether reflected in product prices or policy dividend scales.

Aggregate policy dividends reflect changes in dividend scales, changes in sales mix, and changes in the age of in-force business. Thus, changes in aggregate policy dividends do not necessarily reflect corresponding changes in a company's dividend scales.

For the third consecutive year, a majority 72 of 101 mutuals (71 percent) earned their aggregate policy dividends during each of the last five years (1990 to 1994), the highest ratio in the last eight years.

Excluding 37 smaller mutuals (with nominal dividends), 53 of 64 large dividend-paying mutuals (83 percent) earned their dividends in all five years (1990 to 1994.)

Aggregate policy dividends were earned in all years (1990 to 1994) by 100 percent of 16 companies with increasing aggregate dividends, by 84 percent of 25 companies with relatively constant aggregate dividends, and by 70 percent of 23 companies with decreasing aggregate dividends.

Only 19 of 37 small mutuals (51 percent) earned their dividends in all five years (1990 to 1994), unchanged from 1993, but a sharp improvement over ratios of 19, 22 and 41 percent, respectively, for five-year periods ending 1990 to 1992.

Only 16 of 64 large dividend-paying mutuals experienced a *rising* trend in their aggregate policy dividends from 1990 to 1994, and earned their dividends in all five years.

Companies in this category with over $1 billion of total surplus (surplus, AVR and IMR) include Guardian Life, John Hancock, Metropolitan, Mutual of Omaha, New York Life, Northwestern Mutual and Principal Mutual.

Smaller companies in this category include American Mutual, Berkshire Life, General American, Indianapolis Life, Lafayette Life, Minnesota Mutual, Mutual Trust, Phoenix Home Life and Standard Insurance Co.

Twenty-five of 64 major companies paid relatively *constant* aggregate dividends from 1990 to 1994, and 22 of the 25 companies had surplus funds under $300 million. This may reflect the inability of

(continued)

Insight 10-1 Every Major Mutual Earned Dividends Again in '94, continued

smaller companies to maintain dividend scales, or generate in-force growth.

Four of the 25 companies with relatively constant aggregate policyholder dividends, from 1990 to 1994, failed to earn their dividends in at least one year. State Life Ins. Co. failed to earn its dividends in three of the last five years, but addressed its problems by forming a strategic allegiance with American United in 1994.

Twenty-three of 64 major companies had a downward trend in aggregate dividends from 1990 to 1994, which may reflect a change in business mix, termination of older policies, or a reduction in dividend scales. Twelve of the 23 companies have less than $300 million of surplus funds.

Seven of the 23 companies had pretax operating earnings before policy dividends that were less than policy dividends in at least one year, including State Life Ins. Fund (four years), Unity Mutual (three years), and New England Mutual (two years).

Certain companies, such as New England, have a policy of funding part of their surplus growth and dividends from capital gains. Thus, policy dividend payments could be "earned" despite incurring pretax operating losses.

Source: Adapted from Frederick S. Townsend, "Every Major Mutual Earned Dividends Again in '94," *National Underwriter Life & Health/Financial Services Edition,* No. 4 (January 22, 1996), pp. 4, 20, and 22. Reprinted with permission from *National Underwriter,* © 1996, The National Underwriter Company, *Life & Health/Financial Services Edition,* 1996.

record for each policy's dividend record. The insurer records accounting entries for the total dollar amount of all dividends being applied under each dividend option. After paying a dividend or applying it under an option, the insurer updates the dividend record to provide a detailed history of each policy's dividend transactions. The insurer uses this file to

- Prepare summaries of dividend transactions by state and province for financial reporting purposes
- Prepare lists by policy numbers and branch offices for tracing dividend disbursements in case a policyowner should question whether he or she was sent a dividend
- Facilitate audits by regulatory authorities
- Report interest credited on policy dividends for income tax purposes

Figure 10-2 summarizes the types and uses of data included in the policy dividend record.

Policy Dividend Liabilities

Insurers in the United States must disclose in the Annual Statement how they calculate policy dividends. An insurer includes in the

Figure 10-2. Policy dividend record.

Type of Data	Use of Data
Dividend calculation data, including plan, issue age, amount, and duration of the policy	To calculate the dividend payable each year
Dividend payment data, including policy number, name of policyowner, dividend option elected, amount of dividend, and amount of paid-up additions available	To prepare checks, accounting entries, and dividend notices to the policyowner
Balances held under each option	To determine policy status and liability
History of dividends paid or applied under each option	To provide an audit trail and to respond to policyowner inquiries

Summary of Operations any changes in dividend liabilities between valuation dates. The *Insurance Companies Act* requires Canadian insurers to itemize policy dividends and experience rating refunds on life insurance policies for both participating and nonparticipating policies in the Annual Return. For older policies, Canadian insurers also itemize the amount of current dividends deposited to segregated funds. Recall that *segregated funds* apply to those investments that do not arise from money collected from sales of a company's guaranteed life insurance products. An insurer's liabilities for policy dividends include (1) dividends due and unpaid, (2) dividends payable in the following year, and (3) dividend accumulations. We discuss dividend accumulations under policy dividend payment options.

Policy Dividends Due and Unpaid

Policy dividends due and unpaid are those dividends that were declared by an insurer's board of directors during the year, but that have not yet been paid as of the current financial statement date. For insurance policies that have a monthly premium mode, and for which policyowners have elected to have policy dividends applied to reduce their premiums, insurers typically hold the excess policy dividends and apply them to the next month's premium payment, rather than send the policy dividend to the policyowner. An insurer must establish a liability for policy dividends due and unpaid whenever the policyowner has earned the dividend but has not yet received it or applied it to a dividend option. The typical accounting entry is a debit to Policy Dividends Payable and a credit to Policy Dividends Due and Unpaid:

Policy Dividends Payable	xxx	
Policy Dividends Due and Unpaid		xxx

To record the establishment of estimated policy dividends payable.

Recall that, although an insurer's board of directors can declare a policy dividend at any time, policy dividends are payable on all in-force policies on the policy anniversary date. Under statutory accounting, the insurer reports the entire projected dollar amount of the policy dividend as a liability on the Annual Statement. Under GAAP, however, the insurer reports only that portion of the estimated policy dividend that applies to the reporting period. For example, on October 1, 1997, an insurer's board declares a policy dividend payable on March 31, 1998, the policy anniversary date. The projected amount of the policy dividend is $100,000. In this case, the insurer reports the entire $100,000 as part of its policy dividend liabilities on the 1997 Annual Statement. However, on the insurer's 1997 GAAP-based financial statements, the policy dividend liability is $75,000 ($100,000 × 9/12), which covers the period from April 1, 1997, through December 31, 1997. Below is a timeline that depicts how the insurer reports this policy dividend liability under statutory accounting and GAAP:

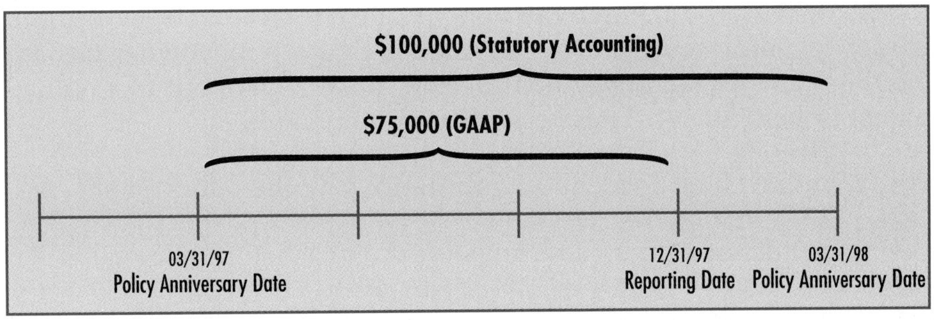

Policy Dividends Payable in the Following Year

Policy dividends payable in the following year, also called *apportioned dividends,* are the estimated amount of all policy dividends that an insurance company's board of directors has declared that are payable in the following year. The insurer's actuaries estimate the amount of this liability because the insurer does not yet know which policies will remain in force on their anniversary dates. Typically, the insurer estimates dividends payable for the entire year, even if the policy anniversary date occurs earlier than December 31. *Policy dividends due and unpaid* apply to the current year. These dividends have met all the criteria for payment, and the exact dollar amount of the dividends is known. On the other hand, *policy dividends payable* apply to the following year, and the exact dollar amount of the insurer's liability is unknown because the payment of a policy dividend depends on whether the policy is in force on its anniversary date, which occurs after the Annual Statement date.

Policy Dividend Payment Options

Five alternatives, called ***policy dividend payment options*** or *dividend payment options,* enable participating policyowners to select the manner in which they want their policy dividends disbursed. Policyowners can choose to have their policy dividends

- Paid in cash
- Applied to reduce the premium due on the policy
- Left with the company to accumulate at interest
- Applied to purchase paid-up additions to the policy
- Applied to purchase one-year term insurance (known as the fifth dividend option)

If any portion of the policy dividend remains after it has been applied to one option, the insurer can apply the balance to another option. Under certain circumstances, dividends that a policyowner has applied under a dividend payment option must be paid out to a policyowner or beneficiary. These circumstances include

- Withdrawal of dividend accumulations by the policyowner
- Surrender of paid-up additions for their cash surrender value
- Termination of the policy by surrender, by death, or as a paid matured endowment

An insurer routinely posts accounting entries for the payment of accumulated dividends held under an option and the cash surrender values of paid-up additions. These transactions involve cash, and the total in an insurer's Cash account must always be current in order to maintain an accurate audit trail. The insurer must also adjust the balance in the dividend record. (We discuss the payment of accumulated dividends later in this section.) To record the surrender of paid-up additions (PUA) for which the cash surrender value is $300, an insurer typically records the following journal entry:

Surrenders Paid—PUA	300	
Cash		300

To record the surrender of paid-up additions.

If the policy terminates by death or as a paid matured endowment, the insurer must also place the dividend record for that policy in a terminated status so future policy dividend transactions do not occur. Later in this chapter, we discuss the accounting entries for recording the termination of a policy at maturity or by surrender or death. In this section, we discuss the primary payment options for policy dividends. Because the fifth dividend payment option is less common than the other four and the accounting process is similar to that for paid-up additions, we consider the fourth and fifth dividend options together.

Policy Dividends Paid in Cash

When a policyowner elects to receive a dividend in cash, an insurer typically updates the dividend record and records the appropriate accounting entries upon payment of the policy dividend. A typical accounting entry to record the payment of $500 in policy dividends is

Policy Dividends Paid	500	
Cash		500

To record the payment of policy dividends.

At the end of the reporting year, the insurer records a change in the liability account for policy dividends:

Change in Policy Dividends	xxx	
Policy Dividends Payable		xxx

To record the change in the liability for policy dividends.

Some companies pay terminal policy dividends upon the termination of a policy. A ***terminal policy dividend,*** or *terminal dividend,* is an extra dividend or pro-rata dividend covering the period between the last policy anniversary date and the termination date of the policy. When a policy matures, becomes a final claim, or is surrendered, the insurer pays any terminal dividends in cash. If a policy lapses and the policyowner elects a nonforfeiture option, the insurer can apply the terminal policy dividend to paid-up additions or to another option. Some participating policies pay a terminal policy dividend that consists of part of the undistributed surplus for that block of policies as well as the annual policy dividend. Policies with this feature may have a terminal dividend that could be as much as $35 per $1,000 of face amount per policy.

Policy Dividends Applied to Pay Premiums

When a policyowner uses a dividend to reduce the policy premium, the insurer deducts the policy dividend from the premium due to determine the amount owed by the policyowner. The insurer records the accounting entry on the policy anniversary date. The policyowner can receive any excess dividend in cash or apply the remainder to another dividend payment option. To record policy dividends applied to pay premiums due, the basic journal entry is a debit to Policy Dividends Applied to Premiums and a credit to Premium Income. Suppose a policyowner owes a quarterly premium of $300 and the insurer declares a $400 dividend that becomes payable at the time the policyowner's premium comes due. If the policyowner wants to apply the dividend to pay the quarterly premium and to receive the balance of the policy dividend in cash, the insurer makes the following journal entry:

Policy Dividends Applied to Premiums	300	
Policy Dividends Payable.	100	
Premium Income		300
Cash		100

To record the application of a policy dividend to pay a current premium and the payment of the balance to the policyowner.

When a dividend is larger than a policy's premium, the policyowner can also apply the unused portion of the dividend to pay subsequent premiums, instead of receiving the balance as a cash payment. In any case, each journal entry should indicate any partial dividends paid to the policyowner or applied to pay premiums in order to provide a clear audit trail. Suppose the policyowner in the above example elects to apply the policy dividend equally to each quarterly premium. In this case, the policyowner would apply $100 for each quarterly premium payment. The quarterly accounting entry for this policyowner's premium payment is

Policy Dividends Due and Unpaid	100	
Cash	200	
Premium Income		300

To record dividends applied to a policy premium.

In this case, the policyowner remits $200, rather than $300, for each quarterly premium payment because $100 of the policy dividend is applied against the quarterly premium. If a policy lapses while a dividend is being held for application under a premium payment option, the dividend is typically applied under a nonforfeiture option in the same manner as a policy dividend paid in cash. We discuss nonforfeiture options in the next section.

Dividend Accumulations

Dividend accumulations result when a policyowner elects to leave policy dividends on deposit at interest with an insurer. The insurer establishes a liability for dividend accumulations and for the accrued interest on those dividends. The insurer also updates the policy dividend record for the current dividend and the accrued interest since the dividend was declared. Interest on policy dividends accrues at a specified rate, which may be stipulated in the policy, plus any additional rate that the insurer may determine. Many insurers record the policy dividend and its accrued interest on the policy anniversary date on which the dividend becomes payable, provided that premiums have been paid to that date. Some insurers record the accounting entry when the policyowner remits the premium payment. A typical entry to record policy dividends left to accumulate at interest is

Policy Dividends Applied to Dividend Accumulations. . .	xxx	
Dividend Accumulations		xxx

To record dividends left to accumulate at interest.

A typical accounting entry to show the amount of interest on dividend accumulations is a debit to Interest on Dividend Accumulations and a credit to Dividend Accumulations. If a policyowner later elects to receive $200 of dividend accumulations, then the insurer makes the following accounting entry to record payment of the dividend accumulations:

Dividend Accumulations.	200	
Cash		200

To record the payment of dividend accumulations.

Policy Dividends Applied to Purchase Additional Insurance

Policyowners can apply their dividends to purchase additional insurance. When a policyowner uses a dividend to purchase paid-up insurance or one-year term insurance, the insurer determines the amount of additional insurance purchased by dividing the dividend by the appropriate net single premium. The insurer can add a rider to the basic policy to indicate the additional insurance coverage or treat paid-up insurance as a separate policy. In either case, the accounting entry to record dividends applied to buy paid-up additions (PUA) is

Dividends to Purchase PUA	xxx	
Single Premiums for PUA		xxx

To record dividends applied to purchase paid-up additions.

Note that the credit for a purchase of paid-up additions is to Single Premiums for PUA, a type of premium income account.

The entry to apply policy dividends to one-year term insurance is similar but the debit and the credit are to One-Year Term Insurance, rather than to Paid-Up Additions. The insurance coverage provided under the fifth dividend option is frequently limited to an amount up to the cash surrender value of the policy. Recall from Chapter 8 that a life insurance policy's *cash surrender value* is the amount, after adjusting for policy loans, premiums due, and other similar factors, that a policyowner will receive if he or she surrenders the policy or allows the policy to lapse. Compare this definition with that of a policy's ***cash value,*** which is the amount stated in the policy, *before* being adjusted for factors such as policy loans or late premiums, that the policyowner will receive if the policyowner allows the policy to lapse or surrenders the policy. The policyowner can also use the fifth dividend option to increase the face value of a term insurance policy. In Canada, applications of either the fourth or fifth policy dividend options are known as ***bonus additions.*** The insurer usually records payments for paid-up additions and one-year term insurance separately to facilitate accounting for tax and financial reporting purposes. A simplified diagram of the process for recording and paying policy dividends is presented in Figure 10-3.

Nonforfeiture Options

When a policy that builds a cash value lapses, the basic insurance contract terminates, except for those rights that the policyowner has under any nonforfeiture options. ***Nonforfeiture options*** are the choices available to a policyowner concerning the methods under which he or she can apply the policy's cash surrender value when the policy expires. Nonforfeiture values may take one of three basic forms: (1) cash surrender, (2) reduced paid-up insurance, or (3) extended term insurance. From an administrative standpoint, many insurers treat cash surrenders as a separate type of nonforfeiture option because no insurance coverage remains under this option. However, we include cash surrender as a nonforfeiture option because it is defined under statute as a nonforfeiture option. The following section presents the accounting procedures for each of these nonforfeiture options. Because the treatment of reduced paid-up and extended term insurance is similar, we discuss these two nonforfeiture options together.

Cash Surrender

When a policyowner decides to terminate his or her policy and has elected the cash surrender value option, insurance protection stops and the insurer calculates the cash surrender value owed to the policyowner. The insurer then remits this amount to the policyowner, and the company has no further obligation under the policy. The basic journal entry to record the surrender is

Surrenders Paid	xxx	
Cash		xxx

To record a policy cash surrender.

Figure 10-3. Process for recording and paying policy dividends.

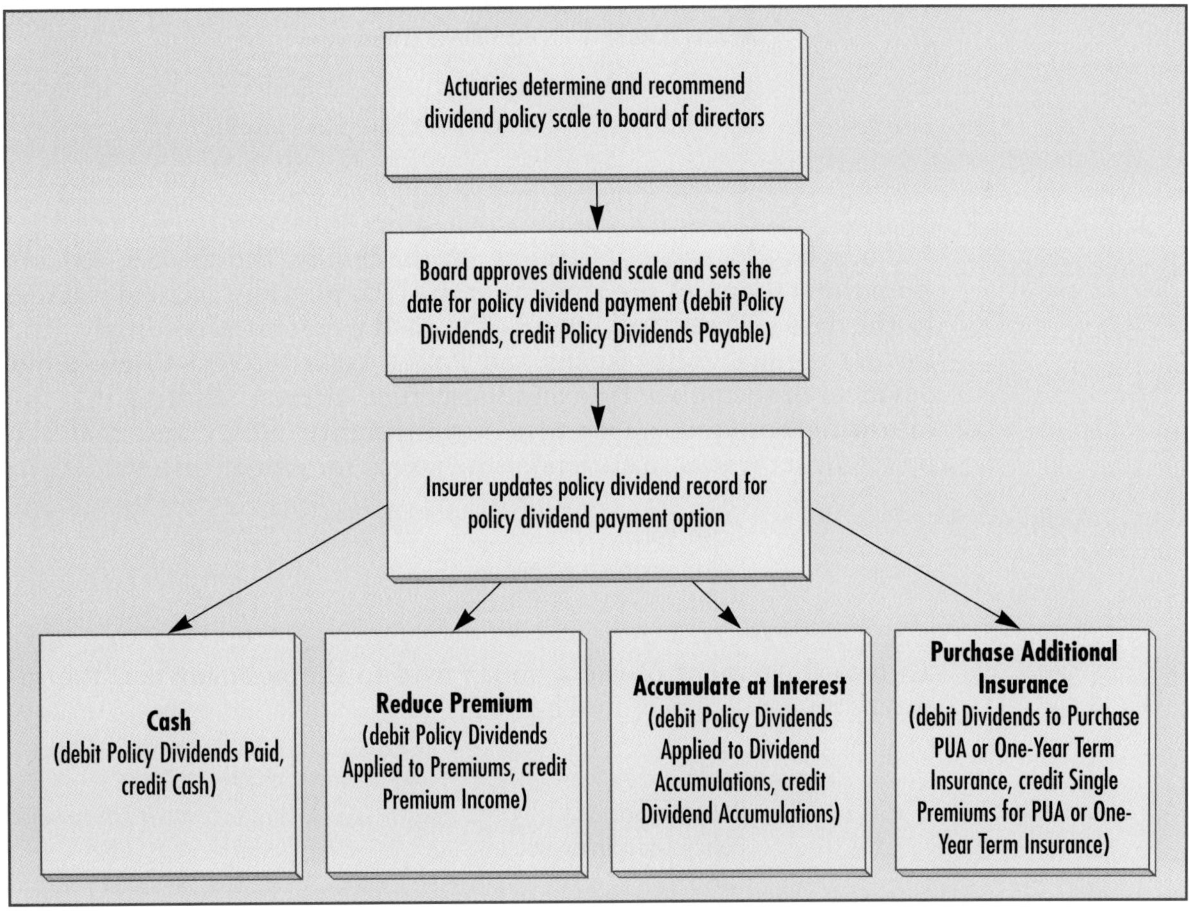

The insurer would typically maintain accounting records for surrenders paid by product type, such as Surrenders Paid—Ordinary, and by participating or nonparticipating policies.

The debit to Surrenders Paid typically decreases the company's surplus because it immediately increases benefits paid, thereby reducing net income. However, a change in the liability for policy reserves occurs simultaneously. As a result, the net effect on surplus is very small or slightly positive because the decrease in surplus from the payment is offset by an increase in surplus resulting from the reserve released. For example, if a policyowner surrenders a policy with a cash surrender value of $3,200, and the reserve released for this policy totals $3,400, then the net effect on surplus is a $200 increase in surplus, all other factors remaining equal. Recall, however, that insurers do not usually make accounting entries each time transactions affect policy reserves. Therefore, the changes caused by the reserve released (shown in the simplified balance sheet that follows) will not be recorded until the insurer's actuaries calculate actual reserves at the end of the accounting period.

Simplified Balance Sheet	
Assets (Cash)	**Liabilities (Reserves)**
–$3,200	–$3,400
	Capital and Surplus (Surplus)
	$ 200

If a policy loan is outstanding on the policy, the insurer deducts from the settlement the amount of the loan plus any accrued interest to the date of lapse and reduces the cash payment accordingly. The insurer credits Policy Loans and Policy Loan Interest to close out payment of the policy loan and its accrued interest. Assume that the following amounts apply to a life insurance policy and that the policyowner wants to surrender the policy for its net cash value:

Cash Value	500
Policy Loan Outstanding	115
Policy Loan Interest Accrued	15

To record payment of the amount paid to the policyowner, the insurer's journal entry would be

	Debit	Credit
Surrenders Paid	500	
Policy Loans		115
Policy Loan Interest		15
Cash		370

To record the payment paid to the policyowner upon policy surrender.

The credit to Cash in this example is the amount paid to the policyowner. If the policyowner had left dividends to accumulate with the insurer, the amount payable to the policyowner would be the policy's cash value plus the amount of the dividend accumulations and their accrued interest, minus policy loans and policy loan interest. If paid-up additions apply to a surrendered policy, the insurer adds the cash value of these additions to the cash cash value of the policy.

Policy loans, dividends, and paid-up additions affect a policy's cash surrender value. Assume that the cash value of a policyowner's ordinary policy is $3,200, the cash value of $100 in paid-up additions is $60, dividend accumulations are $532, and a $2,000 policy loan and $10 of policy loan interest are outstanding. The insurer calculates the total amount payable to this policyowner upon surrender of the policy as follows:

	Cash value of the policy	$3,200
plus	Cash value of the paid-up additions	60
plus	Dividend accumulations	532
	Total	$3,792
minus	Policy loan	2,000
minus	Policy loan interest	10
	Net Payable to Policyowner (cash surrender value)	$1,782

The entry to record this payment would be

Surrenders Paid—Ordinary	3,260	
Dividend Accumulations	532	
Policy Loans		2,000
Policy Loan Interest		10
Cash		1,782

To record the cash surrender of a life insurance policy.

Reduced Paid-Up or Extended Term Insurance

In applying the reduced paid-up or extended term insurance nonforfeiture options, a policyowner receives an equivalent value in the form of paid-up term or extended term insurance, paid-up whole life insurance, or paid-up endowment insurance. When a policy continues under one of these options, with no dividend accumulations or loans outstanding, the insurer need not make an accounting entry. The transaction is simply a transfer of the policy's reserve liability from a premium-paying classification to a paid-up insurance classification. However, the insurer does update the policyowner master file with this information. The insurer makes accounting entries only if there were dividend accumulations or an outstanding policy loan at the time of surrender. For example, if an ordinary policy has a $2,000 cash value, and a $750 outstanding policy loan with $40 interest accrued at the time of surrender, the entry to record the repayment of the policy loan would be

Surrenders Paid—Ordinary	790	
Policy Loans		750
Policy Loan Interest		40

To record the payment of a policy loan.

With this entry, the insurer closes out the policy loan and policy loan interest accounts for this policy before the policyowner converts

Figure 10-4. The accounting process for recording nonforfeiture benefits.

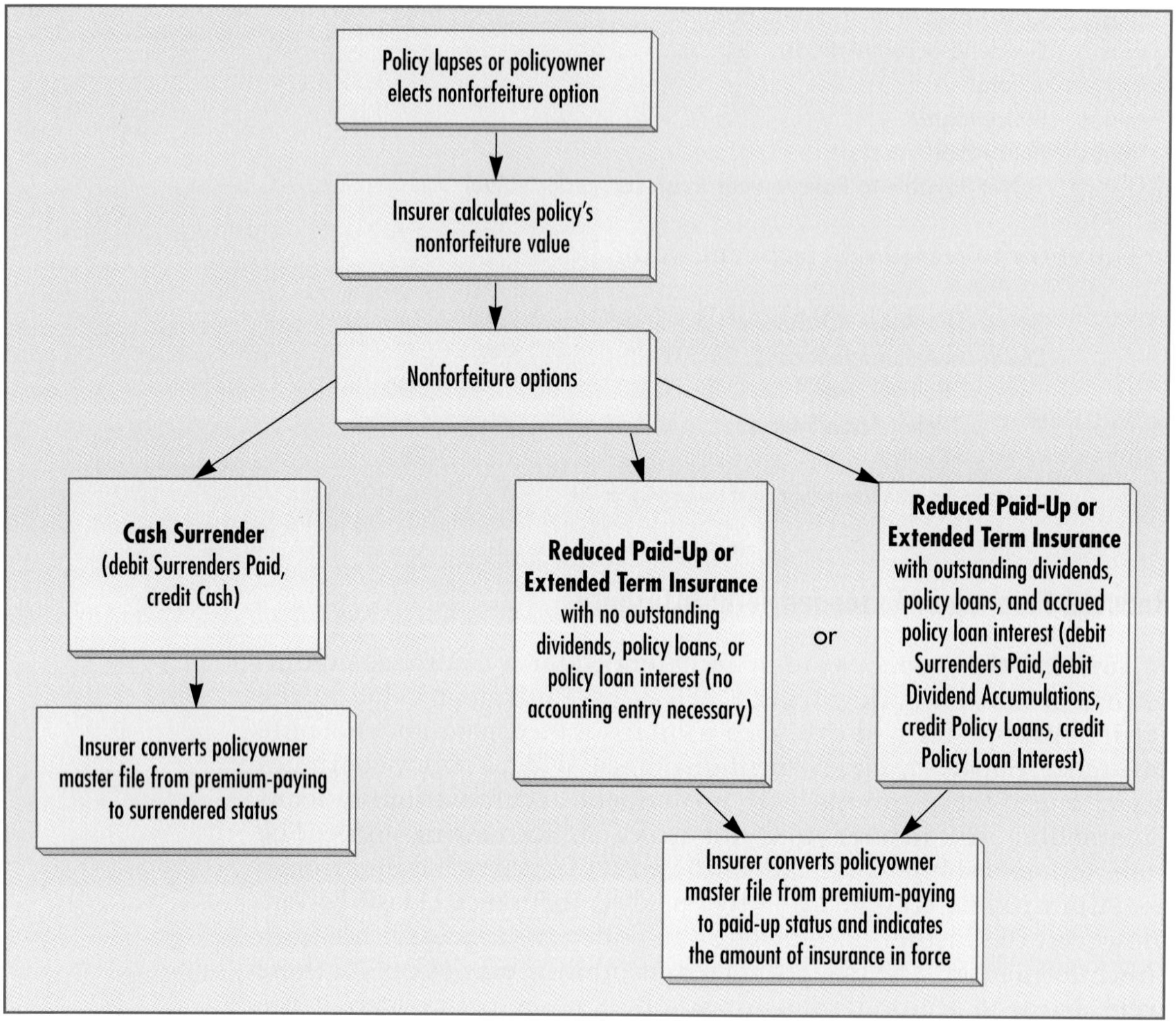

the policy to term insurance. In this example, the cash surrender value applied to the nonforfeiture option is $1,210 ($2,000 cash value minus $790 applied to the repayment of the policy loan and interest). No entry is required for the application of the $1,210 toward establishing a reserve. Concurrently with the entries for nonforfeiture transactions, the insurer converts the policyowner master file from premium-paying status to paid-up status. A simplified flowchart summarizing the procedure for recording nonforfeiture benefits is presented in Figure 10-4.

Claim Settlements

Claims are defined as requests for payments under the terms and conditions of life and A&H insurance policies. Payments on annuities and supplementary contracts, however, are called ***contract payments.*** In this section, we discuss accounting and financial reporting for claim settlements and contract payment liabilities associated with life and A&H insurance policies. Because the amounts of both claims and contract payments are often quite large, insurers carefully examine requests for these payments and approve the claims before disbursement. In many companies, a claim examiner, who is a specialist in investigating claims and is thoroughly familiar with various policy and contract provisions, is the person authorized to approve claim payments. Thus, cooperation between an insurer's claim and accounting functions is critical to timely and accurate claims settlement.

Many insurance companies record journal entries for claim settlements upon approval of the claim. If the policyowner or beneficiary leaves the proceeds with the insurer under a settlement option, the insurer records the accounting entry as soon as it establishes the amounts and conditions of the settlement contract. However, some companies establish a liability for a claim when they receive notice of the claim. A company that has reinsured the risk will simultaneously establish an asset for amounts due from reinsurance companies for outstanding claims. Throughout this chapter, the journal entries associated with death claims refer to ordinary life insurance, unless otherwise noted. In the following sections, we discuss the primary benefit payments for the two major types of claims: (1) life insurance claims and (2) accident and health insurance claims. Figure 10-5 shows an overview of the claim settlement process with typical accounting entries that an insurer records at each step of the process.

Life Insurance Claims

Most life insurance policies provide for payment of the policy's face amount upon the insured's death. Some life insurance policies also provide annuity benefits, endowment benefits, or have a provision or rider for accidental death and dismemberment (AD&D) benefits. The AD&D provision or rider typically provides for an additional benefit amount only if the insured dies or loses any two limbs or the sight of both eyes as a result of an accident. A smaller benefit amount may cover the loss of one limb or the sight of one eye. A typical accounting

Figure 10-5. An overview of the claim settlement process.

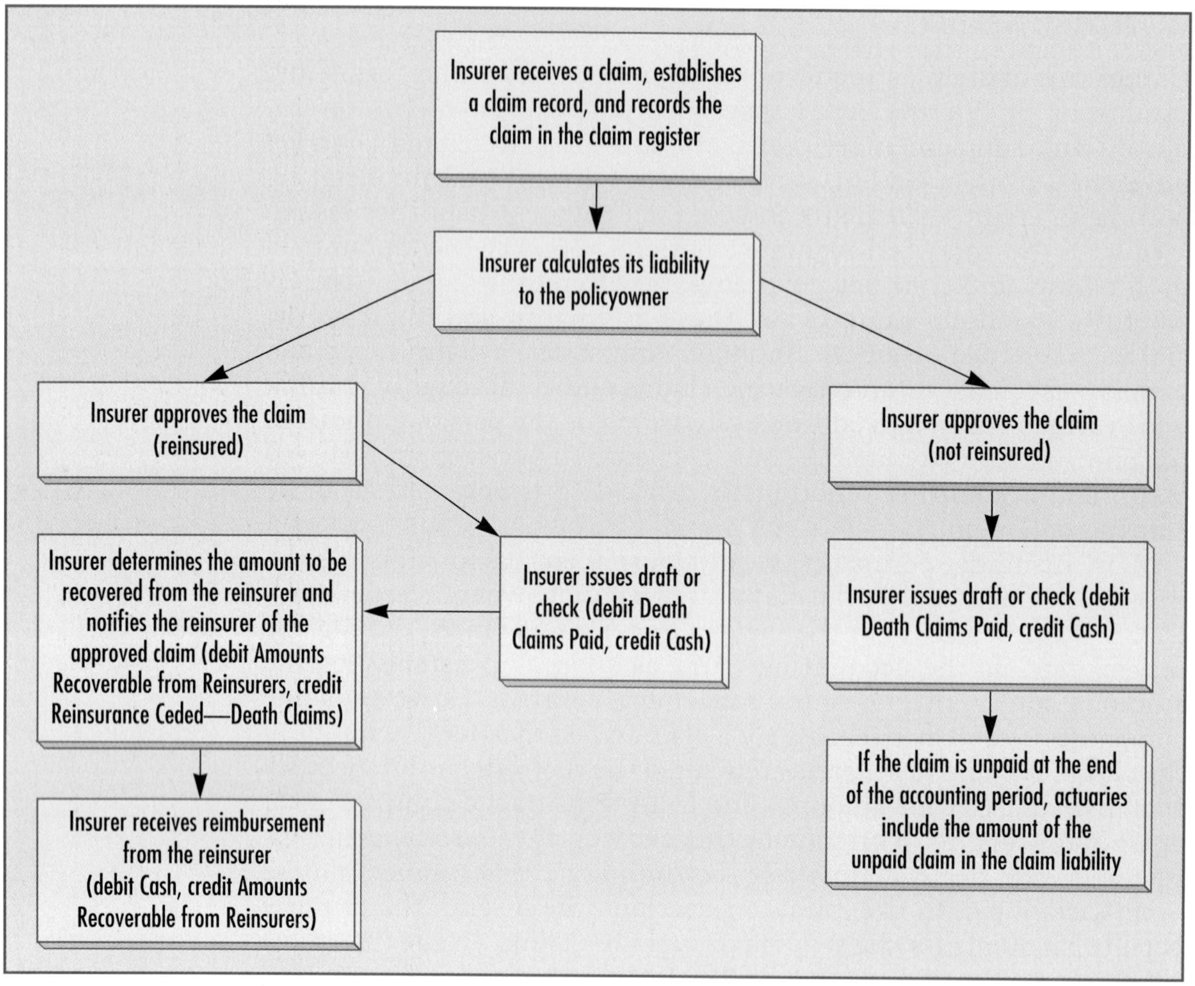

entry for accidental death benefits is a debit to Death Claims Paid, a debit to AD&D Benefits Paid, and a credit to Cash. Although the life insurance policy would terminate upon the death of the insured, the policy would remain in force if the insurer paid a claim against the policy's AD&D rider during the lifetime of the insured. The basic accounting entry to record this transaction is a debit to AD&D Benefits Paid—Ordinary and a credit to Cash.

Universal life insurance products may provide a benefit larger than the policy's face amount. Further, an insurer can make other adjustments to the amount payable to the beneficiary. As a result, the actual amount of death benefit payable often differs from the policy's face amount. The amount of an insurer's liabilities for claims reported in the financial statements usually equals the aggregate amount of all claims. Through debits and credits to other accounts, such as a *claims clearing account,* the insurer makes adjusting entries to the aggregate claim amount. Examples of adjustments that affect the amount of proceeds payable under a death claim appear below. Items that an insurer can *add* to the death benefit include

- Return of premiums that have been paid in advance for periods beyond the next policy anniversary
- Return of the balance on deposit in a premium deposit fund
- Paid-up additions that have been purchased by the policyowner
- Return of premiums paid for the balance of the policy year from the date of the insured's death
- Policy dividends currently payable but not yet paid
- Policy dividends left with the insurer to accumulate at interest
- Unearned policy loan interest paid beyond the date of death
- Interest paid on delayed claims

The final item listed above applies in many states, which require that an insurer pay interest on a claim for which the insurer has postponed claim settlement. The interest typically accumulates between the date of death or the date on which the claim should reasonably have been settled and the date of the claim settlement. The insurer pays this interest to the claimant along with the policy proceeds. Items that an insurer can *subtract* from the death benefit include

- Outstanding policy loans
- Accrued policy loan interest at the date of death
- Premiums due and unpaid if death occurs during the grace period
- Accrued or unpaid premiums (deducted by some companies)

Suppose the insured of a $10,000 ordinary life insurance policy died in an accident and that the policy provided for an AD&D benefit equal to the policy's face amount. Assume also that the policy had a $2,000 outstanding policy loan and $10 of policy loan interest due at the time of the insured's death. The journal entry to record the settlement of this policy would be

Death Claims Paid—Ordinary	10,000	
AD&D Claims Paid—Ordinary	10,000	
Policy Loans		2,000
Policy Loan Interest		10
Cash		17,990

To record the settlement of a life insurance policy.

The $17,990 is the insurer's total liability to the beneficiary ($20,000 in death benefits *minus* the $2,000 outstanding policy loan and the $10 in policy loan interest).

Suppose the insured had died during the policy's grace period and a $100 premium was due and unpaid. The accounting entry would have included a credit to Premium Income or Renewal Premiums for $100 because premium payments must be current before the insurer can settle the claim. For the accounting entry to balance, the insurer would decrease the credit to Cash by $100. In case of death during the grace period, the insurer usually deducts the full premium due from the death benefit, but some companies deduct only a pro-rata fractional premium. Others deduct only enough to pay for one month's coverage during the grace period. Many companies refund any portion of the premium paid beyond the date of death. In this case, the insurer debits Premium Income or Renewal Premiums for the refunded amount and increases the credit to Cash by the same amount.

Sometimes the age of the insured is incorrect in the policy application and not discovered until after the death of the insured. In such cases, the insurer calculates the amount of insurance that could have been purchased with the premiums paid at the insured's correct age. Typically, if the insured was older than the age stated in the application, the policy proceeds are lower than the face amount. Similarly, if the insured was younger than stated in the application, then the proceeds would be higher than the policy's face amount.

Adjustments to the face amount of a policy do not always appear in the accounting entries. For example, a reduction in the face amount payable to correct a misstatement of age on the application requires no separate accounting entry. Also, an insurer does not have to record an accounting entry for the settlement of paid-up additions. Instead, the insurer makes both of these adjustments directly to the amount payable, and the insurer includes them in the debit to Death Claims Paid for the product type. Although maintaining a separate claim account is not necessary for the paid-up additions, some insurance companies use a separate claim account to maintain better control of records regarding changes in paid-up additions. Suppose a $5,000 death claim was incurred on an ordinary policy during the policy's grace period. An age adjustment reduced the amount payable to $4,750. The policy had paid-up additions of $100. A terminal cash dividend of $50 was payable, and the current monthly premium due at the time of death was $15. The entry to record payment of this claim would be

Death Claims Paid—Ordinary	4,850	
Terminal Cash Dividend Paid	50	
Renewal Premiums		15
Cash		4,885

To record the payment of a death claim with paid-up additions and a terminal dividend.

Here, the debit to Death Claims Paid—Ordinary includes both the amount of the age-corrected death claim ($4,750) and the amount of paid-up additions ($100). Note also that the insurer could have credited Premium Income, rather than Renewal Premiums, for $15.

A number of other situations can cause the death claim paid to differ from the policy's face amount. An insurer must adjust the amount of death benefit settlement in case of an insured's suicide within the exclusion period. For example, if an insured commits suicide soon after paying $150 as an initial premium and the ordinary policy provides that the company's liability in such a case consists of an amount equal to the premiums paid, the entry is

Return of Premium—Ordinary	150	
Cash		150

To record the return of initial premium because of suicide of the insured.

Alternatively, an insurance company can treat the return of premium as a reversal of the accounting entry the company made upon receipt of the policy premium:

Premium Income	150	
Cash		150

To record a premium reversal because of suicide of the insured.

If an insurer denies a claim presented during the contestable period because of misrepresentation or fraud in the policy application, the policy is considered to be void from its inception. In this case, the insurer must refund all premiums. Assuming the policy was in its first year and the premium paid was $200, the entry would appear as

Premiums—First Year	200	
Cash		200

To record a premium refund because of a voided policy.

Sometimes a policyowner may have obtained an insurance policy by misrepresenting the state of the insured's health. Because the insurer wishes to avoid a lawsuit, the insurer might make a compromise settlement. The entry for a compromise settlement is similar to the entry for the payment of a full death benefit. To record a $2,000 draft or check paid as a compromise settlement of a $5,000 death claim, the entry is

Death Claims Paid—Ordinary	2,000	
Cash		2,000

To record the payment of a compromise settlement.

Suppose the insurer had reinsured $25,000 of a policy with a $100,000 face amount. At the time a claim for death benefits is presented for this policy, the ceding company would debit Amounts Recoverable from Reinsurers and credit Reinsurance Ceded—Death Claims—Ordinary for $25,000 to record this transaction. The ceding company debits Death Claims Paid—Ordinary and credits Cash upon payment of the death claim. When the insurer receives payment from the assuming company, then the insurer makes the following accounting entry:

Cash	25,000	
Amounts Recoverable from Reinsurers		25,000

To record the receipt of reinsurance ceded on an ordinary policy.

Matured Endowments

Endowment insurance policies can exist in an insurer's ordinary, home service, or group lines of business. Generally, *endowment insurance* is a type of life insurance that provides a benefit in either of two instances: (1) if the insured's death occurs before the policy matures or (2) if the insured is living on the policy's maturity date. A ***matured endowment*** is a type of life insurance policy that has reached the end of its term during the lifetime of the insured and is therefore payable.

Under the first condition above, if the insured dies before the endowment period ends, then the insurer pays the death benefit to the policy's beneficiary. The accounting entry to record the payment of a death benefit to the policy's beneficiary is similar to that for death benefits paid under an ordinary life insurance policy. For example, upon paying the death benefit, the insurer debits Death Claims Paid—Matured Endowments—Ordinary or Death Claims Paid—Ordinary for the product type and credits Cash. Suppose the insured of a $10,000 ordinary endowment policy dies before the maturity date of the policy. In this case, the accounting entry is

Death Claims Paid—Matured Endowments—Ordinary	10,000	
Cash		10,000

To record the payment of a death benefit on an endowment policy.

Under the second condition described above, the insured is living on the policy maturity date, so the insurer would pay him or her the endowment amount. A typical accounting entry to record this transaction would be a debit to Matured Endowments for the product type and a credit to Cash. In our example, the accounting entry would be

Matured Endowments—Ordinary	10,000	
Cash		10,000

To record the payment of a matured endowment.

Should the beneficiary of a matured endowment policy elect to use the policy proceeds to purchase a supplementary contract, then the insurer would debit Matured Endowments Paid—Ordinary, as above, and credit Supplementary Contracts instead of Cash, for the amount of the policy proceeds. Had the insurer reinsured $2,000 of the $10,000 face amount, the insurer would pay the full benefit amount, then establish an account receivable for amounts recoverable from reinsurers. Upon receipt of payment from the reinsurer, the insurer would debit Cash and credit Reinsurance Ceded—Matured Endowments—Ordinary for $2,000.

A few policies provide a series of small annual endowments payable to policyowners. These annual endowments are often in the form of coupons attached to policies that the policyowner can apply in a manner similar to policy dividends. Coupons differ from policy dividends, however, in that both the frequency and the payment amount for coupons are guaranteed. Upon payment of these coupons, an insurer debits Matured Endowments Paid and credits Cash. If the policyowner elects to purchase additional insurance with the coupons, rather than make a separate accounting entry for this transaction, an insurer typically transfers the reserve from one form of life insurance to another at the end of the accounting period. This amount is included in the updated reserve amounts provided by the insurer's actuaries at the end of the accounting period for inclusion in the Annual Statement. However, the insurer may make an accounting entry if the policyowner uses the coupon to purchase an annuity in order to record the change in the line of business.

Waiver-of-Premium Benefits

Most life insurance policies contain a waiver-of-premium rider. The ***waiver-of-premium benefit*** provides premium payments to keep a life insurance policy in force should the insured become disabled and incapable of earning income to pay the premium. Some policies also contain a provision for the insured to receive monthly income upon the disability. Disability benefits are also available under accident and health insurance policies, which we discuss later in the chapter. Upon the disability of the insured, an insurer waives the premium due on the policy according to the terms of the rider. The insurer does not receive cash for the premium, as it would if the insured were able to make ongoing premium payments. However, the insurer credits Premium Income for the amount of the premium waived. The insurer also debits an account such as Waiver-of-Premium Benefits. Suppose the insured under a $10,000 ordinary policy with a waiver-of-premium rider becomes disabled. If the premium due is $150, then the insurer would make the following accounting entry:

Waiver-of-Premium Benefits—Ordinary	150	
Premium Income		150

To record the payment of a waived premium.

Accident and Health Insurance Claims

In this text, the terms *health insurance* and *accident and health (A&H) insurance* are interchangeable. Both terms refer to the type of insurance known in the Annual Statement as "accident and health insurance" and in the Annual Return as "accident and sickness insurance." Health insurance claims vary depending on the type of coverage and the company issuing the policy, but they fall into two major categories: (1) disability claims and (2) medical expense claims. The accounting entries for health insurance claims are similar to entries for life insurance claims. A primary difference between A&H benefits and life insurance benefits is that payment of a health claim does not usually terminate the policy, as payment of a death claim does in the case of life insurance policies. Benefit payments for medical services and long-term disability income benefit payments provided to an insured with a chronic illness can continue for many years.

Accident and health insurance policies state the conditions under which an insurer can refuse to accept further premiums, thereby canceling insurance coverage. To avoid cancellation, a policy can contain certain renewability conditions. These renewability conditions are one of four types: (1) *renewable at the option of the company,* (2) *guaranteed renewable,* (3) *collectively renewable,* and (4) *guaranteed renewable and noncancelable.* The company cannot refuse to continue a guaranteed renewable policy but can increase premium rates for all policies in a particular premium class. If a policy is guaranteed renewable and noncancelable, the company cannot cancel insurance, refuse to renew coverage, or increase premium rates. Insurance companies in the United States must show individual health insurance premiums in the Annual Statement by each of these classifications. Premiums for accident-only coverage appear separately. An insurer maintains accounts for claims paid within each of the renewability classifications and within the principal health insurance classifications of disability claims and medical expense claims. Figure 10-6

Figure 10-6. Schedule H—Parts 2 and 3—U.S. Annual Statement.

ACCIDENT AND HEALTH EXHIBIT									
					Other Individual Policies				
	1 Total	2 Group Accident and Health	3 Credit (Group and Individual)	4 Collectively Renewable	5 Non-Cancelable	6 Guaranteed Renewable	7 Non-Renewable for Stated Reasons Only	8 Other Accident Only	9 All Other
PART 2 — RESERVES AND LIABILITIES									
A. Premium Reserves:									
1. Unearned premiums									
2. Advance premiums									
3. Reserve for rate credits									
4. Total premium reserves, current year									
5. Total premium reserves, previous year									
6. Increase in total premium reserves									
B. Policy Reserves:									
1. Additional reserves									
2. Reserve for future contingent benefits (deferred maternity and other similar benefits)									
3. Total policy reserves, current year									
4. Total policy reserves, previous year									
5. Increase in policy reserves									
C. Claim Reserves and Liabilities:									
1. Total current year									
2. Total previous year									
3. Increase									
PART 3 — TEST OF PREVIOUS YEAR'S CLAIM RESERVES AND LIABILITIES									
1. Claims paid during the year:									
a. On claims incurred prior to current year									
b. On claims incurred during current year									
2. Claim reserves and liabilities, December 31, current year:									
a. On claims incurred prior to current year									
b. On claims incurred during current year									
3. Test:									
a. Lines 1a and 2a									
b. Claim reserves and liabilities, December 31 previous year									
c. Line a minus Line b									

depicts the Annual Statement page on which U.S. insurers itemize their reserves and claim liabilities for A&H insurance.

Accident and health insurance policies protect policyowners from losses as a result of (1) loss of income from a disability, whether temporary or permanent, (2) hospital, surgical, and other medical expenses, and (3) accidental death and dismemberment. These policies can be one of three types: group, credit, and other. The "other" classification includes individual A&H insurance policies. Accident and health benefits include payments an insurer makes to the insured directly or to a medical facility or medical professional for expenses caused by an accident or sickness. The typical accounting entry to record payments made to an insured or his or her designated payee is a debit to Accident and Health (A&H) Claims Paid or Disability Income (DI) Insurance Paid and a credit to Cash on the payment date. For example, if an insurer pays $1,000 in medical expenses for an individual accident and health insurance claim, then the accounting entry to record this transaction would be

A&H Claims Paid—Other	1,000	
Cash		1,000

To record the payment of an individual A&H claim.

If the insurer had reinsured 80 percent of its liability over $700 [80 percent of ($1,000 – 700) = $240], then, upon receipt of payment from the reinsurer for the above claim, the insurer would record the following accounting entry:

Cash	240	
Reinsurance Ceded—A&H Claims—Other		240

To record the receipt of A&H reinsurance.

Disability Benefits

Insurers typically offer two types of disability insurance. Disability income (DI) insurance is a form of A&H insurance that provides a monthly income benefit should the insured become disabled as defined in the policy. The other type of DI insurance commonly offered is a waiver-of-premium benefit that specifies that the insurer will not require premium payments as long as the insured remains disabled. When an insured becomes disabled as defined in a DI policy, he or she becomes eligible for a series of payments that will continue until death or recovery from the disability or until the policy benefit limit is reached. A claim examiner determines whether the insured is still disabled by referring to a disability form. Usually a doctor completes the disability form that specifies the approximate recovery date or date on which the insured can return to work. The claim examiner can investigate the claim annually if recovery seems unlikely. A typical entry for a $400 monthly disability payment is

Disability Claims Paid 400
        Cash. 400
To record the payment of a monthly disability income payment.

Earlier we discussed the waiver-of-premium provision under ordinary life policies. For financial reporting purposes, ordinary life insurance premiums that are waived because of the insured's disability are considered claims against the disability sub-line of business and premium income to the life insurance line of business. The amount recorded in the journal entry for a premium waiver is the amount of the gross premium waived. In a U.S. life and health company, a typical entry to record the waiver of a $110 life insurance premium because of disability is

Waiver-of-Premium—Disability 110
        Premium Income—Life. 110
To record the waiver of a life insurance premium because of disability.

Premiums applicable to supplemental coverage, such as premiums for accidental death benefits, are also waived under the disability waiver provision. If the policyowner in the above example also owed a $5 accidental death benefit premium, the insurer would add the amount of this supplemental coverage premium to the debit and credit entries. Thus, with the waiver of the additional $5 premium, the entry would appear as

Waiver-of-Premium—Disability 115
        Premium Income—Life. 115
To record the waiver of life and accidental death benefit premiums because of disability.

The insurer thus credits a revenue account as though the premium had been paid in cash. Some insurers pay commissions on premiums paid through the waiver-of-premium benefit. Canadian insurers typically post accounting entries for premiums waived as a result of disability to a contra account because the Annual Return excludes these amounts from premium income. In the case of A&H insurance provided by an individual policy, the insurer does not need to make an accounting entry for a waiver of premium because both the income and the disbursement are in the same line of business. Many companies, however, do make such an entry to facilitate claim studies. A typical entry for a health insurance waiver would be the same as for ordinary insurance, with only a change of line of business in the account titles. For example, assume that Tom Shepherd owned an individual A&H insurance policy that provided for a waiver of the $75 premium in the case of his disability as defined in the policy. The entry to record this premium waiver would be

Waiver-of-Premium—Disability—Health	75	
Premium Income—Health.		75

To record the waiver of health insurance premium because of disability.

Medical Benefits

Medical expense insurance pays for the cost of hospital room and board, miscellaneous hospital expenses, surgical expenses, and medical care as set forth in the policy. Major medical insurance, one form of medical expense insurance, provides for a high overall maximum limit on all covered expenses and usually requires that the insured pay a deductible amount and a percentage of the remaining expenses. Normally, these policies pay less than the total costs incurred by the insured. For example, on a $1,000 hospital care bill, the insured might have to pay the first $200 and 20 percent of the remainder. The amount the insurer would pay in this case would be $640 [80 percent of ($1,000 – $200)], and the insured would pay $360 [20 percent of ($1,000 – $200) + $200]. A typical journal entry recording a medical expense claim paid on a group insurance policy is a debit to Hospital Benefits Paid—Group and a credit to Cash. For recording payment to a surgeon, an insurer debits Surgical Claims Paid—Group and credits Cash. Both of these claims could have been debited to just one account, such as A&H Claims Paid—Group. Many companies establish reserves for A&H insurance claims incurred but not yet reported and claims in the process of settlement. In these cases, at the end of the accounting period, the insurer reverses the journal entries for the establishment of these reserves when it pays the claim, thereby releasing the reserve to surplus.

Annuity and Supplementary Contract Payments

Annuity payments are periodic payments of a fixed or variable amount that are made during a fixed period or for the lifetime of one or more people. Annuity contracts are purchased primarily to furnish income to one or more annuitants. Payments from *supplementary contracts,* also called *settlement contracts,* arise from an insurance policy's provisions that allow the insured or the policy beneficiary to select the method of disbursing the proceeds of a life insurance policy. If the proceeds are held at interest or paid in installments over a specified period, the contract is a supplementary contract without life contingencies (WOLC). When the duration of the payment period depends on the lifetime of the beneficiary, the contract is a supplementary contract with life contingencies (WLC).

Annuity Benefits

Recording payments of annuities is relatively simple. The insurer debits Annuity Benefits for the product type and credits Cash for the amount of the payment to the annuitant or beneficiary, as in the following entry:

Annuity Benefits	xxx	
Cash		xxx

To record an annuity payment.

Besides periodic payments for a specified time or amount, some annuities also provide death benefits. If an individual annuitant dies before the annuity payments begin or the specified amounts are paid out, then the insurer provides the contractual death benefit to the annuity's beneficiary. In this case, the accounting entry is a debit to Death Claims Paid—Annuities and a credit to Cash. If the contract enables the annuity's beneficiary to elect to continue receiving annuity payments until the specified benefit period or amount occurs, then the insurer debits Annuity Benefits—Individual and credits Cash upon payment to the beneficiary. The accounting entries associated with annuity payments depend on both the contract type and the beneficiary's option to receive death benefits in a lump sum or over a specified period. Suppose the annuitant of a $6,000 per year annuity with 10 years certain died before receiving the ninth year payment. This annuity has contractual payments of $6,000 per year for 10 years, independent of whether the annuitant is alive to collect each payment. If the annuity's beneficiary elects to receive the death benefit in a lump sum, then the insurer makes the following accounting entry:

Death Claims Paid—Annuity Benefits—Individual . . .	xxx	
Cash		xxx

To record the payment of a lump-sum annuity death claim.

The amount calculated is the present value of the remaining two annuity payments.

On the other hand, if the annuity's beneficiary elects to receive the remaining annuity payments on a monthly basis until the end of the period certain, then the insurer makes the following accounting entry for each payment:

Annuity Benefits—Individual	500	
Cash		500

To record the payment of a monthly annuity payment.

An annuity payment record typically does not show an outstanding balance but describes the type of annuity contract and the payments that have been made or are to be made. This record contains the name of the payee, the amount of each installment, the payment dates, and the installment period. The insurer normally maintains a balance in this account when settlement proceeds are left on deposit at interest and are subject to withdrawal at any time.

Supplementary Contract Payments

Benefit payments for supplementary contracts with or without life contingencies are similar to those for annuities. A major difference between the two, however, is the origin of the contract. A supplementary contract can result from several sources. For example, the owner of a policy that has matured or been surrendered or a policy beneficiary, upon the death of the insured, can request that the policy proceeds be used as a single premium to purchase a series of payments under either of two typical options: (1) a *supplementary contract without (not involving) life contingencies (WOLC),* which provides a specified number of guaranteed payments, or (2) a *supplementary contract with (involving) life contingencies (WLC),* which provides guaranteed payments for the life of the supplementary contract's owner. For the remainder of the contract, the insurer debits the appropriate account, such as Supplementary Contracts—WLC or Supplementary Contracts—WOLC, and credits Cash upon making contractual payments to the owner of a supplementary contract. When a supplementary contract goes into effect, the insurer usually prepares a new set of records. The contract has a different identification number than that of the terminated life insurance policy. Companies usually maintain a record of the initial information on supplementary contracts so they can determine which supplementary contracts are outstanding.

Assume that the Heritage Life and Health Insurance Company sells a $10,000 ordinary life insurance policy with an AD&D rider for the same amount. The insured later dies in an accident, which means that without adjustments, the death benefit is $20,000. However, the policy has dividend accumulations of $532, a policy loan of $2,000, and accrued policy loan interest of $10. In addition, the policy's beneficiary decides to leave $8,000 of the policy proceeds on deposit with Heritage under a supplementary contract that will provide the beneficiary with a monthly income for life. The accounting entry to establish this supplementary contract is

Death Claims Paid—Ordinary	10,000	
Accidental Death Claims Paid—Ordinary	10,000	
Dividend Accumulations	532	
Policy Loans		2,000
Policy Loan Interest		10
Consideration for Supplementary Contracts WLC		8,000
Cash		10,522

To record a life insurance policy settlement option.

Other Liabilities

This section includes a discussion of several liabilities that are unrelated to policy and contract provisions. Insurers typically maintain subsidiary ledgers for these liabilities, which apply to both insurance and non-insurance companies. Other liabilities consist primarily of money that an insurer owes for goods and services. These liabilities include

- Premiums paid in advance
- Premium deposits
- Short-term and long-term debt obligations
- General expenses due or accrued
- Agents' commissions due or accrued
- Taxes, licenses, and fees due or accrued
- Amounts retained by the company as agent or trustee
- Premium suspense accounts
- Dividends to stockholders declared and unpaid

Premiums Paid in Advance

Recall from Chapter 6 that an insurer reports a liability for *premiums paid in advance,* also called *advance premiums,* when an insured pays a premium in one accounting period for coverage that does not begin until the next policy anniversary. This type of liability differs from unearned premium reserves, which we discussed in Chapter 9, in that premiums paid in advance are for coverage that begins in the next policy year. In contrast, unearned premium reserves are for amounts paid in an earlier accounting period for coverage that extends into a later accounting period but not beyond the policy anniversary date. The liability for premiums paid in advance appears on U.S. GAAP, Canadian GAAP, and U.S. statutory financial statements. Suppose the Brick Company pays annual premiums for its group insurance to the Precept Life and Health Insurance Company. On December 30, Brick pays for the next year's coverage. On its Annual Statement dated December 31, Precept establishes a liability for premiums paid in advance equal to the amount of Brick's premiums paid for insurance coverage.

Premium Deposits

Premium deposits are amounts that an insurer's policyowners leave on deposit with the insurer to pay for future premiums. Premium deposits apply to more than one future accounting period and are frequently discounted. Although these amounts are available to the insurer now, the insurer will not apply them to premium income until the premium is due. Instead, the insurer credits these funds to Premium Deposits, a liability account. Because premium deposits represent future premiums, the insurer does not consider the entire amount as premium income during the current accounting period. The insurer only credits Premium Income for the amount of the currently due premium.

Many insurers discount the amount of premium deposits to allow for the interest that will be earned on the amount while it is on deposit with the company. Assume that a policyowner wants to pay the next two $100 annual premiums on a life insurance policy. The first premium is due in one month, just after the financial reporting date. The second premium, however, is not due for over a year. The insurer, in this case, may charge only $94.35 for the premium, if the insurer is anticipating a 6 percent return on premium deposits. At the end of the year, the $94.35 deposit and its interest will have accumulated to approximately $100. The rate of interest that is granted on premium deposits is determined by the insurer's management and usually varies according to market conditions.

Most companies prefer to accept only discounted premiums as premium deposits, although some companies accept for deposit regular contributions that are unrelated to a policy's premiums. Such contributions can be made for the purpose of (1) accumulating an emergency fund that might be used for future premium payments or (2) accumulating an additional amount that can be withdrawn at some future date. The interest paid as a result of the discount on these deposits, however, introduces a new element to premium accounting.

Assume that a $100 renewal premium on an ordinary policy is due and that a policyowner has paid an additional nine years' premiums in advance at a discounted cost of $458.39. (Knowledge of the method of calculating the amounts of discounted premiums is not necessary for the purposes of this discussion.) The typical entry to record receipt of $558.39 ($458.39 + $100) is

Cash	558.39	
Premium Deposits		458.39
Premium Income		100.00

To record the receipt of a premium deposit and the current premium.

Note that the currently due premium is not credited to the Premium Deposit account, a liability account, but instead is credited directly to the Premium Income account. One year later when the next premium comes due, the amount of interest on the total principal of $458.39 is entered as a debit to an expense account, Interest Paid on Policy and Contract Funds. Assuming a 6 percent rate of return on premium deposits, the amount of interest for the first year of the deposit would be $27.50. The full amount of the second year's premium, $100, must be credited to the Premium Income account to record payment of that year's premium. The difference between the $100 premium and the $27.50 interest earned is $72.50, which is transferred from the Premium Deposit account. Most companies record two accounting entries for this transaction, as follows:

Interest Paid on Policy and Contract Funds	27.50	
Premium Deposits		27.50

To record interest paid on a premium deposit.

Premium Deposits	100.00	
Premium Income		100.00

To record the transfer of a premium deposit to premium income.

This process is repeated each year until the amount held in the deposit account for this policy has been reduced to zero.

Short-Term and Long-Term Debt Obligations

Under GAAP, liabilities are commonly divided in a manner similar to that of assets: between short-term (current) and long-term. Recall from Chapter 2 that *short-term liabilities* are those that come due within 12 months. *Long-term liabilities* are those that a company incurs that are payable over time, so they cross several annual accounting periods. For example, an insurer classifies the current portion of the principal due on a long-term bond as a short-term liability. This is known as the *current portion of long-term debt* or *current maturity.* The insurer also treats the current portion of the interest due on the bond as a short-term liability such as Interest Payable. On the other hand, the insurer classifies the principal payments not due within the current accounting period as a long-term liability.

Suppose that, on April 1, 1999, an insurer issues bonds in the amount of $300 million at 8 percent interest with a 30-year maturity. Assume that the insurer has to pay $10 million in principal each year. If this were the insurer's only debt, then the insurer would include the following amounts on its December 31, 1999, balance sheet:

- $18 million under Interest Payable (short-term liability) [$300 million × 8 percent × $\frac{9}{12}$]
- $10 million under Current Portion of Long-Term Debt—8 Percent Bond, due 2028 (short-term liability)
- $290 million under Long-Term Debt—8 Percent Bond, due 2028 (long-term liability) [$300 million – $10 million]

Note that, under GAAP, an insurer accounts for interest and principal separately. Short-term and long-term liabilities are not as clearly differentiated under statutory accounting.

General Expenses Due or Accrued

An insurer estimates its liability for general expenses due or accrued for those goods or services it has received but which the insurer has not yet paid for at the end of the accounting period. Recall that insurers report expenses on the statement of operations and due or accrued expenses as liabilities on the balance sheet. This is analogous to reporting income on the statement of operations and due or accrued income as an asset on the balance sheet. The insurer must exercise a considerable amount of judgment to determine the amount of this liability. The insurer totals all unpaid invoices dated prior to the end of the year. The insurer may add an "adjustment factor" to account for miscellaneous expenses not yet identified. This includes utility bills for the month of December that are not mailed to the insurer until January. An insurer creates a liability for salaries and wages incurred but unpaid because salaries and wages are sometimes partially incurred at the time the Annual Statement is prepared. The insurer must also report liabilities for expenses due and accrued from contributions to employee benefit plans, professional and service fees, utility services used, and investment expenses in the Annual Statement. Further, both agents and home office personnel can order medical examinations and inspection reports. The insurer must estimate the expenses incurred for these items by agents, whose invoices typically do not arrive in the insurer's home office before the end of the current accounting period. Recall that, under U.S. GAAP, an insurer classifies policy-related costs as an asset—deferred policy acquisition costs (DPAC)—and amortizes these costs through income over a specified time.

Agents' Commissions Due or Accrued

A commission is considered due or accrued when the insurer receives a premium too late in the accounting period to process the commission payment to the agent. Commissions generally accrue only on premiums received. Most insurers maintain a subsidiary ledger or file for each agent to track unpaid but owed agent commissions. Agents' Commissions Due or Accrued is a liability account, whereas Agent Commissions Paid is an expense account.

Taxes, Licenses, and Fees Due or Accrued

The liability for *taxes, licenses, and fees due or accrued* includes (1) items billed but not yet paid, such as business or agent licenses, (2) amounts payable but not yet billed, such as property taxes on real estate, and (3) estimates of amounts still owed for premium taxes on premiums collected during the year. An insurer can estimate its premium taxes in each state or province by multiplying the total premiums received from policyowners in each state or province by the state's or province's premium tax rate, then reducing this amount by any prepayments or other reductions. Taxes, Licenses, and Fees Paid is the accompanying expense account. Insurers account separately for due or accrued federal income taxes.

Amounts Retained by the Company as Agent or Trustee

In the normal course of business, life insurance companies act as agents or trustees and retain or keep on deposit funds that will ultimately be paid to others, but which are not related to policy reserves or benefits. Two common liabilities in this category are

1. *Employee payroll deductions* for federal and state income taxes, Social Security taxes, pension plan contributions, and health insurance premiums

2. *Escrow balances* for the payment of property taxes and hazard insurance on mortgaged real estate

Insurers maintain separate accounting records for each liability.

Premium Suspense Accounts

An insurer debits Cash upon receipt of premium payments. This practice not only provides for good accounting control but also makes the funds received available for the insurer to invest. However, the insurer may not be able to determine immediately the credit entry to offset the debit to Cash. In such situations, many insurers use suspense accounts as an interim step. For example, if an insurer receives a premium payment but cannot immediately credit a revenue account, such as Premium Income or Renewal Premiums, then the insurer debits Cash and credits Premium Suspense, a liability account, for the amount of the premium payment. An insurer uses a ***premium suspense account*** to record transactions that are intended as premiums but which the insurer cannot accept as revenue until a particular event occurs. An insurer typically uses suspense accounts for renewal premiums, not initial premiums, if the amount of a premium payment differs from that in the insurer's records, or there is insufficient information (for example, no policy number) for the insurer to account for its receipt.

When using a premium suspense account, an insurer makes the following accounting entry to record receipt of the premium payment:

Cash	xxx	
Premium Suspense		xxx

To record receipt of a premium payment.

Once the particular event occurs (for example, the insurer confirms the correct amount), the insurer can debit the suspense account and credit a revenue account for the premium payment amount:

Premium Suspense	xxx	
Premium Income		xxx

To record the application of a suspensed premium as an actual premium.

Typically, when a policyowner remits a premium in cash to an insurer, the insurer's total assets increase because Cash has increased. However, when the insurer puts the money into a suspense account, the insurer does not update the policyowner master file. Thus, the policyowner master file still shows an uncollected premium, which is an asset for the insurer (for example, Premiums Due or Premiums Receivable). Therefore, when an insurer places a premium in suspense, it must post the premium receipt to a liability account. Otherwise, the amount of the premium is being counted as an asset twice: once as cash and again as an uncollected premium. Many insurers initially suspense all insurance premiums as a matter of procedure. If they do so, insurers must have adequate internal controls in place to ensure that amounts remain only a short time in suspense.

Dividends to Stockholders Declared and Unpaid

Besides the liability for policy dividends on participating business, stock insurance companies must also establish a liability for cash dividends to stockholders as of the date that the insurer's board of directors declares the dividend. The insurer charges dividends to stockholders directly to a surplus account, such as Dividends to Stockholders. The accounting entry to record the dividend liability would be

Dividends to Stockholders	xxx	
Dividends to Stockholders Declared and Unpaid		xxx

To record the declaration of cash dividends to stockholders.

Upon paying the dividend, the insurer would make the following accounting entry:

Dividends to Stockholders Declared and Unpaid	xxx	
Cash		xxx

To record the payment of cash dividends to stockholders.

Financial Reporting Requirements

In Chapter 6, we introduced you to the financial reporting requirements associated with an insurer's liabilities, including policy dividend liabilities, policy and contract claims, and other liabilities. Below is a summary of how U.S. and Canadian insurers report policy benefits and other liabilities on the Annual Statement and Annual Return.

Annual Statement

On its GAAP-based financial statements, a U.S. insurer estimates the present value of all future policy dividends as a component of policy reserves for certain traditional insurance products. However, for statutory accounting purposes, the insurer estimates its policy dividend liabilities for the next year only. Insurers report the total of their policy dividend liabilities on the *Liabilities* page of the Annual Statement. In a separate exhibit, insurers list the dollar amounts of life and accident and health insurance policy dividends that policyowners have applied under each policy dividend payment option. Insurers also disclose the methods used to determine the amount of policy dividend liabilities under each payment option.

Insurers list the total liability for unpaid life insurance claims and unpaid A&H insurance claims on separate lines on the *Liabilities* page of the Annual Statement. An insurer includes unpaid settlement contract installments and unpaid disability benefits provided by life policies with the life insurance claim liability. The Annual Statement filed in each state requires data on A&H insurance claims incurred and paid in that state according to specified methods. For these reasons, insurance companies must maintain a separate statistical record of each claim paid during the year. Companies must also value separately the incurred but unpaid claim liabilities for each state, as well as determine an incurred total for each state in which the company operates. An insurer must report A&H insurance claims and premiums to each state annually on an incurred basis for each plan of in-force A&H insurance. The insurer submits this report, called the A&H Policy Experience Exhibit, separately from the Annual Statement.

Recall from Chapter 6 that the Annual Statement contains policy claim exhibits that show the total claim liability in the following categories: (1) due and unpaid; (2) in course of settlement, divided into "resisted" and "other"; and (3) incurred but unreported. These three categories are known collectively as *incurred and unpaid claims.* Although an insurer does not list the type of claim by product, such as death claim or matured endowment, the column headings provide an approximate classification by general claim categories of ordinary, group, and accident and health. Death claims include matured endowments, although the insurer reports the amounts of matured endowments on both a cash basis and an accrual basis in the footnotes. Claim reserve liabilities appear in a special A&H insurance exhibit that consists of two parts: (1) active life reserve and (2) claim reserve.

If an insurer has ceded a portion of its insurance risk to a reinsurer, then the insurer reduces its claim liabilities by the amount that the insurer expects to recover from the reinsurer, as indicated in the reinsurance agreement. Although the insurer can specifically identify the amounts of reinsurance recoverable from individual policies, the insurer often must estimate this amount for certain group insurance policies. Insurers also disclose their premium deposits, expenses due or accrued, premium suspense accounts, declared and unpaid stockholder dividends, and all other liabilities separately in the Annual Statement.

Annual Return

The Annual Return presents several exhibits of outstanding claims for accident and sickness business. These exhibits (1) itemize an insurer's premiums and claims for accident and sickness insurance according to individual and group policies, (2) present outstanding claims, including a provision for unreported claims for individual policies, and (3) present an analysis of resisted claims that an insurer has encountered during the accounting period.

Conclusion

This chapter concludes our discussion of an insurer's typical liability accounts. Chapter 11, which discusses an insurer's capital and surplus accounts, concludes our presentation of an insurer's typical balance sheet accounts.

Key Terms and Concepts

policy dividends due and unpaid
policy dividends payable in the following year
policy dividend payment options
terminal policy dividend
dividend accumulations
cash value
bonus additions
nonforfeiture options
claims
contract payments
matured endowment
waiver-of-premium benefit
premium deposits
premium suspense account

CHAPTER 11

Accounting for Capital and Surplus

Learning Objectives

After studying this chapter, you should be able to

- List several internal and external sources of capital and surplus for life and health insurance companies
- Describe the major capital and surplus accounts of life and health insurers
- Explain how changes in assets and liabilities affect an insurer's surplus
- Record accounting entries for transactions that affect capital and surplus accounts
- Discuss the effect on surplus of changes in the market value of invested assets

Chapter Outline

Essential Concepts of Capital and Surplus

Internal Sources

External Sources

Capital and Surplus Accounts

Common Stock and Additional Paid-In Capital

Retained Earnings

Treasury Stock

Unrealized Gains and Losses

Special Surplus

Unassigned Surplus

Financial Reporting Requirements

United States

Canada

Life and health insurance companies use premium and investment income to purchase additional invested assets to offset their reserves and other liabilities. A healthy insurer will have more assets than it needs to pay for expected liabilities. This difference is represented by capital and surplus in the basic accounting equation. *Capital* and *surplus* are the terms used in life and health insurance companies for the accounts included in the owners' equity portion of the balance sheet. Specifically, U.S. insurers use capital accounts for GAAP-based financial statements and surplus accounts to satisfy statutory reporting requirements. In this text, when we use the term *capital and surplus,* we mean the insurer's total owners' equity, whether calculated under GAAP or statutory accounting. When we discuss *capital* or *surplus* separately, we are focusing on specific attributes of either capital accounts or surplus accounts, but not both.

The prudent and effective management of capital and surplus is critical to an insurer's solvency and profitability. Because an insurer's capital and surplus accounts represent the amount of investment in the insurer, the insurer must operate profitably to provide its owners, whether they are stockholders or policyowners, with a fair return on their investment. More essentially, though, capital and surplus are available to provide for unexpected events. In this respect, capital and surplus are an insurer's ultimate defense against the threat of insolvency. For example, an insurer's experience may indicate that next year's claims will range from $5 million to $13 million, although either extreme is unlikely to occur. The insurer estimates that $9 million would be the most likely dollar value of claims. The insurer's actuaries thus establish reserves to provide for $9 million of claims. Suppose the insurer's actual claims are $13 million. The insurer's capital and surplus must be sufficient to cover not only the $4 million in obligations that exceed its reserves during the year, but also to continue to meet the minimum statutory surplus requirements established by insurance regulators. When these regulators, as well as rating agencies and independent financial analysts, measure the financial soundness of an insurance company, they pay special attention to the condition of the insurer's capital and surplus accounts.

In this chapter, we present the concepts of capital and surplus, describe the internal and external sources of capital and surplus, discuss an insurer's primary capital and surplus accounts, and explain the disclosure of capital and surplus on the Annual Statement and

Annual Return. Figure 11-1 highlights the capital and surplus section of a typical insurer's balance sheet.

Essential Concepts of Capital and Surplus

Let's review some basic points about capital and surplus accounts as they are used in life and health insurance companies. Remember from Chapter 2 that surplus accounts are specific to the insurance industry. Most other types of businesses classify these accounts as *owners' equity,* as shown in the form of the basic accounting equation presented below:

Assets = Liabilities + Owners' Equity

Insurance companies may also use this form of the basic accounting equation when presenting their GAAP financial statements. Typically, however, the basic accounting equation for insurers is shown in the following form:

Assets = Liabilities + Capital and Surplus

Another way to write the basic accounting equation for insurers is as follows:

Assets = Liabilities + Capital + Surplus

This form of the equation is especially useful when we discuss capital accounts and surplus accounts separately.

The term *capital* has several meanings in business. For example, in economics, capital is one of the factors of production, which also include natural resources, labor, and entrepreneurship. In accounting terminology, *capital* is often used as a synonym for equity, in that a company's capital equals its assets minus its liabilities. Recall from Chapter 2 that *capital* is the amount of money that stockholders have invested in an insurer through the issue of its common stock or preferred stock. As we noted in earlier chapters, capital accounts include Common Stock, Preferred Stock, and Additional Paid-In Capital. Mutual and fraternal life and health insurers do not have capital accounts because they do not issue stock. Instead, mutuals and fraternals raise the funds they need through net gains from operations and by issuing surplus notes. Therefore, the basic accounting equation for a mutual or fraternal insurer can be presented simply as

Figure 11-1. Highlight of the capital and surplus section of a typical insurance company balance sheet.

December 31, 19XX

Assets	
Invested assets:	
Bonds	xxx
Mortgage loans	xxx
Stocks	xxx
Total Invested Assets	xxx
Real estate	xxx
Policy loans	xxx
Investment income due and accrued	xxx
Cash and cash equivalents	xxx
Premiums due	xxx
Deferred policy acquisition costs (GAAP only)	xxx
Reinsurance ceded	xxx
Other assets	xxx
Total Assets	5,000,000

Liabilities and Capital and Surplus	
Liabilities:	
Policy reserves:	
Life insurance	xxx
Annuities	xxx
Accident and health	xxx
Total Policy Reserves	xxx
Claim reserves:	
Life insurance	xxx
Accident and health	xxx
Total Claim Reserves	xxx
Policy dividends due and unpaid	xxx
Unpaid policy claims	xxx
Premium deposits	xxx
Advance premiums	xxx
Interest maintenance reserve	xxx
Asset valuation reserve	xxx
Other liabilities	xxx
Total Liabilities	4,300,000
Capital and Surplus:	
Stock	xxx
Additional paid-in capital	xxx
Special surplus	xxx
Unassigned surplus	xxx
Net unrealized gains (losses)	(xxx)
Treasury stock	(xxx)
Total Capital and Surplus	700,000
Total Liabilities and Capital and Surplus	5,000,000

Assets = Liabilities + Surplus

When U.S. mutual and fraternal insurers prepare GAAP-based financial statements, they assign much of their "surplus" to an account called Retained Earnings. Despite this similarity, however, a U.S. insurer's surplus and its retained earnings are rarely equal because the insurer uses different assumptions and methods for calculating Retained Earnings and Surplus.

For statutory accounting purposes, surplus is the difference between a U.S. insurer's admitted assets and liabilities. For Canadian insurers, surplus is the difference between an insurer's assets and its liabilities, because admitted assets and nonadmitted assets are U.S.-specific terms. Under statutory accounting, surplus accounts include Gross Paid-In and Contributed Surplus, Special Surplus, and Unassigned Surplus. Gross Paid-In and Contributed Surplus is equivalent to Additional Paid-In Capital under U.S. GAAP in that it represents the difference between a stock's par value and its selling price upon issue. Figure 11-2 summarizes the capital and surplus accounts and their equivalent names under U.S. GAAP and statutory accounting. Again, the total in each equivalent account for the same insurer may differ because of the different methods of valuing or calculating each account. With the exception of Additional Paid-In Capital, other designated amounts are typically appropriations of the insurer's Retained Earnings. Because surplus plays an especially significant role in an insurer's statutory and economic solvency, our main focus is on an insurer's surplus accounts.

We begin our discussion with a look at how a life and health insurance company can increase capital and surplus through internal and external sources. Except where noted, the general effects of changes in assets or liabilities on capital and surplus are the same under statutory accounting and GAAP.

An *internal source of capital and surplus* means that capital and surplus are increased by financial transactions that originate in an insurer's core business operations. For example, increases in sales rev-

Figure 11-2. Capital and surplus accounts under statutory accounting and U.S. GAAP.

U.S. Statutory Accounting	U.S. GAAP
Gross Paid-In and Contributed Surplus	Additional Paid-In Capital
Special Surplus	Retained Earnings
Unassigned Surplus	Retained Earnings

enue and decreases in expenses are both internal sources of capital and surplus because they increase net income and they arise from normal business operations. On the other hand, though, an *external source of capital and surplus* means that capital and surplus are increased by financial transactions that originate outside an insurer's core business operations. For example, suppose the Large Life and Health Insurance Company owns several subsidiary companies, including a property/casualty company. If Large sells its property/casualty subsidiary to another company and makes a profit on the sale, then Large increases its capital and surplus through an external source. The next two sections of this chapter discuss internal and external sources of capital and surplus.

Internal Sources

Internal sources of capital and surplus for insurers include net gains from operations and gains from the sale of invested assets (United States only). Internal capital sources may also include decreases in nonadmitted assets (United States only) and decreases in the valuation of policy reserves or claim reserves.

Net Gains from Operations

Life and health insurance companies can increase surplus when their actual experience is more favorable than expected experience, either because revenues are higher than expected or expenses are lower than expected. The primary source of an insurer's capital and surplus is net income, which includes both (1) gains from insurance operations and (2) gains from the sale of assets (United States only). An insurer reports these gains on a net basis in the Annual Statement. Net income is an insurer's revenues *minus* the insurer's total (1) expenses, (2) benefit payments, (3) federal income taxes, and (4) dividends to policyowners.

Many combinations of revenues and expenses can result in a gain from operations. For example, consider the following net income calculations for two insurance companies. Both insurers end the year with a net income of $1.5 million, but both achieve this outcome in different ways. The Assertive Life and Health Insurance Company earns $1 million more in revenues than the Cost Cutting Life and Health Insurance Company. But Cost Cutting spends half as much on operational expenses, such as salaries and commissions, and pays less in benefits, taxes, and policy dividends. What Cost Cutting lacks in revenues it makes up for by reducing its various expenses, thus providing it with the same net income (assuming no capital gains or losses) as Assertive.

Assertive		
Revenues		$5,000,000
Expenses (commissions, salaries, administrative costs, etc.)	$1,000,000	
Benefit payments	1,400,000	
Federal income taxes	375,000	
Policy dividends	725,000	
Net Income		$1,500,000

Cost Cutting		
Revenues		$4,000,000
Expenses (commissions, salaries, administrative costs, etc.)	$ 500,000	
Benefit payments	1,200,000	
Federal income taxes	275,000	
Policy dividends	525,000	
Net Income		$1,500,000

In both cases, each insurer records a closing entry at the end of the accounting period to begin the next accounting period with a zero balance in their revenue accounts and expense accounts. A temporary account such as Income Summary is often used to close out revenue and expense accounts. In this case, an insurer debits all its revenue account balances and credits Income Summary to close out its revenue accounts. Similarly, the insurer debits Income Summary and credits all its expense account balances to close out its expense accounts. Below are the typical closing entries that each insurer would make:

	Debit	Credit
Premium Income	xxx	
Investment Income	xxx	
Income Summary		xxx

To close out revenue accounts.

	Debit	Credit
Income Summary	xxx	
Policy Benefits		xxx
Agent Commissions		xxx
Operating Expenses		xxx
Taxes, Licenses, and Fees		xxx

To close out expense accounts.

Because each insurer earned net income, Income Summary has a credit balance after the closing entries are recorded, so the insurers close out Income Summary to Unassigned Surplus as follows:

Income Summary 1,500,000
Unassigned Surplus. 1,500,000
To close out net income to surplus.

Gains from the Sale of Invested Assets

A U.S. insurer also increases net income by selling invested assets for a net gain. Recall that a *gain* is the positive difference between the book value and the selling price of an invested asset. If the difference between the asset's book value and selling price was negative, then the insurer would experience a loss. Let's consider again the Assertive and Cost Cutting insurance companies. Suppose Assertive sells some of its invested assets and achieves a net capital gain of $750,000. Cost Cutting also sells some of its invested assets. Because of unfavorable market conditions, however, Cost Cutting must sell its invested assets at a net capital loss of $100,000. In this case, the net income calculations that we considered earlier would change as shown below:

Assertive		
Revenues		$5,000,000
Expenses (commissions, salaries, administrative costs, etc.)	$1,000,000	
Benefit payments	1,400,000	
Federal income taxes	375,000	
Policy dividends	725,000	
Net Gain from Operations		$1,500,000
Net Capital Gain		750,000
Net Income		$2,250,000

Cost Cutting		
Revenues		$4,000,000
Expenses (commissions, salaries, administrative costs, etc.)	$ 500,000	
Benefit payments	1,200,000	
Federal income taxes	275,000	
Policy dividends	525,000	
Net Gain from Operations		$1,500,000
Net Capital Gain (Loss)		(100,000)
Net Income		$1,400,000

The closing statutory accounting entries in each case would be:

Assertive Income Summary 2,250,000
Unassigned Surplus. 2,250,000
To close out net income to surplus.

Cost Cutting	Income Summary	1,400,000	
	Unassigned Surplus.		1,400,000
	To close out net income to surplus.		

Canadian insurers amortize the gains on the sale of their invested assets through income, which ultimately affects surplus.

Decreases in Nonadmitted Assets

As we discussed in Chapter 6, admitted assets are those assets that U.S. insurance regulators allow on the *Assets* page of the Annual Statement. Nonadmitted assets—which include furniture, equipment, supplies, stationery, printed matter, and cash advanced to company officers or agents—are those assets that insurers report elsewhere in the Annual Statement. (Although Canadian insurers do not distinguish between admitted assets and nonadmitted assets, they generally list assets that are labeled nonadmitted under U.S. statutory accounting under Goodwill and Other Assets on the *Assets* page of the Annual Return.) Because U.S. insurers do not report nonadmitted assets on the *Assets* page, an increase in the insurer's nonadmitted assets cannot increase its surplus. Rather, increasing nonadmitted assets usually results in a simultaneous decrease in admitted assets. For example, if an insurer purchases office furniture (a nonadmitted asset), and pays for the purchase with cash (an admitted asset), the transaction ultimately results in a decrease in capital and surplus. On the other hand, decreases in nonadmitted assets (such as selling furniture for cash) ultimately increase an insurer's capital and surplus.

Let's consider an example that shows the relationship of admitted assets, nonadmitted assets, and capital and surplus. Suppose the Cost Cutting Life and Health Insurance Company has a total of $4 million in ledger assets, according to statutory accounting. Of these assets, $1 million are considered nonadmitted. Subtracting its nonadmitted assets from its total ledger assets, Cost Cutting has total admitted assets of $3 million, which is the amount used to balance the right side of the simplified statutory balance sheet as shown below:

Ledger assets	$4.0 million	Liabilities	$1.0 million
Nonadmitted assets	− 1.0 million	Capital and Surplus	+ 2.0 million
Total Admitted Assets	$3.0 million	**Total Liabilities + Capital and Surplus**	$3.0 million

Suppose Cost Cutting completes an inventory of its home and branch office buildings and finds that it has an excess of office furniture. Cost Cutting immediately sells this office furniture for $100,000 in cash. This single transaction does not change the value of the insurer's total assets, because the insurer is, in effect, moving amounts from one asset account to another asset account. When this new value for nonadmitted assets is subtracted from total ledger assets, Cost Cutting finds that it has increased its admitted assets by $100,000. This change on the left side of the balance sheet must be matched by an equal change on the right side. Because liabilities are not affected by this transaction, Cost Cutting increases its capital and surplus by $200,000 as shown below:

Ledger assets	$4.1 million	Liabilities	$1.0 million
Nonadmitted assets	– 0.9 million	Capital and Surplus	+ 2.2 million
Total Admitted Assets	$3.2 million	**Total Liabilities + Capital and Surplus**	$3.2 million

Thus, a decrease in nonadmitted assets becomes the source of an increase in capital and surplus.

Decreases in the Valuation of Policy Reserves or Claim Reserves

Policy reserves and claim reserves decrease when reserves are released following the payment of claim benefits. As we mentioned in Chapter 9, reserves are not released after each specific transaction. Instead, an insurance company's actuaries recalculate the company's reserves each accounting period and present these recalculated amounts to the company's accountants, who then make adjusting entries in the company's accounts. The insurer then includes the amount of these changes in calculating the net gain from operations under both GAAP and statutory accounting. Sometimes, however, the amount of the reserves changes, not as a result of the insurer's core business operations, but because the insurer changes its *reserve valuation basis,* which is the method used to value reserves. Under statutory accounting, when a U.S. insurer alters a reserve amount because of a change in the valuation basis of that reserve, the insurer does not treat the amount of the change as a gain from operations, but as a direct change to surplus.

An insurer changes its reserve valuation basis if the insurer had originally used a valuation method that no longer accurately reflects its mortality, morbidity, or interest rate experience. Because policy reserves are liabilities for an insurer, a decrease in policy reserves resulting from a change in the valuation basis increases surplus. On the other hand, an increase in policy reserves decreases surplus. For example, if an insurer is now able to earn higher interest rates than it had assumed when establishing reserves, the insurer can potentially decrease claim reserves, thereby increasing surplus. In Canada, changes in assumptions used to value actuarial liabilities flow through the statement of operations and, thus, indirectly affect surplus or retained earnings.

Under statutory accounting, changes in the asset valuation reserve (AVR), but not the AVR itself, also affect the amount of a U.S. insurer's surplus. The AVR is a liability account, but the account used to report changes in the AVR, typically called Change in the AVR, is a surplus account. Therefore, an increase in the AVR from one accounting period to the next decreases the insurer's available surplus, and a decrease in the AVR increases surplus. The AVR amount before the change remains a liability, however, as its original establishment has already affected the insurer's surplus.

External Sources

External sources of capital and surplus for insurers include (1) ceding insurance risk to a reinsurer, (2) selling a line of business or a subsidiary, (3) issuing stock, (4) issuing surplus notes, (5) changing corporate form, (6) receiving a surplus contribution from a parent company, and (7) issuing bonds. In the following section, we discuss an insurer's primary external sources of capital and surplus.

Reinsurance

A life insurance company can reduce surplus strain and control its exposure to risk by reinsuring the covered amount that exceeds the company's retention limit for that type of policy. Under the terms of certain reinsurance agreements, if a ceding company transfers part of its risk to a reinsurer, then the ceding company maintains policy reserves to cover only the amount of the risk that it has retained. Because the use of reinsurance allows a ceding company to establish a lower amount of policy reserves than it normally would, the ceding company's surplus is higher than it would have been without reinsurance. Because certain reinsurance agreements enable a ceding company to maintain lower levels of reserves, reinsurance also reduces the ceding company's minimum statutory surplus requirements. Despite this advantage, the ceding company must be aware of its potential for residual liability if the reinsurer becomes insolvent. Entering into a reinsurance agreement does not release the ceding insurer from its direct obligations to policyowners. Some reinsurance agreements require the ceding company to maintain policy reserves. Also, only those reinsurance agreements that enable a ceding company to maintain a lower amount of policy reserves than it would have maintained without reinsurance provide an external source of surplus for the ceding company.

An insurer occasionally reinsures some of its business with an *unauthorized company*—that is, a reinsurer that may be licensed in other states, but is unlicensed in the insurer's state of domicile. In such cases, the insurer establishes a specified account, called the ***liability for reinsurance in unauthorized companies,*** or the *liability for reinsurance in unregistered companies* in Canada, which is the excess of the reserve taken on ceded business minus the amounts withheld from or deposits made by the reinsurer. The change in liability for reinsurance in unauthorized companies is the difference between the liability for such reinsurance on the previous year's balance sheet and the liability for such reinsurance on the current year's balance sheet. However, the excess in the reinsurance liability for one reinsurer cannot offset a deficiency for another unauthorized reinsurer.

The purpose of this liability is to protect policyowners by ensuring that the ceding company from which the policyowner purchased his or her policy adequately covers its liabilities. Establishment of the unauthorized reinsurance liability is necessary because the ceding company's domiciliary insurance department has no jurisdiction over the unauthorized reinsurer. As a result, the insurance department has no means by which to make that reinsurer meet its obligations. Life and health insurers in the United States reconcile changes in the liability for reinsurance in unauthorized companies under the Capital and Surplus Account on the *Summary of Operations* page of the Annual Statement.

Both the ceding company and the reinsurer maintain detailed accounting records of their respective obligations, depending on the nature of the reinsurance contract. Generally, the accounting entries for a particular reinsurance transaction for a ceding company are opposite from those made by a reinsurer, because each company is on the opposite side of the reinsurance transaction. Below is a brief description of how specified reinsurance plans affect the accounts of both the ceding company and the reinsurer. Because the details of each reinsurance agreement can vary, we present typical accounting entries for each type of reinsurance plan.

Yearly Renewable Term Reinsurance. Under ***yearly renewable term (YRT) reinsurance,*** also called *risk premium reinsurance (RPR),* a ceding company purchases YRT reinsurance from a reinsurer for the total net amount at risk for a block of insurance policies. The net amount at risk is the difference between a policy's face amount and its terminal reserve. The reinsurer maintains the policy reserve for the net amount at risk. Upon payment of a claim and reimbursement by the reinsurer, the reserve is released, thereby minimizing surplus strain for the ceding company. Suppose a ceding company reinsures, for a premium of $10,000, $250,000 of coverage on a block of life insurance policies. Below are the accounting entries that each company would make to record this transaction:

Ceding Company	Reinsurance Premiums Expense	10,000	
	Cash		10,000
	To record the payment of a reinsurance premium.		

Reinsurer	Cash	10,000	
	Premium Income—Reinsurance Assumed		10,000
	To record the receipt of a reinsurance premium.		

As a result of this transaction, the ceding company is able to decrease its policy reserves by the amount of the reserves established for the $250,000 reinsured. On the other hand, the reinsurer must establish the appropriate amount of policy reserves. Recall that a decrease in policy reserves is an internal source of surplus, so the ceding company's surplus would increase by the amount of the decrease in its policy reserves.

Coinsurance.[1] Under the ***coinsurance*** plan of reinsurance, the ceding company pays the reinsurer part of the premium paid by the insured, minus a proportionate share of the commissions and premium taxes associated with the policy that is being reinsured and a portion of the ceding company's general expenses. The premium paid to the reinsurer is typically higher for coinsurance than it is for YRT reinsurance, but the accounting entries are similar. In return, the reinsurer agrees to pay the ceding company a proportionate part of the death benefit when a claim is filed and to contribute to all other policy benefits, including policy dividends, on a scale determined by the ceding company. The reinsurer also agrees to accumulate the required reserves for the reinsured portion of the policy. The ceding company, on the other hand, accumulates reserves sufficient to cover only the portion of the insurance risk that it has retained. Suppose the ceding company in the above example had originally established policy reserves of $8,000 on the $250,000 of insurance coverage. Under a 100 percent coinsurance plan, the accounting entry that the ceding company and the reinsurer would make to record the change in policy reserves is

Ceding Company	Life Policy Reserves.	8,000	
	Change in Life Policy Reserves		8,000
	To record the decrease in life policy reserves as a result of reinsurance.		

Reinsurer	Change in Life Policy Reserves.	8,000	
	Life Policy Reserves		8,000
	To record the increase in life policy reserves as a result of reinsurance.		

In this case, the reinsurer increases by $8,000 the amount of policy reserves that it reports in the annual report, if applicable, and in the appropriate exhibit of the Annual Statement. The ceding company reports an amount for policy reserves $8,000 less than it otherwise would have without reinsurance.

Modified Coinsurance. A ***modified coinsurance (modco)*** plan of reinsurance uses the basic provisions of coinsurance, except the ceding company, rather than the reinsurer, maintains the entire policy reserve for the reinsured amount. The key difference is that the reinsurer returns part of this reserve amount to the ceding company under a modco plan. At the end of each year, the reinsurer transfers back to the ceding company an amount that equals the increase in the reserve for the reinsured portion of the policy, minus the interest the ceding company earned on the assets that support the reserve for the reinsured portion of the policy. Under a modco plan, a typical account name for premiums ceded is Reinsurance Allowances—Ceded Premiums. A significant difference between the modco and coinsurance plans of reinsurance is that, under the coinsurance plan, the ceding company decreases its aggregate reserves by the amount assumed by the reinsurer. Under the modco plan, the ceding company does not reduce its aggregate reserves.

Again, the premium the ceding company pays to the reinsurer would be higher than that for YRT reinsurance. The ceding company establishes a policy reserve liability, similar to the process of establishing policy reserves under other circumstances, for the amount of the reinsured policy's *net amount at risk,* which is the face amount of a life insurance policy minus the policy's reserve at the end of the policy year. If there is a claim, the reinsurer is responsible for the policy death benefit of the reinsured portion *minus* the reserve credited to the ceding company. Suppose an insurer received a death claim for which $17,000 was reinsured. The reserve credited to the ceding company at the time of the death claim was $4,000. When the insurer paid the claim, it established an asset account for the $13,000 ($17,000 – $4,000) recoverable from the reinsurer. The resulting accounting entry for the ceding company is

Cash	13,000	
Amounts Recoverable from Reinsurers		13,000

To record the receipt of death claim payments reimbursed by the reinsurer.

Figure 11-3 depicts a portion of the reinsurance schedule on which U.S. insurers list all reinsurance ceded for life insurance, annuities, and premium deposits. A separate portion of this schedule lists reinsurance ceded for accident and health insurance.

Selling a Line of Business

An insurer can also increase its capital and surplus through the sale of a line of business. Assume an insurer specializes in life insurance and annuity products but also offers health insurance products. As part of its strategic plan, the insurer decides to remain exclusively in its core business, so it sells its line of health insurance products to

Figure 11-3. Schedule S—Part 3A—U.S. Annual Statement.

Showing Data on Reinsurance Ceded for ALL Life Insurance, Annuities, Deposit Funds and Other Liabilities without Life or Disability Contingencies, and Related Benefits as of December 31, Current Year

NAIC Com-pany Code	Federal ID Number	Effective Date	1 Name of Company	2 Location	3 Type of Reinsurance Ceded	4 Amount in Force at End of Year	Reserve Credit Taken 5a Current Year	 5b Previous Year	6 Premiums	Outstanding Surplus Relief 7a Current Year	 7b Prior Year	8 Modified Coinsurance Reserve	9 Funds Withheld Under Coinsurance
			Affiliates:										
0199999 Totals—Affiliates													
			Non—Affiliates:										
0299999 Totals—Non-Affiliates													
0399999 Totals													

another insurer. If the difference between the assets and reserves released produces a gain, then an insurer's surplus increases. Alternatively, the insurer can use a particular type of reinsurance known as ***assumption reinsurance,*** which is an agreement by which an insurer permanently transfers full responsibility for a block of insurance policies to a reinsurer. Consequently, the insurer no longer maintains the policy reserves for that block of policies. Instead, the reinsurer assumes all obligations and ownership rights associated with the line of business or block of insurance policies. In the event of an insurer insolvency, regulatory authorities may use assumption reinsurance to sell the insolvent insurer's lines of business to protect policyowner interests. The accounting entries for assumption reinsurance, which are typically complex, are outside the scope of this text.

Issuing Stock

A stock insurer increases its capital by issuing common stock or preferred stock. In turn, the insurer decreases capital by retiring stock or purchasing treasury stock. As we discussed in Chapter 5, U.S. insurers separate the value of the stock they issue into two components: (1) the *par value* of the stock, which is the designated legal value assigned to each outstanding share of stock when it is issued, and (2) *additional paid-in capital,* which is the difference between the par value and the selling price of the stock when it was first issued. The par value of the stock is recorded in Common Stock or Preferred Stock. The difference between a stock's par value and its original selling price is recorded in Additional Paid-In Capital (U.S. GAAP) or Gross Paid-In and Contributed Surplus (statutory accounting). Assets and capital both increase as a result of the issue of stock. The basic accounting entry to record the issue of common stock is

Cash	xxx	
Common Stock		xxx
Additional Paid-In Capital		xxx

Under Canadian GAAP, the basic accounting entry is a debit to Cash and a credit to Common Stock because Canadian insurers no longer use par value for financial reporting purposes.

Issuing Surplus Notes[2]

Most businesses have the option of issuing both bonds and stock as a means of raising capital. Stock insurance companies have both of these options available to them, although insurers do not typically issue bonds. Insurers, in fact, are better known as bond *investors* rather than bond *issuers.* Nonetheless, stock insurers can issue both stocks and bonds, whereas mutual and fraternal insurers, which are owned by their policyowners, can issue neither. Thus, mutuals and fraternals have fewer sources for increasing surplus than do stock insurers. However, all U.S. insurance companies can increase surplus through the use of *surplus notes.* Mutuals and fraternals are the most common issuers of surplus notes, but stock insurers sometimes issue surplus notes because they are less expensive to issue than stock.

By definition, ***surplus notes,*** also called *surplus debentures* or *contribution certificates,* are a form of long-term, unsecured debt obligation that provides for the payment of both interest and principal on or before a set maturity date. Unlike typical debt instruments, which are liabilities on a U.S. insurer's balance sheet, surplus notes are classified as surplus accounts under statutory accounting. In other words, issuing surplus notes increases an insurer's surplus, not its liabilities. Surplus notes are a hybrid financial instrument in that they have some of the characteristics of both debt and equity securities. The claims of surplus note holders on an insurer's assets are subordinate to those of the insurer's policyowners and stockholders, state guaranty funds, and other creditors.

The basic accounting entry for the issue of surplus notes is

Cash.	xxx	
Surplus Notes		xxx

To record the issue of surplus notes.

From this simplified accounting entry, you can see that the debit to Cash and the credit to Surplus Notes increases both an insurer's assets and its surplus.

One requirement for surplus notes is that an insurer must receive approval from insurance regulators before making interest or principal payments on its notes. This requirement is the reason that the NAIC allows an insurer to classify its surplus notes as surplus: the repayment of the principal and interest on surplus notes is contingent on regulatory approval. Recall that contingency reserves are also part of a U.S. insurer's surplus. Because surplus notes are part of a U.S. insurer's surplus, the insurer includes surplus notes in the calculation of *risk-based capital,* which we discuss in Chapter 19. In contrast, under U.S. GAAP, the issue of surplus notes is a liability, similar to the issue of bonds or other long-term debt obligations. An insurer must also disclose the nature and extent of the costs and risks associated with its surplus notes in the Management Discussion and Analysis (MD&A) section of the annual report.

Issuing surplus notes improves an insurer's ability to pay claims on a timely basis because the increases in both cash and surplus strengthen the insurer's balance sheet. For this reason, regulatory authorities have approved the issuance of surplus notes. However, some rating agencies subtract surplus notes from capital and surplus when calculating an insurer's surplus. The Internal Revenue Service (IRS) currently allows the deduction of interest paid in cash by U.S.

insurers on surplus notes, as it does for other debt instruments such as bonds.

Changing Corporate Form

In response to increased competition and technological advances in the financial services industry, some insurers have changed their corporate form. For example, an insurer may form a holding company that directly owns various operating companies, thus restructuring itself horizontally. Insurers with foreign subsidiaries might restructure to improve the return on investment in international markets.

To raise capital by changing its corporate form, a well-capitalized insurer can

- Sell non-strategic or unprofitable lines of business
- Merge with another insurer
- Form an alliance or joint venture with a strategic partner
- Demutualize (if a mutual insurer)

We discussed the impact of selling a line of business earlier in this chapter. An insurer usually merges with another company by purchasing that company's outstanding assets or common stock in exchange for cash, stock in the acquiring company, or a combination of cash and stock. After a merger, the combined company typically has higher assets and capital and surplus than either company before the merger. Suppose the Able Life and Health Insurance Company merged with the Bountiful Life and Health Insurance Company. Figure 11-4 shows the balance sheets of both Able and Bountiful before the merger and the Combined Life and Health Insurance Company after the merger.

An insurer can reduce the amount of its own capital required to enter new markets by establishing a strategic partnership or joint venture with another company that has different product lines. Although strategic partnerships and joint ventures encompass a variety of arrangements, typically they involve two or more companies pooling their resources for a specified time to achieve a particular goal, such as developing a new product or service. In turn, each insurer can offer its policyowners a wider range of insurance products and services than would otherwise be possible. The alternative would be for an insurer to purchase outright another insurer's line of business, which would reduce the insurer's cash and increase its statutory reserve and surplus requirements because of the additional liability.

Because mutual insurers have limited access to capital markets, as we mentioned in the section on surplus notes, they must rely primarily on premium income and investment income to raise capital

Figure 11-4. The result of mergin two insurer's capital and surplus.

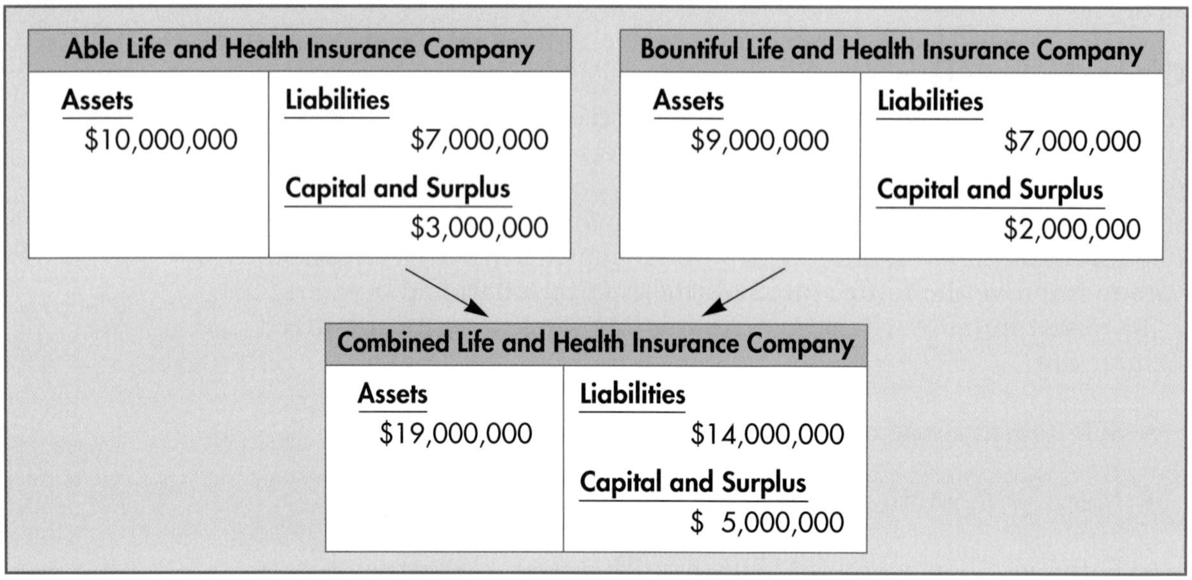

and surplus. As a result, some mutual companies have chosen to demutualize to compete more effectively with the growing number of stock insurers. ***Demutualization*** is the process of converting a mutual insurance company to a stock insurance company. Probably the most complicated step in demutualization is the transfer of ownership rights from a policyowner basis to a stockholder basis. When an insurer demutualizes, it must compensate its policyowners for the value of their ownership rights by offering them (1) stock in the newly forming stock company, (2) cash, or (3) some other form of compensation. Accordingly, the demutualizing insurer uses the GAAP calculation of retained earnings to determine the value of each policyowner's ownership position. During the conversion process, the mutual insurer distributes to its policyowners a large amount of its surplus in exchange for shares of common stock. The result is a partial liquidation of the insurer with no cash inflows to increase capital. Once demutualization is completed, however, the newly created stock company can offer new issues of stock to all potential investors.

Figure 11-5 summarizes the typical internal and external sources of capital and surplus for life and health insurance companies. Insight 11-1 discusses how one state is approaching the demutualization process.

Internal and external *uses* of capital and surplus, which have the opposite effect of an insurer's sources of capital and surplus, decrease an insurer's capital and surplus accounts. Internal uses of capital and surplus may result from (1) a net loss from operations, (2) a net loss

Figure 11-5. Summary of typical internal and external sources of capital and surplus.

Internal Sources of Capital and Surplus	External Sources of Capital and Surplus
• Net gains from operations • Gains from sale of invested assets • Decrease in nonadmitted assets (United States only) • Decrease in the valuation of policy reserves or claim reserves	• Reinsurance • Sale of a line of business • Stock issue • Surplus notes issues (United States only) • Change in corporate form

from the sale of invested assets, (3) a decrease in assets, (4) an increase in liabilities, and, (5) for U.S. insurers, a decrease in admitted assets or an increase in nonadmitted assets. External uses of an insurer's capital and surplus, which would also decrease capital and surplus, may result from (1) assuming insurance risk from a ceding company, (2) purchasing a line of business, (3) purchasing treasury stock, and (4) repaying surplus notes.

Capital and Surplus Accounts

In this section, we introduce you to an insurer's primary capital and surplus accounts. Stock insurers use capital accounts to record the issue or purchase of their own stock. Mutuals and fraternals have no capital accounts. Thus, most business transactions affect an insurer's surplus accounts. The basic accounting equation, solved for surplus, is

<u>**Canadian Insurers**</u>

Surplus = Assets − Liabilities − Capital

<u>**U.S. Insurers**</u>

Surplus = Admitted Assets − Liabilities − Capital

In other words, an insurer's surplus equals its assets, net of its liabilities and capital. As noted earlier, U.S. insurers include only admitted assets in the calculation of surplus, whereas Canadian insurers include total assets. Legal requirements generally prescribe the types and proper valuations of assets and liabilities that can determine surplus. Because the total amount in all surplus accounts represents the cumulative investment in the insurer since its inception, an insurer's surplus is similar to a non-insurance company's retained earnings under GAAP. Unlike a non-insurer's customers, however, an insurer's policyowners have certain ownership rights. Therefore,

Insight 11-1 Demutualization Under New Massachusetts Law

On November 27, 1991, a Massachusetts statute was signed into effect providing for the conversion of mutual life insurance companies organized under the laws of Massachusetts into stock form. Although no Massachusetts-domiciled life insurer has publicly indicated an interest in demutualizing, the new legislation is of particular interest given the number of mutual life insurance companies domiciled in Massachusetts.

In granting to the state commissioner of insurance discretion in approving the amount of consideration which policyholders are entitled to receive in exchange for their membership rights in the mutual insurer, the Massachusetts statute utilizes a broad, flexible approach similar to the Williams Model Act (adopted in many states) and the Michigan demutualization statute.

In 1988, the Maccabees Mutual Life Insurance Co. converted to stock form pursuant to the Michigan statute. Under the conversion plan, Maccabees was reorganized as a stock company, and the newly issued stock was purchased by Royal Financial Services, Inc. The proceeds of the stock sale were distributed to policyholders in cash.

Union Mutual Life Ins. Co. (subsequently renamed UNUM) was demutualized in 1986 under the Maine statute which is based in large part on the Williams Model Act. The UNUM demutualization was followed by a successful public offering of newly authorized stock.

In contrast to the Williams Model Act and similar statutes (including the Massachusetts legislation), the New York demutualization statute permits four alternative conversion methods, two of which set forth mandatory procedures for determining the consideration to be distributed to policyholders.

The board of directors of the Equitable Life Assurance Co. has recently approved a conversion plan under the New York statute. The plan provides for a distribution of stock, cash or policy credits to eligible policyholders following a public offering of stock. Under the plan, the company will not pay out more than 50 percent of the proceeds of the stock offering in cash to policyholders. Groupe AXAS.A., a French insurer, has already made a capital contribution of $1 billion to the insurer to be exchanged for 45 percent equity stake in the company after conversion.

The new Massachusetts statute permits the issuance of stock by either the reorganized insurer or by a parent corporation holding all of the common shares of the reorganized insurer. The plan of conversion must first be approved by the commissioner of insurance, after a public hearing, upon a finding that the plan is not prejudicial either to the policyholders of the insurer or the insurance-purchasing public. In addition, not less than two-thirds of policyholders eligible to vote must approve the plan.

The plan must provide that consideration is to be distributed to those policyholders eligible to participate, and the consideration must be determinable under a fair and reasonable formula approved by the commissioner. The consideration to be distributed may be in the form of cash, securities, additional life insurance coverage or annuity benefits, or other consideration. The amount to be distributed is to be "based upon" the entire surplus of the insurer.

In addition, each eligible policyholder is to be granted preemptive rights permitting him to acquire his proportionate share of the new stock to be issued pursuant to demutualization. The policyholder may elect to apply any consideration he would otherwise receive to such purchase of stock. The conversion plan may provide that preemptive rights with an aggregate subscription price of $2,000 or less will not be honored. Such policyholders must, however, receive their allotted consideration in cash.

No particular provision is made for participating policies under the Massachusetts statute. This is in contrast to the New York statute which provides that, with respect to the two procedures set forth in detail, if the participating business of the mutual insurer is to be continued by the reorganized insurer, that business is to be operated as a closed block of participating business, for dividend purposes only. Although the Maine statute, like the Massachusetts statute, does not require that a closed block be established, UNUM did set up such an account for the benefit of certain participating policies.

Despite the apparent flexibility of the Massachusetts statute, the demutualization procedure remains a technically difficult and costly process with complex actuarial, accounting, legal and tax questions to be addressed. The UNUM and Maccabees experiences indicate, however, that those issues can be successfully resolved.

Source: Thomas R. Bateman, "Demutualization Under New Massachusetts Law," *National Underwriter Life & Health/Financial Services Edition*, No. 1 (January 6, 1992), p. 33. Reprinted with permission from *National Underwriter*, © 1996, The National Underwriter Company, *Life & Health/Financial Services Edition*, 1992.

stockholders and participating policyowners in a stock company, policyowners in a mutual company, and certificate holders in a fraternal benefit society have specified ownership rights to an insurer's surplus. Gross Paid-Up and Contributed Surplus and Policyowners' Surplus are typical accounts that include these policyowner interests.

Surplus gives an insurer adequate funds to meet statutory and regulatory requirements, expand operations, underwrite new business, provide for unforeseen catastrophic events or excess losses, provide funds for investment, and provide policyowners and stockholders with competitive dividends. For this reason, increasing surplus typically improves an insurer's financial position and its current market value. Does this mean that an insurer should accumulate as much surplus as possible? Not necessarily. A company with a large amount of surplus may be missing opportunities to expand its business. Further, most states limit the maximum amount of surplus that an insurer can maintain to ensure that the insurer pays sufficient policy dividends out of its net gain from operations to participating policyowners. Rating agencies, regulatory authorities, company managers, company agents, policyowners, and stockholders often have different ideas about the appropriate level of an insurer's surplus, as shown in Figure 11-6.

Following is a description of an insurer's capital accounts, which include Common Stock, Additional Paid-In Capital, and Retained Earnings, and its surplus accounts, which include Surplus Notes, Special Surplus, and Unassigned Surplus. We also discuss two other accounts that directly affect an insurer's total capital and surplus: Treasury Stock and Unrealized Gains and Losses.

Figure 11-6. Typical interested user concerns about an insurer's surplus.

Rating agencies look at both statutory and GAAP surplus figures to identify an insurer's current surplus. They also use a variety of financial ratios, formulas, benchmarks, and nonquantitative measures of management effectiveness to determine whether an insurer's current surplus is at the right level for financial soundness and profitability.

Regulatory authorities focus on an insurer's statutory solvency and therefore focus on its statutory surplus figures. Each jurisdiction requires a minimum threshold of surplus, which depends on an insurer's size, corporate form, and lines of business. Both U.S. and Canadian regulatory authorities use *risk-based capital formulas* (discussed in Chapter 19) to determine an insurer's threshold capital and surplus. Insurance regulators can restrict the level or scope of an insurer's investments or dividend payments if they believe that the insurer's surplus is too low.

Company managers analyze surplus for the company as a whole and by line of business.

The **board of directors,** which represents the insurer's *stockholders,* evaluates the insurer's management on key capital and surplus ratios, as well as the current market value of the insurer's stock.

Agents' and **policyowners'** concerns typically focus on sufficient surplus to settle policy claims and pay ongoing business expenses.

Common Stock and Additional Paid-In Capital

In Chapter 7, we discussed the basic accounting entries for an insurer's investments in common stock. Earlier in this chapter, we discussed the accounting entries from the point of view of the insurer as stock issuer, rather than stock investor. Recall that a typical accounting entry to record the issue of common stock at par value is a debit to Cash and a credit to Common Stock. If the selling price of the stock issue is greater than the stock's par value, U.S. insurers debit Cash, credit Common Stock for the par value of the stock multiplied by the number of shares issued, and credit Additional Paid-In Capital (U.S. GAAP) or Gross Paid-In and Contributed Surplus (statutory accounting) for the excess of the selling price over the par value. Because Canadian insurers do not record par value, the accounting entry for the issue of common stock, regardless of selling price, is simply a debit to Cash and a credit to Common Stock.

Also in Chapter 7, we discussed cash dividends and stock dividends from the point of view of the insurer as stockholder. Here we discuss them from the perspective of the insurer as stock issuer. An insurer's ability to declare a cash dividend or a stock dividend depends on the amount available in Retained Earnings (GAAP) or Unassigned Surplus (statutory accounting). The distribution of stock dividends does not reduce an insurer's cash, whereas the amount of cash available influences whether an insurer can distribute cash dividends on its common stock. However, if Unassigned Surplus is too low, neither cash dividends nor stock dividends can be declared. Insurers in the United States calculate dividends on a statutory basis, even if the financial statements are prepared under GAAP, because states restrict to a specified percentage of an insurer's statutory earnings or surplus the payment of cash and stock dividends. Under GAAP, the amount available for dividends is also disclosed in the notes to the financial statements.

A stock distribution does not increase a company's cash or capital. When an insurer distributes a *stock dividend,* stockholders receive additional shares of the insurer's stock, expressed as a percentage of the shares that each stockholder owns as of a specified date, called the *date of record.* For example, a stockholder who owns 1,000 shares of common stock in the Dignity Life and Health Insurance Company will receive an additional 100 shares of common stock upon Dignity's distribution of a 10 percent stock dividend (1,000 shares × 10 percent). Suppose Dignity had common stock outstanding of $3,000,000 (300,000 shares × $10 par value per share) and its board of directors declared a 10 percent stock dividend (300,000 shares × 10 percent = 30,000 shares). On the declaration date, Dignity's stock had a market value of $15 per share. The accounting entry for the declaration and distribution of a 10 percent stock dividend follows:

Unassigned Surplus (30,000 × $15) 450,000
Common Stock 300,000
Gross Paid-In and Contributed Surplus (30,000 × $5) 150,000
To record a 10 percent stock dividend on a stock with a $10 par value per share.

To record this transaction under U.S. GAAP, Dignity would debit Retained Earnings instead of Unassigned Surplus, credit Common Stock (a capital account for the stock issuer), and credit Additional Paid-In Capital instead of Gross Paid-In and Contributed Surplus. Note that Dignity does not debit or credit a payable account because an insurer's liabilities are unaffected by the declaration and subsequent distribution of a stock dividend.

The above accounting entry illustrates the primary difference between a stock dividend and a cash dividend in that, unlike a cash dividend, a stock dividend does not transfer a part of an insurer's assets to its stockholders. Stock dividends affect only the company's capital and surplus accounts, not its asset or liability accounts. Under GAAP, the declaration of a stock dividend increases Additional Paid-In Capital and decreases Retained Earnings. It merely transfers funds from one capital account to another, thus maintaining the balance of the basic accounting equation. Therefore, a stock dividend is not a source of capital.

If a U.S. company's board of directors declares a stock dividend of 25 percent or more, then the dividend is called a *stock split,* also known as a *large stock dividend,* and the company values each share of stock at par value, rather than at market value. Suppose an insurer's stockholders own 100,000 shares of the insurer's stock outstanding with a par value of $6. Thus, the insurer has $600,000 (100,000 shares × $6 par value per share) in its Common Stock account. The insurer declares a 2-for-1 stock split. After the stock split, the insurer will still have $600,000 in Common Stock, but twice as many shares (200,000) of stock outstanding. Total capital and surplus does not change and the par value of the stock will be halved to $3 per share ($600,000 ÷ 200,000 shares). Note that this transaction only affects the number of shares outstanding and the par value per share. It does not affect the account totals. Therefore, no accounting entry is necessary. However, insurers typically record a memorandum entry or note to change the par value and the number of shares outstanding on the distribution date. Insurers do this to maintain a record of the par value per share of its stock. Below is an example of a memorandum entry that the insurer would record for the 2-for-1 stock split:

> Called the $6 par value common stock and distributed two shares of $3 par value common stock for each $6 par value share of common stock outstanding.

Again, a stock split is not a source of capital. Recall that an insurer would only increase its total capital and surplus if it were to *issue* additional shares of stock, which would increase both Cash and Common Stock, and perhaps Additional Paid-In Capital. Under U.S. GAAP, in a small stock dividend, Retained Earnings decreases and Additional Paid-In Capital increases. A stock split, however, does not affect Retained Earnings or Additional Paid-In Capital. Instead, it changes only the stock's par value and the number of shares outstanding. Although stock dividends increase the number of shares of stock outstanding as well as the amount of shares owned by each stockholder, they do not change the total dollar value of the stock owned by the insurer or its stockholders.

Retained Earnings

Under U.S. GAAP and the clean surplus theory, only specified transactions can directly increase or decrease Retained Earnings. The *clean surplus theory* states that Retained Earnings consists primarily of the net change in capital and surplus resulting from gains or losses in the company's operations, dividends paid to stockholders, extraordinary items, prior period adjustments (PPAs), and changes in accounting procedures. Canadian GAAP does not adhere to the clean surplus theory.

Treasury Stock

As noted in Chapter 5, *treasury stock* is stock that a U.S. insurer has previously issued, then later repurchased at market prices, with the intention of reselling the stock at a later date. Treasury stock is stock that was issued and outstanding but, upon repurchase, is no longer outstanding. The insurer may resell the stock on a stock exchange or through an employee compensation or pension plan that enables employees to purchase shares of the insurers' stock under specified conditions. Insurers that purchase treasury stock with the intention of later reissuing the stock most often use the *cost method* to account for its purchase. Sometimes, however, an insurer has no intention of reissuing the stock. In such cases, the insurer may use the *par method* to account for the purchase of treasury stock. Both methods are beyond the scope of this text. If the insurer has no intention of reissuing its treasury stock, then the stock is known as ***retired stock.*** In the case of retired stock, the insurer deducts the number of shares and their dollar value, according to the par method, from the capital account.

Increases in the Treasury Stock account ultimately decrease an insurer's total capital because Treasury Stock is a type of contra account, which decreases the amount in its companion account, Common Stock. The amount posted to Additional Paid-In Capital under GAAP or Gross Paid-In and Contributed Surplus under statutory accounting equals the difference between (1) the par value of the retired stock multiplied by the number of shares retired and (2) the purchase price. The purchase of treasury stock for cash reduces the insurer's Cash, an admitted asset. Because the insurer's liabilities and surplus are not affected by this transaction, the insurer must also reduce its capital accounts to maintain the balance in the basic accounting equation. For this reason, insurers typically must obtain statutory approval to purchase treasury stock. Statutory requirements often limit the amount of treasury stock to a specified percentage of the insurer's total capital and surplus or total assets. An insurer's purchase of treasury stock does not decrease the number of total shares of common stock unless the insurer retires the stock. Stock that a company has issued and subsequently purchased as treasury stock is listed separately in the Capital account on the Annual Statement.

Unrealized Gains and Losses

In Chapter 7, we defined realized gains and losses as those that result from the sale of an insurer's invested assets at a price different from the original purchase price. In this section, we focus on accounting for *unrealized gains and losses,* which do not result from the sale of an asset. Recall from Chapter 5 that an *unrealized gain (loss)* is the difference between an asset's book value and its current market value. Often an invested asset gains or loses market value while it is being held by the insurer. Because the insurer still holds the asset, it has not yet generated a *realized* gain or loss. However, the value of these assets has changed from the insurer's original purchase price, and this change affects the insurer's overall financial condition, represented on the balance sheet.

An insurer records an *unrealized loss*—that is, reduces the value of an asset—if the asset's current market value is less than the value recorded in the insurer's accounting records. Because liabilities are not affected by this transaction, a U.S. insurer reports the amount of the decrease in value under its capital and surplus accounts. Except for common stock, insurers do not typically increase the value of an asset. Because insurers maintain accounting records on a conservative basis, an insurer generally does not "write up" an asset that has increased significantly in market value as if the insurer had sold the asset for a realized gain.

An insurer will, however, "write down" the value of an invested asset if the market value of the asset declines significantly and the insurer does not reasonably expect the asset to increase in market value over the long term. Such a long-term decline in value may be the result of the bankruptcy of the asset's issuer or the issuer's continued default on principal and interest payments on its bonds or mortgage loans. Once an insurer determines that an invested asset's market value is not likely to recover, then the insurer classifies that asset as *other-than-temporarily-impaired.* The insurer writes down the asset's value to its *realizable value,* which is the value of an asset as if it had been sold or had matured, even though the insurer still owns the asset. A *write down* is typically a permanent adjustment in the book value of an asset whose market value is deemed to be other-than-temporarily-impaired. The insurer reports the amount of this unrealized loss as a realized loss on the statement of operations. To write down the value of an asset, U.S. insurers debit a realized loss account (for example, Realized Loss on Bonds) and credit the appropriate asset account (for example, Bonds). Canadian insurers debit a credit loss account and credit a contra asset account in such circumstances.

Once an asset has been written down in value, it cannot be written up in value, even if the market value of that asset recovers. On the other hand, an unrealized loss—as opposed to a write down—is a *temporary* recognition of an asset's lower market value. For example, an insurer that owns 1,000 shares of stock in a company that recently declared bankruptcy may choose to permanently write down the value of this stock. Suppose the insurer also owns 1,000 shares of stock in another company that the insurer purchased for $10 per share. If the current market value of the stock is $7 per share, then the insurer reports an unrealized loss of $3,000 [(1,000 × $10 per share) – (1,000 shares × $7 per share)].

Suppose an insurer determines that Bond XYZ, which has a $1,000 par value, is other-than-temporarily-impaired. The insurer estimates that, if the bond were sold, the bond's realizable value would be $450. The insurer would make the following accounting entry to record the realizable value for the par value of this bond:

Realized Loss on Bonds	550	
Bonds		550

To record the realizable value of an other-than-temporarily-impaired bond.

At the end of the accounting period, the insurer would report the value of Bond XYZ as $450 on the balance sheet. The insurer would also report the $550 loss ($1,000 – $450) as a realized loss on the statement of operations. Recall that the effect of a realized loss is to reduce the insurer's net income. As the insurer's net income has decreased in value by $550, retained earnings also ultimately decreases by the same amount on a GAAP-based balance sheet.

Under statutory accounting, a U.S. insurer reports unrealized gains on equity securities in either of two ways, both of which apply directly to accounts on the balance sheet such as the Asset Valuation Reserve (AVR) and Surplus, rather than to accounts on the statement of operations. Insurers in the United States can use the AVR only for its intended purpose: to serve as a buffer for the insurer's surplus by absorbing unrealized gains and losses. Allowing gains and losses to be reflected gradually in capital and surplus minimizes the negative effects of market risk on capital and surplus in a given accounting period. Recall that the AVR is a liability account, whereas Change in the AVR is a surplus account. Alternatively, if an insurance company determines that the unrealized gain or loss on an investment, such as a bond, is the result of changes in market interest rates, rather than the issuer's financial condition, then the company charges the realized gain or loss directly to the Interest Maintenance Reserve (IMR), a liability account.

Under U.S. GAAP, however, accounts on both the balance sheet and the statement of operations are affected by unrealized gains and losses. In the event of an unrealized gain, the insurer records a debit to an asset account and a credit to an unrealized gain account if the market value increases. If the market value decreases, the debit is to an unrealized loss account and the credit is to an asset account. Both accounting entries ultimately affect surplus.

The market value of an insurer's stocks and bonds is reported on a GAAP-based balance sheet if the investments are classified either as available for sale or trading. Under Canadian GAAP, unrealized gains (losses) on stocks, real estate, and other equity securities are amortized into an insurer's income, whereas there is no amortization of these gains and losses on the insurer's fixed-term investments, such as bonds and mortgage loans.

Special Surplus

Special surplus, or *special surplus funds,* consists of the part of a U.S. insurer's surplus that the insurer's board of directors has set aside to (1) meet unforeseen contingencies or (2) pay for certain extraordinary expenses. Special surplus is also known as *assigned surplus, appropriated surplus, earmarked surplus,* and *contingency reserves.* The equivalent accounts for Canadian life and health insurers are liability accounts (for example, contingent liabilities), not surplus accounts. In Chapter 9, we introduced contingency reserves, which are a type of surplus account that, when necessary, supplements a U.S. insurer's other reserves, which are liabilities. Special surplus, which is not available for distribution to stockholders or policyowners, does not replace an insurer's obligation to establish liabilities for expected occurrences. Special surplus can be voluntary or involuntary, depending on statutory requirements. An insurer uses an involuntary special surplus fund only for its specified purposes. In the case of voluntary special surplus funds, an insurer's board of directors can vote to

Figure 11-7. Types of special surplus.

Group annuity contingency reserve*
Participation in separate accounts*
Mortality fluctuation reserve*
Contingency reserve for large risks*
Special contingency reserve*
Reserve for home office remodeling
Group life contingency reserve
Real estate reserve
Currency exchange reserve
Cash value deficiency reserves

* Descriptions of these special surplus funds can be found in Figure 9-11.

re-designate that amount of surplus. Figure 11-7 lists several types of special surplus accounts that an insurer can establish.

One example of an involuntary special surplus fund in most states is the *participation in separate accounts,* which requires all U.S. insurers to allocate a specified amount of their surplus to provide protection for the separate accounts of their policyowners. A typical accounting entry that an insurer uses to establish this special surplus fund is

Unassigned Surplus	xxx	
Participation in Separate Accounts		xxx

To establish a special surplus account for separate accounts.

Unassigned Surplus

Unassigned surplus under statutory accounting is similar to retained earnings under GAAP because this account represents the accumulation of operating income not paid out in dividends. For U.S. life and health insurance companies, ***unassigned surplus,*** also called *unassigned surplus funds, divisible surplus,* or *free surplus,* is the amount of surplus remaining after deducting liabilities, capital, and special surplus from admitted assets. Unassigned surplus is available to meet any contingency that arises, including new business, outstanding debt, or the purchase or retirement of outstanding common stock. An insurer can also use unassigned surplus to satisfy a contingency which has since exhausted the special surplus fund that the insurer originally established for that contingency or to pay operating

Figure 11-8. Accounts that directly affect U.S. unassigned surplus.

Net income
Changes in unrealized capital gains (losses)
Stockholder dividends
Reserve strengthening (destrengthening)
Changes in nonadmitted assets
Changes in the Asset Valuation Reserve (AVR)

expenses when a company experiences a net loss during a year. Whatever remains in unassigned surplus is the accumulation of all gains from operations that an insurer has not used for other purposes. Figure 11-8 lists the primary accounts that directly affect the dollar amount of an insurer's unassigned surplus.

Stockholders typically prefer to receive more and higher dividends. On the other hand, the more dividends an insurer pays to its stockholders, the lower the amount of growth possible in the insurer's Unassigned Surplus. Thus, the insurer cannot declare and pay too high a dividend without risking its financial position. However, an insurer's stockholders must receive a positive return on their investment, so many insurers elect to provide at least a minimum dividend for their stockholders. Most states limit the amount of dividends that a stock insurance company can pay to stockholders. For example, state regulations could limit stockholder dividends to a proportion of the insurer's Unassigned Surplus so the insurer can maintain an adequate level of surplus.

Before declaring stockholder dividends, a company's board of directors uses unassigned surplus as one factor in determining the dividend amount. Laws in an insurer's state of domicile determine the amount of unassigned surplus available for stockholder dividends. Two primary factors in determining the amount of unassigned surplus available for distribution to stockholders are (1) the amount of business that the company writes and (2) the contractual agreements that the company may have, such as loan agreements that might affect the company's future financial situation. Once a stockholder dividend has been declared, it becomes a liability to the insurer, as discussed in Chapter 10.

Financial Reporting Requirements

A debit to Death Claims Paid, an expense account, ultimately decreases surplus because claim payments reduce an insurer's net income. However, because policy reserves are released when a claim is pending, the effect on surplus is lower than the amount paid for the death benefit. Suppose a death claim payment on a policy totals $5,000. If the reserve on the policy is $2,100, the claim will reduce surplus by $2,900 ($5,000 – $2,100). Payment of a claim for accidental death, however, reduces surplus almost to the full extent of that claim because reserves released on accidental death claims are relatively small. An insurer establishes smaller reserves for accidental death claims because of the low incidence of such claims. Group insurance certificates are usually term insurance with little or no reserve released at the time of an insured's death. Therefore, a group term life claim also has a greater impact on surplus than an individual ordinary life claim of the same size. A matured endowment policy does not affect surplus because, with an endowment policy, the combined reserve of the policy and any paid-up additions on the maturity date equals the total amount of the policy plus additions. This reserve is released upon payment of the claim.

Under GAAP, an insurer values its common stock and bonds, other than those held to maturity, at current market value and most of its liabilities at book value. As a result, the insurer's balance sheet can be subject to extreme volatility from year to year because the value of invested assets can change dramatically in the short term. In contrast, an insurer's GAAP liabilities typically remain within a narrow range. If the only change between one year's balance sheet and the next is the change in market value for the insurer's invested assets, then the insurer's asset and surplus accounts change, independent of any other changes that the insurer has made in its balance sheet accounts. Figure 11-9 demonstrates the effect that changes in invested assets have on an insurer's total assets and surplus, given two different scenarios. Note how, between 1998 and 1999, a 40 percent *decrease* in the current market value of the insurer's invested assets results in a 25 percent reduction in total assets and a 33 percent reduction in surplus. On the other hand, if invested assets *increase* by 40 percent, the result is a 25 percent increase in total assets and a 33 percent increase in surplus, without any other changes in the insurer's balance sheet. This type of volatility is difficult to manage in the short term.

An insurer's capital accounts typically do not change in value as a result of the insurer's core business operations. Rather, they change as a result of a specific transaction, such as the issue of stock or the repurchase of treasury stock. On the other hand, the amount of an insurer's surplus can and does change daily as a result of the company's insurance operations. Although the insurer does not record accounting entries each time surplus is affected, it does prepare adjusting entries at the end of the accounting period to report the aggregate effect of these changes on surplus. The amount of an in-

Figure 11-9. The effect of current market value on total assets and surplus.

	Year Ended 1998	Year Ended 1999A (Market Value of Assets *Decreases* by $2 million)	Year Ended 1999B (Market Value of Assets *Increases* by $2 million)
Invested assets	$5,000,000	$3,000,000	$ 7,000,000
Other assets	3,000,000	3,000,000	3,000,000
Total Assets	$8,000,000	$6,000,000	$10,000,000
Liabilities	$2,000,000	$2,000,000	$ 2,000,000
Surplus	6,000,000	4,000,000	8,000,000
Total Liabilities and Surplus	$8,000,000	$6,000,000	$10,000,000

surer's surplus changes because of internal and external sources and uses of capital and surplus, as outlined in this chapter, as well as changes in reserves. The Capital and Surplus Account specifies many types of surplus changes, attributable both to core business operations and to transactions that directly change an insurer's surplus. Outlined below are descriptions of how U.S. and Canadian insurers report changes in surplus.

United States

Life and health insurance companies in the United States have three main surplus accounts under statutory accounting: (1) *unassigned surplus,* (2) *special surplus,* and (3) *gross paid-in and contributed surplus.* They report changes in surplus in the Capital and Surplus Account section of the *Summary of Operations* page of the Annual Statement. To calculate the net annual change in a company's surplus, a U.S. insurer adjusts the total of the previous year's surplus for the factors listed in the *Capital and Surplus Account,* as shown in Figure 6-7. Some of these factors increase an insurer's surplus amount, while others decrease that amount. Changes in surplus associated with an insurer's separate accounts, miscellaneous capital and surplus adjustments, and write-in items are three factors that can change an insurer's surplus.

The *Assets* page and *Liabilities* section of the Annual Statement include the assets and liabilities of any separate accounts that an insurer maintains. Usually, the total assets and liabilities for an insurer's separate accounts are equal. However, when these totals are not equal, the insurer must report the difference in its surplus if the basic accounting equation is to remain in balance. If the assets of the separate accounts exceed the liability totals for those accounts, the amount of excess increases the insurer's surplus. On the other hand, if total liabilities exceed total assets for the separate accounts, the excess decreases surplus.

Stock insurers also include in the Capital and Surplus Account changes in capital that result from the (1) sale of stock, (2) declaration of a stock dividend, and (3) direct transfer of additional paid-in capital to surplus under capital changes. Should any of these changes also affect an insurer's surplus, then the insurer reports the effects under surplus adjustments. Dividends to stockholders include the amount of cash dividends that an insurer has paid to its stockholders as well as any change in stockholder dividends declared but unpaid. The insurer makes payments of cash dividends directly from Unassigned Surplus, which decreases the Capital and Surplus Account.

Insurers use write-in lines to make any necessary capital and surplus adjustments that do not appear separately among the other reconciliation items in the Capital and Surplus Account. Insurers can use these write-in lines to show, for example, corrections of previous years' information or special losses or expenses that should come directly from surplus but which the insurer has not otherwise reported. Among the write-in reconciliation items that can be included in an insurer's Capital and Surplus Account are

- The prior year's federal income tax adjustments
- Adjustments for employee stock ownership plans
- Changes in the reserve valuation basis
- Charitable contributions not reported elsewhere
- Additional contributions to fund pension plans

Canada

A Canadian insurer reports its surplus in the following accounts:

- Capital stock
- Retained earnings
- Currency translation account

Also, Canadian insurers that sell both participating and nonparticipating policies must show surplus separately for each type of business. The accounting treatment and financial reporting requirements for the first two accounts listed above are similar to that for common stock and retained earnings for U.S. insurers.

Until 1994, a Canadian insurer's surplus consisted of both appropriated surplus and unappropriated surplus. These terms are equivalent to special surplus and unassigned surplus in the United States. However, the Minimum Continuing Capital and Surplus Requirements (MCCSR), discussed in Chapter 19, now incorporate amounts that an insurer previously categorized as appropriated surplus. Some Canadian insurers itemize appropriated surplus and unappropriated surplus in a note to the financial statements, as these amounts no longer appear separately in the *Liabilities* section of the Annual Return, as shown in Figure 6-4.

Canadian insurers report changes in surplus in the Annual Return. The method of reconciling surplus changes between reporting years is similar to that used by U.S. insurers. However, under Canadian GAAP, insurers do not differentiate between admitted and nonadmitted assets. To determine total regulatory capital, a Canadian insurer first subtracts liabilities from assets. It then adds deferred realized gains from real estate and certain other items. Finally, it subtracts deferred realized losses and a number of other specified items. The resulting figure is the total regulatory capital.

Conclusion

In this chapter, we focused on the key capital and surplus accounts of life and health insurance companies. We also outlined ways in which an insurer can increase its capital and surplus from both internal and external sources. Chapter 11 concludes our discussion of the major account classifications on the balance sheet of life and health insurance companies. The next two chapters discuss the major account classifications associated with an insurer's statement of operations: revenues and expenses.

Key Terms and Concepts

liability for reinsurance in unauthorized companies
yearly renewable term (YRT) reinsurance
coinsurance
modified coinsurance (modco)
assumption reinsurance
surplus notes
demutualization
retired stock
special surplus
unassigned surplus

References

1. For additional information on coinsurance and modified coinsurance, see *Statutory Accounting: Modified Coinsurance and Coinsurance with Funds Withheld,* Report of the Technical Resource Subgroup to the NAIC (Kansas City, MO: National Association of Insurance Commissioners; September 19, 1994).

2. For an excellent discussion on surplus notes, see Donald F. Behan, "Introduction to Surplus Notes," *The Financial Reporter* (Shaumburg, IL: Society of Actuaries, December 1994), pp. 15–16.

CHAPTER 12

ACCOUNTING FOR REVENUES

LEARNING OBJECTIVES

After studying this chapter, you should be able to

- Identify the main sources of revenues for life and health insurance companies
- Describe the ways to classify income on an accrual basis
- List and describe the different types of premiums
- Discuss the basic objectives of accounting for premium income
- Record the journal entries associated with typical premium income transactions
- List and describe the different types of investment income
- Record journal entries associated with typical investment income
- Discuss the presentation of premium income and investment income on the Annual Statement and Annual Return

CHAPTER OUTLINE

Income Classifications

Premium Income

Premium Accounting Systems

Accounting for Premiums

Accounting for Policy Loan Interest and Policy Dividends

Investment Income

Accounting for Investment Income

Other Sources of Revenues

Financial Reporting of Revenues

Premium Income

Investment Income

With this chapter, we shift our focus from items that appear on the balance sheet to those that appear on the statement of operations. A goal of all companies is to generate revenues, which, as we noted in Chapter 2, are amounts earned from a company's sales of products and services to customers. If a company does not generate sufficient revenues, it will be unable to remain in business for long. When it earns revenues during an accounting period, an insurance company posts the revenues to various revenue accounts. The balances in these accounts represent the amount of revenues that the insurer earned during a particular period. Like all accounts on the statement of operations, revenue accounts are *nominal (temporary)* accounts because they begin each fiscal year with a zero balance. At the end of the accounting period, the insurer records *closing entries* so that the various revenue account balances will be zero at the beginning of the next period.

Although the actual account names can and do vary among insurance companies, most revenue accounts have self-explanatory titles: Premium Income—Life Insurance, Premium Income—Health Insurance, and Investment Income—Common Stock Dividends, for example. Premium income and investment income constitute the largest and most important sources of revenues for most life and health insurance companies. Figure 12-1 highlights the revenues portion of an insurer's statement of operations.

When to recognize revenues is important in accounting and financial reporting. Under GAAP, *accrual-basis accounting* and the *realization principle* require an insurer to recognize revenues when they are earned, rather than when they are received. Under statutory accounting practices, a U.S. insurer typically reports revenues on an accrual basis in the *Summary of Operations,* although the exhibits report amounts on a modified-cash basis. Regardless of the accounting method used, however, an insurer records within the fiscal year the exact amount of revenues received or due from each business transaction. While this chapter focuses on when revenues are recognized by insurance home offices, Insight 12-1 explains when insurance agencies should recognize revenue.

This chapter discusses the accounting and financial reporting requirements associated with an insurer's typical revenue accounts. We focus our discussion on premium income and investment income. To begin, let's first review several income classifications that an insurer can have under accrual-basis accounting. Figure 12-2 categorizes the sources of premium income and investment income for

Figure 12-1. Highlight of the revenues section of a typical insurance company statement of operations.

For the year ended December 31, 19XX	
Revenues	
Premium income	xxx
Net investment income	xxx
Other income	xxx
Total Revenues	1,000,000
Benefits and Expenses	
Policy benefits:	
Life insurance	xxx
Accident and health	xxx
Annuities	xxx
Total Policy Benefits	xxx
Expenses:	
Agent commissions	xxx
Operating expenses:	
Home office salaries	xxx
Rent	xxx
Other operating expenses	xxx
Total Operating Expenses	xxx
Taxes, licenses, and fees:	
Premium taxes	xxx
Guaranty fund assessment	xxx
Other taxes, licenses, and fees	xxx
Total Taxes, Licenses, and Fees	xxx
Total Expenses	xxx
Total Benefits and Expenses	800,000
Income before income taxes	xxx
Income tax expense	50,000
Net Income	150,000

U.S. life and health insurance companies. Figure 12-3 categorizes income for Canadian life and health insurance companies.

Income Classifications

The term *income* can have many different connotations in accounting and finance. For example, you have learned that net income is a

Insight 12-1 Debate on When to Count Premiums as Income

"Don't count your chickens before they hatch" is very old, but very good, advice. It also happens to apply to the quandary faced by insurance agents who are not certain about when they should "count their chickens" for accounting purposes.

The problem encountered by nearly all agents is a decision about when to "recognize" revenue. On the surface, this appears to be a minor detail. Does it really matter when you enter the sale of a policy as income for the agency? This answer is an emphatic "Yes!"

There are two major sources of income for an insurance agency: commissions on premiums (generally a percentage of premiums billed), and fees in lieu of commissions for insurance placement services. Precisely when these funds become revenue has long been a matter of contention and confusion.

This discussion will center on recognizing revenue for financial reporting purposes. Tax accounting is a separate and distinct issue.

The timing of revenue recognition has varied with accounting methods, but generally swings between the effective date of the policy and the billing date of the policy. Obviously, it is in everybody's best interest to standardize revenue recognition for financial reporting. There should be a common financial yardstick. After all, there are other, fairly important people who read your financial statements—like your banker.

But which date is right? Which is better for the agency? Those who read and rely on financial statements should have a common understanding to avoid confusion and misinterpretation.

Here's a strong vote for not recognizing revenue before the effective date of the policy sold. (That is, not before protection is afforded under the policy to the customer.)

Revenue should only be recognized in accordance with the arrangements the agency has for services to be provided to the customer; matching revenue with expense is the common way with which we are all familiar.

Here are some compelling reasons why:

- The effective date is much more than the billing date. In many cases today, the customer is billed directly by the insurance company. The selling agency has no control over when the bill is mailed, and often no knowledge of the billing. On the other hand, when the agency bills, the agency can literally pick and choose the most convenient billing date. While such flexibility may appear to be advantageous, the opportunity for inconsistency and confusion is too great to chance. There is no uncertainty as to the date risk is transferred to the underwriter.
- Advance billing is not income. In fact, advance billing is a liability until the policy becomes effective.
- Figures are actual, not estimated. By the effective date of the policy, the premium amount should be a known quantity. All adjustments and changes to price and premium value should have been complete. Direct billing information should be available via computer link, or be at most a phone call away. If revenue is recognized ahead of the effective date of the policy, financial statements may not be indicative of the agency's true operations for the period in question.
- The effective date offers protection for the agency. When the effective date of the policy is used as the date of revenue recognition, services required for placing the insurance have generally been performed. There may be obligations to perform services after the effective date. The effective date therefore provides an objective starting point for spreading that revenue over the expense period.

The time has come for insurance agencies to standardize the method used for revenue recognition. Let's make financial statements meaningful. It only makes sense that the effective date of the policy should also be the effective date of revenue recognition.

Source: Marshall I. Karp, "Debate on When to Count Premiums as Income," *National Underwriter Life & Health/Financial Services Edition,* No. 46 (November 15, 1993), p. 43. Reprinted with permission from *National Underwriter,* © 1996, The National Underwriter Company, *Life & Health/Financial Services Edition,* 1993.

company's revenues less expenses. Used in another way, however, income is synonymous with revenue; in other words, income is the money earned from the sales of a company's goods or services. In this context, life and health insurance companies are viewed as having two primary sources of income: income from premiums (premium income) and income from investments (investment income). Because

Figure 12-2. Premium income and investment income of U.S. life and health insurance companies.

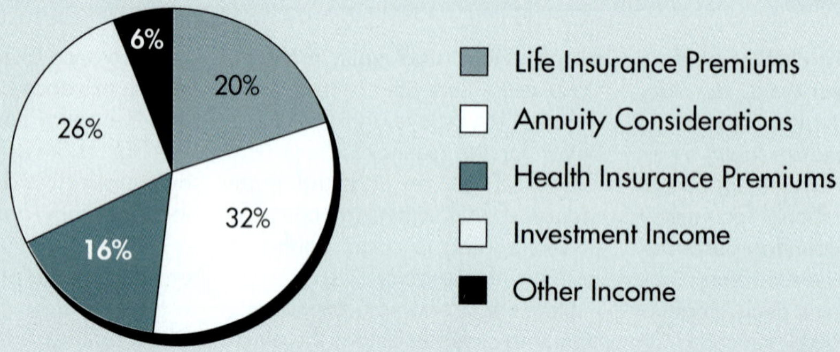

Source: Adapted from the ACLI *1995 Life Insurance Fact Book Update,* p. 31.

of the timing of various reporting requirements, and because U.S. insurers convert from modified cash-basis accounting to accrual-basis accounting for reporting on the Annual Statement, insurers more specifically define income according to when the income is earned, when it is due, and when it is collected. This section describes various ways to classify an insurer's accrual-basis income: *collected income, unearned income, deferred income, uncollected income (due income), accrued income,* and *nonadmitted income.* These terms are not an important distinction for Canadian insurers, which recognize an entire premium received as premium income. The accounting entries that accompany each income classification assume that the fiscal year runs from January 1 through December 31 and that the financial reporting date is December 31.

Figure 12-3. Premium income of Canadian life and health insurance companies.

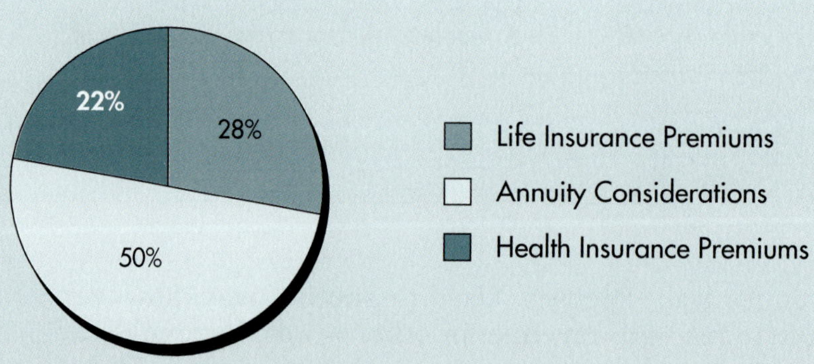

Source: Adapted from the CLHIA *1994 Facts,* pp. 5–6.

- *Collected income* is the amount of income received in cash during a reporting period, including certain adjustments for amortization. For example, premiums collected for the reporting period from January 1 through December 31 constitute collected income.

- *Unearned income,* a subset of collected income, is income that has been collected but not yet earned. For example, an *unearned premium,* also called *unearned premium reserve,* is that portion of the insurance premium received by the statement date and applicable to the insurance coverage to be provided in the following period but before the next policy anniversary. For example, if a quarterly premium payment of $24 for health insurance is due on December 1, then $16 of that premium (⅔ × $24) is applicable to the period from January 1 through February 28 of the following year. On December 31, this premium has an unearned premium liability of $16, so the insurer establishes an unearned premium reserve for this amount. The unearned premium classification usually applies to group life and health insurance premiums and not to individual life insurance premiums or annuity considerations.

- *Deferred income* is income due after the Annual Statement date but before the next policy anniversary. Recall from Chapter 8 that the classification of deferred premiums applies to premium payments made more frequently than annually. For example, deferred premiums, which apply to policies with modal (monthly, quarterly, semiannual) payments, are an asset used to offset an insurer's policy reserves, which are overstated if the insurer uses the mean reserve method to calculate its reserves. The mean reserve method assumes that all premiums are paid annually on the policy anniversary date.

- *Uncollected income (due income)* is income that is scheduled for receipt before December 31, but which the insurer has not received as of December 31. Uncollected premiums, called *outstanding premiums* in Canada, primarily refer to individual life insurance premiums and annuity considerations, whereas due premiums generally refer to accident and health insurance premiums and group life insurance premiums.

- *Accrued income* is income that the insurer has already earned but which is not receivable until a specified date in the next fiscal year (that is, after December 31). For example, suppose an insurer has a particular investment with interest payments scheduled to be paid to the insurer on October 31, January 31, April 30, and July 31. The portion of interest for November and

December is identified as due and accrued investment income until the insurer receives it on January 31. Individual policyowners have no legal obligation to remit policy premium payments; therefore, premium income typically is not accrued because accrued income must be legally collectible.

- *Nonadmitted income* for U.S. insurers consists of an insurer's due income that is overdue for more than a specified period, from three months to two years, as prescribed by state insurance laws. By classifying long overdue income as nonadmitted income, an insurer is implicitly stating that it is not certain whether it will ever be collected.

Figure 12-4 summarizes the different types of income defined above. The primary focus of this chapter is on collected income, which is a revenue account. However, we discuss the other income classifications as well.

Premium Income

Premium income includes premium payments that an insurer receives for individual life insurance, individual accident and health insurance, group life insurance, group accident and health insurance, and disability income insurance. An insurer's premium income also includes annuity considerations, considerations paid on supplementary contracts with or without life contingencies, premiums for reinsur-

Figure 12-4. Types of income.

Type of Income	Received?	Earned?	Account Classification
Collected	Yes	Yes*	Revenue
Unearned	Yes	No	Liability
Uncollected (due)	No	Yes	Asset
Accrued	No	Yes	Asset
Deferred**	No	No	Asset
Nonadmitted (statutory accounting practices only)	No	Yes	Nonadmitted asset

* Collected income may have both an earned and an unearned portion.

** Deferred Premiums is an asset account established to offset the overstated reserve liability.

ance assumed, and deposit funds for retirement accounts such as pension funds. An insurer receives premium payments from a variety of sources, including

- Individual policyowners
- Annuity and supplementary contract owners
- Group policyholders (for example, employers, unions, pension funds)
- Home service agents
- Credit life and health insurance policyowners
- Policy benefits such as paid-up additions

Because a significant portion of an insurer's revenues consists of policy premiums, insurance companies must be aware of the external and internal factors that directly affect the nature, amount, and timing of premium income. External factors include those general economic, industry, and environmental conditions that affect all companies, such as regulatory requirements, accounting standards, interest rates, taxes, existing and potential markets, and competitor actions. Internal factors include those that affect the policy premiums of a particular life and health insurance company, such as product features and benefits, sales distribution system (including agent commissions), investment policy, and management vision and competence. Figure 12-5 illustrates these external and internal factors affecting premium income.

Premium Accounting Systems

An insurer's core business operations depend on the timely receipt of accurate premium payments. For this reason, the maintenance of detailed records of premium transactions, known as *premium accounting* or *policy accounting,* is critical. Premium accounting usually comprises the largest number of an insurer's accounting entries, which can involve millions of transactions a year. Examples of premium transactions include premium billing and collection and accounting for commission payments, claims, policy loans, and policy dividends. We discussed accounting for claims in Chapter 10. We discuss premium billing and collection and briefly review accounting for policy loans and policy dividends later in this chapter. In Chapter 13, we discuss commission payments and other expenses associated with life and health insurance products.

Figure 12-5. External and internal factors affecting premium income.

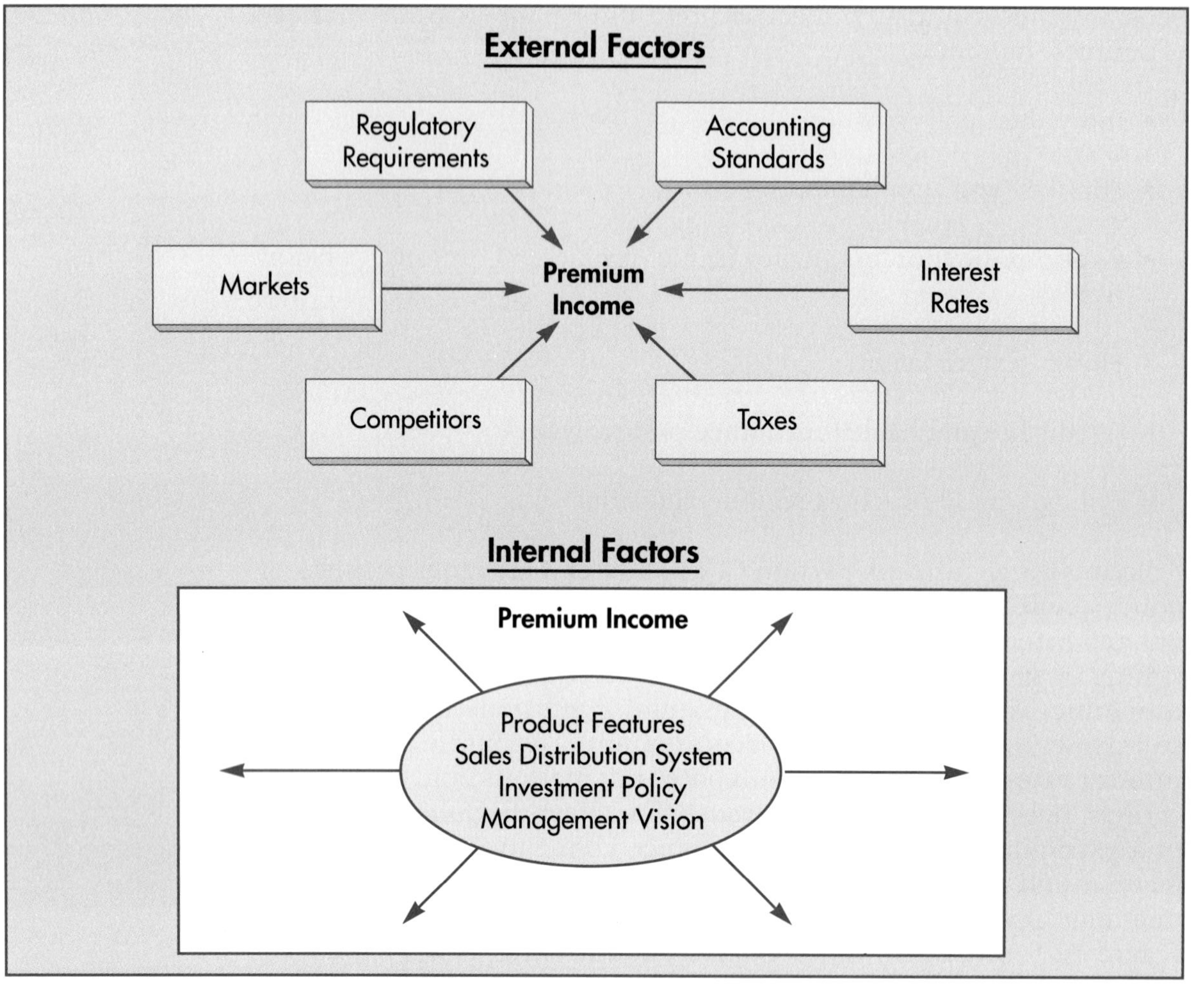

Diversity among premium accounting systems results from differences in company organization, management preferences, and lines of business. For example, some insurance companies centralize premium collections at the home office. Other companies have regional offices or several collection centers throughout their marketing areas. Life and health insurance companies also differ in their preparation of lapse notices and statistical reports. In this text, we describe the common methods of premium billing and collection, although account names and procedures can vary among insurers. Our focus is on accounting for life insurance premiums, although we note the differences, if any, between accounting for life insurance premiums and accounting for other insurance products and annuities.

The primary function of a premium accounting system is to record premium income as soon as the insurer earns it. In addition, an insurer's accounting system must encompass billing, collections, and internal controls associated with premiums. Accuracy in accounting for premium income is essential to conserve insurance business, retain good service standards with policyowners and agents, and fulfill regulatory, tax, and accounting requirements. An insurer's premium accounting system achieves these objectives when it enables the insurer to

- Bill for premiums before the due date, with sufficient lead time between the billing and due dates
- Post a premium payment to the general ledger and to the policyowner's record immediately upon receipt
- Record premium income according to product type and other specified categories so the insurer can use the data to calculate taxable income and prepare financial statements by line of business or product
- Accept no premium payment after the expiration of the grace period, except under circumstances acceptable to the insurer
- Terminate a policy or change the policy from a premium-paying status to a specified nonforfeiture option, if the policyowner has not paid the premium by the end of the grace period

Critical to the financial reporting of premium transactions is the ability of the insurer to record premium income (1) by jurisdiction, for premium tax assessments, (2) by line of business, and (3) by participating and nonparticipating classifications. Further, an effective system for recording and reporting premium transactions facilitates auditing. For example, a sound premium accounting system allows auditors to trace a premium and its related transactions

- From the insurer's bank deposit that included the premium
- To the journal entry used to record the premium payment
- To the policy record to which the insurer credits the premium payment
- To the commission payment associated with the premium

Accounting for Premiums

The accounting effect of the receipt of policy premiums is to increase revenues and assets. As noted earlier, the basic journal entry to record a collected premium is a debit to Cash, an asset account, and a credit to a revenue account, such as Premium Income:

Cash. xxx
    Premium Income xxx
To record the receipt of premium income.

This basic accounting entry for premium income generally does not vary from product to product.

Premium income is often deposited when received. This practice not only provides for good accounting, but also makes the funds received available for investment. However, as we discussed in Chapter 10, some insurance companies do not immediately record a received premium payment as earned income, as happened in the above example. These insurers initially *suspense* a premium received when the premium cannot be accepted as income until a particular event occurs, such as the approval of an application and the issue of a policy. Insurers who first suspense premiums received debit Cash and credit Premium Suspense in the first accounting entry:

Cash. xxx
    Premium Suspense xxx
To record the suspense of a premium payment.

When the reason for holding the premium in suspense no longer applies, as in the case of policy approval, the second entry is to debit Premium Suspense and credit Premium Income:

Premium Suspense xxx
    Premium Income xxx
To record the receipt of premium income.

The insurer does not update the policyowner master file until it debits Premium Suspense and credits Premium Income for the amount of the premium payment. If the insurer declines to issue the policy, then it must return the initial premium to the applicant. A typical accounting entry to record the return of the initial premium is

Premium Suspense xxx
    Cash. xxx
To record the return of an initial premium to the applicant.

An insurer also uses a premium suspense account for incorrect premium amounts, premiums remitted with the incorrect policy number, or other premium payments that render the insurer unable to accept amounts that are intended as premiums until a particular event occurs.

Typically, an insurer maintains premium controls through each *policyowner master file* or *master billing record.* This record contains important information, including the policy's paid-to date. The ***paid-to date*** is the date to which a policy premium provides insurance coverage. The insurer periodically monitors the paid-to date of its policies, which enables the insurer to generate premium notices and past-due warnings, as well as change a policy's status from premium paying to non-premium paying. The insurer processes each premium payment it receives from a policyowner against the master file to maintain current paid-to date information. Figures 12-6 and 12-7 depict the process of accounting for premium payments at policy issue and policy renewal. The accounting treatment of premium income directly affects an insurer's financial reports, particularly the statement of cash flows, which reports all changes in cash from normal business operations.

An insurer's premium accounting system routinely expedites (1) depositing premium payments into the insurer's account, (2) updating

Figure 12-6. An overview of premium accounting at policy issue.

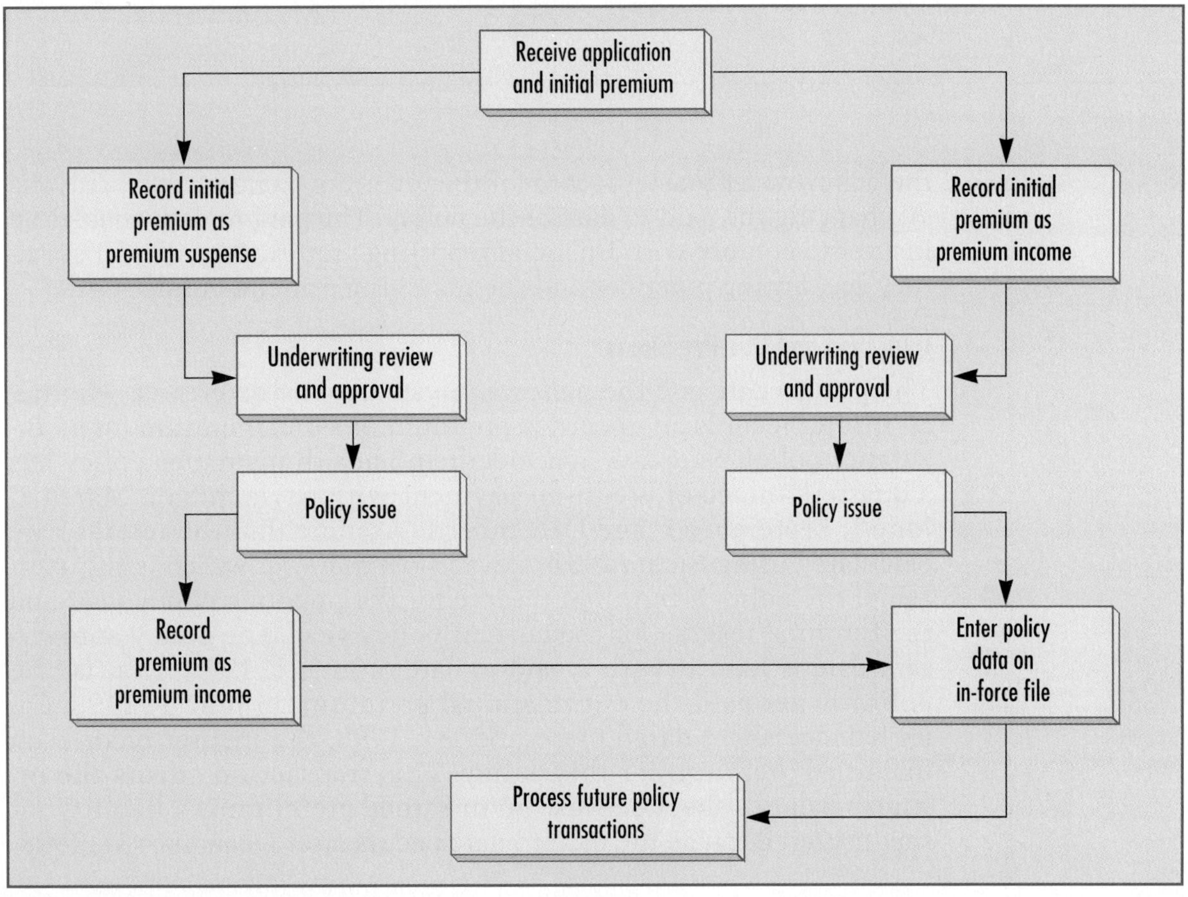

Figure 12-7. An overview of premium accounting at policy renewal.

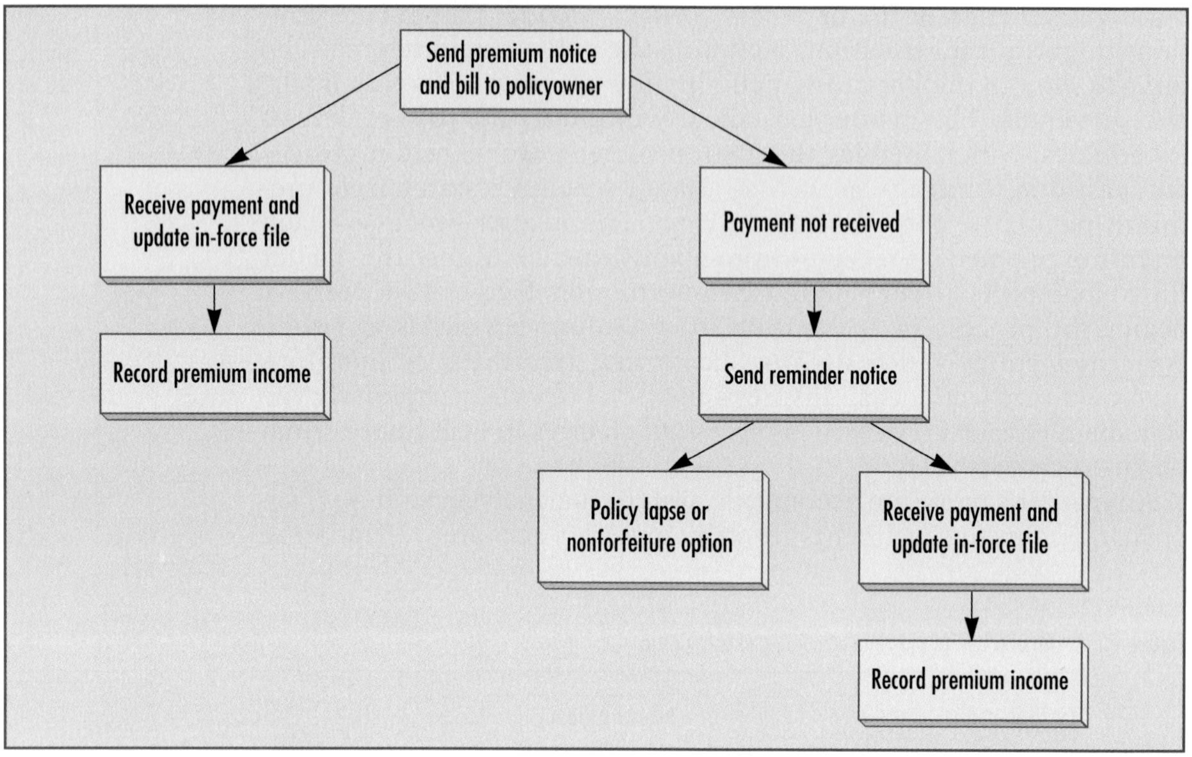

the policyowner master record for the premium payment received, and (3) changing the paid-to date of the policy. The paid-to date enables an insurer to comply with financial reporting requirements under statutory accounting practices and the matching principle under GAAP.

Unearned and Due Premiums

The paid-to date and the policy anniversary date determine whether an insurer records an unearned premium or a due premium for an insurance policy. Suppose an accident and health insurance policy has a quarterly mode of premium payment with payments on March 1, June 1, September 1, and December 1. Assume that the reserves are calculated using the *midterminal reserve method,* which is the average of the policy's terminal reserve for the previous policy year and the terminal reserve for the current policy year. The policy anniversary date is June 1, with a paid-to date of June 1, 1999. That is, the policyowner paid the entire annual premium on June 1, 1998. On its balance sheet dated December 31, 1998, the insurer records an unearned premium for this policy. This transaction affects the insurer's balance sheet because an unearned premium is a liability for the insurer. Because the paid-to date occurs after December 31, 1998, there is no due premium. On the other hand, if the paid-to date were December 1, 1998, and the insurer has not yet received the premium payment, the insurer records a due premium on its December 31 balance sheet, as depicted in the timeline below:

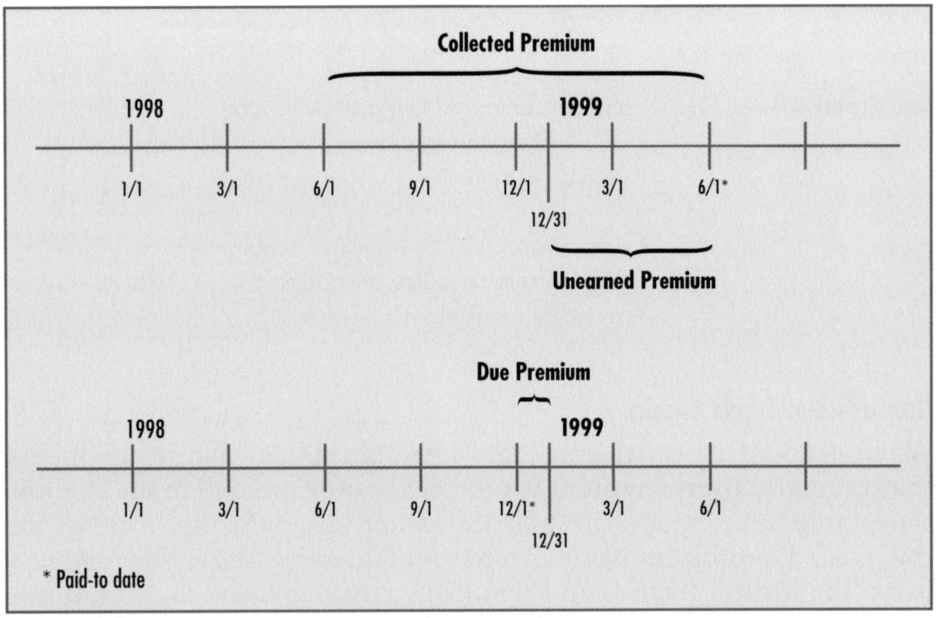

As you can probably guess, unearned premiums and due premiums require accounting treatment that is more complicated than a simple debit to Cash and credit to a revenue account, as is the case with collected premiums. Unearned premiums are liabilities because the insurer has not yet provided the insurance coverage. On the other hand, due premiums are assets, because they represent amounts that the insurer expects to receive. Most premiums are received before the actual coverage period. Therefore, when an insurer receives a premium payment before the beginning date of coverage it has not yet provided, the insurer treats the amount of the unearned revenue as an unearned premium. A typical accounting entry in this instance is a debit to Cash and a credit to Unearned Premiums. Once the insurer has provided the coverage, thus earning the premium payment, the accounting entry is a debit to Unearned Premiums and a credit to Premium Income. Only when an insurer earns an *unearned premium* or receives payment for a *due premium* does the insurer record the amount of the premium in a revenue account such as Premium Income. The following entries compare how an insurer typically records unearned premiums and due premiums:

Unearned Premiums

Cash xxx
    Unearned Premiums xxx
To record the receipt of an unearned premium.

Unearned Premiums xxx
    Premium Income xxx
To record an unearned premium that has been earned.

Due Premiums

Premiums Due and Unpaid xxx
    Premium Income xxx
To record a due premium.

Cash xxx
    Premiums Due and Unpaid xxx
To record the receipt of a due premium.

Nonsufficient Funds Checks

When accounting for the receipt of premiums, an insurer confirms that each premium payment it receives is on time and in an amount acceptable to the insurer. When an insurer discovers that a check for the posted premium payment has not cleared the policyowner's bank, the insurer records an accounting entry to show that it has not received the payment. Recall from Chapter 8 that a typical journal entry indicating an insurer's attempt to collect on a returned policyowner's check after originally debiting Cash and crediting Premium Income is a debit to NSF (Nonsufficient Funds) Checks and a credit to Cash. If the policyowner's check is honored upon the insurer's second attempt at collection, the journal entry that adjusts the debit balance in the suspense account is

Cash. xxx
    NSF Checks. xxx
To record the successful collection on an NSF check.

On the other hand, if the policyowner's bank does not honor the check, the insurer records the following accounting entry:

Premium Income xxx
    NSF Checks. xxx
To record the reversal of premium income because of an NSF check.

This entry reduces the total in both the Premium Income and NSF Checks accounts by the amount of the dishonored check. If the insurer originally suspensed all premium payments, then the above entries would have used Premium Suspense instead of Premium Income. Because the policyowner has not paid the premium, the insurer reviews the policy to see if it has provisions for policy loans or policy dividends to keep the policy from lapsing.

If a policyowner does not pay the premium by the end of the grace period, the insurer either terminates the policy or changes the policy record from premium-paying status to one of the nonforfeiture option classifications. In some cases, a policyowner may request an *automatic premium loan (APL)* from the policy's cash value or from other amounts on deposit with the company. The insurer's accounting system and procedures should be able to accommodate these kinds of transactions.

Premium Payment Methods

Individual policyowners of traditional life insurance products typically remit premium payments to the insurer after receiving premium notices. However, other payment systems are also available. These systems provide convenience both for the policyowner and the insurer. For example, besides using premium notices, many life and health insurance companies also offer a *preauthorized payment system* or a *lock-box system.*

Under a preauthorized payment system, the policyowner signs a two-part authorization form, which is submitted to his or her bank. The first part authorizes the insurer to withdraw due premiums from the policyowner's checking or savings account. The second part of the form authorizes the policyowner's bank to honor these withdrawals. Future withdrawals for premium payments do not require the policyowner's signature. A preauthorized payment system that is implemented by checks drawn against a policyowner's account is called a preauthorized check (PAC) system. Under one variation of the PAC system, a policyowner signs several checks in advance for the premium payments, and the insurer deposits the appropriate check on the date the specified premium amount is due.

Increasingly, preauthorized payments are implemented by an *electronic funds transfer (EFT) system,* in which funds are transferred from the policyowner's bank to the insurer's bank via computer. Under an EFT system, once the policyowner authorizes his or her bank to make the necessary transfers, no additional paper documents are required. The insurer does not mail premium billing notices under either preauthorized payment system because premium payments are made automatically on a specified date. As long as the policyowner's bank account balance is sufficient to cover the amount of the current premium, the insurer will receive premium payments on time and in the correct amount. The policyowner no longer has to worry about accidentally missing payments, and the insurer saves the processing and mailing costs associated with premium billing notices.

Under a ***lock-box system,*** also called *lock-box banking,* policyowners remit premium payments, along with the premium notice stub, to a specified post office box number to which the insurer's bank has access. The insurer's bank opens the premium payment envelopes and immediately deposits them to the insurer's account, then electronically transmits data to the insurer. The insurer uses the information contained on the premium notice stubs to update the policyowner master file. Because the insurer's bank processes the premium payments, these payments are deposited to the insurer's account faster than if the insurer had to process and deposit these amounts.

Group Life and Accident and Health Premiums

The accounting procedures for group insurance premiums depend on whether the billing plan is (1) self administered, (2) insurer administered, or (3) third-party administered. In a ***self-administered plan,*** the group policyholder performs most of the administrative work, including the processing of detailed accounting records of group members and routine requests for name, address, or policy beneficiary changes. Most group policyholders use payroll deductions for employee premium payments and remit the monthly total premium to the insurer. In some cases, the group policyholder even prepares insurance certificates for new group members. The total amount of the premium due on group insurance can change monthly because members join and leave the group. The group policyholder maintains current records of members under a self-administered plan. If the insured group is relatively small in number, then the billing statement typically lists each insured group member and the premium for that member. For a large group of insured members, the statement may show only the number of insureds in each of several classifications and the premium due for each classification. The group policyholder prepares a premium statement that shows the computation of the premium due and sends this statement, along with the premium payment, to the insurer. The insurer periodically audits these computations.

If the group plan is an ***insurer-administered plan,*** the insurer performs the administrative work, which includes calculating the amount of the premium due and mailing a statement to the group policyholder, typically on a monthly basis. Under a ***third-party-administered plan,*** a group policyholder contracts with another organization, called a *third-party administrator (TPA),* to process premium payments for group insurance and remit them directly to the insurer. In an ***administrative services only (ASO) plan,*** an employer hires an outside firm to perform specified administrative services, including claim administration, for a group health insurance program. Premium accounting is similar under each billing plan, although TPAs generally remit premiums on a net basis.

Home Service Premiums

Unlike the premiums for other life insurance products, an insurer's home service agents personally collect policy premiums for home service products such as *industrial insurance.* Home service products typically do not have provisions for policy loans, cash values, or policy dividends. As a result, the policy lapses once the grace period has passed without a premium payment. Historically, insurance companies have used one of two premium accounting systems to account for home service insurance: the cash premium accounting system and the advance and arrears system.

Under the ***cash premium accounting system,*** the home service agent personally collects the premium payments from each policyowner and records each transaction in a *route collection book* or computer. To indicate premium payment, the agent also signs the policyowner's premium receipt book, which is given to the policyowner at policy issue. Then the agent notifies the home office of the premium amount collected on each policy. After the agent remits the amount of the premium to the insurance company, the insurer updates the policyowner master file to record this premium income and prepares new route collection records for the home service agents.

Under the ***advance and arrears accounting system,*** also called the *debit system,* the insurer charges each home service agent with the amount of premium income expected during the month from the agent's policyowners. Few insurers still use the advance and arrears accounting system to account for home service premiums. In this context, advances represent the premium amounts paid in advance and arrears represent the premium amounts due but unpaid. Upon receipt of the premium payments, the insurer reconciles the amount received with the agent's balance.

Accounting for Policy Loan Interest and Policy Dividends

Two additional sources of revenue for life and health insurance companies are interest income on policy loans and policy dividends applied to premiums. Ordinary life insurance policies that build cash value usually have a policy loan provision. Policy loan accounting involves recording the principal and interest on each policy loan. The principal amount of a policy loan plus the interest due or accrued cannot be greater than the policy's cash surrender value. The interest is usually payable on the policy anniversary date, and the amount due is shown on the premium notice. A few companies charge interest in advance. In these cases, a policyowner who repays all or part of the principal during the year is entitled to a partial refund of the interest paid in advance. If the insurer does not receive interest on the policy loan when due, then the insurer adds the amount of the unpaid interest to the policy loan balance, provided the policy's cash value is sufficient to cover both the principal and interest on the loan.

As we discussed in Chapter 10, participating life insurance policies enable policyowners to receive policy dividends. An insurer's board of directors usually declares annual policy dividends to participating policyowners according to a dividend schedule submitted by the chief actuary. The insurer estimates the amount of its policy dividends payable, and it pays the dividends on the policy anniversary date. A policyowner typically can choose from among five dividend options: (1) receive the dividend in cash, (2) apply the dividend to premiums due, (3) leave the dividend with the insurer to accumulate at interest, (4) apply the dividend to purchase paid-up additions, and (5) apply the dividend to purchase one-year term insurance. If the policyowner chooses the second option, the insurer debits Dividends Applied to Premiums and credits Premium Income for the amount of the dividend. If the dividend is not sufficient to cover the entire premium, the policyowner remits cash for the difference.

Only the fourth and fifth options represent additional premium income for the insurer. If the policyowner wishes to apply the dividend to purchase paid-up additions (PUA), the insurer informs the policyowner of the amount of additional insurance purchased under the option. A typical accounting entry to record policy dividends applied to purchase paid-up additions is a debit to Dividends to Purchase PUA and a credit to Single Premiums for PUA. An alternate accounting entry is a debit to Policy Dividends Applied to PUA and a credit to Premium Income—PUA. If the policyowner elects to use the dividend to purchase one-year term insurance, the accounting entry is a debit to Policy Dividends Applied—Term Insurance and a credit to Premium Income—One-Year Term Insurance.

Because of dividend options and policy loan interest, the accounting entry for recording receipt of a renewal premium payment is often a compound entry. Besides recording renewal premium income, this entry can also record payment of (1) the principal and interest on a policy loan, (2) deductions of policy dividends from the amount of cash due from the policyowner, or (3) other policy transactions. To illustrate, assume that the following dollar amounts apply to a life insurance policy:

Renewal premium due	$100
Policy loan interest due	25
Policy dividend payable to policyowner	11

In this case, the policyowner owes the insurance company $100 for the renewal premium and $25 for the loan interest, and the insurer owes the policyowner $11 for the dividend. The proper amount of cash the policyowner pays to the insurer is $114 ($100 premium due + $25 interest due – $11 dividend payable). The insurer's entry to record receipt of this amount is

Cash	114	
Dividends Applied to Premium	11	
Premium Income		100
Policy Loan Interest		25

To record the receipt of premium income and policy loan interest, and the application of policy dividends to premium income.

You have seen how insurance companies record premium payments that arrive on or before the premium due date. When an insurer does not receive a policy premium on time, then the premium is late and the policy's grace period provision takes effect. Life and health insurance policies contain a grace period, typically 30 or 45 days, depending on legal requirements, during which time a policyowner can remit a late premium payment before the policy lapses. Policy coverage remains in force throughout the grace period. If the insurer does not receive the overdue premium payment by the end of the grace period, then the policy's nonforfeiture provisions apply. The insurer determines the amount of the policy's cash surrender value or adjusts the policy to provide for an automatic premium loan (APL) or extended term insurance. The development of automatic premium payments under PAC and EFT has reduced the uncertainty and tardiness of premium payments while providing policyowners with ongoing insurance coverage.

Premium accounting for nontraditional life products, such as universal life insurance or variable life insurance, is similar to that for traditional life products. However, in the case of an unpaid premium for a universal life insurance policy, the insurer continues coverage only if the policy has a sufficient cash value. Automatic premium loans and policy dividends may not be available for nontraditional products.

Investment Income

As defined in Chapter 2, investment income consists of the earnings a company receives on its invested assets. Interest on bonds and mortgage loans, rental income on real estate, and dividends on stock are examples of investment income. Investments play an integral role in the financial operations of life and health insurance companies. In calculating the premium rates that an insurer should charge and the reserves that are needed to pay future policy benefits, actuaries assume that the insurer's investments will earn a certain rate of return. If the actual rate of return falls short of the assumed rate, then the insurer may experience a surplus strain that could prove harmful to operations.

Because investments are the major assets owned by life and health insurance companies, income earned on those investments is usually the second largest source of revenues (after premium income) for a company. In some companies, investment income exceeds premium income. Accounting records for investment income must be up-to-date and accurate because many interested parties, including managers, insurance regulators, and rating agencies, use this information to make decisions. Funds available for investment can be used to acquire bonds, stocks, mortgage loans, and real estate. These funds can also be used to make policy loans and collateral loans and to invest in subsidiary companies. Because of the number of investment alternatives available, the number of investment transactions made by insurers, and the legal restrictions placed on investing, a thorough understanding of accounting for investment income is important. This section introduces the accounting procedures for and reporting of an insurer's investment income.

Accounting for Investment Income

Account titles for investment income vary among insurers, but their purpose is to record and report an insurer's revenues during the accounting period. For example, one insurer may have an account called Bond Interest Income while another insurer has an account called Interest Income—Bonds. Both accounts record bond interest revenue. Regardless of the account title, the account records an insurer's interest income earned and received on the bonds that it owns. For example, an insurer records the following accounting entry for $500 of interest income received on the bonds that it owns:

Cash	500	
Interest Income—Bonds		500

To record interest income received on bonds owned by an insurer that are issued by another company.

Insurers accrue bond interest income unless the bond is in default. Also, an insurer amortizes bond premiums and discounts into income.

Most of an insurer's investment income consists of interest, although it can also include dividends and rental income. However, investment income does not include gains (losses), either realized or unrealized, associated with an insurer's invested assets. Cash dividends on common stock owned by an insurer are reported as due and unpaid once the issuer has declared a dividend on its common stock. Upon receipt of a cash dividend, an insurer debits Cash and credits Dividend Income—Common Stock:

Cash	500	
Dividend Income—Common Stock		500

To record dividend income received by an insurer from common stock issued by another company.

When an insurer rents property to another entity, the accounting entry to record this transaction is a debit to Cash and a credit to Rental Income for the amount of the rental income. An insurer may charge rent to itself for occupancy of its home office building. A typical accounting entry to record this transaction is a debit to Rental Expense and a credit to Rental Income for the rent amount. Note that the insurer does not debit Cash for this rental income because rent that an insurer pays to itself generally has no effect on that insurer's cash balance, net income, or surplus. The amount of rent that an insurer charges itself can be based on either (1) an estimate of the current market rental value of the property or (2) a figure determined by the amount of expenses, taxes, and depreciation on the property plus an amount representing interest on the investment in the home office building.

As noted in Chapter 8, an insurer reports the amount of earned investment income that it has not yet received under Investment Income Due and Accrued, which is an asset account. When the insurer receives the earned income, it records the amount of the income as a debit to Cash and a credit to Investment Income Due and Accrued. The Annual Statement distinguishes between due investment income and accrued investment income.

Other Sources of Revenue

Besides premium income and investment income, an insurer's statement of operations also includes other sources of revenue from its core business operations. For example, an insurer can receive premiums for reinsurance assumed and fee income for services, such as brokerage services, management services from separate (segregated) account business, and third-party administrator (TPA) services. Also, a growing source of revenues for some insurers is management fees related to the side funds associated with universal life insurance and variable annuity products.

Financial Reporting of Revenues

An insurance company complies with accounting and financial reporting requirements by classifying its premium income and investment income according to the following product types: life, accident and health, credit, industrial (home service), and annuities, both individual and group. An insurer therefore typically credits one of several revenue accounts according to the revenue source and the type of policy. For example, when a policyowner remits a renewal premium for a life policy, the journal entry might include a credit to an account entitled Premium Renewal—Life. This specific account enables the insurer to identify this source of revenue by revenue type (premium income) and by line of business (life insurance).

An important difference between a U.S. insurer's preparation of the Annual Statement and a Canadian insurer's preparation of the Annual Return is that U.S. insurers make end-of-year adjustments to convert modified cash-basis revenues to accrual-basis revenues. Recall that accrual-basis accounting attributes income to the period in which the income is earned rather than when the cash is received.

Premium Income

U.S. and Canadian insurers report premium income for each product type as first-year premiums, renewal premiums, or single premiums. They also report participating and nonparticipating policy premiums by line of business and state or province. Proper recording and reporting of these transactions provide an audit trail for a state examiner or other auditor to trace a specific premium payment.

United States

To report premium income on an accrual basis, a U.S. insurer separately identifies premiums as collected premiums, uncollected premiums, deferred premiums, and unearned premiums. The following formula illustrates the mechanics of converting premium income from a modified cash basis to an accrual basis:

  Modified cash-basis premium income
\+ Gross deferred and uncollected premiums at the end of the current period*
− Gross deferred and uncollected premiums at the end of the previous period
− Unearned premiums at the end of the current period
\+ Unearned premiums at the end of the previous period
= Accrual-Basis Premium Income

For example, given the information listed below, the insurer reports $1,075,000 of premiums and annuity considerations on an accrual basis:

* In reporting premium income under accrual-basis accounting, an insurer records deferred and uncollected premiums on a gross premium basis, net of reinsurance. Recall that gross premiums include the amount of loading such as commissions and other policy costs.

Modified cash-basis premium income	$1,000,000
Gross deferred and uncollected premiums at the end of the current period	250,000
Gross deferred and uncollected premiums at the end of the previous period	(100,000)
Unearned premiums at the end of the current period	(175,000)
Unearned premiums at the end of the previous period	100,000
Accrual-Basis Premium Income	$1,075,000

The purpose of this calculation is to determine the amount of premium income that the insurer *earned* during the fiscal year, which generally differs from the amount of premium income the insurer collected during the same period.

Figure 12-8 depicts the Annual Statement exhibit that itemizes premiums and annuity considerations. Note that premiums for the first policy year are shown separately from single premiums and renewal premiums. Statutory authorities analyze an insurer's first-year premiums to determine if the commissions and other first-year costs associated with a block of insurance policies are excessive.

Canada

Exhibits in the Canadian Annual Return show detailed information on an insurer's total premium income in the following three ways:

1. Premiums for an insurer's participating and nonparticipating life insurance business

2. Premiums for an insurer's accident and sickness business by major classification of coverage

3. *Outstanding premiums,* which are equivalent to due premiums for U.S. insurers, for various lines of business (life, annuity, and accident and sickness)

Exhibits also include information pertaining to premium income generated from business transacted outside Canada.

Investment Income

Insurers also recognize investment income on an accrual basis for financial reporting requirements. The accrual-basis amount of *gross investment income* represents the amount of income actually earned during the reporting year. The insurer calculates the amount of investment income using several investment income classifications, outlined below. These income classifications are similar to those discussed earlier in the chapter.

Figure 12-8. Exhibit 1—Part 1—U.S. Annual Statement.

	Premiums and Annuity Considerations										
			Ordinary			Group		Accident and Health			
	1 Total	2 Industrial Life	3 Life Insurance	4 Individual Annuities	5 Credit Life (Group and Individual)	6 Life Insurance	7 Annuities	8 Group	9 Credit (Group and Individual)	10 Other	11 Aggregate of All Other Lines of Business
FIRST YEAR (other than single)											
1. Uncollected											
2. Deferred											
3. Deferred & Uncollected:											
a. Direct											
b. Reinsurance assumed											
c. Reinsurance ceded											
d. Net (Line 1 + Line 2)											
4. Advance											
5. Line 3d – Line 4											
6. Collected during year:											
a. Direct											
b. Reinsurance assumed											
c. Reinsurance ceded											
d. Net											
7. Line 5 + Line 6d											
8. Previous year (uncollected + deferred – advance)											
9. First year premiums and considerations:											
a. Direct											
b. Reinsurance assumed											
c. Reinsurance ceded											
d. Net (Line 7 – Line 8)											
SINGLE											
10. Single premiums and considerations:											
a. Direct											
b. Reinsurance assumed											
c. Reinsurance ceded											
d. Net											
RENEWAL											
11. Uncollected											
12. Deferred											
13. Deferred & Uncollected:											
a. Direct											
b. Reinsurance assumed											
c. Reinsurance ceded											
d. Net (Line 11 + Line 12)											
14. Advance											
15. Line 13d – Line 14											
16 Collected during year:											
a. Direct											
b. Reinsurance assumed											
c. Reinsurance ceded											
d. Net											
17. Line 15 + Line 16d											
18. Previous year (uncollected + deferred – advance)											
19. Renewal premiums and considerations:											
a. Direct											
b. Reinsurance assumed											
c. Reinsurance ceded											
d. Net (Line 17 – Line 18)											
TOTAL											
20. Total premiums and annuity considerations:											
a. Direct											
b. Reinsurance assumed											
c. Reinsurance ceded											
d. Net (Lines 9d + 10d + 19d)											

United States

To reconcile its use of modified cash-basis accounting for investment income to the accrual-basis accounting required for the Annual Statement, a U.S. insurer uses an adjusted income figure from the previous year's Annual Statement and five income classifications for amounts from the current fiscal year: (1) collected income, (2) unearned income, (3) due income, (4) accrued income, and (5) nonadmitted income. Each type of investment does not necessarily result in each of these types of income. To reconcile the amount of accrual-basis income for a given fiscal year, an insurer adds the amounts from the first three classifications, then subtracts the amounts of earned income and nonadmitted income, net of the previous year's accruals. For example, assume that a life insurance company's bond investments yielded the following interest income amounts (unearned income does not apply in this case):

Collected income	$90,000,000
Due income	300,000
Accrued income	10,000,000
Nonadmitted income	50,000
Previous-year adjustment	8,000,000

This insurer calculates accrual-basis gross investment income earned on its bonds as:

Collected income	$ 90,000,000
Due income	300,000
Accrued income	10,000,000
Nonadmitted income	(50,000)
Previous-year adjustment	(8,000,000)
Gross investment income earned during the year	$92,250,000

Insurance companies must show in the Annual Statement the amount of net investment income generated during the year by investment type and category of income: collected, unearned, due, accrued, and nonadmitted. Recall that net investment income is gross investment income minus expenses, taxes, and amortization.

Canada

Canadian insurers also show investment income on an accrual basis. However, a Canadian insurer's earned income need not be calculated on the Annual Return itself. All Canadian insurers keep accounting records on an accrual basis, and thus the amount of earned, due, and accrued investment income can simply be reported on the Annual Return. The Canadian treatment of realized gains and losses

Figure 12-9. *Net Investment Income*—Canadian Annual Return.

NET INVESTMENT INCOME
($'000)

Reference Page			Earned/ Incurred (01)	Accrued at Year End (02)
	Bonds			
	Interest	01		
70.03	Amortization of Net Realized Gains and (Losses)	03		
	Shares:			
	Dividends	10		
70.03	Amortization of Realized and Unrealized Gains and (Losses)	11		
	Mortgage Loans:			
	Interest	20		
70.03	Amortization of Net Realized Gains and (Losses)	23		
	Real Estate:			
	Rental Income Including $ ________ for Company's Own Use	30		
70.03	Amortization of Realized and Unrealized Gains and (Losses) *	31		
	Interest on Policy Loans	38		
	Interest on Deposits and Certificates	41		
	Interest on Overdue Premiums	47		
	Income from Derivative Activities	48		
	Income from Other Investments	50		
	Less:			
70.50	Provision for Losses	53		
70.50	Write-Downs	56		
	Non-Amortizable Capital Gains and (Losses)	60		
	Gross Investment Income	69		
	Less:			
	Investment Expenses (other than Investment Taxes)	70		
	Investment Taxes	79		
	Net Investment Income	89		

* Net income (loss) from subsidiaries as reported on the income statement, page 30.30, line 73 is net of the amount included here in respect of real estate owned by subsidiaries.

on invested assets is different from that under U.S. GAAP and statutory accounting. If a Canadian insurer sells a bond that matures in 10 years, the total gain or loss is amortized into income on the statement of operations over the 10 years. However, the insurer reports the unamortized portion of the bond on the balance sheet. Insurers also itemize the amount of accrued and earned gross investment income from their invested assets, such as bonds, stock, mortgage loans, real estate, and other sources of income, including policy loans. By deducting investment expenses and investment taxes from gross investment income, the insurer obtains net investment income. Figure 12-9 depicts the Annual Return exhibit for a Canadian insurer's net investment income.

Conclusion

Chapter 12 discussed the primary revenue accounts—premiums and interest income—that appear on the statement of operations for life and health insurance companies. In Chapter 13, we conclude our discussion of statement of operations accounts with a closer look at typical expense accounts for life and health insurers. We also discuss the typical accounting entries used to record expense transactions.

Key Terms and Concepts

paid-to date
preauthorized payment system
lock-box system
self-administered plan
insurer-administered plan
third-party-administered (TPA) plan
administrative services only (ASO) plan
cash premium accounting system
advance and arrears accounting system

CHAPTER 13

ACCOUNTING FOR EXPENSES

LEARNING OBJECTIVES

After studying this chapter, you should be able to

- Identify an insurer's major expenses
- Record accounting entries associated with typical expenses incurred in life and health insurance companies
- Describe the objectives of commission accounting
- List and describe an insurer's typical operating expenses
- Identify and describe the various taxes, licenses, and fees of life and health insurance companies
- Discuss how insurers report expenses in the Annual Statement and Annual Return

CHAPTER OUTLINE

Agent Commissions and Salaries

Objectives of Commission Accounting
Factors that Affect Commission Accounting
Accounting for Agent Commissions
Accounting for Agent Salaries

Operating Expenses

Taxes, Licenses, and Fees

Federal Income Taxes
Premium Taxes
Guaranty-Fund Assessments
CompCorp

Financial Reporting of Expenses

In Chapter 12, we discussed the key revenue sources for life and health insurance companies. In this chapter, we discuss an insurer's major expenses. Insurers incur *expenses* while conducting normal business operations. An expense is generated when assets are used to obtain or support the company's revenues during the current reporting period. For auditing and financial reporting purposes, a company establishes a control account for each expense it incurs. A ***control account*** summarizes entries in a subsidiary ledger and serves as a standard of comparison for the amount that is actually reported in the company's financial statements. An insurer's primary expenses are associated with policy and claim benefits, as we discussed in detail in Chapter 10. We will not repeat that discussion in this chapter, but it is critical to understand that policy benefits constitute the largest dollar amount of an insurer's payment obligations. Figure 13-1 highlights an insurer's typical expenses, other than policy benefits.

In the United States, life insurance companies allocate nearly 73 percent of every premium dollar to pay policy benefits. The remaining 27 percent of premiums must cover the insurer's other expenses and allow for a profit. These other expense categories include

- Agent commissions
- Operating (general) expenses
- Taxes, licenses, and fees

Agent commissions typically account for 15 percent of premium dollars, while operating expenses and taxes, licenses, and fees account for 8 percent, leaving 4 percent available for stockholder dividends and net income. Figure 13-2 shows the typical allocation of each 1994 premium dollar for U.S. insurers.

Figure 13-3 shows the allocation of Canadian life insurance companies' total revenues, including premium income and investment income, in 1993. Benefits paid to or invested for policyholders represented approximately 82 percent of 1993 revenues, the latest figures available. General expenses—which in this figure also include commissions, taxes, licenses, and fees—comprised approximately 17 percent of total revenues. The remaining 1 percent of revenues represented stockholder dividends and profit.

This chapter begins with a discussion of accounting for agent commissions and salaries, followed by descriptions of an insurer's operating expenses and its taxes, licenses, and fees. We conclude the chapter

Figure 13-1. Highlight of the expenses section of a typical insurance company statement of operations.

For the year ended December 31, 19XX	
Revenues	
Premium income	xxx
Net investment income	xxx
Other income	xxx
Total Revenues	1,000,000
Benefits and Expenses	
Policy benefits:	
Life insurance	xxx
Accident and health	xxx
Annuities	xxx
Total Policy Benefits	xxx
Expenses:	
Agent commissions	xxx
Operating expenses:	
Home office salaries	xxx
Rent	xxx
Other operating expenses	xxx
Total Operating Expenses	xxx
Taxes, licenses, and fees:	
Premium taxes	xxx
Guaranty fund assessment	xxx
Other taxes, licenses, and fees	xxx
Total Taxes, Licenses, and Fees	xxx
Total Expenses	xxx
Total Benefits and Expenses	800,000
Income before income taxes	xxx
Income tax expense	50,000
Net Income	150,000

with a discussion of financial reporting of expenses for the Annual Statement and Annual Return.

Agent Commissions and Salaries

As noted in Chapter 2, agent commissions are a type of selling expense, and they typically are an insurer's second largest expense after

Figure 13-2. Uses of premium income—U.S. life insurance companies, 1994.

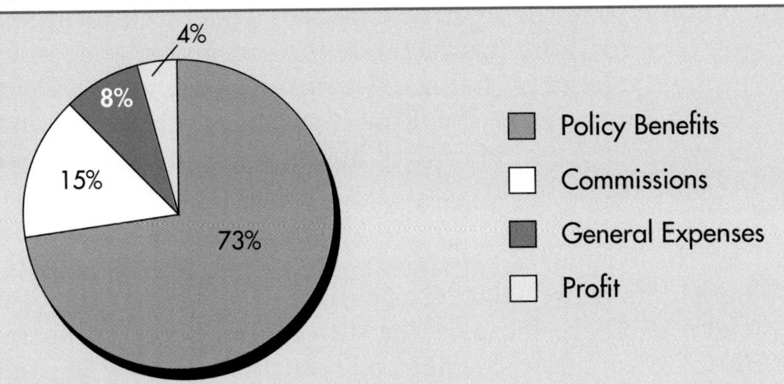

Source: ACLI *1995 Life Insurance Fact Book Update*, p. 37.

policy benefits. An insurer's distribution system determines how the insurer accounts for its selling expenses. Insurers that use an agency distribution system for individual life and health insurance products pay their agents on a commission basis. On the other hand, many group health insurance products and direct response products are sold through a *salaried* group agency system, so salary expense, rather than commission expense, is applicable in these instances. Further, some insurers pay their agents on a salary plus commission basis. Regardless of the distribution system used, the insurer's accounting system reports the appropriate expenses—whether salaries, commissions, or both—in its financial statements.

Insurers, especially those that use a variety of sales distribution systems, must have an accounting system that can accurately record and report salaries and commissions incurred as a result of product

Figure 13-3. Uses of premium and investment income—Canadian life insurance companies, 1993.

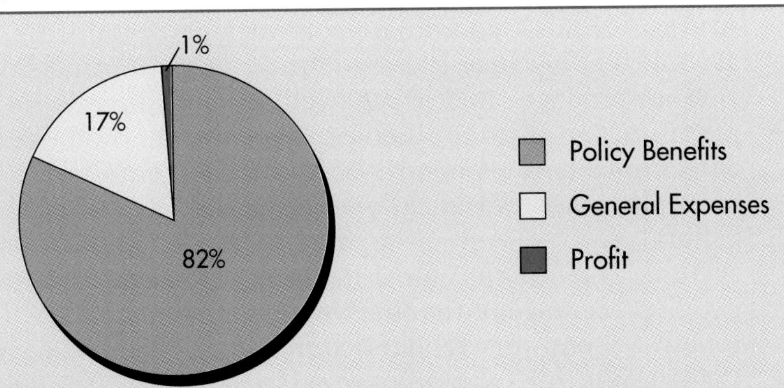

Source: CLHIA *1994 Facts*, p. 6.

sales and service. An insurer's accounting system should also be able to collect and categorize expenses generated by line of business or product for both financial reporting and management accounting purposes. Insurers list agent commissions, which are directly associated with the cost of selling insurance, separately on the statement of operations and by line of business on the Annual Statement. Salaries for administrative and other non-sales employees are only indirectly related to the cost of selling insurance, so an insurer does not list these salaries separately by line of business. Instead, an insurer considers these salaries as part of its operating expenses and reports them as such. Despite the differences between accounting and reporting for agent salaries and commissions, we include salaries paid to agents in this section rather than in the section on operating expenses for two reasons: (1) many agents are paid on a combined salary plus commission basis and (2) discussion of both agent commissions and salaries enables you to more easily compare the differences in their accounting and financial reporting requirements.

Objectives of Commission Accounting

The objectives of commission accounting are to

- Calculate the amount of agent commissions payable on each premium an insurer receives
- Record agent commissions payable to each agent
- Establish an audit trail from the amount of the premium payment to the accounting entry that discloses earned and paid commissions for each agent

Factors that Affect Commission Accounting

An insurer must coordinate commission accounting with premium accounting, because the amount of agent commissions paid for insurance products sold or renewed depends directly on the amount of premiums an insurer receives. Also, the method used to pay agents determines how an insurer accounts for commission payments. For example, insurers typically account for agent commissions under a general agency system separately from those under a brokerage system. The fact that most insurers pay agent commissions that are a high percentage of the first-year premium and a small percentage of renewal premiums renders commission accounting more complex than accounting for employee salaries.

Under traditional commission schedules, first-year commissions can be 55 percent or more of the first-year premium, while renewal commissions typically range from 4 to 5 percent of the premium. After a specified number of years, the company replaces renewal commissions with a 1 or 2 percent persistency fee or service fee to the agent for servicing the account for as long as it remains in force. In some insurance companies, certain agents have a vesting provision in their contract. A ***vesting provision*** allows an agent to continue to receive renewal commissions and service fees for those in-force policies that the agent originally sold, even after the agent leaves the insurer. Renewal commissions, vesting provisions, and service fees provide agents with financial incentives to obtain and retain quality business, thus enabling an insurer to minimize the high costs of policy lapses within the first few policy years. Insight 13-1 discusses the effects of proposed changes in commission accounting rules for agents and brokers.

Insight 13-1 Agents Slam Accounting Rules on Commissions

A proposed change in accounting rules for insurance agents and brokers has raised the ire of some producers who claim it fails to recognize the unique service nature of the insurance business.

The controversy involves an American Institute of Certified Public Accountants exposure draft which outlines a structure for standardized generally accepted accounting principles (GAAP) for producers.

At the heart of the dispute lies the AICPA contention that agency and brokerage commission income should be recognized at the inception of the policy—or in the case of renewals, when the first renewal premium is paid—not as premiums are collected.

"Although certain costs related to a policy may be incurred after the billing or effective date, those costs typically are incurred at the discretion of the broker to retain or increase business with the client and not because the broker is obligated to service the policy in force," according to AICPA.

Some agent leaders are panning that rationale as patently false.

It "fails to recognize that an agent's work begins when a policy is sold and does not end until the policy expires," responded Russell R. Burnett, vice president and treasurer with the Independent Insurance Agents of America, Alexandria, Va.

In discussions with AICPA officials last month, agent representatives contended that the bulk of an agency's expenses are incurred in the servicing of the client, not the sale of the policy.

"We believe that to provide for a proper matching of revenues to expenses, the commission earned should be recognized in the same manner, over the term of the policy," said Mr. Burnett.

The AICPA draft would likely have the most dramatic impact on agents involved in the property-casualty, accident & health and pension/benefits business, with the life business less dramatically affected because of the nature of the contracts and services involved, according to sources familiar with the draft.

Indeed, the draft specifically notes that a "relatively smaller portion of a life insurance broker's effort is devoted to providing services after the effective date of the life policies."

The draft goes on to say that "because all required services have been rendered and the earnings process is complete when the application accompanied by the first premium is accepted by the underwriter, first-year commission on long-duration life insurance policies should be recognized as income when the first premium is paid by the insured and accepted by the underwriter, regardless of whether the first-year premium is paid as a single premium or as a series of monthly, quarterly or semiannual premiums."

Under the AICPA plan, renewal commissions would be recognized when renewal premiums are paid.

Source: Colleen Mulcahy, "Agents Slam Accounting Rules on Commissions," *National Underwriter Life & Health/Financial Services Edition,* No. 22 (June 1, 1992), p. 23. Reprinted with permission from *National Underwriter,* © 1996, The National Underwriter Company, *Life & Health/Financial Services Edition,* 1992.

Accounting for Agent Commissions

Because insurance companies often have hundreds and even thousands of agents, they do not record individual agent transactions in the general ledger. The general ledger typically contains summary information in a control account that shows the total amount of commissions earned by and paid to all agents, while a subsidiary ledger for each agent contains detailed activity for that agent. This control account, sometimes called Agents Ledger Control, includes commissions the insurer owes to agents as well as amounts that agents owe to the insurer. The amount of money owed by an insurer to an agent represents an *account payable,* which is a current liability because the insurer expects to pay the agent within the current accounting period. The amount of money owed by an agent to an insurer, often called Agent Balances Due, is a type of *account receivable* because the insurer expects to receive this amount within the reporting period. Many insurers advance commissions to a new agent during his or her first months with the insurer. Under statutory accounting rules, agent balances due more than a specified length of time are generally a nonadmitted asset for U.S. life and health insurance companies.

Several types of accounting transactions occur frequently in connection with agent commissions. These transactions include (1) recording in the general ledger the total of all agent commissions and bonuses, both earned and paid, (2) crediting each agent's subsidiary ledger account with his or her commissions and bonuses earned and paid, (3) disbursing the proper amounts to agents after deductions such as taxes, and (4) making special charges for services rendered or for premium adjustments. Account balances in the insurer's general ledger must equal the combined account balances in the subsidiary ledgers that show individual agent transactions. For example, when an insurance company's agents earn commissions, the company makes the following journal entry to its general ledger to show that the company has incurred the commission expense and has established a liability for the commission owed:

Commissions Expense	xxx	
Agents Ledger Control		xxx

To record incurred agent commissions expense.

The insurer records the following journal entry upon payment of the earned commission to the agent:

Agents Ledger Control	xxx	
Cash		xxx

To record the payment of agent commissions.

After the insurer records both entries, the Agents Ledger Control account balance is zero. This zero balance indicates that the agent has been paid the full amount that he or she earned for the sale of insurance products. The combined effect of the two transactions is an increase in an expense account (Commissions Expense) and a corresponding decrease in an asset account (Cash). For example, assume the first-year commission rate for an ordinary life insurance policy is 55 percent. When an agent sells an ordinary policy with a $1,200 first-year premium, the insurer makes the following journal entry to the general ledger to record that the company has incurred a $660 commission expense (55 percent × $1,200):

Commissions Expense	660	
Agents Ledger Control		660

To record incurred agent commission expense.

Later, when the insurer pays the commission to the agent, assuming no withholdings, the insurer records the appropriate transaction in the general ledger as follows:

Agents Ledger Control	660	
Cash		660

To record the payment of agent commissions.

Some insurance companies also pay commission bonuses to agents for exceeding target production levels. These bonuses usually represent another commission expense for insurers. The entries to record these commission bonuses in the general ledger are similar to the transactions to record commissions earned and paid. Although most agent commissions and bonuses depend on production, under certain conditions, an insurer may treat such bonuses as an operating expense. For example, if an insurance company's marketing agreement awards a bonus to the general manager whose agency sells the most policies in a specified time frame, the insurer may treat this bonus as an operating expense.

Insurers occasionally refund premiums to policyowners. When a premium is refunded, the agent loses the commission earned on that premium payment. The specific transaction that takes place to reflect an agent's return of a commission varies among insurance companies. For example, an insurer may deduct the "lost" commission from future commission payments.

Reinsurance treaties represent another consideration when accounting for commissions. If an insurance company cedes to an assuming company part of the insurance risk on a block of insurance policies, then the ceding company pays periodic premiums to the assuming company. Besides reimbursing the ceding company for a stated portion of the claims incurred under the reinsurance business, the assuming company usually reimburses the ceding company for commissions, taxes, and other reimbursable expenses under certain reinsurance agreements. Expenses for which the assuming company reimburses the ceding company are commonly known as ***allowances.*** Specific allowances depend on the reinsurance agreement. Commissions that the reinsurer pays to the ceding company are called ***reinsurance commissions,*** which are allowances intended to cover all or part of the ceding company's acquisition costs and other costs related to the reinsured business. In effect, the reinsured business represents new business to the assuming company, and the assuming company pays a commission on this new business, just as any insurer pays a commission to an agent for new business. In this case, the assuming company pays the commission to the ceding company, rather than to an agent.

Suppose an insurer cedes to an assuming company $250,000 of a block of ordinary life policies. If the reinsurance treaty specifies a reinsurance premium of $800 and a reinsurance expense allowance of $600, then the ceding company makes the following journal entry to record payment of the reinsurance premium expense:

	Debit	Credit
Reinsurance Ceded—First-Year Premium Expense	800	
Reinsurance Ceded—Expense Allowance		600
Cash		200

To record the payment of reinsurance premium expense, net of expense allowance.

Note that the ceding company reduces the amount of the reinsurance premium ($800) by the amount of the expense allowance ($600), so that the resulting credit to Cash is $200. The assuming company records the receipt of the reinsurance premium income as follows:

	Debit	Credit
Reinsurance Assumed—Expense Allowance	600	
Cash	200	
Reinsurance Assumed—First-Year Premium Income		800

To record the receipt of reinsurance premium income, net of expense allowance.

Accounting for Agent Salaries

Most life and health insurance companies have a distribution system that relies primarily on commissioned agents. However, some insurers, especially direct response companies and group insurers, rely on salaried agents. Insurers that use a general agency distribution system also have some salaried salespersons. In most cases, salaried agents are first-year agents to whom an insurer provides financial assistance in establishing a client base. Also included in this group are branch or field office managers to whom the insurer provides both a salary and commission overrides for developing an agency office. Such agents are considered employees of the insurer. The insurer usually maintains separate subsidiary ledger accounts for each salaried agent, the same as with its commissioned agents. Also, the insurer maintains separate records for agents that receive a combination of salary and commission payments.

Under Internal Revenue Service (IRS) regulations, most 100 percent commissioned agents are considered independent contractors rather than employees of a U.S. insurer. As a result, the insurer does not withhold taxes for its commissioned agents or for override commissions paid to general agents. The insurer is required, however, to withhold federal, state, local, and Social Security taxes from the earnings of those agents considered to be employees of the company. When withholding taxes from an agent's salary, the insurer typically credits a liability account for the amount withheld for later payment and reporting to governmental authorities. In this section, we address how an insurer accounts for payments to its salaried agents. Again, for financial reporting purposes, an insurer maintains a different accounting record for each salaried agent.

For example, if a salaried agent for a U.S. insurer earns a $100 salary, from which $10 must be withheld for federal income taxes, $5 must be withheld for Social Security (FICA) payments, and $2 must be withheld for state income taxes, the accounting entry establishing the initial liability and the amount payable to the salaried agent is

Salaries Expense	100	
Federal Income Taxes Payable		10
FICA		5
State Income Taxes Payable		2
Salaries Payable		83

To record the establishment of a liability for an agent's salary and the appropriate tax withholdings.

This entry records the insurer's liability for taxes withheld as $17 and records the salary payable to the agent as $83 ($100 – $17). As you can see, the amount payable to the agent equals the salary expense minus any withholdings. When the insurer actually pays the agent's salary, the appropriate accounting entry is

Salaries Payable	83	
Cash		83

To record the payment of an agent's salary.

When the company then pays the state income taxes withheld from the agent's salary, the appropriate journal entry is

State Income Taxes Payable 2
Cash 2
To record the payment of federal income taxes withheld from an agent's salary.

The accounting entries for the payment of federal income taxes and FICA payments are recorded similarly. In both cases, the insurer decreases a liability (Federal Income Taxes Payable and FICA Payable, respectively), and decreases an asset (Cash). Entries such as these are typically restricted to earnings payable to agents who, for tax purposes, are considered to be employees of the insurer. In contrast, insurers do not withhold taxes from amounts paid to commissioned agents. Some salaried agents receive a year-end bonus for generating the new business and maintaining that business. The insurer treats a salaried agent's bonus as part of that agent's salary and withholds the appropriate amounts for tax purposes, as with salary payments.

Operating Expenses

In addition to expenses that are insurance specific, such as agent commissions, insurers also incur expenses that are similar to those incurred by non-insurance companies. As we discussed in Chapter 2, operating expenses, also called *general and administrative expenses,* are expenses a company incurs in the course of conducting business. Figure 13-4 shows typical operating expenses for a life and health insurance company.

An insurer can readily identify the amount of policy benefits and agent commissions incurred by policy type or line of business, but it is more difficult and less precise to determine what portion of an insurer's operating expenses, such as the salaries of home office employees, applies to a particular line of business. On the Annual Statement, U.S. insurers allocate general (operating) expenses by lines of business, usually on the basis of premium income, as in the following example (assume that operating expenses are $20,000):

	Ordinary Life		Group Life		Group A&H		Total
Premium Income	$5,000	+	$35,000	+	$10,000	=	$50,000
Percentage of Premium Income ($50,000)	10%	+	70%	+	20%	=	100%
Allocation of Operating Expenses ($20,000)	$2,000	+	$14,000	+	$4,000	=	$20,000

Figure 13-4. Typical operating expenses for a life and health insurance company.

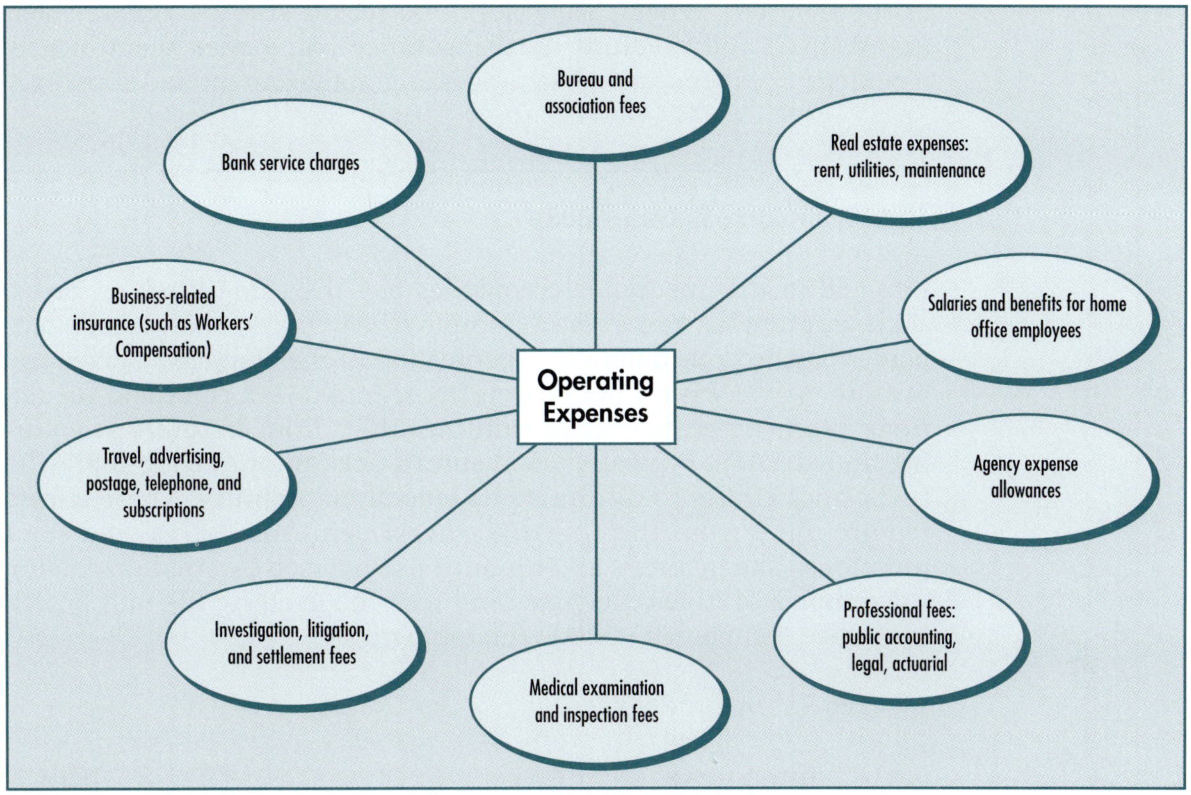

An insurance company typically maintains separate accounting records in its general ledger for each type of operating expense. For example, an insurer may record the salaries of home office employees in a Salaries—Home Office expense account, and bank service charges in a Bank Service Charges expense account. The insurer typically maintains subsidiary ledgers for individuals within each general ledger expense account. An insurer will have a subsidiary ledger for each home office employee showing his or her salary activity. Their aggregate activity is summarized in the Salaries—Home Office general ledger expense account. The insurer pays additional amounts of a specific operating expense by debiting a general ledger expense account and crediting Cash. For example, when an insurer makes payment to a public accounting firm for auditing the insurer's financial statements, a typical journal entry is

Public Accounting Expense	xxx	
Cash		xxx

To record the payment to a public accountant for financial statement auditing.

Because data collection and management are critical to conducting insurance business efficiently, the expenses an insurer incurs for automated database purchases and maintenance are a significant part of the insurer's general expenses. One recent study estimated that many small and medium-sized insurance companies spend nearly 6 percent of expenses on data processing management and support.[1]

Taxes, Licenses, and Fees

Life and health insurance companies pay the same kinds of taxes, such as property taxes and unemployment taxes, that other companies pay. Accountants keep records for all the company's taxes and prepare the necessary tax returns according to tax rules and regulations. (Remember that tax accounting differs from statutory accounting and GAAP.) Typically, an insurer's accountants coordinate the company's efforts to minimize its federal tax liability. These efforts require input from the actuarial, investment, marketing, and sales functions. The insurer's accountants also oversee external tax audits.

Examples of taxes, licenses, and fees incurred by life and health insurance companies include the following:

- Federal income taxes
- Premium taxes
- Municipal taxes in some states
- Other taxes (for example, property taxes and state or provincial income taxes)
- Foreign insurance department licenses, fees for state examinations, and business licenses
- Guaranty-fund assessments (U.S.) or CompCorp (Canada)
- Payroll taxes

In this section, we present an overview of federal income taxes and premium taxes paid by insurers. Figure 13-5 depicts the breakdown of taxes, licenses, and fees, including federal income taxes, that U.S. life and health insurance companies paid in 1994.

Federal Income Taxes

In the United States and Canada, insurers file income tax returns with both federal and some state or provincial taxation authorities.

Figure 13-5. Taxes, licenses, and fees of U.S. life and health insurance companies, 1994.

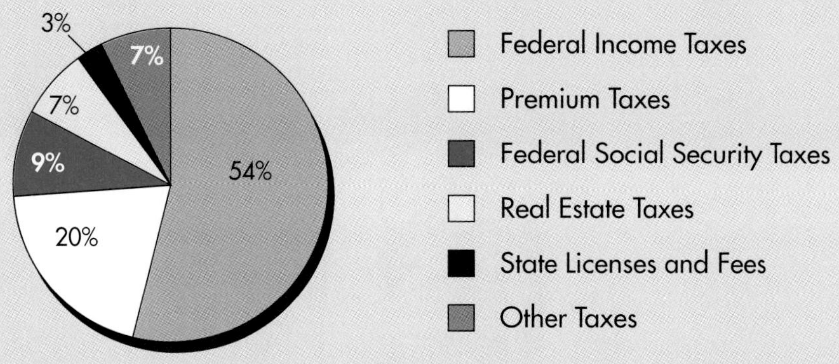

Source: *Statistical Compilation of Annual Statement Information for Life/Health Insurance Companies in 1994,* Summary of Operations and Exhibit 6, National Association of Insurance Commissioners.

Both U.S. and Canadian insurers are subject to federal income taxes. Tax laws and regulations have been the subject of numerous changes in the past 30 years. For example, U.S. insurers must comply with portions of the tax laws that were enacted in 1959, 1984, 1986, 1987, 1988, and 1990. Because life and health insurance companies are corporations, they must pay taxes according to the rules established for corporate income taxes. Canadian insurers are also subject to various taxes. Complying with current laws and regulations is a complex matter for life and health insurance companies. This section presents an overview of the typical federal taxes that apply to life and health insurance companies.

United States

Recall that the Internal Revenue Service (IRS) is the taxation authority in the United States. Federal income taxes on U.S. life insurance companies are specifically addressed in the *Deficit Reduction Act of 1984 (the 1984 Act),* which amended the *Life Insurance Company Income Tax Act of 1959.* The 1984 Act and its amendments made the federal income tax treatment of life insurance companies more closely parallel that of companies in other industries. Insurers also must comply with laws and accounting regulations that affect all U.S. corporations, including accounting standards that provide specific guidance concerning income tax accounting.

To qualify as a life insurance company under the IRS's Internal Revenue Code (IRC), more than half of an insurer's business must come from the issuance of life insurance or annuity contracts or the reinsurance of risks underwritten by life insurance companies during the tax year. In addition, more than 50 percent of the insurer's total reserves must be reserves for life insurance, unearned premiums, and unpaid

Wayne Stayskal, *Tampa Tribune,* © 1990.

losses on noncancelable life, accident, or health insurance policies. The IRS categorizes fraternal benefit societies and other similar benefit associations as tax-exempt insurance companies. A third category consists of insurance companies that do not meet one of the above definitions but still qualify as insurance companies for tax purposes.

It is to an insurer's advantage to comply with the IRS's definition of a life insurance or a tax-exempt insurance company because the tax rules and regulations directly address an insurer's unique business operations. For example, life insurance companies can deduct certain insurance-specific items from gross income to determine their tax liability. However, it is possible for an insurer to meet the definition of a life insurance company according to its state of domicile but not meet the IRS's strict definition of a life insurance company for federal income tax purposes. Insurers that meet the IRS definition of a life insurance company file IRS Form 1120L, the first page of which is shown in Figure 13-6.

Not only must a U.S. insurer meet the tax definition of a life insurance company, but the insurer's products must also meet the tax definition of life insurance products to qualify for tax treatment as life insurance products. For example, modified endowment insurance policies and second-to-die insurance policies that fail to meet specified qualifications are not considered life insurance policies for tax

Figure 13-6. IRS Form 1120L—*U.S. Life Insurance Company Income Tax Return.*

Form **1120-L**
Department of the Treasury
Internal Revenue Service

U.S. Life Insurance Company Income Tax Return

For calendar year 1995 or tax year beginning ...., 1995, ending ...., 19 ..

▶ **Instructions are separate. See page 1 for Paperwork Reduction Act Notice.**

OMB No. 1545-0123

1995

A Check if:
(1) Consolidated return (attach Form 851) ☐
(2) Nonlife insurance companies are included . . ☐

Please print or type

Name

Number, street, and room or suite no. (If a P.O. box, see page 5 of instructions.)

City or town, state, and ZIP code

B Employer identification number

C Date incorporated

D Check applicable box if an election has been made under section(s) ▶ ☐ 953(c)(3)(C) ☐ 953(d)

E Check applicable boxes: (1) ☐ Final return (2) ☐ Change of address (3) ☐ Amended return

Income

Line	Description	Box
1	Gross premiums, etc., less return premiums, etc. Enter balance	1
2	Net decrease, if any, in reserves (see page 5 of instructions)	2
3	10% of any decrease in reserves under section 807(f)(1)(B)(ii)	3
4	3⅓% of yearend balance of reserves under section 807(e)(7)(B)	4
5	Investment income (Schedule B, line 8) (see page 6 of instructions)	5
6	Net capital gain (Schedule D, line 12 (Form 1120))	6
7	Income from a special loss discount account (attach Form 8816)	7
8	Other income (attach schedule)	8
9	Life insurance company gross income. Add lines 1 through 8	9

Deductions (See instructions for limitations on deductions.)

Line	Description	Box
10	Death benefits, etc.	10
11	Net increase, if any, in reserves (Schedule F, line 37)	11
12	10% of any increase in reserves under section 807(f)(1)(B)(i)	12
13	Deductible policyholder dividends (Schedule E, line 7)	13
14	Consideration paid for assumption by another person of liabilities	14
15	Dividends reimbursable by taxpayer	15
16a	Interest ▶ ______ b Less tax-exempt interest expense ______ c Bal ▶	16c
17	Deductible policy acquisition expenses (Schedule G, line 20)	17
18	Additional deduction (attach Form 8816)	18
19	Other deductions (see instructions) (attach schedule)	19
20	Dividends-received deduction (Schedule A, line 16, column (c))	20
21	Operations loss deduction (see page 7 of instructions) (attach schedule)	21
22	**Total deductions.** Add lines 10 through 21	22
23	Gain or (loss) from operations. Subtract line 22 from line 9	23
24	Small life insurance company deduction (Schedule H, line 17)	24
25	Life insurance company taxable income (LICTI). Subtract line 24 from line 23	25
26	Limitation on noninsurance losses (Schedule I, line 9)	26
27	Amount subtracted from policyholder surplus account (Schedule J, Part II, line 10)	27

Tax and Payments (See page 8 of instructions)

Line	Description	Box
28	**Total taxable income.** Add lines 25, 26, and 27; however, the total may not be less than line 27	28
29	**Total tax** (Schedule K, line 10)	29
30a	1994 overpayment credited to 1995	30a
b	Prior year(s) special estimated tax payments to be applied	30b
c	1995 estimated tax payments	30c
d	1995 special estimated tax payments (*Do not include on line 30f*)	30d
e	1995 refund applied for on Form 4466 . . . 30e ( )	30f
g	Tax deposited with Form 7004	30g
h	Credit from regulated investment companies (attach Form 2439)	30h
i	Credit for Federal tax on fuels (attach Form 4136)	30i
j	U.S. income tax paid or withheld at source (attach Form 1042-S)	30j / 30k
31	Estimated tax penalty. Check if Form 2220 is attached ▶ ☐	31
32	**TAX DUE.** If line 30k is smaller than the total of lines 29 and 31, enter AMOUNT OWED	32
33	**OVERPAYMENT.** If line 30k is larger than the total of lines 29 and 31, enter AMOUNT OVERPAID	33
34	Enter amount of line 33 you want: **Credited to 1996 estimated tax** ▶ $ Refunded ▶	34

Please Sign Here

Under penalties of perjury, I declare that I have examined this return, including accompanying schedules and statements, and to the best of my knowledge and belief, it is true, correct, and complete. Declaration of preparer (other than taxpayer) is based on all information of which the preparer has any knowledge.

▶ Signature of officer | Date | ▶ Title

Paid Preparer's Use Only

Preparer's signature ▶ | Date | Check if self-employed ☐ | Preparer's social security no.

Firm's name (or yours if self-employed) and address ▶ | EIN ▶ | ZIP Code ▶

purposes. If an insurer's life insurance products fail to qualify as life insurance products, then the policy benefits may be deemed taxable to the policyowner or beneficiary, which removes an incentive for people to buy the products. Generally, a life insurance product must meet either one of two tests to comply with the tax definition of a life insurance policy: (1) the cash value accumulation test or (2) the guideline level premium and cash value corridor test. Although a discussion of these tests is outside the scope of this text, it is important to note that an insurer may not meet the tax definition of a life insurance company if too many of its products fail either test. In such cases, the insurer will no longer be allowed the specified tax treatment accorded to insurers.

Insurers begin with the amounts reported on the Annual Statement, then convert these statutory totals to obtain taxable income. Because of different definitions and timing differences, amounts shown on the tax return for various revenues and expenses may not be identical to the amounts reported for those items in the insurer's Annual Statement or other financial statements for the same accounting period. Thus, net income on an insurer's statutory or GAAP-based statement of operations will probably differ from the net income reported on the insurer's tax return. The items included in net income and the way net income is calculated varies among statutory accounting, GAAP, and tax accounting.

Another example of this difference is the calculation of an insurer's tax liability. For example, under GAAP, an insurer adds deferred federal income taxes to taxes payable or refundable in the current year to determine its total tax liability for the accounting period. Statutory accounting currently includes only federal income tax expense that is currently payable. Timing differences can occur when an insurer has reported an expense under GAAP but has not yet reported it for tax purposes. Policy dividends payable in the following year are reported in the insurer's current-year Annual Statement, but they have limited deductibility for tax purposes.

Because of the nature of the life insurance industry, there are several unique deductions from income that life insurance companies can take for income tax purposes. These deductions include deductions for (1) increases in life insurance policy reserves, (2) policy dividends, and (3) qualifying as a small life insurance company. The 1984 Act mandated the use of the Commissioners' Reserve Valuation Method (CRVM) for life insurance policies, the Commissioners' Annuity Reserve Valuation Method (CARVM) for annuity contracts, the two-year full preliminary term method for noncancelable accident and health insurance policies, and the use of interest rates, mortality rates, and morbidity rates specified at policy issue to calculate reserves for tax purposes. Before the 1984 Act, life insurance companies were permitted to use the reserve amounts reported on the Annual Statement.

Life insurance companies in the United States determine the amount of income that is subject to federal income taxes by calculating ***life insurance company taxable income (LICTI),*** which is the difference between a life insurance company's gross income and its tax deductions. To calculate LICTI, insurers first determine gross income, then subtract allowable deductions from gross income. Under the 1984 Act, which adjusts for investment-related life insurance products, a tax is imposed on the LICTI of every life insurance company. The IRS includes as gross income of a life insurance company the following amounts:

- *Premiums* on insurance and annuity products, including policy premiums, fees, deposits, and policy proceeds left with the insurer

- *Investment income,* including interest, dividends, and rents

- *Capital gains,* including increases in income resulting from the sale of stock, bond, and real estate investments

- *Decreases in specified reserves,* including life insurance policy reserves, unearned premiums and unpaid losses on guaranteed renewable and noncancelable accident and health insurance policies, dividend accumulations for insurance and annuity products, and certain contingency reserves under group insurance contracts

- *Other income,* consisting of gross income that does not fall into any of the four categories above

For tax purposes, gross income includes advance premiums and excludes deferred and uncollected premiums. Gross income is also adjusted for policy dividends applied under a dividend option other than cash and premiums waived as a result of disability or applied to purchase supplementary contracts. The tax treatment of capital gains is similar for both insurance and non-insurance companies.

Both stock and mutual insurers deduct policy dividends from gross income according to the methods specified by the IRS. Stock insurance companies, which typically sell few participating policies, generally have an unlimited deduction for policy dividends. In contrast, mutual insurers, which offer many of their life products as participating policies, are much more restricted when deducting policy dividends. According to the IRS, the largest portion of a mutual insurer's policy dividend is considered a return of overpaid premiums while a smaller portion is considered a distribution of earnings. Therefore, to provide equitable treatment of policy dividends for both stock and mutual companies, mutuals are allowed to take only a limited deduction for policy dividends.

Reserves are a key factor in determining an insurer's taxable income. Increases in reserves are deductible from an insurer's gross income. A lower gross income results in lower taxable income. On the other hand, decreases in reserves increase gross income, and a higher gross income results in higher taxable income for the insurer. An insurer usually determines the change in its reserves by subtracting its reserve balance at the beginning of the year from its balance at the end of the year. If the difference is positive, then the insurer has experienced an increase in reserves. On the other hand, if the difference is negative, then the insurer has experienced a decrease in reserves. For example, if an insurer's reserves at the beginning of the year are $50 million, and its reserves at the end of the year are $51 million, it has experienced a $1 million increase in reserves. The insurer can then deduct this $1 million difference from its taxable income.

Insurers also adjust expenses reported in the Annual Statement into expenses reportable for tax purposes. Tax rules specify which expenses are deductible from gross income to obtain taxable income. Expense deductions from LICTI include three main categories as follows:

1. *Expenses associated with obtaining income,* including claims, paid or accrued policy dividends and experience rating refunds, agent commissions and insurance expenses, and other benefits associated with life insurance and annuity contracts

2. *Increases in specified reserves* (described above)

3. *General corporate deductions,* including depreciation on long-term assets and amortization of bond premiums

Small insurance companies in the United States—that is, those with less than $500 million in assets calculated under tax rules—also qualify for an additional deduction, called the *small life insurance company deduction.* A company that is eligible for the small life insurance company deduction calculates gross income and subtracts deductible expenses from gross income to obtain tentative LICTI. ***Tentative LICTI*** is the amount of gross income minus deductible expenses before subtracting the small life insurance company deduction, excluding income from non-insurance operations. The insurer must include in gross income only those revenues that arose from its life insurance operations, including investment income to support company liabilities and specified reinsurance transactions. The small life insurance company deduction enables a qualifying insurer to deduct up to 60 percent of its tentative LICTI (up to a maximum $1,800,000), to determine its taxable income according to a specified formula. Canada does not have a tax deduction for small insurance companies.

Many U.S. insurers are also subject to the income taxes imposed by other countries in which they conduct business. For this reason, the Annual Statement requires an insurer to report the type and amount of taxes levied against its income. Mutual life insurance companies, and stock life insurance companies with products similar to those offered by mutuals, or with branches in Canada or Mexico, can, under certain circumstances, exclude branch income from overall taxable income, as long as the companies account separately for each branch. The treatment of foreign tax credits and foreign income tax is outside the scope of this text. However, it is important to note that, in an age of multinational insurance companies, foreign taxes can represent a significant amount of an insurer's tax liability.

Under certain circumstances, U.S. insurers may be subject to the Alternative Minimum Tax (AMT), which could significantly increase the amount of an insurer's taxable income. Briefly, the AMT is a different method of computing a company's tax liability. The company calculates its federal income tax liability under the regular tax method and the method prescribed under the AMT. The company pays the amount of federal income taxes for whichever method results in a higher tax liability.

Canada

Canadian life and health insurers follow the *Canadian Federal Income Tax Act* in reporting their federal income tax liabilities to Revenue Canada, which is equivalent to the IRS in the United States. The federal tax calculation begins with an insurer's financial statements, prepared according to the *CICA Handbook.* Like their U.S. counterparts, Canadian insurers must consider the timing differences associated with amounts reported on the Annual Return and income tax returns. For example, an insurer deducts the excess of reserves calculated for tax purposes from those calculated under the policy premium method (PPM) for the Annual Return. The insurer reports this difference in its current tax return filed with Revenue Canada but does not record this difference in its accounting records until the following year.

One income tax that applies equally to insurance and non-insurance companies is the *business income tax.* To recognize the unique nature of long-term life insurance contracts, the business income tax for insurers applies special taxation provisions. For example, a significant factor in the income taxation of both domestic life insurance companies and all foreign non-life insurance companies is that Canadian taxable income is confined to that which is generated from the company's insurance business in Canada. This tax treatment contrasts with that of other Canadian businesses, including domestic non-life insurance companies, which pay income tax on their worldwide income and receive tax credits for any foreign income tax paid.

Canadian life insurers are subject to minimum taxes payable in the form of the *Federal Capital Tax (FCT).* Although the amount is computed according to the size of an insurer's total capital, the FCT is similar to the AMT in the United States in that both taxes represent minimum tax liabilities. Provincial tax authorities may also impose minimum taxes on either an insurer's total income or its total capital.

For a Canadian life insurance company, the five major items of income are

1. *Premium income,* which consists of insurance premiums and annuity considerations from business in Canada

2. *Gross investment income,* which includes interest, taxable investment dividends, rents, and royalties

3. *Other income,* which includes all other items of taxable income not included elsewhere, such as employee and employer contributions to pension and insurance funds for staff and agents, if these funds are held as a separate liability and not as part of policy reserves

4. *Capital gains,* which is included in income and is taxed at the usual corporate tax rate

5. Profit on the sale of *specified debt obligations (SDOs)*

Tax deductions for Canadian insurers generally consist of (1) insurance benefit costs, (2) interest paid by or credited to the insurer, (3) expenses, (4) increase in reserves, (5) dividends and experience rating refunds, (6) loss on the sale of SDOs, and (7) *capital cost allowances (CCAs),* which are the amounts of depreciation expenses an insurer can deduct in calculating its taxable income. Figure 13-7 summarizes the major components of gross income and tax deductions for U.S. and Canadian life insurance companies.

Premium Taxes

State and provincial governments impose premium taxes on life and health insurance policies issued in that state or province. ***Premium***

Figure 13-7. Gross income components and tax deductions for U.S. and Canadian life insurance companies.

Gross Income Components	Tax Deductions from Gross Income
• Premium income • Investment income • Capital gains • Decreases in specified reserves • Other income • SDOs—profit on sale (Canada only)	• Death benefits, other benefits, and insurance expenses • Increases in specified reserves • Policy dividends and experience-rating refunds • Operating losses and capital losses • Certain reinsurance considerations • General corporate deductions for expenses • Small life insurance company deduction (U.S. only) • Interest paid or credited (Canada only) • Canadian securities—loss on sale and amortization of premium (Canada only) • Capital cost allowances (Canada only)

taxes are taxes on an insurer's premium income earned within a state or province. Taxation authorities calculate these taxes as a percentage of the premium income. Fraternal benefit societies typically are exempt from premium taxes, although many states now impose premium taxes on specific non-profit insurance providers, such as Blue Cross/Blue Shield organizations. Annuity considerations typically are taxed at a lower rate than insurance premiums in those states that impose premium taxes on annuity considerations. Investment income and reinsurance premiums typically are excluded from the formula that determines the amount of premium taxes due from an insurer. Also, most states allow the insurer to deduct policyholder dividends from the amount of premium income used to calculate premium taxes due.

An insurer's incurrence of premium taxes creates a premium tax liability—Premium Taxes Payable—and increases the company's Premium Tax Expense. Thus, when it incurs premium taxes, an insurer makes the following journal entry:

Premium Tax Expense.	xxx	
Premium Taxes Payable		xxx
To record the incurrence of premium taxes.		

The insurer then makes a second entry when it remits payment for its premium tax liability:

Premium Taxes Payable	xxx	
Cash.		xxx
To record the payment of premium taxes.		

For financial reporting purposes, insurers maintain separate accounting records of premiums for each state and province. For example, the accounting entry for premium taxes paid to State A would be called Premium Tax Expense—State A in the insurer's subsidiary ledger. Under an automated accounting system, premium taxes are automatically calculated at year end on the basis of the premium income recorded in each state or province during the year.

Nearly all states and some Canadian provinces have retaliatory tax laws, which are designed to protect domestic companies from unreasonable tax burdens placed upon them by other states or provinces. ***Retaliatory tax laws*** impose premium taxes on a *foreign insurer,* which is an insurer domiciled in another state, at the rate domestic companies in the state of domicile would be taxed by the foreign state, but only if the premium tax rate is higher in the state of domicile. Suppose State A has a premium tax rate of 1.5 percent and a retaliatory tax law and State B has a premium tax rate of 2 percent. Because of State A's retaliatory tax law, an insurer domiciled in State B that also sells insurance in State A is subject to a 2 percent premium tax on business conducted in State A. If both states had the same premium tax rate, then the retaliatory tax law is not needed and, thus, is not imposed. Court decisions in the United States have tended to equalize the rates at which domestic and foreign insurers are taxed. Retaliatory tax laws also apply in some Canadian provinces.

The definition of premium income for tax purposes varies from state to state. Some states impose the tax on gross premiums, while other states allow companies to deduct the amount of policy dividends from the gross premium amount before calculating premium taxes. Some states require that the insurer pay the larger of the premium tax or the state income tax. All Canadian provinces and some U.S. states do not impose taxes on annuity considerations. Premium taxes for Canadian insurers are calculated on premium income collected from life and accident and sickness insurance policies but not on investment income. Also, Canadian insurers deduct policy dividends paid from the amount of collected premiums. Taxes on investment income are determined on the basis of actuarial calculations, which vary from province to province.

Guaranty-Fund Assessments

In Chapter 6, you learned that each state has established a guaranty association to protect policyowners in that state from losses as a result of insurer insolvency. In other words, if an insurance company becomes insolvent, the guaranty association covers the costs of providing benefits to the failed company's policyowners and beneficiaries. A guaranty association collects the money it needs to pay these benefits through ***guaranty-fund assessments,*** which are charges payable by sound insurers to cover the unsupported customer obligations of a failed insurer that had operated in a jurisdiction where the surviving insurer does business. Guaranty-fund assessments represent an expense for sound insurers. An insurance company that fails to pay a guaranty-fund assessment may have its insurance license revoked or suspended.

When a court declares an insurance company insolvent, the guaranty association determines the amount of the required assessment, which is usually the difference between the insolvent company's assets and its policy liabilities. Then, through guaranty-fund assessments to all sound insurance companies in that state, the guaranty association collects the total funds needed to satisfy policyowner obligations, plus a small amount to cover the guaranty association's expenses. The amount assessed to each sound insurer depends on the state and on the percentage of insurance each company writes of the same type or types (life, health, or annuities) for which the guaranty association is collecting. For example, if a state's guaranty association must collect $50 million in assessments for life insurance, and the Foreland Life and Health Insurance Company writes 4 percent of the life insurance business by premium volume in that state, then the guaranty association will assess Foreland $2 million ($50 million × 4 percent) for the insolvency. Each member insurer's guaranty-fund assessment may not exceed a certain sum each year. This sum equals a percentage of the company's premiums written in that state the previous year. A typical assessment limit is between 1 and 4 percent of total premiums written. If, during the year, one state is affected by a large number of insolvencies—or by one unusually large insolvency—the guaranty association may spread the assessment over several years.

In most states, insurers may offset a percentage of their assessments through premium tax reductions. This reduction is usually 20 percent per year for five years, beginning in the year following the assessment, although specific regulations differ from state to state.

CompCorp

While individual guaranty associations in each state protect policyholders and beneficiaries in the United States, the ***Canadian Life and Health Insurance Compensation Corporation (CompCorp)*** protects policyowners and beneficiaries throughout Canada. CompCorp operates similarly to state guaranty associations. The main difference is in coverage limits. Whereas certain state guaranty associations assess insurers in those states up to 4 percent of their premiums written in any one year, CompCorp can assess a single company up to only 0.5 percent of its premium volume in one year. For special circumstances, CompCorp may also borrow money from member companies. Canadian insurance companies are required to be members of CompCorp and to make payments when requested. However, Canadian insurers cannot offset these payments against premium taxes, as U.S. insurers can do with guaranty-fund assessments.

Financial Reporting of Expenses

A life and health insurance company reports its expenses in several ways for GAAP and statutory purposes. Under GAAP, an insurer lists its expenses on the statement of operations. Under statutory accounting in the Annual Statement, an insurer summarizes its expenses on the *Summary of Operations* page. Canadian insurers summarize expenses on the *Income Statement* page in the GAAP-based Annual Return. On each of these statements, an insurance company first lists total commissions, then general expenses, and then taxes, licenses, and fees. The detailed information supporting these summaries is found in numerous other exhibits and schedules that itemize expenses by product type and according to general expense category. In different schedules of the Annual Statement, for example, life and health insurance companies itemize commissions, general expenses, and taxes, licenses, and fees. The *Statement of Cash Flows* also requires summaries of expenses paid during the year. Further, another schedule reports the agent commissions, general expenses, and taxes, licenses, and fees associated with an insurer's accident and health insurance policies. The insurer lists these expenses according to group accident and health, individual and group credit accident and health, collectively renewable group accident and health, and other individual accident and health insurance policies.

The Annual Statement and the Annual Return require life and health insurance companies to report their expenses according to lines of business or particular product types. Figure 13-8 provides a list of the typical lines of business for life and health insurance companies. Within each line of business, an insurer also itemizes expenses associated with participating and nonparticipating policies, if applicable.

Finally, to prepare the Annual Statement, an insurer adjusts paid expenses from a modified cash basis to an accrual basis. To make this adjustment, the insurer starts with the expenses paid during the year, then (1) adds the amount of unpaid expenses at the end of the current year and (2) subtracts the amount of unpaid expenses at the end of the previous year. Assume that expenses paid during the year total $1,000, unpaid expenses at the end of the current year are $150, and unpaid expenses at the end of the previous year were $100. The proper adjusted incurred expense amount for the reporting year is $1,050 ($1,000 + $150 – $100). Figures 13-9 and 13-10 depict the exhibits that report

Figure 13-8. Lines of business for life and health insurance companies for expense reporting purposes.

U.S. Annual Statement	Canadian Annual Return
• Ordinary life insurance • Individual annuities • Ordinary supplementary contracts • Credit life insurance • Group life insurance • Group annuities • Group accident and health insurance • Credit accident and health insurance • Other accident and health insurance	• Individual life insurance • Individual annuities • Group life insurance • Group annuities • Accident and sickness insurance

an insurer's general (operating) expenses and taxes, licenses, and fees on the Annual Statement and Annual Return.

Conclusion

Chapter 13 discussed the primary expenses incurred by life and health insurance companies. With this chapter, we conclude our presentation of insurers' five major account classifications: assets, liabilities, capital and surplus, revenues, and expenses. The next chapter discusses the time value of money. This topic will enable you to interpret the numbers and the interrelationships among account classifications on an insurer's financial statements. For the remainder of the text, we shift our focus to management accounting and the way an insurance company's managers can use the foundations of financial accounting to more effectively manage the company in a changing financial services environment.

Key Terms and Concepts

control account
vesting provision
allowances
reinsurance commissions
life insurance company taxable income (LICTI)
tentative LICTI
premium taxes
retaliatory tax laws
guaranty-fund assessments
Canadian Life and Health Insurance Compensation Corporation (CompCorp)

Figure 13-9. Exhibits 5 and 6—U.S. Annual Statement.

EXHIBIT 5—GENERAL EXPENSES

		Insurance			4	5
		1 Life	2 Accident and Health	3 All Other Lines of Business	Investment	Total
1.	Rent					
2.	Salaries and wages					
3.11	Contributions for benefit plans for employees					
3.12	Contributions for benefit plans for agents					
3.21	Payments to employees under non-funded benefit plans					
3.22	Payments to agents under non-funded benefit plans					
3.31	Other employee welfare					
3.32	Other agent welfare					
4.1	Legal fees and expenses					
4.2	Medical examination fees					
4.3	Inspection report fees					
4.4	Fees of public accountants and consulting actuaries					
4.5	Expense of investigation and settlement of policy claims					
5.1	Traveling expenses					
5.2	Advertising					
5.3	Postage, express, telegraph and telephone					
5.4	Printing and stationery					
5.5	Cost or depreciation of furniture and equipment					
5.6	Rental of equipment					
6.1	Books and periodicals					
6.2	Bureau and association fees					
6.3	Insurance, except on real estate					
6.4	Miscellaneous losses					
6.5	Collection and bank service charges					
6.6	Sundry general expenses					
6.7	Group service and administration fees					
6.8	Reimbursements by uninsured accident and health plans					
7.1	Agency expense allowance					
7.2	Agents' balances charged off (less $ .... recovered)					
7.3	Agency conferences other than local meetings					
9.1	Real estate expenses					
9.2	Investment expenses not included elsewhere					
9.3	Aggregate write-ins for expenses					
10.	General Expenses Incurred					(a)
11.	General expenses unpaid December 31, previous year					
12.	General expenses unpaid December 31, current year					
13.	Amounts receivable relating to uninsured accident and health plans, previous year					
14.	Amounts receivable relating to uninsured accident and health plans, current year					
15.	General expenses paid during year (Lines 10 + 11 − 12 − 13 + 14)					

EXHIBIT 6—TAXES, LICENSES AND FEES (EXCLUDING FEDERAL INCOME TAXES)

1.	Real estate taxes					
2.	State insurance department licenses and fees					
3.	State taxes on premiums					
4.	Other state taxes, incl. $ .... for employee benefits					
5.	U.S. Social Security taxes					
6.	All other taxes					
7.	Taxes, Licenses and Fees Incurred					
8.	Taxes, licenses and fees unpaid December 31, previous year					
9.	Taxes, licenses and fees unpaid December 31, current year					
10.	Taxes, licenses and fees paid during year (Lines 7 + 8 − 9)					

Figure 13-10. *General Expenses and Taxes*—Canadian Annual Return.

GENERAL EXPENSES AND TAXES
(Excluding Investment Expenses and Income Taxes)
($'000)

		Current Year (01)	Prior Year (02)
Rent	20		
Salaries, Wages and Allowances	23		
Employees' and Agents' Welfare	26		
Professional and Service Fees and Expenses	30		
Canadian Life & Health Insurance Compensation Corporation (CompCorp) Assessment	36		
Miscellaneous Expenses	39		
Premium Taxes	40		
Supervision and Examination	43		
Licenses and Fees	46		
Miscellaneous Taxes	50		
Total General Expenses and Taxes	69		

References

1. Louis Sims, "Managing General Expenses in the Age of RBC," *National Underwriter Life & Health/Financial Services Edition,* No. 17 (April 25, 1994), p. 8.

CHAPTER 14

THE TIME VALUE OF MONEY

LEARNING OBJECTIVES

After studying this chapter, you should be able to

- Explain the concept of the time value of money
- Define and explain the concepts of interest and interest rates
- Distinguish between simple interest and compound interest
- Discuss the relationships between nominal, effective, and equivalent interest rates
- Describe the concept of risk and the risk posed by inflation
- Determine the future value of a single amount using the *FVIF* table
- Compare an ordinary annuity to an annuity due
- Determine the future value of an ordinary annuity and an annuity due using the *FVIFA* table
- Determine the present value of a single amount using the *PVIF* table
- Determine the present value of an ordinary annuity and an annuity due using the *PVIFA* table
- Provide examples of how insurance managers use the time value of money when making decisions

CHAPTER OUTLINE

The Time Value of Money

Interest

Risk and Inflation

Calculating Future Value

Calculating Present Value

A Note about Interest Factors

Insurance Operations and the Time Value of Money

If you've taken other courses in the FLMI Program, or if you've worked in insurance or another sector of the financial services industry, you know that many different forces affect an insurance company's operations. Regulatory concerns, competitive influences, and legislative changes are just some of the factors that insurance managers consider when making decisions. Further, managers who make financial decisions are concerned with the *time value of money.* This chapter describes the concept of the time value of money and the reasons that this concept is so important to life and health insurance companies. We describe the time value of money and the key factors that affect it, including interest, interest rates, simple interest, compound interest, risk, and inflation. We also explain some of the most important formulas and calculations used to determine the time value of money, including calculations for the

- Future value of a single payment
- Future value of a series of payments
- Present value of a single payment
- Present value of a series of payments

To conclude the chapter, we describe how insurance companies calculate and forecast the time value of money, and how they apply this concept in the context of their operations.

The Time Value of Money

The ***time value of money*** is the concept that the value of a sum of money at one point in time will differ from its value at another point in time as a result of the effect of interest. Put another way, money in your hand today may have a different value than money promised to you in the future. For example, if you invest money today and your investment turns out to be profitable, then your money will probably have greater value in the future. If, on the other hand, the general level of prices for goods and services increases, this *future value* of your money may be lower than its *present value,* or value today.

The time value of money exerts enormous influence on individuals and businesses. Our beliefs about the time value of money can determine how we use money today and in the future. For example, if you believe that a dollar today is worth more than a dollar will be worth in the future, you might be inclined to spend today's dollar before it loses its value or purchasing power. If, on the other hand, you believe that a dollar in the future will be worth more than a dollar today, you may be more inclined to save today's dollar so you will have more wealth and purchasing power in the future.

Insurance companies spend a great deal of time and effort planning the best ways to use their money so that, in the future, their money will be worth more than it is today. The calculations that insurers use in these planning efforts relate not only to their investments but also to the prices they charge for their products and services. The key factor in understanding and calculating the time value of money is the concept of *interest.* Money invested today can earn interest and, over time, grow to a larger amount. Thus, any amount of money can be said to have a future value equal to the amount that it would be worth at a given point in the future if it were to accumulate at interest. Similarly, any amount of money promised to be paid in the future can be said to have a present value, which is the amount of money that would have to be invested today to accumulate to that future amount. Present value and future value are mathematically linked so that present value can be used to calculate future value, and future value can be used to calculate present value.

In practice, insurance companies' present value and future value calculations are generally performed quickly and easily by computers. Our discussion of the time value of money relies on financial tables, but it also presents the mathematics behind present value and future value calculations so that you can understand these concepts. It is important to note that a given present value can have any number of future values, and a given future value can have any number of present values. The present value or future value of an amount of money is determined by two factors: (1) the assumed interest rate and (2) the length of time between the present and future dates. We discuss interest first.

Interest

Interest, which is the dollar amount earned on an invested amount of money, can be thought of as money paid for the use of money. When we deposit money in a savings account at a bank, we are lending our money to the bank to use. In return for the use of our money, the bank pays us interest. The bank doesn't just hold our money in a vault. Instead, the bank invests it or lends it to other customers. The parties who receive the invested or loaned funds pay the bank interest for the use of the money. Some of the interest payments that the bank makes to us for the use of our money come from the interest the bank receives from other parties. As our money earns interest, the amount of our money grows, thus increasing in value. In this way, the future value of our money will be greater than its present value, thus demonstrating an aspect of the time value of money.

Insurance companies often deal with enormous sums of money, well into the millions or even billions of dollars. Because of this, even the smallest change in interest can mean the difference between making or losing many thousands of dollars. Therefore, insurers carefully calculate the interest they are likely to earn on various investments. With these calculations, they can estimate the present value of their money and forecast its future value.

Interest Rates

Interest is measured in percentages. An ***interest rate*** is the percentage by which an amount of money is multiplied to derive the amount paid for the use of that money. Interest rates are usually expressed in decimal form for ease in calculating interest. A 5 percent interest rate is expressed as 0.05 in decimal form; similarly, a 2½ percent interest rate is expressed as 0.025.

To illustrate the use of interest and interest rates, consider the following scenario: An investor deposits $100 in the bank for one year at an interest rate of 5 percent. Recall that the amount of money originally deposited or invested (in this case $100) is known as the *principal,* and the 5 percent is the *interest rate* or the *rate of return* on the amount of money invested. To find the amount of interest the investor will earn in one year, multiply the principal by the interest rate:

Principal × Interest Rate = Interest Earned

Substituting the figures from our example into the above formula, we obtain the result:

$$\$100 \times .05 = \$5$$

Thus, an investor who deposits $100 into a bank account that pays 5 percent interest will earn $5 interest in one year. The accumulated value of an investment at any time is the principal plus the accumulated interest earned. In the above example, the accumulated value after one year is $105 ($100 principal + $5 interest earned). An important factor that affects the accumulated value is whether the interest is paid as *simple interest* or *compound interest.*

Figure 14-1. $1,000 accumulated at 10 percent simple interest.

{1} Year	{2} Amount Subject to Interest	{3} Interest Earned ({2} × 0.10)	{4} Principal + Interest (previous {4} + {3})
1	$1,000	$100	$1,100
2	$1,000	$100	$1,200
3	$1,000	$100	$1,300
4	$1,000	$100	$1,400
5	$1,000	$100	$1,500

Simple Interest

Simple interest is interest earned on the amount of money originally borrowed or invested. Under simple interest, interest each period is calculated only on the *principal* (the amount of the original investment). Suppose that an insurance company invests $1,000 at 10 percent simple interest. The insurer's investment accumulates as depicted in Figure 14-1. The figure in Column 4 is the sum of the principal plus all accumulated interest. As you can see, interest is earned each year only on the principal amount of $1,000. Thus, at the end of the second year, the $1,200 figure is the sum of the $1,000 principal plus two years of simple interest of $100 per year.

Compound Interest

Unlike simple interest, ***compound interest*** is interest earned on both the principal *and* on the accumulated interest. As an investor, you would prefer to receive compound interest; as a borrower, you would prefer to pay simple interest on your loan. Why do you think this is so? Compound interest results in a higher total payment than simple interest, given the same principal amount, interest rate, and a period greater than one year, because compound interest includes interest on interest.

For example, $1,000 invested at 10 percent compounded annually accumulates as illustrated in Figure 14-2. At the end of the first year, interest is paid on the principal of $1,000. At the end of the second year, interest is paid on the principal plus the $100 of interest that was earned in the first year.

Compare Figures 14-1 and 14-2 and note how much difference there is at the end of five years between the future value (accumulated value) under simple interest and compound interest. Note also that the principal plus interest for both simple interest and compound interest are equal at the end of the first year, because there is no inter-

Figure 14-2. $1,000 accumulated at 10 percent compound interest.

{1} Year	{2} Amount Subject to Interest	{3} Interest Earned ({2} × 0.10)	{4} Principal + Interest ({2} + {3})
1	$1,000	$100	$1,100
2	$1,100	$110	$1,210
3	$1,210	$121	$1,331
4	$1,331	$133	$1,464
5	$1,464	$146	$1,610

est accumulated on interest at this point for amounts that are compounded annually. The accumulated amounts for years 2 through 5 under compound interest are higher than those obtained under simple interest. This example demonstrates how the time value of money can be used to an investor's advantage. The more frequently interest is compounded, the faster the investment grows. From an investor's standpoint, quarterly compounding is preferable to semiannual compounding, which in turn is preferable to annual compounding. On the other hand, from a borrower's standpoint, the less frequent the compounding periods, the less interest the borrower has to pay.

In reality, few institutions pay simple interest. Compound interest is standard in most business transactions, and compounding occurs on a quarterly, monthly, daily, or even a continuous basis. If you have ever earned interest on a savings account or paid interest on an automobile loan, a mortgage loan, or credit card loans, chances are that the interest on these loans was compounded. Typically, insurers borrow and lend money at compound interest rates. Unless otherwise stated, in this text the term *interest* means compound interest.

Risk and Inflation

Frequently, when an insurer must choose between two or more possible uses for its money, other factors besides the interest rate are not equal. Several other factors may be involved. Risk is one of these factors. ***Risk*** is the chance that the actual return on an investment will be less than its expected return. Some investments are riskier than others, and different investments carry different types and levels of risk. Suppose an insurer is trying to decide whether to invest in a new computerized claim administration system. The insurer can calculate that the system will provide a certain rate of return (expressed as an interest rate) based on the improved efficiencies that the system provides. But the insurer must also confront the possible adverse effects of *technology risk.* What if the insurer invests in the new system, and then computer technology changes more quickly than the insurer expects? A better claim administration system could appear on the market. The insurer's competitors could invest in the improved system, and the system that the insurer just bought could lose its competitive edge and become obsolete much more quickly than the insurer had originally estimated.

Another form of risk relates to interest itself. Recall from Chapter 6 that *interest rate risk* refers to the potential problems caused by unpredictable fluctuations in interest rates. Although a company can accurately calculate interest rates, as well as the present value and future value of money based on interest rates, the company is not always guaranteed that it will earn the interest rate it expects to earn. Further, the company can't be guaranteed that the interest rate earned will remain competitive over time with the interest rates on other investments.

Generally, the riskier the investment, the higher the rate of return an insurer will expect from the investment. This is called the *risk-return tradeoff.* Every day businesses are faced with various kinds of risks, and businesses have found ways to analyze and calculate the possible effects of each kind of risk. One particular form of risk relates closely to the time value of money.

Inflation is an increase in the average level of the prices of goods and services. Just as an interest rate is expressed as a percentage, inflation expressed as a percentage is called the *inflation rate,* and the calculations that apply to interest also apply to inflation. Typically, we think of the time value of money as being affected by the amount of interest that we earn on our investments, but inflation also affects the time value of money. When prices are generally rising, a product or service that costs $200 today may cost $220 a few years or even a few months from now.

Inflation risk, also called *purchasing power risk,* refers to the potential problems caused by the increasing prices that occur during inflation, especially when the rate of inflation is hard to predict. Suppose an insurance company decides *not* to buy a new computerized claim administration system this year. Instead, it decides to wait another year and calculates that, by waiting and continuing to use its current system, it can save 10 percent of the cost of the new system. If, however, general inflation in the economy raises prices, including the price of the new system, by 15 percent, then the company is not saving at a rate of 10 percent. Instead, the company is losing 5 percent.

Inflation reduces the future purchasing power of money, and insurers are keenly aware of the risk of inflation. Just like interest rates, inflation rates fluctuate in ways that are not entirely predictable. Just like interest rates, inflation rates affect the present value and the future value of money. While insurers cannot guarantee the inflation rates that will occur in the future, they can calculate the effect of potential inflation on the time value of money. In that way, they can forecast the amount of interest they need to earn or should be willing to pay based on the inflation rate they expect to occur.

While inflation has been a predominant concern for world economies in recent decades, its opposite condition, *deflation,* can also occur. ***Deflation*** is a *decrease* in the average level of the prices of goods and services. Like interest and inflation, deflation can have a profound effect on the time value of money and is calculated using similar formulas.

Calculating Future Value

As we have mentioned, the ***future value (FV)*** of a sum of money is the amount that the sum is expected to be worth at a certain point in the future, given a certain rate of interest. The term *accumulated value* is also used to refer to future value.

Future Value of a Single Amount

When calculating future values, we can substitute the term *present value* for *principal* because, like principal, *present value* refers to an amount of money before it is affected by interest. If present value is represented by *PV* and interest rate is represented by *i,* then the formula for interest earned on a one-year investment can be expressed as follows:

$$\textbf{Interest Earned} = PV \times i$$

Thus, we can calculate the future value of a one-year investment using the following equation:

$$\textbf{Future Value} = \textbf{Present Value} + \textbf{Interest Earned}$$

or

$$FV = PV + (PV \times i)$$

or more commonly

$$FV = PV(1 + i)$$

For example, the future value of a one-year investment of $100 earning 5 percent interest is calculated as follows:

$$FV = \$100\ (1 + 0.05)$$
$$FV = \$100\ (1.05)$$
$$FV = \$105$$

To calculate the future value of an investment earning interest for more than one year, the present value is multiplied by one plus the interest rate $(1 + i)$ once for each period that the investment accumulates interest. In the example discussed above, if the $100 were invested for five years, the formula could be expressed as

$$FV = \$100\ (1.05)(1.05)(1.05)(1.05)(1.05)$$

or

$$FV = \$100\ (1.05)^5$$

Note that $(1.05)^5$ is read "1.05 to the *fifth power.*" *Fifth power* simply means that 1.05 is being multiplied by itself five times. No matter how it is written, the result of the calculation is the same.

$$FV = \$100\ (1.27628)$$
$$FV = \$127.63 \text{ (rounded)}$$

We can use this example to derive a general formula for finding the future value of an investment earning compound interest for more than one year. If the future value after five years is found by multiplying the present value by $(1 + i)$ five times, then the future value after n years is found by multiplying the present value by $(1 + i)$ n times. Thus, the general equation for finding the future value of a single amount can be expressed as follows:

$$FV = PV\,(1 + i)^n$$

Nominal Interest Rates

So far we have assumed that all interest is *compounded*—that is, calculated and applied to the principal and accumulated interest—on an annual basis. An annual interest rate that is quoted independent of the effects of compounding is called a ***nominal interest rate.*** However, it is common for interest to be compounded quarterly, monthly, weekly, daily, or even continuously. Banks often quote nominal interest rates as follows:

4 Percent Annual Interest Rate, Compounded Daily

or

8 Percent Annual Interest Rate, Compounded Quarterly

In such situations and given the equation

$$FV = PV(1 + i)^n$$

n refers to the number of compounding periods, and i is the interest rate per compounding period. To find the interest rate per compounding period when the compounding period is less than a year, divide the annual interest rate by the number of compounding periods per year.

For example, if the nominal interest rate is 8 percent compounded semiannually, then the interest rate for a half-year compounding period is 4 percent (8 percent ÷ 2 compounding periods). A $100 principal amount invested for one year at a nominal 8 percent interest, compounded semiannually, accumulates to $104 ($100 × 1.04) after the first half-year, and it accumulates to $108.16 ($104 × 1.04) after the second half-year. Calculated another way

$$FV = PV(1 + i)^n$$
$$FV = \$100\,(1.04)^2$$
$$FV = \$100\,(1.0816)$$
$$FV = \$108.16$$

What if the nominal 8 percent interest were compounded quarterly? In this case, 8 percent interest divided by four compounding periods equals 2 percent per quarter. Below is the calculation for each of the four compounding periods, which culminates in a future value of $108.24.

End of Quarter	Calculation	Future Value
1	$100 × 1.02	$102.00
2	$102 × 1.02	$104.04
3	$104.04 × 1.02	$106.12
4	$106.12 × 1.02	$108.24

Note that $108.24 (quarterly compounding) is greater than $108.16 (semiannual compounding), which in turn is greater than $108.00 (annual compounding), given a nominal interest rate of 8 percent. This example illustrates that, given the same nominal annual interest rate, the more frequently interest is compounded, the larger the future value.

The value of n can also be calculated by multiplying the number of years over which money accumulates by the number of compounding periods per year. For example, for a 20-year investment with quarterly compounding, n equals 80 (20 years × 4 compounding periods per year).

Effective Interest Rates

When interest is compounded more than once a year, we can find the equivalent annual interest rate that results in the same future value as the given nominal interest rate. This annual interest rate is known as the *effective interest rate.* Recall from Chapter 7 that the *effective interest rate* is the actual interest rate that is earned or paid on principal amounts that are compounded more often than annually. You can obtain the effective interest rate by dividing the interest actually earned or paid for the year by the beginning principal or present value. The general formula for calculating the effective interest rate is

Effective Interest Rate = Interest ÷ Principal

Using the figures obtained from the above example, we can derive the effective interest rate for annual, semiannual, and quarterly compounding to find the *equivalent interest rate* for a given nominal interest rate. For example, the effective annual interest rate that corresponds to a nominal 8 percent interest rate compounded semiannually is 8.16 percent ($8.16 interest ÷ $100 principal). The effective annual interest rate that corresponds to a nominal 8 percent interest rate compounded quarterly is 8.24 percent ($8.24 interest ÷ $100 principal). These interest rates are ***equivalent interest rates*** in that they produce the same future value in the same period. In our example, a nominal 8 percent rate, compounded semiannually, is equivalent to an effective 8.16 percent, compounded annually. Similarly, a nominal 8 percent rate, compounded quarterly, is equivalent to an effective 8.24 percent, compounded annually. These rates are equivalent because they result in the same future values at the end of one year, as shown in the tables that follow:

8 percent, compounded semiannually		8.16 percent, compounded annually
$100 × 1.04^2 = $108.16	=	$100 × 1.0816 = $108.16

8 percent, compounded quarterly	=	8.24 percent, compounded annually
$\$100 \times 1.02^4 = \underline{\underline{\$108.24}}$		$\$100 \times 1.0824 = \underline{\underline{\$108.24}}$

To calculate the effective interest rate in percentage form, subtract 1 from $(1 + i)^n$, then multiply the result by 100.

$$\textbf{Effective Interest Rate} = 100\,[(1 + i)^n - 1]$$

If we use a nominal rate of 8 percent, compounded quarterly, we obtain the following:

$$\begin{aligned}\textbf{Effective Interest Rate} &= 100\,[(1.02)^4 - 1] \\ &= 100\,(1.0824 - 1) \\ &= 8.24 \text{ percent}\end{aligned}$$

For another example, suppose that an insurer's investment department must choose between two investment opportunities, both with similar risk levels. The first investment pays a 6 percent nominal interest rate, compounded quarterly; the second investment pays a 6.12 percent nominal interest rate, compounded semiannually. If you were the insurer's chief investment officer, which investment would you recommend for purchase? The effective rate for the first investment equals 6.14 percent $\{100\,[(1.015)^4 - 1]\}$. The effective interest rate for the second investment equals 6.21 percent $\{100\,[(1.0306)^2 - 1]\}$. Because the effective interest rate on the second investment is higher than that on the first investment, you would recommend the second investment for purchase, all other factors being equal.

Future Value Interest Factors

Calculating the value of $(1 + i)^n$ can be very tedious, especially when the number of compounding periods is as high as 5, 10, or 100. Computers and financial calculators can make such calculations quickly and easily. Tables are also available showing the future value of \$1.00 for numerous interest rates and numbers of compounding periods. The future value of \$1.00 is generally referred to as the ***future value interest factor (FVIF)*** and a table that lists such values is called a *future value interest factor (FVIF) table.* The future value interest factor *(FVIF),* also sometimes called the *compound value interest factor,* can be used to replace $(1 + i)^n$ in the future value equation, so that

$$FV = PV \times FVIF\ (n, i)$$

Note that *FVIF* is not being multiplied by *n* and *i*. The *n* and *i* show the interest rate and number of compounding periods and indicate where the *FVIF* can be found in the *FVIF* table. Figure 14-3 presents a portion of the future value interest factor table that appears in the appendix of this book. To use the *FVIF* table, find the column with the appropriate interest rate *(i)*, then find the row for the appropriate number of compounding periods *(n)*. The cell that represents the intersection of column *i* and row *n* is the correct *FVIF* to use. Thus, you can think of the *(n, i)* notation as the column/row coordinates for the proper cell in an *FVIF* table.

All interest factor tables have the same format: (1) the interest rates shown in the tables represent the interest rates per period, and (2) the periods shown represent the number of compounding periods. In Figure 14-3, the number highlighted, 1.464, is at the row and column intersection of 4 periods and 10 percent interest per period. This could be written *FVIF* (4, 10%) and the number 1.464 is equivalent to 1.10^4. If you have a calculator, you can try raising 1.10 to the fourth power. The result of this calculation is actually 1.4641, but because our table shows only three decimal places, we rounded to 1.464. Note that, because *n* is the number of compounding periods and *i* is the interest rate per period, *FVIF* (4, 10%) could be the *FVIF* for a number of different investments, such as a four-year investment that pays 10 percent interest compounded annually, or a two-year investment that pays 20 percent interest compounded semiannually.

For example, the future value of $5,000 invested for five years at 5 percent interest compounded annually can easily be calculated using the *FVIF* table. First, substitute the information from this problem into the future value equation.

Figure 14-3. *FVIF* table: Future value of $1 at the end of *n* periods, earning interest rate *i*, $\$1(1+i)^n$.

Period	Interest Rate (*i*)			
(*n*)	1%	2%	5%	10%
1	1.010	1.020	1.050	1.100
2	1.020	1.040	1.103	1.210
3	1.030	1.061	1.158	1.331
4	1.041	1.082	1.216	1.464
5	1.051	1.104	1.276	1.611

$$\textbf{\textit{FV}} = \$5{,}000 \times \textbf{\textit{FVIF}}\,(5,\ 5\%)$$

Next, find the appropriate *FVIF* from the *FVIF* table and substitute this *FVIF* in the equation.

$$\textbf{\textit{FV}} = \$5{,}000 \times 1.276$$

Then multiply to obtain the result.

$$\textbf{\textit{FV}} = \$6{,}380$$

Thus, the future value of $5,000 invested at 5 percent interest compounded annually for five years is $6,380.

Suppose you invested $10,000 and expected it to earn interest at an 8 percent annual rate, compounded quarterly for two years. How could you use the *FVIF* table in the appendix to calculate the future value of this investment? First, determine the interest rate per compounding period: 8 percent ÷ 4 compounding periods per year = 2 percent. Then determine the number of compounding periods: 4 periods per year × 2 years = 8. The future value of your $10,000 can then be calculated as follows:

$$\textbf{\textit{FV}} = \$10{,}000 \times \textbf{\textit{FVIF}}\,(8,\ 2\%)$$
$$\textbf{\textit{FV}} = \$10{,}000 \times 1.172$$
$$\textbf{\textit{FV}} = \$11{,}720$$

Standard tables of interest factors depict interest rates from 1 percent to 20 percent or higher, compounding periods from 1 to 50 or more, and interest factors that have been rounded to three or four digits or more beyond the decimal point. If you look at an *FVIF* table, you'll notice three things about *FVIF*s: (1) they are always greater than 1.0 (they would equal 1.0 only if i or n were zero); (2) at a given interest rate (i), the *FVIF*s increase as the number of compounding periods (n) increases; and (3) at a given number of periods (n), the *FVIF*s increase as the interest rate (i) increases.

Most financial services companies use computers and calculators, rather than tables, to calculate interest factors. Time value of money calculations are vital to the operations of such companies, so they use as many compounding periods as a calculation calls for, and, if necessary, base calculations on fractional rates such as 7½ or 7¼ percent. Simplified interest factor tables, however, are acceptable for the purposes of our discussion. You may encounter situations in which you will need to use interest factors for i and n that are fractional or are greater than those available in the tables. However, the sample problems associated with this text can be solved using the set of interest factor tables contained in the appendix of this book.

Future Value of an Annuity

Insurance companies often encounter situations in which they must calculate the future value of a series of payments, rather than the future value of a single amount. In actuarial terminology, an ***annuity*** is any series of equal payments made over equally spaced time periods. Insurers often use the term *annuity* to refer to a specific type of insurance product that makes payments to all surviving members of a group of original contract owners. In fact, these two definitions are not as different as they might seem to be. An annuity *product* is called an annuity because it involves regular, periodic payments to the contract owners. In this section, when we refer to an annuity, we are using the term to mean any series of equal payments. Note that in our discussion of the future value of an annuity, when we refer to interest earned on an annuity, we refer to the interest that could be earned if each annuity payment received were invested at a given interest rate.

The ***future value of an annuity (FVA)*** at a given point in time is the amount that a series of payments plus the interest earned on these payments will grow to by that point in time. Before we begin to explain how the future value of an annuity is calculated, we first review two different types of annuities that you may encounter.

An ***ordinary annuity,*** sometimes called an *annuity immediate* or an *annuity in arrears,* is one for which the payment occurs at the end of each payment period. The semiannual interest paid on most bonds is an example of an ordinary annuity because the first interest payment is made after the bond is issued. Another example of an ordinary annuity is the paycheck a worker receives after each work period has been completed.

An ***annuity due,*** also called an *annuity in advance,* is an annuity for which the payment occurs at the beginning of each payment period. Examples of annuities due include rent, lease payments, and life and health insurance premiums, all of which involve payments made at the beginning of the period concerned. The difference between an ordinary annuity and an annuity due centers on the timing of the payment—whether it occurs at the end of the payment period (ordinary annuity), or at the beginning of the period (annuity due).

In order to visualize a series of periodic payments, it may be helpful for you to draw a simple line diagram. Many actuaries and investment analysts begin their analysis with a line diagram of each investment's expected cash flows. A ***line diagram,*** or *time line,* is a visual device that allows you to see the essential elements of a particular financial transaction. It marks the end of each compounding period, the frequency and amount of each cash flow, and the timing of the valuation date. The ***valuation date*** is the date as of which the value of the financial transaction is determined.

Sometimes it is difficult to determine whether a series of periodic payments is an ordinary annuity or an annuity due. Drawing a line diagram and marking the valuation date makes this determination easier. The future value of an ordinary annuity is evaluated as of the date of the last periodic payment. The future value of an annuity due is evaluated as of the date one period after the last periodic payment.

The future value of an ordinary annuity of $100 per year for three years can be represented by the following line diagram:

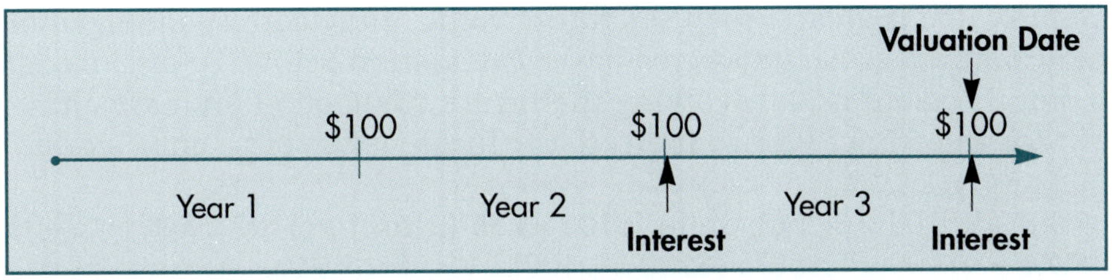

Note that the interest accrues twice for the ordinary annuity. No interest accumulates in Year 1 of the ordinary annuity, because the first payment does not occur until the end of Year 1. Compare the diagram of the ordinary annuity just presented with that of an annuity due, which follows:

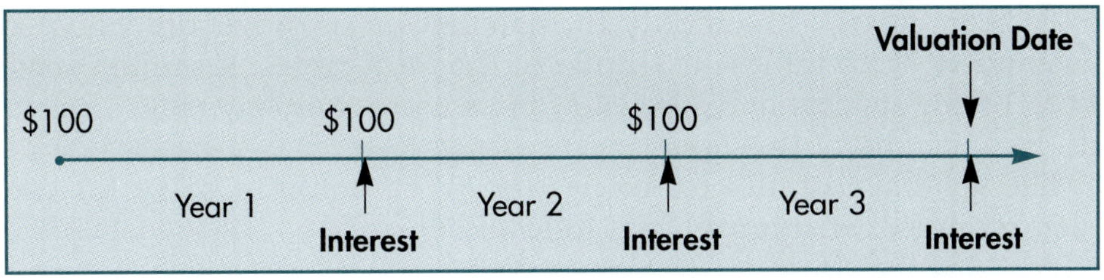

For the annuity due, the first payment occurs at the beginning of Year 1 and interest accrues in each of the three periods.

Future Value of an Annuity Interest Factors

The future value of an annuity *(FVA)* can be calculated by adding together the future values of each periodic payment. For a three-year ordinary annuity of $100 earning 5 percent interest compounded annually, the future value can be calculated as shown here (refer to Figure 14-3 to see the values of the *FVIF* table):

$$\begin{aligned}
\mathbf{FVA} &= [\$100 \times \mathbf{FVIF}(2, 5\%)] + [\$100 \times \mathbf{FVIF}(1, 5\%)] + \$100 \\
\mathbf{FVA} &= (\$100 \times 1.103) + (\$100 \times 1.050) + \$100 \\
\mathbf{FVA} &= \$110.30 + \$105.00 + \$100.00 \\
\mathbf{FVA} &= \$315.30
\end{aligned}$$

For this ordinary annuity, the first $100 payment earns two years of interest and thus is multiplied by *FVIF* (2, 5%). The second $100 payment earns one year's interest, and so is multiplied by *FVIF* (1, 5%). The final payment is made on the valuation date, and so it earns no interest.

If the annuity in this example were an annuity due instead of an ordinary annuity, the first payment earns interest for three full years, the second payment earns interest for two years, and the final payment earns interest for one year. As a result, the future value of the annuity due is greater than the future value of the corresponding ordinary annuity, as demonstrated in the calculation below. To distinguish it from a calculation involving the future value of an ordinary annuity, we are using *FVAd* to indicate the future value of an annuity due.

$$\mathbf{FVAd} = [\$100 \times \mathbf{FVIF}\,(3, 5\%)] + [\$100 \times \mathbf{FVIF}\,(2, 5\%)] + [\$100 \times \mathbf{FVIF}\,(1, 5\%)]$$
$$\mathbf{FVAd} = [\$100 \times 1.158] + [\$100 \times 1.103] + [\$100 \times 1.050]$$
$$\mathbf{FVAd} = \$115.80 + \$110.30 + \$105.00$$
$$\mathbf{FVAd} = \$331.10$$

When an annuity involves a large number of compounding periods, calculating the future value of the annuity by adding together the future value of each payment can be laborious and time-consuming. Consequently, ***future value interest factor of an annuity (FVIFA)*** tables have been created to simplify the calculation of the future value of an annuity. Such tables are similar to the *FVIF* tables. A sample of an *FVIFA* table appears in Figure 14-4, and a more complete table appears in the appendix of this book.

The general formula for using the *FVIFA* table to solve for the future value of an annuity is as follows:

Future Value of an Annuity = Periodic Payment × *FVIFA (n, i)*

or

FVA = PP × FVIFA (n, i)

The future value of the three-year ordinary annuity earning 5 percent interest described in the previous example can be calculated using the *FVIFA* table as follows:

$$\mathbf{FVA} = \$100 \times \mathbf{FVIFA}\,(3, 5\%)$$
$$\mathbf{FVA} = \$100 \times 3.152$$
$$\mathbf{FVA} = \$315.20$$

Figure 14-4. *FVIFA* table: Future value of a $1 annuity per period for *n* periods at *i* interest.

Period (*n*)	Interest Rate (*i*) 1%	2%	5%	10%
1	1.000	1.000	1.000	1.000
2	2.010	2.020	2.050	2.100
3	3.030	3.060	3.152	3.310
4	4.060	4.122	4.310	4.641
5	5.101	5.204	5.526	6.105

Substituting the single value from the *FVIFA* table shown in Figure 14-4, we get $315.20, which is almost the same result as we found using multiple values from the *FVIF* table. The $0.10 difference is a result of rounding.

The factors in *FVIFA* tables are calculated for ordinary annuities. To use the *FVIFA* table to find the future value of an annuity due, we need to use a slightly different method than the one described above. The future value of an annuity due is equal to the future value of a corresponding ordinary annuity of one additional period, minus the amount of one payment. To find the future value of an annuity due of *n* periods, we first need to find the *FVIFA* for the current interest rate and *n* + 1 periods. Then we subtract 1—remember that the interest factor tables are based on a $1.00 payment—from this factor and multiply the periodic payment by the result. The method of calculating the future value of an annuity due using the *FVIFA* table can be summarized in the following equation (recall that we are using *FVAd* to indicate the future value of an annuity due):

$$FVAd = PP \times [FVIFA\,(n + 1, i) - 1]$$

As an example, how would we calculate the future value of a four-payment $1,000 annuity due earning 10 percent interest? In this example, *n* is 4, *i* is 10%, and *PP* is $1,000. Substituting these numbers into the *FVAd* equation yields the following results:

$$\begin{aligned} FVAd &= \$1{,}000 \times [FVIFA\,(4 + 1, 10\%) - 1] \\ FVAd &= \$1{,}000 \times [FVIFA\,(5, 10\%) - 1] \\ FVAd &= \$1{,}000 \times (6.105 - 1) \\ FVAd &= \$1{,}000 \times (5.105) \\ FVAd &= \$5{,}105 \end{aligned}$$

Note that the techniques we have described for calculating the future value of an annuity using the *FVIFA* table apply only to annuities for which the length of the annuity payment period and the length of the compounding period are the same. It is possible to calculate the future value of annuities involving payment periods and compounding periods of different lengths, but such calculations are extremely complicated and are not covered in this chapter.

Future Value of an Uneven Stream of Payments

What is the future value of an investment project earning 5 percent interest if the expected cash flows are uneven—say $12,000 at the end of Year 1, $13,000 at the end of Year 2, $11,000 at the end of Year 3, and $10,000 at the end of Year 4? Remember that future value of an annuity formulas apply only to periodic payments of equal amounts and an evenly spaced number of periods. Normally, the way to calculate the future value of an uneven stream of cash flows using interest factor tables is to calculate the future value of each payment separately using the *FVIF* table and then add these future values together. In this example, assuming that each payment is made at the end of the compounding period, interest accumulates on the first payment for three years, on the second payment for two years, on the third payment for one year, and the final payment accumulates no interest because it is made on the valuation date. Thus, we calculate the future value of this stream of cash flows as follows:

$$
\begin{aligned}
\$12{,}000 \times \textbf{FVIF}\,(3, 5\%) &= \$13{,}896 \\
\$13{,}000 \times \textbf{FVIF}\,(2, 5\%) &= \$14{,}339 \\
\$11{,}000 \times \textbf{FVIF}\,(1, 5\%) &= \$11{,}550 \\
\$10{,}000 &= \underline{\$10{,}000} \\
&= \underline{\underline{\$49{,}785}}
\end{aligned}
$$

Calculating Present Value

In many situations, an insurance company knows or can predict the amount of a future cash flow. For example, insurers often estimate the amount and timing of future profits, expenses, benefit payments, and premium income. But because a sum of money payable in the future is not equivalent to that same sum today, insurers typically need to calculate the present value of such future cash flows. By definition, the ***present value (PV)*** of a future sum is the amount of money that, if invested at a specified interest rate on a certain date, called the *valuation date,* would grow to equal that future sum. Because the present value of a sum is generally less than its future value, the present value is often called the *discounted value.* Theoretically, all other factors being equal, it makes no difference to a company whether it receives the present value of a sum on the valuation date, or the future value at the specified point in the future.

Present Value of a Single Amount

Finding present value is similar to finding future value, and the formula used to determine present value can be derived from the formula used to calculate future value. Recall the basic formula for calculating the future value of a one-period investment:

$$FV = PV(1 + i)$$

From this equation, we can solve for *PV* to come up with the following formula for calculating present value when the future value is known:

$$FV = PV(1 + i)$$
$$FV \div (1 + i) = PV$$

which is most commonly expressed as

$$PV = FV\left(\frac{1}{1 + i}\right)$$

Suppose you knew you were going to have to pay $1,050 one year from now and that you could earn 5 percent interest, compounded annually, on an investment. How much would you need to invest today to have $1,050 one year from now? We know the future value ($1,050) and the interest rate (5 percent), so we can use our present value formula to find the answer.

$$PV = \$1,050\left(\frac{1}{1.05}\right)$$
$$PV = \$1,050\ (0.9524)$$
$$PV = \$1,000.02$$

In this equation we have *discounted* $1,050 to its present value of $1,000.02 (note that if we had not rounded 1 ÷ 1.05 to 0.9524, the present value would be exactly $1,000). ***Discounting,*** which can be considered the opposite of compounding, is the process of converting a future value to its present value.

Suppose the $1,050 payment wasn't due until two years in the future. We can use the same formula as before, except that, because two discounting periods are involved, we must perform the calculation as demonstrated below:

$$PV = \$1{,}050\ [(1 \div 1.05)(1 \div 1.05)]$$

which is mathematically equivalent to

$$PV = \$1{,}050\ [1 \div (1.05)(1.05)] \text{ or}$$
$$PV = \$1{,}050\ [1 \div (1.05)^2]$$
$$PV = \$952.38$$

The general formula for determining the present value of a future sum when more than one discounting period is involved is

$$PV = FV\left[\frac{1}{(1+i)^n}\right]$$

Present Value Interest Factors

As with future value, tables can simplify the calculation of present value. Called *present value interest factor tables,* such tables show the value of the present value interest factor for many possible interest rates and numbers of periods. The ***present value interest factor (PVIF)*** is the present value of $1.00 discounted at an interest rate of i for n periods. The *PVIF* can be substituted for $[1 \div (1 + i)^n]$ in the present value equation. Thus, the present value of an amount to be paid at a specified later time can be calculated by multiplying that amount by the appropriate *PVIF* from the *PVIF* table as shown in the following equation:

$$PV = FV \times PVIF\ (n, i)$$

A sample *PVIF* table appears in Figure 14-5, and a more complete *PVIF* table appears in the appendix of this book. Notice that all of the numbers in the *PVIF* table are less than 1. The reason is that the present value of any amount is generally less than its future value. Thus, the present value of a future value of $1.00 is generally less than $1.00. The only time this would not be the case would be if the investment in question were expected to earn no interest or to lose money. An investment that earns no interest would have a future value *equal* to its present value. An investment that loses money would have a negative interest rate and future value that is less than the present value. In looking at a *PVIF* table, you'll also notice that, at a given interest rate, the *PVIF*s decrease as the number of dis-

Figure 14-5. *PVIF* table: Present value of $1 [1 ÷ (1 + i)^n].

Period (n)	Interest Rate (i) 1%	2%	5%	10%
1	0.990	0.980	0.952	0.909
2	0.980	0.961	0.907	0.826
3	0.971	0.942	0.864	0.751
4	0.961	0.924	0.823	0.683
5	0.951	0.906	0.784	0.621

counting periods increases, and that, at a given number of compounding periods, the *PVIF*s decrease as the interest rate increases.

We can use the present value interest factor to determine the present value of the $1,050 future amount from our earlier example.

Assuming a 5 percent interest rate and two compounding periods, the present value can be found as follows:

$$\textbf{PV} = \$1{,}050 \times \textbf{PVIF}\,(2, 5\%)$$
$$\textbf{PV} = \$1{,}050 \times 0.907$$
$$\textbf{PV} = \$952.35$$

The present value we calculated using the *PVIF* table ($952.35) is very close to the amount we calculated using exponents ($952.38). The difference of $0.03 results from the rounding of the factors in the *PVIF* table.

Present Value of an Annuity

Insurance companies and other businesses often need to calculate the present value of a series of payments, evenly spaced over a specified time period. In such cases, the value being calculated is the present value of an annuity. The ***present value of an annuity (PVA)*** is the amount that must be invested now in order to provide for a specified series of equal future payments, given a specified interest rate and a specified number of periods. The present value of an annuity also represents the amount that, if invested at a given interest rate, would, as of the end of the last annuity period, produce a future value equal to the sum of the future values of each periodic payment. As we have discussed, the sum of the future values of each periodic payment of an annuity is equal to the future value of that annuity. Thus, the mathematical relationship between the present value and future value of an annuity can be expressed as follows:

$$PVA \times FVIF(n, i) = FVA$$

Our discussion of the present value of an annuity applies both to a series of payments *received* and to a series of payments *paid out.*

The valuation date for the present value of an ordinary annuity occurs at the beginning of the first period, which is one period before the first payment is made.

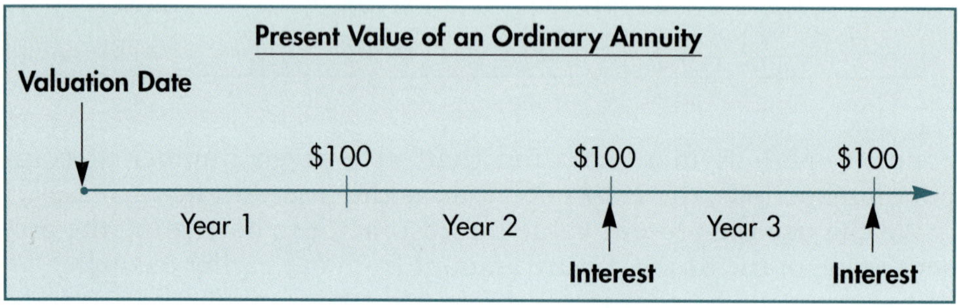

For an annuity due, the valuation date is the beginning of the first period, which corresponds to the timing of the first payment.

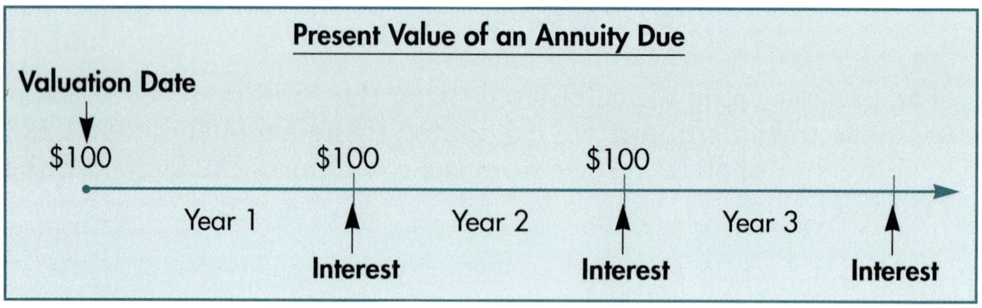

Present Value of an Annuity Interest Factors

The present value of an annuity can be found by adding together the present values of each individual payment. This process is similar to finding the future value of an annuity by summing the future values of each payment. Calculating the present value of an annuity by separately calculating the present value of each payment is a time-consuming process. Therefore, tables are available that provide the ***present value interest factor of an annuity (PVIFA).*** A sample *PVIFA* table is shown in Figure 14-6, and a more complete *PVIFA* table appears in the appendix of this book. As with the *FVIFA* table discussed earlier, the numbers in the *PVIFA* table apply only to ordinary annuities. Using the *PVIFA,* the formula for calculating the present value of an ordinary annuity is

Figure 14-6. *PVIFA* table: Present value of a \$1 annuity per period for *n* periods at interest rate *i*.

Period	Interest Rate (*i*)			
(*n*)	1%	2%	5%	10%
1	0.990	0.980	0.952	0.909
2	1.970	1.942	1.859	1.736
3	2.941	2.884	2.723	2.487
4	3.902	3.808	3.546	3.170
5	4.853	4.713	4.329	3.791

$$PVA = PP \times PVIFA\ (n, i)$$

Applying this formula, we can determine the present value of an ordinary annuity of \$1,000 for three periods at 5 percent interest.

$$PVA = \$1{,}000 \times PVIFA\ (3, 5\%)$$
$$PVA = \$1{,}000 \times 2.723$$
$$PVA = \$2{,}723$$

The present value of an *annuity due*—for which we substitute *PVAd*—is equal to the present value of a corresponding ordinary annuity of one less period plus the amount of one periodic payment. Using the *PVIFA* table to find the present value of an annuity due, we first find the *PVIFA* factor for the interest rate and $(n - 1)$ compounding periods. Then we add 1 to the appropriate interest factor and multiply by the amount of the periodic payment. The following equation illustrates this process:

$$PVAd = PP \times [PVIFA\ (n - 1, i) + 1]$$

Suppose you wanted to know the amount you would have to invest today in a 5 percent single-premium annuity due in order to receive \$15,000 per year for the next five years. You could use the *PVIFA* table to calculate the amount of the lump sum payment needed now in order to achieve your goal:

$$PVAd = \$15{,}000 \times [PVIFA\ (5 - 1, 5\%) + 1]$$
$$PVAd = \$15{,}000 \times (3.546 + 1)$$
$$PVAd = \$15{,}000 \times 4.546$$
$$PVAd = \$68{,}190$$

As with the techniques we described for calculating the future value of an annuity, the techniques we have described for calculating the present value of an annuity apply only to annuities for which the length of the annuity payment period and the length of the compounding period are the same.

Present Value of an Uneven Stream of Payments

If you needed to calculate the present value of a stream of uneven cash flows, you could not use the *PVIFA* table. Normally, this calculation would be made by calculating the present value of each payment separately. For example, if an investment project were expected to yield $500 at the end of its first year, $600 at the end of its second year, and $200 at the end of its third year, and the going interest rate were 10 percent, the present value of this investment's cash flows could be calculated as follows:

$500 × **PVIF** (1, 10%)	=	$ 454.50
$600 × **PVIF** (2, 10%)	=	$ 495.60
$200 × **PVIF** (3, 10%)	=	$ 150.20
	=	$ 1,100.30

A Note about Interest Factors

The style of notation we have used to represent the various interest factors we have discussed is designed to help you remember and understand the mathematical concepts underlying these interest factors. Actuaries use a different style of notation. The following table compares the notation used in this chapter with the equivalent actuarial notation:

Textbook Notation	Actuarial Notation
FVIF (n, i)	$(1 + i)^n$
FVIFA (n, i)	$s_{\overline{n}\rceil i}$
PVIF (n, i)	v^n
PVIFA (n, i)	$a_{\overline{n}\rceil i}$

Insurance Operations and the Time Value of Money

At the beginning of this chapter, we said that the time value of money is an important concept to any business that is engaged in long-range planning. How does the time value of money specifically affect life and health insurance operations? Death claim and disability claim benefits, annuity payments, premium rates, cash surrender values, policy reserves, and policy dividends are some insurance-related calculations affected by the time value of money. Further, many insurance products—especially life insurance and deferred annuities—are based on future financial obligations that insurers are responsible for and must calculate accurately.

Discounting future value back to present value is critical in life and health insurance because insurers must have the equivalent values now in order to provide promised future benefits. Typically, the calculation for these amounts is the function of the insurer's actuaries. They must be able to predict the various costs associated with each insurance product and the income the insurer expects to receive from the sale of these products and its investments. Also, many insurance-related calculations, such as premiums, are in the form of an annuity due—a series of payments that occur at the beginning of the compounding period. In the next sections, we discuss specific applications of the time value of money concept in life and health insurance company operations, including establishing premium rates, investing premium income and cash, meeting future expenses, and determining life insurance coverage.

Establishing Premium Rates

The job of insurance company actuaries, assisted by investment specialists, includes establishing prices for new life insurance and annuity products, either to take advantage of higher interest rates or to maximize returns when interest rates fall. To calculate premium rates, actuaries use mortality tables and interest rate tables. Mortality tables report the probabilities of living and dying at specified ages. To calculate premium rates for health insurance products, actuaries use morbidity tables and interest rate tables. Morbidity tables help actuaries determine the probabilities associated with injury or illness, given certain circumstances. Actuaries make interest rate assumptions by studying the interest rates that the company has earned in the past and asking investment personnel what the company expects to earn in the future, given the context of the internal and external forces that affect the insurer's solvency and profitability.

Premiums and estimated claim payments are calculated using the concept of present value. For example, assume that an insurance company expects to pay $1,000,000 in claims one year from today. The actuaries calculate the amount of money the company needs to invest today at a certain interest rate in order to have $1,000,000 one year from today. Present value is also used to calculate the loading that applies to the gross premium. The present values of the expenses, contingencies, and any policy dividends associated with a block of life insurance policies are included in the loading formula as one step in the process of determining the gross premium for the block of policies.

Investing Premium Income

Consider one of an insurance company's biggest sources of cash: premium income. What happens to all the money that flows into an insurance company, and where does all the money come from to pay policyowners, stockholders, and beneficiaries? In order to fund the payment of claims and benefits in the future, insurers invest part of their premium income so that interest can accumulate on the money in time to fulfill their claim and benefit obligations. An insurer's investment department uses the time value of money to value stocks, bonds, real estate, and other investments. The income generated from investments is used to pay ongoing and future expenses and benefits. Prudent investing on the part of an insurer keeps premium costs lower than would otherwise be possible, and it ensures that the insurer can meet its obligations for operating expenses, benefits, and claims.

An insurer's investment department uses the concept of present value in determining which bonds to purchase. Suppose that, as the insurer's portfolio manager, you are considering the purchase of a five-year bond with a *par value* (principal) of $100,000. Interest is payable semiannually at an annual rate of 10 percent. The current interest rate is also 10 percent and the bond's current market price is $100,000. Is this a reasonable price to pay for this bond? To arrive at your solution, you first use the *PVIF* table for determining the present value of a single amount—in this example, the $100,000 principal amount to be received at the end of five years at the current interest rate, which in this case equals the interest rate on the bond. The *PVIF* for 10 compounding periods (5 years × 2 compounding periods per year) at 5 percent (10 percent ÷ 2 compounding periods) is 0.614. The result of multiplying $100,000 by 0.614 is $61,400, which is the present value of $100,000 to be received in five years.

Next, you would use the *PVIFA* table to calculate the present value of an annuity of $5,000 ($10,000 ÷ 2) at the end of each period for 10 periods at 5 percent interest. The *PVIFA* for 5 percent interest and 10 periods is 7.722. Multiplying $5,000 by 7.722 equals $38,610. To determine the total present value of the bond, add the present value of the principal to the present value of the interest payments: $61,400 + $38,610 = $100,010, which approximates the current par value of the bond.

Theoretically, the bond's present value should equal its current market value as well as its par value because the current market interest rate equals the bond's stated rate of interest. An insurer generally would be willing to pay no more than the present value of an

Figure 14-7. Bond valuation—present value.

Cash Flows	*PVIF* (5%, 10 periods)	*PVIFA* (5%, 10 periods)	Present Value
$100,000 principal	0.614		$ 61,400
$5,000 semiannual interest payments		7.722	38,610
Total Present Value			$100,010

investment—be it a bond, real estate, or a major piece of equipment—all other factors remaining equal. In theory, the current market price of an asset should equal the present value of the asset's cash flows at the current interest rate. Figure 14-7 summarizes the bond valuation.

Investing Cash

An insurance company always keeps some of its assets in cash or cash-equivalent instruments such as money market funds. For a large company, this amount may be quite significant, perhaps in the tens of millions of dollars. Money is needed for the daily operations of the company. Life insurers specifically need cash to pay policy proceeds to beneficiaries and policy dividends or cash surrender values to policyowners as they become due. Recall that cash on hand generally means cash equivalents, which are invested to earn interest, rather than hard currency. In a time of inflation, money that is not earning interest is actually losing value in terms of purchasing power. By investing a company's cash holdings and receiving interest on them, insurance managers offset the negative effects of inflation by making sure that the purchasing power of the company's cash is not diminished over time.

Meeting Future Obligations

The time value of money is considered in budgeting and planning when a manager tries to determine how much money is needed to meet specific future obligations. For example, an insurer sets aside a reserve for future claim payments, known as the *present value of amounts not yet due on claims.* This reserve is an amount an insurer sets aside for future payments on claims currently being paid in installments, as in the case of disability income coverage and waiver-of-premium benefits. By applying the concept of present value, the insurer can calculate the approximate amount of money needed to meet its obligations as they come due.

Conclusion

The time value of money is used extensively in several functions of a life and health insurance company, including the accounting, actuarial, investment, claim processing, and customer service functions. In addition, determining the present value or future value of cash flows is associated with many management decisions, such as whether to lease or purchase equipment or real estate, purchase or sell financial investments, or develop a new insurance product or service. In upcoming chapters, we discuss management decision making, which relies on an understanding of the time value of money in evaluating the best use of a company's limited resources.

Key Terms and Concepts

time value of money
interest
interest rate
simple interest
compound interest
risk
inflation
inflation risk
deflation
future value (*FV*)
nominal interest rate
equivalent interest rates
future value interest factor (*FVIF*)
annuity
future value of an annuity (*FVA*)
ordinary annuity
annuity due
line diagram
valuation date
future value interest factor of an annuity (*FVIFA*)
present value (*PV*)
discounting
present value interest factor (*PVIF*)
present value of an annuity (*PVA*)
present value interest factor of an annuity (*PVIFA*)

CHAPTER 15

MANAGEMENT ACCOUNTING

LEARNING OBJECTIVES

After studying this chapter, you should be able to

- Explain the purpose of management accounting
- List the four functions of management and describe how management accounting applies to each function of management
- Identify the similarities and differences between financial accounting and management accounting

CHAPTER OUTLINE

Functions of Management and Management Accounting

Four Functions of Management

The Role of Management Accounting

Financial Accounting vs. Management Accounting

Intended Audience

Time Focus

Statutory and GAAP Requirements

Level of Precision

Use of Non-Monetary Information

Elective Nature

To this point in the textbook, we have concentrated on financial accounting, which involves the reporting of life and health insurance company financial data to external parties, including state and provincial regulatory agencies, taxation authorities, policyowners, and stockholders. But accounting information is also important to an insurer's internal managers who are charged with ensuring the company's solvency and profitability. Managers determine a company's financial condition and make decisions about the company by analyzing various aspects of operations. The purpose of management accounting is to provide information to meet the needs of internal managers.

Imagine if managers in a large insurance company had to make decisions by analyzing the thousands of accounting transactions that take place in an ordinary day. It would be impractical to study only this accounting ***data,*** or raw, unprocessed facts. Managers are more productive when supplied with accounting ***information,*** which is data that has been processed and placed in a meaningful and useful context for the user. When using accounting information, rather than raw data, to manage operations, a company's internal management is reaping the benefits of management accounting. Recall from Chapter 1 that *management accounting* is the process of identifying, measuring, analyzing, and communicating financial information to allow for informed decision making regarding the acquisition and use of a company's resources.

Let's examine the components of this definition. *Information* is the key output of the management accounting function. To be valuable for management purposes, the information provided by management accounting must be timely, relevant, reliable, and concise. Information that is not timely or relevant to the operations of the company has no value because it does not assist management in any way. Information that is relevant but is lost among an overabundance of information—a condition known as *information overload*—also fails as a management tool. *Identifying* involves recognizing all information that is relevant for management use. A management accountant must be able to distinguish between raw data that requires processing and information that is ready for a manager to absorb. *Measuring* encompasses estimating the numeric value of things or events. It is the management accountant's responsibility to measure data. What is the cost of labor, the income of an investment, or the economic benefit of selling one type of insurance product instead of another? The management accountant must put these costs, revenues, and benefits into monetary units so that managers can evaluate all courses of action to determine which are most appropriate for the company. *Analyzing* is examining the information to determine the nature and tendencies of the subject matter. Through analysis, the accountant can best organize the information so that he or she can *communicate* it to management. Useful information that is not clearly communicated to the appropriate manager is wasted.

The effectiveness of management accounting information hinges on the way it affects management's behavior.[1] Suppose a certain report is designed to indicate whether the total expenses of an insurer's claims department came in under budget for the most recent accounting period. If the report does not provide the necessary information to make this determination, then management can make no effective response. The information will not affect management's behavior and therefore will fail as a management accounting tool. Management accountants work closely with top management to ensure that information is communicated in an appropriate form for management's purposes. In most cases, top management generally is not interested in minute details, so accounting reports developed for top management should focus on summary information. In most small and medium-sized insurers, the company's accountants perform both financial accounting and management accounting functions. Some large insurance companies have separate personnel for these two types of accounting.

This chapter introduces you to the basic concepts of management accounting in life and health insurance companies. We begin this chapter with a discussion of the four functions of management—*planning, organizing, leading,* and *controlling*—and relate them to the perpetual management act of decision making. We then examine how management accounting information allows managers to perform these functions. Lastly, we compare in detail financial accounting to management accounting.

Functions of Management and Management Accounting

Management is a process of actions undertaken to accomplish a stated goal, such as providing a service, making a profit, or achieving a desired market share. In this text, we identify four core functions of management: (1) planning, (2) organizing, (3) leading, and (4) controlling.

Four Functions of Management

Briefly, the ***planning*** function involves establishing objectives and then formulating the strategies, tactics, and other supporting activities needed to achieve those objectives. During planning, a manager decides where the company should be at some point in the future and how it should get there. Planning is the beginning point for the entire management process; without the setting of goals and the desired path toward their attainment, there is no need for management. ***Organizing*** is the process of ensuring that the necessary resources—human, economic, and physical—are available to carry out the plan and achieve the desired goals. During the organizing function, the manager groups tasks into departments or other subdivisions and assigns staff members to each task. ***Leading*** means influencing others to carry out the activities that will result in the achievement of organizational goals. Leading, which encompasses behavioral skills such as communicating, motivating, and coaching, is often synonymous with management. ***Controlling*** is ensuring that performance results in the achievement of the desired goals. To control operations, managers need ***feedback,*** which are accounting reports and information that enable managers to identify problems and opportunities. Using feedback, managers engage in the central controlling activity: comparing actual results to expected results.

Implicit within the four management functions is ***decision making,*** which is the process of identifying and selecting a course of action to solve a problem or take advantage of an opportunity. We can divide decision making into three general steps: (1) identifying a problem or opportunity, (2) evaluating alternatives, and (3) choosing the most appropriate alternative. Managers constantly make decisions about what to sell, whom to hire, what to charge, how to motivate, and so on. In the planning phase, for example, managers decide the best course of action to achieve the company's goals. During organizing, managers decide which employees will be responsible for which activities. During leading, managers decide how best to motivate employees toward carrying out the company's plans. During controlling, managers decide whether performance is meeting standards and, if not, what changes they should make to improve future performance.

Although the four functions of management have distinct characteristics, they are interrelated and often difficult to distinguish in actual practice. For example, managers often use performance standards during the controlling function. But establishing standards is an inherent part of planning and is also used in leading and motivating employees. Moreover, the four functions do not necessarily occur in the linear sequence presented here. Combinations of these functions take place simultaneously in all organizations. In fact, the relationship among the four management functions is circular, rather than linear, in nature, with decision making being intricately involved with all four. Figure 15-1 illustrates the circular relationship of the four management functions. Note that each function is itself represented by a circle, because within each function, management

Figure 15-1. The circular relationship of the functions of management.

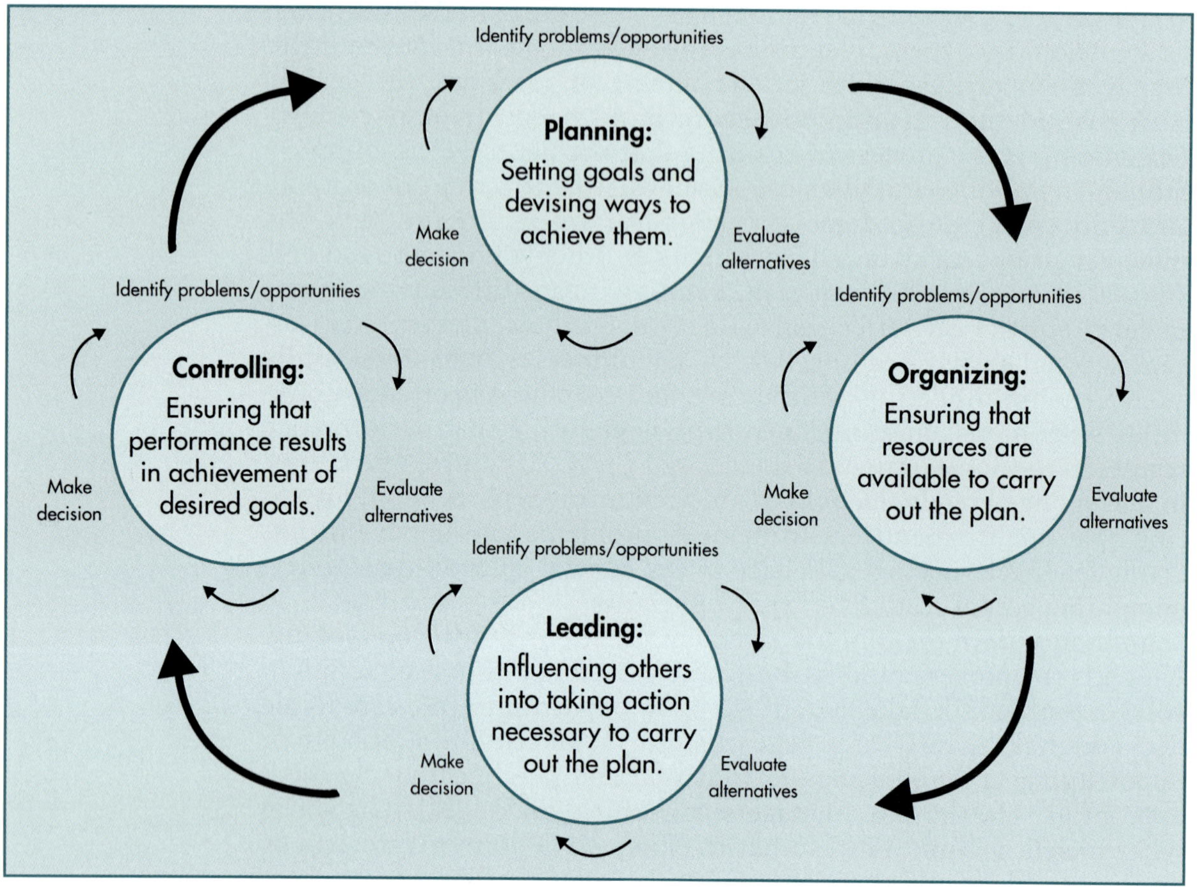

identifies problems or opportunities, evaluates alternatives, and makes decisions before moving on to the next function. For example, one outcome of a controlling activity may be that actual performance does not match planned performance, such as when net premiums written are below budget. The cause of this poor performance is a problem for management to identify. Three possible alternatives might be to (1) expand the agency distribution system by contracting with additional agents, (2) review the original budget to determine how and if it should be modified, and (3) remain on course and hope that policy sales improve. Decision making requires management to select and implement one of these alternatives.

The Role of Management Accounting

In order to make effective decisions about a company, a manager needs information. The continued success of the company depends on the accuracy and availability of information. For example, a manager might need to know how much money the company paid in commissions to agents last year, the rate of persistency for a particular insurance product, or the economic effects of installing a new computer system. The purpose of management accounting is to provide managers with the information necessary to assist them in making decisions. Management accounting provides information at the level of planning, organizing, leading, and controlling necessary for the company to achieve its objectives. With management accounting information, managers can hire an appropriate number of employees, price products and services to cover costs and produce a desired profit, accurately forecast premium and investment income, pay claims as they come due, and so on.

Management accounting information is most useful in the management functions of planning, organizing, and controlling. In the next section, we discuss the ways in which management accounting, in the context of insurance company operations, enhances these three management functions and decision making. Because it provides the information needed to plan, organize, and control a company's operations, management accounting also helps a manager lead his or her company by providing him or her with a certain level of confidence from which to motivate and coach employees. Without such information, a manager would be in a much weaker position from which to lead.

Planning

Constant changes in the financial services environment have made life and health insurance companies aware of the importance of comprehensive planning in achieving and maintaining growth, financial stability, and profitability. More than ever, the survival and ultimate success of an insurer depends on its ability to adapt to a changing environment and plan for its future. The planning activity consists of

- Setting goals
- Determining policy in accordance with company philosophy
- Anticipating changes that can affect performance
- Devising the strategies, methods, and procedures necessary to achieve the desired results

Because the environment in which insurers operate has become increasingly complex, comprehensive planning is more important than ever. Insight 15-1 focuses on planning and the future of financial management.

Typical planning activities in a life and health insurance company include the study of costs, budgeting for short-term and long-term

Insight 15-1 The Future of Finance

What will the corporate finance department look like in the twenty-first century? Will it be staffed by CPAs, MBAs, computer information specialists? Will it even exist—absorbed instead by other departments? These were some of the tough questions 40 senior financial executives (from companies such as General Motors and Control Data), accounting educators (from schools such as Vanderbilt University, New York University and Senshu University in Japan) and CPAs (from accounting and consulting firms such as KPMG Peat Marwick, Price Waterhouse and Arthur Andersen & Co.) wrestled with for two days last April at a workshop in New York sponsored by the American Institute of CPA's management accounting executive committee.

The goal of the workshop, mapping the future of financial management, was to help the committee envision the future of the finance function in businesses and thus help the Institute prepare its members for that future. As an opener, participants shared their views on the future of finance management by voting on various business management scenarios. Those with similar views were grouped in panels that constituted the management of a fictitious company; each panel member assumed a leading management role in the organization.

Then each panel was asked to focus on its unique scenario, or "endstate," and to develop a business plan for that endstate; the economic and business conditions that created and support it, the problems and opportunities it faces as it strives to survive, the tools it needs to prosper and the role of the finance department in this enterprise.

Each panel then had to rationalize its endstate to the others in the workshop, defend its positions from the challenges and report the weaknesses uncovered by working through the exercise.

The five endstates were

1. Shareholder advocate—a back-to-basics focus on costs designed to boost shareholder wealth in the short run—even at the expense of future growth. The major role of the finance department is to root out activities that fail to produce immediate returns.

2. Business team—the management style is team oriented and the corporate goal is gaining market leadership by responding to market demand and customer needs. The role of finance is to dismantle excessive controls that paralyze meaningful analysis.

3. Managing risk—management recognizes it must confront multiple risks, including swiftly changing technology and severe business cycle and financial market swings. The principal role of finance is to act as a combination of internal hedge- and venture-fund managers.

4. Outsourcing—many of the corporation's finance functions, from payroll to general ledger and tax, are handled by outside organizations. The role of the finance department is no longer routine processing; it now is focused on control and standard-setting.

5. Decentralization—core business units are run relatively independently. Finance provides high-level analytical support.

When the exercise was over, some of the participants came away with more than their original vision. In developing strategies and then being forced to defend them, some participants found their finance management views had changed somewhat. Some recognized advantages in endstates they had dismissed before. Others felt their original views were bolstered. And still others said they were considering shifting their allegiances or seeking to combine some endstate features with others.

The bottom line: For some participants, the two-day exercise forced them to lay down some long-held views, recognizing that the future often is not a straight-line extension of the past.

Coming to Consensus

As a final exercise, participants were reassigned to different panels so they had to work with new colleagues—most of whom supported different endstates. Their new assignment was to search for common ground and create accommodations for their divergent views so they could agree on a new endstate.

Discussions became animated when participants who supported, for example, a shareholder-advocate endstate had to negotiate a common ground with participants who championed teamwork or decentralization. Again, the underlying goal was not so much to work out a solution to the conflicts as it was to experience the process of rethinking advocacy positions.

While the participants certainly did not fully agree on the role of tomorrow's finance departments, most did find consensus on the following future scenarios:

- Transaction processing will become more automated than most in the profession think possible.
- Outsourcing of some finance management functions will become widespread.
- Operating managers will continue to lose confidence in the traditional reporting system.
- There will be general agreement among managers that no one

(continued)

Insight 15-1 The Future of Finance, continued

financial report will meet everyone's needs.

- Data will no longer be stored separately by departments; instead, companies will create one central data warehouse, accessible companywide.
- The finance staff will become information specialists, providing others in the organization with analysis of all the accumulated data.
- The traditional financial report will never be an effective performance indicator and thus will never be the exclusive basis for business decisions.
- The title of CFO (chief financial officer) could become CAO (chief analytical officer) with a bigger role in modeling the whole business operation; the CAO's motto will be "close is good enough."
- The controller will no longer run the "backroom" accounting transaction "factory" but will take a more active role as a business partner.

As one participant summed up the two-day exercise: "Times are changing. Today operating managers are telling us, 'Thanks very much, but the beans have already been counted. We need different information—information that will help us steer our business confidently into tomorrow.' We must be prepared for that change if we want to survive."

Source: Stanley Zarowin, "The Future of Finance," *Journal of Accountancy* (August 1995), pp. 47–49. Reprinted with permission from the *Journal of Accountancy*,

expenditures, and evaluating potential acquisitions or divestitures. Planning occurs at all levels of a company, and the accounting function is an integral part of the process. Planning typically involves an analysis of a specified set of conditions. Moreover, it is essential for the information to be accurate and timely. Otherwise, management's decisions could be made on the basis of inaccurate or outdated financial information. For example, reported dollar totals must be correct at the beginning of the planning process so that the following period's budget projections are based on realistic amounts. In addition, proper accounting procedures throughout the planning process ensure that management can determine whether the company's financial plans are being met. Generally, we can divide a company's planning activities into two major segments: *strategic planning* and *operational planning.*

Strategic planning is the process of determining how to pursue long-term goals with available resources. Strategic planning studies the company's current performance, identifies the company's position in the market, predicts future trends, and creates a plan of development for the company's future. The long-term period in strategic planning typically is from two to five years but varies from company to company. ***Operational planning*** is the process of determining how to accomplish specific tasks with available resources. Operational planning is primarily concerned with the short-term, day-to-day activities of a company. Most insurers restrict the scope of their operational planning to one or two years or less. Regardless of time frames covered by a company's strategic and operating plans, certain activities and goals are typical of each type of plan. Figure 15-2 lists some

Figure 15-2. Applications of an insurer's strategic planning and operational planning for different functional areas.

Function	Strategic Planning	Operational Planning
Marketing	• Market identification and penetration • Agency development strategy • Product development	• Advertising plans and promotions • Agent commission plans • Product introduction • Annual sales forecasts
Risk Selection	• Underwriting strategy • Underwriting standards analysis	• Underwriting targets and guidelines • Reinsurance policies
Customer Service	• Desired service levels	• Policy issue procedures • Service standards • Policy processing alternatives
Financial Planning	• Economic research and forecasting • Capital adequacy • Allocation of capital	• Cash flow planning • Product profitability goals • Monthly forecast of expenses • Tax planning
Investments	• Investment strategy • Risk analysis • Legal restrictions	• Performance planning • Legal restrictions • Liquidity planning
Human Resources	• Long-term personnel requirements • Personnel policies	• Current-year recruiting plans • Fiscal-year wage and salary plans • Job design and analysis
Electronic Data Processing	• Systems architecture • Long-term capacity requirements	• Software needs • Personal computer and hardware requirements • Short-term capacity requirements

areas that are often associated with and that influence strategic planning and operational planning for an insurer's major functional areas.

Note that overlap can exist between the topics covered by the two types of planning. For example, the legal restrictions placed on a company's investments are topics in both strategic and operational planning. Also, both types of planning involve the preparation of budgets. Approaches to planning and budgeting activities are numerous and diverse, as we discuss in Chapter 17.

Organizing

During the organizing function, management takes explicit actions to ensure achievement of the corporate plan. Among these actions are assigning responsibility for specific operations to specific individuals. Assignment of responsibility is the first step in the management accounting concept of *responsibility accounting.* For example, an insurer's responsibility accounting system should ensure that the senior vice president for the life insurance product line knows exactly which employees and operational duties are under his or her authority and for which he or she will be held accountable. Once all managers and employees are organized in such a way that each employee understands the span of accountability, the company can more easily control its operations.

Controlling

Controlling involves ensuring that the actions of employees are moving the organization toward its stated goals. A company's internal controlling activities involve (1) establishing standards of performance, (2) measuring and evaluating actual performance against the standards, (3) detecting deviations from the standards, and (4) determining appropriate action to correct deviations. Responsibility accounting is an important component of control.

The most complete managerial control would consist of close physical supervision of each employee. However, because this type of control is not usually practical or desirable, managers rely on the concept of ***management by exception,*** which states that managers should be informed about operational progress only when results or activities differ from expected norms by a certain amount or percentage. Such information comes from accounting reports that indicate deviations or exceptions. A manager can then investigate these exceptions to learn the causes behind them. For example, one accounting report could show the budgeted costs and actual costs for the investment department. Instances where the actual costs differ from the budgeted costs are known as ***variances.*** One way to gauge the performance of the investment department is to examine these variances. A report of variances is an example of *feedback* that informs management how well the organization is achieving its plan. Accurate and timely feedback is essential for effective management control. Providing feedback is one of the most important purposes of management accounting. Feedback allows managers to locate the sources of financially successful and unsuccessful operations and to indicate why certain areas of the company perform well while others do not.

Decision Making

As we have seen, decision making is inseparable from other management functions. In order to make a sound decision, a manager needs financial information that is relevant, reliable, and comparable across accounting periods and departments. Management accounting provides this information. It also provides analytical techniques that help managers understand the implications of a decision. For example, if management decides to launch a new health insurance product, management accounting analysis can tell managers how many policies the company must sell and what level of persistency it must maintain to achieve a desired contribution to surplus during an accounting period. Management accounting analysis can also indicate the cost savings and useful life required of a new piece of equipment for the company to recover the cost of the equipment. We discuss specific analysis techniques in the remaining chapters of this book. The information provided by management accounting does not itself solve the problems that managers face. Rather, the information allows managers to weigh the consequences of various actions so that they can make well-informed decisions.

Financial Accounting vs. Management Accounting

Financial accounting and management accounting each deal with economic events and attempt to quantify the results of those events in terms that are understandable and accurate. Both are concerned primarily with revenues, expenses, assets, liabilities, and capital and surplus. Both make use of the same accounting information system and the same accounting data. But financial accounting and management accounting serve different purposes. In planning, organizing, leading, controlling, and making decisions about their organizations, managers require different information than that used for financial accounting and reporting. In this text, we identify six specific differences between financial accounting and management accounting: (1) intended audience, (2) time focus, (3) statutory and GAAP requirements, (4) level of precision, (5) use of nonmonetary information, and (6) elective nature.

Intended Audience

As stated earlier in the chapter, financial accounting and management accounting are intended for two different audiences. Generally, financial accounting governs the reporting of financial information for individuals and organizations *outside* a company. In contrast, management accounting typically exists for the benefit of those individuals *inside* a company who are responsible for managing the company's operations.* Management accounting re-configures financial account-

* A parent company, which in this text we consider an internal audience, is also interested in the financial accounting reports of its subsidiaries.

ing data in ways that best suit management's purposes. The form and content of this management accounting information typically is irrelevant to the needs of regulators, policyowners, and stockholders.

Time Focus

Financial accounting focuses primarily on historical events. The external users of financial accounting may use financial statements to prepare their own projections, but financial accounting is not concerned with forecasting. Management accounting, on the other hand, has a forward-looking time focus, because many of an internal manager's responsibilities are concerned with planning for the future. Therefore, except for financial statements that compare budgeted to actual amounts, management accountants put a great deal of effort into providing *pro forma*, or projected, financial statements, which estimate the company's financial condition at the end of an accounting period.

Figure 15-3 illustrates the differences between the way internal and external parties use accounting information. Column 1 shows the Popular Life and Health Insurance Company's 1999 statement of operations. An external party, such as a policyowner or stockholder, examines this absolute data to judge how the company performed during the past year. An internal manager, however, needs more information to make decisions about the direction of the company. Thus, as shown in Column 2, a management accounting report might display each line of the statement of operations as a percentage of total revenue. (We discuss this process, known as vertical analysis, in Chapter 19.) The management accountant might then compare the actual absolute and percentage results from 1999 with the 1999 budgeted absolute and percentage figures shown in Columns 3 and 4, respectively. You should recognize this comparison as being part of the controlling function of management. Using these figures, a manager can then determine, for instance, that actual total benefits and expenses were a larger percentage of total revenue than was budgeted (99.1 percent to 96.7 percent in Columns 2 and 4, respectively). The higher-than-expected benefits and expenses are the primary reasons that the net income for the period is below the budgeted figure. Lastly, the management accountant can help prepare the pro forma statement of operations for 2000, which is shown in absolute and percentage terms in Columns 5 and 6, respectively. This pro forma information shows that one of management's goals for 2000 is to reduce total benefits and expenses to 92.7 percent of revenue. As you can see, the pro forma information is a planning mechanism for the beginning of the accounting period and will be useful for control purposes at the end of the period.

Figure 15-3. Financial accounting and management accounting uses of the statement of operations for the Popular Life and Health Insurance Company.

December 31, 1999						
	Financial Accounting Information	**Management Accounting Information**				
	1 **1999 Actual**	**2** **Percent of Total Revenues**	**3** **1999 Budgeted**	**4** **Percent of Total Revenues**	**5** **2000 Pro Forma**	**6** **Percent of Total Revenues**
Revenues						
Premiums	$593,200	71.4%	$590,000	71.9%	$625,000	71.7%
Net investments income	221,800	26.7%	215,000	26.2%	230,500	26.4%
Other	15,400	1.9%	16,000	1.9%	16,500	1.9%
Total Revenues	$830,400	100.0%	$821,000	100.0%	$872,000	100.0%
Benefits and Expenses						
Life and annuity benefits	$361,500	43.5%	$350,000	42.6%	$358,000	41.1%
Amount set aside for future payments	341,800	41.2%	335,000	40.8%	340,000	39.0%
Operating expenses	110,150	13.3%	99,700	12.1%	100,100	11.5%
Premium and other taxes	8,800	1.1%	9,500	1.2%	9,600	1.1%
Total Benefits and Expenses	$822,250	99.1%	$794,200	96.7%	$807,700	92.7%
Income before income taxes	$ 8,150	0.9%	$ 26,800	3.3%	$ 64,300	7.3%
Income taxes	2,853	0.3%	9,380	1.1%	22,505	2.6%
Net Income	$ 5,297	0.6%	$ 17,420	2.2%	$ 41,795	4.7%

Statutory and GAAP Requirements

As you have learned in the financial accounting portion of this text, certain U.S. insurance company financial statements must be prepared according to statutory accounting practices or generally accepted accounting principles (GAAP), depending on the type of company and the type of statement. By requiring insurers to abide by these accounting guidelines, external analysts are assured of viewing statements that are prepared under a common set of rules, thereby reducing the misunderstanding and misrepresentation of data, and improving the comparability and consistency of data from one company to another and from period to period.

The financial statements and reports prepared for internal managers are under no such restrictions. Management accountants are free to prepare these internal reports in any form or fashion and to include or omit any information to best accommodate the needs of the manager. For example, the Annual Statement requires that, for one exhibit, insurance companies group lines of business in a specific way. In a management accounting report, however, a company may group its lines of business in any way it chooses. Generally, however, the guiding principles behind the preparation of management accounting reports are that the information be accurate and relevant, that the information is consistent with the financial data (or that it notes the reasons for any discrepancies), and that the reports be prepared consistently across accounting periods. Moreover, accountants should not arbitrarily change the way they prepare management accounting reports from period to period, so that comparisons between periods remain meaningful and accurate.

Level of Precision

Financial accounting compiles transactions from a company's basic accounting system into detailed, precise financial statements. Depending on the size of the company, the preparation of this type of report can take days or weeks and occupy many employees. When making decisions, managers rarely have that much time to wait for such detailed reports. Exact figures down to the last dollar are generally unnecessary. Also, many management accounting reports deal with future events for which estimates are needed. Therefore, management accounting is less concerned with the exact precision required of financial accounting.* Management accounting strives to provide managers with reports containing sound estimates in a timely fashion. These reports enable managers to make the quick decisions so often required in the business world.

* The U.S. Annual Statement does require some financial accounting estimation, such as for incurred but not reported (IBNR) claims.

Use of Non-Monetary Information

The information provided by financial accounting is primarily monetary. Financial statements contain supplemental notes, but these are explanatory notes that serve to clarify the accounting practices and procedures used to compute the amounts in the statements. The scope of management accounting extends beyond simply providing managers with financial reports so that managers can formulate their own decisions. Non-monetary information is also of considerable importance. For example, while financial accounting provides data on premium income earned by an insurer, management accounting may also describe the size of the distribution force required to generate that income. Management accountants furnish other non-monetary information that decision makers need to manage effectively, such as persistency rates, the number of policy applications approved and rated, and the number of claims processed and denied.

Elective Nature

Insurance companies are required to compile certain financial statements for external agencies. For example, all insurance companies document their financial transactions in the Annual Statement (U.S.) or the Annual Return (Canada). Stock insurance companies prepare an annual report for stockholders. Financial statements are also required by the Internal Revenue Service, Revenue Canada, the Securities and Exchange Commission, and other government agencies. Financial accounting supports the production of these mandatory financial reports. Insurance companies are under no such obligation to prepare any accounting reports for internal management use. Although management accounting reports make good business sense and allow for informed management decision making, they are purely elective. For example, a key element of the planning process is preparing budgets. Virtually all companies engage in budgeting, but few are required to do so. Figure 15-4 summarizes the general differences between financial accounting and management accounting.

Figure 15-4. Differences between financial accounting and management accounting.

Issue	Financial Accounting	Management Accounting
Audience →	• Primarily external	• Internal
Time focus →	• Current and historical	• Current and future
Accounting standards →	• Statutory and GAAP	• Selected by company
Precision →	• Highly exact	• Permits estimates
Non-monetary information →	• Little	• Extensive
Reporting obligations →	• Mandatory	• Mostly optional

Conclusion

This chapter introduced you to the basic concepts of management accounting. You learned about the four functions of management—planning, organizing, leading, and controlling—and the decision making that is required in each of them. You also learned how management accounting information applies to each management function and how management accounting differs from financial accounting.

We devote the next three chapters to discussing individual management accounting concepts. Chapter 16 covers cost accounting, which is a system that accumulates and analyzes cost data to control costs and price products and services. Managers closely analyze costs in order to plan, organize, and control operations. In Chapter 17, we explain the budgeting process within life and health insurance companies. Budgeting includes creating a financial plan of action that an organization believes will help it achieve its goals. Budgeting is the central planning activity. In Chapter 18, we examine responsibility accounting, which is a system of policies and procedures that allows for costs and revenues to be assigned to the individual or the level of the organization having responsibility for them. The emphasis of responsibility accounting is on assigning responsibility to individuals and on measuring and evaluating performance based on the areas within each individual's span of responsibility. Thus, responsibility accounting encompasses the organizing and controlling aspects of management accounting.

Key Terms and Concepts

data
information
management
planning
organizing
leading
controlling
feedback
decision making
strategic planning
operational planning
management by exception
variances

References

1. *Accounting & Finance for Managers in Insurance* (Cambridge, England: The Chartered Insurance Institute, 1991), sec. 5, p. 2.

CHAPTER 16

Cost Accounting

Learning Objectives

After studying this chapter, you should be able to

- Explain the primary uses of cost accounting in life and health insurance companies
- Identify and distinguish costs that are classified by description, by behavior, and by measurement
- Discuss how costs are accumulated by type, by line of business, by cost center, by function, and by project
- Describe three basic methods of service department cost allocation and three basic methods of time analysis
- Compare the three methods of analyzing costs: change analysis, functional cost analysis, and activity-based cost analysis
- Determine the break-even point on a cost-volume-profit (CVP) graph and discuss what the break-even point means

Chapter Outline

Uses of Cost Accounting

Basics of an Effective Cost Accounting System

Cost Classifications

Costs Classified by Description

Costs Classified by Behavior

Costs Classified by Measurement

Cost Perspectives

Cost Accumulation and Cost Allocation

Cost Accumulation

Cost Allocation

Analyzing Costs

Change Analysis

Functional Costing

Activity-Based Costing

Cost and the Pricing of Products

Cost-Volume-Profit Analysis

One management accounting subject of considerable interest and concern to organizations and managers is cost. Just about everything—materials, labor, buildings, advertising, even time—carries a cost. Before a company can estimate what it can produce, how much it can produce, and what it can charge for its products and services, the company must know the cost of doing business. For example, an insurer determines the minimum premium or price that it can charge for a policy by examining the costs it incurs in developing, distributing, and administering the product, as well as the cost of the product's future benefits. Generally, the selling price of a product must be high enough to cover all the product's costs. The gathering of cost information is therefore critical for determining an appropriate selling price.

In Chapter 4, we defined *cost* as the amount of a company's resources (assets) used for any purpose. Specifically, a *cost* is an expenditure incurred to obtain an economic benefit or extinguish an obligation. This expenditure can result from a direct decrease in an asset or an increase in a liability, the payment of which ultimately decreases a company's assets. ***Cost accounting*** is a system that accumulates expense data which facilitates effective cost control and accurate pricing of products and services. A cost accounting system defines, describes, accumulates, records, and assigns all the costs incurred by a company. The system enables a company's managers to plan operations, organize employee work loads, and evaluate current financial performance so that the company is best prepared to make decisions.

Generally, companies have the freedom to establish cost accounting systems that satisfy their unique needs. Thus, there is great variety in cost accounting systems among companies, and possibly even between different divisions of the same company. Before extensive automation of the accounting function, costs had to be recorded, accumulated, and allocated through numerous manual operations. The arrival of automated accounting systems, however, has enabled insurers to more easily identify expenses that apply to specific products, functions, or lines of business. When an insurer prepares its financial reports at the end of an accounting period, it can program the cost accounting system to allocate expenses to a specified division, segment, product, or customer. Also, the insurer can design its cost accounting system to provide information in a variety of formats, including GAAP and statutory presentation, and for a variety of purposes, including internal and external reporting.

We begin this chapter with an overview of the uses and purposes of cost accounting. Next we classify some of the many types of costs and describe the methods companies use to capture and allocate these costs. Then, we explore ways to analyze costs. Last, we discuss the importance of cost accounting in pricing and describe how insurers make decisions using cost-volume-profit analysis.

Uses of Cost Accounting

An insurer uses cost accounting to

- Determine the costs of creating, marketing, and servicing its products so they are priced appropriately
- Match the costs incurred during a given accounting period to the income earned in or attributed to that same period
- Determine the costs incurred during a given accounting period by product type, line of business, or by subsidiary or affiliate
- Provide managers with useful information for analyzing problems in less productive functional areas
- Budget resources in line with strategic goals such as maintaining market share or expanding, contracting, or changing the focus of normal business operations
- Determine premium and dividend scales for its products
- Maintain and exercise control over operations by evaluating the efficiency of corporate procedures and personnel

Basics of an Effective Cost Accounting System

One essential element of an effective cost accounting system is accurate and complete accounting data. Before an insurer can develop an effective cost accounting system, it must already have in place an accounting system that produces reliable financial data at the appropriate level of detail. The information provided by cost accounting is only as reliable as the historical and current data on which the cost accounting system is based. Another necessary element is the identification of costs by product line, line of business, division, and function. Many accounting systems provide basic cost information, usually by department or product line. As cost identification becomes more specific, the overall effectiveness of a company's cost accounting system increases. An insurer can develop a cost accounting system to analyze and plan for many different types of costs that reflect its ongoing operations and financial performance. The remainder of this chapter describes the different ways of classifying costs, the methods of identifying costs under each classification, and the methods of analyzing costs.

Cost Classifications

The first step toward analyzing costs is classifying them in practical ways. It is important to describe all costs as precisely as possible because the general term *cost* can be vague. To help overcome this vagueness, management accountants use several classifications of cost. These classifications assist insurers in recording cost data so the insurer's cost accounting system produces useful management reports. It is important to remember that the definition ascribed to a cost depends on both the attributes of the cost and the circumstances surrounding the cost. In the sections that follow, we classify costs into three categories: by description, by behavior, and by measurement. Note that many of these costs have similar or overlapping characteristics. Where appropriate, we provide synonymous terms and describe shared characteristics.

Costs Classified by Description

The most basic way to classify costs is by their descriptive characteristics. Because many cost classifications have an opposing classification, you can better understand costs if you think of them in pairs. Figure 16-1 summarizes the most common classifications for pairing costs by description.

Direct Costs and Indirect Costs

A ***direct cost,*** also called a *traceable cost,* is incurred for or physically traceable to one specific product, line of business, department, function, or other cost object. A ***cost object*** is any purpose for which an insurer measures costs. A simple way to determine whether a cost is a direct cost of a particular cost object is to decide if the cost would disappear if the cost object disappeared. For example, the salary of the manager of the group health insurance line of business is a direct cost of that line because the salary cost disappears if the group health insurance line disappears.

Figure 16-1. Summary of costs classified by description.

Direct Cost Cost that is physically traceable to a single cost object	**Indirect Cost** Cost that is not physically traceable to any single cost object
Controllable Cost Cost over which one individual has power and influence	**Noncontrollable Cost** Cost over which one individual does not have power and influence
Differential Cost Future cost that changes as a result of a future decision	**Sunk Cost** Past cost that does not change as a result of a future decision
Committed Cost Cost that results from a prior management decision that cannot be changed quickly	**Discretionary Cost** Cost that results from periodic management decisions that change as conditions change

A cost that is not incurred for or cannot be physically traced to one specific cost object is considered an ***indirect cost.*** Indirect costs are sometimes called *common costs* or *shared costs.* We can apply the same test as described above to determine which costs are indirect. For example, the salary of the vice president in charge of all group insurance—life and health—is an indirect cost of the group health insurance line because that salary cost would not disappear if the insurer phased out its health insurance operations. A familiar type of indirect cost is an ***overhead cost,*** which is a cost incurred during normal business operations and which is not directly associated or identifiable with a specified product or service. Examples of overhead costs are utilities, property taxes, depreciation on facilities, repairs, maintenance, and rent.

Controllable Costs and Noncontrollable Costs

A ***controllable cost*** is a cost over which a particular manager or level of management has power and influence. Every manager has the ability to incur or not incur costs that are controllable and to determine the amount of controllable expense that is incurred for any given time period. For example, the cost of supplies, travel, and overtime within a department are controllable costs because the department's manager can decide whether or not these costs are incurred. A cost over which a particular manager or level of management has no power or influence is considered a ***noncontrollable cost.*** Examples of noncontrollable costs are rent and depreciation on equipment. Depreciation on equipment is charged to the department "owning" the equipment, and a manager cannot control the rent paid or the portion of rent allocated to his or her department.

Differential Costs and Sunk Costs

Differential costs and sunk costs often result from management decisions. A ***differential cost*** associated with a decision is a future cost that changes as a result of that future decision. A ***sunk cost*** is a past cost that does not change as the result of a future decision. Assume that a life and health insurance company plans to design and implement a new decision support system for its investment department. To complete this project, the company must add new computer equipment and software to existing equipment and it must hire consultants to design the system's software and train its employees. All costs that are incurred as a result of deciding to proceed with this project are differential costs. All costs that are already committed but that were not originally committed to benefit this project are sunk costs. Thus, the costs of the new computer equipment and software and the costs of the consultants are differential costs. The cost of the existing equipment will not change as a result of the decision to go ahead with the project, so this cost is a sunk cost.

Committed Costs and Discretionary Costs

Committed costs are costs that result from prior management decisions that cannot be changed quickly. Committed costs include the cost of facilities, equipment, systems development, and executive salaries. Actions taken to control committed costs require long-term focus and an explicit tie to a company's strategic plan. ***Discretionary costs*** are costs that result from periodic management decisions that can change as conditions require. Discretionary costs include the cost of product advertising, promotional campaigns, and employee training. Discretionary costs can more easily be changed to reflect shifting market conditions.

Costs Classified by Behavior

Time and volume are the defining factors when classifying cost by behavior. Some costs change as the amount of time needed to complete an activity changes. Other costs change as the volume of activity changes. Many costs change with both time and volume, and some costs are not affected by time or volume at all. Costs that can be defined by behavior are most commonly classified as *fixed costs, variable costs,* and *semi-variable costs.*

Fixed Costs

A ***fixed cost*** is a cost that remains constant for all levels of operating activity or production. Examples of an insurer's fixed costs are rent on a branch office, fire insurance on the home office facility, and depreciation on computer equipment. Whether an insurance company sells one policy or one million policies during a given period, these fixed costs remain the same. We can further categorize fixed costs as either committed costs or discretionary costs, which we described earlier.

Variable Costs

The amount of a ***variable cost*** fluctuates in direct proportion to changes in the level of operating activity. An example of a variable cost is agent commissions. If an insurer sells no insurance policies, there are no agent commission costs. However, as sales volume increases, the cost of commissions also increases. Another variable cost is the cost of premium processing. The higher the sales volume, the more premium processing costs the insurer incurs. Figure 16-2 graphically demonstrates the difference between fixed costs and variable costs. Note that fixed costs remain the same for all levels of sales volume, while variable costs increase as the volume of sales increases.

Semi-Variable Costs

A ***semi-variable cost,*** also called a *mixed cost,* contains elements of both fixed and variable costs. A semi-variable cost is comprised of a fixed cost component plus the amount of a variable component over time and at each volume level. Semi-variable costs include electricity, heat, repair, telephone, and building maintenance costs. For ex-

Figure 16-2. Characteristics of fixed costs and variable costs.

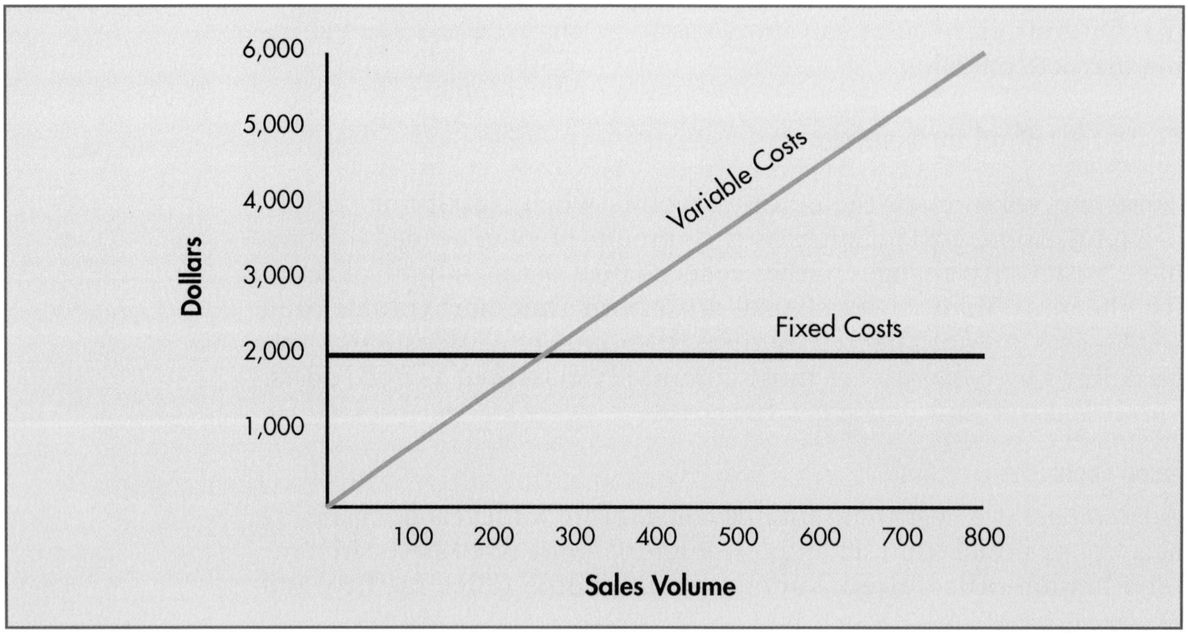

Figure 16-3. Characteristics of semi-variable electricity costs.

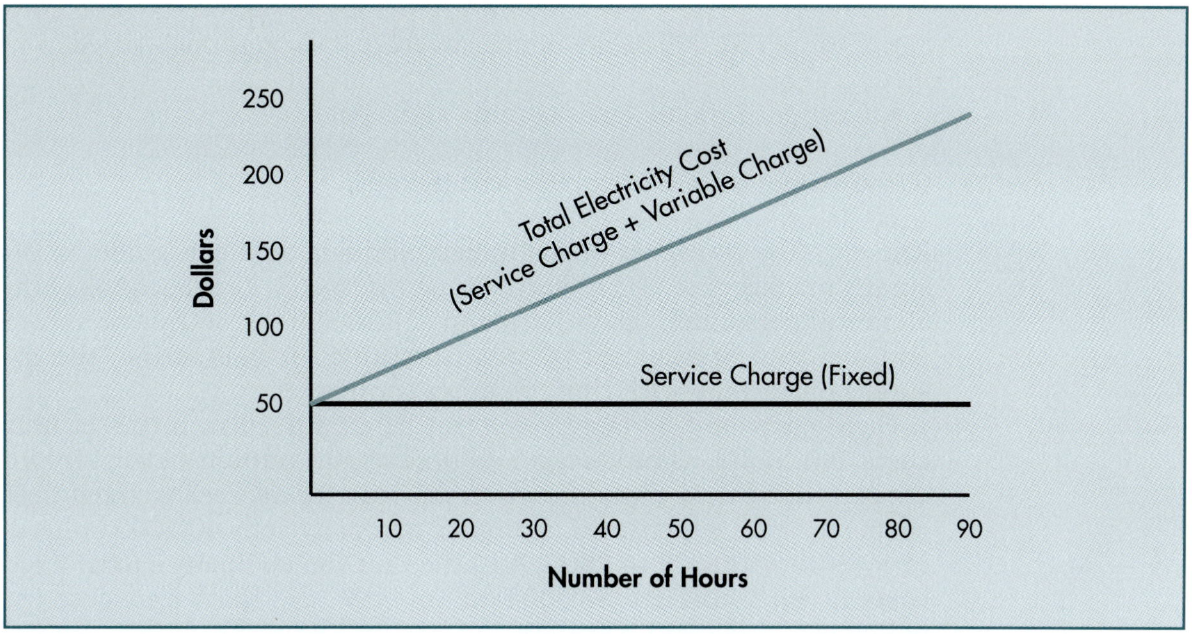

ample, the cost of electricity involves a basic monthly service charge to have electricity available for use. This charge is the fixed cost component, and it remains the same each month regardless of how much electricity the insurer uses. The variable component of the insurer's electricity cost includes the number of kilowatt-hours of electricity the company uses. If the insurer shuts off all of its office lights every night, it will use fewer kilowatt-hours of electricity—and therefore incur a lower variable electricity cost—than if it keeps its lights on all night. Figure 16-3 graphically depicts the characteristics of an insurer's total electricity costs. Note that, even when the insurer uses no electricity, there is still a fixed cost for the basic service.

Costs Classified by Measurement

The third cost classification considers a cost's measurement attributes. These costs are especially helpful for management reports and for cost-volume-profit analysis, which we describe later in this chapter. Costs classified by measurement include unit costs, marginal costs, and opportunity costs.

Unit Costs

Unit cost is the basic measurement in cost accounting. A ***unit cost*** is the incurred expense attributable to a single measured amount of work. Examples of unit costs are

- Cost per policy issued
- Cost per $1,000 of insurance coverage (face amount) issued
- Cost per $100 of agent commissions paid
- Cost per $1,000 of investment income

Knowing the unit cost of insurance products sold can guide an insurer's managers in (1) predicting future costs, (2) evaluating the efficiency of personnel, operations, and equipment, (3) setting premium and dividend scales, and (4) benchmarking, or comparing, the insurer's operations with those of other companies.

Fixed costs and variable costs can be expressed in terms of unit costs. Normally, as production volume or the amount of activity *increases,* fixed unit costs *decrease.* As volume *decreases,* fixed unit costs *increase.* Suppose an insurance company sells 400,000 policies in 1999 and 500,000 in 2000. Assume that the company's total fixed costs in each year are $8,000,000. In 1999, the fixed unit cost per policy is $20 ($8,000,000 ÷ 400,000). In 2000, the fixed unit cost decreases to $16 ($8,000,000 ÷ 500,000). This example demonstrates that fixed unit costs decrease as volume increases.

Unit costs are often used to express ***standard costs,*** which are predetermined costs expected to be incurred for particular items during normal business operations. Many companies establish a standard cost for each item against which they later compare the actual cost. Two important standard unit costs for insurance companies are the unit cost of processing one claim and the unit cost of maintaining one policy. An insurer establishes a standard unit cost for processing one claim and then compares that standard cost with the actual unit cost of processing the claim. As stated in Chapter 15, an instance where the actual cost deviates from the standard cost is known as a *variance.* Analyzing variances is an important step in the control process of management accounting.

Marginal Costs

A ***marginal cost,*** which is also called an *incremental cost* or a *differential cost,* is the additional total expense incurred as a result of producing one additional unit of a product or service. For example, if an agent submits 50 new applications per year at a total cost of $40,000, and the total cost of processing 51 new applications is $40,500, then the marginal cost of the 51st application is $500 ($40,500 – $40,000). A similar marginal cost study could be performed on the costs of processing the 52nd and 53rd applications, and so on.

Marginal cost information is essential for making production decisions because it helps managers to determine the monetary effect of a specific action, and, in certain cases, whether an action should or should not be taken. Once a certain sales volume has been reached, the decision whether to produce or sell additional units involves different cost considerations than the earlier decision to produce or sell the initial amount. Some of the costs involved in processing the initial amount may not apply to the additional production. In the previous example, the agent's submission of the 51st application would probably not cost as much as 1/50th of $40,000, because most of the total expenses, such as advertising, office supplies, office space, etc., are committed or sunk costs and thus are unaffected by the processing of a single additional application. Alternatively, the additional submission may incur costs not required for the initial amount of processing. Thus, the marginal cost of each additional unit is different from the unit cost of the initial amount produced. To help make production decisions, managers consider the ***marginal unit cost,*** which is the increase or decrease in the unit cost as a result of an additional unit of a good or service.

Figure 16-4 depicts an example of the marginal costs and marginal unit costs incurred in an insurer's policy issue department. For simplicity, the example assumes that salaries do not increase during the period of study. In Year 1, 50 employees issue 20,000 policies. The policy issue department incurs total costs of $7,000,000, including $1,500,000 for employee-related items (such as salaries, employee benefits, workspace, etc.), and $5,500,000 in other expenses (such as supplies, policy forms, and computer run time). Thus, the Year 1 unit cost per policy issued is $350 ($7,000,000 ÷ 20,000) as seen in Column 6. In Year 2, policies issued increases by 300 to 20,300. The

Figure 16-4. Unit costs and marginal costs for an insurer's policy issue department.

	1 Number of Policies Issued	2 Number of Employees	3 Employee-Related Expenses	4 Other Policy Expenses	5 Total Expenses {3} + {4}	6 Unit Cost {5} ÷ {1}
Year 1	20,000	50	$1,500,000	$5,500,000	$7,000,000	$350.00 *
	300			10,000	10,000 **	$ 33.33 ***
Year 2	20,300	50	$1,500,000	$5,510,000	$7,010,000	$345.32 *
	300	1	35,000	10,000	45,000 **	$150.00 ***
Year 3	20,600	51	$1,535,000	$5,520,000	$7,055,000	$342.48 *

* Unit cost for each policy
** Marginal cost for additional 1,000 policies
*** Marginal unit cost for each additional policy

department's manager believes that the current staff can handle the extra workload. The expected additional costs incurred are $10,000 in other expenses. In this case, the marginal cost for the additional 300 policies is $10,000, and the marginal unit cost per policy for each additional policy is $33.33 ($10,000 ÷ 300). Note that the unit cost per policy for all policies drops from $350 in Year 1 to $345.32 in Year 2.

In Year 3, the department issues an additional 300 policies, bringing the cumulative total that year to 20,600. The department's manager believes that more staff will be required to handle this increase, so another employee is added at an employee-related cost of $35,000. In addition, the department incurs $10,000 in other expenses, bringing the total additional costs incurred during Year 3 to $45,000. This $45,000 represents the marginal costs for the newest 300 policies. When the manager faces the situation of processing an additional 300 policies in Year 3, the marginal unit cost per policy for the 300 additional policies jumps to $150 ($45,000 ÷ 300) as a result of hiring an additional employee. The unit cost per policy for all 20,600 policies is $342.48.

As you may have guessed, marginal cost information is useful to managers when determining the optimal level of production relative to the resources available. When deciding to employ additional resources, a prudent manager should also consider marginal unit costs associated with other alternatives. In our example, the policy issue department manager should, in Year 3, also consider the effects of *not* hiring an additional employee. Although the manager could avoid the cost of one additional full-time salary and benefits, the manager might have to pay current employees overtime pay, an action that would increase the marginal unit cost of issuing additional policies. Also, employees working these extra hours may be more prone to errors, and correcting them may ultimately result in increased costs.

Opportunity Costs

In making decisions about expenditures, most managers are aware of ***out-of-pocket costs,*** which are costs that require outlays of cash or other resources. However, they sometimes overlook the opportunity costs associated with a decision. An ***opportunity cost*** is the benefit that is forfeited in choosing one decision alternative over another. Managers must be aware that all out-of-pocket costs carry associated opportunity costs. Suppose a life and health insurance company is considering introducing a new universal life product. The company estimates that the out-of-pocket cost of this project will be $1 million for research, actuarial work, systems, and marketing. What are the opportunity costs associated with this project? The company could use the $1 million to enhance its current universal life operating systems. These improved existing systems may provide a return that equals or exceeds the return offered by the new product alone.

The company could also use the $1 million to purchase assets to generate investment income.

The difficulty with opportunity costs is that there is no definitive way to capture them in the accounting system because there is no transaction involved—no exchange of money or value of service to record. Managers should therefore analyze various business scenarios to determine the cost of making each business decision. In the above example, the project manager would make revenue and expense projections associated with (1) undertaking the new product, (2) enhancing the existing operating systems, and (3) investing in income-producing assets.

Cost Perspectives

By now it should be clear that there are many varieties of costs, and that a single cost can be classified in several different ways, depending on the point of view of the individual analyzing the cost and the point of view of the individual or department incurring the cost. For example, the salary of an insurer's vice president of marketing is (1) a *direct* cost of the marketing division as a whole, (2) an *indirect* cost with respect to the individual life insurance marketing department within the marketing division, (3) a *fixed* cost that remains unchanged regardless of the activity of the division, (4) a *controllable* cost to the chief executive officer of the company, (5) a *committed* cost that resulted from a prior management decision regarding the operation of the company, and (6) a *sunk* cost that has already been incurred and cannot be avoided.

Similar multiple-characterizations can be made for virtually every other cost incurred by an insurer. A function of management accounting is classifying costs in different ways to better analyze company operations. Useful cost classification also promotes proper cost accumulation and cost allocation.

Cost Accumulation and Cost Allocation

Ideally, a cost accounting system should provide each manager with sufficient information to make informed decisions about the operations for which he or she is accountable. But the information generated from the cost accounting system is only as useful as the information originally input. To be a valuable management tool, the cost accounting system should accumulate costs and allocate costs accurately and fairly. ***Cost accumulation*** is the process of capturing all of a company's costs and categorizing them in meaningful ways. Once the company accumulates the total amount of costs, it can allocate them to departments, products, and lines of business relative to management needs. Specifically, the cost accounting system should ensure that each cost is charged to the area of the company that is responsible for generating the cost.[1]

Cost Accumulation

An insurer's general ledger provides the first instrument for accumulating cost data. The general ledger system should be well organized for capturing and categorizing data so that appropriate cost reports are available for management review. Four methods of accumulating cost data are by (1) type of cost, (2) line of business, (3) department or cost center, and (4) function. Many life and health insurance companies accumulate costs by more than one of these methods to learn whether the costs associated with one classification, line of business, department, or function, are greater than or less than expected.

Accumulating Costs by Type

The most basic level of cost accumulation in the general ledger is by cost type, such as salaries, advertising, commissions, and so on. On this level, costs are accumulated without regard to the specific area of the company that incurs the expense. For example, all company costs relating to salaries can be accumulated in one "Salaries" classification rather than be associated with a particular department or line of business. Accumulating costs by type enables companies to satisfy financial reporting requirements for compiling financial statements and corporate tax returns. Also, accumulating costs by type assists managers in studying which types of costs are rising and falling over time. However, accumulating costs by type does not explain which areas of the company incur each cost and, therefore, who or what is responsible for changes in cost levels.

Accumulating Costs by Line of Business

When accumulating costs by line of business, all costs that are associated with the sale and administration of a particular line are charged to that line. Recall from Chapter 6 that a *line of business (LOB)* is a segment that differs from other segments with respect to sales approach or policyowner service, for example. In the context of cost accounting, a *line of business (LOB)* is a segment of products that has a cost pattern distinct from that of other product segments. The product segment's methods of distribution and service usually determine its cost patterns. Examples of an insurer's lines of business include individual life insurance and group accident and health insurance. After entering a cost in the general ledger, such as under "Salaries," the insurer also codes the cost to a line of business, such as group accident and health insurance. Cost accumulation by line of business may include all the costs associated with a particular line or with individual products within a line. This method of cost accumulation helps management (1) make pricing decisions, (2) analyze the profitability of products and lines of business, and (3) complete the *Analysis of Operations by Lines of Business* section of the Annual Statement and the equivalent exhibit on the Annual Return. For example, a certain product may be draining more of a company's resources than its other products. If the company accumulates costs by line of business, its managers are better able to identify the problem and take appropriate action to address the issue through either price increases or re-engineering of processes to reduce costs.

Accumulating Costs by Department or Cost Center

The third level of cost accumulation is by department or cost center. A ***cost center*** is a department or other business segment to which costs can be charged. Examples of an insurer's cost centers are the accounting department, legal department, and claims department. To provide accurate cost information, cost centers should accumulate their costs according to the various levels of accumulation, such as type and function. An insurer establishes cost centers to facilitate the budgeting process and to identify the total cost of operating various areas. When accumulating costs by cost center, the costs of departments at each level of a company can be "rolled into" the cost reports for departments at higher levels in the organization. This type of accumulation enables management to judge the performance of individual cost centers.

Accumulating Costs by Function

When costs are accumulated by function, they are directed to the company operation that generates the costs. A ***function*** consists of a series of activities that serve a specific purpose. For example, policy maintenance is a typical insurance company function, and all the costs associated with the maintenance of in-force policies should be charged to that function. Activities within this function include collecting renewal premiums, processing agent commissions, administering policy loans, and processing policy surrenders. The accumulated costs of the activities involved within a certain function, without regard to departmental lines, are known as ***functional costs.*** Within each function are the costs of salaries, supplies, equipment, and so on. Figure 16-5 shows the accumulation of costs for the policy maintenance function for the individual life insurance line of business in one life and health insurance company. Note that the company accumulates its functional costs by line of business and cost center.

Accumulating costs by function is more complicated than accumulating costs by type or cost center. Functional cost accumulation

Figure 16-5. Accumulation of policy maintenance costs by line of business and cost center.

Policy Maintenance Function
Individual Life Insurance
$000 omitted

	Salary	Benefits	Operations	Overhead	Subtotal
Cost Center 1: Premium Collection	$200	$20	$100	$ 50	$ 370
Cost Center 2: Commission Processing	175	35	90	70	370
Cost Center 3: Policyowner Service					
Activity A: Policy Administration	210	25	140	60	435
Activity B: Surrender Administration	100	10	80	30	220
Subtotal	$310	$35	$220	$ 90	$ 655
Total Policy Maintenance Costs	$685	$90	$410	$210	$1,395

involves identifying and measuring all the activities involved in a given function. Some activities may be involved in more than one function. In this case, it is necessary to allot the correct portion of an activity's cost to each function that uses the activity.

Cost Perspectives

Again, we can classify a single cost in different ways. For instance, the cost of underwriting applications for a new term life insurance product is (1) an underwriting cost when accumulated by *type,* (2) a term life insurance cost when accumulated by *line of business,* (3) an underwriting department cost when accumulated by *cost center,* and (4) a policy acquisition cost when accumulated by *function.*

Cost Allocation

Once a company accumulates all costs, it should assign them to the department, function, and line of business that was responsible for generating them. By assigning costs to various cost centers, functions, and lines of business, the company's managers have a better understanding of the sources of company costs. Figure 16-6 shows how one company allocates the cost of salaries first to cost centers and then to functions by line of business. Note that this company incurs $3,000 in salary costs, so the total amount it allocates to cost centers and functions is $3,000.

It is usually straightforward to charge direct costs to the appropriate cost object. *Charging* a cost refers to assigning a cost to the cost center that is most responsible for generating the cost. For example, if the marketing department spends $300 for dedicated telephone lines for its department's fax machines, the cost of the lines is

Figure 16-6. Allocation of salary costs to cost centers and to functions by line of business.

Total salary costs incurred: $3,000

1. Allocate salary costs to cost centers

Cost Center	**Total Allocations**
#1000: Individual Premium Collection	$1,000
#2000: Individual Commissions	1,000
#3000: Individual Policyowner Service	1,000
Total Salary Costs	$3,000

2. Allocate salary costs to functions by line of business

	Allocations
#1000: Individual Premium Collection	
A. Individual Life New Business	$ 200
B. Individual Health New Business	100
C. Individual Annuities New Business	100
D. Individual Life Policy Maintenance	300
E. Individual Health Policy Maintenance	200
F. Individual Annuities Policy Maintenance	100
Subtotal	$1,000
#2000: Individual Commissions	1,000
#3000: Individual Policyowner Service	1,000
Total Salary Costs	$3,000

charged to the marketing department. Unfortunately, assigning indirect costs is less straightforward. In the past, many insurers chose not to assign indirect costs. Instead, they lumped several indirect costs into an overhead category that was excluded from the analysis of each department's operations. Yet these costs were still part of the final cost of the company's products and services and needed to be assigned accordingly. Excluding them yielded an inaccurate portrait of operating results and could lead to managers making poor decisions. To correct this problem, insurers turned to ***cost allocation,*** which is the accounting process of assigning or distributing an indirect cost according to a method or formula. To help ensure an equitable allocation of indirect costs, insurers seek an ***allocation base,*** or measure of use, that exhibits a proportional relationship between the indirect cost and the cost center being allocated a portion of that cost. Common allocation bases are the amount of square footage, number of employees, and percentage of direct costs:

- **Amount of square footage:** This allocation base assumes that indirect costs should be allocated according to the size of a cost center's workspace. Costs such as utility bills are often allocated to cost centers according to square footage. If one cost center uses 12 percent of an insurer's office space and another uses 8 percent, the total amounts of the insurer's utility bills are allocated to each cost center according to these percentages.

- **Number of employees:** This allocation base assumes that indirect costs should be assigned according to the relative size of each cost center's staff. The more employees a cost center requires, the larger its allocated share of indirect costs. For example, a cost center with 63 percent of an insurer's employees is allocated 63 percent of the insurer's indirect costs.

- **Percentage of direct costs:** This allocation base assumes that cost centers should be allocated indirect costs in proportion to the level of direct costs they generate. For example, if the new business department incurs direct costs of $2 million each year, which amounts to 17 percent of an insurer's direct costs, the company allocates 17 percent of all indirect costs to the new business department.

Different allocation methods and allocation bases are typically appropriate for various types of costs. In this section, we discuss common methods for allocating indirect salary costs, expenses other than salaries, and service department costs.

Indirect Salaries

Salaries usually represent the largest percentage of indirect costs in a life and health insurance company. For example, the salary of the vice president of the group insurance division is a direct cost of the entire division, but it is an allocable indirect cost to each of three departments within the group insurance division: the group underwriting department, the group new business department, and the group claims department. The allocation of the vice president's salary to each department must be as precise as possible if the company allocates other expenses in proportion to salaries. Most companies allocate indirect salary costs by using ***time analysis,*** which determines the percentage of time a manager spends with different departments or activities. Three common methods of time analysis are estimated time, actual time, and standard time.

Estimated Time Analysis. Through *estimated time analysis,* managers estimate the percentage of their time they spend on the activities of each cost center under their control. These percentages then become the base for allocating the manager's salary. For example, suppose Bert Hudson is the vice president of the individual insurance division. He estimates that he spends 20 percent of his time supervising the individual underwriting department, 40 percent of his time with the individual new business department, and 40 percent of his time with the individual claims department. The company allocates Mr. Hudson's salary to each department according to the same percentages. The company could further break out the costs by function or line of business within each cost center. Estimated time is the simplest and least expensive time analysis method, and it is most effective in cost centers where work is fairly repetitive in nature. However, it can be inaccurate because it does not account for the true amount of time spent on each department's activities.

Actual Time Analysis. *Actual time analysis* requires managers to record the amount of time spent on various activities during a given period, usually two weeks to one month. The period under study should be representative of normal conditions. The recorded times are converted into percentages that become the base for the allocation of management salaries to various functional areas or cost centers. This method lends itself best to cost centers that are involved in less repetitive, project-type work. The actual time method is the most accurate time analysis method, but it also requires the most management effort and cooperation.

Standard Time Analysis. *Standard time analysis* uses standard times for various activities and functions that have been developed by work measurement analysts. In effect, these standard times indicate how much time a manager *should* be spending on a given function or activity. These times are converted to percentages that become the base of the salary cost allocation. To accurately reflect a particular manager's actual experiences, the standard times must be based on current actual times and must be reviewed regularly.

Indirect Expenses Other than Salaries

Indirect expenses other than salaries include rent and utilities, institutional advertising, association dues, medical fees, and data processing services. A decision whether to distribute nonsalary expenses among cost centers depends on a company's size, cost control program, and the level of information that its management requires. Methods of allocating indirect expenses other than salaries are somewhat arbitrary and differ from company to company. Typically, a company allocates certain costs in the same proportion as the directly chargeable salary costs for that department or function. Thus, when a number of cost centers are involved in one function, indirect costs are allocated based on each cost center's share of the total payroll. For example, assume that Cost Centers A, B, C, and D have the following percentages of salaries for personnel involved in a particular function:

Cost Center	Percent of Salaries
A	60
B	20
C	15
D	5

If direct usage of office supplies is not tracked, the accountants can allocate the office supply expense in the same proportion as the salary expense: 60 percent to Cost Center A, 20 percent to Cost Center B, 15 percent to Cost Center C, and 5 percent to Cost Center D.

Service Department Costs

A department that engages in an insurance company's revenue-generating activities is often called a ***production department*** or an *operating department.* Revenue-generating activities are sometimes referred to as *line functions.* The marketing, underwriting, policy issue, premium collection, policyowner service, and claim administration departments are typical operating departments in an insurance company. All costs incurred by an operating department are directly traceable to that department. On the other hand, a ***service department*** provides support services to operating departments and to other service departments but does not itself generate revenue. The services provided by service departments are often called *staff functions.* Examples of service departments include accounting, actuarial, human resources, legal, and information services. A service department's costs are indirect costs, which should be allocated to the cost centers that use the services. Most companies use one of three methods of allocating service department costs: the direct method, the step method, or the reciprocal method.

Direct Method. In the context of cost allocation, the ***direct method*** of allocating service department costs assumes that a service department benefits production departments only. There is no consideration given to services provided by one service department to another. All service department costs are allocated directly to production departments using an appropriate allocation base. Assume that a life and health insurance company has two production departments, underwriting and premium collection, and two service departments, accounting and human resources. Collectively, the four departments have incurred total costs of $1,000,000 during the accounting period. The breakdown of costs incurred by each department is as follows:

Department	Costs
Underwriting	$ 170,000
Premium collection	700,000
Accounting	60,000
Human resources	70,000
Total Costs	$ 1,000,000

The task is to allocate the costs of the accounting and human resources departments to underwriting and premium collection in a way that reflects the amount of service these two departments received. Assume that the company's management has decided the allocation base should be the percentage of direct costs that each production department generates. The total amount of costs generated by the two production departments is $870,000 ($170,000 + $700,000). Thus, the company should allocate approximately 20 percent ($170,000 ÷ $870,000) of each service department's costs to underwriting and 80 percent ($700,000 ÷ $870,000) of each service department's costs to premium collection.

Figure 16-7 shows the service department cost allocation using the direct method.* Note that the total costs incurred by the entire company before allocation are $1,000,000 (top line). Next, 20 percent of the $60,000 of Accounting costs is allocated to underwriting, and the remaining 80 percent is allocated to premium collection. Lastly, 20 percent of the $70,000 of human resources costs is allocated to underwriting and the remaining 80 percent is allocated to premium collection. After the allocation of service department costs, total

* For ease of display, in Figures 16-7 and 16-8 we have rounded calculations and omitted decimal places. For example, in Figure 16-7, the actual allocation base for underwriting is 19.54% rather than 20%. All calculations in these figures are based on the rounded amounts.

Figure 16-7. Allocation of service department costs using the direct method.

	Service		Production		
	Accounting	Human Resources	Underwriting	Premium Collection	Total Costs
Direct costs	$ 60,000	$70,000	$170,000	$700,000	$1,000,000
Allocation base (Percentage of production costs)			20%	80%	
Allocation of Accounting	$(60,000)		$ 12,000	$ 48,000	$ 0
Allocation of Human Resources		(70,000)	14,000	56,000	0
Total Allocations	$ 0	$ 0	$196,000	$804,000	$1,000,000

costs are still $1,000,000 (bottom line), but the entire amount has been divided among the two production departments, underwriting and premium collection.

Step Method. The ***step method*** of cost allocation, also called *step-down allocation,* assumes that service departments perform services for production departments and for other service departments. For instance, the human resources department performs personnel functions for the accounting department, as well as for the underwriting and premium collection departments. Under the step method, a service department's costs are allocated to other benefiting service departments first, and then to benefiting production departments.

To illustrate, let's return to the insurance company from the previous example. Assume that the company's management has decided to allocate accounting costs based on the percentage of the company's total costs that each department incurred. The allocation base for human resources costs is the number of employees in each department as a percentage of the total employees in the company. The costs incurred by and the number of employees in each department are given as follows:

Department	Cost	Employees
Underwriting	$ 170,000	10
Premium collection	700,000	40
Accounting	60,000	7
Human resources	70,000	8
Total	$1,000,000	65

Because there is more than one service department, management must next decide which service department's costs to allocate first. The order will ultimately affect the amount of costs that are allocated to each production department. Some companies follow guidelines in selecting the order of allocation. They begin with the service department that serves the most other service departments, or they arrange departments based on the percentage of their services that are used by other service departments. Let's assume in our example that the company's managers allocate the $60,000 of accounting costs first.

Figure 16-8 illustrates the step method. In Part 1, we allocate the accounting costs to the human resources, underwriting, and premium collection departments following the allocation base guidelines. Note that total costs incurred by the four departments are still $1,000,000, but the $60,000 of accounting costs has been properly distributed to the three remaining departments. In Part 2 of Figure 16-8, the company allocates the human resources costs to the two production departments. In making this allocation, the company uses the new human resources total of $74,800, which includes $4,800 of accounting costs

Figure 16-8. Allocation of service department costs using the step method.

1. Allocate the $60,000 of Accounting costs

	Human Resources	Underwriting	Premium Collection	Total
Direct costs	$70,000	$170,000	$700,000	$940,000
Allocation base (Percentage of total costs)	8%	18%	74%	100%
Allocation of Accounting	4,800	10,800	44,400	60,000
Total after Allocation	$74,800	$180,800	$744,400	$1,000,000

2. Allocate the $74,800 of Human Resources costs

	Underwriting	Premium Collection	Total
Costs after allocation of Accounting	$180,800	$744,400	$ 925,200
Employees	10	40	50
Allocation base (Percentage of total employees)	20%	80%	100%
Allocation of Human Resources	14,960	59,840	74,800
Total after Allocation	$195,760	$804,240	$1,000,000

3. Summary of the Step Method

	Service		Production		
	Accounting	Human Resources	Underwriting	Premium Collection	Total Costs
Direct costs	$ 60,000	$70,000	$170,000	$700,000	$1,000,000
Allocation of Accounting	(60,000)	4,800	10,800	44,400	0
Allocation of Human Resources		(74,800)	14,960	59,840	0
Total Allocations	$ 0	$ 0	$195,760	$804,240	$1,000,000

allocated to human resources in Part 1. The company allocates the human resources cost based on the number of employees in each department. Keep in mind that once it allocates a service department's costs, the company does not allocate other service department costs back to it. Thus, in Part 2 it does not allocate any of the human resources cost to accounting. Part 3 summarizes the step method. Notice that the total cost listed on the bottom lines of Parts 2 and 3 remains \$1,000,000. Again, no additional costs are added; the current costs are simply rearranged to provide more useful information regarding a company's cost structure.

Reciprocal Method. The ***reciprocal method*** of service department cost allocation fully recognizes the services that service departments perform for each other. Also called the *simultaneous method,* the reciprocal method is regarded as more accurate than either the direct method or the step method. Unlike the other methods, the reciprocal method requires the allocation of costs back and forth between all service departments. In the step method example, we allocated accounting costs to the human resources department, but human resources costs were not allocated back to accounting. Such is not the case with the reciprocal method. The reciprocal method requires the use of simultaneous algebraic equations and is beyond the scope of this text. Applying the reciprocal method to the previous example yields the following allocations: \$26,026 to underwriting and \$103,974 to premium collection. Again, the total allocations of \$130,000 (\$26,026 + \$103,974) equal the combined direct costs for accounting and human resources, and the total cost remains \$1,000,000. These facts reiterate that service department cost allocation methods do not *add* any new costs. They simply redistribute costs.

Chargebacks

A relatively new method of allocating costs has helped alleviate some of the arbitrariness of traditional cost allocation systems. Using this method, known as ***chargeback,*** a department allocates its indirect costs to departments based on usage. Chargebacks can be thought of as internal billing. When one department performs work for another department, the first department bills the second department. In most cases, service departments bill production departments, although chargebacks can work the other way if a production department performs a service for a service department. Chargebacks are most common for corporate service functions such as data processing, building services, accounting, human resources, and office services. The area that uses any of these services is held financially responsible for the usage.

Suppose the premium billing department uses 20 hours of mainframe computer processing time, and the information services (IS) department's computer chargeback rate is \$70 per hour. The IS department charges premium billing \$1,400 (20 hours × \$70). Chargeback methods provide for the equitable distribution of costs to the areas that use the services. Chargebacks also require service providers and service users to plan for their needs. The provider areas must be able to project staff needs, and the user areas must be able to budget for chargebacks. One drawback of chargebacks is that departments may not always agree on the appropriate billing rates for each service. It is therefore essential that service areas communicate extensively when determining the appropriate billing rate.

Analyzing Costs

Originally, most cost accounting systems for life and health insurance companies were established to meet statutory reporting requirements, not management information needs. In recent years, however, changing factors in the business environment have affected the insurance industry and brought about refinements in cost accounting systems. These environmental factors include

- More complex pricing assumptions as a result of inflation and interest rate changes
- Increased competition from other financial services firms, such as banks, mutual fund companies, and brokerage firms
- Increased competition within the industry
- Consumer awareness of alternative investments to life insurance
- Economic pressures on traditional distribution systems

These environmental factors have led to an assortment of new and complex insurance products, declining profit margins, and other pressures. As a result, insurance companies have become more aware of the need for accurate cost data and analysis. In this section, we describe three methods used to analyze costs for internal management purposes: *change analysis, functional costing,* and *activity-based costing (ABC).*

Change Analysis

Insurers analyze the way costs change over time to spot trends in costs. ***Change analysis*** involves the comparison of cost in one period to the same cost in a different period, such as comparing this month's cost to last month's cost or this month's cost to the same cost six months ago, one year ago, or several years ago. Figure 16-9 shows an example of an insurance company's change analysis. This example compares operating costs for the current period with the same period in the previous year.

Figure 16-9. Change analysis showing six-month expenses in current year and previous year.

Expenses for 6-Month Period Ending June 30, 2000 000 omitted				
	2000 Actual	1999 Actual	Dollar Change	Percent Change
Policy benefits	$ 4,298	$ 4,275	$ 23	0.5%
Commissions	1,633	1,900	(267)	(14.1%)
Salaries	3,707	3,935	(228)	(5.8%)
Maintenance	2,353	2,100	253	12.0%
Research and development	921	400	521	130.3%
General and administrative	445	475	(30)	(6.3%)
Taxes	992	828	164	19.8%
Total Expenses	$14,349	$13,913	$436	3.1%

Analyzing cost trends helps management spot fluctuations, peaks, and valleys in the company's operations. It also helps predict future costs. However, change analysis does not indicate what causes the fluctuations. For example, if the mix of products significantly changed during the periods under study, resources may or may not have changed proportionately. Change analysis would not consider this alteration in product mix. Thus, change analysis is useful for identifying what costs have changed but not why they changed.

Functional Costing

Functional costs are the accumulated costs of the activities involved within a certain function, without regard to departmental lines or cost centers. A functional cost accounting system analyzes all the component costs of particular functions. For example, we can determine the cost of collecting renewal premiums by gathering cost data from all departments involved in the collection process, not just from the cashiers' area that receives and records premiums. Other costs incurred in receiving premiums include printing and postage expenses, machine costs for preparing and mailing premium notices, and the indirect costs of other departments involved in premium collection. The costs of all these operations are included in a functional cost analysis of the renewal premium collection process.

A functional cost accounting system allows an insurer's top management to analyze costs as they apply to workflow rather than to organizational structures. Functional costing is especially helpful when insurers make pricing and staffing decisions. Using functional cost accounting, management can analyze relatively small functions, such as file maintenance or policy issue by product line, all the way up to complex functions, such as total selling costs. Having functional cost data in addition to departmental data helps an insurance company to

- Price products
- Monitor and control current operational procedures
- Identify trends that are not recognizable with conventional analyses
- Project more accurate plans and budgets for future operations
- Benchmark operations against other companies

For example, management can pinpoint the inefficient or unnecessary functions within a department and cut costs accordingly without harming the more efficient, useful functions within the department.

Development of a Functional Cost Accounting System

Developing an effective functional cost system with an appropriate level of detail requires identifying and defining each business function within the company—marketing, claim processing, data processing, underwriting, etc.—as well as each line of business or product offered. These functions, lines, or products may or may not coincide with the departmental units of the company. For example, mail handling is a function that is likely to be the responsibility of one department in the company's organizational structure, but the policy change function could be administered by a single subdivision of one department, or it could span over two or more departments.

When developing a functional cost accounting system, system designers must be careful to include all activities and costs—and only those activities and costs—that are relevant to the specific function under study. Two other important considerations include flexibility and special needs capabilities. The entire functional cost accounting system should be flexible enough to change commensurate with company growth or diversification. The system should also be able to provide for exceptions and peculiarities within any function or line of business. It is important to remember that the information provided by the system is only as reliable as its input data.

Functional Unit Costs

One of the most useful ways to analyze functional costs is unit costing. A functional unit cost is found by dividing the total functional cost by an appropriate base unit, such as number of claims or the amount of premiums collected. The appropriate unit of measure to

Figure 16-10. Typical insurance company functions and functional unit cost units of measure.

Function	Unit of Measure
Sales	First-year premiums New policies issued
Selection and issue	Policies issued New business (face amount)
Policy maintenance	Policies in force Renewal premiums
Research and development	Premiums Policies in force (face amount)
Underwriting	Per application Per policy issued
Writing agent's compensation	First-year premiums Renewal premiums

use in calculating unit costs depends on the function itself and the line of business being monitored. Units of measure may be monetary or non-monetary. More than one unit of measure may be used so that costs can be examined from different viewpoints. For example, policy issue costs can be expressed in terms of the number of policies issued, the number of applications submitted, or the face amount of insurance (per $1,000) issued. Figure 16-10 shows some typical insurance company functions and the units of measure that may be used to express the functional unit cost.

Unit costing adds perspective to functional costs and places emphasis on the efficiency of the operations based on unit cost ratios. By comparing functional costs on a unit cost basis, for example, management is able to monitor the effectiveness of each department involved in that function. In other words, unit costing gives a reasonable indication of the productivity and profitability of departments and products. The ratio of expenses to premiums is one example of unit cost information in which senior management is keenly interested. Middle managers examine additional cost ratios, such as first-year distribution expense to premiums or selling costs to premiums.

Unit costing is also meaningful when comparing the functional unit cost of a particular product in one year with the functional unit cost of the product in previous years or with another product's functional unit costs. For example, if the unit cost to issue one insurer's policy is $30, and the unit cost to issue a similar policy at another company is $20, this could indicate a problem for the first insurer. In many cases, the total costs of a product may appear to be modest until they are calculated on a unit-cost basis. The effect of volume may also be overlooked until the insurer's accountants develop unit cost information. A significant movement in functional unit costs from one year to the next serves as a warning that something has changed which may warrant investigation.

Activity-Based Costing

While managers use functional cost analysis to assign a cost to each company function, activity-based costing goes a step further. ***Activity-based costing (ABC)*** links costs to products based on the activities consumed in producing the products or services. In other words, ABC first traces costs to activities and then traces activity costs to products or lines of business. For example, whereas functional costing helps determine the cost of processing claims, ABC identifies the cost of each activity within the claim processing function and assigns the activity costs to the insurance products for which claims are processed. Once purely a manufacturing concept, activity-based costing is gaining acceptance in the insurance industry. Insight 16-1 discusses activity-based budgeting as a growing trend.

Traditional costing systems assume that products generate costs. ABC assumes that activities generate costs. To provide products and services for customers, a company engages in a variety of activities. These activities consume resources—labor, supplies, computer time, etc.—and produce outputs, such as a check for an approved claim. ABC identifies units of activity, calculates the costs of performing each unit of activity, and then assigns the cost of each unit of activity to products or lines of business. By analyzing the cost of each activity, a company's managers are able to identify which activities add value to products and which do not. A ***value-added activity*** is one that makes the product or service more valuable to the customer. A ***non-value-added activity*** is an activity that does not make the product or service more valuable to the customer. Generally, non-value-added activities are wasteful and should be minimized or eliminated. The primary benefits of ABC are that it allows management to identify wasteful areas of operations, and it provides a solid base for assigning costs to products.

At this point it is helpful to define a few key terms associated with activity-based costing. An ***activity*** is any procedure that generates work. Activities within a life and health insurance company include processing a policy application, sending a premium due notice, and investigating a claim. An ***activity driver*** is the output of an activity being performed. It is what drives the activity. For example, if the activity is application processing, the activity driver would be a processed application. A *cost object,* as we defined earlier in the chapter, is any purpose for which costs are measured, such as a product, business unit, or cost center. Figure 16-11 offers a simple comparison of costs accumulated in a traditional way and costs accumulated by activity. Note that the bottom line is the same. In other words, total

Insight 16-1 Generally Accepted Practice?

Even if you'd never think of calling your company a zoo, you probably regard the budget you toil over as an 800-pound gorilla that's going to do whatever it wants. Indeed, at one multinational, budgeting reportedly consumed the equivalent of a year's work—for 800 people. Any one of these people—worn out and put upon—would likely get a sympathetic hearing from New York–based Stephen J. Lukens, principal consultant in Price Waterhouse LLP's change-integration group. Although he's not for junking budgets altogether, Lukens does advocate dramatic reform.

Discard, he urges, "bottom-up" budget creation, the (to him) anachronistic and expensive practice of repeatedly passing numbers up through successive layers only to have them come to rest with some senior executives who had pretty much predetermined what figures would be acceptable. Instead, Lukens counsels, have the top people in a business unit set targets for such things as revenue growth and profit margins and then ask the folks on the next level down whether they're consistent with the strategic plan and the economic environment. Once that exercise is finished companywide and the CEO is satisfied, "You then lay in a budget for the entire organization as far down as you want," Lukens says.

He's not the only one producing reform in a process that's still popularly identified with the green-eye-shaded cost accountants who made business life miserable for functional managers in industry 40 years ago. And the most intriguing of the changes now being touted is activity-based budgeting.

"In activity-based budgeting, essentially what we're saying is that we're going to avoid the classic approaches to trying to manage costs and organization," explains James Reeve, professor of accounting at the University of Tennessee College of Business, Knoxville. Instead of concentrating on the cost of such items as salaries, supplies, and insurance, activity-based budgeting focuses on the processes integral to a business.

For example, Reeve recalls that a bank's COO (chief operating officer) recently came to him complaining that classic cost-based budgeting had left him with very little understanding of the businesses the bank was in. One result was that the COO, responsible and accountable for the bank's financial performance, was not able to intelligently "push back" on budget numbers with his direct reports.

In contrast to the bank executive's situation, a major plus of activity-based budgeting, contends Reeve, is that it concentrates on what an organization does—that it deals with what Reeve dubs the action "verbs" of the organization.

In addition, he claims activity-based budgeting helps companies distinguish between those actions that add value for customers and those that do not—such as processing customer returns and performing machinery setups. "As a manager, I can begin to look at . . . performance and I can target improvements, because I now have names to attach" to the actions. "What I'm doing is moving from a cost-control perspective to a cost-reduction perspective."

U.S. automakers are among firms that Reeve regards as eager to reduce their costs by better managing their activities. "All the Big Three (Detroit automakers) are looking at these approaches. It's a competitive marketplace, and that whole industry has got to be cost-competitive. There is no choice."

Reeve sees activity-based budgeting having wide on-the-job application. "This concept, in a manufacturing facility, goes beyond the manufacturing function itself. It certainly gets into the channel-related activities—the sales (and the) marketing-related activities. In fact, that's where I'm seeing the biggest move right now."

What's more, says Reeve, service companies—such as banks, hospitals, and insurance companies—are embracing activity-based management and budgeting. Reason: "Traditionally there have been very weak cost-management and cost-planning tools in these environments. They are, in effect, captives of department-based budgeting. Example: If you ask a CFO (chief financial officer) of a hospital what's the cost of anything, he can't answer that question."

However, Reeve guesses that Microsoft Corp. "does not spend one minute" thinking about activity-based budgeting. The fabled computer software producer, he says, is one of several firms not experiencing margin squeezes, companies where "cost just isn't as important" as it is in other firms. Microsoft makes "money hand-over-fist, and the name of the game there," says Reeve, "is get the software out and onto the shelves."

Although activity-based budgeting probably can't be written off as a fad, it remains to be seen whether this now-emerging technique will more than ripple the surface of the pool of management tools.

"Everyone we're working with today is moving to (activity-based

(continued)

Insight 16-1 Generally Accepted Practice?, continued

costing) in some form or fashion," states Philadelphia-based Jim Bramante, a partner in Coopers & Lybrand Consulting. But that "doesn't mean everyone is there."

The big plus, according to Bramante: "Once you start to view your costs from an activity-and-process standpoint, you begin to realize that building budgets from the bottom up by cost accounts is not the way to go." Instead of playing numbers games with costs, "you begin to focus on what the work is in the business and how that's being done to support your strategies," Bramante stresses.

However, Brandt R. Allen, a professor and associate dean at the University of Virginia's Darden Graduate School of Business Administration in Charlottesville, views activity-based costing as a "very helpful" driver of the business-decision process that runs in parallel with the budget process, "rather than the budget process itself."

Finally, a fundamental shortcoming of budgets is that they are only for the short term, insists Richard Balaban, a Mercer Management Consulting vice president and head of the Lexington, Mass.-based firm's London office. "You need ways of thinking about the evolution of the business that are by definition more flexible than a budget by my definition can be."

Budgeting "is what a lot of companies still do when they think about business planning—and even they think about strategy development," he believes. But budgeting, by his reckoning, is "a short-term description of the business you expect to have in a time frame around which you ought to have a lot of certainty"—a time frame of a year or maybe two. "But beyond that, when you get into periods of uncertainty, the word *budget* no longer applies, because the level of certainty that you're using to create that budget, by definition, has to go down."

Balaban, consequently, likes to think in terms of business scenarios, business plans, and (then) budgets. Scenarios, he says, are descriptions of the ways the business environment say "evolve, and grow, and change." Business plans deal with the ways companies allocate their human and financial assets to try to gain competitive advantage "over a reasonable period of time." And a budget, Balaban says, focuses on the initial, tangible slice of time, the period for which both management and operating units need targets and measures.

"I don't do much work with clients on their budgeting. (But) I do a lot of work with clients on their plans and scenarios," Balaban relates. That's not because the budget lacks importance, but "the problem is that too many people build budgets without business plans."

Source: Adapted from John S. McClenahen, "Generally Accepted Practice?" *Industry Week,* Vol. 244, No. 20 (November 6, 1995), pp. 13–14. Reprinted with permission from *Industry Week,* 1995. Copyright Penton Publishing, Inc., Cleveland, Ohio.

costs incurred do not change. The use of ABC, however, allows management to report the cost of performing specific tasks. In turn, accountants will be able to charge these costs to products more accurately than with traditional systems, resulting in more appropriate pricing and more effective cost control.

Establishing an ABC system is essentially a four-step process: (1) identifying the activities within a company, (2) identifying the activity drivers, (3) matching costs to each activity, and (4) tracing activity costs to products.

1. **Identify the activities within a company:** There are literally hundreds of activities performed in an insurance company every day. Because tracking all of these activities is not practical, most companies, when establishing an ABC system, group individual tasks into activity pools. For example, an activity pool for verifying a claim could contain separate tasks such as making telephone

Figure 16-11. Comparison of traditional costing and activity-based costing.

Traditional Costs (by Category)	
Salaries	$500,000
Supplies	70,000
Rent	60,000
Computer	55,000
Miscellaneous	25,000
	$710,000

Activity-Based Costs	
Underwrite applications	$185,000
Process approved applications	90,000
Process claims	95,000
Issue claim checks	75,000
Service policyowner requests	130,000
Manage departments	80,000
File statements with regulators	55,000
	$710,000

calls, photocopying, preparing affidavits, and many others. Activity pools are then assigned to activity centers, which are similar to cost centers in a traditional cost system.

2. **Identify activity drivers:** The next step is to identify all the activity drivers for each activity. Examples of these activity drivers are policies issued, premiums paid, and policies changed. It is during this step where managers may begin to see the relationships between activities and the costs associated with them.

3. **Match costs to each activity:** This step is often the most time consuming. It involves determining a unit cost for each activity driver. Assume the activity driver is applications approved, and the activity caused by the driver is the underwriting process. Management first totals the actual costs involved in the underwriting process. This means tracking the time involved in underwriting and accumulating all the associated salary costs, equipment costs, and supply costs. Next, management determines the unit cost of underwriting one policy by dividing the total costs of underwriting by the number of applications underwritten. If the activity driver for the underwriting department is approved, applications, the number of applications submitted during the period is 350, and the total underwriting costs are $43,750, the unit cost for underwriting one application is $125 ($43,750 ÷ 350). Management may then compare this actual unit cost to a standard or budgeted unit cost.

4. **Trace activity costs to products:** The final step is for each activity cost to be assigned to its lowest meaningful level, such as to a product type or line of business. Management can then use

this information to determine which products are profitable and unprofitable and which are efficient and inefficient.

Cost and the Pricing of Products

Cost is a major area influencing the pricing of products. A product's cost sets the lower limit for the product's price because, in the long run, no organization can expect to survive if it sells products below what it costs to produce and sell them. The pricing of insurance products is much more complicated than the pricing of most other products because the premiums charged for insurance products have to be established long before other costs are known. The sum of the costs associated with a block of policies is never known until all the premiums on that block have been collected and all the claims and expenses associated with it have been paid. Nevertheless, companies establish projected costs for products before they can price the products. Depending on policy provisions, a specific insurance product's premium income, plus any earned interest, may have to cover many different types of costs, including

- *Policy benefit costs,* such as death claims, annuity payments, disability payments, medical claims, surrender benefits, matured policy endowments, and payments on supplementary contracts

- *Operating costs,* such as product development costs, policy acquisition costs, distribution costs, policy maintenance costs, termination costs, general administrative costs, and income taxes

- *Unexpected costs* associated with contingencies

Because many factors—such as mortality or morbidity rates, interest rates, and inflation—may affect these costs, an insurer carefully establishes the assumptions on which it bases a product's estimated costs. Understanding the behavior of costs is essential to estimating a product's costs. Some costs may decrease over time as a company gains product and marketing experience. Costs can also escalate rapidly, particularly in times of high inflation, and quickly reduce or even eliminate the profit expected from a particular product. As a company gains experience in developing, marketing, and servicing a product, the company's cost accumulation data helps management understand and project the costs associated with that product. Companies can apply this knowledge when pricing similar new products or when adjusting pricing factors, such as mortality charges, on current products. One tool that managers in all companies use to help analyze the appropriateness of its pricing decisions is cost-volume-profit analysis.

Cost-Volume-Profit Analysis

Arguably the three most important elements in business decisions are cost, volume, and profit. Analysis of these elements is a powerful management accounting tool. ***Cost-volume-profit (CVP) analysis,*** sometimes called *break-even analysis* or *profit-volume analysis,* is the study of the effects of changes in product prices, sales volume, fixed costs, variable costs, and the mix of products. The use of CVP analysis assists managers in budgeting and planning and it helps answer such questions as, "Which products and services should we sell?" "What price should we charge?" and "What level of sales should we strive for?"

Contribution Margin

Cost-volume-profit analysis makes use of costs that are classified by behavior—fixed costs, variable costs, and semi-variable costs—and unit costs. (We discussed each of these types of costs earlier in the chapter.) Fundamental to CVP analysis is the concept of ***contribution margin,*** which is the difference between a product's selling price and its variable costs. To calculate a product's contribution margin, an insurer must separate the product's fixed costs (for example, salaries, rent, and utilities) from its variable costs (for example, commissions and selling expenses). The term *contribution* is used because this amount is available to (1) cover fixed costs and (2) contribute to profit. If a product's contribution margin is less than its fixed costs, the company suffers a loss on the product. Otherwise, the company breaks even or experiences a gain. Two ways to express contribution margin are as a total, and on a per-unit basis. We calculate these two variations as follows:

Total Contribution Margin = Sales Revenue – Total Variable Costs

Unit Contribution Margin = Unit Price – Unit Variable Cost

Determining unit price figures for insurance products is complicated and outside the scope of this text. Insurers typically state the unit price of an insurance product as the price per $1,000 of coverage or the price per policy. In this discussion, we assume that the insurer has already calculated its unit price figures.

Break-Even Point

The contribution margin is important to CVP analysis because it indicates the impact of changes in net gain caused by changes in costs, selling price, volume, or a combination of the three. Assume that a whole life insurance product sold by Value Life and Health Insurance Company has a unit premium (sales price) of $1 per $1,000 of face amount of insurance and a unit variable cost of $0.60 per $1,000 of face amount. The unit contribution margin for this product is $0.40 ($1.00 – $0.60). If Value sells 2,000,000 units of the product in one month and has $400,000 in fixed costs per month, the net gain for the month is $400,000, as shown on the following contribution statement of operations:

	Per Unit	Total
Sales revenue (2,000,000 units)	$1.00	$ 2,000,000
Less: Variable costs	0.60	(1,200,000)
Contribution margin	$0.40	800,000
Less: Fixed costs		(400,000)
Net gain (loss)		$ 400,000

If Value sells just enough units of the product to experience neither a net gain nor a loss—in other words, net income of $0—it will *break even.* The level of revenue at which a company just breaks even is called the ***break-even point.*** At the break-even point, total revenue equals total costs, and fixed costs equal the contribution margin. In the above example, the break-even point is at 1,000,000 units sold:

	Total
Sales revenue (1,000,000 units)	$1,000,000
Less: Variable costs	(600,000)
Contribution margin	$ 400,000
Less: Fixed costs	(400,000)
Net gain (loss)	$ 0

Once it reaches the break-even level of sales, Value will begin to experience a net gain equal to the contribution margin for each additional unit sold. Thus, if Value sells 1,000,001 units, or one more unit above its break-even point, its net gain is 40 cents, as follows:

	Total
Sales revenue (1,000,001 units)	$1,000,001.00
Less: Variable costs	(600,000.60)
Contribution margin	$ 400,000.40
Less: Fixed costs	(400,000.00)
Net gain (loss)	$ 0.40

The break-even point could be found by trial and error. However, it is much simpler to use a break-even formula, in which fixed costs are divided by the unit contribution margin:

$$\textbf{Break-Even Point} = \frac{\textbf{Fixed Costs}}{\textbf{Unit Contribution Margin}}$$

For clarity, this equation is often re-written as

$$\textbf{Break-Even Point} = \frac{\textbf{Fixed Costs}}{\textbf{Unit Price} - \textbf{Unit Variable Cost}}$$

Substituting the appropriate values into this equation verifies that Value's break-even point for the example product is 1,000,000 units:

$$\text{Break-Even Point} = \frac{\$400{,}000}{(\$1.00 - \$0.60)} = 1{,}000{,}000 \text{ units}$$

The Cost-Volume-Profit Graph

Companies often prepare CVP data graphically. The ***cost-volume-profit (CVP) graph,*** sometimes called a *break-even chart,* highlights CVP relationships over a wide range of sales levels. The CVP graph gives managers another way to see the point at which net gain begins. On the CVP graph, we plot sales volume in units along the horizontal (x) axis, and we plot dollars along the vertical (y) axis. Preparing the CVP graph is a three-step process:

1. Plot fixed costs as a straight horizontal line at the appropriate level for the period.

2. Draw a total cost line (fixed + variable) by applying the variable unit cost to the number of units produced. Note that at zero sales, total cost will equal fixed costs.

3. Draw a sales revenue line, again by applying the number of units sold to the selling price.

For steps two and three, you need to plot only a few points before you are able to determine the correct slope of each line. The point at which the total cost line and the sales revenue line intersect is the break-even point. If a company achieves a level of sales to the left of (or less than) that point, it experiences a net loss on the product. If

Figure 16-12. CVP graph for the Value Life and Health Insurance Company.

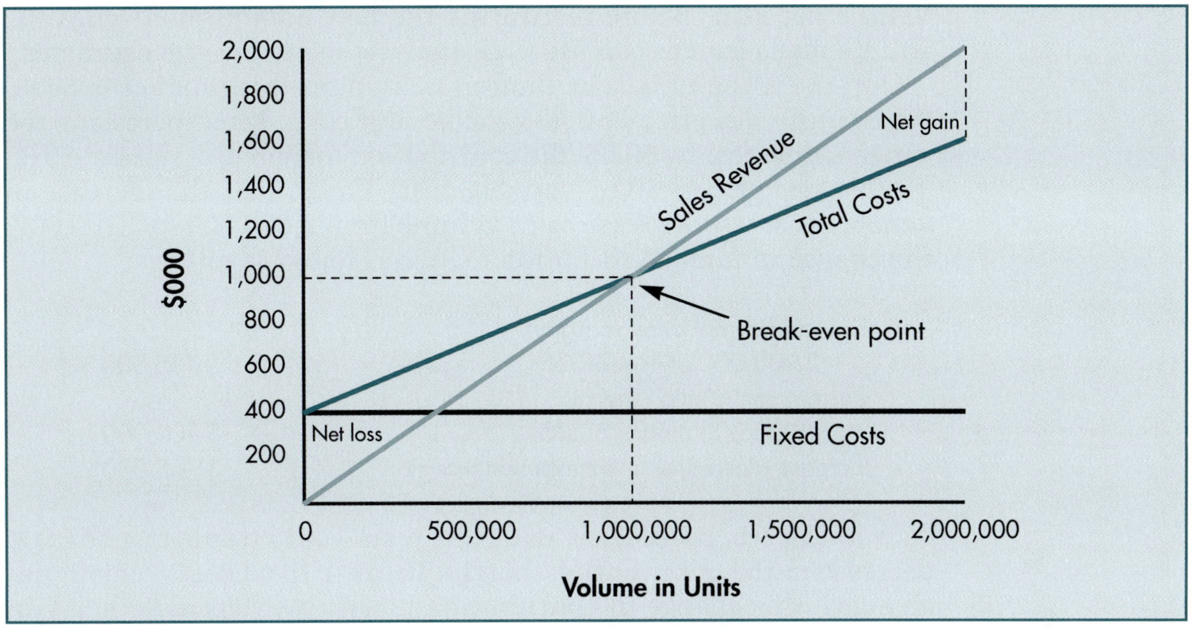

sales reach a level to the right of (or greater than) the break-even point, then the company experiences a net gain.

Figure 16-12 shows the CVP graph for the Value Life and Health Insurance Company product discussed earlier. Note that the total cost line and the sales revenue line intersect when the volume of sales is 1,000,000 units. This is the same break-even point that we calculated using the break-even formula. At each volume of sales to the right of the break-even point, the vertical distance between the sales revenue line and the total cost line is the amount of net gain realized at that volume. Likewise, to the left of the break-even point, the vertical distance between the total cost line and the sales revenue line is the amount of net loss realized at that volume.

Uses of Cost-Volume-Profit Information

After reading this overview, you may imagine that there are many applications of CVP analysis for management accounting. This analysis allows managers to test scenarios using different cost, volume, and price assumptions for each product so they can maximize the net gain to the company. Suppose the Value Life and Health Insurance Company is currently selling 2,000,000 units of its insurance product per month, and Value's management is looking for ways to increase its net gain from operations. One suggestion is to increase the commission schedule on the product so that agents will sell more units of the product each month. Management predicts that a $0.05 increase in the variable unit cost (from the higher commissions) will result in an increase in sales of 100,000 units, which should increase Value's net gain. Before instituting the new commission schedule, Value's management can use CVP analysis to confirm its estimates.

Currently, the unit contribution margin on this product is $0.40 ($1.00 unit sales price – $0.60 variable unit cost). After increasing the variable unit cost by $0.05, the contribution margin decreases to $0.35 ($1.00 sales price – $0.65 variable cost). Given that the increase in variable cost will increase sales volume from 2,000,000 to 2,100,000, the change in total contribution margin is found as follows:

Expected contribution margin:	
2,100,000 units × $0.35	$735,000
Current contribution margin	
2,000,000 units × $0.40	$800,000
Increase (decrease) in contribution margin	$ (65,000)

As you can see, proceeding with this plan would result in a $65,000 decrease in the contribution margin. Because fixed costs remain unchanged, this change in contribution margin will decrease net gain by $65,000. Value should therefore *not* institute this new commission schedule.

The previous example is one of many possible applications of CVP analysis. CVP analysis seeks the most profitable combination of fixed cost, variable cost, sales volume, and product price. Managers study changes in any or all of these variables to maximize the performance of their products, product lines, and organizations. Contribution margin is an important consideration in these analyses. Sometimes, a company can improve net gain by reducing contribution margin, but only if it reduces fixed costs by a greater amount. Otherwise, an increase in net gain comes through an increase in contribution margin. There are many ways to increase contribution margin, such as reducing selling price to increase sales volume, increasing fixed costs to increase sales volume, or trading off fixed and variable costs to achieve appropriate changes in volume. The process is more complex when companies sell many products. In that case, improving net gain comes from finding the right mix and right amount of each product to sell.

Conclusion

In this chapter, you learned that cost is the backbone of management accounting, incorporating the tenets of planning, organizing, and controlling to facilitate decision making. As we discuss in the next two chapters, cost is a vital concept in budgeting operations and monitoring performance. In Chapter 17, we explore how companies use budgets to plan for costs. Chapter 18 explains the concept of responsibility accounting and describes how organizations hold individual managers accountable for costs.

Key Terms and Concepts

cost accounting
direct cost
cost object
indirect cost
overhead cost
controllable cost
noncontrollable cost
differential cost
sunk cost
committed costs
discretionary costs
fixed cost
variable cost
semi-variable cost
unit cost
standard costs
marginal cost
marginal unit cost
out-of-pocket costs
opportunity cost
cost accumulation
cost center
function
functional costs
cost allocation
allocation base
time analysis
production department
service department
direct method
step method
reciprocal method
chargeback
change analysis
activity-based costing (ABC)
value-added activity
non-value-added activity
activity
activity driver
cost-volume-profit (CVP) analysis
contribution margin
break-even point
cost-volume-profit (CVP) graph

Reference

1. Portions of the remaining sections of the cost accumulation and cost allocation section have been adapted from the *Cost Accounting Manual* (Atlanta, GA: LOMA, 1996).

CHAPTER 17

BUDGETING

LEARNING OBJECTIVES

After studying this chapter, you should be able to

- List the benefits and drawbacks of budgeting
- State the ways pro forma financial statements differ from other financial statements
- Identify the relative strengths of top-down budgeting, bottom-up budgeting, and zero-based budgeting
- Distinguish between static and flexible budgets, short-term and long-term budgets, and rolling and period budgets
- Itemize the various components of a master budget
- Discuss the fundamentals of cash inflows and cash outflows for a life and health insurance company
- Analyze an insurer's cash budget
- Describe the purpose of capital budgeting
- Describe the factors that affect capital budgeting decisions

CHAPTER OUTLINE

Why Budget?

The Master Budget

The Budgeting Process

Approaches to Budgeting

Who Prepares Budgets?

Types of Budgets

Classifications of Budgets

Operational Budgeting

Revenue Budgets

Expense Budgets

Pro Forma Statement of Operations

Cash Budgeting

Elements of Cash Flows

The Cash Budget

Pro Forma Statements

Capital Budgeting

Capital Budgeting Process

Selecting the Appropriate Discount Rate

Capital Budgeting Methods

Factors Affecting Capital Budgeting Decisions

In Chapter 15, we noted that planning involves setting goals and determining how to achieve them. In one sense, a company examines and enumerates its goals during budgeting. ***Budgeting*** is a management accounting process that includes creating a financial plan of action that an organization believes will help it achieve its goals. In the cyclical management functions of planning, organizing, and controlling, budgeting is one of the central planning activities, and budgets are an important instrument in the controlling process. A ***budget*** is a financial plan of action, expressed in monetary terms, that covers a specified time period, such as one year. A budget can be used to plan for something as minor as the office supplies the underwriting department will use in a given month, or as major as the premium income and investment income the company expects for the entire year. Through budgeting, a company affirms its goals and establishes expected performance levels for its management team. Once a budget is in place, the company uses it to monitor performance and ensure that behavior is consistent with the direction of its goals. As such, the budget essentially forms the cornerstone of the controlling aspect of management accounting.

Budgets are estimates. They reflect management's expectations of performance and provide a plan that a company uses to guide it into the future. Budgets cannot anticipate future conditions precisely, but they do provide a company with a point of reference. By comparing its actual results to its budgeted expectations, a company can evaluate and control its overall performance and the performance of individual departments and employees. Through such comparisons, a company gains insights that help it plan new courses of action.

In this chapter, we provide an overview of the budgeting environment for life and health insurance companies. We describe the benefits and the drawbacks of budgeting. We then lead you through the budgeting process, discussing the way insurers budget and the types of budgets they produce. We separate budgeting into operational budgeting, financial budgeting, and capital budgeting, and we discuss how an insurer combines these individual budgets into a master budget, which becomes the basis for *pro forma,* or expected, financial statements.

Why Budget?

Managing a company without budgeting is like driving to an unfamiliar place without a map. You may have an idea where you want to go, but you won't be certain how you will get there. For this reason, all companies budget, however informally. Budgets outline an organization's plans for the acquisition and allocation of financial and other resources. Further, a budget is one of many management accounting reports that a company uses to make decisions about its product lines, target markets, and future expectations. Budgets are most often used to

- Monitor and evaluate financial operations
- Evaluate managerial performance
- Assist in financial planning
- Control and reduce expenses
- Communicate information throughout the various levels of a company
- Motivate personnel

Regardless of its ultimate use, sophistication, or complexity, a budget should systematically project for a given department, division, or line of business the anticipated expenses and income for a given period of time.

Budgets indicate whether managers are meeting the goals set for the company. Insurance company managers are evaluated on the basis of their ability to control the costs, revenues, or investments that are under their supervision. Almost all companies have control and expense analysis units that review each area's actual operating expenses and compare them with the budgeted operating expenses. These units generally conduct such reviews monthly and base them on computer-generated reports. If an area's actual expenses vary significantly from its budgeted amounts, then the area's manager will meet with the analysis unit's personnel to discuss the variance so as to explain the variance and develop an action plan to ensure the adequate control of expenses.

Although the drawbacks of budgeting are not important enough to keep companies from using budgets, you should be aware of what those drawbacks are. First, the budgeting process can be very time-consuming and can involve everyone from entry-level personnel to senior vice presidents. During the budgeting process, insurance company personnel forecast, among other things

- The number of policies the company will sell in the coming year
- The speed with which the company will process applications for those policies

- The level of resources the company should spend on technology during the coming year
- The number of people it will take to fulfill the company's objectives
- The amount of money to be spent for recruiting new employees and the determination of what their salaries and benefits packages will be

All this time is spent away from doing the actual work that generates the revenue that keeps the company in business. Another drawback is that if the company makes a material change in its plan for the year, or if expected market conditions change considerably, the company has to revise its budgets, which may involve considerable work. However, budgeting is work that must be done, because invariably it will improve an insurer's probability of achieving its goals.

The budgeting process has a behavioral drawback: A manager may try to manipulate the budgeting process in order to improve or protect his or her status in the company. For example, because many companies evaluate managers on a comparison of actual results to the managers' budgets, a manager may develop a budget with revenues that are lower than he or she really expects to earn. Thus, the manager makes it easier to achieve revenue goals. Two other examples of budget manipulation are padding and excessive end-of-year spending. Both problems affect expense budgets and occur when a manager behaves in a way to avoid losing budgeted expense levels. Padding occurs when managers budget for more expenses than they actually expect to incur. Managers may pad their budgets to guarantee that their departments will have enough funds to cover unexpected expenses. Excessive end-of-year spending occurs when managers believe they must spend all budgeted funds in order to guarantee that they will receive the same expense budget in the next accounting period.

These behavioral problems are detrimental to the success of a company. As a result of these drawbacks, managers may receive better-than-deserved evaluations, and the company will not be in position to make the most informed judgments regarding its investments. Unfortunately, these drawbacks reflect the company's own corporate culture. If the budgeting process is well monitored and if managers are not rewarded for underestimating revenues or for padding expense budgets, then these behaviors are less likely to occur. As is reflected in Figure 17-1, which summarizes the benefits and drawbacks associated with budgeting, the benefits of budgeting outweigh the drawbacks.

Producing a thorough, accurate budget requires considerable cooperation among company managers and other employees. This cooperation between different departments and functional areas allows a company to prepare a comprehensive planning document known as a master budget.

Figure 17-1. Benefits and drawbacks of budgeting.

Benefits of Budgeting	Drawbacks of Budgeting
• Provides management with an effective control system by keeping company personnel accountable for their actions • Provides an accepted basis for evaluating performance • Helps a company manage expenses • Provides a means of communicating and consolidating plans throughout an organization • Ensures consistency of organizational behavior with strategic and financial plans • Helps formalize the planning process by forcing management to focus on financial expectations for the future • Promotes good decision making by encouraging management to make careful analyses before making projections • Assists in pricing new products and evaluating new ventures • Provides a strongly positive motivating force in the company, when used effectively	• Process is often time-consuming, cutting into otherwise "productive" time • May promote overspending because it creates a desire to spend entire budget even when unnecessary • Budgets may not always be realistic • Some managers may be inclined to pad budgets to make it easier to meet budget goals • May restrict management by discouraging innovative solutions to changing market conditions

The Master Budget

Large companies usually draw up a network of separate budgets and schedules, each reflecting operating and financial plans for specific segments of the company. When integrated, this group of budgets becomes the ***master budget,*** which shows the overall operating and financial plans for the company during a specified period, often one year. Different companies refer to the master budget by many different names, such as *operating budget, comprehensive budget, corporate budget, performance plan,* or simply the *budget.* In this text, we use the term *master budget.* The master budget begins with a forecast of revenues, then shows the company's budgeted expenses, cash flows, and capital investment activities. The master budget can be thought of as a *profit plan,* because the achievement of the company's goals outlined in the budget typically will result in a profit for the company. Most companies compile the master budget annually and update it semi-annually.

Pro Forma Statements

The master budget culminates in a set of *pro forma financial statements.* A *pro forma statement* projects what a company's financial condition will be at the end of a budgeting period, assuming the company achieves all of its budgetary objectives. At the close of the budget cycle, most insurers draft a pro forma statement of operations, statement of cash flows, and balance sheet. Figure 17-2 shows the relationships among the various components of the master budget, including the pro forma statements for a typical insurance company. Notice that supporting budgets interweave to complete the master budget.

At the end of the accounting period, the company compares its actual financial statements to the pro forma statements to determine

Figure 17-2. Relationships among the financial components of the master budget for a life and health insurer.

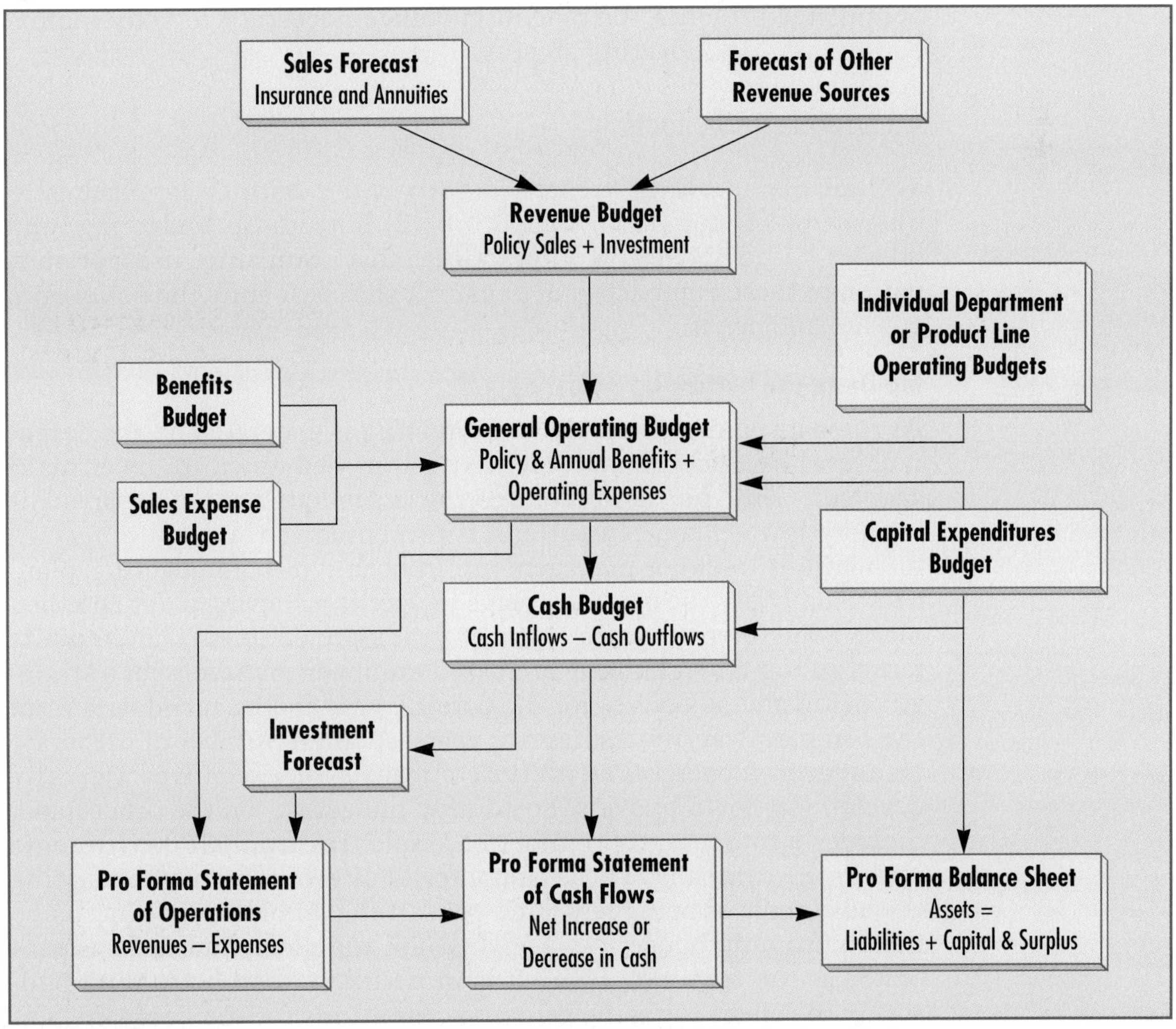

whether it has met its goals. Top management and the board of directors use the variances between the pro forma statements and the actual statements to evaluate the performance of the company and its management team.

The Budgeting Process

While budgeting is a key planning function of management accounting, budgeting itself requires a great deal of planning to be successful. In many companies, a budget committee formed by top executives and managers from the company's functional areas oversees the budgeting and financial planning process. The budget committee reviews proposed plans for reasonableness and works toward integrating all supporting budgets into the master budget. Ultimately, the budget committee provides the overall guidance necessary to coordinate a company-wide budgeting process.

Approaches to Budgeting

Technically speaking, we can identify three distinct approaches to budgeting: (1) top-down budgeting, (2) bottom-up budgeting, and (3) zero-based budgeting. In practice, most companies use a combination of these approaches in a manner that best suits the company's culture and needs.

Top-Down and Bottom-Up Budgeting

As the names imply, ***top-down budgeting*** is generated on the corporate level by upper management and is passed down to lower management, while ***bottom-up budgeting*** is generated at the department level by lower management and is presented in the form of recommendations to upper management. In both types of budgeting, planners usually use the previous year's budget as a starting point and then make adjustments for the current year's projections. The amounts found in top-down budgets are based on upper management's strategic vision and objectives for the coming year and financial data from the company's activities in prior years. A small number of corporate planners, in cooperation with the company's top executives, typically develop top-down budgets. Bottom-up budgeting, on the other hand, includes a much larger number of employees from all departments within the company. These characteristics give top-down budgeting the advantage of being less time consuming and less labor intensive than bottom-up budgeting. And, because top-down budgeting is generated at the corporate level, it is more likely than bottom-up budgeting to reflect top management's intentions for the company. On

DILBERT reprinted by permission of United Feature Syndicate, Inc.

the other hand, because budgets developed from the bottom up usually reflect the input and participation of the employees who will be responsible for achieving the budgetary goals, bottom-up budgeting is more likely to reflect the realities of day-to-day operations. In addition, bottom-up budgeting often has more grassroots support among company employees than does top-down budgeting.

Zero-Based Budgeting

Companies can apply top-down and bottom-up budgeting approaches to both income and expense budgets. Zero-based budgeting generally applies only to expense budgets. Zero-based budgeting differs from other budgeting approaches in that, for every accounting period, each organizational line of business must justify its continued operation. In other words, with ***zero-based budgeting (ZBB),*** the company begins with the premise that no resources will be allocated for the following period unless and until each dollar to be spent is justified and is shown to be in accord with departmental plans and corporate goals and objectives. Thus, ZBB treats each activity as though it is a new project under consideration and does not automatically assume that the current levels of spending are reasonable starting points for developing next year's budget.

Many of the positive results of zero-based budgeting come from the financial analysis and planning requirements that are imposed on all levels of management in order to carry out this budgeting process. Every operation is evaluated in terms of efficiency and need. Lower-level employees play a key role in ZBB because they are often called upon to provide details to accurately assess the importance and financial requirements of each activity. Other benefits of ZBB are the breadth and quality of information contained in the budgets and the training and education employees receive as part of their contribution to the process.

Figure 17-3. Advantages and disadvantages of budgeting approaches.

Budgeting Approach	Advantages	Disadvantages
Top-Down	• Minimal preparation time • Reflects management's intentions	• Possible lack of commitment of lower-level employees • Less reflective of operational realities than other methods • Limited information to assess internal or external changing forces
Bottom-Up	• Budget information based on realistic data • Increased likelihood of employee support and cooperation	• Time-consuming • May fail to meet top management's objectives • May result in over-estimation as each management level builds its contingencies
Zero-Based	• Provides detailed examination of company efficiency/effectiveness • Extensive employee participation • High-quality informational input • Likely to hold expenses down	• Most time-consuming of the budgeting approaches • May not include sufficient input from upper management

The main drawback of ZBB is that it is costly and time consuming. A great deal of the work associated with ZBB involves collecting and analyzing data in order to justify each item and prepare contingency budgets. Thus, many companies do not really have pure ZBB, but more of a modified ZBB. With a modified ZBB approach, either the budgetary approach is only partially zero-based, or the zero-based process is performed irregularly and not at each accounting period. Figure 17-3 summarizes the three approaches to budgeting.

Who Prepares Budgets?

The preparation of an insurer's budgets typically involves many individuals from throughout the company. The actual participation depends on the way a company budgets. Often, the work of creating a budget is truly participative in nature—a joint effort of top management, lower-level managers, and other employees. Typically, each department or line of business submits its own budget. The budget committee then assembles these budgets into one master budget, and the chief executive officer (CEO) gives final approval to the company's budget. The budgeting process in most companies involves both the financial management and the accounting units. The budgeting process often begins months before the deadline for submitting budgets to the CEO for approval.

In many life and health insurance companies, the accounting function or department coordinates the budgeting process, and it assembles and reports financial information for each department or line of business. The accounting department works with other departments to estimate, for a specified period, (1) the amount of income the company expects to earn, (2) the amount of work required to generate that income, and (3) the cost of doing that work. Responsibility for overseeing the budget process is often delegated to the accounting department because the budget is compiled almost exclusively from financial information contained in accounting reports and statements. However, the success of the budgeting process depends on the input of several different departments. For example, the marketing and actuarial departments provide estimates of the premium income the company should receive during the following year. The actuarial department also estimates the impact of those premiums on policy reserves. The underwriting department estimates the cost of evaluating policy applications. The claims department estimates the volume of claims and claim expenses. These and other estimates are used to allocate appropriate funding to the budget of each department, product line, or line of business.

Types of Budgets

Companies typically produce four types of budgets: *operational budgets, cash budgets, supporting budgets,* and *capital budgets.* In this section, we present overviews of these types of budgets. Later in this chapter, we discuss operational budgets, cash budgets, and capital budgets in greater detail.

A budget covering part or all of a company's operations is referred to as an ***operational budget.*** Operational budgets set forth the income or expenses that a company expects over a definite period of time. Figure 17-4 presents an example of an insurance company's operational budget. The format and content of operational budgets vary widely among companies. To help ease decision making, the company in Figure 17-4 has chosen to present comparative data showing prior-year budgeted, actual, and variance figures next to the upcoming year's budget. This information shows planned and actual income and expense amounts for 1999 as well as planned amounts for 2000. This format is useful for planning and controlling in that it allows the reader to see the future expense level (2000) relative to the prior periods, and to access the adequacy of expense controls by reflecting the variance between the 1999 actual and budgeted amounts.

Cash budgets project a company's beginning cash balance, inflows, outflows, and ending cash balance. Cash budgets assist with investment strategy determination and management decision-making. Figure 17-5 is an example of an insurer's annual cash budget broken down by quarter.

Figure 17-4. An operational budget.

Operational Budget
$000 omitted

	1999			2000
	Actual	Budget	Variance	Budget
Net premiums written	$ 15,030	$ 17,225	$(2,195)	$ 17,430
Investment income	6,408	6,365	43	7,002
Total Income	$ 21,438	$ 23,590	$(2,152)	$ 24,432
Policyholder benefits	$ (7,797)	$ (9,177)	$(1,380)	$ (8,813)
Change in reserves	(1,664)	(2,643)	(979)	(1,750)
Commissions and fees	(2,013)	(1,815)	198	(1,822)
Policyholder dividends	(192)	(255)	(63)	(157)
Total Benefits and Expenses	$(11,666)	$(13,890)	$(2,224)	$(12,542)
Income before income taxes	$ 9,772	$ 9,700	$ 72	$ 11,890
Federal income tax	(3,909)	(3,880)	(29)	(4,756)
Net Income	$ 5,863	$ 5,820	$ 43	$ 7,134

Capital expenditure budgets show a company's plans for the financial management of long-term investment proposals, sometimes called capital investment proposals. *Capital investments* include, for example, purchasing another insurance company, launching a new insurance product, purchasing computer equipment, or purchasing a building for additional office space. An insurer establishes such budgets to help it monitor the financial status of these investments. ***Capital budgeting*** is the vehicle companies use to analyze decisions about investing in long-term projects. Because of their long-term nature, capital expenditure budgets frequently are used in strategic planning, although they are also useful for the planning of capital purchases and their relative expense impact during the upcoming accounting period. Figure 17-6 is an example of a capital expenditure budget for an insurer's proposed new facility.

Supporting budgets provide details of the projections and objectives found in a company's master budget. Supporting budgets are generally classified by subject matter. Examples of supporting budgets for a life and health insurance company include the

- *Revenue budget* or *sales budget* to project first-year and renewal premium income

- *Investment budget* to project the types of investments to be made and the amounts of expected investment-related income

Figure 17-5. A cash budget.

Cash Budget
$000 omitted

	Quarter 1	Quarter 2	Quarter 3	Quarter 4
Receipts				
Policy receipts:				
Individual premiums & annuities	$ 6,420	$ 6,790	$ 6,607	$ 6,733
Group premiums	360	1,803	2,750	3,840
Total Policy Receipts	$ 6,780	$ 8,593	$ 9,357	$10,573
Investment receipts:				
Long-term security sales	$ 968	$ 1,230	$ 980	$ 984
Short-term security sales	2,730	2,081	3,010	3,320
Mortgage income	1,020	1,130	1,454	1,344
Total Investment Receipts	$ 4,718	$ 4,441	$ 5,444	$ 5,648
Total Cash Receipts {1}	$11,498	$13,034	$14,801	$16,221

	Quarter 1	Quarter 2	Quarter 3	Quarter 4
Disbursements				
Insurance disbursements:				
Claims	$ 2,151	$ 3,323	$ 2,755	$ 2,210
Annuities	3,322	3,143	3,419	3,140
Commissions	691	551	593	663
Leases	142	142	142	142
Payroll	3,130	3,130	3,130	3,130
General	1,500	1,500	1,500	1,500
Total Insurance Disbursements	$10,936	$11,789	$11,539	$10,785
Investment disbursements:				
Short-term security purchases	$ 843	$ 987	$ 1,344	$ 1,060
Long-term security purchases	1,608	774	1,013	1,625
Mortgage purchases	456	187	1,249	573
Total Investment Disbursements	$ 2,907	$ 1,948	$ 3,606	$ 3,258
Total Cash Disbursements {2}	$13,843	$13,737	$15,145	$14,043
Net change in cash {1} – {2}	$ (2,345)	$ (703)	$ (344)	$ 2,178
Beginning cash balance	5,322	2,977	2,274	1,930
Ending cash balance	$ 2,977	$ 2,274	$ 1,930	$ 4,108

Figure 17-6. A capital expenditure budget.

Design and Construction Summary Budget for a Proposed New Facility	
Demolition	$ 70,000
General construction ($30.50 per square foot)	11,250,000
Mechanical	2,090,600
Electrical	1,577,450
Vertical transportation	875,750
Construction manager fee	425,950
Sitework (including landscaping and surface parking)	1,700,000
Parking deck	1,050,600
Renovation of existing building	1,100,000
Architect/engineers	1,000,000
Construction contingency reserve	650,000
Estimated Total	$21,790,350

- *Operating expense budget* to project benefits and general and administrative expenses

- *Cash receipts budget* and *cash disbursements budget* to estimate the cash flows during the period

Supporting budgets can show information by department, line of business, functional area, or any other classification that might accommodate management's decision-making needs.

Classifications of Budgets

Each of the four types of budgets can be classified in three ways: (1) as a *static* or *flexible budget,* (2) as a *short-term* or *long-term budget,* and (3) as a *rolling* or *period budget.*

Static vs. Flexible Budgets

When budgets are classified by the degree of variability inherent in them, they are often referred to either as static budgets or flexible budgets. The amounts in a ***static budget,*** also known as a *fixed budget* or a *fixed-amount budget,* are generally not subject to change unless management has approved the changes. As a result, static budgets are of limited managerial usefulness if projected amounts of revenues and expenses are uncertain. Static budgets provide no alternative financial predictions when actual experience differs from the assumptions underlying the budgeted figures.

Static budgets are most useful when a budget's objective is to reduce or limit expenses. For example, if a company allocates $10,000,000 for expenses for the coming month, the company generally cannot spend more than this fixed amount. The company, of course, could spend less than the budgeted amount. Figure 17-7 presents an example of a monthly static expense budget for each functional area of this insurance company.

In contrast, a ***flexible budget,*** also known as a *flexible-amount budget,* a *dynamic budget,* or a *variable budget,* provides alternative sets of figures to use under the different circumstances that may arise during a budgeting period. Managers use flexible budgets to test assumptions. When an insurer cannot predict accurately its income and expenses for a given period—such as during the introduction of a new product or line of business—the insurer might prepare separate budgets for levels of activity that approximate different projected dollar amounts of insurance sold. For example, assume that a company is trying to budget for the coming year's first-year commission expenses for a new product. Because the company cannot forecast with certainty the exact amount of sales, the company might prepare multiple budgets under different sales projections. A flexible-amount budget might show three columns of possible first-year commission expenses based on a low or pessimistic sales figure of $22,000,000 of new premium income, a middle or expected figure of $25,000,000, and a high or optimistic figure of $28,000,000. In each case, the amount budgeted for commissions differs. Figure 17-8 is an example of this flexible budget.

Figure 17-7. A static expense budget.

Expenses by Functional Area $000 omitted			
	Budgeted Amount	**Actual Amount**	**Variance**
Functional Area			
Marketing	$ 1,833	$1,853	$ (20)
Investments	973	944	29
Actuarial	237	248	(11)
Underwriting	1,613	1,677	(64)
Claim administration	442	401	41
Accounting	247	229	18
Legal	377	296	81
Customer service	772	778	(6)
Human resources	1,746	1,705	41
Information systems	1,760	1,727	33
Total Expenses	$10,000	$9,858	$142

Figure 17-8. A flexible expense budget showing first-year commission expense.

Commission Expense Budget $000 omitted			
	Range of Sales		
	Pessimistic	Expected	Optimistic
Budgeted sales revenue	$22,000	$25,000	$28,000
Sales level relative to expected	88%	100%	112%
First-year commission expense	$12,100	$13,750	$15,400

Short-Term vs. Long-Term Budgets

Budgets can cover almost any time frame. A ***short-term budget*** generally addresses a period of one year or less and relates mainly to a company's operations during that period. Often, the budget is further divided into quarterly, monthly, weekly, or even daily budgets. A ***long-term budget*** addresses periods of more than one year. Many firms produce long-term budgets covering the next 5 to 10 years. Budgets projecting that far into the future allow for income and expenditures that correspond to the company's strategic planning objectives. For example, long-term budgets are often used to plan for the large capital purchases that will be necessary for the future operations of the company. Long-term budgets have less detail than short-term budgets because budgetary predictions are less accurate over multiple years. The most current year of the long-term budget should be the current period's operating budget. Thus, a long-term budget incorporates a company's short-term budgets.

Rolling vs. Period Budgets

A ***rolling budget,*** also known as a *continuous budget,* allows a company to continually maintain projections for a certain time period into the future. A company with a six-month rolling budget updates the budget at the end of each month so that the projections always apply to the coming six-month period. This rolling budget forces management to constantly consider the upcoming six months regardless of the current point in the fiscal year. In contrast, a ***period budget*** covers a specific time frame, such as one month or one year, and expires at the end of that time frame. The figures in a period budget do not change during the time frame covered by the budget. Because it is updated regularly based on the results of the most recent period, a rolling budget can maintain a higher measure of accuracy than a period budget. However, maintaining a rolling budget generally requires more resources than a period budget.

To illustrate, assume that an insurance company creates a rolling budget for the period January 1 to June 30. If the company updates

Figure 17-9. A rolling, six-month sales revenue budget.

Sales Revenue $000 omitted										
	Jan	Feb	Mar	Apr	May	Jun	Jul	Aug	Sep	6-month Total
Sales revenue	$500	$525	$535	$495	$505	$520	–	–	–	$3,080
After 1st month Sales revenue	–	$530	$540	$500	$510	$530	$535	–	–	$3,145
After 2nd month Sales revenue	–	–	$536	$500	$505	$525	$530	$510	–	$3,106
After 3rd month Sales revenue	–	–	–	$512	$515	$535	$540	$520	$540	$3,162

the budget monthly, then it presents a new budget on February 1 to reflect the six-month period from that date until July 31. The company repeats this procedure for March 1 to August 31, April 1 to September 30, and so on. Each new budget reflects revised projections for the coming six-month period. Figure 17-9 depicts a rolling sales revenue budget based on this scenario.

Now that you have a general understanding of budgeting in an insurance company, we devote the remainder of this chapter to discussing in detail (1) operational budgeting, (2) cash budgeting, and (3) capital expenditure budgeting.

Operational Budgeting

Operational budgeting covers all or part of a company's operations. In fact, the *master budget* is sometimes called the *operating budget* because it reflects all of a company's operations. The foundation of a company's operational budget is the achievement of the company's profitability objectives. The operational budget reflects the financial steps the company will take during the coming year to achieve those objectives. Two basic types of operational budgets are revenue budgets and expense budgets.

Revenue Budgets

A ***revenue budget*** indicates the amount of income from operations—policy sales and investments—that the company expects in the coming budget period. The revenue budget determines the limits of the other budgets and must be prepared before them. Some insurers divide the revenue budget into the *sales budget* and the *investment budget*. A ***sales budget*** projects first-year and renewal premium income. The company bases its estimates on historical data, reviews of the marketplace, and premium rates charged by competitors, among other factors. An ***investment budget*** projects the types of investments the company will make and the expected amount of investment-related income for each type. Because the cash flow can have a significant impact on investment strategy, the investment budget is not finalized until after the completion of the cash budget.

Sales and Investment Forecasts

Anyone who has ever prepared a personal budget knows that the first step is to project the amount of income you expect to earn during the budgeting period. Until you determine that figure, you cannot establish limits on your spending for housing, utilities, food, clothing, entertainment, and any other items. The same principle is true for insurance companies: all operational budgets begin with a forecast of sales revenue and investment income. The ***sales forecast*** is an estimate of insurance and annuity sales for a particular period. The ***investment forecast*** is an estimate of the performance of bonds, stocks, mortgages, and other invested assets a company owns. A company estimates how much money it will earn from sales and investments so that it has a reasonable idea of how much money it will have available.

For large companies, developing sales and investment forecasts is complex and time consuming. Sales forecasts require analysis of all internal and external variables that can affect sales. Internal variables include product prices, distribution systems, and advertising outlays. External variables include the general economic climate and consumer preferences. Investment forecasts also require analysis of specific types of investment vehicles and analysis of market conditions. Methods of projecting sales and investment performance can range from relatively simple estimates based on prior experience to more complex forecasts based on computer simulations. A few of the forecasting techniques that insurers use include qualitative methods, trend predictions, and regression analysis:

- *Qualitative methods* rely on the judgment of managers, who use their own experience and understanding of current economic conditions to make predictions.

- *Trend predictions* rely on historical data to reveal sales and investment trends, and then use these trends to predict future performance.

- *Regression analyses* rely on the knowledge of how the fluctuations of a known, dependent variable, such as disposable income, impacts an unknown variable, such as sales.

Some companies make several different forecasts that reflect different assumptions, such as fluctuations in interest rates. Companies can then use the different tentative sales or investment forecasts to devise a single composite forecast. This compromise or the ***expected value*** is found by assigning a probability to each individual forecast and then calculating the weighted average of the forecasts. The sum of the assigned probabilities must add up to 1. To find the expected value, multiply each forecast by its assigned probability, and then add together the resulting values. For example, if managers feel that there is a 15 percent probability that policy sales during the period will be $10,000,000, a 50 percent probability that policy sales will be $12,000,000, and a 35 percent probability that policy sales will be $14,000,000, the expected value will be $12,400,000, calculated as follows:

(a) Sales Forecast	(b) Probability	(a × b) Expected Value
$10,000,000	.15	$ 1,500,000
$12,000,000	.50	6,000,000
$14,000,000	.35	4,900,000
	1.0	$12,400,000

Personnel in an insurer's sales and actuarial areas provide management with estimates of the amount of premium income the company can expect. Sales managers in the home office usually check the sales forecasts for reasonableness. The investment department estimates the amount of investment income the insurer expects to earn during the next period.

The sales budget is often broken down by product type (such as life insurance and annuities), and the investment budget is broken down by investment vehicle (bonds, mortgage loans, stocks, and so forth). For example, assume that the Quality Life and Health Insurance Company sells individual life insurance, group life insurance, and individual annuities. Figure 17-10 shows Quality's annual revenue budget, divided into its sales and investment components, and broken down by quarter.

Expense Budgets

Following the revenue budget, the next step in completing the operational budget is preparing expense budgets. An ***expense budget*** is a schedule of expenses expected during the given period. An expense budget (1) helps control expenses, (2) increases cost awareness among managers, (3) measures management performance, and (4) assigns responsibility for expenses. Three types of insurance company expense budgets are the benefits budget, sales expense budget, and general and administrative expense budget:

Figure 17-10. Quality Life and Health Insurance Company annual revenue budget by quarter.

$000 omitted					
	Quarter				
	1	2	3	4	Total
Premium Income					
Individual insurance	$ 5,008	$ 5,298	$ 5,404	$ 4,899	$20,609
Individual annuities	4,427	4,500	4,805	5,233	18,965
Group insurance	3,606	3,004	2,752	3,844	13,206
Total Premium Income	$13,041	$12,802	$12,961	$13,976	$52,780
Investment Income					
From long-term securities	$ 1,926	$ 1,993	$ 1,930	$ 1,929	$ 7,778
From short-term securities	2,735	2,730	2,804	2,737	11,006
Mortgage income	1,127	1,132	1,134	1,135	4,528
Total Investment Income	$ 5,788	$ 5,855	$ 5,868	$ 5,801	$23,312
Total Revenues	$18,829	$18,657	$18,829	$19,777	$76,092

- The ***benefits budget*** indicates the amount of money a company expects to pay for claims, cash surrenders, and policy dividends during the next period. Actuaries typically are responsible for developing the benefits budget.

- The ***sales expense budget*** is based primarily on the costs incurred in selling insurance. In addition to commission costs, these expenses include the costs of advertising, promotion, travel, branch office operations, and salaries for marketing personnel. The marketing and agency departments typically are responsible for developing the sales expense budget.

- The ***general and administrative expense budget*** includes the other expenses needed to operate the company. Usually, this budget is the sum of all departmental expense budgets. The general and administrative expense budget also includes such company-wide expenses as depreciation on buildings, computer equipment costs, and administrative salaries. Each functional area of the company usually prepares its own expense budget.

Expense budgets can describe either variable or fixed expenses. The benefits budget and the sales expense budget describe variable expenses because the amounts budgeted depend on the figures contained in the sales budget. In most cases, the more policies the company sells, the more commission payments and benefit payments it

Figure 17-11. Quality Life and Health Insurance Company annual expense budget by quarter.

$000 omitted

	Quarter 1	2	3	4	Total
Benefits					
Individual insurance	$ 2,324	$2,346	$ 2,318	$ 2,344	$ 9,332
Individual annuities	1,755	1,409	1,419	1,805	6,388
Group insurance	1,373	1,245	1,290	1,214	5,122
Total Benefits	$ 5,452	$5,000	$ 5,027	$ 5,363	$20,842
Commissions	$ 2,831	$2,939	$ 3,063	$ 3,040	$11,873
General and Administrative					
Leases	$ 145	$ 145	$ 145	$ 145	$ 580
Payroll	1,134	1,134	1,134	1,134	4,536
General	705	705	705	705	2,820
Depreciation	22	22	22	22	88
Total General and Administrative	$ 2,006	$2,006	$ 2,006	$ 2,006	$ 8,024
Total Expenses	$10,289	$9,945	$10,096	$10,409	$40,739

makes. The general and administrative expense budget contains most of the company's fixed expenses, such as home office salaries, rent, and depreciation.

Figure 17-11 shows Quality's annual expense budget by quarter. This budget includes elements of the benefits budget, the sales expense budget, and the general and administrative expense budget.

The concept of *allowable expenses* is important for insurance company expense budgets. ***Allowable expenses*** are the expenses assumed in calculating the price of an insurance product. Companies use pricing models to run simulations that determine the amount of total expenses allowed for each of its products. The company can then compare the total amount of allowable expenses to the combined total of expense budgets submitted by individual departments. If the allowable expenses exceed the total departmental expenses, the company appears in line to earn a profit. If departmental expenses exceed allowables, the company must reconsider the pricing of its products or look for ways to trim departmental expenses.

Pro Forma Statement of Operations

Having prepared the revenue and expense budgets, a company can then draft the ***pro forma statement of operations,*** also called the *budgeted income statement,* which estimates the net income for the entire

Figure 17-12. Quality Life and Health Insurance Company pro forma statement of operations.

Statement of Operations $000 omitted	
Revenue	
Premium income	$52,780
Investment income	23,312
Total Revenue	$76,092
Benefits and Expenses	
Insurance and annuity benefits	$20,842
Change in reserves for future benefits	17,473
Total Benefits	$38,315
Commissions	11,873
General and administrative expenses	8,024
Total Benefits and Expenses	$58,212
Income before income taxes	$17,880
Income tax expense	7,152
Net Income	$10,728

company. If the master budget is for a period of one year, the pro forma statement of operations may show only the end-of-period data, or it can be divided into quarterly or monthly columns and show the end-of-period totals. To prepare this statement, the company simply transfers the total monthly (or quarterly or annual) amounts of each revenue budget and expense budget onto the appropriate lines of a statement of operations. Managers use this pro forma statement to obtain board approval for the budget and then monitor overall progress during the year. Figure 17-12 shows Quality's pro forma statement of operations. The statement indicates that Quality should achieve a net income of $10,728,000 for the year, if the company's budgeting and forecasting are accurate.

Cash Budgeting

Insurers use cash to make many types of payments, such as policy benefits, salaries, commissions, operating expenses, and cash dividends to stockholders and participating policyowners. A goal for many companies is to have on hand just enough cash to make these payments as they come due. A shortage of cash means that the company could be delinquent on some of its payments, leading to problems with policyowners, stockholders, or employees. The company may also have to sell investments at an inopportune time and incur a loss. But excess cash is also problematic. While it provides a sense of security, excess cash is unproductive because it sits idly and earns little or no return. A large amount of excess cash therefore has a high opportunity cost because the company could, by using that money elsewhere, earn additional income and improve profitability.

Budgeting for cash helps companies plan for cash shortages and cash excesses. ***Cash budgeting*** anticipates the flows of cash into and out of a company during a given period. As stated earlier, a cash budget shows all expected cash inflows, outflows, and ending cash during a period. Many companies prepare an annual cash budget that is broken down into quarterly, monthly, weekly, and even daily budgets to monitor cash flow more closely. In conjunction with, and sometimes instead of, a formal cash budget, some insurers have the accounting department submit a daily cash report to the investment department. The investment department uses the cash report to determine the additional funds available to invest each day.

Elements of Cash Flows

Specific cash inflows and outflows are unique to each company, but assumptions can be made about these flows for a particular industry. Similar to revenue forecasting, insurers can project cash receipts and disbursements using qualitative methods, trend predictions, and regression analysis.

Cash Receipts

Most individual life insurance policy premiums are due on an annual, semiannual, quarterly, or monthly basis according to due dates specified in each policy. The majority of policyholders pay premiums by the due date to avoid losing coverage. Investment income for insurers is relatively stable because, even though some investments are volatile by nature, insurers invest in relatively low-risk assets that provide guaranteed, regular income. An example is a bond investment with semiannual interest payments. Nevertheless, when forecasting for investments, insurers must consider the overall economic outlook, statutory requirements, tax factors, and the company's investment strategy. A company plans for its cash inflows through a ***cash receipts budget,*** which is a schedule of cash receipts expected during the period. To predict both the timing and amount of its cash receipts, a company constructs the cash receipts budget using data from the sales and investments forecasts. Figure 17-13 shows Quality's annual cash receipts budget broken down by quarter. Note that the company divides this budget into receipts from sales of insurance and annuity products and receipts from investments.

Figure 17-13. Quality Life and Health Insurance Company annual cash receipts budget by quarter.

$000 omitted	Quarter 1	2	3	4	Total
Policy Receipts					
Individual premiums and annuities	$ 9,435	$ 9,798	$10,209	$10,132	$39,574
Group premiums	3,606	3,004	2,752	3,844	13,206
Total Policy Receipts	$13,041	$12,802	$12,961	$13,976	$52,780
Investment Receipts					
Long-term securities income	$ 1,926	$ 1,993	$ 1,930	$ 1,929	$ 7,778
Short-term securities income	2,735	2,730	2,804	2,737	11,006
Mortgage income	1,127	1,132	1,134	1,135	4,528
Total Investment Receipts	$ 5,788	$ 5,855	$ 5,868	$ 5,801	$23,312
Total Cash Receipts	$18,829	$18,657	$18,829	$19,777	$76,092

For simplicity, Figure 17-13 assumes that there is no timing difference between income and cash receipts. In other words, the revenue forecast equals cash.

Cash Disbursements

Unlike its cash receipts, an insurer's cash disbursements take a variety of forms. Among the common disbursements most insurers make are benefit payments to policyowners, salary payments to employees, commission payments to sales employees, payments for the purchase of new securities, dividend payments to stockholders and participating policyowners, reinsurance premium payments to reinsurers, tax payments to government agencies, and payments for an array of general and administrative expenses such as office supplies, travel, and utilities. Certain non-recurring cash disbursements result from capital budgeting decisions, such as the purchase of new office equipment. Insurers generally experience heavy cash outflows in the first few working days of each month because most monthly payments are due on the first of the month. These payments include annuities, leases, and utilities. Throughout the year, insurers process claims and policy surrenders on a relatively regular basis.

An insurer attempts to estimate the timing and amount of all of its cash disbursements in the ***cash disbursements budget.*** Estimating cash disbursements for fixed expenses such as salaries is made with relative ease and accuracy, compared to estimating the cash disbursements for variable expenses such as benefit payments and commissions. The accuracy of variable expense predictions depends in large

Figure 17-14. Quality Life and Health Insurance Company annual cash disbursements budget by quarter.

$000 omitted					
	Quarter				
	1	2	3	4	Total
Insurance Disbursements					
Variable items:					
Insurance claims	$ 3,697	$ 3,591	$ 3,608	$ 3,558	$14,454
Annuity benefits	1,755	1,409	1,419	1,805	6,388
Commissions	2,831	2,939	3,063	3,040	11,873
Total Variable Items	$ 8,283	$ 7,939	$ 8,090	$ 8,403	$32,715
Fixed items:					
Leases	$ 145	$ 145	$ 145	$ 145	$ 580
Payroll	1,134	1,134	1,134	1,134	4,536
General	705	705	705	705	2,820
Total Fixed Items	$ 1,984	$ 1,984	$ 1,984	$ 1,984	$ 7,936
Computer equipment purchase			1,001		1,001
Total Insurance Disbursements	$10,267	$ 9,923	$11,075	$10,387	$41,652
Investment Disbursements					
Short-term security purchases	$ 9,302	$ 984	$ 1,340	$ 1,065	$12,691
Long-term security purchases	1,601	773	1,013	1,626	5,013
Mortgage purchases	450	183	1,244	573	2,450
Total Investment Disbursements	$11,353	$ 1,940	$ 3,597	$ 3,264	$20,154
Total Cash Disbursements	$21,620	$11,863	$14,672	$13,651	$61,806

part on the accuracy of the sales forecast. Figure 17-14 shows Quality's cash disbursements budget. Quality divides this budget into disbursements for insurance and annuities, and disbursements for investments. The company subdivides the disbursements for insurance and annuities into a fixed component and a variable component. Also, note the one-time purchase of computer equipment during the third quarter.

The Cash Budget

Once the cash receipts budget and the cash disbursements budget are complete, the next step is to draft the cash budget. The important pieces of information contained in the cash budget are (1) the beginning cash balance, (2) the cash available for the period, (3) the minimum cash balance, (4) the cash needed for the period, (5) the excess or deficiency of cash, (6) the effects of financing, and (7) the ending cash balance. The beginning cash balance for one period equals the ending cash balance from the prior period. The cash available for the period is beginning cash plus cash receipts. The cash needed for the period is the cash disbursements plus the minimum cash balance. The cash available for the period minus the cash needed equals the excess or deficiency of cash. A positive result indicates an excess of cash and a negative result indicates a deficiency of cash. The excess or deficiency of cash plus any financing activity (borrowing or repayment) yields the period's ending cash balance.

Minimum Cash Balance Policies

The minimum cash balance is of great importance in cash budgeting. The ***minimum cash balance*** is the amount of cash that an insurer determines is necessary to pay all obligations in a given budgeting period without needlessly tying up excess funds. As you can imagine, arriving at this figure requires a great amount of research and estimation from a company's accounting manager, financial manager, and other executives. Setting this figure too low raises the risk of running out of cash. Setting this figure too high carries a high opportunity cost. Companies that wish to set a lower minimum balance and keep more of their cash "at work" in the company's productive assets usually arrange for a line of credit from a bank. A ***line of credit,*** also called a *bank line,* is a prearranged agreement whereby a company can borrow money on demand up to a specified amount. This short-term borrowing becomes necessary whenever a company encounters a cash shortage. Some insurers make arrangements with banks whereby the insurer keeps funds in interest-bearing accounts and the bank automatically transfers money to the company's checking account as needed.

An insurer can use many methods to derive its minimum cash balance. A rule of thumb is to set the minimum balance equal to the budgeted cash disbursements for one month. More sophisticated techniques involve computer spreadsheet simulations. It is important to note that the decision is significant and involves a great amount of judgment and experience.

By examining the cash budget, an insurer can estimate the timing and amount of cash deficiencies that will require additional financing or cash excesses that allow for investment in relatively liquid assets. Recall that *liquidity* is the ease with which an asset can be converted into cash for an approximation of its true value. The more liquid an asset, the more easily it can be converted into cash if the need for that cash arises. Insurers invest excess cash in liquid assets, such as money market mutual funds, government securities money funds, certificates of deposit (CDs), commercial paper, and U.S. Treasury bills, so that, when necessary, they can retrieve cash quickly. Figure 17-15 shows Quality's cash budget. As you can see, the company has set its quarterly minimum cash balance at $3,250,000.

Figure 17-15. Quality Insurance Company annual cash budget by quarter.

$000 omitted					
	Quarter				
	1	2	3	4	Total
Beginning Cash Balance	$ 4,020	$ 3,729	$ 9,210	$12,055	$ 4,020*
Total Cash Receipts	18,829	18,657	18,829	19,777	76,092
Total Cash Available {1}	$22,849	$22,386	$28,039	$31,832	$80,112*
Cash disbursements:					
For insurance and annuities	$10,267	$ 9,923	$10,074	$10,387	$40,651
For investments	11,353	1,940	3,597	3,264	20,154
For computer equipment			1,001		1,001
Total Cash Disbursements {2}	$21,620	$11,863	$14,672	$13,651	$61,806
Minimum cash balance	3,250	3,250	3,250	3,250	3,250*
Total Cash Needed	$24,870	$15,113	$17,922	$16,901	$74,806
Excess (deficiency) of cash	$ (2,021)	$ 7,273	$10,117	$14,931	$ 5,306*
Short-term financing:					
Borrowing	$ 2,500				$ 2,500
Repayment		$ (1,250)	$ (1,250)		(2,500)
Interest (10% annnually)		(63)	(62)		(125)
Total Effects of Financing {3}	$ 2,500	$ (1,313)	$ (1,312)	$ 0	$ (125)
Ending Cash Balance {1}−{2}+{3}	$ 3,729	$ 9,210	$12,055	$18,181	$18,181*

* Not a total of four quarters.

Notice from Figure 17-15 that Quality anticipates that, by the end of the first quarter, it will encounter a cash shortage of $2,021,000. It therefore has planned for a short-term loan in the amount of $2,500,000.* The company expects to be able to repay the loan plus interest in the fourth quarter. Such estimated financing activity is usually included in the cash budget.

Pro Forma Statements

Once the cash budget is complete, the company can prepare two more pro forma financial statements: the statement of cash flows and the balance sheet.

* As an alternative to borrowing money, the company may decide to sell investments to cover the cash shortage.

Pro Forma Statement of Cash Flows

Like the end-of-period statement of cash flows described in Chapter 5, the ***pro forma statement of cash flows*** estimates the cash inflows and outflows for the entire company. The important figure on the statement of cash flows is the net increase or decrease in cash expected during the period. Data from the cash receipts and cash disbursements budgets, the cash budget, and the pro forma statement of operations are transferred to the pro forma statement of cash flows.

The pro forma statement of cash flows categorizes budgeted cash receipts and disbursements into three activities: (1) cash flows from operating activities, such as policy sales, benefit payments, and investment income; (2) cash flows from investing activities, which, for insurance companies, are *capital* investing activities such as the purchase or sale of securities; and (3) cash flows from financing activities, such as issuing stock, borrowing funds, or repaying a debt. Figure 17-16 shows a pro forma statement of cash flows for the Quality

Figure 17-16. Quality Insurance Company pro forma statement of cash flows.

$000 omitted		
Cash flows from operating activities		
Net income		$10,728
Depreciation of equipment	$ 88	
Increase in future insurance benefits	4,826	
Increase in future annuity benefits	4,065	
Decrease in unpaid claims	(1,262)	
		7,717
Net cash flows from operating activities		$18,445
Cash flows from investing activities		
Increase in securities	$(1,080)	
Increase in mortgages	(2,078)	
Purchase of computer equipment	(1,001)	
Net cash flows used by investing activities		(4,159)
Cash flows from financing activities		
Borrowed funds	$ 2,500	
Repayment of borrowed funds	(2,500)	
Interest on borrowed funds	(125)	
Net cash flows from financing activities		(125)
Net increase (decrease) in cash		$14,161
Cash at beginning of year		4,020
Cash at end of year		$18,181

Life and Health Insurance Company. Notice that the net increase in cash ($14,161,000) equals the difference between the ending and beginning total cash balances ($18,181,000 – $4,020,000) on the cash budget in Figure 17-15.

Pro Forma Balance Sheet

The ***pro forma balance sheet*** predicts the change in asset, liability, and stockholders' equity accounts based on information contained in the rest of the company's budgets. This statement is a snapshot of the company's financial position at the end of the budget period assuming that all goes according to plan. Figure 17-17 shows Quality's pro forma balance sheet.

The pro forma balance sheet reflects the various period changes of items contained in the pro forma statement of operations, pro forma statement of cash flows, and the cash budget. To illustrate the integrative properties of these statements, assume that the cash balance on Quality's most recent end-of-period balance sheet is $4,020,000. The cash balance on the pro forma balance sheet in Figure 17-17 is $18,181,000, which is the same as the ending balance of the cash

Figure 17-17. Quality Life and Health Insurance Company pro forma balance sheet.

$000 omitted	
Assets	
Securities	$312,788
Mortgage loans	58,694
Cash	18,181
Other assets	5,960
Total Assets	$395,623
Liabilities and Stockholders' Equity	
Liabilities:	
Policy reserves	$288,645
Provision for future claims	38,350
Other liabilities	6,356
Total Liabilities	$333,351
Stockholders' equity:	
Capital stock	$ 5,354
Unrealized gain (loss) on investments	(2,240)
Retained earnings	59,158
Total Stockholders' Equity	$ 62,272
Total Liabilities and Stockholders' Equity	$395,623

budget in Figure 17-15. The difference of $14,161,000 is indicated as the net increase in cash near the bottom of the pro forma statement of cash flows in Figure 17-16.

Capital Budgeting

Company executives are always considering ways to make their firms grow or become more productive. In many cases, growth or increased productivity requires investing in new assets, which sometimes means a large outlay of funds. To prepare for such outlays, companies undertake capital budgeting, which, as we noted earlier, refers to the analysis of decisions about investing in long-term *capital assets.* Buildings, automobiles, and computer equipment are examples of capital assets that a firm plans to hold for 3 to 20 years or more. Capital assets are sometimes referred to as *long-lived assets, long-term assets, plant assets,* or *fixed assets.* For insurance companies, the launch of a new insurance product may be another major capital investment project if it requires a large amount of up-front capital for development and marketing. A trait common to all capital expenditures is that they are expected to produce income or other benefits for more than one year.

Capital Budgeting Process

Because a capital budget is long-term in nature, it is used extensively in strategic planning. A company's top management is closely involved in developing a company's capital budget. A capital budget generally incorporates projected new investments, major repairs to or remodeling of already-owned capital assets, acquisitions of other companies, legislatively mandated safety and environmental improvements, cost reduction projects, and revenue expansion projects. The capital budgeting process often includes many steps. In this text, we identify four important steps: (1) generating capital budgeting ideas, (2) classifying each capital investment proposal, (3) estimating cash flows for each proposal, and (4) evaluating and selecting proposals.

Generating Ideas

All capital expenditures begin as ideas. For example, an employee identifies a need or an opportunity that requires a significant outlay of cash which could have long-term benefits for the company. Individuals in any functional area of an insurance company can generate an idea. For instance, the marketing or actuarial department may suggest a new insurance product. The claim administration department may recommend upgrading outdated equipment to enable more effective claim processing. The investment department may request a new decision support computer system to generate a higher return on investments. Or the company president may decide that the organization is outgrowing its office space and propose investing in additional space or extensive remodeling.

Classifying Each Proposal

In compiling the master budget, a company determines the resources (funds, personnel, etc.) it can devote to proposed capital investments. Because there are often multiple functional areas requesting capital resources, it is helpful to classify each capital expenditure proposal so that managers can better analyze each one and gauge its potential usefulness to the firm. Specific classifications can vary between companies, but some typical classifications are new projects, replacement investments, cost reduction programs, and safety and regulatory expenditures:

- *New projects* include new assets or new uses for existing assets. Examples of this category are new insurance products or the purchase of another company or one or more of its product lines.

- *Replacements* include new assets that will be used to replace old or defective assets. An example is replacing an outdated mainframe computer with a new computer system.

- *Cost reduction* includes assets that reduce the cost of operations. An example is purchasing a printer to handle in-house print jobs that previously had been outsourced.

- *Safety and regulatory expenditures* address employee safety concerns or are required by legal regulations. An example is the purchase of a new fire alarm and sprinkler system for an office building.

Estimating Cash Flows

Once capital expenditure ideas have been generated and classified, the next step is to estimate the cash flows of each project. Estimating each project's cash flows quantifies its benefits and drawbacks and facilitates the evaluation of each project. Capital projects have cash outflows and cash inflows. Management should consider only ***incremental cash flows,*** which are the additional costs or revenues that result from a capital project. Suppose an insurer's salary expenses are $1,000,000 before undertaking a capital budget. The insurer estimates that its salary expenses will be $1,200,000 after the project. In this case, the incremental cash outflow associated with this project is $200,000.

Almost all capital expenditures begin with an initial investment in equipment or other assets. In subsequent years, some capital projects will require cash outflows for repairs and maintenance or incremental operating costs. The cash inflows of a capital expenditure are usually in the form of incremental revenues or a reduction in costs. For capital budgeting purposes, a reduction in costs is equivalent to an increase in revenues. The cash inflows can be *even,* in which case the same inflow is expected during each year of the asset's useful life, as with an annuity, or *uneven,* in which case the amount of the inflow varies each year. In the case of a replacement proposal, the salvage value of an old or terminated asset is treated as a cash inflow. ***Salvage value*** is the residual value or selling price of an asset at the end of its useful life. Keep in mind that the projected cash flows are estimates and are therefore arbitrary by nature. The accuracy of the capital project evaluation techniques will depend on the accuracy of the cash flow estimates.

Evaluating and Selecting Proposals

Once the relevant cash flows of each proposed capital investment have been calculated, the final step in capital budgeting is to evaluate the proposals and decide which, if any, to accept and implement. Companies can use a number of evaluation methods, four of which are described later in this section. Each method attempts to quantify the value of each proposed investment, thus making it easier to compare proposals with each other or with some predefined decision-making benchmark.

Most proposed investments are accepted or rejected based on their financial attributes. However, some proposals are accepted even if their profit evaluations suggest unacceptability. For example, companies implement safety and regulatory projects, despite their lack of profitability, because they are required by law. On the other hand, a company is not required to approve all proposed capital investments that receive a favorable evaluation. For example, a certain proposal may not fit the company's strategic goals, or the company may not have the resources to undertake all acceptable proposals. In this situation, known as *capital rationing,* the company ranks all proposals and accepts only those with the highest rankings. We discuss capital rationing and ranking proposals later in this section.

A manager analyzing the benefits and drawbacks of a particular capital expenditure should consider other possible outcomes of the project, asking questions such as the following:

- Will the project reduce or offset the company's tax liability?
- How will depreciation of a capital investment, such as a building, affect the company's financial statements?

- Is there a required rate of return on the investment?
- Does the expenditure and its risk level fit in with corporate strategy and goals?
- Is the expenditure subject to any regulatory restrictions?
- How will the operations of each department be affected by the expenditure?

The time value of money is critical to capital budgeting decisions because such decisions require the company to invest money in the present so it can generate more money in the future. As we discussed in Chapter 14, the value of one dollar earned today is different from that of one dollar earned three years from today. Analysts should also be aware of the opportunity cost of capital budgeting decisions; by committing money today, the company is giving up the opportunity to make other investments in the future.

Selecting the Appropriate Discount Rate

Because of the importance of the time value of money, some capital budgeting methods involve discounted cash flows. For example, the *net present value method* states all of a proposed investment's cash flows in terms of their present value and applies that discount rate. It is therefore vital that the company choose an appropriate rate to discount these cash flows to their present value and apply that rate consistently to each project. For example, the discount rate used in capital budgeting may represent a company's cost of capital.

Cost of Capital

In the business world, there is no free money. All financing carries a price. The "price" that a company pays collectively for its various sources of financing is called its ***cost of capital.*** The cost of capital, expressed in percentage terms, is not simply the interest rate that is charged on borrowed funds. It is the rate of return the company could earn if it chose a different investment with equivalent risk. One way to determine the cost of capital is to find the *weighted average* cost of all sources of debt capital (primarily bank loans and bond issues) and equity capital (common stock, preferred stock, and retained earnings). Each component's costs are measured in terms of interest payments, bond amortizations, dividend payments, and the opportunity cost of retained earnings (or surplus).

A complete analysis of the way a company derives its cost of capital is beyond the scope of this text, but a simple example using the Main Line Life and Health Insurance Company, a stock insurer, should help illustrate the concept. Assume that 60 percent of Main Line's total capital comes from surplus and 40 percent comes from a new issue of common stock. Moreover, assume that the financial managers of Main Line have calculated the cost of surplus to be 13 percent and the cost of the common stock issue to be 18 percent. The company's cost of capital is the weighted average of these two sources of financing, calculated as follows:

Type of Financing	(a) Cost of Financing	(b) Weight	(a × b) Weighted-Average Cost of Capital
Surplus	13%	60%	7.8%
Common stock	18%	40%	7.2%
		100%	15.0%

The weighted average of Main Line's cost of capital is 15 percent. Therefore, an appropriate discount rate for Main Line to use when applying each capital budgeting method is 15 percent.

Capital Budgeting Methods

Capital budgeting methods serve a *screening* function. That is, they evaluate proposed capital investments to determine which ones meet a minimum standard of financial acceptability. In this section we discuss four methods of analyzing the worthiness of a capital investment: (1) payback, (2) discounted payback, (3) net present value, and (4) internal rate of return. In Chapter 19, we discuss return on investment and residual income, which also may be used to evaluate the worthiness of a capital investment. Admittedly, capital budgeting is imprecise because the process requires an analyst to estimate expected cash inflows and outflows. Therefore, analysts often use more than one capital budgeting method to minimize the chance of making incorrect decisions about investment proposals. Analysts apply company-defined *decision rules* to the results of one or more of these analyses to decide whether to accept or reject a particular capital investment proposal. Instead of emphasizing the mathematical calculations inherent in these methods, the following sections highlight the decision rules that a company may use and the way these methods assist in decision making.

Payback Method

The basic ***payback method*** is a capital budgeting technique that calculates how long it will take a company to recover its investment. This recovery time is called the *payback period.* The payback method compares the initial investment with the additional cash expected to come into the company as a result of the investment. If the annual revenues or savings are expected to remain constant each year, the payback method calculation is relatively simple: divide the actual cost of the expenditure under consideration by the annual cash inflow. To illustrate, assume that the Main Line Life and Health Insurance Company is considering the purchase of 20 new laser printers at a cost of $75,000 (a cash outflow). The new printers will enable Main Line to print all of its forms in-house. Under the current system, Main Line spends $25,000 a year to have forms printed by a local printing company. Thus, by purchasing the new printers, Main Line should save $25,000 a year (a cash inflow).* To compute the payback period, we divide the investment by the annual inflow and find that Main Line's payback period is three years ($75,000 ÷ $25,000). If Main Line's decision rule is to accept all proposed capital investments with payback periods of four years or less, then it would accept this proposal. If the decision rule requires a payback period of less than three years, then Main Line would reject the proposal.

The main benefit of the payback method is its simplicity. Also, the payback method suggests a degree of risk in the proposed investment: a longer payback period indicates a greater risk because the initial investment may not be recovered. The basic payback method has several drawbacks, however. First, it does not measure profitability, as no information is provided about the rate of return on the investment. Second, the payback method ignores the time value of money. Third, the payback method ignores all cash inflows and outflows that occur after the payback period. For example, the new printers may reduce Main Line's expenses by $25,000 for each of the first three years (the payback period), but what about cash flows in the fourth and succeeding years? Because of these limitations, many companies supplement the payback method with another analysis method. Many companies use payback only as an initial screening device, because the payback period alone is not enough justification for undertaking a proposed capital expenditure.

Discounted Payback Method

Similar to the payback method is the discounted payback method, which overcomes one drawback of the payback method by taking into account the time value of money. The ***discounted payback method*** calculates, in terms of discounted dollars, how long it will take a company to recover its initial investment. For example, assume again that the Main Line Life and Health Insurance Company is considering the purchase of the 20 printers at an initial cost of $75,000, and that the savings (cash inflow) provided by the

---

* In reality, the $25,000 cash inflow figure would change from year to year as the cost of external printing increases or decreases and as the volume of printing increases or decreases. For simplicity, we have ignored these factors.

printers will be $25,000 per year. Assume the company selects a 15 percent discount rate based on its cost of capital as calculated earlier. The cash inflows for each year, discounted to their present value, are as follows:

Year	Cash Inflow	Discounted Cash Inflow (15 %)	Running Total
Year 1	25,000	$21,750	$21,750
Year 2	25,000	18,900	$40,650
Year 3	25,000	16,450	$57,100
Year 4	25,000	14,300	$71,400
Year 5	25,000	12,425	$83,825
		$83,825	

According to the discounted payback method, Main Line recovers only $57,100 of its investment after Year 3 and $71,400 after Year 4. It is not until Year 5 that Main Line recovers the entire $75,000 initial investment. Therefore, consideration of only discounted cash flows has increased the payback period to more than 4 years (actually 4.29 years).* Main Line would not approve this proposal if its decision rule is to accept all projects with payback periods of 4 years or less. Because it considers the time value of money, the discounted payback method is superior to the payback method. However, the discounted payback method also fails to measure profitability and ignores cash flows beyond the payback period.

Net Present Value Method

A third method of evaluating proposed capital expenditures is the ***net present value (NPV) method,*** which evaluates a proposal based on its *net present value (NPV),* or the difference between the present value of a project's cash inflows (revenues, cost savings, and interest income) and the present value of its cash outflows (investment cost and expenses). As you can tell from its name, an obvious benefit of the NPV method is that it takes into account the time value of money. The NPV calculation involves determining the proposed capital investment's useful life and selecting an appropriate discount rate from present value interest tables. Again, an appropriate discount rate is the company's cost of capital. The general decision rule for approving a proposal according to the net present value method is that the present value of cash inflows must exceed the present value of the investment itself. In other words, the net present value *must be greater*

* In Year 5, Main Line needs $3,600 ($75,000 – $71,400), and it receives $12,425. Main Line will earn the $3,600 in .29 of a year, calculated as $3,600 ÷ $12,425. Thus, the entire payback period is 4.29 years.

than zero. Companies may establish other specific decision rules, such as the net present value must be greater than or equal to $100, $500, or $1,000, for a proposal to be acceptable.

Assuming a five-year useful life and a 15 percent discount rate, the net present value for Main Line's printer proposal is $8,825, which is calculated as follows:

	Initial Cash Outflow	
Year 0	(75,000)	
	Cash Inflow	**Discounted Cash Inflow (15%)**
Year 1	$25,000	$21,750
Year 2	$25,000	18,900
Year 3	$25,000	16,450
Year 4	$25,000	14,300
Year 5	$25,000	12,425
		$83,825

Net Present Value = PV of Cash Inflows – PV of Cash Outflows
Net Present Value = $83,825 – $75,000
Net Present Value = $8,825

If we assume that Main Line's decision rule is to accept all capital proposals with a net present value greater than zero, then the printer proposal is acceptable.

Net present value has many advantages. It considers profitability, because the net present value can be thought of as additional wealth to the firm. NPV also takes into account the time value of money, and it considers all cash flows during a capital investment's useful life, including those after the payback period. The drawbacks of NPV are that it requires the firm to determine its cost of capital, which is a complex process, and that a direct NPV comparison of two or more capital proposals is misleading unless the proposals require equivalent amounts of capital investment.

Internal Rate of Return Method

Another useful, although complex, evaluation method is the internal rate of return. Sometimes called the *time-adjusted rate of return method,* the ***internal rate of return (IRR) method*** determines the discount rate at which the net present value of the capital investment equals zero. The internal rate of return results from analyzing the proposed investment, the yearly cash inflows resulting from the investment, and an interest factor to calculate the present value of the

Figure 17-18. Summary of capital budgeting methods for Main Line Life and Health Insurance Company's capital project proposal.

Capital Budgeting Method	Result	Accept/Reject*
Payback	3.0 years	Accept
Discounted payback	4.29 years	Reject
Net present value	$8,825	Accept
Internal rate of return	19.87%	Accept

* Assumes that (1) acceptable payback period is 4 years or less, (2) acceptable net present value is greater than 0, and (3) the cost of capital is 15 percent

cash inflows. The internal rate of return for Main Line's printer proposal, assuming a useful life of five years, is 19.87 percent.*

The decision rule for the internal rate of return method involves comparing the company's cost of capital to the proposed investment's internal rate of return. If the internal rate of return exceeds the cost of capital, then the investment's benefits should exceed its costs, and the proposal should be accepted. Otherwise, the proposal should be rejected. Main Line's printer project is acceptable because the internal rate of return of 19.87 percent exceeds the company's cost of capital of 15 percent. If Main Line compares this capital investment with another, the investment with the *higher* internal rate of return should be accepted.

Figure 17-18 summarizes the four capital budgeting methods we discussed and the evaluation each one provided for Main Line's proposed capital investment.

Factors Affecting Capital Budgeting Decisions

As you can see from Figure 17-18, different capital budgeting methods may yield conflicting evaluations of the same proposal. For example, the decision rule for the discounted payback period indicates that the company should reject the proposal, while the other three methods indicate acceptance. Therefore, companies consider other factors when deciding which capital investment proposals to accept and reject. We describe some of these factors next.

* To find an approximate internal rate of return (IRR), divide the amount of the investment by the annual net cash inflows to achieve a present value interest factor. In our example, $75,000 investment ÷ $25,000 annual inflows = 3.0. Next, from a table of present value interest factors for an annuity (*PVIFA*), find the discount rate, at the appropriate number of periods, that is closest to 3.0. From the *PVIFA* table in the appendix, you will see that, at five periods (for a five-year useful life), the factor closest to 3.0 is between 19 percent and 20 percent. Thus, we can say that the IRR of the Main Line proposal is between 19 and 20 percent. Calculating an exact IRR requires a mathematical technique known as interpolation, which is outside the scope of this text.

Investing Decisions and Financing Decisions

A golden rule of capital budgeting is that investing decisions (what to purchase) should be kept separate from financing decisions (how to purchase). Combining the two can lead to inaccurate capital budgeting evaluations. For example, assume that a company with a 15 percent cost of capital uses the net present value method to evaluate a capital investment that will be financed through a long-term bank loan carrying an interest rate of 10 percent. It might seem logical for the company to set the discount rate for the NPV calculation equal to the interest rate on the loan: 10 percent. This would be inappropriate, however, because it could lead the company to accept a proposal whose return is less than the *entire company's* cost of capital, even if the return may be greater than the cost of a *specific form* of financing, such as the 10 percent bank loan.

Mutually Exclusive Alternatives

When a company considers multiple capital investment proposals, it must be aware of whether the proposals are independent or mutually exclusive. ***Independent proposals*** have cash flows that are unrelated. The acceptance of one independent proposal does not automatically eliminate any others. ***Mutually exclusive proposals*** involve investment choices that perform essentially the same function. The acceptance of one proposal automatically eliminates all others from consideration. A company can accept any number of independent proposals but only one in a group of mutually exclusive proposals. For example, if a U.S. insurer wished to move its home office to Atlanta, Charlotte, or Miami, the acceptance of one of these mutually exclusive alternatives automatically eliminates the other two.

Capital Rationing

A company may find that it has more acceptable capital proposals than it has available resources to fund them all. In such situations, the company chooses which proposals to accept and which to reject. In this case, the company ranks the proposals according to their expected return. The process of allocating limited resources to ranked capital investment proposals is known as ***capital rationing.*** There are several ways to rank all acceptable proposals. If the firm relies on the internal rate of return to screen capital proposals, it ranks them by their expected IRR. For example, assume that a company has four acceptable capital proposals with internal rates of return as follows:

Proposal	Internal Rate of Return	Rank
A	16%	3
B	15%	4
C	22%	1
D	18%	2

If this company has resources to accept only two proposals, it should choose Proposals C and D because they have the highest internal rates of return.

Unlike IRR, the net present value method does not allow for direct comparison of proposed capital investments, unless they require an equal amount of investment. Companies that use the net present value method compute a profitability index in order to rank their proposals. The ***profitability index (PI)*** is the ratio of the present value of future cash flows to the amount of investment, or

$$\text{Profitability Index} = \frac{\text{Present Value of Future Cash Flows}}{\text{Investment}}$$

With an initial investment of $75,000 and a present value of future cash flows of $80,000, Main Line's printer investment has a profitability index of 1.07. A profitability index of 1.0 means that the investment's net present value is zero. Thus, projects with a PI of less than 1.0 should always be rejected. If several investments are being considered, the one with the highest profitability index should receive the highest ranking, with other investments ranked accordingly.

Sensitivity Analysis

To this point in our discussion of capital budgeting, we have made decisions assuming perfect knowledge of the future. We do not have such knowledge of the future, of course. Any number of assumptions could be wrong. In the Main Line example, the printers could provide only $15,000 of cash inflows per year instead of $25,000, or the printers could be usable for only four years instead of five. If either or both happened, would this capital investment proposal still be acceptable?

Managers apply sensitivity analysis to help answer this type of question. ***Sensitivity analysis*** tests the amount of latitude that is built into the estimates a company makes during capital budgeting. Sensitivity analysis determines "worst-case" scenarios by calculating how far reality can vary from estimates without invalidating the accept/reject screening decision. For example, sensitivity analysis reveals that Main Line must receive cash inflows of *at least* $22,375 per year for five years for the proposal to "break even."* Main Line's managers should also perform a similar calculation to determine the cushion in the estimate of the printers' useful life. In light of the new information, the managers should assess the likelihood that the proposal will actually meet the company's investment thresholds.

* The task is to determine the break-even amount of cash flows at a minimum rate of 15 percent and five years. Divide the cost of the investment by the present value interest factor at 15 percent and five years: $75,000 ÷ 3.352 (PVIFA for 15% and 5 years) = $22,375.

Conclusion

This chapter introduced various topics in the important management accounting concept of budgeting. In the next chapter, we discuss responsibility accounting and the ways insurers monitor and evaluate the performance of employees. As you will see, budgets are one of the most important tools in a responsibility accounting system.

Key Terms and Concepts

budgeting
budget
master budget
top-down budgeting
bottom-up budgeting
zero-based budgeting (ZBB)
operational budget
cash budgets
capital expenditure budgets
capital budgeting
supporting budgets
static budget
flexible budget
short-term budget
long-term budget
rolling budget
period budget
operational budgeting
revenue budget
sales budget
investment budget
sales forecast
investment forecast
expected value
expense budget
benefits budget
sales expense budget
general and administrative expense budget
allowable expenses
pro forma statement of operations
cash budgeting
cash receipts budget
cash disbursements budget
minimum cash balance
line of credit
pro forma statement of cash flows
pro forma balance sheet
incremental cash flows
salvage value
cost of capital
payback method
discounted payback method
net present value (NPV) method
internal rate of return (IRR) method
independent proposals
mutually exclusive proposals
capital rationing
profitability index (PI)
sensitivity analysis

CHAPTER 18

Responsibility Accounting

Learning Objectives

After studying this chapter, you should be able to

- Differentiate among the terms *responsibility accounting, responsibility center,* and *responsibility manager*
- Identify the distinguishing features of a cost center, profit center, and investment center
- Compare the performance of different profit centers using segment reporting
- Measure an investment center's performance using the return on investment (ROI) method and the residual income (RI) method
- Describe variance analysis and how it is applied in responsibility reports that detail budget variances
- Discuss the factors that should be considered when evaluating a responsibility center's performance
- Describe three ways life and health insurance companies allocate investment income to the investment centers that earn the income

Chapter Outline

Goal Congruence

Management by Objectives

Effectiveness vs. Efficiency

Responsibility Centers

Cost Centers

Profit Centers

Investment Centers

Performance Measurement and Evaluation

Performance Evaluation Issues

Problems with Evaluation Criteria

Cost Allocation

Revenue Allocation

Transfer Pricing

As we have noted in earlier chapters, management accounting information is most useful for three management functions: planning, organizing, and controlling. During the planning phase, a company sets goals and uses budgets to make decisions on how best to achieve those goals. Then, by comparing actual results to its budgets, the company is able to control operations. If performance is better than expected, management offers recognition and reward to those employees responsible. Likewise, management can identify the individuals responsible for poor performance and take steps to improve their performance. The easier it is for management to identify its weak and strong areas and those individuals responsible for performance, the better that management is able to control operations.

In this chapter, we continue our discussion of management control, and we also explore the organizing function, which involves arranging the company's human, economic, and physical resources so that the company's plans can be carried out. A central activity of organizing is assigning responsibility for specified operations to company individuals. In management terminology, *responsibility* is an employee's obligation to perform assigned duties. If employees are to assume responsibility, then a company should be organized in such a way as to enable all employees to understand precisely their areas of responsibility.

Responsibility accounting, sometimes called *profitability* accounting, is a people-oriented system of policies and procedures that allows for revenues and costs to be assigned to an individual employee or to the organizational level that is accountable for them. Responsibility accounting is used to prepare and monitor budgets and to analyze performance. However, responsibility accounting is not a replacement for financial accounting. Financial accounting is still necessary to record transactions and prepare financial statements that comply with accounting principles and standards. Through responsibility accounting, a company uses its financial data to report internally on the status of operations and on specific areas of managerial responsibility.

In responsibility accounting, the person who has the most influence over an area—the manager of a department, function, activity, or product—is held accountable for the operations of that area. When a manager has control of, and thus responsibility for, an organizational unit of the company's business, the unit is commonly known as a ***responsibility center.*** The manager of a responsibility center, called a ***responsibility manager,*** is evaluated according to the responsibility center's performance. The responsibility manager should have (1) goals that are consistent with the company's goals, (2) a clear understanding of the responsibility center's goals, and (3) the necessary authority to establish formal reporting and budgeting control over the resources required to meet those goals. By assigning responsibility to specific individuals, an insurer's top management has a tool for controlling revenues and costs and an objective means of evaluating its managers and supervisors. The basic tenet of responsibility accounting is that responsibility managers should be held accountable for only the costs and revenues over which they have direct control. Keep this in mind as you read this chapter.

In discussing responsibility accounting, we first define *goal congruence.* Then we categorize the three types of responsibility centers, and we describe methods of measuring and evaluating the performance of responsibility centers and responsibility managers. Last, we discuss various factors that can impact performance evaluations.

Goal Congruence

Managers and other employees have many motivations. Among these motivations are the achievement of personal goals such as salary increases, promotions, and self-actualization. Businesses are also motivated to achieve goals, such as increased revenues, reduced expenses, and growth. Successful life and health insurance companies are those that create an operational condition called ***goal congruence,*** in which the goals of a company and the goals of its managers are mutually supportive. When the business goals of a company are congruent with the personal goals of the company's managers, the managers are motivated to make decisions that are in the best interest of the company. The managers can achieve their own goals by helping the company achieve its goals. ***Goal incongruence*** occurs when managers' goals and the company's goals are in conflict, when they are not mutually achievable. For example, if an underwriting department manager allows significant increases in the amounts his or her staff is spending on travel at a time when the company's senior management is encouraging departments to limit expenses, the effect is goal incongruence. Responsibility accounting encourages goal congruence by making managers accountable only for those operations they can control. Each manager can then be rewarded for the achievements over which he or she has direct control. Responsibility managers believe that their company's responsibility accounting system is fair and that it will accurately interpret their performance. Likewise, the evaluation system is based on criteria that are under the managers' control.

Management by Objectives

Responsibility managers manage with the intention of achieving stated goals, a process known as *management by objectives (MBO).* A typical goal for a responsibility manager is to meet a budget. Management by objectives also includes the establishment and achievement of nonmonetary goals, such as improved customer service or more favorable responses on an opinion survey of the responsibility center's employees. In successful MBO programs, senior management and responsibility managers collaborate on developing objectives, and these objectives support the company's overall objectives. Objectives that are devised by a third party and then imposed on the responsibility manager have a lesser chance of being realized.

When the objectives of responsibility managers conflict, the situation can interfere with goal congruence. An insurer's senior management would typically review such conflict to reach a compromise plan. For instance, one goal of an insurer's marketing development manager may be to reach a certain level of sales for a new insurance product. However, the actuarial and underwriting departments may argue that the marketing manager's objective conflicts with the company's profit objectives because of high first-year expenses. In this case, the insurer's management would analyze the effects of increased sales on profit and recommend a course of action.

Effectiveness vs. Efficiency

All responsibility centers share a common goal: to be both effective and efficient. ***Effectiveness*** (doing the right things) for a responsibility center is the extent to which it is able to establish and achieve appropriate objectives. The ***efficiency*** (doing things right) of a responsibility center is the extent to which it is able to achieve objectives with a minimum of waste.[1] While effectiveness generally fosters goal congruence, efficiency, on its own, does not. In other words, it is possible to have an efficient responsibility center whose goals do not support the company's goals. For example, an investment department that executes investment transactions on time and at a low cost is *efficient.* But if the investments that the department makes result in a low investment return for the company, the department has not met its goal of maximizing investment return and is therefore not *effective.* The responsibility accounting system should incorporate methods—such as comparing actual results to budgets—of simultaneously measuring both effectiveness and efficiency. If the responsibility accounting system offers fair evaluation criteria, provides practical feedback, and strives for both effectiveness and efficiency, then it promotes goal congruence. The first step in implementing such a responsibility accounting system is to establish responsibility centers.

Responsibility Centers

A responsibility center defines the sphere of its manager's responsibility. In other words, only those items, such as investments, revenues, and costs that can be directly attributable to a responsibility center are the responsibility of that center's manager. A responsibility center can be a department, division, line of business, or any other business segment. To establish and evaluate distinct responsibility centers, a company must distinguish controllable costs from noncontrollable costs and direct costs from indirect costs. Remember from Chapter 16 that a controllable cost is a cost over which a particular manager or level of management has power and influence. On the other hand, a cost over which a particular manager or level of management has no power or influence is considered a noncontrollable cost. A direct cost is incurred for or physically traceable to one specific product, line of business, department, or other cost object. However, a cost that is not incurred for or cannot be physically traceable to one specific product, line of business, department, or other cost object is considered an indirect cost. For example, the salary of a responsibility manager is a direct cost of that center. However, depreciation on an insurer's home office facility is an indirect cost, and the same responsibility manager should not be held accountable for it.

By designating costs as controllable or noncontrollable and direct or indirect, senior management can evaluate a responsibility center fairly by considering only those costs that are directly traceable to the center and under the control of the manager. As we describe later in this chapter, some companies allocate indirect costs to specific responsibility centers. But in evaluating responsibility centers, management focuses on the direct costs charged to each responsibility center. Responsibility centers typically are divided into three types: cost centers, profit centers, and investment centers. We differentiate among these centers based on the extent of operational control accorded to the manager. The degree of control ranges from lowest in a cost center to highest in an investment center.

Cost Centers

We first described cost centers in our discussion of cost accounting in Chapter 16. Recall that the manager of a cost center has control only over the costs incurred therein. Cost centers do not directly generate revenues or control the assets used to earn a profit. A cost center manager's main objective is to minimize costs while maintaining effective and efficient operations. The human resources department and the accounting department in a life and health insurance company are examples of cost centers.

Profit Centers

In a ***profit center,*** a manager is responsible for both costs and revenues. As its name implies, a profit center is evaluated based on its profitability, that is, the extent to which its revenues exceed its expenses. In an insurance company, lines of business typically are regarded as profit centers. For example, a company's ordinary life insurance line and its group life insurance line would be considered profit centers. The manager of a profit center has control over most aspects of the center except decisions regarding the company's assets invested in the center.

Investment Centers

In an ***investment center,*** a responsibility manager has control over costs, revenues, and the assets or investment funds used to meet operating needs. An investment center has the authority to make capital management decisions, to purchase new fixed assets, and to supply the resources necessary to meet the operating needs of all the company's or the investment center's functional areas. The corporate headquarters for a life and health insurance company is generally considered an investment center. If a company has a major division that has control over investment in the division's physical plant and equipment and all its costs, revenues, marketing and other functions, then that division is usually regarded as an investment center.

Figure 18-1 shows the organization of responsibility centers in one life and health insurance company. Assume that the managers of the individual insurance division and the group insurance division have control over the capital used by the respective divisions.

Note that in many companies, the distinction between a profit center and an investment center is blurred. Therefore, some companies use the term *profit center* to refer to both investment centers and profit centers. In this text, we maintain the distinction between the two.

Performance Measurement and Evaluation

Responsibility managers know what aspects of a company's operations they are responsible for and understand how their performance is judged. In theory, the characterization of success and failure is a two-step process: (1) measuring performance and (2) evaluating performance. *Measuring* performance involves quantifying the responsibility center's results. *Evaluating* performance involves assessing those results. Together, measuring and evaluating performance answer two questions: What did the manager or center achieve? and What do the achievements mean? Responsibility accounting requires the establishment of procedures for fairly and accurately measuring and evaluating the performance of responsibility centers and responsibility

Figure 18-1. Responsibility centers in a typical life and health insurance company.

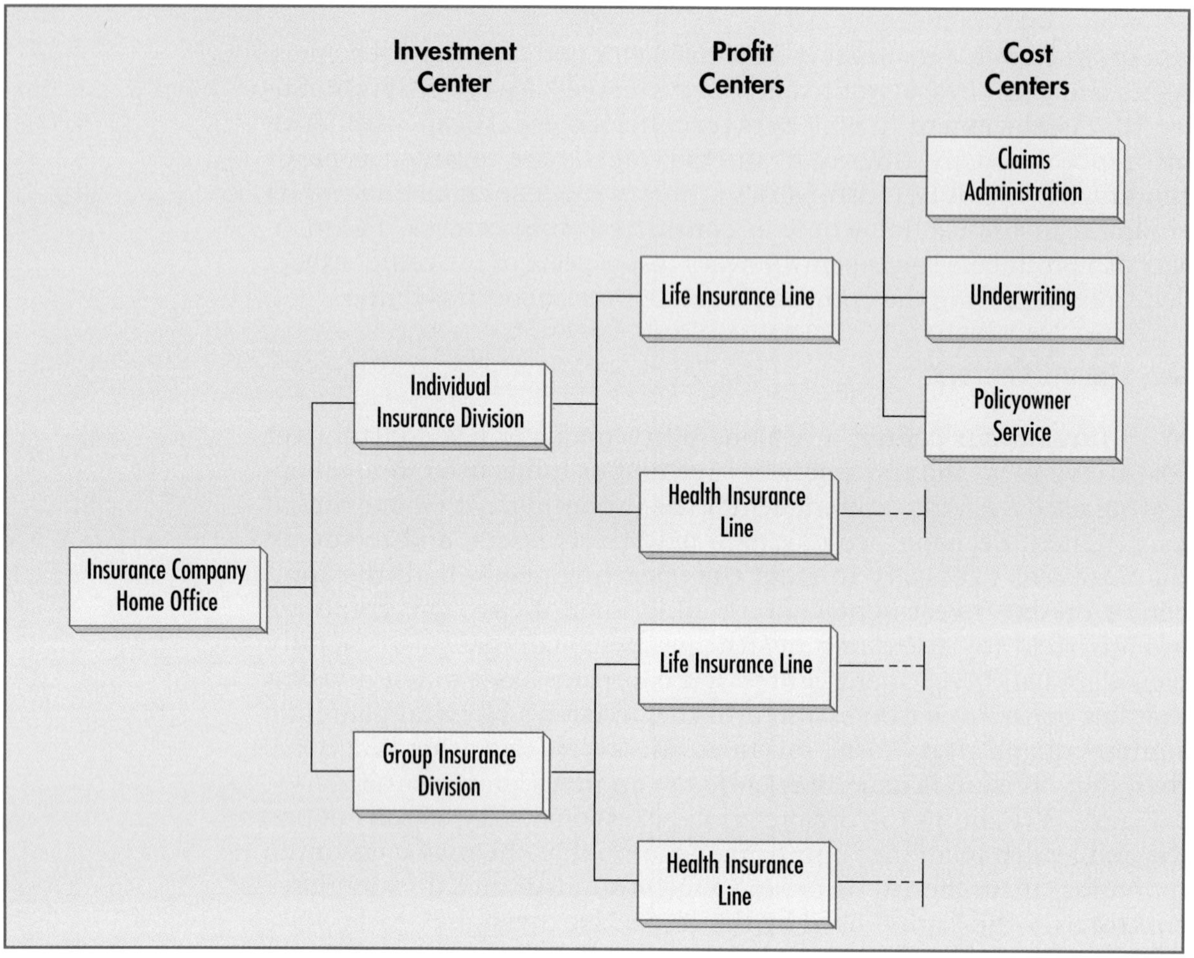

managers. Distinguishing between performance measurement and performance evaluation can be difficult. Measurement and evaluation are interwoven and not easily separated. Additionally, specific tools for performance measurement and evaluation differ for each type of responsibility center. However, one basic technique applicable to any responsibility center is *variance analysis.*

Variance Analysis

A basic concept of controlling in management accounting is using a standard or expected result as a benchmark against which actual performance is compared. An instance where the actual result differs from the standard or expectation is called a *variance.* We first introduced variances in our discussion of standard costs in Chapter 16. Budgets are often used to pinpoint variances. For example, if an amount budgeted for an item is $10,000, and the actual result for this item is $12,000, the budget variance is $2,000 over budget. Generally, positive variances, or variances in which actual amounts exceed expected amounts, are considered favorable for revenue items because the responsibility center earned more revenues than it anticipated. In contrast, positive variances are unfavorable for expense items, because the center incurred more expenses than anticipated. Similarly, negative variances, in which actual amounts are less than expected amounts, are usually considered favorable for expense items and unfavorable for revenue items.

When using budgets to study variances, some degree of variance is not unusual because budgets and actual experience are rarely the same. ***Variance analysis*** is the study of the difference between expected results and actual results. Variance analysis is helpful for monitoring and evaluating performance because variances quantify the unexpected results under the control of a responsibility manager. The management accounting concept of management by exception, which we introduced in Chapter 15, encompasses variance analysis. According to management by exception, a manager is alerted only when results or activities differ from expected norms by a certain minimum amount or percentage. An effective variance system focuses on matters that require management's attention. Budget variance analysis directs a manager's attention to the differences between budgeted and actual results. Management by exception allows a manager to isolate the problem areas, but it does not suggest solutions to problems. Most companies conduct monthly or quarterly reviews of their operating expenses and compare actual expenses to budgeted expenses. Large variances are a matter of concern, or at least interest, to upper management. Large variances can lead to revised budgets or changes in a company's operations. An important aspect of responsibility accounting is that managers explain budget variances that are under their control.

We can categorize variances as either *rate variances* or *usage variances.* The sum of the two equals the total variance. The ***rate variance*** is the difference between a product's actual rate (or unit cost or price) and the budgeted rate, multiplied by the actual number of units sold or processed. The ***usage variance*** is the difference between the actual quantities to be sold or processed and the budgeted quantities sold or processed, multiplied by the budgeted rate. Assume that the claims department's budget includes the following information on the cost of processing claims:

Budgeted rate (unit cost of processing one claim)	$ 40
Budgeted usage (number of claims processed)	× 1,200
Budgeted claim cost	$48,000

Suppose the actual results show that the cost center processed 1,300 claims at a total cost of $54,600. The total variance between budgeted cost and actual cost is $6,600 ($54,600 – $48,000). Figure 18-2 highlights the rate and usage components of this variance. Alternately,

Figure 18-2. Variance analysis of the cost of processing claims.

Actual rate (unit cost per claim)				$ 42
Actual usage (number of claims)				× 1,300
			(a)	$54,600
Budgeted rate				$ 40
Actual usage				× 1,300
			(b)	$52,000
Budgeted rate				$ 40
Budgeted usage				× 1,200
			(c)	$48,000
Rate variance	(a – b)	$2,600		Unfavorable
Usage variance	(b – c)	+ 4,000		Unfavorable
Total variance		$6,600		Unfavorable

you could obtain the $2,600 rate variance by subtracting the budgeted rate from the actual rate ($42 – $40), then multiplying the result by 1,300. This analysis indicates that not only did the center process more claims than expected, but the unit cost of processing each claim was more than budgeted. The result is both an unfavorable rate variance and an unfavorable usage variance, which lead to an unfavorable total variance of $6,600. In other words, the cost center spent more money to process claims than it had anticipated in its budget.

Variance analysis normally studies budgeted and actual results, but managers can also use it to compare other data. Managers can analyze variances between numbers from different areas or reporting periods by comparing a responsibility center's operating results from a current accounting period with those from a prior period. For example, a marketing manager may compare the level of new policies written during the current three-month period to new policies written during the previous three-month period or during the same three-month period the previous year. Another version of variance analysis compares actual costs with standard costs. Recall that standard costs are predetermined costs that are expected to be incurred for particular items during normal business operations.

Typical budgets that lend themselves to variance analysis are sales budgets, expense budgets, and investment budgets. An investment budget has many opportunities for variance analysis. An insurer may begin its investment planning process with a matrix of possible interest rates or an interest rate forecast. From this forecast and from a projection of the insurer's expected business, managers set out the insurer's investment objectives. At the end of the reporting period, managers can compare their interest rate forecast to actual interest rates. Also, top management uses variance analysis to gauge whether the investment department achieves the rate of return required to meet the insurer's current and future contractual obligations.

Responsibility Center Reports

The budget variances for each responsibility center are usually listed in a regular report that is used to measure and evaluate performance. This ***responsibility center report,*** or *responsibility report,* itemizes budgeted and actual amounts and the corresponding variance for each revenue or cost category. Responsibility reports include only revenue or cost items under the responsibility manager's sphere of control. Items that a manager cannot control are either omitted from the report or listed separately. For example, a cost center report lists only the costs that are under the control of its responsibility manager. Responsibility center reports serve two primary functions: (1) to assist senior management in controlling the performances of responsibility centers and (2) to enable a responsibility manager to uncover information about the center's operations, such as clues for improving cost control during the next operating period. A responsibility center report often contains segmented information about a high organizational level responsibility center and the lower-level centers contained within it. The performance reports for the lower managerial levels become a part of the performance reports for levels above.

To illustrate the association among responsibility accounting, responsibility centers, and responsibility reports, look at Figures 18-3 and 18-4. The Emerald Life and Health Insurance Company's organizational chart is shown in Figure 18-3. This company is organized by function. The policyowner service function has been condensed and highlighted, although you may assume that all other functional areas are organized similarly. Each unit of the organizational chart is a responsibility center that controls all units directly below it. The senior vice president of policyowner service is responsible for the East and the West divisions of policyowner service. The assistant vice president in charge of the West division of policyowner service is responsible for five departments in that division. Each policyowner service department manager is responsible for his own department. Figure 18-4 shows the monthly responsibility reports for the policyowner service centers at three different levels. Policyowner service is a cost center; therefore, this report includes only costs. The report examines cost items under each manager's control and compares budgeted amounts to actual amounts.

The report for each level of responsibility includes all the costs of the responsibility centers below it. For instance, the report for the manager of the West division reinstatements department contains a figure of $13,800 budgeted for salaries and bonuses. This amount is included in the $30,435 on the "Reinstatements" line of the West division assistant vice president's report, even though specific reference

Figure 18-3. The Emerald Life and Health Insurance Company's organizational chart highlighting the policyowner service function.

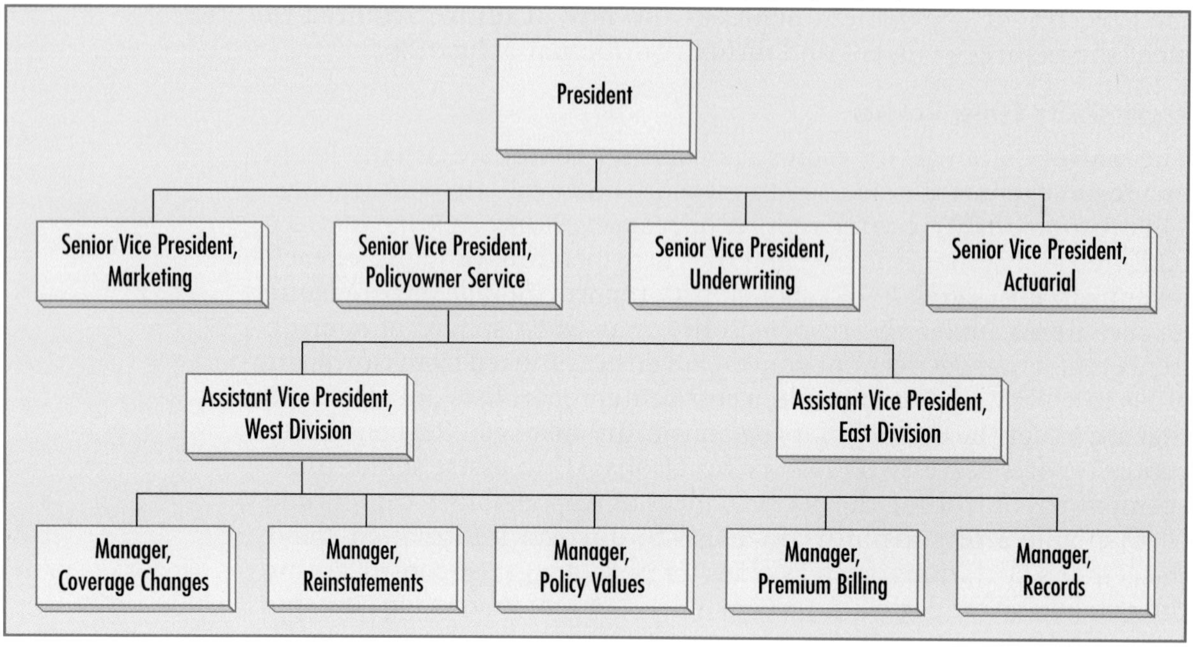

to salaries is lost. Similarly, the report for the senior vice president for policyowner service includes data from both the West and the East divisions. Because that information is condensed in the senior vice president's report, individual line items within each division are lost.

Note that the report for each level of management includes both the direct *and* indirect costs of all the managers. As the segments become more narrow, direct and indirect costs are allocated accordingly within each segment, just as they were in the segment above. However, a direct cost can be divided only so finely before arbitrary allocation becomes necessary. Thus, when one report is divided into smaller segmented reports, certain direct fixed costs from the larger statement can become indirect fixed costs on a smaller statement. Therefore, the total cost attributable to one manager is *greater* than the sum of the direct costs attributable to the individual departments under that manager's supervision.

For example, the report for the assistant vice president in charge of the West division in Figure 18-4 includes the direct costs incurred by the five departments within the West division, and it also includes $16,000 in budgeted costs that are common to the five departments. A portion of this $16,000 could be the assistant vice president's salary. This point emphasizes the concept of controllable costs under responsibility accounting. The assistant vice president's salary is not under the control of any of the five policyowner service departments and, therefore, should not be the responsibility of any single department.

Figure 18-4. Monthly responsibility reports generated for Emerald's policyowner service cost centers.

Senior Vice President, Policyowner Service

	Actual	Budget	Variance
Direct divisional costs:			
West Division	$153,621	$153,935	$ 314
East Division	135,227	138,900	3,673
Total direct costs	$288,848	$292,835	$3,987
Indirect costs to divisions	90,213	87,450	(2,763)
Total costs	$379,061	$380,285	$1,224

Assistant Vice President, West Division

	Actual	Budget	Variance
Direct departmental costs:			
Coverage changes	$ 31,622	$ 33,425	$1,803
Reinstatements	34,530	30,435	(4,095)
Policy values	21,845	20,950	(895)
Premium billing	23,338	24,575	1,237
Records	26,436	28,550	2,114
Total direct costs	$137,771	$137,935	$ 164
Indirect costs to departments	15,850	16,000	150
Total costs	$153,621	$153,935	$ 314

Manager, West Division Reinstatements

	Actual	Budget	Variance
Direct costs:			
Salaries and bonuses	$14,250	$13,800	$ (450)
Office supplies	195	235	40
Toll-free phone lines	10,037	6,000	(4,037)
Policyowner service training	2,825	2,900	75
Total direct costs	$27,307	$22,935	$(4,372)
Indirect costs	7,223	7,500	277
Total costs	$34,530	$30,435	$(4,095)

Segment Reporting for Profit Centers

The evaluation of a profit center should be based on the profits earned by the center. One way to monitor profit centers is to prepare a statement of operations for each profit center. Preparing statements of this type is sometimes referred to as ***segment reporting.*** A segment report is required in certain situations, such as the *Analysis of Operations by Lines of Business* exhibit in the Annual Statement. Also, the Financial Accounting Standards Board (FASB) requires that the GAAP-based annual reports to the stockholders of large U.S. companies include revenues and operating profit for each significant business segment.

A segment report for a profit center details activity for each level of management, including condensed information from operations subordinate to each managerial level. Thus, as we move downward from one level to the next, we examine a smaller portion of the company. Like the segment report for cost centers, the segment report for profit centers separates direct costs from indirect costs for each level of management, and it allows top management to gain new insight by viewing the company's operations from many different angles. Unlike the segment report for cost centers, the segment report for profit centers includes revenues, and it further divides direct costs into fixed and variable components.

The segment report begins with the total revenues (premium income plus investment income) attributable to each level of profit center, then subtracts, in order, the variable costs and fixed costs incurred by each segment. After all variable costs have been assigned to the proper segments, we can calculate a contribution margin. Recall from Chapter 16 that the contribution margin for a product is the difference between its selling price and its variable costs. Similarly, the contribution margin for a segment is the difference between total revenues and total variable costs. Fixed costs are divided into direct fixed costs and indirect fixed costs to allow for the calculation of a segment margin for each segment of the company. A ***segment margin*** is the portion of the contribution margin that remains after a segment has covered its direct fixed costs. The segment margin is found by subtracting the segment's direct fixed costs from its contribution margin.

Figure 18-5 shows segmented statements of operations for the Responsible Life and Health Insurance Company. The entire company is first segmented by product line—group life insurance and ordinary life insurance. Then the ordinary life insurance line is segmented by product form—term life and whole life—sold within the line. Then the whole life product form is segmented by product item—traditional whole life and universal life. This report may show actual amounts, budgeted amounts, and variances. For simplicity, Figure 18-5 shows only actual amounts. As with a cost center report, the direct cost attributable to one manager is more than the sum of the direct costs of the responsibility centers under his supervision. For example, in the top segment—segmentation by product line—ordinary life insurance has $217,984 in direct fixed costs. But when this segment is divided into two product forms (whole life and term life), total direct costs from ordinary life are only $161,445. The difference of $56,539 appears under indirect fixed costs for ordinary life.

In segment reporting of profit centers, managers pay close attention to the segment margin, which is an indicator of a segment's profitability. A segment margin incorporates only those costs and revenues attributable to the segment. If the segment cannot cover its own costs, it is not profitable and should be investigated. Responsible's

Figure 18-5. Segmented report for the Responsible Life and Health Insurance Company's profit centers.

Product Line Segments of Responsible Life and Health Insurance Company	Total Company	Group Life	Ordinary Life
Total revenues	$6,949,176	$4,308,489	$2,640,687
Less: Variable costs:			
Variable policy benefits	3,207,111	2,151,479	1,055,632
Other variable costs	244,476	171,133	73,343
Total Variable Costs	$3,451,587	$2,322,612	$1,128,975
Contribution margin	$3,497,589	$1,985,877	$1,511,712
Less: Direct fixed costs	622,811	404,827	217,984
Product line segment margin	$2,874,778	$1,581,050	$1,293,728
Less: Indirect fixed costs	1,692,314		
Income Before Taxes	$1,182,464		

Product Form Segments of Ordinary Life Product Line	Ordinary Life	Term Life	Whole Life
Total revenues	$2,640,687	$422,510	$2,218,177
Less: Variable costs:			
Variable policy benefits	1,055,632	190,014	865,618
Other variable costs	73,343	24,203	49,140
Total Variable Costs	$1,128,975	$214,217	$ 914,758
Contribution margin	$1,511,712	$208,293	$1,303,419
Less: Direct fixed costs	161,445	32,289	129,156
Product form segment margin	$1,350,267	$176,004	$1,174,263
Less: Indirect fixed costs	56,539		
Product Line Segment Margin	$1,293,728		

Product Item Segments of Whole Life Product Form	Whole Life	Traditional Whole Life	Universal Life
Total revenues	$2,218,177	$1,774,542	$443,635
Less: Variable costs:			
Variable policy benefits	865,618	675,182	190,436
Other variable costs	49,140	34,398	14,742
Total Variable Costs	$ 914,758	$ 709,580	$205,178
Contribution margin	$1,303,419	$1,064,962	$238,457
Less: Direct fixed costs	87,872	73,813	14,059
Product item segment margin	$1,215,547	$ 991,149	$224,398
Less: Indirect fixed costs	41,284		
Product Form Segment Margin	$1,174,263		

segments presented in Figure 18-5 are profitable because the segment margin value for each segment is greater than zero. Segment margins and contribution margins are also useful for performance evaluation when put in ratio form. The ***segment margin ratio*** is the segment margin divided by the segment's total revenues, or

$$\textbf{Segment Margin Ratio} = \frac{\textbf{Segment Margin}}{\textbf{Segment's Total Revenues}}$$

This ratio measures a segment's efficiency of operating performance. The ***contribution margin ratio*** is the contribution margin divided by the segment's total revenues. This ratio is also a measure of segment performance:

$$\textbf{Contribution Margin Ratio} = \frac{\textbf{Contribution Margin}}{\textbf{Segment's Total Revenues}}$$

These two ratios allow for the comparison of segments of different sizes. For example, from Figure 18-5, the segment margin ratios and contribution margin ratios for Responsible's term life and whole life product forms are

	Segment Margin Ratio		**Contribution Margin Ratio**	
	Ratio	Percentage	Ratio	Percentage
Term Life	$\frac{\$\ 176{,}004}{\$\ 422{,}510}$	41.7%	$\frac{\$\ 208{,}293}{\$\ 422{,}510}$	49.3%
Whole Life	$\frac{\$1{,}174{,}263}{\$2{,}218{,}177}$	52.9%	$\frac{\$1{,}303{,}419}{\$2{,}218{,}177}$	58.8%

The whole life segment is considerably larger than the term life segment in absolute terms. In addition, the whole life segment has higher segment margin and contribution margin ratios and is, in relative terms, the more profitable segment.

Measuring Investment Center Performance

Unlike profit centers, investment centers are evaluated on the effective use of assets employed to earn a profit. The simplest measure of an investment center's performance is the amount of net income listed on the investment center's statement of operations. Traditional thinking indicates that the best-run segment of the company is the one with the highest net income, but this is not necessarily true. First, net income includes income tax expense, which violates the maxim of responsibility accounting: managers should be held accountable only for items they can control. Taxes are beyond the control of an investment center manager. Also, a small, well-managed investment center may have lower net income than a large, poorly managed investment center. We should not compare these two responsibility centers only by net income, because such a comparison does not adequately interpret their respective performances.* This idea is similar to using a straight contribution margin or segment margin to compare profit centers of different sizes. Comparing responsibility centers by the amount of income they generate should not be completely dismissed, however. Two common measures of investment center performance, *return on investment (ROI)* and *residual income (RI)*, both incorporate income. Therefore, income should be used in the process of performance measurement, although not as the sole basis.

Return on Investment. Return is a measure of financial performance. Generally, *return* is the profit made on an exchange of goods or services and is found by dividing the income generated by the capital invested to generate that income. In Chapter 19, we show how return on assets and return on equity measure the performance of an entire company. To measure the performance of an investment center, many companies use ***return on investment (ROI)***, which is the ratio of operating income to controllable investment. The ROI ratio is calculated as follows:

$$\text{Return on Investment (ROI)} = \frac{\text{Operating Income}}{\text{Controllable Investment}}$$

Operating income, which can also be called *net gain from operations before taxes*, is income before subtracting income taxes. ***Controllable investment*** includes all balance sheet items controlled by the manager of the investment center. Controllable investment is found by subtracting *controllable liabilities* from *controllable assets*. Sometimes insurers substitute *controllable surplus* for controllable investment in the denominator of the ROI ratio. The operating income used in the ROI calculation can be determined according to statutory accounting or GAAP. Generally, the higher the ROI, the better the performance of the investment center.

Return on investment is a better performance measure than net income because ROI overcomes the problem of comparing investment centers of different sizes. Like the segment margin ratio and the contribution margin ratio, ROI presents a result in percentage terms rather than in absolute terms. This is not to suggest that absolutes are unimportant. Absolute size is still a consideration in determining

* Some insurance companies compare investment centers' income before income taxes, although this still does not overcome the problem of comparing investment centers of different sizes.

an investment center's contribution to the company as a whole. However, a large absolute can unintentionally prejudice an evaluator against a smaller investment center. Calculating ROI for each investment center helps level the playing field.

Assume that Investment Center A of a company earns \$10,000,000 in operating income on controllable investments of \$60,000,000. The ROI for this investment center is 16.7 percent (\$10,000,000 ÷ \$60,000,000). Assume also that the company's Investment Center B earns \$1,000,000 in operating income on \$4,000,000 controllable investments. The ROI for Center B is 25 percent (\$1,000,000 ÷ \$4,000,000). Center B's operating income is only 1/10th that of A's (\$1,000,000 versus \$10,000,000), yet Center B achieves a much higher return on its available resources (25 percent versus 16.7 percent).

Besides being valuable as an evaluation tool, ROI can assist company executives in searching for ways to improve an investment center's performance. Such assistance arises when the ROI formula is expanded into a return on revenue component and an investment turnover component. ***Return on revenue*** measures management's ability to control operating expenses in relation to total revenues, which includes premium income and investment income. Return on revenue is found by dividing operating income by total revenue:

$$\textbf{Return on Revenue} = \frac{\textbf{Operating Income}}{\textbf{Total Revenue}}$$

Investment turnover is a measure of the revenue that can be generated for each dollar invested by the responsibility manager. We calculate investment turnover by dividing total revenue by controllable investment:

$$\textbf{Investment Turnover} = \frac{\textbf{Total Revenue}}{\textbf{Controllable Investment}}$$

The expanded ROI formula is the product of return on revenue and investment turnover:

$$\begin{aligned}\textbf{ROI} &= \textbf{Return on Revenue} \times \textbf{Investment Turnover}\\ &= \frac{\textbf{Operating Income}}{\textbf{Total Revenue}} \times \frac{\textbf{Total Revenue}}{\textbf{Controllable Investment}}\\ &= \frac{\textbf{Operating Income}}{\textbf{Controllable Investment}}\end{aligned}$$

Figure 18-6. Return on investment (ROI) comparison of the East and West divisions of the Sturdy Life and Health Insurance Company.

	East	West
Total revenues (a)	$5,950,000	$10,395,000
Less: Policy benefits	2,950,000	5,175,000
Less: Operating expenses	2,001,000	3,900,000
Operating income (b)	$ 999,000	$ 1,320,000
Controllable investment (c)	$4,250,000	$ 8,850,000
Return on revenue (b ÷ a)	16.8%	12.7%
Investment turnover (a ÷ c)	1.40	1.17
Return on investment (b ÷ c)	23.5%	14.9%

We can see from the expanded ROI that an increase in total revenue alone will not increase ROI because total revenue appears in both the numerator and denominator of the combined ratio.

Figure 18-6, which helps to clarify ROI, presents data for the East and West divisions of the Sturdy Life and Health Insurance Company. Each division is considered to be an investment center. Total revenue for the West division is nearly twice that of the East division, yet West's ROI is much lower than East's. Why? Notice that the East division earned a much better return on revenue than West, and East also had a significantly higher investment turnover. These two factors led to a much more impressive ROI, which, all other factors being equal, could earn East's manager a better performance evaluation than West's manager.

How can the West division attain an ROI similar to the East's? As stated earlier, an increase in total revenue alone is not the answer. Generally, ROI increases in one or more of the following ways: (1) by reducing expenses to increase operating income, (2) by reducing controllable investment, or (3) by increasing total revenue, accompanied by a proportionate increase in operating income. Figure 18-7 details these possibilities. Column 1 restates the current data for Sturdy's West division. The goal is to increase ROI from the current 14.9 percent to the 23.5 percent achieved by the East division. In Column 2, we reduce the West division's operating expenses from $3,900,000 to $3,140,000. This reduction in expenses increases operating income, which increases return on revenue and ultimately increases ROI to the target 23.5 percent. In Column 3, we retain the current levels of total revenue and operating income and reduce the investment from $8,850,000 to $5,620,000 to generate an ROI of 23.5 percent. And in Column 4, an increase in total revenue from $10,395,000 to $11,155,000, along with a corresponding increase in operating income, increases ROI to 23.5 percent. Notice that the increase in operating income (the differences between Column 1 and Columns 2 and 4) required to raise ROI to 23.5 percent is only $760,000. But the decrease in controllable investment (between Column 1 and Column 3) necessary to achieve the same ROI is $3,230,000. Because either of these changes results in the same improvement in ROI, it would seem to be much easier for the West division to improve its ROI by either decreasing expenses or increasing revenue (and operating income) by a relatively small amount than it would be to operate at the current level using far fewer invested assets. In fact, a current trend in all industries is to cut expenses, otherwise known as "trimming fat," to improve operating results.

Some insurers require that their investment centers earn a specified ROI. Incentive programs often encourage responsibility managers to strive for higher returns on investment. Managers of these investment centers consider a variety of actions that could increase ROI, such as expansion, capital improvements, and even the sale or discontinuance of a lagging business.

Figure 18-7. Three methods of increasing ROI.

	1 West	2 West	3 West	4 West
Total revenues (a)	$10,395,000	$10,395,000	$10,395,000	**$11,155,000**
Less: Policy benefits	5,175,000	5,175,000	5,175,000	5,175,000
Less: Operating expenses	3,900,000	**3,140,000**	3,900,000	3,900,000
Operating income (b)	$ 1,320,000	$ 2,080,000	$ 1,320,000	**$ 2,080,000**
Controllable investment (c)	$ 8,850,000	$ 8,850,000	**$ 5,620,000**	$ 8,850,000
Return on revenue (b ÷ a)	12.7%	20.0%	12.7%	18.6%
Investment turnover (a ÷ c)	1.17	1.17	1.85	1.26
Return on investment (b ÷ c)	14.9%	23.5%	23.5%	23.5%

Here, operating expenses are reduced to $3,140,000.

Here, controllable investment is reduced to $5,620,000.

Here, total revenues increase to $11,155,000. This increases operating income to $2,080,000.

Residual Income. Some companies measure the performance of investment centers using residual income. ***Residual income (RI),*** also called *economic value added (EVA),* is the amount of income an investment center earns above a certain minimum required rate of return on investment. As we learned in our discussion of capital budgeting in Chapter 17, the minimum required rate of return reflects the company's cost of capital, which is the future cost of raising capital through issues of stock and debt. To earn a positive return on investment and to foster growth, companies establish a required rate of return that is higher than their cost of capital. Residual income is found by subtracting the product of (1) an investment center's minimum required rate of return and (2) its controllable investment from the center's operating income. The minimum required rate of return times controllable investment is sometimes called the *capital charge.* The entire residual income calculation is

$$\text{Residual Income (RI)} = \text{Operating Income} - \left(\text{Minimum Required Rate of Return} \times \text{Controllable Investment}\right)$$

or

$$\text{RI} = \text{Operating Income} - \text{Capital Charge}$$

Assume that an investment center's operating income is $450,000, its controllable investment is $2,000,000, and its minimum required rate of return is 15 percent. We calculate the center's residual income as follows:

$$\text{Operating Income} - \text{Capital Charge } (\$2 \text{ million} \times 15\%) = \text{Residual Income}$$
$$\$450{,}000 - \$300{,}000 = \$150{,}000$$

The $150,000 in residual income represents the amount of income that the investment center manager is able to earn in excess of the firm's minimum required rate of return. When using residual income to compare two or more investment centers, the investment center with the largest amount of residual income generally has the best financial performance.

Return on Investment and Residual Income Compared. Goal congruence is a key consideration when a company implements a performance measurement system for its investment centers. Performance measurement systems can affect the behavior of managers and thereby affect whether the decisions they make are the right ones for the company. Ideally, the evaluation system draws managers toward goal congruence. The RI method of evaluation demands greater goal congruence from managers than ROI. Evaluation by ROI requires only that investment center managers achieve an acceptable return on investment, but residual income encourages managers to accept investment opportunities that have rates of return greater than the cost of capital. One drawback of ROI is that managers being evaluated by ROI may be reluctant to accept new investments that might lower their center's current ROI, even though the investment would be in the best interest of the entire company. This practice defies goal congruence.

Figure 18-8 reveals these behavioral characteristics of ROI and RI. Assume that an insurer requires its investment centers to achieve an ROI of 20 percent. The actual results of one investment center, as seen in the top portion of Figure 18-8, are $610,000 of operating income on $3,000,000 of controllable investment. As you can see, the ROI of 20.3 percent indicates that the center's manager has met the insurer's target ROI. Suppose that this manager has the opportunity to invest $500,000 in a project that will provide a 17 percent annual return or $85,000 (17 percent × $500,000). The insurer's minimum required rate of return is 15 percent.* It is in the insurer's best interest for the manager to invest in this project because the project's return exceeds the insurer's minimum required rate of return and the project will generate an additional $85,000 of operating income per year. However, this manager, whose performance evaluation is based on achieving an ROI of 20 percent, might be reluctant to make the investment because it would lower the investment center's ROI from 20.3 percent to 19.9 percent, as is exhibited in the middle section of Figure 18-8. This goal incongruence is induced by the use of ROI.

What if the investment center is evaluated by residual income? The bottom portion of Figure 18-8 demonstrates an acceptance of the project. As you can see, because the project's 17 percent return exceeds the company's 15 percent minimum required rate of return, the project will increase residual income from $160,000 to $170,000. This additional residual income will not only improve the investment center manager's evaluation, it is also in the best interest of the insurer. Thus, the use of residual income as a performance evaluation method induces goal congruence.

The major disadvantage of RI is that it is a dollar amount and not a ratio, so it tends to favor larger investment centers. Residual income can be converted to a ratio, however, to enable comparisons between investment centers of different sizes. A disadvantage of both ROI and RI is that, if emphasized too greatly, they can lead to decisions that improve short-term profits at the expense of long-term goals. As shown in Figure 18-7, ROI and RI can be improved by reducing expenses. It

* Note that the minimum required return will be different for different projects to reflect the level of risk presented by each project.

Figure 18-8. Comparison of ROI and RI.

Investment Center Evaluation by ROI	
Controllable investment (a)	$3,000,000
Operating income (b)	$ 610,000
ROI (b ÷ a)	20.3%

Investment Center and New Project Evaluation by ROI	**Investment Center**	**New Project**	**Total with New Project**
Controllable investment (a)	$3,000,000	$500,000	$3,500,000
Operating income (b)	$ 610,000	$ 85,000	$ 695,000
ROI (b ÷ a)	20.3%	17.0%	19.9%

Investment Center and New Project Evaluation by ROI	**Investment Center**	**New Project**	**Total with New Project**
Controllable investment	$3,000,000	$500,000	$3,500,000
Operating income (a)	$ 610,000	$ 85,000	$ 695,000
Capital charge, 15% (b)	450,000	75,000	525,000
Residual income (a – b)	$ 160,000	$ 10,000	$ 170,000

is therefore possible that a manager may forego some important expenditures for the sake of a higher ROI or RI. For example, an insurer's policyowner service division may need additional staff, but the division manager might not hire the necessary employees because the extra salary expense would decrease the division's ROI or RI. However, overworked employees could make mistakes and cause such delays in service that dissatisfied policyowners would allow their current policies to lapse, then purchase insurance from a competing insurance company. In the long run, this would be more costly to the insurer than hiring additional employees in the first place. Figure 18-9 lists the advantages and disadvantages of return on investment and residual income.

Performance Evaluation Issues

In the previous section, we examined the ways in which a company's top management monitors the performance of its various responsibility centers. In actual practice, however, achieving an accurate

Figure 18-9. Advantages and disadvantages of return on investment and residual income.

	Advantages	Disadvantages
ROI	• Is useful for comparing investment centers of different sizes • Assists managers in searching for ways to improve an investment center's performance • Encourages managers to seek the optimal level of investment given the profit potential of the investment center	• Misuse may encourage investment center managers to avoid investment opportunities that could benefit the company in the long run • Misuse can lead to decisions that improve short-run profits at the expense of long-run goals
RI	• Encourages investment center managers to make investment decisions that are in the best interest of the company	• Unless converted to a ratio, is not useful for comparing investment centers of different sizes • Misuse can lead to decisions that improve short-run profits at the expense of long-run goals

summary of performance is rarely so straightforward as preparing one report or calculating a simple ratio. For example, a premise of responsibility accounting is that responsibility managers should be accountable for only the costs that they directly control. But few costs are clearly the responsibility of only one individual. Most costs have varying degrees of controllability. The purpose of responsibility management is identifying the individual most directly responsible for incurring each cost. Several related issues must also be considered before giving a final "grade" to a responsibility center or its manager. Some of these issues are problems inherent in the evaluation process. Other issues may affect a responsibility center's performance, and, if not considered, may lead to an inaccurate appraisal of the center. In this section, we list potential problems surrounding performance evaluation criteria. Then we describe mitigating factors, such as cost allocation, revenue allocation, and transfer pricing, that can influence performance results.

Problems with Evaluation Criteria

The underlying motive behind responsibility accounting is measuring and evaluating the performance of responsibility centers and responsibility managers. These evaluations guide upper management in allocating future resources to each business segment, making decisions about segments, and compensating and promoting responsibility managers. But the evaluation criteria can be as important to the final evaluation as the actual performance that is being evaluated. Potential problem areas include (1) relying too heavily on variance analysis, (2) using only one evaluation criterion, (3) using inappropriate evaluation criteria, (4) setting unattainable goals, and (5) judging a responsibility manager's performance solely on the basis of the responsibility center's performance.

Overemphasis on Variance Analysis

Isolating budget variances is a simple and common method for evaluating performance. Variances, however, can be misleading. For example, when analyzing budget variances, management has a tendency to pay attention only to unfavorable variances. However, seemingly favorable variances should also receive close scrutiny to determine whether they are indeed favorable to the company. A department may have been budgeted $38,000 for a given activity but spent only $29,000. On the surface, this variance appears to be favorable. Upon reviewing the figures, however, management attempts to determine the reason for the seemingly superior performance. The favorable variance may have resulted from overly pessimistic projections, indicating that what at first appeared to be performance that exceeded expectations was actually an indication of poor judgment in making budget estimates. Favorable variances can also occur as a result of overzealous or shortsighted actions that include lowering quality standards, disregarding training, or altering operating procedures to reduce expenses. For example, a dramatic increase in new business that might appear to be a favorable budgetary variance could actually be the result of using lax underwriting standards that could result in extensive losses for the insurer at a later date.

Variance analysis can also mislead when evaluators consider budget variances that are beyond the control of a responsibility manager. This uncontrollability often arises when one variance causes a second variance. Assume that an insurance company spends $30 to process each life insurance claim. The actuarial department estimates that the company will receive 7,000 claims in April. Thus, the claims department's budgeted claim processing costs for April are $210,000 (7,000 claims × $30 per claim). If the claims department actually processes 10,000 claims that month, the claim processing costs are $300,000, exceeding the budgeted amount by $90,000. Thus, a variance in actual experience—which is beyond the control of the claims manager—causes a variance within the claims department. This fact should not be overlooked during the final evaluation of the claims department or its manager.

Use of a Single Evaluation Criterion

Another evaluation problem occurs when evaluators reduce a responsibility manager's performance evaluation into a single, all-encompassing measure. This practice usually emphasizes only one goal of the company and ignores all others. Suppose that the loan officers of a bank are evaluated solely on the number of loans they approve. If the bank bases the loan officers' job stability and promotions on this one criterion, the loan officers might approve every loan application that comes across their desks, regardless of the level of credit risk presented by each applicant. Eventually, the bank would lose money on defaulted loans. Therefore, managers evaluate the performance of loan officers on other criteria besides the quantity of approved loans. The same idea applies in the insurance industry. For example, the manager of an insurer's marketing department is evaluated on whether the company's marketing efforts are generating the budgeted quantities of policies, at budgeted marketing costs, and of a quality that meets the company's established underwriting standards. The manager of the information systems department is evaluated on whether that department has provided adequate computer support for the company's other departments and met its budgeted costs.

Use of Inappropriate Criteria

A related evaluation criteria problem is using performance measures that fail to reflect an insurer's objectives or its employees' responsibilities. As you saw during the discussion of return on investment and residual income, emphasizing profits in the short run without consideration of long-term consequences can negatively affect a company's financial performance. Nonetheless, some companies base management evaluations only on short-term results, such as a quarterly target ROI. Therefore, managers can be tempted to forsake long-term goals and overuse resources to maximize short-term returns if it is the only way to earn a satisfactory performance evaluation. Such companies may find themselves with insufficient resources in the future.

Unattainable Goals

Evaluation problems can arise when performance standards are not attainable by responsibility managers. For example, a responsibility manager may be evaluated unfavorably for failing to achieve goals that are unrealistic. Evaluators can avoid this problem by becoming aware of how the budgets and other standards are determined and to what extent controllability is considered in the comparison of budgeted to actual amounts. A company can reduce the problem of unattainable goals by involving responsibility managers in the preparation of their centers' budgets. Managers tend to react more favorably toward budgets that they helped prepare.

Responsibility Managers vs. Responsibility Centers

Senior management evaluates responsibility managers apart from their responsibility centers. A manager may be doing an acceptable job even though the results of the center are unsatisfactory. This situation can happen to the manager of a business segment in a declining market. Conversely, a business segment in a growing market may be thriving through no special accomplishment of the manager. In either case, senior management looks carefully at the situation and asks: What should this responsibility center be able to accomplish? Then senior management can determine whether the performance of the manager has affected the performance of the segment, or whether the results are a function of the segment's environment.

Cost Allocation

In Chapter 16, we defined cost allocation as the accounting process of assigning or distributing an indirect cost or expense according to a method or formula. Examples of indirect costs that can be allocated include service department costs and the salaries of managers in charge of more than one responsibility center. However, cost allocation is arbitrary to some degree. Therefore, when conducting performance evaluations, management considers whether indirect costs are allocated and by what method they are allocated. Sometimes, responsibility managers believe they are being allocated costs that do not apply to their centers. In this respect, cost allocation is much like income taxes: everyone thinks he or she is paying too much. Problems with improper or unfair cost allocation can occur because of internal influences (company politics), insufficient data to properly allocate costs, or a flawed allocation system.

Cost allocations violate a basic principle of responsibility accounting because responsibility managers feel they are being held accountable for costs they do not incur in their responsibility centers. For the purposes of internal reporting and evaluations, some companies delete cost allocations from their accounting systems. In such cases, the system for monitoring the performance of individual managers is part of the complete accounting system. Other companies fully allocate indirect costs to all responsibility centers but concentrate only on direct costs during performance evaluations.

The cost allocation process includes the development of reasonable allocation methods. Essentially, indirect costs are allocated to responsibility centers in relation to the benefits received by each center. At the very least, any cost allocation method should be unambiguous and justifiable. The method should also divide all costs that are available to be allocated. These guidelines apply to all methods of cost allocation. The allocation of service department costs is a particularly complex issue for life and health insurance companies, because insurers generally have a large number of service departments providing a variety of support functions. Keep in mind that the choice of cost allocation method, and the selection of allocation bases for each method, will impact the results of an insurer's responsibility centers. In turn, these results could affect the performance evaluations of the managers of these centers.

Revenue Allocation[2]

The performance of an insurer's responsibility centers cannot be measured and evaluated fairly unless revenues are accurately allocated to the centers that control the revenues. Moreover, overstating or understating revenues allocated to a particular responsibility center can impair management's ability to make decisions about that center. The two primary ways that insurance companies generate revenues are through the sale of insurance policies and annuities and through assets that earn investment income. Allocating premium income to the appropriate responsibility center is generally straightforward because premium revenues are easily identifiable by product. However, it is much more difficult to allocate investment income to particular products or product lines. Currently, insurance companies use several investment income allocation methods. Three of these methods are the mean liabilities method, the investment year method, and the investment segmentation method.

Mean Liabilities Method

The simplest investment income allocation method is the ***mean liabilities method,*** which allocates investment revenues to lines of business based on the reserves attributable to each line. For example, if 40 percent of an insurer's reserves are attributable to group life insurance business, then group life is allocated 40 percent of the company's investment income. This method may be simple, but its accuracy is questionable. One problem is that newer lines of business share in the investment income of older, high-yielding investments that were purchased before the new products were even established. Second, this method ignores the surplus required to support the line that also contributes to investment income. Last, this method fails to match the duration of specific assets with the duration of specific liabilities.

Investment Year Method

The ***investment year method*** of allocation overcomes a basic problem of the mean liabilities method by forming separate investment pools that contain the investments made during each year. A share of the investment pool each calendar year is allocated to each product line or line of business. Each line's share of investment revenue is determined by the investable funds generated by that line each year. ***Investable funds*** consist of (1) net income before taxes, (2) investment income received on prior investments, and (3) the maturities of principal on prior investments. The advantage of the investment year method is that newer product lines with low amounts of accumulated funds and larger cash flows from current operations receive relatively larger shares of investment revenue from newer investments. Older lines with larger reserves will receive larger shares of investment revenues from older investments. The disadvantage of the investment year method is its complexity.

Investment Segmentation Method

In the ***investment segmentation method*** of investment revenue allocation, the cash flows of a particular product line or line of business are used to purchase specific investments for that line. In essence, each line is treated as if it owns certain investments. The investment income from each investment is allocated to the line that acquired the investment. The advantage of this method is that separate investment strategies can be developed for different lines. This versatility is important because cash flow patterns and the interest income requirements of different lines vary significantly. For example, the cash flows of health insurance business are quite different from the cash flows of ordinary life business.

The choice of which investment revenue allocation method to use depends on the insurer's objectives. If the major objective is merely to allocate investment income for line of business reporting on the Annual Statement, then the mean liabilities method is adequate. But for more accurate evaluation of responsibility centers, the insurer should use a more sophisticated investment income allocation method such as the investment year method or the investment segmentation method.

Transfer Pricing

Evaluating the performance of profit and investment centers can be difficult when transfer pricing is involved. A ***transfer price*** is the price of a good or service that one segment of a company charges another segment of the same company. Unlike inter-company transactions in which prices are determined by supply and demand factors, transfer pricing arrangements are established by a company's management. Transfer pricing is especially important for insurance companies with subsidiaries, or insurers that are themselves subsidiaries.

Several methods are used to set transfer prices, including cost, market price, and negotiated price. The transfer pricing method a company selects is critical, because transfer prices directly influence the profits for which managers of profit or investment centers are held responsible. An inappropriate transfer price might provide a misleading picture of a responsibility center's true performance and, even worse, might motivate the center's manager to initiate actions that are not in the best interest of the company.

- **Cost-Based Transfer Prices:** A transfer price that is set at cost is the price that it actually costs the selling center to manufacture the product or provide the service. In this case, because the selling center's "revenues" are equal to its costs, it earns no profit. Some cost-based transfer-pricing systems use cost plus a markup, and the selling center earns a profit on each internal transfer. In either case, it can be argued that the selling center has little incentive to operate efficiently and control costs under this method of transfer pricing.

- **Market-Based Transfer Prices:** Companies that use a market-based transfer pricing system exchange products at their external market value. This system is common when the selling center is viewed as a distinct business and has both internal and external markets. The advantage of this system is that the selling center receives its deserved profit, and the buying center does not overpay for the good or service. The disadvantage of the market-based system is that competitive market prices do not exist for all products, or the prices available may not be representative of the transfer situation.

- **Negotiated Transfer Prices:** Individual buying and selling centers sometimes negotiate the price of transferred products. Negotiated transfer pricing is effective if both sides can agree on a price. Negotiated prices should not be set below the variable costs of the goods or services—so that the seller does not take a loss on the sale—and should not be higher than the market price, if one exists. In some cases, managers of highly autonomous centers can ignite an inflationary spiral of price increases to other investment centers.

Conclusion

In this chapter, we discussed how life and health insurance companies use a responsibility accounting system to organize and control operations. Through variance analysis, an insurer can evaluate the financial performance of all its responsibility centers. Return on investment and residual income also are key measures of insurers' investment centers. In Chapter 19, we discuss additional methods used to analyze an insurer's financial performance.

Key Terms and Concepts

responsibility accounting
responsibility center
responsibility manager
goal congruence
goal incongruence
effectiveness
efficiency
profit center
investment center
variance analysis
rate variance
usage variance
responsibility center report
segment reporting
segment margin
segment margin ratio
contribution margin ratio
return on investment (ROI)
operating income
controllable investment
return on revenue
investment turnover
residual income (RI)
mean liabilities method
investment year method
investable funds
investment segmentation method
transfer price

References

1. Peter F. Drucker, *Management: Tasks, Responsibilities, Practices* (New York: Harper & Row, 1973), pp. 45–46.

2. The discussion of revenue allocation methods has been adapted from *GAAP Accounting and Financial Analysis for Life and Health Insurance Companies*, Section 1, (Atlanta, GA: LOMA; and New York: Ernst & Young; 1995), pp. 8–10.

CHAPTER 19

FINANCIAL STATEMENT ANALYSIS

LEARNING OBJECTIVES

After studying this chapter, you should be able to

- Differentiate between external analysis and internal analysis
- Apply horizontal and vertical analysis to financial statements
- Analyze trends using an index number trend analysis
- List and apply the information contained in a common-size statement
- Explain how to use the statement of cash flows to reveal financial information
- List and apply liquidity, activity, leverage, and profitability ratios under generally accepted accounting principles (GAAP)
- List and apply statutory liquidity, capital, leverage, and profitability ratios
- Identify Insurance Regulatory Information System (IRIS) ratios and describe their use by state insurance regulators
- Discuss the relationship between an insurer's capital levels and its solvency
- Recognize and apply key financial ratios for health insurers

CHAPTER OUTLINE

External and Internal Analysis

External Analysis

Internal Analysis

Horizontal and Vertical Analysis

Horizontal Analysis

Vertical Analysis

Benchmarking

Analysis of the Statement of Cash Flows

Ratio Analysis

GAAP Ratios

Statutory Ratios

Regulatory Analysis of Financial Statements

IRIS Ratios

Financial Analysis and Solvency Tracking System

Monitoring Capital and Surplus Requirements

Health Insurance Financial Analysis

Financial statements provide glimpses of a company's past performance and current condition, and they can be one of the tools used to predict its future success. Financial statements are also the primary means for an insurance company to communicate information to various audiences, such as regulators, stockholders, creditors, managers, and policyowners. But financial statements require interpretation. Otherwise, they are nothing more than columns of numbers. If you are unskilled in the techniques needed to decipher these numbers, the numbers themselves will have little or no meaning. You might as well be reading a foreign language. In this chapter, we help you translate all those numbers into meaningful information by leading you through the basics of financial statement analysis. ***Financial statement analysis*** assesses an insurance company's financial performance and position and compares the company with other companies within and outside the insurance industry. The financial statements that analysts study most often are the balance sheet, the statement of operations, and the statement of cash flows.

We begin this chapter by reviewing the external and internal parties who are interested in an insurer's financial statements. We then discuss various techniques for analyzing the financial statements. These techniques include horizontal analysis, vertical analysis, and benchmarking. Next, we discuss the unique aspects of analyzing the statement of cash flows. We then define ratio analysis and present the important financial ratios in two parts: ratios that are important for analyzing statements prepared according to generally accepted accounting principles (GAAP), and then ratios important for analyzing statements prepared under statutory accounting practices. Finally, we discuss the methods regulatory agencies use to monitor the financial condition of insurers.

External and Internal Analysis

Many different people and organizations analyze an insurance company's financial statements. Each party has different goals and purposes for conducting these analyses. We separate these parties into external and internal analysts. Both types of analysts use some or all of the following techniques: horizontal analysis, vertical analysis, common-size statements, benchmarking, and ratio analysis.

External Analysis

External analysis is financial analysis performed by someone outside the company being analyzed. The most common external analysts are regulatory authorities, rating agencies, investment firms, public accounting firms, and policyowners. State and provincial insurance regulators analyze insurance company financial statements to monitor the solvency of insurers and to ensure that insurers remain reliable providers of financial security. Independent rating agencies—such as A.M. Best Company, Moody's Investors Service, Duff & Phelps, and Standard and Poor's Insurance Rating Services—monitor insurance companies on behalf of insurance buyers and investors, and they incorporate financial statement analysis into their evaluations of insurance companies. Brokerage houses and other investment firms analyze financial statements to determine which insurance companies are good investments. Public accounting firms examine financial statements as part of the auditing process, which involves examining and evaluating company records and procedures to ensure the reliability of the company's accounting reports.

Policyowners are interested in financial statements to determine an insurer's financial strength and to verify its ability to continue operating, to pay claims as they come due, and to make policy loans. Policyowners of mutual insurance companies have additional interest in financial statements if the company decides to demutualize. During demutualization, the company's policyowners receive stock, cash, or other consideration for their ownership interests. These policyowners and other potential investors in the demutualized company use financial statement analysis to view the effects of demutualization on the insurer's balance sheet and to determine if the insurer is a worthy investment.

Internal Analysis

Internal analysis is financial analysis undertaken by employees of the company being analyzed. Usually, a company's managers conduct internal analysis (1) to maintain awareness of the needs and interests of all external parties and (2) to determine where to allocate their resources to support growth and ongoing business operations. While external analysts have available to them only published reports and financial statements, internal analysts can access many additional operational reports and data that are never released to the public. Internal analysis can be more detailed and more specific than external analysis. Some types of internal analysis compare two or more accounting periods to determine trends in performance. Other types of internal analysis compare one company's performance with the performances of other companies or evaluate the performance of specific management personnel and individual departments.

Horizontal and Vertical Analysis

Figures on a financial statement do not always tell a complete story when viewed in isolation. Additional insight can be gained by relating one set of numbers to another set of numbers or analyzing the change in one or more numbers over a period of time. Two types of financial statement analysis that accomplish these tasks are *horizontal analysis* and *vertical analysis.* Financial statements that are analyzed horizontally or vertically are known as ***comparative financial statements,*** which are financial statements that present data for two or more accounting periods side by side. In this way, an analyst can review the changes in individual statement items from one year to the next. The most important factors revealed in comparative financial statements are the direction and velocity of trends. *Direction* refers to whether a trend displays an increase or decrease in account amounts. *Velocity* refers to whether the increase or decrease in an account is gradual or rapid. Further analysis enables you to compare trends in related items. For example, a year-to-year increase in premium income of 10 percent is fine unless it is accompanied by a 20 percent annual increase in policy benefit payments. This disparity is revealed through comparative financial statements and would likely trigger an investigation by management. Comparative financial statements often present the year-to-year changes in absolute amounts as well as percentages. An analyst should consider both. A large percentage change in an item is significant only if the amount of the item is consequential. For example, a 50 percent decrease in petty cash may be insignificant, but a 50 percent decrease in total revenues is cause for alarm.

Horizontal Analysis

Horizontal analysis measures the amount that corresponding items change from one financial statement to another over consecutive accounting periods. Both GAAP- and statutory-prepared balance sheets, statements of operations, and statements of cash flows can be analyzed horizontally. Horizontal analysis shows the absolute amount of the increase or decrease in an item along with the percent of the increase or decrease. The earliest period being used in the analysis is known as the ***base period.*** We compute the percentage change by subtracting the base period amount from the amount of the period being studied and dividing that result by the base period amount. Finally, multiply the total by 100 to put the answer in a percent form:

$$\text{Percentage Change} = \frac{(\text{Period Under Study} - \text{Base Period Amount}) \times 100}{\text{Base Period Amount}}$$

Figure 19-1. Grand Life and Health Insurance Company GAAP-based consolidated balance sheets.

December 31	2000	1999
Assets		
Securities available for sale		
Debt securities	$12,204,000	$11,225,000
Equity securities	500,380	1,066,800
Total Securities Available for Sale	$12,704,380	$12,291,800
Policy loans	1,392,580	824,995
Cash and cash equivalents	634,696	718,200
Property and equipment	93,404	66,283
Total Assets	$14,825,060	$13,901,278
Liabilities and Stockholders' Equity		
Liabilities:		
Policy liabilities:		
Future policy benefits:		
Life	$ 7,018,245	$ 6,983,486
Health	3,315,422	3,055,782
Unpaid claims	122,894	104,800
Total Policy Liabilities	$10,456,561	$10,144,068
Accounts payable	193,732	94,380
Due to reinsurers	124,730	120,019
Dividends payable to stockholders	272,511	243,100
Long-term liabilities	123,558	89,543
Total Liabilities	$11,171,092	$10,691,110
Stockholders' Equity:		
Common stock, $0.02 par value; 6,000,000 shares authorized; 1,000,000 outstanding	$ 20,000	$ 20,000
Additional paid-in capital	641,356	641,356
Unrealized capital gain (loss), net	112,230	100,950
Retained earnings	2,880,382	2,447,862
Total Stockholders' Equity	$ 3,653,968	$ 3,210,168
Total Liabilities and Stockholders' Equity	$14,825,060	$13,901,278

To illustrate percentage changes, Figure 19-1 shows the consolidated balance sheets of Grand Life and Health Insurance Company, a U.S. stock insurer that sells nonparticipating life and health insurance products. Notice that Grand had total assets of $13,901,278 in 1999 and total assets of $14,825,060 in 2000. The focus of horizontal analysis is the percentage change between the two periods. In this case, the year 1999 is the base period; the period under study is the year 2000. The computation of the percentage change in total assets from 1999 to 2000 is

$$\frac{(\$14{,}825{,}060 - \$13{,}901{,}278)}{\$13{,}901{,}278} = 0.066 \times 100 = 6.6\%$$

Thus, the company experienced a 6.6 percent increase in total assets from 1999 to 2000. Next, notice from Grand's consolidated statements of operations in Figure 19-2 that Grand paid $205,888 in commissions and fees in 1999 and $189,074 in commissions and fees in 2000. Once again, the base period is 1999. The percentage change in commissions and fees expense is

$$\frac{(\$189{,}074 - \$205{,}888)}{\$205{,}888} = -0.082 \times 100 = -8.2\%$$

In this case, the base period amount is greater than the succeeding amount, so the resulting percentage change is a decrease, which is represented by a negative percent.

Similar calculations can be made for every category on two or more GAAP- or statutory-based financial statements. The Annual Statement and the Annual Return show the current year's and at least the previous year's financial information, providing a basis for horizontal analysis. Companies frequently prepare comparative balance sheets, statements of operations, and statements of cash flows for two or more accounting periods. Figure 19-3 illustrates a format Grand might use to analyze its comparative balance sheets and comparative statements of operations.

One form of horizontal analysis is trend analysis. ***Trend analysis,*** also called *trend percentages* or *index-number trend analysis,* involves the calculation of percentage changes in financial statement figures over several successive accounting periods, rather than over just two periods. Trends are an important indicator of the direction and nature of business developments over time. To conduct trend analysis, you first select a base period and assign it an index number of 100. The use of an *index number* provides a statistical method for measuring the change in a variable. Then you compute a series of index numbers by reference to the base period. If the amount of a subsequent accounting period is higher than that of the base period, then the resulting

Figure 19-2. Grand Life and Health Insurance Company GAAP-based consolidated statements of operations.

Years Ended December 31:	2000	1999
Revenues		
Premiums:		
Life	$3,656,220	$3,278,658
Health	1,509,458	1,104,616
Net investment income	1,758,592	1,499,764
Other	24,906	8,582
Total Revenues	$6,949,176	$5,891,620
Benefits and Expenses		
Policy benefits:		
Death benefits and other policy benefits	$2,151,479	$1,672,986
Health benefits	1,055,632	921,951
Increase in liability for future policy benefits	55,402	189,362
Total Benefits	$3,262,513	$2,784,299
Expenses:		
Commissions and fees	$ 189,074	$ 205,888
Salaries	922,811	854,138
Other operating expenses	1,392,314	996,200
Total Expenses	$2,504,199	$2,056,226
Total Benefits and Expenses	$5,766,712	$4,840,525
Earnings before interest and taxes	$1,182,464	$1,051,095
Interest expense	7,413	5,373
Earnings before income taxes	$1,175,051	$1,045,722
Income tax expense (40%)	470,020	418,289
Net Income	$ 705,031	$ 627,433
Earnings per share of common stock:		
Net earnings per share	$ 0.71	$ 0.63

index number will be greater than 100. Otherwise, the resulting index will be less than 100. An index number of 120 indicates a 20 percent increase, whereas an index number of 80 indicates a 20 percent decrease, from the base period to the period being studied.

To illustrate trend analysis, assume that an insurer recorded the following amounts for life insurance premium income received and life insurance benefits paid during the past five years:

($000 omitted)

	1996	1997	1998	1999	2000
Premium income	$2,300	$3,700	$3,500	$4,400	$6,000
Benefits paid	1,467	2,295	2,201	3,018	4,020

Figure 19-3. Excerpts of Grand Life and Health Insurance Company GAAP-based comparative balance sheets and GAAP-based comparative statements of operations using horizontal analysis.

BALANCE SHEET

			Increase (Decrease)	
	2000	**1999**	**Amount**	**Percentage**
Total Assets	$14,825,060	$13,901,278	$923,782	6.6

STATEMENT OF OPERATIONS

Commissions and Fees	$189,074	$205,888	$ (16,814)	(8.2)

We can see from this data that, during the five-year period, premium income and benefits paid increased every year except 1998. But it is difficult to determine how rapidly premium income increased (or decreased) and how those trends compare with the increases or decreases in benefits paid. Trend analysis can help. In this example, 1996 is the base year. To determine the index number for each year for premium income, divide the current year balance by the base year balance of $2,300, then multiply this result by 100. To determine the index numbers for benefits paid, divide the current year balance by the base period figure of $1,467, then multiply this result by 100. Finally, add this amount to 100, the base index number, to obtain the index number for the period under study. The index numbers for premium income and benefits paid for the five-year period are

	1996	1997	1998	1999	2000
Premium income	100	161	152	191	261
Benefits paid	100	156	150	206	274

From this analysis, we can see that, in 1997 and 1998, premium income outpaced benefits paid relative to the base period. The trend reversed in 1999 and 2000, however. Management would likely investigate the reasons behind this trend.

External financial analysts and insurance company managers use trend analysis to identify financial statement accounts or other items that appear unusual. A few words of caution, however. First, we cannot express fluctuations between negative amounts and positive amounts as index numbers. For example, index numbers cannot describe the change in net income from –$1,000 (a net loss) in one period to $1,000 (net income) in the next. Second, when three or more base periods are being analyzed, index numbers are relevant only when compared with the base amount. For instance, in the previous example, the percentage change in premium income between the base year and 1998 is 52 percent (index 152 – index 100 = 52). However, the percentage change between 1998 and 1999 is *not* 39 percent as you might assume from a direct comparison (index 191 – index 152). The percentage change between these two years can be found *only* by computing the change with reference to 1998 as the "new" base year. In doing so, we discover that the true percentage change between 1998 and 1999 is 26 percent ($4,400 ÷ $3,500 = index 126), not 39 percent.

Vertical Analysis

While horizontal analysis highlights changes in a financial statement item over time, ***vertical analysis*** reveals the relationship of each financial statement item to another financial statement item. To conduct vertical analysis of the balance sheet, divide each asset item by total assets, and divide each liability or stockholders' equity item by total liabilities and stockholders' equity (or total liabilities and capital and surplus on a statutory balance sheet). The combined percentage totals of all asset accounts or liabilities and stockholders' equity accounts should equal 100. On the statement of operations, each item is stated as a percentage of total revenues. In other words, divide each item by total revenues.

For instance, the consolidated balance sheets for the Grand Life and Health Insurance Company in Figure 19-1 list the asset account Debt Securities with a balance of $12,204,000 in 2000. Because total assets equal $14,825,060, debt securities represent 82.3 percent ($12,204,000 ÷ $14,825,060) of total assets. Figure 19-4 displays a vertical analysis of Grand's consolidated balance sheets. Note from Figure 19-4 that debt securities (mainly bonds and mortgages) represent a large percentage of Grand's total assets: 82.3 percent in 2000 and 80.7 percent in 1999. This asset allocation is common among insurance companies because insurance regulators limit the amount of high-risk investments insurers can make. As noted in Figures 7-3 and 7-4 in Chapter 7, higher-risk equity investments, such as common stocks and real estate, traditionally account for a low percentage of insurance asset holdings. Grand's equity holdings dropped from 7.7 percent in 1999 to 3.4 percent in 2000, which represents the greatest relative change on the assets portion of the balance sheet between 1999 and 2000. On the liabilities and stockholders' equity side, health insurance policy benefits experienced a modest relative increase. Overall, there were no major relative changes in any balance sheet account.

Care should be taken when determining the significance of vertical analysis percentages of different years. For example, the percentage of total securities relative to total assets declined from 88.4 percent in 1999 to 85.7 percent in 2000. Yet, the absolute dollar amount of total securities increased by $412,580. This change indicates that, although

Figure 19-4. Vertical analysis of Grand Life and Health Insurance Company GAAP-based consolidated balance sheets.

	2000 Amount	2000 Percent	1999 Amount	1999 Percent
Assets				
Securities available for sale:				
Debt securities	$12,204,000	82.3%	$11,225,000	80.7%
Equity securities	500,380	3.4%	1,066,800	7.7%
Total Securities Available for Sale	$12,704,380	85.7%	$12,291,800	88.4%
Policy loans	1,392,580	9.4%	824,995	5.9%
Cash and cash equivalents	634,696	4.3%	718,200	5.2%
Property and equipment	93,404	0.6%	66,283	0.5%
Total Assets	$14,825,060	100%	$13,901,278	100%
Liabilities and Stockholders' Equity				
Liabilities:				
Policy liabilities:				
Future policy benefits:				
Life	$ 7,018,245	47.3%	$ 6,983,486	50.2%
Health	3,315,422	22.4%	3,055,782	22.0%
Unpaid claims	122,894	0.8%	104,800	0.8%
Total Policy Liabilities	$10,456,561	70.5%	$10,144,068	73.0%
Accounts payable	193,732	1.3%	94,380	0.7%
Due to reinsurers	124,730	0.9%	120,019	0.9%
Dividends payable to stockholders	272,511	1.9%	243,100	1.7%
Long-term liabilities	123,558	0.8%	89,543	0.6%
Total Liabilities	$11,171,092	75.4%	$10,691,110	76.9%
Stockholders' Equity:				
Common stock, par	$ 20,000	0.1%	$ 20,000	0.1%
Additional paid-in capital	641,356	4.3%	641,356	4.7%
Unrealized capital gain (loss), net	112,230	0.8%	100,950	0.7%
Retained earnings	2,880,382	19.4%	2,447,862	17.6%
Total Stockholders' Equity	$ 3,653,968	24.6%	$ 3,210,168	23.1%
Total Liabilities and Stockholders' Equity	$14,825,060	100%	$13,901,278	100%

total securities increased, other assets also increased, slightly altering the percentage mix of Grand's total assets for 2000.

Vertical analysis uses percentages to relate different financial statement items to a specified, total amount on the statement. We can also use vertical analysis to compile a ***common-size statement,*** which is a statement that consists of the percentages obtained from vertical analysis. Common-size statements display only percentages; there are no dollar figures for each item. Balance sheets and statements of opera-

Figure 19-5. Grand Life and Health Insurance Company GAAP-based common-size consolidated balance sheets.

December 31	2000	1999
Assets		
Securities available for sale:		
Debt securities	82.3%	80.7%
Equity securities	3.4%	7.7%
Total Securities Available for Sale	85.7%	88.4%
Policy loans	9.4%	5.9%
Cash and cash equivalents	4.3%	5.2%
Property and equipment	0.6%	0.5%
Total Assets	100%	100%
Liabilities and Stockholders' Equity		
Liabilities:		
Policy liabilities:		
Future policy benefits:		
Life	47.3%	50.2%
Health	22.4%	22.0%
Unpaid claims	0.8%	0.8%
Total Policy Liabilities	70.5%	73.0%
Accounts payable	1.3%	0.7%
Due to reinsurers	0.9%	0.9%
Dividends payable to stockholders	1.9%	1.7%
Long-term liabilities	0.8%	0.6%
Total Liabilities	75.4%	76.9%
Stockholders' Equity:		
Common stock, par	0.1%	0.1%
Additional paid-in capital	4.3%	4.7%
Unrealized capital gain (loss), net	0.8%	0.7%
Retained earnings	19.4%	17.6%
Total Stockholders' Equity	24.6%	23.1%
Total Liabilities and Stockholders' Equity	100%	100%

tions are often exhibited as common-size statements. Figure 19-5 presents Grand's common-size consolidated balance sheets for 1999 and 2000. Each line item is expressed as a percentage of total assets or total liabilities and stockholders' equity. In other words, total assets is the "common size" to which we relate the balance sheet's other asset amounts, and total liabilities and stockholders' equity is the common size to which we relate the balance sheet's liabilities and stockholders' equity.

As shown in Figure 19-5, analysts use a common-size statement to compare percentages associated with a company's current and previous accounting periods. In addition, common-size statements allow a company to compare itself to another company or to industry averages of the percentages found in common-size statements. Because all amounts are stated in relative terms rather than absolutes, common-size statements also facilitate comparison of companies of different sizes in the same industry and facilitate somewhat the comparison of companies in different industries, which is especially valuable to potential investors. For example, assume that in comparing the statements of operations of two companies, you notice that Company A's net income is three times as great as Company B's net income. It would be easy to conclude that Company A is the more profitable company. However, if you look at common-size statements of operations of the two companies, you might discover that Company B's net income represents a greater *percentage* of its total revenues than that of Company A. So, although Company B's net income is lower, we can deduce from this one comparison that, all other factors being equal, Company B appears to be operating more efficiently than Company A.

Benchmarking

Common-size statements are a useful tool for ***benchmarking,*** which is a process by which a company compares its own performance, products, and services with those of other organizations that are recognized as the best in a particular category. Benchmarking measures an organization's performance and practices and helps identify those practices that will lead to superior performance. Insurers commonly benchmark against other insurance companies, against other financial services institutions, such as banks and mutual fund companies, and even against companies in other industries.

There are four keys to implementing a successful benchmarking program for an insurance company.[1] *First* is to recognize the difference between benchmarking and rating. In rating, a specific "grade" or quality rating is assigned to a life and health insurance company by an independent rating agency. The public uses these ratings to make investment and insurance buying decisions. Benchmarking, on the other hand, helps an analyst assess performance areas that require improvement. *Second,* insurance companies must realize that one company may not be the best in every area. Therefore, the insurer should not use only one company as a benchmark for every operation or category. *Third,* life and health insurance companies must realize that the best companies for benchmarking are not always direct competitors or industry giants. The ideal benchmarking candidates are those companies with similar asset size, business mix, and ownership structure, as well as a high level of performance in the area being studied. *Fourth,* an insurer engaged in benchmarking should set specific goals to improve its performance over a specific time horizon. Goals should be as explicit as possible. Rather than setting a general goal of reducing operating expenses, the company should select as a benchmark a similar-sized firm that is known as an industry leader in operating expense cost control. Using vertical analysis, the insurer could then set the goal of equaling the benchmarked company's percentage of operating expenses to revenue by the end of the following accounting period.

Analysis of the Statement of Cash Flows

To this point, we have discussed financial analysis as it pertains to the balance sheet and the statement of operations. However, the statement of cash flows should be analyzed along with the balance sheet and statement of operations to gain a complete understanding of a company's financial condition. The statement of cash flows serves two primary purposes: (1) to reflect increases and decreases in cash so that trends or patterns in cash flow can be determined, and (2) to help isolate the way the company's operations and investment activities affect its liquidity. Analysis of the statement of cash flows helps answer questions such as the following:

- Are changes in the amount of cash and short-term investments caused by revenue or expense levels, or are they the result of changes in the company's financing or investing activities?

- Is the company relying on the internal generation of profits to finance growth, or is it obtaining funds through the sale of additional equity?

Thus, the statement of cash flows can be a valuable aid in determining the company's future direction.

Recall from Chapter 5 that the statement of cash flows details the sources and uses of cash by segregating the statement into cash flows from operating activities, investing activities, and financing activities. Within operating activities for most insurance companies, the principal sources of cash (cash inflows) are premium income and investment income, while the principal uses of cash (cash outflows) are policy benefit payments, agent commissions, operating expenses, and taxes, licenses, and fees. Within investment activities, the major sources of cash are the sale or maturity of investments and the sale of a subsidiary or a line of business, and the primary uses of cash are the purchase of investments, the purchase of equipment, and the purchase of another company. Within financing activities, the main sources of cash are the sale of capital stock or surplus notes, while the main use of cash is the payment of stockholder dividends.

Analysis of the statement of cash flows reveals financial changes that are not apparent in either the balance sheet or the statement of operations. These changes are important for internal and external analysis. For example, policyowners and investors typically prefer that a company's sources of cash be from operating activities because this indicates that a company's core business operations are healthy and active. Consider the following three circumstances in which a company can acquire a $250,000 net cash inflow:

- Higher sales volume (operating activity)
- The sale of a line of business (investing activity)
- A stock issue (financing activity)

If you were a potential creditor, under which circumstance would you prefer to lend money to this company, all other factors remaining equal? You would probably prefer the company that obtained most of its net cash inflow from operating activities, rather than from investing or financing activities. This scenario indicates soundness in the company's core business operations and increases the likelihood that the company will be able to repay the loan. As a potential investor, you would probably prefer to invest in a company that has increasing sales revenue, again because it increases the likelihood that the company will be profitable. You might be uneasy about investing in a company that just incurred additional debt or diluted the potential value of your stock by issuing additional shares of stock. The insurance company whose statement of cash flows is depicted in Figure 19-6 has net cash flows from operating activities of $78,142. This amount far exceeds the cash flows used for investing or financing activities and is indicative of a solvent company. Generally, this company would be more attractive to a policyowner or an investor than a company that generated the majority of its net cash flows from financing or investing activities. This brief analysis is

Figure 19-6. Insurance company GAAP-based statement of cash flows.

Cash flows from operating activities:		
Net income		$88,753
Add increase in benefits payable	$ 53,047	
Subtract increase in securities	(63,658)	
Net cash flow from operating activities		$78,142
Cash flows from investing activities:		
Cash payment for acquisition of equipment	$ (4,400)	
Net cash flow used for investing activities		(4,400)
Cash flows from financing activities:		
Cash payment for stockholder dividends	$(22,709)	
Net cash flow used for financing activities		(22,709)
Net cash flows		$51,033
Beginning cash balance		35,750
Ending cash balance		$86,783

admittedly simplistic. The point of this illustration is to provide you with a preview of how you might begin to use financial analysis in order to make rational decisions about a company's financial well-being. Generally, the larger the cash inflows from operating activities, the better able a company will be to pay its obligations and to weather unfavorable changes in the economy.

Ratio Analysis

One of the most widely used methods of financial statement analysis is ratio analysis. ***Ratio analysis*** consists of comparing various financial statement values for the purpose of assessing a company's financial performance or condition. A ***ratio*** is a comparison of two or more numbers in fraction form. Several of the preceding chapters mentioned ratios, such as unit cost ratios, the segment margin and contribution margin ratios, and return on investment. The number on the top part of the fraction is the *numerator* and the number in the bottom part of the fraction is the *denominator.* For example, the *current ratio* for a company is the ratio of current assets to current liabilities. We calculate this ratio as current assets (the numerator) divided by current liabilities (the denominator). If a company has current assets of $2,500,000 and current liabilities of $1,000,000, its current ratio is

$$\textbf{Current Ratio} = \frac{\$2{,}500{,}000}{\$1{,}000{,}000} = 2.5$$

This ratio can also be written as 2.5:1, which is read as "two point five to one."

The relationships created by ratio analysis help to highlight an entity's strengths and weaknesses and reveal areas needing further research. A company's short-term assets may appear to be adequate on the balance sheet, but only when they are applied in the current ratio can their adequacy be confirmed or contradicted. You can relate any bit of financial statement data to any other, which makes for a large number of potential ratios. But only a limited number of ratios are meaningful, and not all ratios are applicable to all types of businesses. Ratios should be used with a general understanding of the company being studied and its environment. Acceptable ratio results for a clothing manufacturer are going to be quite different from the acceptable ratio results for a public accounting firm. Ratios can answer a company's yes/no questions, such as whether short-term debts can be paid on time and whether a firm is efficiently using its assets to generate profits. Ratios do not answer "why" questions such as: *why* are current liabilities exceeding current assets and *why* is an insurer unable to meet all its claims to policyowners. For this reason, meaningful ratios serve best only to point out changes or trends in operating performance and help illuminate the hazards or opportunities associated with normal business operations.

Before proceeding further, a few words of caution. First, there are no standards guiding the preparation of ratios. For example, you may find a slightly different calculation for the same ratio in another textbook. Consequently, this chapter cannot provide an exact description for every financial ratio used in every analysis. Instead, we review some commonly used ratios and indicate the type of information typically provided by these ratios. You should be aware that the calculations in this text represent only one way of describing each ratio. Next, because of the nature of the insurance industry, not all traditional financial ratios are applicable to insurance companies. For the most part, insurance companies do not have inventories, make purchases or sales on an installment basis, or acquire large amounts of fixed assets. Therefore, ratios involving inventories, accounts payable, accounts receivable, and fixed assets, which are common in most industries, lose meaning when applied to insurers.

As we have seen, insurance companies in the United States generally prepare financial statements under two different bases: GAAP and statutory accounting. Therefore, in this text we present two sets of financial ratios. The first set contains traditional financial ratios that apply to an insurer's GAAP-based statements that appear in an annual report. The second set consists of insurance industry-specific ratios and modifications of the traditional ratios that apply to the insurer's statutory-based statements that appear in the Annual Statement.

GAAP Ratios

This section describes traditional financial ratios that analysts use to study a company's GAAP-based financial statements. It is important for insurers to be familiar with these ratios because (1) insurers need to be able to analyze the financial statements of non-insurance companies in which they are considering investing, and (2) insurers should be able to analyze the information contained in their own and other insurers' annual reports. In this section we categorize ratios as liquidity ratios, activity ratios, leverage ratios, and profitability ratios. We apply each ratio to the Grand Life and Health Insurance Company, whose balance sheet and statement of operations are shown in Figures 19-1 and 19-2, respectively.

Liquidity Ratios

Liquidity ratios measure a company's ability to meet its maturing short-term obligations. Recall from earlier discussions that short-term obligations (liabilities) are those that are expected to come due within one year. For insurers, liquidity is a commonly used predictor of potential trouble because a sufficient amount of cash and other liquid assets must be available when needed to pay claims and general business expenses. However, short-term assets produce little, if any, return, so too great an amount of liquidity damages profits. Thus, the goal for insurance companies is to maintain as low a level of liquidity as possible while at the same time ensuring that short-term obligations can be met.

The ***current ratio,*** which was mentioned earlier, measures a company's short-term debt-paying ability. A company's current ratio is found by dividing its current (short-term) assets by its current (short-term) liabilities:

$$\text{Current Ratio} = \frac{\text{Current Assets}}{\text{Current Liabilities}}$$

Because all of its invested assets are available for sale, Grand considers all assets except Property and Equipment current, while all liabilities except Long-Term Liabilities are current. Therefore, the current ratio for Grand in 2000 is

$$\frac{\$14{,}731{,}656}{\$11{,}047{,}534} = 1.3$$

There is no standard current ratio result for all business in all industries. An average current ratio in the life insurance industry is 2.9.[2] A ratio of 1.0 means that the corporation theoretically has exactly enough current assets to cover all of its current liabilities. The higher the current ratio, the greater the liquidity of the company and the greater the ease with which it can cover its short-term obligations. A ratio that falls below 1.0 generally indicates that a company's liquidity may be too low, and, in an emergency, the company could be forced to sell long-term assets to cover current liabilities. The more predictable the company's cash flows, the lower the acceptable current ratio. This guideline holds true for most companies.

Other versions of the current ratio are the *quick ratio* and the *cash ratio.* A company calculates the quick ratio by subtracting inventory from current assets and dividing the result by current liabilities. For companies, like many insurers, that do not have inventories, the quick ratio equals the current ratio. The cash ratio is the ratio of cash to current liabilities. Finally, the elements of the current ratio in subtraction form (Current Assets – Current Liabilities) equal *net working capital,* which is another common measure of liquidity. Net working capital also provides an indication of the amount of excess cash a company may consider using for investment purposes. We discussed the investment of excess liquid assets in the cash budgeting section of Chapter 18.

Activity Ratios

Activity ratios, also called *operating efficiency ratios,* measure the speed with which various financial statement account totals are converted into sales or cash. Activity ratios gauge the productivity and efficiency of a company. One activity ratio, *asset turnover,* is a standard activity measure in most industries, including insurance. There are several versions of the asset turnover ratio, each of which is found by dividing total revenues by some measure of assets, such as cash, invested assets, or fixed assets. An important asset turnover ratio for insurance companies is ***total asset turnover,*** which measures how efficiently a company has used its total assets to generate revenues, as follows:

$$\textbf{Total Asset Turnover} = \frac{\textbf{Total Revenues}}{\textbf{Total Assets}}$$

In this text, the total assets amount used in the denominator is from the end of the accounting period. Other sources may use *average* total assets. In the numerator, we use total revenues because, for an insurance company, generating investment income is part of its core business operations.

Generally, the higher a firm's total asset turnover, the more efficiently it has used its assets. For example, assume that the total asset turnover for Company A is 1.0 and the total asset turnover for Company B is 2.0. Company B has generated $2 for each dollar invested in total assets, while Company A has generated only $1 for each dollar invested in total assets. Thus, we could infer that Company B has used its assets more efficiently.

Grand's total asset turnover in 2000 is

$$\frac{\$6{,}949{,}176}{\$14{,}825{,}060} = 0.47$$

Thus, Grand turned its total assets over .47 times, which is better than the insurance industry average of .30.

Financial Leverage Ratios

Leverage is an important concept in finance. ***Leverage,*** also called *trading on the equity,* is a financial effect in which the use of fixed-cost funds magnifies both risks and returns to a company's owners. There are three main types of leverage: total leverage, operating leverage, and financial leverage. We are most interested in ***financial leverage,*** which involves financing company assets with debt or other borrowed funds. If the assets in which a company's borrowed funds are invested earn a rate of return greater than the fixed rate of return required by the suppliers of borrowed funds, the result is ***positive financial leverage.*** This positive difference boosts overall returns for the company's owners. On the other hand, if the assets in which the borrowed funds are invested earn a rate of return lower than the fixed rate required by lenders, the result is ***negative financial leverage.*** The difference between the cost of borrowing the funds and the return earned using these funds is called the ***margin,*** also called the *spread, marginal return,* or *profit margin.* For example, assume that a company can borrow money at 9 percent interest. If the company earns an 11 percent return on those borrowed funds, it has realized positive financial leverage with a margin of 2 percent.

The preceding example illustrates the ***leverage effect,*** or the effect that fixed costs have on magnifying risk and return. The borrowed funds are a fixed cost that the company must pay. The leverage effect applies to all companies, including insurers. An important aspect of the leverage affect is that, as leverage increases, the potential rewards increase but so does the company's exposure to risk. Likewise, as leverage decreases, the potential risks and rewards decrease as well. Traditional leverage ratios compare some measure of a company's liabilities, or amounts owed, to some indicator of the firm's financial strength. For many non-insurance companies, liabilities on the balance sheet consist largely of accounts payable and long-term debt (bonds or notes payable). For insurers, most liabilities are policy reserves and other contractual obligations. In either case, the purpose of leverage ratios is to measure a company's debt burden in relation to the assets it owns to cover its debts. For this reason, leverage ratios are sometimes called *solvency ratios.* Two important GAAP ratios that apply to all companies, including insurers, are the debt ratio and the debt-to-equity ratio.

Debt Ratio. Companies use the ***debt ratio*** to measure the proportion of total assets financed with liabilities. Specifically for insurers, the debt ratio measures the proportion of total assets against which policyowners have legal claims, such as future policy benefits, unearned premiums, and unpaid policy claims. The higher the debt ratio, the greater the company's financial leverage. The debt ratio is a balance sheet ratio that is found by dividing total assets into total liabilities:

$$\text{Debt Ratio} = \frac{\text{Total Liabilities}}{\text{Total Assets}}$$

Grand's debt ratio in 2000 is

$$\frac{\$11{,}171{,}092}{\$14{,}825{,}060} = .75 = 75 \text{ percent}$$

A debt ratio of about 85 percent is considered average for a life insurance company. Grand's debt ratio is therefore below the insurance industry average.

Debt-to-Equity Ratio. For most non-insurance companies, the debt-to-equity ratio measures the relationship between the amount of assets provided by the company's *creditors* and the amount of assets provided by its stockholders. For a stock insurance company, the ***debt-to-equity ratio*** measures the relationship between the amount of liabilities to policyowners and the amount of equity provided by stockholders. The higher the debt-to-equity ratio, the more the company relies on borrowed or owed funds to cover future and current benefit payments, to pay for ongoing business operations, and to finance growth. The debt-to-equity ratio is calculated as total liabilities divided by stockholders' equity, as follows:

$$\text{Debt-to-Equity Ratio} = \frac{\text{Total Liabilities}}{\text{Stockholders' Equity}}$$

Grand's debt-to-equity ratio in 2000 is

$$\frac{\$11{,}171{,}092}{\$3{,}653{,}968} = 3.06$$

The insurance industry average for this ratio is about 5. For a mutual insurance company, this ratio would be called the *debt-to-surplus* ratio and would be found by dividing total liabilities by total surplus. Insurance companies usually have high debt-to-equity ratios because policy reserves represent such a large portion of a company's liabilities, and these reserves must be balanced by assets.

Profitability Ratios

Companies are in business to earn a profit. ***Profitability ratios*** measure profitability by relating the returns of a company to sales, total revenues, assets, stockholders' equity, capital and surplus, or stock share price. Stockholders, rating agencies, policyowners, and the company's managers pay close attention to a company's profitability ratios for two reasons: (1) to judge if management has operated the business efficiently enough to cover costs and still provide a return for owners to compensate them for the risk of their investment, and (2) to measure the efficiency with which management has used the company's assets and owners' equity to generate revenues. The first of these tasks is completed by relating net income to revenues. Common-size statements, described earlier in this chapter, are a handy tool for evaluating profitability in relation to revenues. For example, a frequently cited profitability ratio that can be found in the common-size statement of operations is net profit margin. The second task is completed by comparing income to the assets and the stockholders' equity used in generating that income. Two useful ratios for this task are return on assets (ROA) and return on equity (ROE). In this section, we also describe several other measures of

DILBERT reprinted by permission of United Feature Syndicate, Inc.

profitability: earnings per share (EPS), the price/earnings (P/E) ratio, and the dividend payout ratio.

Net Profit Margin. ***Net profit margin,*** also called *rate of return on net sales,* or *return on sales,* shows how much after-tax profit is generated by each dollar of total revenue. This ratio is found by dividing net income, sometimes called *net gain from operations,* by total revenues:

$$\textbf{Net Profit Margin} = \frac{\textbf{Net Income}}{\textbf{Total Revenues}}$$

An average net profit margin for an insurance company is 2.8 percent. Grand's net profit margin in 2000 is

$$\frac{\$705{,}031}{\$6{,}949{,}176} = .101 = 10.1 \text{ percent}$$

Grand's management has therefore operated efficiently enough to cover expenses and still adequately compensate stockholders for putting their capital at risk.

Return on Assets (ROA). The ***return on assets (ROA)*** ratio measures a company's success in using its assets to earn a profit. ROA is an indicator of management's efficiency and is one of the most widely used measures of a company's overall success. ROA indicates the productive use of business resources and is often used to rank companies within the same industry. The higher a company's ROA, the better. There are several variations of the ROA ratio, such as return on *total* assets and return on *invested* assets. In addition, different companies employ different valuations of assets to make this calculation. In this section, we calculate ROA for GAAP statements as return on *total* assets using the *book value* (the end-of-period value shown on the company's books) of the assets, as follows:

$$\textbf{Return on Assets (ROA)} = \frac{\textbf{Net Income}}{\textbf{Total Assets}}$$

Grand's ROA in 2000 is

$$\frac{\$705{,}031}{\$14{,}825{,}060} = .048 = 4.8 \text{ percent}$$

The insurance industry average for return on assets is 2.1 percent. Therefore, Grand has achieved a strong return on all its financial resources.

Return on Equity (ROE). The ***return on equity (ROE)*** ratio, also called the *return on stockholders' equity,* measures the rate of return on the book value of the stockholders' investment in the firm. The higher a company's ROE, the better for the company's stockholders. To compute ROE, divide net income by the stockholders' equity as of the end of the period. ROE is calculated as follows:

$$\text{Return on Equity (ROE)} = \frac{\text{Net Income}}{\text{Stockholders' Equity}}$$

Grand's ROE for 2000 is

$$\frac{\$705{,}031}{\$3{,}653{,}968} = .193 = 19.3 \text{ percent}$$

An average ROE for an insurance company is 5.3 percent. If Grand were a mutual insurer, this ratio would be the *return on surplus,* and policyowners' surplus would replace stockholders' equity in the denominator of the ratio.

Earnings per Share (EPS). Investors purchase shares of a company's stock to realize a return in the form of cash dividends and ***capital gains,*** which is the amount by which the selling price of an asset exceeds its purchase price. The company's net income (earnings) form the basis for dividend payments and any future increases in stock values that will provide for capital gains. Therefore, a company's reported earnings per share of stock is one of the most important ratios to investors. ***Earnings per share (EPS),*** also called *earnings per share of common stock,* is the amount of net income per share of the company's common stock. To calculate EPS, divide net income available to common stockholders by the number of common shares outstanding (outstanding common stock):*

$$\text{Earnings per Share (EPS)} = \frac{\text{Net Income} - \text{Preferred Stock Dividends}}{\text{Number of Common Shares Outstanding}}$$

Note that preferred stock dividends are subtracted from net income to determine the amount of income available to common stockhold-

* Because the number of common shares outstanding can fluctuate during the year, many companies use a *weighted average method* to determine the denominator of the EPS ratio. Suppose that on January 1, the Acme Company had 100,000 common shares outstanding, and on July 1 it issued another 50,000 shares. The original 100,000 shares were outstanding for a full year and the additional 50,000 shares were outstanding for half a year. The year-end weighted average number of common shares for Acme is (100,000 × 1) + (50,000 × ½) = 100,000 + 25,000 = 125,000. If Acme earns $75,000 during the year, it's earnings per share is $75,000 ÷ 125,000 = $0.60.

ers. Insurance companies generally do not issue preferred stock, so for most insurers, the numerator for this ratio is simply net income. The EPS is the only ratio that companies must include in their financial statements. It appears in the statement of operations in the annual report. Grand's EPS in 2000 is already listed on the last line of the statement of operations in Figure 19-2. It was calculated as follows:

$$\frac{\$705{,}031}{1{,}000{,}000} = \$0.71$$

Grand's earnings per share figure for 1999 was $0.63, so the company experienced a 12.7 percent increase in EPS in 2000. Most companies strive to increase EPS by 10 to 15 percent annually, although upward trends generally will encounter an occasional down year.

Earnings per share can be affected by extraordinary items and by convertible securities. Great care should be taken with these factors when computing earnings per share. Recall from Chapter 5 that an extraordinary item, also called an *extraordinary gain (loss)*, is an item that is unusual or infrequent, such as damage caused by fire at a company's home office. An insurer that reports an extraordinary item on its statement of operations also reports two EPS figures. The first is calculated using earnings before the extraordinary item, and the second is calculated using earnings after the extraordinary item. For example, assume that a company had earnings after interest and taxes of $1,560,000, a $600,000 (net) extraordinary gain, and 1,200,000 shares of common stock outstanding. Figure 19-7 demonstrates the correct way to report the earnings per share before and after the extraordinary gain. By computing the EPS both ways, the company avoids artificially inflating its EPS, which would have overstated its normal income-producing ability.

Price/Earnings (P/E) Ratio. An often-quoted relationship between a company's earnings per share and the current market price of its stock is

Figure 19-7. Earnings per share treatment of an extraordinary item on the statement of operations.

Income before extraordinary item	$1,560,000
Extraordinary gain, net of tax	600,000
Net income after extraordinary item	$2,160,000
Earnings per share on common stock:*	
On net income, before extraordinary gain	$ 1.30
On net extraordinary gain	0.50
Net earnings per share	$ 1.80

* Based on 1,200,000 shares of common stock outstanding

the ***price/earnings (P/E) ratio,*** also called the *earnings multiple.* The P/E ratio represents the amount of money that investors are willing to pay for each dollar of the firm's earnings. The P/E ratio is found as follows:

$$\textbf{Price/Earnings Ratio} = \frac{\textbf{Market Price per Share of Common Stock}}{\textbf{Earnings per Share}}$$

There is a wide range of interpretations of the P/E ratio, but, generally, the higher the P/E ratio, the greater the investor confidence in a company. Assume that as of December 31, 2000, Grand's common stock had a market price of $7.50 per share. It follows that Grand's 2000 P/E ratio is

$$\frac{\$7.50}{\$0.71} = 10.6$$

That is, Grand's stock is selling for about 10.6 times its current earnings per share. Stated another way, investors are willing to pay $10.60 for each dollar of Grand's earnings. The P/E ratio is used by investors as a general guideline for valuing companies for purposes of buying stock or acquiring a company. Price/earnings ratios vary widely among companies and industries and are most meaningful when compared to selected industry groups or market averages so that comparisons of relative performance can be made. An average P/E ratio for a stock insurance company is between 10 and 15.

Dividend Payout Ratio. Investors hold shares of stock for two reasons: (1) to realize current income in the form of cash dividends and (2) to realize appreciation in stock market values. Some investors prefer that a company not pay any cash dividends and retain all earnings and reinvest them internally to support company growth. In the long run, this strategy should result in a rising stock price. The stocks of such companies are generally referred to as *growth stocks.* Investors who prefer to receive regular cash dividends invest in companies with consistent dividend policies. The stocks of these companies are called *income stocks.* Traditionally, the stocks of most stock insurers have been considered income stocks because insurers regularly pay dividends to their stockholders. The ***dividend payout ratio*** represents the proportion of earnings (net income) paid out to stockholders in the form of cash dividends. This ratio, which is presented in percentage terms, is computed as follows:

$$\textbf{Dividend Payout Ratio} = \frac{\textbf{Dividends per Share}}{\textbf{Earnings per Share}}$$

Because the numerator and denominator are in per share terms, we can simplify this ratio to

$$\textbf{Dividend Payout Ratio} = \frac{\textbf{Dividends}}{\textbf{Earnings}}$$

In this case, Earnings are equivalent to Net Income.

One function of a stock company's board of directors is to determine the portion of net income, if any, to pay out in dividends to stockholders. To make this decision, the board must balance stockholders' expectation of dividends with the company's need for capital. The board of directors of the Grand Life and Health Insurance Company has decided to pay $272,511 in dividends to stockholders. We can now calculate Grand's dividend payout ratio for 2000:

$$\frac{\$272{,}511}{\$705{,}031} = 0.386 = 38.6 \text{ percent}$$

Investors who seek growth in a company want this figure to remain small, because a low dividend payout means that the company has retained most of its earnings to fund future growth. Investors who seek current income prefer the dividend payout ratio to be larger. The dividend payout ratio tends to be somewhat similar for many firms within a particular industry. A typical dividend payout ratio for an insurance company is within the range of 35 to 40 percent.

Summary of GAAP Ratio Analysis

By applying ratio analysis to the GAAP statements of Grand Life and Health Insurance Company, we are able to make several observations:

- With a current ratio of 1.3, Grand will have to monitor its cash closely to ensure that it has enough cash and cash equivalents to pay obligations as they are due.
- Grand's total asset turnover of .47 is higher than the industry average.
- Grand's debt ratio of 75 percent and debt-to-equity ratio of 3.06 are both below industry averages, indicating that Grand maintains lower reserves in relation to total assets and stockholders' equity than the average insurance company. Grand's management may ask its actuaries to consider an increase in policy reserves.
- Grand's net profit margin (10.1 percent), return on assets (4.8 percent), and return on equity (19.3 percent) are strong, indicating

that the company has been managed effectively and has used its assets efficiently.

- Grand's earnings per share (EPS) on common stock is $0.71, a respectable 12.7 percent increase over the previous year.
- Grand's P/E ratio of 10.6 and dividend payout ratio of 38.6 percent are both in line with the industry.

Statutory Ratios

Earlier we stated that many traditional financial ratios cannot be applied directly to the statutory financial statements that appear in the U.S. Annual Statement. Therefore, many traditional ratios have been modified for insurance purposes. In some cases, new ratios were created specifically for analysis of statutory insurance company statements. These "statutory ratios" are commonly divided into four categories: liquidity ratios, capital and surplus ratios, leverage ratios, and profitability ratios. It is important to note that these insurance-specific ratios are also applied to an insurer's GAAP-based financial statements. However, in this text we refer to these financial ratios as "statutory ratios" because we apply them to an insurer's statutory financial statements.

Liquidity Ratios

Two primary liquidity ratios are quick liquidity and current liquidity. The quick liquidity ratio is similar to the traditional GAAP quick ratio. ***Quick liquidity*** compares an insurer's liquid assets (cash and other readily marketable assets such as short-term investments) to contractual reserves, which are reserves for current insurance and annuity contracts. Contractual reserves do not include other miscellaneous reserves. Quick liquidity is calculated as follows:

$$\text{Quick Liquidity} = \frac{\text{Liquid Assets}}{\text{Contractual Reserves}}$$

The usual range for this ratio is between 10 and 20 percent.[3]

The ***current liquidity*** ratio is similar to the traditional current ratio in that current liquidity compares all of an insurer's total assets not invested in its affiliates to all the insurer's total liabilities, not just its reserves. The current liquidity ratio is calculated as follows:

$$\text{Current Liquidity} = \frac{\text{Total Assets Not Invested in Affiliates}}{\text{Total Liabilities}}$$

The average range for this ratio is 95 to 120 percent. A ratio lower than 95 percent is considered below the accepted norm.

Capital and Surplus Ratios

Insurance companies measure their financial strength using ***capital and surplus ratios,*** which are sometimes referred to as simply *capital* ratios for stock companies and *surplus* ratios for mutual companies. The basic capital and surplus ratio for an insurer is

$$\textbf{Capital and Surplus Ratio} = \frac{\textbf{Capital and Surplus}}{\textbf{Total Liabilities}}$$

Generally, the greater the value of this ratio, the stronger the insurer's financial position. The average industry range is between 4 and 12 percent. An insurer's capital and surplus position can weaken because of (1) poor profitability, (2) payment of excessive dividends relative to the insurer's actual profit, (3) excessive capital losses from investments, and (4) reserve valuation changes that increase the insurer's reserves. A weakness of the basic capital and surplus ratio is that it is an unweighted ratio which fails to recognize the factors that can cause significant changes to a company's capital position. To obtain a more accurate measure of solvency and financial strength, insurers, regulators, and rating agencies use capital ratios that are weight-adjusted to account for different levels of capital risk and different reserving practices that are unique to each insurer. These specialized capital ratios are known as the Risk-Based Capital (RBC) ratios in the United States and the Minimum Continuing Capital and Surplus Requirements (MCCSR) ratios in Canada. We discuss RBC and MCCSR later in this chapter.

Financial Leverage Ratios

Financial leverage ratios compare an insurer's obligations to its ability to meet those obligations. In the context of insurance, obligations can be measured in terms of contractual reserves alone or contractual reserves plus other miscellaneous reserves and liabilities. Leverage ratios typically relate an insurer's liabilities to its capital. The ***insurance leverage ratio,*** also called the *gross leverage ratio,* relates contractual reserves to capital and surplus. This ratio is similar to the traditional debt-to-equity ratio, which is the ratio of long-term debt to total equity. A low result for this ratio is more desirable than a high result, within a normal range. However, there is no absolute standard for determining what is too low and what is too high for all insurers. The insurance leverage ratio is found as follows:

$$\text{Insurance Leverage} = \frac{\text{Contractual Reserves}}{\text{Capital and Surplus}}$$

Profitability Ratios

Profit for a U.S. insurance company is reported in the *Summary of Operations* in four ways: (1) as net income from operations before dividends to policyowners and federal income taxes, (2) as net income from operations after dividends to policyowners and before federal income taxes, (3) as net income from operations after dividends to policyowners and federal income taxes and before realized capital gains (losses) and (4) as net income. In this last context, *profit* and *net income* are used interchangeably. Specialized profitability ratios are available to meet the needs for diverse measures of an insurer's profitability. Some of these ratios evaluate the insurer's overall results on a gross basis or a net basis. These ratios include the *gross profit ratio* and the *return on capital ratio.* The *statutory return on assets (ROA)* and *investment yield ratios* measure investment profitability, and the ratio of *net gain to total income* analyzes profitability in relation to net income.

Gross Profit Ratio. The ***gross profit ratio*** provides a simple measure of the growth of an insurance company's capital and surplus. This ratio compares the insurer's profit before interest expenses and taxes for the period to its beginning capital and surplus. The gross profit ratio is calculated as follows:

$$\text{Gross Profit Ratio} = \frac{\text{Gross Gain from Operations}}{\text{Beginning Capital and Surplus}}$$

For a mutual insurance company, the gross profit ratio is

$$\text{Gross Profit Ratio} = \frac{\text{Gross Contributions to Surplus}}{\text{Beginning Surplus}}$$

Contributions to surplus is similar to net income in that it represents the excess income not needed to pay for the cost of providing insurance.

Return on Capital Ratio. The return on capital ratio is similar to the traditional return on equity (ROE) ratio. Whereas ROE is stated as the ratio of net income to stockholders' equity, the ***return on capital ratio*** is the ratio of net gain from operations to beginning capital and surplus. This ratio indicates the company's overall success in generating returns to owners. The return on capital ratio for insurers is calculated as follows:

$$\text{Return on Capital Ratio} = \frac{\text{Net Gain from Operations}}{\text{Beginning Capital and Surplus}}$$

The result of the return on capital ratio indicates how efficiently an insurer's managers are employing capital and surplus to earn a return for its owners. The average industry range for this ratio is 8 to 14 percent.

Statutory Return on Assets (ROA). The ***statutory return on assets (ROA)*** ratio is the ratio of an insurer's net gain from operations to its average invested assets. This ratio is similar to the GAAP return on assets, which is a company's net income divided by its total assets. However, statutory ROA considers only gains from an insurer's normal business operations, like premium income and investment income, and only the insurer's invested assets. The statutory ROA ratio is:

$$\text{Statutory Return on Assets (ROA)} = \frac{\text{Net Gain from Operations}}{\text{Average Invested Assets}}$$

To determine an insurer's average invested assets, add its beginning-of-year invested assets balance to the end-of-year balance and divide the sum by two. The statutory return on assets ratio shows how efficiently the company's managers are employing the investment portfolio to earn a return for the company's owners.

Investment Yield Ratio. The ***investment yield ratio,*** also called *net yield,* measures how effectively an insurance company's investment managers can earn adequate or higher returns on the company's investment portfolio. The calculation for this ratio is a version of the traditional ROA ratio, as follows:

$$\text{Investment Yield Ratio} = \frac{\text{Investment Income}}{\text{Average Invested Assets}}$$

An insurer's investment yield is an important indicator of potential returns. Investment managers seek an investment yield that is neither too high nor too low, although a definition of these extremes varies among companies. An average range for this ratio is 7 to 9 percent. An unusually high investment yield could indicate excessively risky investments, while a low yield probably indicates inadequate returns.

Net Gain to Total Income. To measure the share of operating income, that is, operating revenues less operating expenses, that represents net profit, insurers apply the ***net gain to total income*** ratio. In this context, net gain means *net gain from operations,* which is the net gain before dividends to policyowners and federal income taxes. This ratio also highlights the share of the insurer's income that is not used to cover expenses. The net gain to total income ratio is found as follows:

$$\text{Net Gain to Total Income} = \frac{\text{Net Gain from Operations}}{\text{Total Income} + \text{Realized Capital Gains and Losses}}$$

A result of less than zero for this ratio could indicate that the insurer is performing poorly. The usual industry range is 1.5 to 6.0 percent. Figure 19-8 compares the traditional ratios used to analyze GAAP-prepared financial statements with the ratios used to analyze statutory-prepared statements.

Regulatory Analysis of Financial Statements

Insurance company financial statements come under intense scrutiny from regulators, possibly more than any other industry. In this section, we describe three regulatory measures of financial statement analysis that apply to most insurers operating in the United States: the *NAIC Insurance Regulatory Information System (IRIS),* the *Financial Analysis and Solvency Tracking (FAST) system,* and *Risk-Based Capital (RBC)* requirements. To continue operating, Canadian insurers must meet solvency requirements known as the *Minimum Continuing Capital and Surplus Requirements (MCCSR),* which are similar to the RBC requirement for U.S. insurers. These requirements—IRIS, RBC, and MCCSR—are designed to flag impaired companies that may require regulatory intervention and to help determine the extent of that intervention.

IRIS Ratios

While ratio analysis is a valuable tool for analyzing the strength and stability of any business concern, U.S. insurance regulators use a set of specific financial ratios to monitor life and health insurance companies. This system, developed by the National Association of Insurance Commissioners (NAIC) and the A.M. Best Company, is called

Figure 19-8. Comparison of GAAP ratios and statutory ratios.

GAAP	Statutory
Liquidity Ratios	***Liquidity Ratios***
$\text{Current Ratio} = \frac{\text{Current Assets}}{\text{Current Liabilities}}$	$\text{Quick Liquidity} = \frac{\text{Liquid Assets}}{\text{Contractual Reserves}}$ $\text{Current Liquidity} = \frac{\text{Total Assets Not Invested in Affiliates}}{\text{Total Liabilities}}$
Activity Ratios	***Capital Ratios***
$\text{Total Asset Turnover} = \frac{\text{Total Revenues}}{\text{Total Assets}}$	$\text{Capital and Surplus Ratio} = \frac{\text{Capital and Surplus}}{\text{Total Liabilities}}$
Financial Leverage Ratios	***Financial Leverage Ratios***
$\text{Debt Ratio} = \frac{\text{Total Liabilities}}{\text{Total Assets}}$ $\text{Debt-to-Equity Ratio} = \frac{\text{Total Liabilities}}{\text{Stockholders' Equity}}$	$\text{Insurance Leverage Ratio} = \frac{\text{Contractual Reserves}}{\text{Capital and Surplus}}$
Profitability Ratios	***Profitability Ratios***
$\text{Net Profit Margin} = \frac{\text{Net Income}}{\text{Total Revenues}}$	$\text{Gross Profit} = \frac{\text{Gross Gain from Operations}}{\text{Beginning Capital and Surplus}}$
$\text{Return on Assets (ROA)} = \frac{\text{Net Income}}{\text{Total Assets}}$	$\text{Return on Capital} = \frac{\text{Net Gain from Operations}}{\text{Beginning Capital and Surplus}}$
$\text{Return on Equity (ROE)} = \frac{\text{Net Income}}{\text{Stockholders' Equity}}$	$\text{Return on Assets (ROA)} = \frac{\text{Net Gain from Operations}}{\text{Average Invested Assets}}$
$\text{Earnings per Share (EPS)} = \frac{\text{Net Income} - \text{Preferred Stock Dividends}}{\text{Common Shares Outstanding}}$	$\text{Investment Yield} = \frac{\text{Invested Income}}{\text{Average Invested Assets}}$
$\text{Price/Earnings (P/E) Ratio} = \frac{\text{Market Price per Share of Common Stock}}{\text{Earnings per Share}}$	$\text{Net Gain to Total Income} = \frac{\text{Net Gain from Operations}}{\text{Total Income} + \text{Realized Capital Gains and Losses}}$
$\text{Dividend Payout Ratio} = \frac{\text{Dividends per Share}}{\text{Earnings per Share}}$	

the ***Insurance Regulatory Information System (IRIS).*** State insurance departments are assisted by the IRIS in identifying companies most likely to experience financial difficulty. Insurers that conduct business in the United States submit to the IRIS tests. IRIS consists of two phases. The first is a *statistical phase* that uses 12 standardized financial IRIS ratios to flag companies that show results outside of a *usual* (normal) range. A result outside the usual range is called an *exception.* The second phase is an *analytical phase* in which a team of financial examiners analyzes the Annual Statements and ratio results of flagged companies. An insurer with four or more ratios outside the usual range undergoes an analytical review. It is important that insurance companies calculate and monitor these ratios on at least a semiannual basis so a company's management can take corrective measures before an unfavorable review by insurance regulators becomes necessary.

The NAIC calculates the 12 IRIS ratios using statutory data extracted from the Annual Statement, then provides the results of these tests in a report to state insurance departments and to each insurance company. This report indicates the ratios calculated for the company and the percentile ranking of all life and health insurance companies. Figure 19-9 describes each of the IRIS ratios. The first eight ratios are tests of an insurance company's solvency and profitability. The final four IRIS ratios are tests of a company's stability. These ratios identify wide swings in operational results, such as changes in premium income or reserve positions. If these ratio results do not fall within the normal range, they may raise questions about the company's ability to manage its operations.

Financial Analysis and Solvency Tracking System

Large insurance companies—those that write business in at least 17 states and have gross premiums greater than $50 million—must submit their financial statements to a solvency analysis known as the ***Financial Analysis and Solvency Tracking (FAST) system.*** The FAST system uses two types of analysis to examine these insurers' financial statement information:

1. Ratio analysis of the insurer's most recent financial statements.

2. Analysis of the five-year history of specific aspects of the insurer's financial statements. The aspects to be analyzed are chosen by the NAIC on a case-by-case basis.

If the examiners find unusual results during the FAST analysis, the NAIC contacts the insurer's state of domicile for further information about the insurer's financial condition and to learn about any new

Figure 19-9. IRIS ratios.

Ratio	Calculation	Purpose	Usual Range
1. Net Change in Capital and Surplus	Changes in Capital and Surplus between the Prior and Current Year, Net of any Capital and Surplus Paid-In / Prior Year Capital and Surplus	Measures the general improvement or deterioration in a company's financial condition	−10% to 50%
1A. Gross Change in Capital and Surplus	Change in Capital and Surplus from the Prior Year to the Current Year / Prior Year Capital and Surplus	Also measures the general improvement or deterioration in a company's financial condition	−10% to 50%
2. Net Income to Total Income	Net Income from Operations / Total Income (Including Realized Capital Gains or Losses)	Measures profitability	Greater than 0%
3. Commissions and Expenses to Premiums and Deposits (discontinued)			
4. Adequacy of Investment Income	Net Investment Income / Interest Required	Determines whether the company's investment income is adequate to meet the interest requirements of its reserves	125% to 900%
5. Nonadmitted to Admitted Assets	Nonadmitted Assets / Admitted Assets	Measures the degree to which the insurer has acquired nonproductive investments	Less than 10%
6. Total Real Estate and Total Mortgage Loans to Cash and Invested Assets	Real Estate / Cash and Invested Assets	Measures the degree to which real estate may be overstated	Less than 30%
7. Total Affiliate Investments to Capital and Surplus	Total Affiliate Investments / Capital and Surplus	Identifies excessive investments in affiliates	Less than 30%
8. Surplus Relief	Net Commissions and Expense Allowances on Reinsurance / Capital and Surplus	Measures the company's trend in utilizing reinsurance to control capital and surplus levels	(a) −10% to 10% (b) −99% to 30%
9. Change in Premium Revenue	Change in Premium Revenue / Prior Year Total Premium Revenue	Measures the percentage change in premium revenue from the prior year to the current year	−10% to 50%
10. Change in Product Mix	Sum of the Differences between the Current Year and Prior Year Percentages of Premiums / Number of Product Lines	Measures the average change in the percentage of total premium revenue from each product line during the year	Less than 5%
11. Change in Asset Mix	Sum of the Differences between the Current Year and Prior Year Percentages of Cash and Invested Assets / Cash and Invested Assets	Measures the percentage shift in invested assets from one investment vehicle to another	Less than 5%
12. Change in Reserving Ratio	Aggregate increase in reserves for individual life insurance taken as a percentage of renewal and single premiums for individual life insurance	Represents the difference between the reserving ratio for current and prior years	−20% to 20%

(a) Companies with capital and surplus equal to or less than $5 million
(b) Companies with capital and surplus greater than $5 million

Source: *Insurance Regulatory Information System Ratio Results—1995* (Kansas City, MO: National Association of Insurance Commissioners, 1996), pp. 35–65.

regulatory action the state has taken against the insurer. If the NAIC determines that the state has taken appropriate action toward the insurer, then the NAIC may either end its involvement in the case or continue to monitor the insurer. If the NAIC finds that the state's regulatory action toward the insurer is inadequate, then the NAIC will recommend further action. If the state does not follow the NAIC's recommendation, then the NAIC notifies the other states in which the insurer does business and coordinates all the states' actions toward the insurer.

Monitoring Capital and Surplus Requirements

By selling insurance products and investing funds, insurance companies assume a great deal of risk that unforeseen events could significantly impact their financial condition. Capital and surplus help to protect insurers from the risks inherent in their normal business operations. In the past, insurance regulators required all insurance companies, regardless of size and type of risks undertaken, to maintain a target amount of capital and surplus. But in the 1980s, a few large insurance companies failed after overinvesting in assets too risky to be supported by their levels of capital and surplus. In response, regulators adopted rules that require insurers to set aside capital amounts that reflect the riskiness of their unique asset mix and operations. These requirements are called Risk-Based Capital (RBC) requirements in the United States and Minimum Continuing Capital and Surplus Requirements (MCCSR) in Canada. Both requirements follow a similar philosophy: the more volatile an insurer's assets or insurance products—in other words, the more *risky* the company—the more capital and surplus it must maintain. Insight 19-1 describes the impact of these requirements on insurers, and how insurers have responded.

Risk-Based Capital Requirements[4]

In 1993, the NAIC drafted the ***Risk-Based Capital (RBC) requirements*** for evaluating, based on an insurer's size and risk profile, the adequacy of the insurer's capital and surplus. The principle behind RBC is that an insurer that exposes itself to more risk, such as by investing in low-grade bonds, should maintain more capital and surplus than an insurer that invests primarily in investment-grade bonds and thus exposes itself to less risk. The RBC requirement includes a formula to quantify the threshold amount of capital and surplus that each insurer should set aside based on the risks it incurs. Regulators use the RBC formula to evaluate an insurer's reported statutory capital and surplus so they can identify companies with inadequate capital and surplus levels. In determining the threshold amount of capital and surplus for each insurer, the RBC formula incorporates

Insight 19-1 Will Insurers Buy This Policy?

It's one of the biggest things to hit the life insurance industry in years, causing companies to sell or restructure billions of dollars of assets and often to rethink their business strategy.

The cause of this turmoil is a seemingly arcane accounting concept called "risk-based capital" (RBC). New regulatory measures require life insurers to report to regulators annually the riskiness of their assets and lines of business. The higher the risk levels, the more capital an insurer must have on its balance sheet to support the risks.

The primary reason for the new requirements is the rash of insurer collapses in recent years. The information on risk provided by the companies, regulators say, will be a big help in spotting solvency problems. Adjusting to the guidelines could have a profound effect on the products and pricing offered to insurance consumers.

The RBC requirements were created by the National Association of Insurance Commissioners (NAIC), a group of state insurance commissioners that works to craft uniform standards for the industry. A company's RBC ratio is calculated by dividing its total capital by an index of the riskiness of its assets and lines of business.

Side Effects

Insurers are on a tight schedule. Life and health insurers had to report their RBC ratios to state insurance departments by March 15; property-casualty insurers have another year before their numbers must be filed.

Some industry executives warn that the RBC guidelines could have unfortunate side effects. Because the guidelines require large amounts of capital to be held against higher-yielding, more volatile assets such as common stocks, junk bonds, real estate, and mortgages, insurers are reducing such holdings. That could lead to serious damage to the private-placement, real estate, and junk-bond markets. Jerry M. de St. Paer, Equitable Cos.' chief financial officer, says RBC "could have a major economic impact" on the private-placement market for small companies.

Cutting back on higher-yielding assets, in turn, is reducing investment returns, which may force insurers to cut costs and raise premiums, says Larry G. Mayewski, a senior vice president with rating agency A.M. Best Co. Jeffrey R. Schuman, an analyst with Conning & Co., complains that "this cautious investing . . . will hurt company earnings as well as policy values."

That is producing a flurry of deals that may not always make the best business sense. "You're seeing a catch-up and new analysis looking at a whole new universe of transactions that can be done primarily for RBC, not for economics," says Dennis P. Yeskey, a principal with accounting firm Kenneth Leventhal & Co. Down the road, RBC is expected to help spur a major industry shakeout. "If you like change, it'll be fun," says Sanford I. Weill, chairman of Hartford-based Travelers Inc.

Insurers are finding ways to offset some of the negative consequences of the RBC guidelines. Rather than dump all their junk bonds and mortgages to lessen capital charges, many insurers have simply pooled mortgage loans and created less risky, securitized bonds. Phoenix Home Life Mutual Insurance Cos., for example, securitized $400 million in commercial mortgage loans, pooling the loans and turning them into higher-rated bonds.

Rich Parent

Other insurers are increasing their RBC numbers by raising capital, sometimes without even tapping into the public markets. Take Equitable Life Assurance Society of the United States. Because its 100 percent holding of the outstanding common stock of Donaldson, Lufkin & Jenrette Inc. would have resulted in an enormous capital charge, the insurer's parent company, Equitable Cos., stepped in and purchased about 61 percent of the company from its subsidiary. That brought down the capital charge considerably and gave the subsidiary an $800 million cash infusion.

As insurers vie to come up with the best possible RBC ratios, they're debating whether the numbers ought to be more widely disseminated to the public. Some companies fear they will lose business if they don't look as good as their competitors. The model law crafted by the NAIC prohibits agents or insurance companies from using an RBC ratio as a marketing tool—by, say, taking out a full-page ad boasting about their RBC number.

Still, the industry remains fearful that RBC ratios will be viewed by the public as a new ranking system, when, in fact, they exclude such important qualitative issues as quality of management and distribution channels. It's a legitimate concern, for in the end, human capital may be the best gauge of a company's staying power.

Source: Adapted from Suzanne Woolley, "Will Insurers Buy This Policy?" *Business Week* (March 28, 1994), p. 152. Reprinted from March 28, 1994 issue of *Business Week* by special permission,

four classifications of risk, called ***contingency risks,*** or ***C risks,*** that are intrinsic to an insurer's invested assets and the products it underwrites:

- **C1 risk (asset risk):** The risk of default for debt assets (bonds and mortgages) and the risk of loss of market value for equity assets (real estate and stocks).

- **C2 risk (insurance risk):** The risk that claims might be larger or more numerous than expected or that products might be inadequately priced to meet expected claims.

- **C3 risk (interest rate risk):** The risk of loss caused by changes in market interest rate levels. This is the risk of securities not performing as expected to keep up with the interest rates that the company must pay to policyowners.

- **C4 risk (general business risk):** This risk incorporates several kinds of risks, such as risks from fraud, mismanagement, market competition, or a guaranty-fund assessment resulting from the failure of another insurer.

The calculation of the Risk-Based Capital formula is beyond the scope of this text. However, the formula involves three main steps: (1) calculating the Authorized Control Level RBC, (2) calculating the Total Adjusted Capital (TAC), and (3) comparing the two in ratio form. All asset, premium, reserve, and net amount at risk items are evaluated and assigned a risk-based capital *factor* based on their level of exposure to the four C risks. The sum of the risk amounts is the insurer's *Authorized Control Level RBC,* which is a quantitative measure of the risk inherent in the business. The Authorized Control Level RBC is compared with available capital, also known as *Total Adjusted Capital (TAC),* which is the sum of (1) the company's statutory capital and surplus, (2) asset valuation reserve (AVR), (3) voluntary investment reserves, and (4) half of the liability for policy dividends. When the TAC and Authorized Control Level RBC are placed in ratio form, known as the ***Risk-Based Capital ratio,*** regulators are able to identify companies whose level of capital and surplus is insufficient to support their relative risk. For example, assume that Noble Life and Health Insurance Company has a Total Adjusted Capital of $200,000,000 and an Authorized Control Level RBC of $110,000,000. Noble's RBC ratio is

$$\frac{\textbf{Total Adjusted Capital}}{\textbf{Authorized Control Level RBC}} = \frac{\$200{,}000{,}000}{\$110{,}000{,}000} = 1.8 = 180\%$$

Regulators compare RBC ratios with trigger points to determine if regulatory intervention is necessary, and, if so, to what degree. The four levels of regulatory intervention are listed below:

- *Level 1: Company Action,* in which an insurer must submit a proposal for corrective actions to the insurance commissioner in the state of domicile
- *Level 2: Regulatory Action,* in which the insurance commissioner initiates the corrective actions for the insurer
- *Level 3: Authorized Control,* in which the insurance commissioner has the authority to place the insurer under either a plan of rehabilitation or liquidation
- *Level 4: Mandatory Control,* in which the insurance commissioner seizes the insurer for rehabilitation or liquidation

Figure 19-10 summarizes the RBC ratio result cut-off points for each level of regulatory intervention. Note that if the RBC ratio percentage is greater than 200, then no action is taken unless the company's results reflect a negative trend.

Recall from our earlier example that the RBC ratio for Noble yielded a result of 180 percent. Therefore, the company is subject to Level 1 (Company Action) intervention and is required to submit a financial plan identifying the cause of the capital and surplus shortage and proposals to correct it. Risk-based capital requirements add another layer of solvency regulation and provide an additional set of enforcement tools for insurance regulators. Because risk-based capital is the *minimum* threshold capital required, insurance companies should aim to have a significantly higher amount of statutory surplus—in effect, a safety cushion—than is otherwise required using the RBC formula.

Figure 19-10. Risk-based capital (RBC) ratio percentages and levels of regulatory intervention.

Level	Regulatory Intervention	RBC Ratio Percentage
Level 1	Company Action	150% to 200%
Level 2	Regulatory Action	100% to below 150%
Level 3	Authorized Control	70% to below 100%
Level 4	Mandatory Control	Below 70%

Minimum Continuing Capital and Surplus Requirements[5]

Like RBC requirements in the United States, the Canadian ***Minimum Continuing Capital and Surplus Requirements (MCCSR)*** mandate that Canadian insurers maintain at least a minimum level of capital and surplus that reflects the riskiness of their assets and operations. The MCCSR allows regulators to evaluate the adequacy of an insurer's capital and to provide an early warning tool for measuring the solvency of insurers. The MCCSR formula is not identical to RBC, although it is similar. One difference is that the MCCSR's definition of *available capital,* which is the Canadian version of the Total Adjusted Capital, is more complex than TAC. This MCCSR calculation, which is outside the scope of this text, is similar to the capital provisions governing U.S. depository institutions, such as banks, in that capital falls into two categories: Tier 1 (core) capital and Tier 2 (supplementary) capital. Another difference between RBC and MCCSR is that MCCSR has no explicit allowance for C4: general business risk. Instead, it has a component for ***interest margin pricing risk,*** which is the risk relating to interest margin losses from future investment and pricing decisions on in-force insurance business. Life insurers operating in Canada file an MCCSR calculation each quarter. As with RBC, the MCCSR calculation shows the ratio of available capital to required capital.

Health Insurance Financial Analysis

Besides the financial ratios that are important to all companies and the IRIS ratios that are important to most insurers, health insurers track other ratios and financial data relating specifically to health business written. Among the most important ratios for health insurance are the loss ratio and the expense ratio. The ***combined ratio,*** which is a profitability ratio, is the sum of the loss ratio and the expense ratio and, as such, indicates whether the premiums being collected are sufficient to pay both the claims to policyowners and the company's expenses. Stated as a formula, the combined ratio is

Combined Ratio = Loss Ratio + Expense Ratio

The ***loss ratio*** is the percentage of incurred claims to earned premiums. The ***expense ratio*** measures the percentage of health insurance expenses paid for each dollar of premium income. If the combined ratio is less than 100 percent, then the premium contains a margin for profit or adverse risk. To the extent that the combined ratio exceeds 100 percent, the company must rely on investment income to avoid losses.

The loss ratio is one of the most important measures of the capital and surplus of health insurers. It is a simple tool for measuring overall claims levels. Insurers use the loss ratio to determine if the benefits provided by its policies are in line with the premiums charged. Companies calculate the loss ratio as follows:

$$\textbf{Loss Ratio} = \frac{\textbf{Incurred Claims}}{\textbf{Earned Premiums}}$$

Because the denominator of the loss ratio is earned premiums, the loss ratio automatically adjusts for growth in business. There are several variations of the loss ratio. One is the *paid loss ratio,* which is based on paid claims rather than incurred claims. However, paid loss ratios can be misleading because they can be unusually low for new or rapidly growing blocks of business. It is therefore difficult to determine with certainty the profitable and unprofitable blocks of business using only paid loss ratios.

Another variation of the loss ratio is the *tolerable loss ratio (TLR),* also called the *acceptable loss ratio,* which is used to indicate the ratio of losses the insurer can tolerate without losing money on a particular block of business. If the overall loss ratio exceeds the tolerable loss ratio, then profits may disappear. Further, health insurance companies that offer a new product form or that apply for a rate increase for an existing product must calculate the *lifetime loss ratio,* which measures the ratio of losses for the entire lifetime of the policies, including the future lifetime of the policies from the date of the rate revision.

In 1978, the NAIC modified existing guidelines for the approval of premium rates for individual health insurance policies sold in the United States. These guidelines established minimum criteria for the reasonableness of benefits in relation to premiums. For example, a loss ratio of 60 percent may be required over the lifetime of certain policies. The company's actual experience plus projected future results are compared with this 60 percent standard before a rate increase is approved.

As stated earlier, the loss ratio is often used in tandem with the expense ratio, which is found as follows:

$$\textbf{Expense Ratio} = \frac{\textbf{Health Insurance Expenses}}{\textbf{Earned Premiums}}$$

The expense ratio can also be somewhat misleading if the company has a new or growing block of business, because expenses are generally higher in the first year of a sale. It is therefore necessary to track the expense ratio over a number of years if the level of earned premiums varies from year to year.

Conclusion

This chapter reviewed the key financial ratios used to analyze an insurer's GAAP-based and statutory financial statements for financial strength and profitability. Chapter 20, the final chapter in this text, discusses an insurer's internal controls and the auditing function, which help to preserve the credibility of amounts reported in the insurer's financial statements.

Key Terms and Concepts

financial statement analysis
external analysis
internal analysis
comparative financial statements
horizontal analysis
base period
trend analysis
vertical analysis
common-size statement
benchmarking
ratio analysis
ratio
liquidity ratios
current ratio
activity ratios
total asset turnover
leverage
financial leverage
positive financial leverage
negative financial leverage
margin
leverage effect
debt ratio
debt-to-equity ratio
profitability ratios
net profit margin
return on assets (ROA)
return on equity (ROE)
capital gains
earnings per share (EPS)
price/earnings (P/E) ratio
dividend payout ratio
quick liquidity
current liquidity
capital and surplus ratios
financial leverage ratios
insurance leverage ratio
gross profit ratio
return on capital ratio
statutory return on assets (ROA)
investment yield ratio
net gain to total income
Insurance Regulatory Information System (IRIS)
Financial Analysis and Solvency Tracking (FAST) system
Risk-Based Capital (RBC) requirements
contingency risks (C risks)
Risk-Based Capital ratio
Minimum Continuing Capital and Surplus Requirements (MCCSR)
interest margin pricing risk
combined ratio
loss ratio
expense ratio

References

1. John L. Ward, "Cost Allocation Methodology," *Life Insurance Accounting* (Durham, NC: Insurance Accounting & Systems Association, Inc., 1994), p. 14-10.

2. All industry averages in the GAAP ratios section are extracted from *Almanac of Business and Industrial Financial Ratios,* 26th Anniversary Edition (Englewood Cliffs, NJ: Prentice-Hall, 1995), p. 283.

3. All industry averages in the section on statutory ratios were extracted from *Best's Insurance Reports, Life-Health United States* (Oldwick, NJ: A.M. Best, 1996), p. xvii.

4. Portions of the section on risk-based capital requirements were adapted with permission from *Risk-Based Capital Requirements for Insurers: A New Solvency Tool for Consumer Protection* (Kansas City, MO: National Association of Insurance Commissioners, 1994), pp. 1–4 and 8–9.

5. The section on minimum continuing capital and surplus requirements has been adapted with permission from *Risk-Based Capital in the Life Insurance Industry* (Atlanta, GA: LOMA, 1994), pp. 57–62.

CHAPTER 20

INTERNAL CONTROL AND AUDITING

LEARNING OBJECTIVES

After studying this chapter, you should be able to

- List the primary goals of internal control
- Describe several elements of an effective system of internal controls
- Differentiate between internal and external auditing
- Identify the primary types of internal and external auditing

CHAPTER OUTLINE

Internal Control

Preventive Controls and Detective Controls

Managing the Limitations of Internal Controls

Compliance and Monitoring

Key Participants in the Internal Control System

Elements of Effective Control

Examples of Internal Controls

Auditing

Internal Auditing

External Auditing

Types of Internal and External Audits

The activities associated with accounting and financial reporting are an integral part of an insurer's *control function*, which serves to measure and monitor all of an insurer's transactions as it pursues its corporate objectives, including statutory solvency, profitability, and quality service to policyowners. Two key aspects of an insurer's control function that directly affect all of an insurer's operations are internal control and auditing. ***Internal control*** consists of the steps a company takes to (1) protect its assets, (2) monitor the accuracy of its accounting records, and (3) encourage both operational efficiency and adherence to the company's management policies. ***Auditing*** is the process of examining and evaluating company records and procedures to ensure that the company's accounting records and financial statements are presented fairly and reasonably, that quality assurance is maintained, and that operational procedures and policies are effective. Auditing can be thought of as a form of external control.

Typically, the internal control and auditing functions are separate from the duties of the accounting department. To perform their analysis effectively and without bias, audit and control personnel must maintain a high degree of independence and objectivity regarding other departments. Figure 20-1 provides examples of specific activities for which insurers establish internal controls and which internal and external auditors review. Besides these examples, an insurer also establishes internal controls for premium taxes, insurance claims by product type, invested assets, investment income, and others.

In this chapter, we begin by discussing internal control. We discuss the individuals and areas that establish and conduct internal control activities. We discuss specific types of accounting controls, the advantages and limitations of internal controls, the elements of effective control, and examples of internal controls. We conclude the chapter with a discussion of internal and external auditing, describing in detail financial auditing, compliance auditing, and performance auditing.

Internal Control

Internal controls are divided into two general types: administrative controls and accounting controls. ***Administrative controls,*** also called *operating controls,* are the procedures and policies that guide employees in conducting their normal day-to-day tasks. An example of

Figure 20-1. Insurance activities and the control function.

Functional Area	Internal Controls and Auditing ensure that . . .
Premium Income	• Duties for premium collection and premium accounting are segregated. • Premium notices have correct premium amounts. • Preauthorized checks (PACs) and electronic funds transfers (EFTs) have proper authorization and correct amounts. • The policyowner master file has current and correct policy paid-to dates. • Procedures are established for advance premiums, automatic premium loans (APLs), policy lapses, and policy surrenders.
Reinsurance	• Reinsurance is obtained in accordance with the insurer's retention limits. • Reinsurers are billed promptly for recoverable benefits. • Ceding company records are routinely compared with reinsurer records.
Agent Commissions	• Procedures for determining agent balances due are established. • Procedures for proper authorization and accurate payment of agent commissions on individual and group insurance products are followed. • Commission payments are routinely compared with premium income and insurance company products. • Chargeback procedures for agent commissions upon policy lapse or policy surrender are established.
Policy Reserves	• Adequate policy reserves are maintained. • Reserve valuation procedures comply with regulatory requirements and applicable accounting principles and practices. • Routine comparisons of in-force policies and the reserves for each policy type are conducted.
Benefit Payments	• Duties for claim processing and claim disbursement are segregated. • Proper authorization and approval of benefit payments are documented. • Disbursement records with prenumbered checks are compared routinely. • Approved claims and claim disbursements are reconciled routinely.
Treasury Operations (cash management)	• Duties for cash receipts, cash disbursements, and bank reconciliation are segregated. • Collections procedures are efficient. • Management of cash flows is effective and efficient. • Appropriate and consistent controls for authorization, check security, and accounting records for cash disbursements are maintained.

Source: *LOMA Internal Audit Manual*, Seventh Edition (Atlanta, GA: LOMA, 1995), various pages.

an administrative control is the policy that requires a manager to check three business references before hiring an employee. On the other hand, ***accounting controls,*** also called *financial controls,* are the policies and procedures used to authorize financial transactions, safeguard assets, and provide reliable, timely, and fairly presented financial information about a company. Accounting controls in a life and health insurance company generally include the preparation and analysis of financial statements, internal auditing, responsibility accounting, the establishment of standard costs, variance analysis, overhead analysis, and other measures of financial performance. By adhering to accounting controls, an insurer can be reasonably certain that only authorized personnel

- Record accounting entries for the insurer's financial transactions
- Prepare financial statements that comply with GAAP, statutory accounting practices, or other regulatory requirements
- Access the insurer's assets
- Compare the insurer's assets with its accounting records for those assets

While both administrative and accounting controls have their own unique qualities, they are sometimes difficult to distinguish in actual practice. The American Institute of Certified Public Accountants (AICPA) recognizes this difficulty and indicates in its *Statement of Auditing Standards No. 1* that the two types of internal control are not mutually exclusive. For example, personnel records are an internal control that provide wage and salary information that is useful as an accounting control. However, personnel records also provide performance evaluation information that is used as an administrative control. In this text, we focus on internal controls that are associated with accounting and financial reporting.

Generally, internal controls are designed to prevent or reduce losses arising from (1) mistakes and irregularities in the processing of transactions and the handling of assets and (2) unexpected losses or contingencies. One of the responsibilities of an insurer's management team is to determine the level of risk associated with various kinds of losses and develop safeguarding controls accordingly. For example, the risks associated with office furniture are lower than those for handling cash, because someone can more easily divert cash to personal use. Therefore, the internal controls for handling cash are typically stricter than the controls for dealing with office furniture. Similarly, while natural disasters, such as floods or fires, occur infrequently, the loss from such disasters can be catastrophic. Therefore, most insurers have developed business disaster recovery plans as internal controls for dealing with natural disasters. On the other hand, internal controls are not intended to protect a company from the risk of loss arising from the company's own strategic decisions, such as the cost of developing and trying to sell an unprofitable product, or losses that result from normal business operations.

Preventive Controls and Detective Controls

An insurer's internal controls should include both preventive and detective controls. ***Preventive controls,*** as the name implies, are designed to keep an error or a problem from occurring. Normally, preventive controls are steps that must be taken before a transaction occurs. Examples of preventive controls are the requirement that a claim administration employee must obtain proper authorization before disbursing a benefit payment check and that two signatures are required on checks written over a certain dollar amount. ***Detective controls*** are intended to identify problems after they occur. Most detective controls are undertaken after a series of transactions have taken place. An example of a detective control is an insurer's monthly review of the claim disbursements it made during the preceding month. Preventive controls are usually more effective at reducing problems than detective controls, but they are also more expensive than detective controls. As with any other expense, the value of establishing and maintaining internal controls is based on the benefits that they return to a company. Therefore, companies do regular cost-benefit analyses to make sure their internal controls are providing benefits that are worth their costs.

Managing the Limitations of Internal Controls

While internal controls are a necessary part of insurance company operations, and while some internal controls, such as internal audits, are required by regulatory agencies, no system of internal controls is infallible. All systems have their limitations, which may be exposed by

- Employee error
- Criminal acts
- Poor design
- Changing economic and regulatory conditions

An insurance company's internal controls are designed in part to reduce or avoid employee error. However, employees can make mistakes in implementing the internal controls themselves, and improperly implemented controls are unlikely to detect the problems they were designed to detect. The two most common tactics for overcoming the problem of employee errors are (1) to hire the best qualified people available and (2) to train employees thoroughly in the proper use of established internal controls. Another possible tactic for reducing employee error is to involve employees in the development of internal controls. By participating in the process, employees not only become more knowledgeable about the controls, but they often gain a sense of ownership in the system itself and are more likely to follow it accurately.

As with employee error, internal controls are designed to eliminate the possibility of criminal acts, such as theft, vandalism, or embezzlement. However, no system is perfect, and a determined individual can occasionally circumvent a company's internal controls. While the possibility of an undeterred criminal act remains a limitation of any system of internal controls, most such criminal acts are eventually detected.

Of course, if a system of internal controls is poorly designed to begin with, the controls have little hope of being effective. Proper design, the elements of which we discuss later in this chapter, is essential for reducing the limitations of any system of internal control. To design internal controls, company employees or outside consultants must examine and evaluate all company policies and procedures. They must then develop controls that fit the company's actual operations. Controls must be workable from an operational point of view, and, as noted earlier, they must provide greater benefits than they cost.

Finally, internal controls are designed to be used in certain conditions. As conditions change, the controls must be changed to adapt to the new conditions. Change can come from outside the company or from within. For example, the federal income tax code changes frequently, and these changes sometimes require insurers to make changes in their operating procedures. As procedures change, the internal controls used to monitor those procedures must also change. Further, when a company introduces a new product, internal controls for the administration of that product must be developed. Similarly, when a company modifies an old product, old internal controls must be changed to match modified procedures.

Compliance and Monitoring

As we indicated above, an insurer must be able to adjust its internal controls to accommodate changes in laws, regulations, and accounting practices, as well as changes in its strategic plans. The internal control system must also facilitate employee training, communication of policies and procedures, and warning signals for prompt error detection and correction. In recent years, *compliance* has focused on the market conduct of an insurer's agents as well as the insurer's financial reports. An insurer could be subject to fines and other penalties for noncompliance with statutory and regulatory requirements. The payment of fines decreases an insurer's net income and ultimately its surplus. For example, the IRS and Revenue Canada impose fines and penalties for noncompliance with tax regulations. Also, a state or provincial insurance department can impose a fine on an insurer that continues to file late quarterly financial statements. To minimize the risk of noncompliance, an insurer implements a strong system of internal controls. Some insurers have a compliance officer or a cross-divisional team of employees to address compliance issues.

An internal control system must enable an insurer to monitor progress toward its corporate goals. Monitoring involves an evaluation of the kind of measurement tools used to track progress as well as the effectiveness of the progress to date. Many insurers use information system controls to monitor claims processing, underwriting, user access to files, and budget variances. Other monitoring methods include

- Physical counts of computer workstations and other property and comparison of those counts with accounting records to identify discrepancies in the amount or description of an insurer's assets

- Specialized controls for determining the accuracy and timeliness of automated accounting and policyowner information

- Bank reconciliation, which monitors the insurer's checking account balance on a monthly basis

- Procedures for resolving policyowner complaints, which provide the insurer with valuable feedback on the quality of its services and products

Insight 20-1 discusses the role of effective internal controls in reducing an insurer's risk.

Key Participants in the Internal Control System

The proper implementation of internal controls demands solid ethical support and communication at all organizational levels, including an insurer's board of directors, audit committee, internal auditors, and managers and other employees. We introduced these key participants in Chapter 1, in the context of internal users of an insurer's accounting records and financial reports. Briefly outlined below are the typical roles these key participants assume in achieving corporate objectives while adhering to internal controls.

Insight 20-1 Internal Control Systems Help Insurers Reduce Risk

With hundreds of millions of dollars lost on lawsuits, penalties, and reputational damage, the insurance industry is faced with an urgent need to reassess business risks and to devise adequate means of controlling them. The key is to understand how to adapt controls to the accelerating pace of change dominating the industry. This need is particularly acute for sales practices and product development areas not typically covered by traditional controls but which have caused significant erosion in consumer confidence. A response that is working in many companies calls for an integrated framework of control that adapts to continuous industry change.

Many efforts are currently under way including:

- The American Council of Life Insurance drafting a proposal to recognize insurers who embrace a code of ethical market conduct.
- The National Association of Insurance Commissioners sponsoring a joint effort among the industry, agents and regulators to develop model regulations for sales illustrations and disclosure.
- The National Association of Life Underwriters convening a task force on replacement sales.

In addition, the New York Insurance Department held a hearing in October 1995 on the relationship of agent commissions to "churning."

This groundswell of activity creates a sense of urgency that makes management get their houses in order. But irresistible forces are changing traditional insurance markets and undermining management control efforts. These changes include:

- Lower regulatory boundaries between banks, broker-dealers, and insurers.
- Growing customer demands for speed and service, requiring localized decisions at the expense of centralized controls.
- Restructurings and downsizings that eliminate much of the "institutional memory" that previously kept problems in check.

The only aspects of the business that haven't changed are the customers' needs for suitable products and the knowledge that an insurer has enduring financial strength.

Traditional Controls

Insurers are responding to competitive pressures by using new technology, downsizing, and reengineering existing operations, and expanding into new lines and products. These changes are necessary not just to remain competitive, but in many cases to survive. However, these changes aren't tied to a commensurate reengineering of controls. Business conduct is being fundamentally rethought, but control thinking remains essentially static.

Managers are adding procedures and personnel in a patchwork attempt to "have enough control." They add compliance monitors and internal auditors to cover problem areas, write voluminous policy and procedure manuals and generate more management reports. With this expensive and far-from-seamless approach, new risks still fall between the cracks and problems grow.

Examining the characteristics of traditional insurance control systems exposes the gaps:

- Traditional controls are vested in the chief financial officer and are delegated to staff and support functions at the back end of business processes. Control occurs after the sale.
- Policies and procedures are perceived as overwhelming business impediments by the people on the "front lines," and thus are skirted or ignored.
- Investigations into problems are inherently flawed by a focus on symptoms rather than on root causes.

Once a problem is noticed, an investigation confirms its existence and assesses the extent of wrongdoing. Then blame is apportioned. Changes are made but don't normally go far enough into the business process. The key question often isn't asked: "Are the findings symptomatic of underlying root causes for control deficiencies?" Further, little time exists for proactive analysis: "If nothing happened, could it happen and what can be done to control the risk?"

Structural problems demonstrate why traditional controls are ineffective. Traditional controls deal with yesterday's risks and provide a "detection" function after a problem has occurred. In today's highly sensitized climate, providing a "prevention" function and containing risks before problems occur are critical.

Redefining the Scope

A review of recent corporate breakdowns reveals that many of the biggest problems occur in nonfinancial areas where risks can be substantial but oversight and control aren't as formal. Financial statement inaccuracies aren't a big insurance risk because the control environment is highly developed. On the other hand, poor sales practices and faulty product design have caused major reputational damage partly because the control environment is substantially less developed. A review of the broader spectrum of risks previously ignored by the

(continued)

Insight 20-1 Internal Control Systems Help Insurers Reduce Risk, continued

scope of traditional control would include:

Customer risk. For example, agents not adequately trained in the products they are selling, particularly in relation to discretionary investment and taxation features.

Performance risk. When product profitability is compromised because the product design process lacks discipline and/or isn't aligned to profitability assumptions included in business plans.

Compliance risk. For instance, agents using unapproved or misleading product illustrations and sales material.

Solving deficiencies across the full spectrum of the business requires a new way of thinking about internal control. Fortunately, there is a new, broader view that mandates a comprehensive and unified approach to assessing and controlling business risk. Under this approach, control and risk assessment are embedded into the management of the company.

This approach was articulated with the 1992 issuance of the Internal Control-Integrated Framework which was sponsored by the Committee of Sponsoring Organizations of the Treadway Commission and authored by Coopers & Lybrand. This broader view is commonly referred to as the COSO model and has become the benchmark for effective internal control systems adopted by several large insurers.

The new view isn't to spend more money on additional reviewers and control procedures but rather to change the nature of control. When the focus is on integrating control throughout a business process, fewer controls are required. When everyone in the company views control as an individual responsibility, fundamental changes in culture and behavior occur. For example, an agent sees the value of training that not only focuses on selling skills but also addresses product risks, benefits, and compliance requirements. The branch manager becomes more vigilant in reviewing product sales with individual agents to ensure specific customers have been well served.

Obviously, changes like these take time and require fundamental shifts, including adjustments in employee incentives, hiring practices and corporate communication. But the emerging standards of corporate governance demand that organizations anticipate and control business risks and not accept breakdowns as random bad luck.

The new and integrated view goes well beyond the traditional model and introduces several new concepts:

- Internal control is a continuous process, not an after-the-fact activity for internal audit or compliance departments.
- People throughout an organization are responsible and accountable for managing risk on a daily basis.
- Internal control is a positive concept that enhances efficiency and the achievement of corporate objectives.

The COSO model describes five interrelated components of control that must be embedded within the management and business processes of the entity control: environment, risk assessment, control activities, information and communication, and monitoring.

Control environment. The core of any control framework is the integrity, ethical values and competence of employees and the environment in which they operate. Practices that encourage business risk assessment and control include communicating purpose, values, and objectives, hiring and developing the best people and establishing clear boundaries of acceptable behavior.

Perhaps the most fundamental control environment issue faced by insurers is the cultural divide between management and the agents and, to a lesser extent, people in field operations closest to the customer. In the past, management actively encouraged agents' entrepreneurial behavior. Now agents find insurance companies wanting to direct their activities. Ultimately, management wants to support agent entrepreneurship while demonstrating that agents do their jobs better with good control. The goal is to forge a stronger partnership between the agency force and management.

For example, good control can make products more competitive by building into the new product development activities that increase the likelihood the new product will be competitive and in compliance with laws and regulations. This also will help the agent sell more products and see the personal benefit of sharing the customer relationship with the organization. The burden is squarely on executive management to articulate clearly how each employee fits into the structure, what they are accountable for and how they will be measured.

Management can use hiring, training, discipline and compensation to reinforce values and purpose. In a control context, they are a critical test of how management demonstrates leadership. For example, if a

(continued)

Insight 20-1 Internal Control Systems Help Insurers Reduce Risk, continued

top seller breaches the code of conduct and management ignores the violation, a clear message is sent to the field that control isn't a top priority. Instead, management could reinforce the importance of controlling business risk by basing agent compensation on policy longevity and new production.

Risk assessment. COSO is based on the proposition that for integrated control to become reality, risk assessment must become a natural part of people's daily activities. There are many risks associated with the insurance sale. These include inadequately trained agents, use of misleading sales material, faulty product design, sale of the wrong insurance product to the customer and inadequate systems information about sales practices. From the agent's perspective, the biggest risk is erosion of personal reputation.

By adopting an integrated, systematic approach to identifying and assessing risks and building controls into the sales process, the organization will better meet its strategic objectives, including increasing customer satisfaction.

Control activities. Consider the following controls that will mitigate risk if integrated with sales practices:

- Recruiting procedures that emphasize hiring agents who share the company's values.
- Sales scripts that incorporate minimum standards of conduct, including what can and cannot be said.
- Case development tools that list risks and benefits associated with particular products.
- Sales presentations that include providing the customer with sensitivity analyses (impact of changes in interest rates, expenses, etc.) and show how the product coincides with identified customer needs.

Information and communication. Those in the field who are responsible for monitoring agents' activities must have sufficient and timely information. Unless systems and procedures facilitate effective monitoring before transactions are processed, management must rely on informal mechanisms such as ad hoc conversations between field personnel and agents. Transaction reports produced after a sale are reactive; all that can be done is an investigation. Late reports can never check behavior such as misrepresentation, inadequate disclosure or unsuitable sales. Integrated internal control means the right person exercises control at the right point in the process (i.e., where the risk is highest).

Effective communication must occur throughout the organization. Ineffective communication can result in differing views about compliance. Consider the gaps between the messages communicated to agents by different controlling influences:

- Branch managers: compliance means National Association of Security Dealers regulations.
- Internal auditors: compliance means following policies and procedures.
- Legal: compliance means not breaking the law.
- Chief executive: compliance means doing the right thing.

Communication throughout the organization needs to be concise, easy to understand and written to consider the agents' point of view. Simplicity in communication is fundamental.

Monitoring. Monitoring assesses the quality of the control system's performance over time and improves it. Examples of good monitoring controls include the branch manager reviewing weekly reports of replacement sales or having regular meetings with agents to discuss their selling practices. One instance of how monitoring can improve the system's performance is a field visit by a compliance manager who educates agents on how to interpret regulations.

Linking these five components creates an integrated system that reacts dynamically to changing conditions.

Regaining Respect

There is no doubt that the insurance industry has suffered from a recent spate of bad publicity. The need for a zero-defect culture in compliance is indisputable because the downside is unacceptable. Those in the industry need to know that the values, policies and directives of senior management and the board of directors are being carried out at the customer level. If internal control is properly integrated into business processes, insurers can better achieve objectives in a constantly changing environment. They also can better meet the customer's need for suitable products. Integrating internal control into the fabric of the business will help insurers regain control and restore public trust.

Source: Adapted from William C. Jennings and Peter C. Sutherland, "Internal Control Systems Help Insurers Reduce Risk," *Best's Review, Life/Health Edition* (January 1996), pp. 71–75. Reprinted by permission of the publisher.

Board of Directors and the Audit Committee

An insurer's board of directors has a duty to (1) support the insurer's internal controls as a proper way of conducting business and (2) communicate to all employees the importance of adhering to strong internal controls. The board of directors is influential in establishing broad forms of internal control, including a company-wide code of ethics or code of professional conduct and a corporate policy for identifying and dealing with conflicts of interest. The board of directors is also influential in enforcing appropriately conservative accounting standards and practices as well as establishing severe penalties for violations of corporate policies.

A prime component of effective internal control is an insurer's audit committee. The audit committee, which consists of members of the insurer's board of directors, oversees the activities of the company's internal and external auditors. The ongoing duties of the insurer's audit committee include

- Monitoring the internal controls developed for financial operations
- Supervising and meeting with internal auditors to discuss their activities and findings
- Hiring and meeting with external auditors to discuss their activities and findings
- Reporting the committee's activities to the board of directors
- Reporting the committee's activities in the annual report to stockholders and policyowners

An effective audit committee works independently of the insurer's organizational chart and typically reports its findings directly to the board of directors. Further, members of the audit committee are usually outside directors, rather than employees, of the insurer. For example, a Canadian company's members of the audit committee cannot be affiliated with the company.

Internal Auditors

Internal auditors are typically insurance company employees who are often assigned to the company's accounting department. Department managers provide internal auditors with their day-to-day assignments and receive reports on the auditors' daily activities. To do their work effectively, however, internal auditors must be assured an appropriate level of independence from all company departments. Therefore, internal auditors usually report their findings directly to the audit committee and are accountable to the board of directors for the accuracy and integrity of their work. Small insurance companies that do not have a full-time internal auditing staff sometimes assign department managers to serve as internal auditors as the need arises. Under such circumstances, these companies must be extremely careful to ensure that the temporary auditors exercise independent and unbiased judgment in their auditing assignments, especially in companies whose internal auditors prepare documents for the insurer's external auditors.

Managers and Other Employees

From the standpoint of internal control, an insurer's managers ensure that all employees under their supervision follow the company's methods and procedures in order to support the financial and operating decisions made by management. Specifically, the insurer's management team

- Communicates to employees the importance of adhering to the insurer's internal controls
- Monitors the costs and benefits associated with internal controls in each responsibility center
- Resolves discrepancies revealed by employees and the internal control system

Successful use of internal controls enables management to respond quickly and positively to changing regulatory and economic conditions. Successful internal controls are often those that are developed with the cooperation of other company employees. Actively soliciting employee suggestions and giving these suggestions serious consideration reinforces and encourages employee compliance with established procedures.

Elements of Effective Control

Any internal accounting control system relies on certain methods to be effective. Some critical elements of an effective system of accounting controls are the

- Segregation of duties
- Execution of transactions as authorized
- Recording of transactions as executed
- Safeguarding of assets
- Physical comparison of recorded amounts

Segregation of Duties

The ***segregation of duties*** provides for the checking of one person's work against that of another person. An effective system of internal controls may require, for example, that one employee be responsible for authorizing a transaction, another employee be responsible for recording that transaction, and a third employee be responsible for custody of the assets involved in the transaction. These duties are ***incompatible functions,*** which are job duties that, when combined, place any person in a position to commit an illegal act or to conceal errors or irregularities in the normal course of his or her employment. Incompatible functions require segregation of duties so that a system of checks and balances safeguards assets and ensures the accuracy and timeliness of accounting records and financial statements. One example of segregation of duties is that an insurer's internal auditors typically report directly to the audit committee of the board of directors rather than to the controller, who oversees the insurer's accounting function. This way, the auditors of the accounting records are independent of the person ultimately responsible for recording the insurer's transactions.

Another example of the segregation of duties is that the responsibility for cash receipts and cash disbursements is usually divided between two employees. In many insurance companies, the treasurer is responsible for cash management and the controller is responsible for the accounting records associated with cash transactions. Similarly, one employee should receive premium payments from policyowners, another employee should record the premium payments in the insurer's accounting system, and a third employee should deposit the premium payment in the insurer's bank account. In other words, an effective internal control separates the custodial, authorization, and accounting tasks associated with assets. *Custodial* in this context applies not only to the physical handling of assets, but also to the electronic handling of assets. Therefore, an investment department employee who assumes custody of securities as the insurer purchases them should not be the same employee who maintains the accounting records associated with these securities, nor should either employee be authorized to sell or otherwise dispose of these securities. Segregating these duties among employees provides an environment in which an insurer can more likely detect and correct errors and irregularities quickly. Thus, the procedures used to detect errors and irregularities should be performed by persons other than those who are in a position to cause or contribute to the errors.

A matter that has added a new dimension to the segregation of duties is the trend toward employee empowerment and start-to-finish processing by one employee, both of which require more frequent, random internal audits of an insurer's transactions. Many companies are delegating authority to employees at the lowest possible level in specified functional areas or responsibility centers. In some cases, this results in a blurring of incompatible functions. For example, an insurer may authorize its claim processors to approve claims *and* disburse the claim payments to policyowners up to a specified dollar amount. Similarly, a screening staff in underwriting typically can approve policy applications up to a specified dollar amount if the insured is a standard risk. Because prompt claim payments and accelerated policy issue are value-added services to policyowners and agents, the insurer establishes dollar limits for routine financial transactions. Typically, someone outside each functional area oversees the accounting records for that area. In cases that involve employees who oversee particularly sensitive areas, such as investment management or treasury operations (cash management), the insurer may purchase a *fidelity bond,* which covers the risk of violations of internal controls by employees who work in that functional area. Some insurers purchase fidelity bonds on all employees.

Execution of Transactions as Authorized

In a life and health insurance company, many different types of transactions, such as purchasing and selling securities, issuing policies, paying benefits, and paying operating expenses, take place each day. Whatever the type of transaction, good internal control dictates that a manager authorize each transaction. For example, a claim examiner may have to obtain specific authorization from the claim manager to make any benefit payment of $50,000 or more. Although the same claim examiner may have the authority to make payments of lesser amounts according to established operating procedures, this is one form of internal control. Regardless, no transaction should occur without some form of authorization.

The ***execution of transactions as authorized*** is the element of the internal control system that concerns the delegation of authority to perform specified tasks and the communication of that authority. Authorization levels should be realistic and a company should communicate them clearly. Whatever the type of transaction, a manager authorizes each transaction at the appropriate level. Each level of authorization should reflect the significance of the transaction and the experience and responsibility of the employee concerned. For example, a claim examiner with only two months experience may have to obtain management approval for all claims over $2,500, while an experienced examiner may approve claims up to $50,000, within specified guidelines, without management approval.

Recording of Transactions as Executed

A significant internal control is the ***recording of transactions as executed,*** which means that a company records its transactions as they occur in the correct accounting period, so that the company can summarize all transactions for that period in its financial statements. For example, an insurer records premium income when it is earned. The accounting entry includes the proper amount of the receipt as posted to the correct record in the policyowner master file and the correct bank account. The proper recording of transactions as executed requires the following:

- **Valid transactions:** An insurer records all authorized and executed transactions in its accounting records. The receipt of a premium payment is an example of a valid transaction.

- **Correct accounts:** An insurer records all accounting entries in the correct accounts. For example, the insurer should record the purchase of a large computer by debiting an asset account rather than an office supplies expense account. Similarly, the insurer records a policy loan to a policy loan account, rather than to a policy benefit expense account.

- **Correct amounts:** An insurer records all transactions in their correct amounts. If the insurer purchases municipal bonds for $100,000, including brokerage commissions, it should debit the appropriate asset account for $100,000 and credit Cash for $100,000.

- **Timely recording:** An insurer should record all transactions in the proper accounting period. For example, an insurer records and reports the sale of a line of business in December 1998 as part of its 1998 financial transactions. Failure to record transactions in the correct accounting period could result in the omission of the transaction and an unfair presentation of the insurer's financial position as of the reporting date.

- **Timely reporting:** An insurer should summarize transactions within a reasonable time frame after the end of an accounting period for inclusion in an insurer's financial statements, which summarize all transactions executed during the reporting period.

Communicating the policies and procedures necessary to document a financial transaction is an essential part of recording transactions as executed. Employee training sessions, prenumbered checks and purchase orders, and written procedures manuals help support the documentation of an insurer's financial transactions.

Safeguarding of Assets

The ***safeguarding of assets*** is the process of (1) limiting access to offices, documents, and records, (2) storing negotiable documents in vaults to which no person has sole access, (3) maintaining written business disaster recovery plans and off-premises storage of back-up files for all critical records, (4) investigating the integrity of employees hired to fill sensitive positions, (5) counting all assets and comparing this count to a written record, and (6) reviewing the adequacy of insurance coverage, given the company's risk exposure. Safeguarding assets requires sensitive handling. Certain assets should be sufficiently accessible so the company's operations can be carried out. At the same time, the company should restrict access to these assets to authorized persons. Threats to an insurer's assets include theft, destruction, waste, and deterioration. An insurer's computer system may be safeguarded, for example, by

- Requiring the use of passwords before users are allowed access to the software itself
- Restricting access to the system's physical location
- Maintaining adequate property and liability insurance and service contracts on the system
- Requiring employees to follow appropriate virus protection procedures
- Providing back-up copies of critical records and housing them in an off-site facility
- Separating the incompatible functions between those who program the database software and those who enter records into the database

An insurer can safeguard its invested assets, such as bonds, common stock, and other securities, in one of three typical ways: (1) physical settlement, (2) central depository, and (3) book-entry safekeeping. ***Physical settlement*** of invested assets includes the tangible exchange of funds and securities and the clearing of account balances between the buyer and seller of the securities. Technological developments in automating securities exchanges have rendered physical settlement largely unnecessary. Safeguarding securities through ***central depository safekeeping*** involves contracting with a centralized safekeeping facility to house and safeguard the insurer's securities, except for those issued by the federal government. ***Book-entry safekeeping*** is similar to central depository safekeeping, except no physical security exists. In other words, the exchange of securities between buyer and seller is transacted without the physical exchange of the securities being traded. Instead, electronic record keeping systems at central depositories safeguard an insurer's securities. Federal government securities are typically handled through book-entry safekeeping.

Physical Comparison of Recorded Amounts

The ***physical comparison of recorded amounts*** means that a company counts its assets, income, and disbursements on a periodic basis and compares this count to the recorded amounts. Perhaps the best example of a physical comparison is the annual inventory of equipment and furniture that many companies conduct. A company typically identifies each piece of furniture and equipment with a unique identification number. The company compares this number to its accounting records, then it investigates and reconciles any discrepancies between the two. In many companies, internal or external auditors, or employees from other functional areas, conduct physical counts of furniture and equipment. In other companies, employees responsible for maintaining assets conduct the inventory for those assets. An independent group then tests and checks the inventory.

Examples of Internal Controls

Up to this point, the discussion of internal controls has been general. You should recognize that the specific controls actually in use vary widely from company to company. However, the types of controls used are universal. Below are examples of different types of controls that might be found in a life and health insurance company.

- **Approval, review, checking, or recalculation:** Examples of this type of internal control are requirements that senior management approve all claim payments over a certain amount, random recalculation of premiums charged to policyowners, and the completion of checklists indicating that the insurer has received all required documents prior to paying a claim or making a policy loan.

- **Comparing information on independently generated documents:** Examples of this type of control are comparing information from a policy application to the policyowner master file and comparing the amount of a policy loan requested by a policyowner to the loan check generated before mailing the check.

- **Prenumbering:** Examples of this category include prenumbering checks and purchase orders, and numbering applications and claims when received. An insurer uses or processes these documents in numerical order and must explain any numbers that are missing or out of sequence.

- **Maintenance of control totals:** This type of control includes listing all policy loans separately and reconciling the total of the listing to the total policy loans on the general ledger. Another example is the use of batch totals on premium receipts. When an insurer receives premium checks, it groups them together and totals the amounts to obtain a *batch total.* When the insurer enters these receipts in the computer, the batch total appears first. If the total of the checks entered does not equal the batch total, then the employee entering the figures must identify and correct the error.

- **Comparison with third-party information:** This type of control includes bank reconciliation, reconciliation of internally generated listings of securities held in safekeeping with listings provided by the custodian of the securities, reconciliation of notes payable with statements provided by owners of the notes, and the resolution of discrepancies and unreconciled differences between the two sets of records.

- **Soliciting third-party information:** This type of control includes periodically sending agents or policyowners statements that request notification of errors in payment or policy records or confirmation of amounts receivable from persons or companies owing the insurer. For example, some companies routinely send letters to policyowners asking them to confirm that the information concerning their policies matches their records or that actual benefits paid under an annuity or an accident and health (A&H) provision or rider coincides with the insurer's records.

- **Cancellation of documentation:** This method requires defacing documents in some way so that they cannot be sent through normal channels of processing. For example, an insurer should void, rather than discard, a check that contains an error. Also, the insurer should include an indication of claim payment so that it does not issue the same disbursement check twice.

- **Timeliness of operation:** An insurer should process all transactions promptly. For example, it may require daily deposits of cash receipts, monthly reviews of the claim register for unresolved claims, and periodic reviews of the new business register with subsequent resolution of insurance policies that have neither been issued nor denied after a specified time.

Figure 20-2 is a partial list of questions that an external auditor, such as a state examiner, may ask when evaluating an insurer's internal controls associated with an insurer's bond and stock investments.

Auditing

When you think of the word "auditing," you probably think of the Internal Revenue Service (IRS) or Revenue Canada contacting you about your federal income tax return, and you probably don't have a

Figure 20-2. Internal controls questionnaire.

Bonds and Stocks

A. Does the company maintain adequate facilities for safekeeping securities?
   1. Are all company-held securities kept in a vault, safe, or safety deposit box?
   2. Do all custodial agreements provide the necessary safeguards and controls?
   3. Is the evidence of ownership in the form of book entries?
B. Does the board exercise tight control over securities transactions?
   1. Trace a representative sample of securities purchases and sales from Schedule D to the board minutes.
   2. Investigate transactions not appearing in the minutes.
C. Are authorization policies and procedures for gaining access to securities adequate?
   1. Are employees with access to securities independent of those with securities recordkeeping functions?
   2. Are two or more authorized individuals required to be present for access to securities?
   3. Is removal of securities from the vault or room containing the safe prohibited?
   4. Must everyone seeking access to securities sign a permanent log?
   5. Are bearer securities handled with sufficient safeguards and controls? (e.g., same as cash?)
D. Are securities periodically audited internally?
   1. How often?
   2. Are surprise audits taken?
   3. Are audit procedures adequate?
E. Do procedures exist for following up on securities that have been written off?

Source: *Financial Condition Examiners Handbook,* Volume 1, Part 2. Internal Controls (Kansas City, MO: National Association of Insurance Commissioners, 1991), p. 2-1.

very pleasant picture in mind. However, all companies undergo periodic accounting audits, also called examinations, by both *internal auditors,* who are company employees, and *external auditors,* who are not employees of the company, such as public accounting firms or federal, state, or provincial regulators.

Both internal and external auditors typically have the following major responsibilities:

- Verifying that a company's assets are accounted for and that they are safeguarded from loss
- Assessing the soundness and the application of the company's administrative and accounting controls
- Ensuring that employees follow specified policies and procedures
- Verifying the reliability of the company's accounting records and financial reports
- Evaluating the effectiveness and efficiency of specified operating procedures

An insurer undertakes an audit to determine the degree of correspondence between certain standards and the company's actual financial and operational actions and to communicate the results to interested parties. The following statements can also be made about auditing:

- **Auditing is planned:** An auditor generally develops a program of the procedures that should be performed in order to achieve specified objectives before scheduling and conducting an audit.

- **Auditing has a purpose:** The purpose of an audit is to gather information that either supports or refutes an assertion. For example, governmental taxation authorities perform tax audits to determine if the amount of income tax that a company claims it owes is correct. Independent audits of an insurer's financial statements performed in the United States by Certified Public Accountants (CPAs) and in Canada by Chartered Accountants (CAs), are intended to determine if the amounts reported in those statements are in accordance with defined accounting principles. In the United States, this type of audit is based on criteria established by the National Association of Insurance Commissioners (NAIC) and the Financial Accounting Standards Board (FASB). In Canada, the criteria are established by the Office of the Superintendent of Financial Institutions (OSFI) and the Canadian Institute of Chartered Accountants (CICA).

- **The parties interested in the results of an audit are varied:** Interested parties may include the stockholders, policyowners, creditors, and suppliers of a company, as well as various governmental agencies. The results of an audit are reported to company management through the board of directors. In this way, management can evaluate the financial condition of the company.

In addition to audits of accounting records and financial statements, activities that may be audited include those processes, systems, or functional areas with specified objectives that support a company's strategic plans. Specific examples of auditable activities for a life insurance company include claims processing, agent commission payments, and wire transfers of cash. All insurance company managers establish internal controls to monitor the activities in their departments, product lines, or responsibility centers. These controls ensure compliance with corporate policies and procedures, accurate record keeping, and the protection of assets. One role of the auditor is to verify that these controls exist and are in use throughout a company to minimize the risks associated with the company's normal business operations.

Internal Auditing

By definition, an ***internal audit*** is performed by company employees who assess and evaluate their company's system of internal controls to assist the company's managers in effectively discharging their responsibilities. Typically, an internal audit, which is a type of internal control, focuses on an insurer's

- Accounting records
- Cash receipts and cash disbursements
- Regulatory compliance
- Policyowner records
- External auditor findings
- Tax reporting
- Operating efficiency with respect to corporate policies and procedures

To remain objective and independent, internal auditors should not directly supervise the areas being audited, should have unrestricted access to all the records, files, and reports that concern the scope of the audit, and should report to a high-level executive or the audit committee of the board of directors. Internal auditors in the United States should comply with generally accepted auditing standards (GAAS) established by the AICPA. Canadian auditors often comply with GAAS developed by the Canadian Institute of Chartered Accountants (CICA), although they are not required to do so.

The internal auditing function may be organized according to regional offices, distribution system, or by line of business, depending on a company's size and its products. To conduct a thorough internal audit of a particularly technical area, such as real estate or variable annuities, internal auditors may consult with a specialist in that technical area. Internal auditors normally have unrestricted access to all of the insurer's accounting records and financial reports, as well as access to interview key employees. The role of an insurer's internal auditors focuses on evaluating the effectiveness, efficiency, and quality of the insurer's internal control system. The activities undertaken by internal auditing staff include

- Reviewing and appraising the soundness and adequacy of accounting, financial, and other operating controls

- Investigating the extent to which company assets are accounted for and are safeguarded from all types of losses
- Ascertaining the reliability of statistical data and other managerial data that have been developed internally
- Reporting the results of audits objectively, making recommendations for corrections or improvements, and following up on their implementation
- Coordinating internal auditing activities with those of external auditors
- Investigating areas of suspected irregularity
- Conducting systems or security audits to ensure that proper internal controls are in place

Internal auditors also look for and examine any evidence of fraud or the unintentional presentation of false information to another party. ***Fraud*** is the intentional use of false information to mislead another party. A critical component of an effective system of internal controls is the opportunity for an auditor to isolate any breach of control and bring it to the attention of the manager, audit committee, or board of directors, depending on the severity of the infraction. However, while an insurer's internal controls may be effective against fraud committed by one person, they may be less effective at detecting fraud that arises from ***collusion,*** which is a secret agreement entered into by two or more persons to perpetrate an illegal act. One device used to uncover irregularities in a company's accounting records is an ***audit trail,*** which is a chronological and sequential set of accounting records and reports from the beginning to the end of a business transaction. Examples of steps in an audit trail include posting accounting entries to the appropriate accounts in the correct amounts on a timely basis and the proper authorization and approval of all company disbursements.

By examining an insurer's audit trails for a variety of financial transactions, an internal auditor can also identify the overall strengths and weaknesses of the insurer's system of internal controls. For example, a sound premium accounting system enables an auditor to trace a premium and its related transactions

- From the journal entry that recorded receipt of the premium payment
- To the insurer's bank deposit that included the premium payment

- To the policyowner master file to which the insurer credited the premium payment

- To the accounting entries and activities generated under commission accounting for commission payments to an agent

An internal auditor spends several weeks or even months within a specified area of the company, examining not only all its financial records, but all operating and reporting procedures associated with its accounting records and financial reports. The internal auditor then submits a report to management or to the audit committee. This report may describe every function of that area, whether the functions are carried out efficiently or inefficiently, and what improvements should be made. Figure 20-3 is a flowchart of typical activities involved in conducting an internal audit.

A typical activity during an internal audit is a review of an insurer's suspense accounts. Insurers may have a number of suspense accounts to indicate unidentified or pending transactions. For example, some insurers debit Cash and credit Premium Suspense whenever there is

Figure 20-3. Typical internal audit activities.

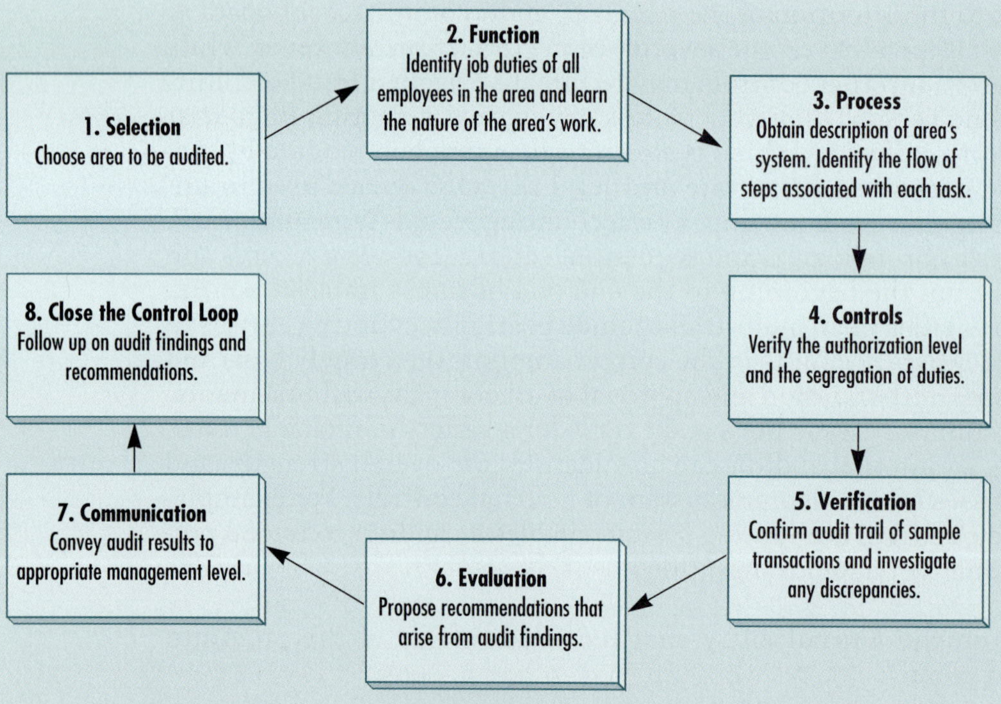

Source: *Establishing an Internal Audit Function in a Life Insurance Company,* Financial Planning and Control Report No. 24 (New York: LOMA, 1972), pp. 13–14.

incomplete or inaccurate information about a cash receipt for premium payment, whenever there is a lock-box arrangement, or when the insurer's accounting system cannot handle cash entries. After a reasonable period of time, the insurer should have uncovered the correct and complete information needed to debit Premium Suspense and credit the appropriate premium income account for the amount of the premium payment.

Sometimes, however, prompt follow-up and resolution of an amount in Premium Suspense does not occur, so the audit trail stops at the debit to Cash and the credit to Premium Suspense. An internal audit of the premium collection function can determine whether the insurer is pursuing the prompt identification and resolution of amounts posted to this account as well as monitoring routine transactions involved in premium collection. An insurer conducts frequent internal audits of its suspense accounts because they are an internal control for numerous cash transactions, and many financial transactions are posted to the insurer's suspense accounts. Figure 20-4 presents a sample of activities involved in an internal audit of an insurer's premium suspense account. These steps are identified with the accompanying activity labels from Figure 20-3.

Although internal audits are not required by law or by regulation, most companies conduct them as a preventive measure, to uncover potential problems or to discover ideas for improving a particular process. Sometimes the main purpose of an internal audit has little to do with accounting records or even financial information. An example is an internal audit conducted on a process or procedure, such as what happens to a claim form from the time it arrives at a life insurance company until a check for policy proceeds is mailed to the beneficiary. Conducting this type of audit may or may not involve a review of the accounting records, because the main goal is to discover a better and perhaps faster way of processing claims. Nonaccounting personnel, such as the members of a quality improvement task force, often are assigned to conduct such audits. When we discuss audits in this text, however, we are referring specifically to the audits associated with accounting records and financial information.

External Auditing

An ***external audit,*** also called an *independent audit,* is the process of (1) issuing an opinion as to whether a company's financial statements present fairly, in all material respects, the company's operations through adherence to GAAP, statutory accounting, or other accounting principles, (2) reviewing and recommending changes to a company's system of internal control, and (3) preparing reports of audit findings for the company's audit committee or board of directors. An external audit is conducted primarily for the benefit of interested third

Figure 20-4. Specific activities for an internal audit of premium suspense.

Selection	Review the definition and purpose of Premium Suspense and the circumstances, including turnaround time requirements, specified for transactions to be posted to Premium Suspense.
Function	Describe the job duties and authorization levels of all employees who post entries to Premium Suspense.
Process	Develop a flowchart and narrative for documenting Premium Suspense, including who and when employees handle checks for premium payments, the account's audit trail, procedures for posting accounting entries to the account, and the account's aging schedule (that is, how long do transactions remain in the account and how often do the same transactions get cleared, then re-posted to the account).
Controls	Indicate in the flowchart and narrative the control points and authorizations required to approve entries to Premium Suspense.
Verification	Confirm the balance in Premium Suspense with the general ledger balance for that account. Thoroughly review the audit trail, including source documents from other areas, for a sample of financial transactions involving Premium Suspense.
Evaluation	Note discrepancies between established controls and what actually occurs in Premium Suspense. Cite items that have remained too long in suspense and need to be cleared. Compare the number of cited items with historical records to determine if there is a trend toward higher numbers of questionable items. Make recommendations for improvements in internal controls and operating efficiencies in this area.
Communication	Provide audit findings to senior management team that oversees premium collection.
Close the Control Loop	Follow up in 60 to 90 days to determine if cited items have been resolved and recommendations have been implemented.

Source: Adapted from *Establishing an Internal Audit Function in a Life Insurance Company,* Financial Planning and Control Report No. 24 (New York: LOMA, 1972), pp. 13–14.

parties, including the insurer's board of directors, stockholders, policyowners, creditors, regulators, and others who rely on the information contained in the insurer's financial statements, and is performed in accordance with generally accepted auditing standards (GAAS).

External audits are required for all companies that file annual reports for stockholders. Therefore, undergoing an external audit is a normal business operation for all publicly traded companies. Typically, an insurer's external audit focuses on statutory solvency, regulatory compliance, or proper tax reporting. The findings of an external audit are of particular interest to an insurer's policyowners, stockholders, and creditors, all of whom rely on the accuracy of the insurer's financial statements because they do not have direct access to the insurer's financial transactions. External audits are primarily concerned with an insurer's accounting and financial reporting functions.

Companies retain the services of public accounting firms, usually CPA firms in the United States and CA firms in Canada, to conduct annual independent audits of their financial information. The use of independent auditors helps ensure that a company's financial performance is evaluated impartially. The auditors examine the company's financial statements and accounting records to determine whether these statements and records present fairly, in all material respects, the company's financial position and operating results. Because of the complicated nature of the financial information contained in the annual report, external auditors may contract with specialists in particular areas. For example, an external auditor may hire an environmental engineer to conduct an independent review of an insurer's exposure to environmental risks. Also, the external auditor could have an actuary on staff or hire an outside actuary with expertise in developing actuarial assumptions for employee benefits to examine the insurer's actuarial assumptions for its defined benefit plan. The external auditor, however, retains full accountability for preparing and signing the auditor's report.

Publicly traded companies in the United States and all federally licensed companies in Canada are required to hire independent external auditors, at least on an annual basis, to perform audits of financial information that will be included in the annual report. All U.S. companies reporting to the SEC must have their GAAP-based financial statements audited by a CPA firm. In Canada, all federally licensed companies are required to file independent auditor's reports. In addition, in some provinces, all foreign life insurers with a branch in Canada file an independent auditor's report. External auditors also prepare and sign the auditor's opinion or report that is found at the end of an insurer's annual report. The auditor's report indicates that the insurer's financial statements are fairly presented, in all material respects, and that the audit was conducted in accordance with GAAS. Figure 20-5 shows an independent auditor's report of a U.S. life and health insurance company's GAAP-based financial statements.

Examining every operation and verifying every financial transaction within a company is impractical and costly. Instead, auditors rely on a system of *statistical sampling* in which they examine a portion of the accounts, transactions, or operations in a company. The samples are chosen according to sound statistical methods, giving the auditor a reasonable level of confidence that all the accounts, transactions, or operations are as valid as those in the sample. In many cases, the auditor reviews transactions at only two or three key points in the processing system. This review indicates whether

Figure 20-5. Independent auditor's report.

Independent Auditor's Report

The Shareholders and Board of Directors
XXX Incorporated

We have audited the accompanying consolidated balance sheets of XXX Incorporated and its subsidiaries as of December 31, 2000 and 2001, and the related consolidated statements of earnings, stockholders' equity and cash flows for each of the years in the two-year period ended December 3, 2001. These consolidated financial statements are the responsibility of management. Our responsibility is to express an opinion on these consolidated financial statements based on our audits.

We conducted our audits in accordance with generally accepted auditing standards. Those standards require that we plan and perform the audit to obtain reasonable assurance about whether the financial statements are free of material misstatement. An audit includes examining, on a test basis, evidence supporting the amounts and disclosures in the financial statements. An audit also includes assessing accounting principles used and significant estimates made by management, as well as evaluating the overall financial statement presentation. We believe that our audits provide a reasonable basis for our opinion.

In our opinion, the consolidated financial statements referred to above present fairly, in all material respects, the financial position of XXX Incorporated and its subsidiaries at December 31, 2000 and 2001, and the results of their operations and their cash flows for each of the years in the two-year period ended December 31, 2001, in conformity with generally accepted accounting principles.

other transactions within the system have been processed accurately. Figure 20-6 is a flowchart of the external audit process.

Auditors conclude an annual report with one of several different types of auditor's reports (see Figure 20-7). The type most desired by an audited insurer is the *unqualified opinion* or *clean opinion* (called a *standard audit opinion* in Canada), which is the type of report depicted in Figure 20-5. An ***unqualified opinion*** means that an insurer's financial statements were prepared in accordance with GAAP, or in special circumstances, in conformity with statutory accounting practices, and that the presentation is free of material misrepresentations, given the insurer's financial condition. However, an insurer can obtain an unqualified opinion and still have financial difficulties, such as declining profitability or losses on the sale of invested assets. Also, an unqualified opinion does not guarantee that fraud has not occurred within the scope of the audit.

Some U.S. insurers receive a ***modified report,*** which contains explanatory language concerning inconsistencies resulting from a change in accounting principles or practices. Explanatory language is necessary only if the change in accounting principle affects the materiality

Figure 20-6. Flowchart of an external audit.

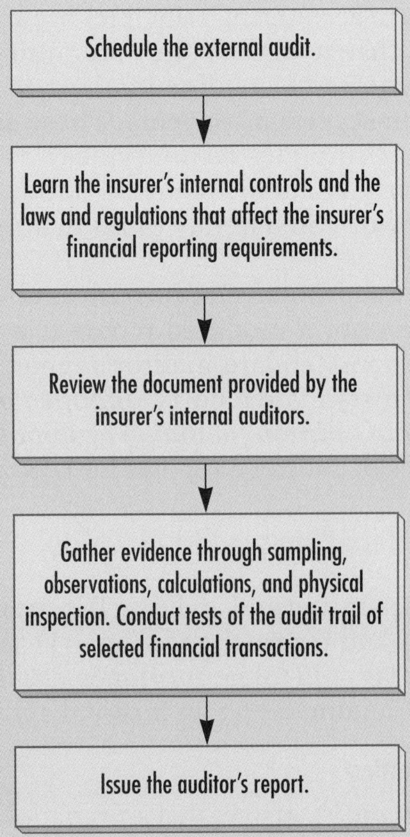

Source: Adapted from *Reports Prepared by Chartered Accountants—What Do They Mean?* (Toronto: Chartered Accountants of Canada, n.d.), p. 4.

and comparability of an insurer's financial statements. Numerous regulatory and industry changes in accounting principles and practices have resulted in a prevalence of modified reports among U.S. insurers in the recent past. Although no longer required to do so, external auditors of U.S. companies may also include an explanatory paragraph that emphasizes other uncertainties, such as matters of materiality unrelated to consistency, that an insurer has fully disclosed in its financial statements.

Recall that a *material* change is one that causes a company's financial information—especially income amounts, asset values, and capital and surplus amounts—to alter significantly. *Consistency* is violated when a company changes its accounting principles and practices. *Comparability* enables an interested user to identify similarities and differences in financial information across accounting periods and between different companies. The modified auditor's report reinforces the impact of these changes because it specifically addresses the effects of these changes on materiality and consistency.

Changes in accounting principles occur less frequently in Canada, but the recent change to the policy premium method (PPM) of calculating reserves required Canadian insurers to restate their financial statements from several prior years. These and other required changes in accounting principles do not typically result in a non-standard audit opinion for Canadian insurers, but such changes often affect the materiality or consistency of an insurer's previous financial statements.

There are additional circumstances under which neither an unqualified opinion nor a modified report is possible. Under these circumstances, a non-standard auditor's report is required. There are three types of non-standard reports: ***qualified opinion, adverse opinion,*** and ***disclaimer of opinion (denial of opinion).*** Figure 20-7 explains the different types of auditor's reports for U.S. and Canadian companies.

Types of Internal and External Audits

Current accounting and auditing literature identifies three major types of external and internal auditing—(1) *financial auditing,* (2) *compliance auditing,* and (3) *performance auditing.* All three types of auditing can be conducted on an internal and external basis.

Financial Auditing

A ***financial audit,*** also called a *financial statement audit* or an *attest audit* (because the result is an auditor's report that attests to the fairness of a company's financial statements), is the traditional auditing of financial information and includes both the overall examination of a company's financial statements and the examination of individual accounts and accounting records. A financial audit can be limited in scope (for example, an examination of commission accounting) or cover all financial transactions in an accounting period (for example, an audit of the insurer's Annual Statement). Financial audits are generally performed by CPAs or CAs, internal auditors, and auditors from various governmental agencies.

Financial audits by independent CPAs or CAs are generally made to determine whether the financial statements of a company are presented fairly and in conformity with either GAAP or statutory accounting practices. The SEC requires that all U.S. companies registered with the SEC be audited annually to determine whether their financial statements conform to GAAP. On the other hand, life and health insurance companies that are not registered with the SEC may be audited to determine if their financial statements conform to statutory accounting practices, which serves as the basis for financial reporting to state insurance departments. A CPA's opinion on a nonpublic company's internal controls must also be submitted.

Figure 20-7. Types of auditor's reports.

United States

- **Unqualified opinion** (standard report or clean opinion): Indicates that the financial statements present fairly, in all material respects, the financial position, results of operations, and cash flows of the entity in conformity with GAAP or, for "special purpose" financial statements, in accordance with statutory accounting practices
- **Modified opinion** (modified unqualified consistency report): Contains explanatory language concerning specific circumstances, such as material inconsistencies resulting from a change in accounting principles or practices

Non-standard auditor's reports:

- **Qualified opinion:** States the area of exception to an otherwise unqualified opinion (for example, the insurer has a large pending lawsuit for a disputed claim for which the amount of the claim liability is material and under contention)
- **Adverse opinion:** States that the financial statements do not fairly present the company's financial condition
- **Disclaimer of opinion:** Indicates that the auditor has no opinion on the financial statements

Source: Adapted from *AICPA Professional Standards, Volume 1, U.S. Auditing Standards, Attestation Standards* (New York: American Institute of Certified Public Accountants, 1995), pp. 654–655.

Canada

- **Standard audit opinion:** Indicates that the financial statements present fairly, in all material respects, the financial position, results of operations, and changes in financial position of the entity in accordance with GAAP

Non-standard auditor's reports:

- **Qualified opinion:** Complies with requirements of standard audit opinion except in specified areas referred to in the report
- **Adverse opinion:** States that the financial statements do not fairly present the company's financial condition
- **Denial of opinion:** Indicates that the external auditor is unable to provide an audit opinion

Source: *Reports Prepared by Chartered Accountants—What Do They Mean?* (Toronto: Chartered Accountants of Canada, n.d.), pp. 3–4.

Financial audits of public and non-public insurers by state authorities are performed at least every three to five years, depending on the state. In the case of insurers considered by regulatory authorities to be large and stable, these examinations may be performed every five years. If an insurer is having financial difficulties, these examinations may take place annually. Considering internal audits, regulatory examinations, and independent audits, life insurance companies are generally subject to at least two and often three financial audits annually. The different groups of auditors sometimes rely on certain aspects of each others' work to minimize duplication of effort.

A significant part of a financial audit is a ledger audit. The purpose of the ledger audit is to determine if an account's balance is fairly stated. Ledger audits are particularly useful if fraud is suspected, because a ***ledger audit*** starts with the balance in the general ledger and validates either all amounts or at least the major amounts in the account being audited. A typical ledger audit traces each ledger entry back to the respective *source document* such as an invoice, cash receipt listing, or deposit slip. An insurer reconciles any discrepancies between ledger entries and source documents discovered in the ledger audit.

Compliance Auditing

The distinction between financial auditing and compliance auditing is that the focus of financial auditing is to render an opinion as to the fairness of the presentation of financial statements, while the thrust of ***compliance auditing,*** also called *regulatory auditing,* is to verify adherence to the laws, regulations, policies, and procedures prescribed by internal or external authorities. Compliance auditing is being expanded to focus on the market conduct of an insurer's agents. Examinations of an insurance company by state regulatory authorities include compliance auditing because one purpose of such examinations is to determine whether the company has complied with applicable laws and regulations. External auditors in the United States use the AICPA's *Compliance Attestation* standard as a guideline in conducting a compliance audit. Canadian insurers refer to the *CICA Handbook* section on compliance auditing. Another type of compliance audit is a tax audit conducted by representatives of the IRS or Revenue Canada. The purpose of such a tax audit is to determine whether a company has followed the instructions for completing the federal tax return and paid the correct amount of tax. Tax auditors prepare auditor's reports for companies being audited for income tax reasons. Reports of both compliance and financial audits are reports of facts and transactions that have occurred and, thus, are reports of past events. However, as we discuss in the next section, past performance is not always the subject of the auditing function.

Performance Auditing

By definition, ***performance auditing,*** also called *operational auditing,* is the examination of a particular operations area to measure and evaluate progress toward achieving management objectives for that area. The results of a performance audit are presented to company management. A performance audit typically includes a description of the audit's purpose, followed by an explanation of the processes uncovered in the audit and a report of the auditor's findings and his or her recommendations for improvement. Performance audits require more subjective judgment than financial or compliance audits because the purpose of a performance audit is to measure departmental efficiency or effectiveness, rather than adherence to an established set of accounting principles. Two types of performance auditing are *management auditing* and *program results auditing.*

Management Auditing. The focus of ***management auditing,*** also known as *economy and efficiency auditing,* is on improving the effectiveness and efficiency of a company's operations. Management audits are performed to identify areas in which costs can be reduced and improvements in operations can be made. Alternatively, such audits can be described as evaluations of management effectiveness and efficiency. Management auditing includes reviews of operational controls and the formulation of possible improvements and cost reductions. Depending on the needs of the company, the scope of management audits can vary widely, addressing a single area or undertaking a review of all company operations.

One example of a management audit is a ***departmental audit,*** which evaluates and tests the performance of a department's personnel by first identifying the responsibilities involved in each person's job and then determining if those responsibilities are being met. To conduct this type of audit, an auditor must become familiar with the company's policies and procedures and the department's system of internal controls. For this reason, the auditor reads all departmental reports for accuracy and usefulness. The auditor can then report its findings to management. Figure 20-8 is a list of potential areas for company audits.

Program Results Auditing. In many companies, certain operations take the form of goal-oriented sets of activities called *programs.* For example, programs might include such activities as an insurer's quality service or employee teamwork initiatives. The purpose of ***program results auditing,*** or *effectiveness auditing,* is to determine whether the results or benefits desired from a particular program are actually being achieved. Such an audit typically indicates whether the program's goals and objectives are realistic and well defined and whether the desired results could be achieved at a lower cost. A fairly recent offshoot of program results auditing is known as *social auditing,* which attempts to determine how a corporation's actions affect society. Areas evaluated under social auditing may include the impact of corporate actions on employee diversity, local communities, and the environment.

Figure 20-8. List of potential areas for company audits.

Note: The following list is not intended to be a complete listing of areas in a life insurance company that are subject to audits. The list is shown, however, as a representative example.

Financial Division

Bank Reconciliation
Bonds and Stocks
Dividends Received on Stocks
Home Office Building and Real Estate
Interest Received on Bonds
Mortgage Loans
Petty Cash
Real Estate Purchased for Income
Security Vault Control
Separate Accounts

Ordinary Division

Accident and Health Reserves
Agency Expense Allowance
Agents' Benefit Plans
Agents' Financing
Commissions Due and Unpaid
Commissions Paid
Death Claims Paid
Death Claims Due and Unpaid
Disability Claims
Dividend Accumulations
Dividends Paid to Policyowners
Inspection Report Fees
Medical Examination Fees
Periodic Annuity Payments
Policyowner Master File
Policy Loans
Policy Reserves
Premiums
Surrender Benefits

Other

Agency Offices
Equity Investments
Mortgage Loan Correspondents
Subsidiaries

Group Division

Accident and Health Benefits
Accident and Health Claims
Agency Expense Allowance
Agents Benefit Plans
Agents' Financing
Claim Drafts Payable
Commissions Due and Unpaid
Commissions Paid
Contingency Reserve
Death Claims
Death Claims Due and Unpaid
Dividends to Policyowners
Inspection Report Fees
Medical Examination Fees
Periodic Annuity Payments
Policy Reserves
Premiums
Service Fees
Unearned Premium Reserves—Accident and Health

Corporate

Advertising
Data Processing
Employee Benefit Plans
Furniture and Equipment
Home Office Budgets
Loans
Operating Expenses
Payroll
Postage and Expenses
Rent Paid
Rental of Equipment
Stock
Taxes
Telephone
Travel

Source: *Establishing an Internal Audit Function in a Life Insurance Company,* Financial Planning and Control Report No. 24 (New York: LOMA, 1972), p. 32.

Conclusion

Internal control and auditing are components of both financial accounting and management accounting. Although the traditional focus of auditing has been on the specific requirements of accounting and financial requirements, a growing trend associated with both internal and external auditing is to place less emphasis on serving only in an enforcement function and more emphasis on consultative, partnership relationships with the companies they audit. For example, if an insurer and its auditors were to jointly assess risks in the insurer's lines of business, they could develop action plans that already include the appropriate internal controls to address risks associated with a particular line of business.

This last chapter unites and supports the material contained in the earlier chapters. It demonstrates the importance of established accounting principles to enable an insurer to present and use the information contained in its financial transactions to help achieve its corporate objectives. This concludes our discussion of accounting and financial reporting for life and health insurance companies. We hope you have obtained a better understanding of the purpose and role of accounting and financial reporting in conducting an insurer's normal business operations.

Key Terms and Concepts

internal control
auditing
administrative controls
accounting controls
preventive controls
detective controls
segregation of duties
incompatible functions
execution of transactions as authorized
recording of transactions as executed
safeguarding of assets
physical settlement
central depository safekeeping
book-entry safekeeping
physical comparison of recorded amounts
internal audit
fraud
collusion
audit trail
external audit
unqualified opinion
modified report
qualified opinion
adverse opinion
disclaimer of opinion (denial of opinion)
financial audit
ledger audit
compliance auditing
performance auditing
management auditing
departmental audit
program results auditing

Appendix

Figure A-1. Future Value Interest Factor Table, FVIF (*n, i*).

# of periods	Interest rate (*i*)									
(*n*)	1%	2%	3%	4%	5%	6%	7%	8%	9%	10%
½	1.005	1.010	1.015	1.020	1.025	1.030	1.034	1.039	1.044	1.049
1	1.010	1.020	1.030	1.040	1.050	1.060	1.070	1.080	1.090	1.100
1½	1.015	1.030	1.045	1.061	1.076	1.091	1.107	1.122	1.138	1.154
2	1.020	1.040	1.061	1.082	1.103	1.124	1.145	1.166	1.188	1.210
2½	1.025	1.051	1.077	1.103	1.130	1.157	1.184	1.212	1.240	1.269
3	1.030	1.061	1.093	1.125	1.158	1.191	1.225	1.260	1.295	1.331
3½	1.035	1.072	1.109	1.147	1.186	1.226	1.267	1.309	1.352	1.396
4	1.041	1.082	1.126	1.170	1.216	1.262	1.311	1.360	1.412	1.464
4½	1.046	1.093	1.142	1.193	1.246	1.300	1.356	1.414	1.474	1.536
5	1.051	1.104	1.159	1.217	1.276	1.338	1.403	1.469	1.539	1.611
5½	1.056	1.115	1.177	1.241	1.308	1.378	1.451	1.527	1.606	1.689
6	1.062	1.126	1.194	1.265	1.340	1.419	1.501	1.587	1.677	1.772
6½	1.067	1.137	1.212	1.290	1.373	1.460	1.552	1.649	1.751	1.858
7	1.072	1.149	1.230	1.316	1.407	1.504	1.606	1.714	1.828	1.949
7½	1.077	1.160	1.248	1.342	1.442	1.548	1.661	1.781	1.909	2.044
8	1.083	1.172	1.267	1.369	1.477	1.594	1.718	1.851	1.993	2.144
8½	1.088	1.183	1.286	1.396	1.514	1.641	1.777	1.924	2.080	2.248
9	1.094	1.195	1.305	1.423	1.551	1.689	1.838	1.999	2.172	2.358
9½	1.099	1.207	1.324	1.451	1.590	1.739	1.902	2.077	2.268	2.473
10	1.105	1.219	1.344	1.480	1.629	1.791	1.967	2.159	2.367	2.594
10½	1.110	1.231	1.364	1.510	1.669	1.844	2.035	2.244	2.472	2.720
11	1.116	1.243	1.384	1.539	1.710	1.898	2.105	2.332	2.580	2.853
11½	1.121	1.256	1.405	1.570	1.753	1.954	2.177	2.423	2.694	2.992
12	1.127	1.268	1.426	1.601	1.796	2.012	2.252	2.518	2.813	3.138
12½	1.132	1.281	1.447	1.633	1.840	2.072	2.330	2.617	2.937	3.292
13	1.138	1.294	1.469	1.665	1.886	2.133	2.410	2.720	3.066	3.452
13½	1.144	1.306	1.490	1.698	1.932	2.196	2.493	2.826	3.201	3.621
14	1.149	1.319	1.513	1.732	1.980	2.261	2.579	2.937	3.342	3.797
14½	1.155	1.333	1.535	1.766	2.029	2.328	2.667	3.052	3.489	3.983
15	1.161	1.346	1.558	1.801	2.079	2.397	2.759	3.172	3.642	4.177

Figure A-2. Future Value Interest Factor of an Annuity Table, FVIFA (*n*, *i*).

# of periods	Interest rate (*i*)									
(*n*)	1%	2%	3%	4%	5%	6%	7%	8%	9%	10%
½	0.499	0.498	0.496	0.495	0.494	0.493	0.492	0.490	0.489	0.488
1	1.000	1.000	1.000	1.000	1.000	1.000	1.000	1.000	1.000	1.000
1½	1.504	1.507	1.511	1.515	1.519	1.522	1.526	1.530	1.533	1.537
2	2.010	2.020	2.030	2.040	2.050	2.060	2.070	2.080	2.090	2.100
2½	2.519	2.538	2.557	2.575	2.595	2.614	2.633	2.652	2.671	2.691
3	3.030	3.060	3.091	3.122	3.152	3.184	3.215	3.246	3.278	3.310
3½	3.544	3.588	3.633	3.679	3.724	3.770	3.817	3.864	3.912	3.960
4	4.060	4.122	4.184	4.246	4.310	4.375	4.440	4.506	4.573	4.641
4½	4.579	4.660	4.742	4.826	4.910	4.997	5.084	5.173	5.264	5.356
5	5.101	5.204	5.309	5.416	5.526	5.637	5.751	5.867	5.985	6.105
5½	5.625	5.753	5.884	6.019	6.156	6.296	6.440	6.587	6.737	6.891
6	6.152	6.308	6.468	6.633	6.802	6.975	7.153	7.336	7.523	7.716
6½	6.681	6.868	7.061	7.259	7.464	7.674	7.891	8.114	8.344	8.580
7	7.214	7.434	7.662	7.898	8.142	8.394	8.654	8.923	9.200	9.487
7½	7.748	8.006	8.273	8.550	8.837	9.135	9.443	9.763	10.095	10.438
8	8.286	8.583	8.892	9.214	9.549	9.897	10.260	10.637	11.028	11.436
8½	8.826	9.166	9.521	9.892	10.279	10.683	11.104	11.544	12.003	12.482
9	9.369	9.755	10.159	10.583	11.027	11.491	11.978	12.488	13.021	13.579
9½	9.914	10.349	10.807	11.287	11.793	12.324	12.882	13.468	14.084	14.730
10	10.462	10.950	11.464	12.006	12.578	13.181	13.816	14.487	15.193	15.937
10½	11.013	11.556	12.131	12.739	13.382	14.063	14.783	15.545	16.351	17.203
11	11.567	12.169	12.808	13.486	14.207	14.972	15.784	16.645	17.560	18.531
11½	12.123	12.787	13.495	14.249	15.052	15.907	16.818	17.789	18.823	19.924
12	12.683	13.412	14.192	15.026	15.917	16.870	17.888	18.977	20.141	21.384
12½	13.245	14.043	14.900	15.818	16.804	17.861	18.996	20.212	21.517	22.916
13	13.809	14.680	15.618	16.627	17.713	18.882	20.141	21.495	22.953	24.523
13½	14.377	15.324	16.347	17.451	18.644	19.933	21.325	22.829	24.453	26.208
14	14.947	15.974	17.086	18.292	19.599	21.015	22.550	24.215	26.019	27.975
14½	15.521	16.630	18.837	19.149	20.577	22.129	23.818	25.655	27.654	29.828
15	16.097	17.293	18.599	20.024	21.579	23.276	25.129	27.152	29.361	31.772

Figure A-3. Present Value Interest Factor Table, PVIF (*n*, *i*).

# of periods	Interest rate (*i*)									
(*n*)	1%	2%	3%	4%	5%	6%	7%	8%	9%	10%
½	0.995	0.990	0.985	0.981	0.976	0.971	0.967	0.962	0.958	0.953
1	0.990	0.980	0.971	0.962	0.952	0.943	0.935	0.926	0.917	0.909
1½	0.985	0.971	0.957	0.943	0.929	0.916	0.903	0.891	0.879	0.867
2	0.980	0.961	0.943	0.925	0.907	0.890	0.873	0.857	0.842	0.826
2½	0.975	0.952	0.929	0.907	0.885	0.864	0.844	0.825	0.806	0.788
3	0.971	0.942	0.915	0.889	0.864	0.840	0.816	0.794	0.772	0.751
3½	0.966	0.933	0.902	0.872	0.843	0.816	0.789	0.764	0.740	0.716
4	0.961	0.924	0.888	0.855	0.823	0.792	0.763	0.735	0.708	0.683
4½	0.956	0.915	0.875	0.838	0.803	0.769	0.738	0.707	0.679	0.651
5	0.951	0.906	0.863	0.822	0.784	0.747	0.713	0.681	0.650	0.621
5½	0.947	0.897	0.850	0.806	0.765	0.726	0.689	0.655	0.623	0.592
6	0.942	0.888	0.837	0.790	0.746	0.705	0.666	0.630	0.596	0.564
6½	0.937	0.879	0.825	0.775	0.728	0.685	0.644	0.606	0.571	0.538
7	0.933	0.871	0.813	0.760	0.711	0.665	0.623	0.583	0.547	0.513
7½	0.928	0.862	0.801	0.745	0.694	0.646	0.602	0.561	0.524	0.489
8	0.923	0.853	0.789	0.731	0.677	0.627	0.582	0.540	0.502	0.467
8½	0.919	0.845	0.778	0.717	0.661	0.609	0.563	0.520	0.481	0.445
9	0.914	0.837	0.766	0.703	0.645	0.592	0.544	0.500	0.460	0.424
9½	0.910	0.829	0.755	0.689	0.629	0.575	0.526	0.481	0.441	0.404
10	0.905	0.820	0.744	0.676	0.614	0.558	0.508	0.463	0.422	0.386
10½	0.901	0.812	0.733	0.662	0.599	0.542	0.491	0.446	0.405	0.368
11	0.896	0.804	0.722	0.650	0.585	0.527	0.475	0.429	0.388	0.350
11½	0.892	0.796	0.712	0.637	0.571	0.512	0.459	0.413	0.371	0.334
12	0.887	0.788	0.701	0.625	0.557	0.497	0.444	0.397	0.356	0.319
12½	0.883	0.781	0.691	0.612	0.543	0.483	0.429	0.382	0.341	0.304
13	0.879	0.773	0.681	0.601	0.530	0.469	0.415	0.368	0.326	0.290
13½	0.874	0.765	0.671	0.589	0.518	0.455	0.401	0.354	0.312	0.276
14	0.870	0.758	0.661	0.577	0.505	0.442	0.388	0.340	0.299	0.263
14½	0.866	0.750	0.651	0.566	0.493	0.430	0.375	0.328	0.287	0.251
15	0.861	0.743	0.642	0.555	0.481	0.417	0.362	0.315	0.275	0.239

Figure A-4. Present Value Interest Factor of an Annuity Table, PVIFA (*n*, *i*).

# of periods	Interest rate (*i*)									
(*n*)	1%	2%	3%	4%	5%	6%	7%	8%	9%	10%
½	0.496	0.493	0.489	0.485	0.482	0.479	0.475	0.472	0.469	0.465
1	0.990	0.980	0.971	0.962	0.952	0.943	0.935	0.926	0.917	0.909
1½	1.481	1.463	1.446	1.428	1.411	1.395	1.379	1.363	1.347	1.332
2	1.970	1.942	1.913	1.886	1.859	1.833	1.808	1.783	1.759	1.736
2½	2.457	2.415	2.374	2.335	2.297	2.259	2.223	2.188	2.154	2.120
3	2.941	2.884	2.829	2.775	2.723	2.673	2.624	2.577	2.531	2.487
3½	3.423	3.348	3.276	3.207	3.140	3.075	3.012	2.952	2.893	2.836
4	3.902	3.808	3.717	3.630	3.546	3.465	3.387	3.312	3.240	3.170
4½	4.379	4.263	4.152	4.045	3.942	3.844	3.750	3.659	3.572	3.488
5	4.853	4.713	4.580	4.452	4.329	4.212	4.100	3.993	3.890	3.791
5½	5.326	5.160	5.002	4.851	4.707	4.570	4.439	4.314	4.194	4.080
6	5.795	5.601	5.417	5.242	5.076	4.917	4.767	4.623	4.486	4.355
6½	6.263	6.039	5.827	5.626	5.435	5.255	5.083	4.920	4.765	4.618
7	6.728	6.472	6.230	6.002	5.786	5.582	5.389	5.206	5.033	4.868
7½	7.197	6.901	6.628	6.371	6.129	5.901	5.685	5.482	5.289	5.107
8	7.652	7.325	7.020	6.733	6.463	6.210	5.971	5.747	5.535	5.335
8½	8.110	7.746	7.406	7.087	6.789	6.510	6.248	6.002	5.770	5.552
9	8.566	8.162	7.786	7.435	7.108	6.802	6.515	6.247	5.995	5.759
9½	9.020	8.574	8.161	7.776	7.419	7.085	6.774	6.483	6.211	5.956
10	9.471	8.983	8.530	8.111	7.722	7.360	7.024	6.710	6.418	6.145
10½	9.921	9.387	8.894	8.439	8.018	7.627	7.265	6.929	6.616	6.324
11	10.368	9.787	9.253	8.760	8.306	7.887	7.499	7.139	6.805	6.495
11½	10.812	10.183	9.606	9.076	9.588	8.139	7.724	7.341	6.987	6.658
12	11.255	10.575	9.954	9.385	8.863	8.384	7.943	7.536	7.167	6.814
12½	11.696	10.964	10.297	9.688	9.132	8.622	8.154	7.723	7.327	6.962
13	12.134	11.348	10.635	9.986	9.394	8.853	8.358	7.904	7.487	7.103
13½	12.570	11.729	10.968	10.277	9.649	9.077	8.555	8.077	7.640	7.238
14	13.004	12.106	11.296	10.563	9.899	9.295	8.745	8.244	7.786	7.367
14½	13.435	12.480	11.619	10.843	10.142	9.507	8.930	8.405	7.926	7.489
15	13.865	12.849	11.938	11.118	10.380	9.712	9.108	8.559	8.061	7.606

Glossary

account. The basic storage unit used to record, group, and summarize similar types of business transactions. (2)

account form. A form of presenting a company's balance sheet under which the asset items appear on the left and liabilities and owners' equity appear on the right. (5)

accounting. A system or a set of rules and methods for collecting, recording, summarizing, reporting, and analyzing a company's financial operations. (1)

accounting controls. Also known as *financial controls,* the policies and procedures used to authorize financial transactions, safeguard assets, and provide reliable, timely, and fairly presented financial information about a company. (20)

accounting cycle. The sequence of steps that occur during one accounting period, usually a calendar year or a fiscal year. (3)

accounting entry. Also known as a *journal entry,* the record of a business transaction in a company's journal. (2)(3)

accounting period. A specified length of time during which a company's business transactions are recorded, summarized, and reported. (4)

accrual-basis accounting. A system in which a company records revenues when they are earned and expenses when they are incurred, even if cash has not actually changed hands. (4)

accrued income. Income that an insurer has already earned, but which is not receivable until a specified date in the next accounting period—that is, income that is due *after* the insurer's financial reporting date. (8)(19)

accumulated cost of insurance. The amount that an insurer has paid in benefits since the beginning of the contract, accumulated with interest. (9)

accumulated value of net premiums. The amount of net premiums received since the beginning of a contract, plus interest. (9)

active life reserves. Also known as *additional reserves,* a type of policy reserve for accident and health insurance. (9)

activity. Any procedure that generates work. (16)

activity-based costing (ABC). A cost accounting method that links costs to products based on the activities consumed in producing the products or services. (16)

activity driver. The output of an activity being performed. (16)

activity ratios. Also known as *operating efficiency ratios,* calculations that measure the speed with which various financial statement account totals are converted into sales or cash. (19)

actuarial assumptions. Conjectures made by insurers when they calculate the amounts to report in their reserve accounts. Interest rates, mortality or morbidity rates, withdrawal rates, and reserve methods are used to calculate policy reserves. The actuarial assumptions that an insurer chooses to use determines how conservative the insurer's policy reserves will be. (9)

additional paid-in capital. An account that records the difference per share between the issue price and the par value when a U.S. company issues stock for a price above its par value. (5)

adjusting entries. A method used to correct accounting errors or to account for transactions that apply to more than one accounting period. (3)

administrative controls. Also known as *operating controls,* the procedures and policies that guide employees in conducting their normal day-to-day tasks. (20)

administrative services only (ASO) plan. A plan in which an employer hires an outside firm to perform specified administrative services, such as claim administration for a group health insurance program. (12)

admitted assets. In the United States, those assets that state insurance law permits to be included on the *Assets* page of the Annual Statement. (6)

advance and arrears accounting system. Also known as the *debit system,* a system in which the insurer charges each home service agent with the amount of premium income expected during the month from the agent's policyowners. (12)

* The number(s) in parentheses after glossary entries indicate the chapter(s) in which the term is discussed.

advance premiums. Also known as *premiums paid in advance,* the total of life insurance premiums received by the company before the statement date, but which are due on or after the next policy anniversary date. (6)

adverse opinion. A type of non-standard auditor report which states that the financial statements do not fairly present the company's financial condition. (20)

allocation base. A measure of use that exhibits a proportional relationship between the indirect cost and the cost center being allocated a portion of that cost. (16)

allowable expenses. The expenses assumed in calculating the price of an insurance product. (17)

allowances. In terms of reinsurance agreements, expenses for which the assuming company reimburses the ceding company. (13)

American Institute of Certified Public Accountants (AICPA). A professional association of Certified Public Accountants (CPAs) in the United States. (1)

amortization. The accounting process by which an insurer periodically and systematically adjusts the book value of an investment so that, on the maturity date, the book value equals that investment's par value. (7)

amortized cost. An asset's historical cost net of any adjustment to the asset's book value. (7)

amounts temporarily held for disposition. Amounts covering items that represent most of the company's liabilities associated with cash transactions on the *Liabilities* page of the Annual Statement. (6)

annual report. The publication that a company's management sends to its stockholders and other interested parties to report on the company's performance during the past year. (3)

Annual Return. A document that presents information about a Canadian insurer's operations and financial performance, with an emphasis on demonstrating the insurer's solvency. (6)(1)

Annual Statement. A document that presents information about a U.S. insurer's operations and financial performance, with an emphasis on demonstrating the insurer's solvency. (6)

annuity. Any series of equal payments made over equally spaced time periods. (14)

annuity due. Also known as an *annuity in advance,* an annuity for which the first payment occurs at the beginning of each payment period. (14)

asset/liability management (ALM). An activity that coordinates the administration of an insurer's investment portfolios with the administration of its policy liabilities to achieve the best possible financial effects. (7)

assets. A major account classification on the balance sheet, representing items of readily determinable value owned by a company. (2)

asset valuation reserve (AVR). A reserve that appears only on the U.S. Annual Statement and that minimizes the effects of credit-related capital gains and losses realized on the sale of an insurer's invested assets, including bonds, stocks, mortgages, and real estate. (6)

associating cause and effect. An accounting approach whereby costs that can be recognized as having a direct relationship to certain future earnings or specific elements of revenue are charged to earnings of future accounting periods instead of being charged to the current accounting period. (4)

assumption reinsurance. An agreement by which a ceding company permanently transfers to a reinsurer full responsibility for a block of insurance policies. (11)

auditing. The process of examining and evaluating company records and procedures to ensure that the company's accounting records and financial statements are presented fairly and reasonably, that quality assurance is maintained, and that operational procedures and policies are effective. (20)

auditor's report. Also known as the *accountant's report,* a statement by independent public accountants who have audited the annual report. (5)

audit trail. A chronological and sequential set of accounting records and reports from the beginning to the end of a business transaction. (20)

automatic premium loan (APL). A nonforfeiture option that allows the insurer to pay overdue premiums on a policy by establishing a loan against the policy's cash value. An APL does not require a special loan agreement. (8)

balance. The amount in an account as of a specified date. (2)

balance sheet. Also known as a *statement of financial position* or *statement of financial condition,* a financial statement that shows a company's financial status as of a particular date. (2)

bank reconciliation. The process of identifying and explaining the difference between the balance presented in the bank statement and the balance in the insurer's general ledger. (8)

base period. In terms of horizontal analysis, the earliest period being used in the analysis. (19)

basic accounting equation. The mathematical expression of the dual concept that is fundamental to the accounting function: *Assets + Liabilities = Owners' Equity.* (2)

benchmarking. A process by which a company compares its own performance, products, and services with those of other organizations that are recognized as the best in a particular category. (19)

benefits budget. An expense budget that indicates that amount of money a company expects to pay for claims, cash surrenders, and policy dividends during the next year. (17)

bond. A certificate of indebtedness issued by a corporation, government, or other legal entity. (7)

bonus additions. In Canada, applications of either the fourth and fifth policy dividend payment options. (10)

book-entry safekeeping. A method of possessing securities similar to central depository safekeeping, except no physical security exists. In other words, the exchange of securities between buyer and seller is transacted without the physical exchange of the securities being traded. (20)

book value. The value at which an asset is recorded or carried in the company's accounting records, specifically its general ledger. (4)

bottom-up budgeting. A budget generated at the department level by lower management and presented in the form of recommendations to upper management. (17)

break-even point. The level at which a company's revenues equal its costs. (16)

budget. A financial plan of action, expressed in monetary terms, that covers a specified time period, such as one year. (17)

budgeting. A management accounting process that includes creating a financial plan of action that an organization believes will help it achieve its goals. (17)

business transaction. A transaction to which a company must assign an objective monetary value, whether the impact on the company is large or small, actual or contingent. (2)

Canadian Institute of Chartered Accountants (CICA). A professional accounting association in Canada that develops GAAP pronouncements. (1)

Canadian Life and Health Insurance Compensation Corporation (CompCorp). A federally incorporated, nonprofit company established by the Canadian Life and Health Insurance Association (CLHIA) to protect policyholders against loss of benefits in case a life or health insurance company becomes insolvent. (13)

capital. The money that a company's owners have invested in a stock insurance company. (2)

capital and surplus ratios. A method by which insurance companies measure their financial strength. (19)

capital budgeting. The vehicle companies use to analyze decisions about investing in long-term projects. (17)

capital expenditure budgets. Sometimes known as *capital investment proposals,* budgets that show a company's plans for the financial management of long-term investment proposals. (17)

capital gains. The amount by which the selling price of an asset exceeds its purchase price. (19)

capitalization. The process of deferring the recognition of expenses until future accounting periods. (4)

capital rationing. The process of allocating limited resources to ranked capital investment proposals. (17)

cash. The amount of currency on hand or on deposit at an insurer's bank. (7)

cash accounting. A type of accounting that relates to the management and maintenance of records for all cash transactions, namely funds deposited or withdrawn from an insurer's bank accounts. (8)

cash-basis accounting. A system in which a company recognizes revenues or expenses only when it receives or disburses cash. (4)

cash budgeting. Budgeting that anticipates the flows of cash into and out of a company during a given period. (17)

cash budgets. Budgets that project a company's beginning cash balance, inflows, outflows, and ending cash balance. (17)

cash disbursement. The payment of cash by a company to a recipient such as a policy beneficiary. (4)

cash disbursements budget. A budget that attempts to estimate the timing and amount of all of a company's or department's cash disbursements. (17)

cash dividend. A dividend that a company pays in the form of cash. (5)

cash equivalents. A type of short-term asset that can be converted into cash within 90 days with little or no risk of losing value. (7)

cash inflow. A *source* of funds. (5)

cash outflow. A *use* of funds. (5)

cash premium accounting system. A system in which a home service agent personally collects premium payments from each policyowner and records each transaction in a route collection book or computer. (12)

cash receipt. A check, money order, electronic funds transfer (EFT), or other cash transaction that is remitted to a company as some form of payment. (4)

cash receipts budget. A schedule of cash receipts expected during a given period. (17)

cash surrender value. Also known as the *net cash value,* the amount of money, after adjusting for policy loans, premiums due, and other similar factors, that a policyowner will receive if he or she surrenders the policy or allows the policy to lapse. (8)

cash value. The amount of money, *before* being adjusted for factors such as policy loans or late premiums, that the policyowner will receive if the policyowner allows the policy to lapse or surrenders the policy. (10)

central depository safekeeping. A method of housing and safeguarding an insurer's securities, except for those issued by the federal government, through a centralized safekeeping facility. (20)

Certified General Accountant (CGA). A Canadian accounting designation that requires a university-level course of study as well as practical experience. (1)

Certified Management Accountant (CMA). An accounting designation which indicates that an accountant has met certain educational and experience requirements, is competent in financial accounting and management accounting practices, has passed a uniform national examination on management accounting practices, and has fulfilled certain practical experience requirements. (1)

Certified Public Accountant (CPA). The major U.S. accounting designation that all accountants must earn to work in public accounting. (1)

change analysis. The comparison of a cost in one period to the same cost in a different period. (16)

chargebacks. A method of allocating costs in which a department allocates its indirect costs to departments based on usage. (16)

Chartered Accountant (CA). The major professional accounting designation in Canada. (1)

chart of accounts. Also known as a *system of accounts,* a numbered or alphabetical list of all the company's account names. (2)

claim reserves. Also known as *disabled life reserves,* liabilities that identify the amounts that an insurer will pay in the future on claims that have been reported to the insurer before the date of the financial statement but have not yet been paid in full. (9)

claims. Requests for payments under the terms and conditions of life and accident and health insurance policies. (10)

claims in the course of settlement. Claims that have been reported to an insurer and that are being investigated. (6)

closing costs. The charges incurred in transferring property from seller to buyer, including legal fees and title search fees. (7)

closing entries. Accounting entries that a company makes at the end of the year to start the next annual accounting period with a zero balance. (3)

coinsurance. A form of reinsurance in which the ceding company pays the reinsurer part of the premium paid by the insured, minus a proportionate share of the commission and premium taxes associated with the policy that is being reinsured and a portion of the ceding company's general expenses. In return, the reinsurer agrees to pay the ceding company a proportionate part of the death benefit when a claim is filed and to contribute to all other policy benefits, including policy dividends, on a scale determined by the ceding company. (11)

collateral. Something of value, usually a portion of a bond issuer's assets, which the bondholder will receive if the bond issuer fails to make the contracted interest and principal payments on the bond. (7)

collateralized mortgage obligations (CMOs). Mortgage-backed bonds secured by a pool of residential mortgage loans. (7)

collusion. A secret agreement entered into by two or more persons to perpetrate an illegal act. (20)

combined ratio. A calculation that indicates whether the premiums being collected are sufficient to pay both the claims to policyowners and the company's expenses; the summation of the loss ratio and the expense ratio. (19)

committed costs. Costs resulting from prior management decisions that cannot be changed quickly. (16)

common-size statement. A statement that consists of the percentages obtained from vertical analysis. (19)

common stock. A unit of ownership that typically entitles the owner to vote on the selection of directors and on other important company matters and also entitles the owner to receive dividends. (5)(7)

comparability. The feature of a company's financial statements that enables an interested party to identify similarities and differences in financial information across accounting periods and between different companies. (4)

comparative financial statements. Financial statements that present data for two or more accounting periods side by side. (19)

compliance auditing. A type of auditing that verifies adherence to the laws, regulations, policies, and procedures prescribed by internal or external authorities. (20)

compound accounting entry. An accounting entry that involves more than two accounts. (2)

compound interest. Interest earned on both the principal and on the accumulated interest. (14)

conservatism. The choice of a financial reporting method that results in the projection of lower values for a company's assets, higher values for its liabilities and expenses, and a lower level of net income than would be the case if a company used a more optimistic reporting method. (4)

consistency. The characteristic of a company's financial statements that use the same accounting policies and procedures from one accounting period to the next, unless there is a sound reason for changing a policy or procedure. (4)

consolidated financial statements. Financial statements that combine the assets, liabilities, owners' equity, revenues, and expenses of a subsidiary company with those of its parent company. (5)

contingency reserves. Reserves created by U.S. insurers as a cushion against various special risks. (9)

contingency risks (C risks). Four classifications of risk that are intrinsic to an insurer's invested assets and the products it underwrites. (19)

contra account. A type of account that accompanies a specified account and that has a normal balance, which is the opposite of the specified account's balance. (8)

contra asset account. A ledger account used to deduct specified amounts from a company's asset account. (8)

contract payments. Payments on annuities and supplementary contracts. (10)

contribution margin. The difference between a product's selling price and its variable costs. (16)

contribution margin ratio. The contribution margin divided by the segment's total revenue. (18)

control account. An account that summarizes entries in a subsidiary ledger and serves as a standard of comparison for the amount that is actually reported in the company's financial statements. (13)

controllable cost. A cost over which a particular manager or level of management has power and influence. (16)

controllable investment. All balance sheet items controlled by the manager of an investment center. (18)

controller (comptroller). A title which reflects the fact that a primary function of a company's accounting activities is to control the company's operations and protect its resources and wealth. (1)

controlling. Ensuring that performance results in achievement of corporate goals. (15)

conventional mortgage loans. Mortgage loans that are not insured or guaranteed by a government agency. (7)

conventional policy loan. A loan made to a policyowner when he or she uses the policy as security for the loan. (8)

cost. The amount of a company's resources (assets) consumed or used for any purpose. (4)(16)

cost accounting. A system that accumulates expense data that facilitates effective cost control and accurate pricing of products and services. (16)

cost accumulation. The process of capturing all of a company's costs and categorizing them in meaningful ways. (16)

cost allocation. The accounting process of assigning or distributing an indirect cost according to a method or formula. (16)

cost center. A department or other business segment to which costs can be charged. (16)

cost concept. Also known as the *historical-cost concept, initial-recording concept,* or the *acquisition-cost concept,* the accounting concept which states that companies should post items on the balance sheet and the statement of operations according to their actual cost at their time of purchase. (4)

cost object. Any purpose for which an insurer measures costs. (16)

cost of capital. The "price" that a company pays collectively for its various sources of financing. (17)

cost-volume-profit (CVP) analysis. Also known as *break-even analysis* or *profit-volume analysis,* the study of the effects of changes in product prices, sales volume, fixed costs, variable costs, and the mix of products. (16)

cost-volume-profit (CVP) graph. Also known as a *break-even chart,* this graph highlights CVP relationships over a wide range of sales levels. (16)

credit. A change made to the *right* side of an account. (2)

credit-balance accounts. An account for which its normal balance appears in the credit column. (2)

credit risk. The financial risk that an obligation will not be paid. (6)

current liquidity. A ratio that compares all of an insurer's total assets not invested in its affiliates to all the insurer's liabilities, not just its reserves. (19)

current market value. Also known as the *fair market value,* the price at which an asset can be sold under current economic conditions. (4)

current ratio. A ratio that divides a company's current assets by its current liabilities to measure its short-term debt-paying ability. (19)

data. Unprocessed information consisting of raw facts. (15)

debenture. An unsecured bond, backed only by the bond issuer's creditworthiness. (7)

debit. A change made to the *left* side of an account. (2)

debit-balance accounts. An account for which its normal balance appears in the debit column. (2)

debt ratio. A ratio used by companies to measure the proportion of total assets financed with liabilities. (19)

debt security. An investment in the debt of one or more entities. A bond is a type of debt security. (7)

debt-to-equity ratio. A ratio that measures the relationship between the amount of liabilities to policyowners and the amount of equity provided by stockholders. (19)

decision making. The process of identifying and selecting a course of action to solve a problem or take advantage of an opportunity. (15)

default. To fail to pay the contracted interest and principal amounts on a loan of any type. (7)

deferred policy acquisition costs (DPAC). An asset account allowed under U.S. GAAP that enables an insurer to capitalize certain costs associated with a block of new products and/or new business and amortize these costs over the premium-paying periods of traditional insurance products. (8)

deferred premiums. Premiums that are due after the date of the Annual Statement, but before the next policy anniversary date and the next Annual Statement. (6)

deflation. A *decrease* in the average level of the prices of goods and services. (14)

demutualization. The process of converting a mutual insurance company to a stock insurance company. (11)

departmental audit. A type of audit that evaluates and tests the performance of a department's personnel by first identifying the responsibilities involved in each person's job and then determining if those responsibilities are being met. (20)

depreciation. The process of spreading (allocating) the cost of an asset over the asset's estimated useful life. (4)

derivative. A financial instrument that obtains (derives) its value from the underlying security on which it is based. (8)

detective controls. Controls that are intended to identify problems after they occur. (20)

differential cost. A future cost that changes as a result of a future decision. (16)

direct cost. Also known as a *traceable cost,* a cost incurred for or physically traceable to one specific product, line of business, department, function, or other cost object. (16)

direct financial interest. An interest in a company expressed by either an individual or an organization that can gain or lose money as a result of the company's financial performance. (1)

direct method. 1. A method of determining net cash flow from operating activities by taking a company's major types of operating cash receipts and then subtracting each major type of cash disbursement. The difference between the cash receipts and the disbursements is the net cash for the period (5); 2. A method of service department cost allocation that allocates all of a service department's costs directly to production departments using an appropriate allocation base. (16)

disclaimer of opinion (denial of opinion). A type of non-standard auditor's report that indicates that the auditor has no opinion on the financial statements. (20)

discontinued operations. One-time transactions that result from ending operations through the sale or other disposition of a business segment. (5)

discount. The difference between the sales price and the par value of a bond when an insurer pays less than par value for a bond. (7)

discounted payback method. A method that calculates, in terms of discounted dollars, how long it will take a company to recover its initial investment. (17)

discounting. The process of converting a future value to its present value. (14)

discretionary costs. Costs that result from periodic management decisions that can change as conditions require. (16)

dividend accumulations. Amounts resulting when a policyowner elects to leave policy dividends on deposit at interest with an insurer. (10)

dividend payout ratio. The proportion of earnings (net income) paid out to stockholders in the form of cash dividends. (19)

dividends. Distributions of earnings that the company pays to stockholders. (5)

divisible surplus. The amount of an insurer's surplus that is available for distribution to owners of participating policies. (6)

double-entry accounting. An accounting concept which requires that every business transaction affecting at least two accounts must have at least one debit and one credit for each transaction, and the sum of the debits must equal the sum of the credits for each transaction. (2)

dual concept. An accounting concept which states that every business transaction has two aspects that always offset and balance each other. (2)

due and unpaid claims. Claims that have been approved by an insurer but have not yet been paid to the policy beneficiary. (6)

due income. Income that was expected by the insurer before the reporting date but that has not yet been received. (8)

dynamic measure. The movement or flow of business transactions over a specified accounting period. (2)

earnings per share (EPS). Also known as *earnings per share of common stock,* the amount of net income per share of the company's common stock. (19)

economic solvency. Also known as *technical solvency,* the ability of a company to meet financial obligations as they come due. (6)

effective interest rate. Also known as the *effective rate of return* or the *true rate of return,* the actual rate of interest paid on a bond or other investment with interest compounded more often than annually. This may differ from the stated rate of return if a price other than par is paid. (7)

effectiveness. The extent to which a responsibility center is able to establish and achieve appropriate objectives. (18)

efficiency. The extent to which a responsibility center is able to achieve objectives with a minimum of waste. (18)

entity. The basic economic unit for which a company maintains distinct accounting records and reports. (4)

entity concept. Also known as the *accounting-entity concept* or the *business-entity concept,* an accounting concept which states that a company must account separately for the business activities of each economic unit. (4)

equity-based insurance products. Products in which the cash value and the benefit level fluctuate according to the performance of a portfolio of equity investments, such as stocks. (1)

equivalent interest rates. Interest rates that produce the same future value in the same period. (14)

escrow account. A trust account used to pay property taxes, insurance premiums, and other expenses related to a mortgaged property. (7)

ex-dividend date. The date that determines whether a shareholder is eligible to receive a declared dividend. (7)

execution of transactions as authorized. The element of the internal control system that concerns the delegation of authority to perform specified tasks and the communication of that authority. (20)

expected value. An investment forecast used to account for possible fluctuations in interest rates and other assumptions in order to devise a single "compromise" forecast. (17)

expense budget. A schedule of expenses expected during the given period used to help control expenses, increase cost awareness among managers, measure management performance, and assign responsibility for expenditures. (17)

expense ratio. A ratio that measures the percentage of health insurance expenses paid for each dollar of premium income. (19)

expenses. A major account classification on the statement of operations that constitutes the amount of one or more assets a company uses to receive a certain benefit or service. (2)

experience rating refund. In the context of reinsurance, the portion of a reinsurance premium that is returned to the ceding company when claims experience is better than had been expected at the time the premium was calculated. (9)

external analysis. The financial analysis performed by someone outside of the company being analyzed. (19)

external audit. Also known as an *independent audit,* the process of issuing an opinion as to whether a company's financial statements present fairly, in all material respects, the company's operations through adherence to GAAP, statutory accounting, or other accounting principles; reviewing and recommending changes to a company's system of internal control; and preparing reports of audit findings for the company's audit committee or board of directors. (20)

extraordinary item. A non-core business transaction that is unusual, rare in occurrence, and not based primarily on management decisions. (5)

feedback. Information such as accounting reports that enables managers to identify problems and opportunities. (15)(18)

financial accounting. The type of accounting that primarily focuses on reporting a company's financial information to meet the needs of the company's external users. (1)

Financial Accounting Standards Board (FASB). A private organization, funded by the accounting profession and companies with an interest in accounting, whose purpose is to establish and promote generally accepted accounting principles (GAAP) in the United States. (1)

Financial Analysis and Solvency Tracking (FAST) system. A system by which financial statement information is evaluated to determine insurers' financial condition. (19)

financial audit. Also known as a *financial statement audit* or an *attest audit* (because the result is an auditor's report that attests to or verifies the fairness of a company's financial statements), the traditional auditing of financial information that includes both the overall examination of a company's financial statements and the examination of individual accounts and accounting records. (20)

financial leverage. A type of leverage that involves financing company assets with debt or other borrowed funds. (19)

financial leverage ratios. Ratios that compare an insurer's obligations to its ability to meet those obligations. (19)

financial statement analysis. A method of analysis that assesses an insurance company's financial performance and position and compares the company with other companies within and outside the insurance industry. (19)

financial statements. Statements, including the *balance sheet,* the *statement of operations,* the *statement of cash flows,* and the *statement of stockholders' equity* or *policyowners' equity,* that report major financial events and transactions of a company. (1)

financing activities. Transactions involving borrowed funds and cash payments to or from owners of the company. (5)

first mortgage. The original mortgage secured by a piece of real estate. (7)

fiscal year. The 12-month accounting period, which may or may not coincide with the calendar year, chosen by a company for financial reporting purposes. (4)

fixed cost. A cost that remains constant for all levels of operating activity or production. (16)

flexible budget. Also known as a *flexible-amount budget,* a *dynamic budget,* or a *variable budget,* a budget used to test assumptions by providing alternative sets of figures that can be used under the different circumstances that may arise during a budgeting period. (17)

floor rate. A minimum guaranteed rate of return. (7)

footing. The process of calculating an account's ending balance as of a particular date. (3)

foreclosure. A legal procedure by which a lender recovers an unpaid loan balance by gaining title to the real estate offered as collateral if the borrower defaults in the obligation to meet the terms of the loan. (7)

foreign exchange risk. The risk exposure to changes in the exchange rate between two currencies, such as the U.S. dollar and the Japanese yen. (8)

fraud. The intentional use of false information to mislead another party. (20)

full-disclosure concept. Also known as the *adequate-disclosure concept,* an accounting concept which states that financial statements must contain all material information about a company and that the company must disclose any additional information or fact that, by its omission, could mislead an interested user. (4)

full preliminary term method. A modified reserving method according to which the first-year reserve is equal to the end-of-year reserve of a one-year term policy, which is $0. (9)

function. A series of activities that serve a specific purpose. (16)

functional costs. The accumulated costs of the activities involved within a certain function, without regard to departmental lines. (16)

future value (*FV*). Also known as *accumulated value,* the amount that a sum of money is expected to be worth at a certain point in the future, given a certain rate of interest. (14)

future value of an annuity (*FVA*). At a given point in time, the amount that a series of payments plus the interest earned on these payments will grow to by that point in time. (14)

future value interest factor (*FVIF*). The future value of $1.00 compounded at interest rate *i* for *n* periods. (14)

future value interest factor of an annuity (*FVIFA*). Interest factors arranged in a table to simplify the calculation of the future value of an annuity. (14)

gain. Income obtained by a transaction other than a core business function. (5)

general account. An undivided account in which life and health insurers maintain funds from guaranteed insurance products such as ordinary life insurance. (6)(8)

general and administrative expense budget. A type of budget that is the sum of all departmental expense budgets. (17)

general ledger. A summary of all accounts with their current balances. (3)

generally accepted accounting principles (GAAP). A set of financial accounting standards that all U.S. stock companies and all Canadian companies follow when preparing financial statements. (1)

goal congruence. An operational condition in which the goals of a company and the goals of its managers are mutually supportive. (18)

goal incongruence. An operational condition in which managers' goals and the company's goals are in conflict, and they are not mutually achievable. (18)

going-concern concept. The accounting concept which states that accounting processes are typically based on the assumption that a company will continue to operate for an indefinite period of time. (4)

gross premium. The amount that policyowners must pay for their insurance coverage, equal to the net premium plus the loading. (6)

gross profit ratio. A ratio that provides a simple measure of the growth of an insurance company's capital and surplus by comparing the insurer's profit before interest expenses and taxes for the period to its beginning capital and surplus. (19)

guaranteed interest contract (GIC). Also known as a *guaranteed income contract* or a *guaranteed investment contract,* a funding vehicle in which an insurer accepts a deposit from a pension plan sponsor for a specified period of time, such as five years, and holds the deposit at a specified rate of interest. At the end of the period, the insurer returns the deposited funds, including accumulated interest, to the pension plan sponsor, who in turn can reinvest the plan assets with the same insurer or with another financial institution. (6)

guaranty-fund assessments. Charges payable by sound insurers to support the customer obligations of a failed insurer that had operated in a jurisdiction where the surviving insurers conduct business. (13)

hedge. An investment strategy undertaken to protect a future (unrealized) gain, to minimize a potential loss on invested assets, or to reduce costs or increase current investment income. (8)

historical cost. The actual amount paid for an asset. (4)

horizontal analysis. A method of financial analysis that measures the amount that corresponding items change from one financial statement to another over consecutive accounting periods. (19)

immediate recognition. An accounting concept that recognizes all costs as expenses during the current accounting period. (4)

incompatible functions. Job duties that place any person in a position to commit an illegal act or to conceal errors or irregularities in the normal course of his or her employment. (20)

incremental cash flows. Additional costs or revenues that result from a capital project. (17)

incurred but not reported (IBNR) claims. Claims that were incurred during an accounting period, but that have not been reported to the insurer as of the Annual Statement date. (6)(10)

independent proposals. Proposals that contain unrelated cash flows. (17)

indirect cost. Also known as *common cost* or *shared cost,* a cost that is not incurred for or cannot be traced to one specific cost object. (16)

indirect financial interest. An interest in a company that is expressed by either an individual or an organization that is seeking financial information about the company on behalf of others. (1)

indirect method. Also known as the *reconciliation method,* a method of financial reporting that begins with the net income figure as reported on the statement of operations, and then reconciles this amount to operating cash flows through a series of additions and subtractions. (5)

inflation. An increase in the average level of the prices of goods and services. (14)

inflation risk. Also known as *purchasing power risk,* a risk regarding the potential problems caused by the increasing prices that occur during inflation, especially when the rate of inflation is hard to predict. (14)

information. Accounting data that has been processed and placed in a meaningful and useful context for the user. (15)

insurance leverage ratio. Also known as the *gross leverage ratio,* a calculation that relates contractual reserves to capital and surplus. (19)

Insurance Regulatory Information System (IRIS). A set of specific financial ratios used to monitor the financial well-being of life and health insurance companies. (19)

insurer-administered plan. A group insurance plan in which the insurer performs the administrative work, which includes calculating the amount of the premium due and mailing a statement to the group policyholder, typically on a monthly basis. (12)

intangible asset. An asset, such as a bond, stock, or other security, that does not have physical substance. (7)

interest. The dollar amount earned on an invested amount of money. (14)

interest maintenance reserve (IMR). A reserve that absorbs the realized net gains and losses, caused by changes in the economy, from the sale of fixed-income securities by U.S. life and health insurance companies. (6)

interest margin pricing risk. The risk relating to interest margin losses from future investment and pricing decisions on in-force insurance business. (19)

interest rate. The percentage by which an amount of money is multiplied to derive the amount paid for the use of that money. (14)

interest rate risk. Risk regarding the potential problems caused by unpredictable fluctuations in interest rates. (6)

internal analysis. The financial analysis undertaken by employees of the company being analyzed. (19)

internal audit. A type of internal control performed by company employees who assess and evaluate their company's system of internal controls to assist the company's managers in effectively discharging their responsibilities. (20)

internal control. The steps a company takes to protect its assets, monitor the accuracy of its accounting records, and encourage both operational efficiency and adherence to the company's management policies. (20)

internal rate of return (IRR) method. A capital budgeting method that determines the discount rate at which the net present value of the capital investment equals zero. (17)

Internal Revenue Service (IRS). The U.S. federal government agency that controls the taxation of businesses as well as individuals. (1)

investable funds. Funds generated by a product line, which consist of net income before taxes, investment income received on prior investments, and the maturities of principal on prior investments. (18)

investing activities. Transactions that involve the purchase or sale of long-term assets and the lending of funds to another entity. (5)

investment accounting. An accounting function that is typically responsible for recording all accounting entries related to invested assets in an insurer's portfolio. (7)

investment budget. A budget that projects the types of investments the company will make and the expected amount of investment-related income for each type. (17)

investment center. Sometimes known as a *strategic business unit (SBU),* an insurance company area that has control over costs, revenues, and the assets or investment funds used to meet operating needs. (18)

investment forecast. An estimate of the performance of bonds, stocks, mortgages and other invested assets a company owns. (17)

investment-grade. A characteristic of bonds that are classified by the NAIC as either highest quality or high quality. (7)

investment segmentation method. A system wherein cash flows of a particular product line or line of business are used to purchase specific investments for that line. (18)

investment turnover. A measure of the revenue that can be generated for each dollar invested by the responsibility manager; calculated by dividing total revenue by controllable investment. (18)

investment year method. The forming of separate investment pools that contain the investments made during each year. (18)

investment yield ratio. Also known as *net yield,* a ratio that measures how effectively an insurance company's investment managers can earn adequate or higher returns on the company's investment portfolio. (19)

journal. An accounting record that contains all the original, chronological records of a company's financial transactions. (3)

leading. The process of influencing others to carry out the activities that will result in the achievement of organizational goals. (15)

ledger. A set of account books (manual system) or electronic records (automated system) that provides detailed information on the dollar amounts in each of a company's accounts. (3)

ledger audit. An audit that starts with the balance in the general ledger and validates either all amounts or at least the major amounts in the account being audited. (20)

leverage. Also known as *trading on the equity,* a financial effect in which the use of fixed-cost funds magnifies both risks and returns to a company's owners. (19)

leverage effect. The effect that fixed costs have on magnifying risk and return. (19)

liabilities. A major account classification on the balance sheet representing a company's current and future obligations. (2)

liability for premium and other deposit funds. Amounts left with an insurer to accumulate at interest, including guaranteed interest contracts and other contract deposit funds. (6)

liability for reinsurance in unauthorized companies. An account established by an insurer when it reinsures some of its business with a company that is not licensed within the insurer's state of domicile; an account that represents the excess of the reserve taken on ceded business minus the amounts withheld from or deposits made by the reinsurer. (11)

life insurance company taxable income (LICTI). The difference between a U.S. life insurance company's gross income and its tax deductions. (13)

line diagram. Also known as a *time line,* a device that allows visualization of the essential elements of a particular financial transaction, marking the end of each compounding period, the frequency and amount of each cash flow, and the timing of the valuation date. (14)

line of business (LOB). A segment of the insurance market that is distinctively different from other segments, often because of sales approaches or policyowner service functions. (6)

line of credit. A prearranged agreement whereby a company can borrow money on demand up to a specified amount. (17)

liquidation. The process of converting a company's assets to cash, usually to pay off the company's liabilities. (4)

liquidity. The ease with which an asset can be converted into cash. (2)

liquidity ratios. Ratios that measure a company's ability to meet its maturing short-term obligations. (19)

loading. A charge that an insurer adds to the net premium to cover the insurer's operating expenses, compensate for the loss of income when policies lapse, provide contingency funds in the event of unexpected events like natural disasters, and provide margins for profits and contributions to the insurer's surplus. (6)

lock-box system. Also known as *lock-box banking,* a system in which policyowners remit premium payments, along with the premium notice stub, to a specified post office box number to which the insurer's bank has access. (12)

long-term assets. Assets that are less liquid, and not directly or easily converted into cash, that a company plans to retain for a long time to generate income. (2)

long-term budget. A budget that addresses periods of more than one year. (17)

long-term liabilities. Liabilities that do not have to be paid in full during the current accounting period. (2)

loss. The event that occurs when a company loses money on an activity that does not arise from normal business operations. (5)

loss ratio. The percentage of incurred claims to earned premiums. (19)

lower of cost or market (LCM) rule. A U.S. accounting method which states that insurers should report values at historical cost, amortized cost, or current market value, whichever is lowest. (7)

management. A process consisting of planning, organizing, and controlling actions undertaken to accomplish a stated goal, such as providing a service, making a profit, or achieving a desired market share. (15)

management accounting. Also known as *managerial accounting,* a type of accounting in which the process of identifying, measuring, analyzing, and communicating financial information to allow for informed decision making by internal managers regarding the acquisition and use of a company's resources. (1)

management auditing. Also known as *economy and efficiency auditing,* a type of auditing that focuses on improving the effectiveness and efficiency of a company's operations. Audits performed to identify areas in which costs can be reduced and improvements in operations can be made. (20)

management by exception. A type of control which states that managers should be informed about operational progress only when results or activities differ from expected norms by a certain amount or percentage. (15)

Management Discussion and Analysis of Financial Condition and Results of Operations (MD&A). The analysis and interpretation of a company's financial statements and company performance from management's point of view. (5)

margin. The difference between the cost of borrowing funds and the return earned using these funds. (19)

marginal cost. Also known as an *incremental cost* or a *differential cost,* the additional total expense incurred as a result of producing one additional unit of a product or service. (16)

marginal unit cost. The increase or decrease in unit cost as a result of an additional unit of a good or service. (16)

master budget. Also known as the *comprehensive budget* or *operating budget,* a budget that shows the overall operating and financing plans for the company during a specified period, often one year. (17)

matching principle. An accounting principle which states that a company should recognize expenses when the company earns the revenues related to those expenses, regardless of when the company receives cash for revenues earned. (4)

materiality. An accounting concept requiring companies to disclose all significant information in their financial statements. (4)

matured endowment. An endowment insurance policy that has reached the end of its term during the lifetime of the insured and is therefore payable. (10)

maturity date. The date on which a bond issuer must pay principal to the bondholder. (7)

mean liabilities method. A method that allocates investment revenues to lines of business based on the reserves attributable to each line. (18)

measuring-unit concept. Also known as the *stable-monetary-unit concept,* the *unit-of-measurement concept,* or the *stable-dollar concept,* an accounting concept which states that a company should record the amounts associated with its business transactions in monetary terms, such as U.S. or Canadian dollars. (4)

minimum cash balance. The amount of cash that an insurer determines is necessary to pay all obligations in a given budgeting period without needlessly tying up excess funds. (17)

Minimum Continuing Capital and Surplus Requirements (MCCSR). A mandate that Canadian insurers maintain at least a minimum level of capital and surplus that reflects the riskiness of their assets and operations. (19)

minimum reserve requirements. An NAIC mandate that U.S. insurers use the prospective method to calculate reserves and that they specify the mortality tables, interest rates, and other factors that are used to calculate their policy reserves. (9)

modified cash-basis accounting. A combination of cash-basis and accrual-basis accounting. (4)

modified coinsurance (modco). A type of reinsurance that uses the basic provisions of coinsurance, except that the ceding company, rather than the reinsurer, maintains the entire policy reserve for the reinsured amount. (11)

modified report. A report that contains explanatory language concerning inconsistencies resulting from a change in accounting principles or practices. (20)

modified reserve method. A method for calculating policy reserves that creates smaller first-year statutory reserves than those calculated using the net level premium approach. (9)

mortgage correspondents. Firms that service mortgage loans for a fee, usually a percentage of the unpaid loan balance. (7)

mortgage loan. A type of loan under which a person, business, or other entity borrows money from a lender and offers some specific piece of real estate, such as a house, farm, or office building, to the lender as collateral. (7)

moving average market method (MAMM). A method that Canadian insurers use to systematically adjust, over a period of years, unrealized gains (losses) that result from changes in current market value of equity investments. (7)

multiple-step statement of operations. A statement of operations that draws out subtotals for each category of revenues or expenses. (5)

mutual funds. Diversified, professionally managed portfolios that invest in a variety of debt and/or equity securities. (8)

mutually exclusive proposals. Proposals that involve investment choices that perform essentially the same function. (17)

National Association of Insurance Commissioners (NAIC). An association of state insurance commissioners created to promote consistent insurance regulation. (1)

negative financial leverage. The result when the assets in which a company's borrowed funds are invested earn a rate of return lower than the fixed rate required by lenders. (19)

net basis. In accounting for the sale of a bond, a method of recording both bond sale price and purchase price to reflect adjustments for expenses incurred in the purchase and sale of bonds. (7)

net book value. An asset's historical cost less accumulated depreciation. (7)

net GAAP reserves. A U.S. insurer's GAAP policy reserves minus the insurer's deferred acquisition costs. (9)

net gain to total income. A measurement of the share of operating income—that is, operating revenues less operating expenses—that represents net profit. (19)

net income. The excess of total revenues over total expenses. (5)

net level premium approach. A method used by U.S. insurers to calculate life insurance policy reserves, which assumes that a policy's net premiums do not increase or decrease during the life of the policy. (9)

net loss. The excess of total expenses over total revenues. (5)

net premium. The amount of money needed to provide life insurance benefits for a policy; calculated by using an assumed interest rate and a tabular mortality rate, independent of the loading. (6)

net present value (NPV) method. A method of evaluating proposed capital expenditure based on its *net present value (NPV);* the difference between the present value of a project's cash inflows (revenues, cost savings, and interest income) and the present value of its cash outflows (investment cost and expenses). (17)

net profit margin. Also known as *rate of return on net sales,* or *return on sales,* a margin that shows how much after-tax profit is generated by each dollar of total revenues. (19)

nominal interest rate. An annual interest rate that is quoted independent of the effects of compounding. (14)

nonadmitted assets. Assets that state insurance law prohibits from being included on the *Assets* page of the Annual Statement. (6)

noncontrollable cost. A cost over which a particular manager or level of management has no power or influence. (16)

nonforfeiture options. The choices available to a policyowner concerning the methods under which he or she can apply the policy's cash surrender value when the policy expires. (10)

nonsufficient funds (NSF) check. A check that has "bounced" when the payor did not have enough money in its checking account to pay the amount of the check. (8)

non-value-added activity. An activity that does not make the product or service more valuable to the customer. (16)

normal balance. The side of the account in which *increases* to the account are recorded. (2)

notes to the financial statements. Factual disclosures of the details behind some of the amounts presented in the financial statements, usually accompanying or immediately following the financial statements in a company's annual report, that enable users to understand some of the more complex items in the published financial statements. (5)

Office of the Superintendent of Financial Institutions (OSFI). The agency primarily responsible for overseeing Canadian insurance companies and ensuring compliance with federal laws. (1)

operating activities. Activities associated with a company's major lines of business involving transactions that directly determine a company's net income. (5)

operating efficiency. A company's ability to manage the relationship between revenues and expenses. (5)

operating expenses. Expenses that occur as a result of undertaking certain activities in the course of normal business operations to generate sales revenues. (2)

operating income. Also known as *net gain from operations before taxes,* the amount of income before subtracting income taxes. (18)

operational budget. A budget covering part or all of a company's operations. (17)

operational budgeting. Budgeting that covers all or part of a company's operations. (17)

operational planning. The process of determining how to accomplish specific tasks with available resources. (15)

opportunity cost. The benefit that is forfeited in choosing one decision alternative over another. (16)

ordinary annuity. Also known as an *annuity immediate* or an *annuity in arrears,* an annuity for which the payment occurs at the end of each payment period. (14)

organizing. The process of ensuring that the necessary resources—human, economic, and physical—are available to carry out the plan and achieve the desired goals. (15)

out-of-pocket costs. Costs that require outlays of cash or other resources. (16)

outstanding checks. Checks that the insurer has written, deducted from its book balance, and sent to payees, but that have not yet cleared the bank. (8)

outstanding stock. Stock that has been issued. (5)

overhead cost. A cost incurred during normal business operations that is not directly associated or identifiable with a specific good or service. (16)

owners' equity. Also known as stockholders' equity, a major balance sheet account classification that represents the owners' investment in a company. (2)

paid-to date. The date to which a policy premium provides insurance coverage. (12)

par value. 1. The designated legal value assigned to each outstanding share of common stock. 2. Another name for the principal amount of a bond. The par value for a bond is generally $1,000. (5)(6)(7)

payback method. A capital budgeting technique that calculates how long it will take a company to recover its investment. (17)

performance auditing. Also known as *operational auditing,* the examination of a particular operations area to measure and evaluate progress toward achieving management objectives for that area. (20)

period budget. A budget that covers a specific time frame, such as one month or one year, and that expires at the end of that time frame. (17)

permanent accounts. Accounts included in the basic accounting equation: *Assets = Liabilities + Owners' Equity.* (3)

physical comparison of recorded amounts. The process of a company counting its assets, income, and disbursements on a periodic basis and comparing this count to the recorded amounts for these items. (20)

physical settlement. The tangible exchange of funds and securities and the clearing of account balances between the buyer and seller of the securities. (20)

planning. A function that involves establishing objectives and then formulating the strategies, tactics, and other supporting activities needed to achieve those objectives. (15)

policy acquisition costs. Costs, such as commissions that insurers pay to their agents, that are directly attributable to the production of new business. (4)

policy and contract claims. Liabilities for all types of insurance policy and annuity contract claims that must be settled. (6)

policy dividend. Also known as *policyowner dividend* or *policyholder dividend,* a policyowner's share of an insurer's divisible surplus. (6)

policy dividend liabilities. Liabilities for all policy dividends that have been declared by a company's board of directors, but which are not yet payable. (6)

policy dividend payment options. Also known as *dividend payment options,* options that enable participating policyowners to select the manner in which they want their policy dividends disbursed. (10)

policy dividends due and unpaid. Dividends that were declared by an insurer's board of directors during the year, but that have not yet been paid as of the current financial statement date. (10)

policy dividends payable in the following year. Also known as *apportioned dividends,* the estimated amount of all policy dividends that an insurance company's board of directors has declared that are payable in the following year. (10)

policy loan. A loan made to a policyowner and secured by a policy's cash surrender value. (8)

policy premium method (PPM). A reserve method for Canadian insurers that uses gross premiums instead of net premiums, using the following equation: *Policy Reserve = Present Value of Future Benefits – Present Value of Future Gross Premiums.* (9)

policy reserves. Liability accounts that identify the amount that, together with the insurer's future expected premiums and investment income earned from in-force policies, the insurer expects will be sufficient to pay future benefits on in-force policies. (6)

portfolio. A collection of financial assets such as stocks and bonds. (6)

positive financial leverage. The result when the assets in which a company's borrowed funds are invested earn a rate of return greater than the fixed rate of return required by the suppliers of borrowed funds. (19)

posting. The process of transferring the amounts listed in a journal to the appropriate accounts in a ledger. (3)

posting reference. Also known as a *journal reference,* a code that links an accounting entry in a journal to one or more source documents associated with a business transaction. (3)

power of sale. The method by which Canadian insurers can recover unpaid loan balances on defaulted loans by allowing the lender to settle the mortgage debt through a sale of the property on behalf of the owner of the property's legal title. (7)

preauthorized payment system. A premium payment system under which the policyowner signs a two-part authorization form, which is submitted to his or her bank. The first part authorizes the insurer to withdraw due premiums from the policyowner's checking or savings account. The second part of the form authorizes the policyowner's bank to honor these withdrawals. (12)

predictive quality. A feature of financial information that enables interested users to develop a reasonably accurate estimate of a company's financial strength or earnings potential if the users analyze the company's financial statements. (4)

preferred stock. A unit of ownership that does not ordinarily carry the voting rights of common stock, but does carry a stated dividend rate or amount that has a priority over common stock. (5)(7)

premium. The excess amount paid when an insurer pays more than par value for a bond. (7)

premium deposits. Amounts that an insurer's policyowners leave on deposit with the insurer to pay for future premiums. (10)

premiums due. Uncollected premiums for accident and health insurance and group life insurance. (6)(8)

premiums outstanding. In Canada, life insurance premiums and annuity considerations that are due on or before the Annual Return date but that the insurer has not received by that date. (6)

premium suspense account. An account used by insurers to record transactions that are intended as premiums but which insurers cannot accept as revenue until a particular event occurs. (10)

premium taxes. Taxes on an insurer's premium income earned within a state or province. (13)

prepaid expenses. Expenditures that the insurer expects will provide a future value or benefit. (8)

present value (*PV*). The amount of money that, if invested at a specified interest rate on a certain date, called the *valuation date,* would grow to equal a future sum. (14)

present value interest factor (*PVIF*). The present value of $1.00 discounted at an interest rate of *i* for *n* periods. (14)

present value interest factor of an annuity (*PVIFA*). Interest factors arranged in a table to simplify the calculation of the present value of an annuity. (14)

present value of an annuity (*PVA*). The amount that must be invested now in order to provide for a specified series of equal future payments, given a specified interest rate and a specified number of periods. (14)

present value of future benefits. The net single premium at the insured's attained age for the remaining policy benefits. (9)

present value of future net premiums. The present value of a life annuity due, assuming whole life policies rather than limited-pay policies. (9)

preventive controls. Controls designed to keep an error or a problem from occurring. (20)

price/earnings (P/E) ratio. The relationship between a company's earnings per share and the current market price of its stock. (19)

principal. An amount of money originally borrowed, deposited, or invested. (7)(14)

prior period adjustments. Corrections or adjustments related to previous accounting periods. (5)

private placements. Bonds offered by the bond issuer directly to specific financial institutions, including insurance companies. (7)

pro forma balance sheet. A balance sheet that predicts the change in asset, liability, and stockholders' equity accounts based on information contained in the rest of a company's budgets. (17)

pro forma statement of cash flows. A statement that estimates the cash inflows and outflows for a company. (17)

pro forma statement of operations. Also known as a *budgeted income statement,* a statement of operations that estimates the net income for a company. (17)

production department. A department that engages in an insurance company's revenue-generating activities. (16)

profit. Extra income that is not needed to pay for the cost of providing insurance, and which contributes to the insurer's surplus. (5)(16)

profitability index (PI). The ratio of the present value of future cash flows to the amount of investment. (17)

profitability ratios. The relationship of a company's returns to sales, total revenues, assets, stockholders' equity, capital and surplus, or stock share price. (19)

profit center. A line of business that is evaluated on its profitability and that incorporates the responsibilities of a cost center and a revenue center and is responsible for both costs and revenues. (18)

program results auditing. A type of audit that determines whether the results or benefits desired from a particular program are actually being achieved. (20)

prospective method. A method of calculating policy reserves that looks ahead at a policy's future premiums and benefits and calculates policy reserves using the following equation: *Policy Reserve = Present Value of Future Benefits – Present Value of Future Net Premiums.* (9)

provision for adverse deviation. A safety margin created to allow for unfavorable variations from actuarial assumptions. (9)

public offering. The sale of bonds to the general public. (7)

purchase money mortgage. A mortgage in which the seller of the property grants credit to the purchaser, and the purchaser uses the real estate being purchased as collateral for the mortgage loan. (7)

qualified opinion. A type of non-standard auditor report that states the area of exception to an otherwise unqualified opinion. (20)

quick liquidity. A ratio that compares an insurer's liquid assets (cash and other readily marketable assets such as short-term investments) to contractual reserves, which are reserves for current insurance and annuity contracts. (19)

quota share method of reinsurance. In terms of reducing surplus strain, a reinsurance method that requires a ceding company to reinsure a percentage of the premium amount and the claim dollars incurred on a block of insurance policies, typically accident and health or disability income policies. (9)

rate variance. The difference between a product's actual rate (or unit cost or price) and the budgeted rate, multiplied by the number of units sold or processed. (18)

ratio. A comparison of two or more numbers in fraction form. (19)

ratio analysis. Financial analysis that compares various financial statement values for the purpose of assessing a company's financial performance or condition. (19)

real estate. A type of asset that includes both buildings and undeveloped land. (8)

realization principle. Also known as the *revenue principle* or *revenue recognition principle,* an accounting principle which states that a company should recognize revenue when it is earned. (4)

realized gain (loss). In the sale of an asset, the difference between the asset's net sales proceeds and its book value. (7)

reciprocal method. Regarding service departments, a cost allocation method that fully recognizes the services that service departments perform for each other. (16)

recognition. The process of classifying an item in a financial statement as an asset, liability, owners' equity, revenue, or expense account. (4)

record. To enter or input the appropriate accounting entries for each transaction into a company's accounting system. (2)

recording of transactions as executed. A significant internal control where a company records its transactions as they occur in the correct accounting period, so that the company can summarize all transactions for that period in its financial statements. (20)

reinsurance. A transaction between two insurance companies in which one company—called the *assuming company* or the *reinsurer*—agrees to take on (or assume) some of the insurance risks of another insurance company—called the *ceding company* or the *direct insurer.* (6)(8)

reinsurance commissions. Commissions that the reinsurer pays to the ceding company and which are allowances intended to cover all or part of the ceding company's acquisition costs and other costs related to the reinsured business. (13)

released reserve. A policy reserve that was originally established in connection with an in-force policy but that is no longer required. (9)

relevance. A quality of accounting information that is useful, timely, and likely to affect an interested user's decisions about a company. (4)

reliability. A quality of accounting information when that information is accurate, objective, and free from bias and misrepresentation. (4)

report form. A form of balance sheet presentation under which asset, liability, and owners' equity accounts are listed in order vertically. (5)

reserve destrengthening. The process of revaluing and decreasing policy reserves, resulting in an increase in surplus. (6)(9)

reserves. Estimates of the amounts of money that an insurer needs to pay future business obligations or to help absorb the financial impact of realized or unrealized gains and losses on the insurer's invested assets. (9)

reserves for future contingent benefits. Additional reserves used for deferred maternity benefits or medical expense policies with high deductibles for which the deductible has nearly been satisfied. (9)

reserve strengthening. The process of revaluing and increasing policy reserves, resulting in a decrease in surplus. (6)(9)

residual income (RI). Also known as *economic value added (EVA),* the amount of income an investment center earns above a certain minimum required rate of return on investment. (18)

resisted claims. Also known as *contested claims* or *disputed claims,* claims that the company has refused to pay, but which it may have to pay in the future. (6)

responsibility accounting. Also known as *profitability accounting,* a people-oriented system of policies and procedures that allows for costs and revenues to be assigned to an individual employee or to the organizational level that is accountable for them. (18)

responsibility center. A company's business unit over which a manager has control and responsibility. (18)

responsibility center report. Also known as a *responsibility report,* a report that itemizes budgeted and actual amounts and the corresponding variance for each revenue or cost category. (18)

responsibility manager. The manager of a responsibility center. (18)

retained earnings. The cumulative amount of a company's earnings that has been kept (retained) in the company over time in order to finance its continuing operations. (5)

retaliatory tax laws. Laws that impose premium taxes on a *foreign insurer,* which is an insurer domiciled in another state, at the rate domestic companies in the state of domicile would be taxed by the foreign state, but only if the premium tax rate is higher in the state of domicile. (13)

retention limit. The highest amount of risk that an insurance company will assume on a single policy without reinsurance. (8)(11)

retired stock. Treasury stock that an insurer has no intention of reissuing. (11)

retrospective method. A method of calculating policy reserves that looks back at a policy's past premiums and benefits to determine policy reserves and that defines the policy reserve for a block of policies according to the following equation: *Policy Reserve = Accumulated Value of Net Premiums – Accumulated Cost of Insurance.* (9)

return on assets (ROA). A ratio that measures a company's success in using its assets to earn a profit. (19)

return on capital ratio. The ratio of net gain from operations to beginning capital and surplus. (19)

return on equity (ROE). Also known as the *return on stockholders' equity,* the rate of return on the book value of the stockholders' investment in the firm. (19)

return on investment (ROI). A ratio that measures the performance of an investment center by calculating the relationship between operating income and controllable investment. (18)

return on revenue. A ratio that measures management's ability to control operating expenses in relation to total revenue, which includes both premium income and investment income, by dividing operating income by total revenue. (18)

revenue budget. A budget which indicates the amount of income from operations—policy sales and investments—that the company expects in the coming budget period. (17)

Revenue Canada. The governmental agency that is responsible for enforcing the provisions of the *Canadian Income Tax Act.* (1)

revenues. A major account classification on the statement of operations, the amounts earned from a company's sales of products and services to its customers. (2)

risk. The chance that the actual return on an investment will be less than its expected return. (14)

Risk-Based Capital ratio. The ratio of an insurer's total adjusted capital to its authorized control level risk-based capital (RBC). (19)

Risk-Based Capital (RBC) Requirements. A system used for evaluating the adequacy of a U.S. insurer's capital and surplus based on the insurer's size and risk profile. (19)

risk-return tradeoff. The relationship between risk and return that applies to all investments and all types of risk: as risk goes up, return goes down. (7)(14)

rolling budget. Also known as a *continuous budget,* a type of budget that allows a company to continually maintain projections for a certain time period into the future. (17)

safeguarding of assets. The process of 1. limiting access to offices, documents, and records; 2. storing negotiable documents in vaults to which no person has sole access; 3. maintaining written business disaster recovery plans and off-premises storage of back-up files for all critical records; 4. investigating the integrity of personnel hired to fill sensitive positions; 5. counting all assets and comparing this count to a written record; and 6. reviewing the adequacy of insurance coverage. (20)

sales budget. A budget that projects first-year and renewal premium income. (17)

sales expense budget. Budgets based primarily on the costs incurred in selling insurance. Besides commission costs, these expenses include the costs of advertising, promotion, travel, branch office operations, and salaries for marketing personnel. (17)

sales forecast. An estimate of insurance and annuity sales for a particular period. (17)

salvage value. The residual value or selling price of an asset at the end of its useful life. (17)

scenario analysis. In Canada, analysis that is required in calculating policy reserves for annuity products, which involves altering assumptions to see how changes in assumptions affect results. (9)

second mortgage. A mortgage loan taken on a piece of property on which one mortgage loan already exists. (7)

secured bond. A bond where the issuer pledges collateral to guarantee the safety of the bondholder's investment. (7)

Securities and Exchange Commission (SEC). A U.S. federal government agency that regulates the investment industry. (1)

segment margin. The portion of the contribution margin that remains after a segment has covered its direct fixed costs. (18)

segment margin ratio. The segment margin divided by the segment's total revenues. (18)

segment reporting. Statements of operations prepared by each individual profit center to provide management with a means of evaluating each separate unit. (18)

segregated funds. In Canada, accounts maintained outside a life insurance company's general account to help manage funds placed in nonguaranteed insurance products, such as equity-based or variable products. (6)

segregation of duties. An accounting control that provides for the checking of one person's work against that of another person. (20)

self-administered plan. A plan in which the group policyholder performs most of the administrative work, including the processing of detailed accounting records of group members and routine requests for name, address, or policy beneficiary changes. (12)

selling expenses. Expenses related to the marketing and sale of a company's products and services. (2)

semi-variable cost. Also known as a *mixed cost,* a type of cost that contains elements of both fixed and variable costs. (16)

sensitivity analysis. A type of analysis that tests the amount of latitude that is built into the estimates a company makes during capital budgeting by determining "worst-case" scenarios that calculate how far reality can vary from estimates without invalidating the accept/reject screening decision. (17)

separate accounts. In the United States, accounts maintained outside a life insurance company's general account to help manage the funds placed in nonguaranteed insurance products such as equity-based or variable products. (6)(8)

service department. A department that provides support services to operating departments and to other service departments but does not itself generate revenue. (16)

short-term assets. Assets that a company expects to use up or convert to cash during the current operating period, generally one year. (2)

short-term budget. A budget which generally addresses a period of one year or less and relates mainly to a company's operations during that period. (17)

short-term investments. Investments, such as *money market funds* and *Treasury bills,* that a company expects to turn into cash within one year. (7)

short-term liabilities. Debts that must be paid in one year or less. (2)(10)

simple accounting entry. An accounting entry that affects only two accounts. (2)

simple interest. Interest earned on the amount of money originally borrowed or invested. (14)

single-step statement of operations. A statement of operations that depicts one step in subtracting total operating expenses from total revenues. (5)

source documents. Various business papers and electronic forms that contain original information about a company's daily business transactions. (2)

special surplus. Also known as *assigned surplus, appropriated surplus, earmarked surplus,* and *contingency reserves,* the part of an insurer's surplus that the insurer's board of directors has set aside to meet unforeseen contingencies or pay for certain extraordinary expenses. (11)

standard costs. Predetermined costs that are expected to be incurred for particular items during normal business operations. (16)

stated rate. Also known as *coupon rate* or *nominal rate,* the rate of interest specified on a bond certificate. (7)

statement of cash flows. Also known as a *cash flow statement,* a financial statement which provides information about a company's cash receipts (inflows) and cash disbursements (outflows) during a given accounting period. (3)

statement of operations. A financial statement which reports on profit or loss for a given period by summarizing the company's revenue and expense accounts for that period. (2)

statement of stockholders' equity. Also known as the *statement of owners' equity* or *statement of shareholders' equity,* a financial statement that shows the changes which occurred in stockholders' equity during the accounting period. (3)

static budget. Budgets classified by the degree of variability inherent in them. Amounts in these budgets generally are not subject to change unless management has approved the changes. (17)

static measure. A snapshot of a company's financial position on a specified date. (2)

statutory accounting practices. A set of financial accounting standards that all U.S. life and health insurers must follow when preparing the Annual Statement and certain other financial reports. (1)

statutory reserves. Reserves established to satisfy the requirements of state insurance regulators. (9)

statutory return on assets (ROA). The ratio of an insurer's net gain from operations to its average invested assets. (19)

statutory solvency. An insurer's ability to maintain at least the minimum amount of capital and surplus specified by insurance regulators. (3)(6)(19)

step method. Also known as *step-down allocation,* a cost accounting method which assumes that service departments perform services for production departments and for other service departments. (16)

stock. An asset that represents a stockholder's ownership interest in a company. (5)(7)

stock dividend. A dividend that a company pays in the form of additional shares of the company's stock. (5)(7)(11)

stockholder. Anyone who owns shares of stock in a company. (7)

strategic planning. The process of determining how to pursue long-term goals with available resources. (15)

subsidiary ledgers. Ledgers that contain more detailed sub-accounts within the account categories listed in the general ledger. (3)

sunk cost. A past cost that does not change as the result of a future decision. (16)

supporting budgets. Budgets that provide detail to the projections and objectives found in a company's master budget. (17)

surplus. The amount that remains when an insurer subtracts its liabilities and capital from its assets. (2)

surplus notes. Also known as *surplus debentures* or *contribution certificates,* a form of long-term, unsecured debt obligation that provide for the payment of both interest and principal on or before a set maturity date. (11)

surplus strain. Also known as *issue strain* or *new business strain,* the decrease in an insurer's surplus caused by the high first-year costs and the reserving requirements associated with new products. (9)

systematic and rational allocation. A method of matching revenues and expenses that expenses an asset's cost over its estimated useful life, regardless of when the company realizes revenues from using the asset. (4)

T-account. An account presentation that shows the activities in an account during a given accounting period. (2)

tangible asset. An asset that has physical substance, such as an insurer's home office building or computer equipment. (7)

temporary accounts. Also known as *nominal accounts,* accounts that are listed on the statement of operations, do not have a cumulative balance from one year to the next, and are closed out to permanent accounts at the end of each annual accounting period. (3)

tentative LICTI. The amount of gross income minus deductible expenses before subtracting the small life insurance company deduction, excluding income from non-insurance operations. (13)

terminal policy dividend. Also known as *terminal dividend,* an extra dividend or pro-rata dividend covering the period between the last policy anniversary date and the termination date of the policy. (10)

third-party-administered (TPA) plan. A plan in which a group policyholder contracts with another organization, called a *third-party administrator (TPA),* to process premium payments for group insurance and remit them directly to the insurer. (12)

time analysis. A method of determining the percentage of time a manager spends with different departments or activities. (16)

time-period concept. Also known as the *concept of periodicity,* an accounting concept which states that a company's financial statements should report the company's business operations during a specified time period, called an *accounting period.* (4)

time value of money. The concept that the value of a sum of money at one point in time will differ from its value at another point in time. (14)

top-down budgeting. A method of budgeting that generates a budget on the corporate level by upper management and then passes the budget down to lower management. (17)

total asset turnover. A measure of how efficiently a company has used its total assets to generate revenues. (19)

transaction processing. Also known as *bookkeeping,* the recordkeeping aspect of the accounting function. (2)

transfer price. The price of a good or service that one segment of a company charges another segment of the same company. (18)

treasury stock. A type of stock that represents an insurer's purchase of its own outstanding stock. (5)

trend analysis. Also known as *trend percentages* or *index-number trend analysis,* a method of financial statement analysis that involves the calculation of percentage changes in financial statement figures over several successive accounting periods, rather than over just two periods. (19)

trial balance. A listing of all ledger accounts with their debit or credit balances. (3)

unassigned surplus. Also known as *unassigned surplus funds, divisible surplus,* or *free surplus,* the amount of surplus remaining after deducting liabilities, capital, and special surplus from admitted assets. (11)

uncollected premiums. In the United States, individual life insurance premiums and annuity considerations that are due on or before the

Annual Statement date but that the insurer has not received by that date. (6)

unearned income. A subset of collected income, including advance premiums and investment income, that was received by the insurer during the reporting period but that will not be earned until a later period and is, thus, applicable to the later period. (6)(12)

unearned premiums. Also known as *unearned premium reserves,* the portion of an insurance premium received by the statement date, applicable to the insurance coverage to be provided in the following period, but before the next policy anniversary date. (6)

unit cost. The incurred expense that can be attributed to a single measured amount of work. (16)

unqualified opinion. An auditing statement which shows that an insurer's financial statements were prepared in accordance with GAAP, or in special circumstances, in conformity with statutory accounting practices, and that the presentation is free of material misrepresentations. (20)

unrealized gain (loss). For invested assets, such as certain stocks, bonds, and mortgages, the difference between the asset's book value and its admitted value (statutory accounting) or its current market value (GAAP). (5)

unrecorded deposits. Deposits that the insurer added to its book balance after the closing date on the bank statement and, therefore, that the bank has not yet added to its account balance. (8)

usage variance. The difference between the budgeted quantities to be sold or processed and actual quantities sold or processed, multiplied by the budgeted rate. (18)

valuation date. The date as of which the value of a financial transaction is determined. (14)

value-added activity. An activity that makes the product or service more valuable to the customer. (16)

variable cost. A cost that fluctuates in direct proportion to changes in the level of operating activity. (16)

variance analysis. The study of the difference between expected results and actual results. (18)

variances. Instances in which actual amounts differ from budgeted amounts. (15)

vertical analysis. A type of analysis that reveals the relationship of each financial statement item to another financial statement item. (19)

vesting provision. A provision of an agent's contract that allows the agent to continue to receive renewal commissions and service fees for in-force policies that the agent originally sold, even after the agent has left the insurer. (13)

waiver-of-premium benefit. A life insurance policy benefit that provides premium payments to keep a life insurance policy in force should the insured become disabled and incapable of earning income to pay the premium. (10)

writing down. The process of recording a permanent decrease in the value of an asset. (7)

yearly renewable term (YRT) reinsurance. Also known as *risk premium reinsurance (RPR),* a type of reinsurance in which the ceding company purchases reinsurance from a reinsurer for the total net amount at risk for a block of insurance policies. (11)

zero-based budgeting (ZBB). A method of budgeting under which an organizational line of business must justify its continued operation for every accounting period. (17)

Index

A

A&H insurance. *See* accident and health insurance.
ABC. *See* activity-based costing.
acceptable loss ratio, 629
accident and health (A&H) insurance, 328
  Annual Statement reporting, 342
  claims, 328–332
  financial analysis, 628–629
  group premiums, 396
  premiums due and unpaid, 147
  renewability conditions, 328
  reserves, 283–287
accident and sickness insurance, 328
accidental death and dismemberment (AD&D) benefits, 321–323
account, 36
account classification. *See* assets, balance sheet, expenses, liabilities, owners' equity, revenues, statement of operations.
account form, 113
accountant's report. *See* auditor's report.
accounting
  defined, 3
  fields of, 10–15
  manual vs. automated system, 59
  practitioners, 15–19
  principles, 11–13
  profession, 28–30
  purpose of, 4–6
  regulation of, 19–27
  as service activity, 5
  system, 5–6
  users of information, 6–9
accounting basis. *See* accrual-basis accounting, cash-basis accounting, modified cash-basis accounting.
accounting concepts. *See* cost concept, entity concept, expense recognition, full-disclosure concept, going-concern concept, matching principle, realization principle, measuring-unit concept, revenue recognition, time-period concept.
accounting controls, 635
accounting cycle, 59, 60. *See also* adjusting entries, closing entries, journals, ledgers, trial balance.
accounting department, 17, 18
  responsibility in budgeting, 529
accounting elements, 96
accounting entity concept. *See* entity concept.
accounting entry, 33, 59
  compound, 56
  defined, 33
  simple, 56
accounting information, 6–9
  in centralized vs. decentralized environment, 7
  consolidation of, 7
  external users of, 7–9
  internal users of, 6–7
  quality of, 6, 82–90, 91
accounting period, 94
accounting profession. *See* Certified General Accountant, Certified Management Accountant, Certified Public Accountant, Chartered Accountant.
accounting records, 59–70. *See also* accounting entries, adjusting entries, closing entries, journals, ledgers, trial balance.
accounting regulation, 19–27. *See also* regulation.
accounting, types of
  private, 16–19
  public, 9, 16, 19
accounts
  classification of, 33–46
accounts payable, 39
  money owed to agents, 414
accounts receivable
  as assets, 37, 38
  money owed by agents, 414
accrual-basis accounting, 100, 101–102, 103, 381
accrued income, 385–386
  investment, 147
accumulated cost of insurance, 277
accumulated value. *See* future value.
accumulated value of net premiums, 276
acquisition-cost concept. *See* cost concept.
active life reserves, 284–286
activity, 509
activity driver, 509–513
activity ratios, 607–608
activity-based costing (ABC), 509–513
actual time analysis, 499
actuarial assumptions, 271–272
actuarial liabilities. *See* policy reserves.
actuarial reserves. *See* policy reserves.
AD&D benefits. *See* accidental death and dismemberment benefits.
additional paid-in capital, 359
  as owners' equity account, 41, 128–129
additional reserves, 285–286
adequate-disclosure concept. *See* full-disclosure concept.
adjusting entries, 67–68
adjustments to accounting records, 85
administrative controls, 633–635
administrative services only (ASO) plan, 396
admitted assets, 143–148, 184
  policy loans, 237
  See also Annual Statement assets.
admitted value (bonds), 200
advance and arrears accounting system, 397
advance premiums, 39, 154–155
adverse opinion, 660
agent commissions
  accounting for, 414–418
  due or accrued, 339
  and salaries, 410–418
Agents' Ledger Control, 414–415
AICPA. *See* American Institute of Certified Public Accountants.
allocation base, 497–498
allowable expenses, 539
allowances, 416

ALM. *See* asset/liability management.
Alternative Minimum Tax, 427
A.M. Best, 9, 592
  IRIS ratios, 620
American Accounting Association, 25
American Institute of Certified Public Accountants (AICPA), 8, 21, 29, 662
  Statement of Auditing Standards, 635
amortization
  bonds, 196–200
  mortgage loans, 216
amortized cost, 113–114, 187
amounts retained by the company as agent or trustee, 339
amounts temporarily held for disposition, 155–156
Analysis of Income by Line of Business (Can.), 173–174
Analysis of Operations by Lines of Business (U.S.), 173–174
  segment reporting in, 571
analytical phase (IRIS), 622
Annual Information Form (Can.), 73
annual report, 11, 70–73, 107–138
  auditor's report, 71, 108, 134–135
  balance sheet, 110–114
  financial highlights, 71, 108–109
  financial statement integration, 135–138
  financial statements, 71, 108, 109–131
  impact on inflation reported in, 93
  letter to stockholders, 71, 108–109
  mutual companies and, 107
  notes and supplementary information, 71, 131–134
  as promotional document, 108
  statement of cash flows, 119–125
  statement of operations, 114–119
  statement of owners' equity, 125–131
Annual Return (Can.), 11, 26, 70, 75, 141–177
  balance sheet, 142–158
  bonds, 200–201
  capital and surplus account, 162–166, 374–375, 376–377
  exhibits and schedules, 174–177
  income statement, 75, 158–162
  liabilities, 342
  mortgage loans, 218
  policy loans, 241
  real estate, 229–232
  reconciliation of surplus, 75
  reinsurance, 250
  revenues, 403, 405–407
  short-term investments, 241
  statement of assets, 75
  statement of liabilities, policyholders' and shareholders' equity, 75
  stocks, 208–211
  use of GAAP in, 12
Annual Statement (U.S.), 11, 20, 70, 73–75, 141–177
  admitted assets, 146–148
  analysis of operations by lines of business, 74, 173–174, 571
  assets, 74, 143–150, 187, 200–201, 208–211, 218, 229–232
  balance sheet, 142–158
  bonds, 200–201
  capital and surplus account, 74, 162–166, 374–376
  cash flow statement, 74, 170–173
  exhibits and schedules, 174–177
  five-year historical data, 74, 174
  liabilities, 341–342
  liabilities, surplus and other funds, 74, 150–158
  mortgage loans, 218
  nonadmitted assets, 74, 143, 148–149
  notes to the financial statements, 74
  policy loans, 240–241
  real estate, 229–232
  reinsurance, 250
  revenues, 401–405
  separate accounts, 149–150
  short-term investments, 241
  statement of operations, 158–162
  statutory accounting practices used in, 12–13
  statutory to GAAP reconciliation, 167–170
  stock account in, 128
  stocks, 208–211
  summary of operations, 74, 158–162, 163–164
  valuation of securities, 184
annuity
  distinguishing between types of, 451
  due, 450–453
  future value of, 450–451
  ordinary, 450–453
  policy reserve for, 281–283
  present value of, 457–458
annuity benefits, 333
annuity due, 450–453
  present value of, 459
annuity immediate. *See* ordinary annuity.
annuity in advance. *See* annuity due.
annuity in arrears. *See* ordinary annuity.
annuity payments (as liabilities), 332–334
APL. *See* automatic premium loan.
Appointed Actuary report (Can.), 108
apportioned dividends. *See* policy dividends payable in the following year.
appropriated surplus. *See* contingency reserves.
appropriation of retained earnings, 131
ASO plan. *See* administrative services only plan.
assets, 37–38, 181–257
  admitted, 143–148
  amount of in U.S. industry, 3
  in Annual Statement/Annual Return, 143–150, 187, 200–201, 208–211, 218, 229–232, 240–241, 250
  bonds, 188–201
  cash, 241–247
  classification and valuation, 183–188
  as debit balance accounts, 52

assets (continued)
deferred, due, and accrued income, 146–147, 248
deferred policy acquisition costs, 254–255
deferred premiums, 146
depreciation of, 99–100
derivatives, 232–236
effect of increase in revenues, 44
effect on premiums and reserves, 181
electronic data processing equipment, 255
intangible, 184
invested, 146, 181–218, 351–352
investment-grade, 148
long-term, 38, 247
mortgage loans, 211–218
nonadmitted, 143, 148–149, 352–353
partially admitted, 148
policy loans, 236–241
premiums due, 248–249
prepaid expenses, 249
real estate, 223–232
reinsurance ceded, 146, 250–254
safeguarding of, 646–647
separate accounts (segregated funds), 256–257
short-term, 38, 241–249
stocks, 201–211
tangible, 183–184
types of, 37–38
asset fluctuation reserves
See asset valuation reserve, interest maintenance reserve.
asset offset account. *See* contra asset account.
asset turnover, 607
Asset Valuation Reserve (AVR), 156–157, 166, 187, 300–301
changes in, 353–354, 370–371
asset/liability management (ALM), 181
Assets, 143–150
assigned surplus. *See* contingency reserves.
Associate, Insurance Accounting and Finance (AIAF), 30
associating cause and effect, 98–99
Association for Investment Management and Research, 25
assuming company. *See* reinsurer.
assumption reinsurance, 359
attest audit. *See* financial audit.
audit committee, 642
audit trail, 35, 653
linking of posting references to accounting entries, 64
for premium accounting, 389
auditing, 633, 649–664
compliance, 662
external, 9, 19, 82
financial, 660–662
independent auditor's report, 71, 73
internal, 642–643, 652–655
management, 663
noting consistency of accounting policies and procedures, 85
performance, 662–663
program results, 663
reliance on reliability of accounting information, 82
auditor's report, 71, 134–135
authorized control level RBC, 626
automatic premium loan (APL), 237–239, 395
available capital (MCCSR), 628
AVR. *See* asset valuation reserve.

B

balance, 36
balance sheet, 11, 37–42
account form, 113
accounts presented in ledgers, 63
in annual report, 110–114
Annual Statement, 142–158
carrying forward accounts in, 68
permanent accounts, 68
presentation of assets, 38
presentation of liabilities, 39–40
report form, 113
balance sheet equation. *See* basic accounting equation.
bank line. *See* line of credit.
bank reconciliation, 36, 243–247
banker's acceptances, 241
base period, 593
basic accounting equation, 41, 47–50, 53–54
in annual report, 113
at end of accounting cycle, 69–70
for fraternals and mutuals, 347–348
including statement of operations accounts, 53
surplus and revenues in, 288
See also balance sheet.
batch total, 649
benchmarking, 601–602
in variance analysis, 566
benefits budget, 538
bonds, 38
accounting for purchase and sale of, 192–193
accrued interest income, 193–194
Annual Return (Can.) presentation, 200–201
Annual Statement (U.S.) presentation, 184–186, 200–201
discounts, 189–190, 194–200
income from, 399–401
premiums, 189–190, 194–200
bonus additions, 316
book balance, 243–247
book value, 92
book-entry safekeeping, 647
bookkeeping. *See* transaction processing.
bottom-up budgeting, 526–527
break-even analysis. *See* cost-volume-profit (CVP) analysis.
break-even chart. *See* cost-volume-profit (CVP) graph.
break-even point, 515–516
budget, 521
capital expenditure, 530
cash, 529
cash disbursement, 532
cash receipts, 532
classifications of, 532–536
expense, 537–539
flexible, 533
investment, 530–532, 536
long-term, 534

manipulation of, 523
master, 524–526
operating expense, 532
operational, 529, 535
period, 534–535
pro forma statements, 525–526, 539–540, 546, 548
revenue (sales), 530, 535–536
rolling, 534–535
short-term, 534
static, 532
supporting, 530–532
types of, 529–532
See also master budget.
budgeted income statement. *See* pro forma statement of operations.
budgeting, 521–558
bottom-up, 526–527
capital, 548–558
cash, 540–548
reasons for, 521–523
time value of money used in, 463
top-down, 526–527
use of ledger information to monitor, 65
zero-based, 527–528
business entity concept. *See* entity concept.
business income tax, 427
business transaction, 33

C

C risks. *See* contingency risks.
C1 risk, 626
C2 risk, 626
C3 risk, 626
C4 risk, 626
CA. *See* Chartered Accountant.
calendar year, 95
calls, 235
Canadian GAAP, 10, 11–12, 26–27, 86, 141
and expense recognition, 99
requirement of comparative financial statements, 86
and reserves, 281
Canadian Institute of Actuaries, 26, 280
Canadian Institute of Chartered Accountants (CICA), 8, 26–27, 651
and GAAP, 11
See also *CICA Handbook*.
Canadian Life and Health Insurance Association, 27
Canadian Life and Health Insurance Compensation Corporation. *See* CompCorp.
capital, 41, 346
capital account
absence in mutuals and fraternals, 41
capital and surplus, 157–158, 162–166, 345–377
accounts, 363–373
external sources of, 349, 354–363
financial statement presentation of (Can.), 162–166, 376–377
financial statement presentation of (U.S.), 162–166, 373–376
internal sources of, 348–354
types of accounts. *See* additional paid-in capital, capital, common stock, gross paid-in and contributed surplus, retained earnings, special surplus, surplus, surplus notes, treasury stock, unassigned funds (surplus), unrealized gains and losses.
Capital and Surplus Account, 162–166
capital and surplus ratios, 617
capital assets. *See* long-term assets.
capital budgeting, 530, 548–558
factors affecting, 556–558
methods of, 552–556
process of, 548–551
capital charge, 579
capital cost allowances, 428
capital expenditure budgets, 530
capital gains, 93, 166
capital investments, 530
capital rationing, 550, 557–558
capital ratios. *See* capital and surplus ratios.
Capital Stock Issued and Paid, 128
Capital Stock Paid, 128
capitalization, 81, 99
bonds, 193
caps, 235
CARVM. *See* Commissioners' Annuity Reserve Valuation Method.
cash, 241–247
investing of, 183, 241, 463
uses of, 540
cash accounting, 242–243
vs. investment accounting, 242
cash budget, 529, 543–545
cash budgeting, 540–548
elements of cash flows, 541–543
minimum cash balance policies, 544–545
pro forma statements, 545–548
cash disbursement, 36, 103, 542–543
cash disbursements budget, 542–543
cash dividend, 127, 204
cash equivalents, 183, 463
Cash Flow, 170
cash flow, 541–548
analysis of, 602–604
of capital expenditure projects, 549
effects of positive or negative, 120–121
elements of, 541–543
estimating, 549–550
identified by investment accounting, 181
See also cash inflow, cash outflow.
cash flow statement (annual report). *See* statement of cash flows.
cash inflow, 121–124, 541
cash management, 242
cash outflow, 121–124, 542–543
cash premium accounting system, 397
cash ratio, 607
cash receipt, 36, 102–103, 541
cash receipts budget, 541
cash surrender nonforfeiture option, 316–319
cash surrender value, 236–241, 316
cash value, 236–241, 316
adjustments to, 318
cash-basis accounting, 101, 102–104
modified, 104

CCA. *See* capital cost allowances.
CD. *See* certificates of deposit.
ceding company, 289
central depository safekeeping, 647
certificate loan. *See* policy loan.
certificates of deposit, 241
Certified General Accountant (CGA), 30
Certified Internal Auditor, 30
Certified Management Accountant (CMA), 28, 29
Certified Public Accountant (CPA), 28–29, 651
  adherence to GAAP, 24
CGA. *See* Certified General Accountant.
change analysis, 505–506
chargeback, 504–505
charging (a cost), 496–497
chart of accounts, 35–36, 51
Chartered Accountant (CA), 27, 29, 651
CICA. *See* Canadian Institute of Chartered Accountants, *CICA Handbook.*
CICA Handbook, 26–27
  and accrual-basis accounting, 102
  and annual report, 73, 116–117
  bond valuation, 200
  and compliance auditing, 662
  derivatives, 236
  and entity concept, 80
  and quality of accounting information, 82
  and statement of changes in financial position, 119
  stock valuation, 208–209
  tax calculation, 427
claim fluctuation reserves, 295
claim liabilities. *See* policy and contract claims.
claim reserves, 39, 286–287
  decreases in valuation of, 353–354
claim settlements (liabilities), 153, 320–332
claims, 320
  accident and health insurance, 328–332
  life insurance, 321–328
  matured endowments, 326–327
  statutory exhibits, 177
  waiver-of-premium benefits, 327–328
claims clearing accounts, 323
claims in the course of settlement, 153
clean opinion. *See* unqualified opinion.
clean surplus theory, 368
closing costs, 215
closing entries, 68–70, 381
CMA. *See* Certified Management Accountant.
CMOs. *See* collateralized mortgage obligations.
codification, 14–15
coinsurance plan of reinsurance, 356–357
collateral, 188
collateralized mortgage obligations (CMOs), 212, 232
collected income, 385
collusion, 653
combined ratio, 628
commercial paper, 241
commission accounting, 410–418
  coordination with premium accounting, 412
  and expense recognition, 98–99
  factors affecting, 412–413
  objectives of, 412
  salaries of agents, 411–412
Commissioners' Annuity Reserve Valuation Method (CARVM), 424–425
Commissioners' Reserve Valuation Method (CRVM), 291, 424–425
commissions, 410–418
  as example of variable cost, 488
  as expenses, 45
  objectives of accounting for, 412
  payable, 39
committed costs, 487
common costs. *See* indirect cost.
common stock, 127–128
  and additional paid-in capital, 359
  and derivatives, 234–235
  as owners' equity account, 41
  See also stock.
common-size statement, 599–601, 610
comparability, 85–86, 659
comparative financial statements, 593
CompCorp, 8, 431–432
compliance, 638
compliance auditing, 662
compound accounting entry, 56
compound interest, 440–441
compound value interest factor. *See* future value interest factor.
comprehensive budget. *See* master budget.
comptroller. *See* controller.
concept of periodicity. *See* time-period concept.
conservatism, 89–90, 145–146
  and reserve valuation, 271
consistency, 83–85, 659
  adjustments affecting, 85
consolidated basis, 110
consolidated financial statements, 110
contested claims. *See* resisted claims.
contingency reserves, 296–297. *See also* special surplus.
contingency risks, 626
continuous budget. *See* rolling budget.
contra account, 225
contra asset account, 218
  for real estate, 225
contra benefit account, 252
contra owners' equity account, 129
contract payments, 320
  See also annuity, supplementary contract.
contributed capital accounts, 126
contribution certificate. *See* surplus notes.
contribution margin, 514, 572
contribution margin ratio, 574
contributions to surplus, 618
control account, 409
control function, 633
controllable assets, 575
controllable cost, 486
controllable investment, 575
controllable liabilities, 575
controllable surplus, 575

controller (comptroller), 16–17
responsible for chart of accounts, 36
controlling, 469, 475
conventional mortgage loans, 212
conventional policy loan, 237–239
corporate budget. *See* master budget.
corporate form, changes of, 361
cost, 96, 483
cost accounting, 483–518
analyzing costs, 505–513
basics of, 484–485
classifications of costs, 485–493
cost accumulation, 493–496
cost allocation, 496–505
product pricing, 513–518
uses of, 484–485
cost accumulation, 493–496
by department or cost center, 495
by function, 495–496
by line of business, 494–495
by type, 494
cost allocation, 496–505
chargebacks, 504–505
common allocation bases, 498
direct method, 500–502
to indirect expenses other than salaries, 499–500
to indirect salaries, 498–499
reciprocal method, 504
and responsibility accounting, 585–586
to service departments, 500–504
step method, 502–504
cost center, 495, 564
cost concept, 91–92
assumption of reliability, 92
cost object, 485, 509
cost of capital, 551
cost-based transfer price, 588
costing
activity-based, 509–513
functional, 506–509
costs
accumulation of, 493–496
allocation of, 496–505
analysis of, 505–513
classified by behavior, 487–489
classified by description, 485–487
classified by measurement, 489–493
committed, 487
controllable, 486
differential, 487
direct, 485
discretionary, 487
fixed, 487–488
functional, 495–496, 506–509
indirect, 486
marginal, 490–492
marginal unit, 491–492
noncontrollable, 486
operating, 513
opportunity, 492–493
out-of-pocket, 492
overhead, 486
policy acquisition, 98, 167
policy benefit, 513
and product pricing, 513–518
and responsibility accounting, 564
semi-variable, 488–489
service department, 500–504
standard, 490
sunk, 487
unexpected, 513
unit, 489–490
variable, 488
cost-volume-profit (CVP) analysis, 514–518
cost-volume-profit (CVP) graph, 516–517
coupon payments, 192
coupon rate. *See* stated rate.
CPA. *See* Certified Public Accountant.
credit, 51
credit risk, 156–157
credit-balance accounts, 52
CRVM. *See* Commissioners' Reserve Valuation Method.
current asset. *See* short-term asset.
current basis, 85
current liquidity ratio, 616–617
current market value, 91–92
current maturity. *See* current portion of long-term debt.
current portion of long-term debt, 338
current ratio, 606–607
CVP. *See* cost-volume-profit analysis.

D

DAC. *See* deferred acquisition cost.
data vs. information, 467
date of record, 366
death claims, calculation of, 323–326
fraud, 325
misrepresentation, 325–326
reinsurance, 326
suicide, 325
debenture, 188
debit, 51
debit system. *See* advance and arrears accounting system.
debit-balance accounts, 52
debt instrument. *See* debt security.
debt obligations, 337–338
debt ratio, 609
debt security, 188, 216
debt-to-equity ratio, 609–610
debt-to-surplus ratio, 610
decision making, 469, 475–476
default, 190
default component, 300
deferred acquisition costs. *See* deferred policy acquisition costs.
deferred, due, and accrued income, 146
deferred income, 385
deferred policy acquisition costs (DPAC), 254–255, 339
and limited surplus strain, 292–293
deferred premiums, 146–147
deferred realized gains (losses) (Can.), 201, 299
deflation, 443
demutualization, 362
and financial statement analysis, 592
denial of opinion. *See* disclaimer of opinion.
departmental audit, 663
deposits in transit. *See* unrecorded deposits.
depreciation, 96, 99–100
and real estate, 223–227, 232
straight-line method, 99–100
derivative, 232–236
detective controls, 636

differential cost, 487. *See also* marginal cost.
direct changes in surplus, 163–166
direct cost, 485, 570
direct financial interest, 7–8
direct method, 124, 500
direction (of trends), 593
disabled life reserves. *See* claim reserves.
disability benefits, 330–332
disability income (DI) insurance, 330
disclaimer of opinion (denial of opinion), 660
discontinued operations, 117, 118
discount, 189–190, 194–200
discount rate
  and capital budgeting, 551
discounted payback method, 553–554
discounted value. *See* present value.
discounting, 455
discretionary costs, 487
disputed claims. *See* resisted claims.
dividend accumulations, 314–315
dividend payment options. *See* policy dividend payment options.
dividend payout ratio, 614–615
dividends, 126–127, 166
  See also cash dividend, policy dividend, stock dividend.
dividends to stockholders declared and unpaid, 341
divisible surplus, 153–154
double-entry accounting, 46–56
  account balances, 51–56
  basic accounting equation, 47–50
  debits and credits, 50–51
  entries, 56
  origins of, 48
DPAC. *See* deferred policy acquisition costs.
dual concept, 46–47
dual-aspect concept. *See* dual concept.
due and unpaid claims, 153
due income, 146
due premiums. *See* premiums due.
Duff and Phelps, 592
dynamic budget. *See* flexible budget.
dynamic measure, 42, 68, 120
  statement of operations as, 42, 131

E

earmarked surplus. *See* contingency reserves.
earnings multiplier. *See* price/earnings (P/E) ratio.
earnings per share (EPS), 612–613
  effect of treasury stock on, 129
economic solvency, 142–143
  vs. statutory solvency, 142
economic value added (EVA). *See* residual income (RI).
economy and efficiency auditing. *See* management auditing.
effective interest rate, 145, 446–447
effective rate of return. *See* effective interest rate.
effectiveness, 563
effectiveness auditing. *See* program results auditing.
efficiency, 563
electronic data interchange, 34
electronic data processing (EDP) equipment, 255
electronic funds transfer (EFT) system, 214, 395
encumbrances, 229
endowment insurance, 326
entirely nonadmitted asset, 148
entity, 79
entity concept, 79–80
EPS. *See* earnings per share.
equity component, 300
equity method, 208
equity securities, 201
equity-based insurance products, 21–22, 256
equivalent interest rates, 446
escrow account, 213–215
estimated time analysis, 498–499
ex date. *See* ex-dividend date.
exception, 622
ex-dividend date, 206
execution of transactions as authorized, 645
expected value, 537
expense budget, 537–539, 568
expense loading. *See* loading.
expense ratio, 628
expense recognition, 95, 97–100
  associating cause and effect, 98–99
  immediate recognition, 100
  systematic and rational allocation, 99–100
expenses, 45–46, 409
  agent commissions and salaries, 410–418
  as debit balance accounts, 52
  as expired costs, 96
  financial reporting of (Can.), 432–433
  financial reporting of (U.S.), 432–433
  and matching principle, 97–100
  operating, 46, 418–420
  selling, 45
  statutory exhibits, 177
  taxes, licenses, and fees, 420–432
experience rating refund, 253–254, 290
expired cost, 96
extended term insurance, 319–320
external analysis, 591–592
external audit, 655–656
extraordinary item, 177–179, 613

F

face value. *See* principal.
fair market value. *See* current market value.
FASB. *See* Financial Accounting Standards Board.
FAST. *See* Financial Analysis and Solvency Tracking (FAST) system.
FCT. *See* Federal Capital Tax.
Federal Capital Tax, 428
feedback, 469, 475
fee income, 44
fidelity bond, 645
financial accounting, 11–13
  vs. management accounting, 476–480
Financial Accounting Standards Board (FASB), 8, 22–25, 134, 651

and accrual-basis accounting, 102
and derivatives, 236
and DPAC, 254
and entity concept, 80
and GAAP, 11, 21
and GAAP for mutuals, 107
pronouncements, 22, 71
and quality of accounting information, 82
segment reporting required by, 571
and statement of cash flows, 119
supplementary information requirements, 134
Financial Analysis and Solvency Tracking (FAST) system, 622–624
financial audit, 660–662
financial controls. *See* accounting controls.
Financial Executives Institute, 25
financial highlights, 71, 108–109
financial information
examples of, 5
financial interest
direct, 7–8
indirect, 8–9
financial leverage, 608
financial leverage ratios
debt ratio, 609
debt-to-equity ratio, 609–610
GAAP, 608–610
statutory, 617–618
Financial Review. *See* Management Discussion and Analysis of Financial Condition and Results of Operations.
financial statement analysis, 591–629, 635
benchmarking, 601–602
external, 591–592
GAAP ratios, 606–616
health insurance, 628–629
horizontal, 593–598
internal, 591–592
ratio analysis, 604–620
regulatory analysis of, 620–628
solvency tracking system, 622–624
statutory ratios, 616–620
vertical, 593, 598–601
financial statement audit. *See* financial audit.
financial statement concepts. *See* cost concept, entity concept, expense recognition, full-disclosure concept, going-concern concept, matching principle, realization principle, measuring-unit concept, revenue recognition, time-period concept.
financial statements, 11, 70–75, 109–131
format of, 110
integration of, 135–138
interim, 95
use of GAAP in, 11–12
See also annual report, Annual Return (Can.), Annual Statement (U.S.), balance sheet, statement of cash flows, statement of operations (income statement), statement of stockholders' (owners') (policyowners') equity.
financial transaction. *See* business transaction.
financing activities, 123
first mortgage, 211–212
fiscal year, 95
fiscal-year basis, 95
Five-Year Historical Data, 174
fixed assets. *See* long-term assets.
fixed budget. *See* static budget.
fixed costs, 487–488
fixed-amount budget. *See* static budget.
flexible budget, 533
flexible-amount budget. *See* flexible budget.
flexible-premium deferred annuities (FPDAs), 281–282
floor rate, 212
floors, 235
footing, 65, 69
foreclosure, 216–217, 227–229
foreign exchange risk, 232
foreign insurer, 430
forward contracts, 234
fraternal societies
annual report requirements, 71
exemption from premium taxes, 429
refund accumulations (refunds due and unpaid), 13
fraud, 653
full preliminary term method, 273, 291
full-disclosure concept, 86–88, 94
function, 495
functional costing, 506–509
functional costs, 495–496, 506–509
future value (*FV*), 437, 443
calculation of, 443–454
interest factor (*FVIF*), 447–449
interest factor of an annuity (*FVIFA*), 451–454
of an annuity (*FVA*), 450–451
of a single amount, 443–447
of an uneven stream of payments, 454
future value interest factor (*FVIF*), 447–449
future value of an annuity (*FVA*), 450–451
futures, 235
FV. See future value.
FVA. See future value of an annuity.
FVIF. See future value interest factor.
FVIFA. See future value interest factor of an annuity.

G

GAAP. *See* generally accepted accounting principles.
GAAP reserves, 274–275, 279
GAAP-statutory hierarchy, 13, 23, 24
gain
in annual report statement of operations, 117
gains from the sale of invested assets, 351–352
general account, 149
general and administrative expense budget, 538
general expenses. *See* operating expenses.
general expenses due or accrued, 339

general ledger, 62
as basis for cost data, 494
generally accepted accounting principles (GAAP), 10, 11–12
and annual report, 70–71, 74, 107–138
annuity reserves, 283
approaches to expense recognition, 98–100
and comparability of financial statements, 85–86
conservatism of, 89–90
deferred policy acquisition costs, 254–255
and derivatives, 236
exclusion of prior period adjustments, 131
in financial statements, 11–12
limiting surplus strain under, 292–294
and noncash transactions, 104
prepaid expenses, 249
ratio analysis, 606–616
reserve assumptions, 274–275, 279
SEC filings, 22
statutory to GAAP reconciliation, 167–170
use in financial statements vs. statutory accounting, 84
generally accepted auditing standards (GAAS), 21, 652, 656, 657
in annual report, 134
GIC. *See* guaranteed interest contract.
goal congruence, 562–563, 579–580
goal incongruence, 562, 580
going-concern concept, 81, 94
reflected in annual report, 113
Goodwill and Other Assets (Can.), 149
gross leverage ratio. *See* insurance leverage ratio.
gross paid-in and contributed surplus, 158
gross premium, 147–148, 295
gross profit ratio, 618
group insurance premiums, 396
growth stocks, 614
guaranteed income contract (GIC). *See* guaranteed interest contract.
guaranteed interest contract (GIC), 154
guaranteed investment contract (GIC). *See* guaranteed interest contract.
guaranty-fund assessments, 430–431

H

health insurance, 328. *See also* accident and health (A&H) insurance.
hedge, 232
historical cost, 91, 113–114
home service premiums, 397
horizontal analysis, 593–598

I

IBNR. *See* incurred but not reported claims.
immediate recognition, 100
IMR. *See* interest maintenance reserve.
income, 382–386
accrued, 385–386
collected, 385
deferred, 385
nonadmitted, 386
uncollected, 385
unearned, 154–155
income and expense statement. *See* statement of operations.
Income Statement (Can.), 158–162, 432
income statement (U.S.). *See* statement of operations.
income stocks, 614
income taxes payable, 39
incompatible functions, 644
incremental cash flows, 549
incremental cost. *See* marginal cost.
incurred and unpaid claims, 342
incurred but not reported (IBNR) claims, 153, 265, 286–287
independent audit. *See* external audit.
independent proposals, 557
index number, 595–596
index-number trend analysis. *See* trend analysis.
indirect cost, 486, 570
indirect financial interest, 8–9
indirect method, 124–125, 135
industrial insurance, 397
inflation, 93, 442
inflation rate, 442
inflation risk, 442–443
information, 6–9
vs. data, 467
success dependent on, 470–471
information overload, 467
initial-recording concept. *See* cost concept.
insolvency
capital and surplus as protection against, 345
Institute of Management Accountants, 25
Insurance Accounting and Systems Association, 25
Insurance Companies Act of 1992 (Canada), 25, 73
and Annual Return, 141
itemization of policy dividends and experience rating refunds, 310
insurance leverage ratio, 617–618
Insurance Regulatory Information System (IRIS), 620–622
insurer-administered plan, 396
intangible asset, 184
interest, 438–441
compound, 440–441
rates, 439
simple, 440
interest income (checking accounts), 244–245
interest maintenance reserve (IMR), 156–157, 187, 298–300, 371
interest margin pricing risk, 628
interest method of amortization, 197
interest rate, 439
effective, 444–446
equivalent, 446
nominal, 446
and reserves, 279
interest rate risk, 156, 442
interest rate swaps, 234
interim financial statements, 95
interim reports. *See* interim financial statements.
internal analysis, 591–592
internal audit, 635, 652–655

internal control, 633–649
compliance and monitoring, 637–638
elements of, 643–648
examples of, 648–649
participants in, 638–643
internal rate of return (IRR) method, 555–556
Internal Revenue Service (IRS), 8, 20–21
change of accounting procedures, 84
definition of life insurance company, 421–424
employee status of agents, 417
international accounting standards, 87–88
investable funds, 586–587
invested assets, 146
gains from the sale of, 351–352
investing activities, 123
investment accounting, 181–218
bonds, 180–210
vs. cash accounting, 242
mortgage loans, 211–218
reporting of income, 403–407
on statutory statements, 177
stocks, 201–211
investment budget, 530–532, 568
investment center, 565
evaluating performance of, 574–581
investment income, 44, 399–401
due and accrued, 248
investment segmentation method, 587
investment turnover, 576
investment year method, 586–587
investment yield ratio, 619–620
investment-grade, 148
bonds, 191
IRIS. *See* Insurance Regulatory Information System (IRIS).
IRR method. *See* internal rate of return method.
IRS. *See* Internal Revenue Service.
issue strain. *See* surplus strain.

J-K

journal, 36, 60–62
general vs. specialized, 62
journal entry. *See* accounting entry.
journal reference. *See* posting reference.

L

lapses, 279
large stock dividend. *See* stock split.
LCM. *See* lower of cost or market rule.
leading, 469
ledger, 36, 62–65
general, 62
subsidiary, 62–63
use of accounting information in budgeting, 65
ledger audit, 662
legal reserves. *See* policy reserves.
letter to stockholders, 71, 108–109
Level 1: Company Action, 627
Level 2: Regulatory Action, 627
Level 3: Authorized Control, 627
Level 4: Mandatory Control, 627
leverage, 608
leverage effect, 608–609
liabilities, 38–40, 263–342
advance premiums, 154–155
agents' commissions due and accrued, 339
amounts retained by the company as agent or trustee, 339
amounts temporarily held for disposition, 155–156
annuity payments, 332–334
asset valuation reserve, 156–157, 166, 187, 300–301
claim settlements, 153, 320–332
as credit-balance accounts, 52
debt obligations, 337–338
dividends to stockholders declared and unpaid, 341
financial reporting requirements, 341–342
general expenses due and accrued, 338–339
interest maintenance reserve, 156–157, 187, 298–300
long-term, 40, 337
net actuarial, 150
nonforfeiture options, 316–320
policy dividends, 305–316
policy dividends due and unpaid, 153–154
for premium and other deposit funds, 154
premium deposits, 154, 336–337
premiums paid in advance, 335–336
premium suspense accounts, 340
reserves, 150–153, 156–157, 263–301
short-term, 40, 337
supplementary contract payments, 332, 334–335
taxes, licenses, and fees due and accrued, 339
types of, 39
unearned income, 154–155
unearned premiums, 155
Liabilities, Policyholders' and Shareholders' Equity, 75, 150
Liabilities, Surplus and Other Funds, 74, 150–158
liability for premium and other deposit funds, 154
liability for reinsurance in unauthorized (unregistered) companies, 354–355
LICTI. *See* life insurance company taxable income.
life insurance claims, 321–328
matured endowments, 326–327
waiver-of-premium benefits, 327–328
life insurance company
defined for tax purposes, 421–424
life insurance company taxable income (LICTI), 425–427
lifetime loss ratio, 629
Life Insurance Institute of Canada, 27
life insurance product
defined for tax purposes, 20, 27, 424
line diagram, 450
line functions, 500
line of business (LOB), 173, 494–495
as proft center, 565
selling of, 357–359
line of credit, 544

liquid assets. *See* short-term assets.
liquidation, 81
liquidity, 38, 544
liquidity ratios, 606–607
 cash, 607
 current, 604–605, 606–607
 quick, 607
loading, 147–148
 present value in calculations, 461–462
LOB. *See* line of business.
lock-box banking. *See* lock-box system.
lock-box system, 396
long-lived assets. *See* long-term assets.
long-term assets, 38, 548
long-term budget, 534
long-term liabilities, 40, 337
loss
 in annual report statement of operations, 113–114
loss on sale, 192
loss ratio, 628
lower of cost or market (LCM) rule, 114, 187, 191

M

major medical insurance, 330
MAMM. *See* moving average market method.
management, 468
 functions of, 468–476
management (managerial) accounting, 13, 15, 467–629
 budgeting, 521–558
 cost accounting, 483–518
 vs. financial accounting, 476–480
 financial statement analysis, 591–629
 focus on summary information, 468
 use of non-monetary information, 480
 responsibility accounting, 561–588
 role of, 13, 470–476
 statutory and GAAP requirements, 479
Management Accounting Practice (MAP) statements, 29
management auditing, 663
management by exception, 475
 and variance analysis, 567
management by objectives (MBO), 563
Management Discussion and Analysis of Financial Condition and Results of Operations (MD&A), 73, 83, 360
 in annual report, 134
managerial accounting. *See* management accounting.
margin, 608
marginal cost, 490–492
marginal return. *See* margin.
marginal unit cost, 491–492
market-based transfer price, 588
market value. *See* current market value.
master billing record, 391
master budget, 524–526
matching principle, 95, 97–100
 and accrual-basis accounting, 101–102
materiality, 86–89
matured endowment, 326–327
maturity date, 188
maturity value. *See* principal.
MCCSR. *See* Minimum Continuing Capital and Surplus Requirements.
MD&A. *See* Management Discussion and Analysis of Financial Condition and Results of Operations.
mean liabilities method, 586
mean reserve method, 249
measurability, 467
 and recognition, 96
measuring-unit concept, 92–93
medical benefits, 332
medical expense insurance, 332
midterminal reserve method, 392
Message to Stockholders, 83
minimum cash balance, 544
Minimum Continuing Capital and Surplus Requirements (MCCSR), 166, 377, 617, 628
minimum reserve requirements, 278
mixed cost. *See* semivariable cost.
modco plan of insurance. *See* modified coinsurance plan of reinsurance.
modal premium payment, 146, 385
Model Standard Valuation Law, 283, 291
modified cash-basis accounting, 104
modified coinsurance (modco) plan of reinsurance, 357
modified report, 658
modified reserve method, 291
money market funds, 183, 241
Moody's, 9, 148, 592
 bond ratings, 190
morbidity rates, 272–273, 284
 adjustments, 150
 effect of conservatism on assumptions, 90
mortality rates, 272–273, 279
 adjustments, 150
 effect of conservatism on assumptions, 90
mortgage correspondents, 215
mortgage loan, 38, 211–218
 accounting for, 212–216
 foreclosure, 211, 216–217
 presentation on Annual Return (Can.), 218
 presentation on Annual Statement (U.S.), 218
moving average market method (MAMM), 209, 225, 229
multiple-step statement of operations, 115
mutual funds, 256–257
mutually exclusive proposals, 557

N

NAIC. *See* National Association of Insurance Commissioners.
National Association of Insurance Commissioners (NAIC), 8, 20, 651
 and Annual Statement, 20, 73–74
 effect on foreign insurers, 20
 FAST system, 622–624
 IRIS ratios, 620
 minimum reserve requirements, 278

reserves for annuities, 282–283
Securities Valuation Office, 148, 184, 190
natural business year, 95
negative financial leverage, 608
negative-asset account. *See* contra asset account.
negotiated transfer price, 588
net actuarial liabilities, 150. *See also* policy reserves.
net amount at risk, 357
net basis, 193
net book value, 188
net cash value. *See* cash surrender value.
net change in cash, 122
net GAAP reserves, 293
net gain from operations before taxes. *See* operating income.
net gain to total income, 620
net gains from operations, 349–351
net income, 42, 618
closed to owners' equity accounts, 69–70
effect on owners' equity, 119, 349
and investment center performance, 574–575
in statement of operations, 114
net investment income, 159
net level premium approach, 273, 275
net loss, 42, 135
closed to owners' equity accounts, 69–70
in statement of operations, 114
net premium, 147–148
net present value, 554
net present value (NPV) method, 554–555
net profit margin, 610–611
net yield. *See* investment yield ratio.
new business strain. *See* surplus strain.
nominal accounts. *See* temporary accounts.
nominal interest rate, 444–446
nominal rate. *See* stated rate.
nonadmitted assets, 143, 148–149, 167, 184, 352–353
changes in, 166
decreases in, 352–353
prepaid expenses, 248
nonadmitted income, 386
noncontrollable cost, 486
noncurrent asset. *See* long-term asset.
nonforfeiture options, 316–320
cash surrender, 316–319
extended term insurance, 319–320
reduced paid-up insurance, 319–320
nonsufficient funds (NSF) check, 243, 245, 394–395
non-value-added activity, 509
normal balance, 52
notes payable, 39
notes and supplementary information, 71, 131–134
notes to the financial statements, 131–134
NPV method. *See* net present value method.
NSF. *See* nonsufficient funds check.

O

objectivity, 82
Office of the Superintendent of Financial Institutions (OSFI), 8, 25–26, 141, 651
operating activities, 123
operating budget. *See* master budget.
operating controls. *See* administrative controls.
operating cost, 513
operating department. *See* production department.
operating efficiency, 119
operating efficiency ratios. *See* activity ratios.
operating expenses, 45, 46, 418–420
operating income, 575
operational auditing. *See* performance auditing.
operational budget, 529
operational budgeting, 535
operational planning, 473–474
opportunity cost, 492–493
ordinary annuity, 450–453
organizing, 469, 474–475
OSFI. *See* Office of the Superintendent of Financial Institutions.
OSFI-54. *See* Annual Return (Can.).
OSFI-85, 150
other admitted assets, 146
other-than-temporarily impaired, 370
out-of-pocket costs, 492
outstanding checks, 244
outstanding premiums. *See* premiums outstanding.
outstanding stock, 126
overhead cost, 486
owners' equity, 41–42 *See also* capital, surplus.
as credit-balance account, 52
effect of net income (loss) on, 69–70
events that cause changes in, 126
types of accounts, 41

P

paid loss ratio, 629
Paid-In Capital, 128
paid-in capital in excess of par. *See* Additional Paid-In Capital.
paid-to date, 391
paid-up additions, 312, 315, 398
par method, 368
par value (bond). *See* principal.
par value (stock), 128, 359
partially admitted asset, 148
participation in separate accounts, 372
payables
as liabilities, 38, 40
payback method, 552–553
payback period, 552
P/E ratio. *See* price/earnings ratio.
performance auditing, 662–663
performance measurement and evaluation, 565–581
investment center performance, 574–581
issues and problems with, 581–585
segment reporting for profit centers, 571–574
variance analysis, 566–570

performance plan. *See* master budget.
period budget, 534–535
permanent accounts, 68
physical comparison of recorded amounts, 648
physical settlement, 647
PI. *See* profitability index.
planning, 468, 469, 471–474
  operational, 473–474
  strategic, 473
  time value of money used in, 463
plant assets. *See* long-term assets.
policy accounting, 387
policy acquisition costs, 98, 167
policy benefit costs, 513
policy benefits, 45
  on *Summary of Operations,* 159
policy and contract claims, 153
  in the course of settlement, 153
  due and unpaid, 153
  incurred but not reported, 153
  resisted, 153
  unpaid, 39, 153
policy dividends, 153–154, 305–316
  accounting for, 397–399
  declaration of, 307
  due and unpaid, 153–154, 310–311
  liabilities for, 309–316
  payable in the following year, 311
  statutory vs. GAAP treatment, 154
policy dividend payment options, 312–316, 398–399
  applied to pay premiums, 313–314
  applied to purchase additional insurance, 315–316
  cash, 313
  dividend accumulations, 314–315
policy dividends due and unpaid, 310–311
policy dividends payable in the following year, 311
policy loan, 236–241
  accounting for, 238–239, 397–399
  admitted vs. nonadmitted asset, 240–241
  interest, 239–240, 397–399
  presentation on the Annual Return (Can.), 241
  presentation on the Annual Statement (U.S.), 237, 240–241
policy premium method (PPM), 150, 273, 280, 286, 296, 427, 659–660
  effect on surplus strain, 289
policy reserves, 39, 150–153
  for annuities, 281–283
  decrease in valuation of, 353
  increase in *Summary of Operations,* 159
  for life insurance, 275–281
  statutory vs. GAAP, 278–280
policyholder dividend. *See* policy dividend.
policyowner dividend. *See* policy dividend.
policyowner master file, 391
portfolio, 157
positive financial leverage, 608
posting, 63
posting reference, 61
power of sale, 211
PPM. *See* policy premium method.
preauthorized payment system, 214, 395–396
predictive quality, 79
preferred stock
  as owners' equity account, 41
premium (bond), 189, 194–200
premium (policy)
  accident and health insurance due and unpaid, 147
  accounting systems for, 387–397
  advance, 39, 154–155
  deferred, 146–147
  distinction between advance and unearned, 155
  due, 147, 249, 392–394
  gross, 147
  group accident and health, 396
  group life, 396
  home service, 397
  income, 386–399
  net, 147
  nonsufficient funds checks, 243, 245, 394–395
  payment methods, 395–396
  and realization principle, 97
  refunds, 415
  reporting of income, 402–403
  sources of income, 387
  statutory exhibits, 177
  on *Summary of Operations,* 159
  time value of money used in calculating rates, 461–462
  time value of money used in investing income, 462–463
  uncollected, 147
  unearned, 155, 392–394
premium accounting, 387–397
  coordination with commission accounting, 412
premium assets, 147
premium deficiency reserves, 295–296
premium deposits, 154, 336–337
premiums due, 147, 249, 392–394
premium income, 44, 386–399
  accounting systems, 387–397
  amount of in U.S. industry, 3
premium on common stock. *See* Additional Paid-In Capital.
premium suspense account, 340
premium taxes, 428–430
premiums outstanding (Can.), 147, 385, 403
premiums paid in advance, 335–336. *See also* advance premiums.
prepaid expenses, 249
present value (*PV*), 437, 454–455
  of amounts not yet due on claims, 463
  of an annuity (*PVA*), 457–458
  calculation of, 454–460
  of future benefits, 276, 279
  of future net premiums, 276
  interest factor (*PVIF*), 456–457
  interest factor of an annuity (*PVIFA*), 458–460
  of a single amount, 455–456
  of an uneven stream of payments, 460
present value of an annuity (*PVA*), 457–458
present value interest factor (*PVIF*), 456–457
present value interest factor of an annuity (*PVIFA*), 458–460
preventive controls, 636

price/earnings (P/E) ratio, 613–614
pricing
  influence of costs on, 513–518
principal, 188, 439–440
principle of duality. *See* dual concept.
prior period adjustments, 131
private accounting, 16–19
private placements, 189
pro forma balance sheet, 525, 547–548
pro forma financial statements, 525–526
  defined, 477
pro forma statement of cash flows, 525, 546–547
pro forma statement of operations, 525, 539–540
production department, 500
profit. *See* net income.
profit
  on statement of operations, 115–116
  See also net income.
profit center, 565
  segment reporting for, 571–574
profit and loss statement. *See* statement of operations.
profit margin. *See* margin.
profit on sale, 192
profit plan. *See* master budget.
profit-and-loss statement. *See* statement of operations.
profit-volume analysis. *See* cost-volume-profit (CVP) analysis.
profitability accounting. *See* responsibility accounting.
profitability index (PI), 558
profitability ratios
  dividend payout ratio, 614–615
  earnings per share, 612–613
  GAAP, 610–616
  net proft margin, 610–611
  price/earnings ratio, 613–614
  return on assets, 611
  return on equity, 612
  statutory, 618–620
program results auditing, 663
property taxes, 227–229
prospective basis, 85
prospective method, 275–276, 286
provision for adverse deviation, 280
provision for future policy benefits. *See* policy reserves.
public accounting, 16, 19
public offering, 188–189
purchase money mortgage, 218
purchasing power risk. *See* inflation risk.
put option, 234, 235
PV. See present value.

Q

qualified opinion, 660
quick liquidity, 616
quick ratio, 607
quota share method of reinsurance, 289

R

rate of return. *See* interest rate.
rate of return on net sales. *See* net profit margin.
rate variance, 567–568
rating agencies, 8, 9
  reliance on annual reports, 109
  See also A.M. Best, Duff and Phelps, Moody's, Standard and Poor's.
ratio, 604
ratio analysis, 604–620
  activity, 607–608
  current, 604–605, 606–607
  dividend payout, 614–615
  financial leverage, 608–610
  GAAP, 606–616
  investment yield, 619–620
  IRIS, 620–622
  liquidity, 606–607
  net gain to total income, 620
  price/earnings (P/E), 613–614
  profitability, 610–615
  return on assets, 611, 619
  return on capital, 618–619
  statutory, 616–620
ratios. *See* ratio analysis.
RBC requirements. *See* risk-based capital requirements.
real estate, 38, 223–232
  accounting for purchase and sale of, 223–227
  foreclosure, 227–229
  income from, 401
  presentation on the Annual Return (Can.), 229–232
  presentation on the Annual Statement (U.S.), 229–232
  property taxes, 227–229
  rental expense, 229
  rental income, 229
  subsidiary ledger, 62–63
realizable value, 370
realization principle, 95–97, 381
  and accrual-basis accounting, 101–102
realized gain (loss), 192
reciprocal method, 504
recognition, 95–100
reconciliation method. *See* indirect method.
Reconciliation of Surplus, 75
record (a transaction), 33
recording of transactions as executed, 645–646
reduced paid-up insurance, 319–320
refund accumulations, 153
refunds due and unpaid, 153
regression analyses, 536
regulation, 19–27. *See also* American Institute of Certified Public Accountants (U.S.), Canadian Institute of Chartered Accountants (Can.), Financial Accounting Standards Board (U.S.), Internal Revenue Service (U.S.), National Association of Insurance Commissioners (U.S.), Office of the Super-intendent of Financial Institutions (Can.), Revenue Canada (Can.), Securities and Exchange Commission (U.S.).
regulatory auditing. *See* compliance auditing.
regulatory financial analysis, 620–628
reinsurance, 146, 289, 354–357
  amounts recoverable from reinsurers, 146, 250–253
  on Annual Return/Annual Statement, 250
  assumption, 359
  ceded, 250–254
  coinsurance, 356
  commissions, 146, 416

reinsurance (continued)
commissions and expense allowances due, 253
effects on capital and surplus, 354–357
effects on commissions payable, 415
expense allowances, 146
experience rating and other refunds due, 146, 253–254, 290
journalizing death claims with, 326
modified coinsurance, 357
quota share method, 289
reducing surplus strain, 289–291
other refunds, 146, 253–254
yearly renewable term, 355–356
reinsurance ceded, 250
reinsurer, 289
released reserve, 268
relevance, 82–83
conflict with reliability, 82–83
and recognition, 96
reliability, 82
conflict with relevance, 82–83
and cost concept, 92
and recognition, 96
report form, 113
required reserves. *See* policy reserves.
reserve destrengthening, 166, 274–275
reserve strengthening, 166, 274–275
reserve valuation basis, 353
reserves, 263–301
for accident and health insurance, 283–287
active life, 284–286
actuarial assumptions, 271–272
additional, 285–286
for annuities, 281–283
asset fluctuation, 297–301
effect of cash surrender nonforfeiture option, 317
claim, 39, 265, 286–287
claim fluctuation, 295
contingency, 296–297
destrengthening, 274–275
full preliminary term method, 291–292
for future contingent benefits, 286
GAAP annuity, 283
GAAP life, 278–280
impact on surplus, 263, 353–354
interest rates for, 272
for life insurance (Can.), 280–281
for life insurance (U.S.), 275–280
modified reserve method, 291–292
morbidity rates for, 272–273
mortality rates for, 272–273
net GAAP, 293
policy, 39, 150–153, 265
premium deficiency, 295–296
released, 268
effect on solvency and profitability, 270–275
statutory, 269–270
statutory annuity, 282–283
statutory exhibits, 177
statutory vs. GAAP, 269–270, 278–280
strengthening of, 274–275
limiting surplus strain under GAAP, 292–294
limiting surplus strain under statutory accounting, 291–292
tax calculation of, 294–295
unearned premium, 155, 285
valuation, 267
valuation method, 273
withdrawal rates, 273
reserves for future contingent benefits, 286
residual claim, 129
residual income (RI), 579–581
residual value. *See* salvage value.
resisted claims, 153
responsibility, 561
responsibility accounting, 475, 561–588, 635
vs. financial accounting, 581
goal congruence, 562
problems with evaluation criteria, 582–585
responsibility centers, 561
responsibility center, 561, 564–581
cost centers, 564
investment, 565
profit centers, 565
performance measurement and evaluation, 565–581
responsibility center report, 569–570
responsibility manager, 561–562
responsibility report. *See* responsibility center report.
restricted retained earnings, 130
retained earnings, 130, 368
appropriation of, 131
as owners' equity account, 41, 130–131, 348
restricted, 130
retaliatory tax laws, 430
retention limit, 252
retired stock, 368
retroactive basis, 85
retrospective method, 276–277
return, 575
return on assets (ROA), 611
statutory, 619
return on capital ratio, 618–619
return on equity (ROE), 612
return on investment (ROI), 575–581
return on revenue, 576
return on sales. *See* net profit margin.
return on stockholders' equity. *See* return on equity.
revenue allocation, 586–587
investment segmentation method, 587
investment year method, 586–587
mean liabilities method, 586
revenue budget, 530
Revenue Canada, 8, 27
change of accounting procedures, 84
taxation, 427–428
revenue principle. *See* realization principle.
revenue recognition, 95–97
revenue recognition principle. *See* realization principle.
revenues, 44–45, 381–407
as credit-balance accounts, 52
financial reporting of (Can.), 401–403, 405–407
financial reporting of (U.S.), 401–405

income classifications, 382–386
investment income, 399–401
premium income, 386–399
and realization principle, 97
types of, 44
RI. *See* residual income.
rights, 235
risk, 441–443
contingency, 626
and inflation, 441–443
interest rate, 442
technology, 442
tradeoff with return, 442
risk premium reinsurance. *See* yearly renewable term (YRT) reinsurance.
risk-based capital, 360
Risk-Based Capital ratio, 626–627
Risk-Based Capital (RBC) requirements, 166, 617, 624–627
risk-return tradeoff, 190, 442
ROA. *See* return on assets.
ROE. *See* return on equity.
ROI. *See* return on investment.
rolling budget, 534–535
route collection book, 397

S

safeguarding of assets, 646–647
sales budget, 536, 568
sales expense budget, 538
sales forecast, 536
salvage value, 550
scenario analysis, 280–281, 283
SCFP. *See* Statement of Change in Financial Position.
SDO. *See* specified debt obligation.
SEC. *See* Securities and Exchange Commission.
second mortgage, 212
secured bond, 188
securities. *See* invested assets.
Securities and Exchange Commission (SEC), 8, 21–22
annual report requirements, 72–73, 116
and GAAP, 11, 25
Integrated Disclosure System, 73
10–K reports, 73
10–Q reports, 73
segment margin, 572
segment margin ratio, 574
segment reporting, 571–574
segregated funds (Can.), 149–150, 256–257, 310
Annual Return, 257
purpose of, 149
segregation of duties, 644–645
self-administered plan, 396
selling expenses, 45
semi-variable cost, 488–489
sensitivity analysis, 558
separate accounts (U.S.), 149–150, 256–257
Annual Statement, 256–257
purpose of, 149
service charges, 244
service department, 500
costs, 500–504
settlement contract. *See* supplementary contract.
shared cost. *See* indirect cost.
shareholder. *See* stockholder.
short-term assets, 38
short-term budget, 534
short-term investments, 183
short-term liabilities, 40, 339
simple accounting entry, 56
simple interest, 440
simultaneous method. *See* reciprocal method.
single-premium deferred annuities (SPDAs), 282
single-premium immediate annuities (SPIAs), 282
single-step statement of operations, 115
slides, 66
small life insurance company deduction, 426
small stock dividend, 207
social auditing, 663
Society of Management Accountants, 27
solvency. *See* economic solvency, statutory solvency.
solvency ratios. *See* leverage ratios.
source documents, 34
source of funds, 121
special surplus, 371–372
special surplus funds. *See* special surplus. *See also* contingency reserves.
specified debt obligations, 428
spread. *See* margin.
staff functions, 500
Standard and Poor's, 9, 148, 592
bond ratings, 190
standard audit opinion. *See* unqualified opinion.
standard costs, 490, 635
standard report. *See* unqualified opinion.
standard time analysis, 499
stable-dollar concept. *See* measuring unit concept.
stable-monetary-unit concept. *See* measuring unit concept.
state guaranty funds, 8
state insurance departments, 8
stated rate, 192
statement of cash flows, 11, 71, 119–125, 391
analysis of, 602–604
in annual report, 119–125
direct method, 123–124
expenses reported on, 432
effect of financing activities, 123
indirect method, 123–124, 135
information obtained for balance sheet and statement of operations, 121
effect of investing activities, 123
effect of operating activities, 123
statement of change in financial position (SCFP) (Can.), 119, 170–173
statement of financial condition. *See* balance sheet.
statement of financial position. *See* balance sheet.
statement of operations, 11, 42–44, 381, 401
accounts in ledgers, 63
in annual report, 114–119
closing accounts in, 68
multiple-step, 115
reporting for accounts on, 381–433
single-step, 115
containing temporary accounts, 68–69
statement of owners' equity, 126
in annual report, 125–131
See also statement of stockholders' equity.

statement of policyholders' equity. *See* statement of owners' equity.
statement of shareholders' equity. *See* statement of stockholders' equity.
statement of stockholders' equity, 11, 71
Statements of Financial Accounting Standards, 22, 23
Statements of Position, 21, 71
statement value (bonds), 200
static budget, 532
static measure, 42, 131
 in annual report, 120
 balance sheet as, 37, 42
 and closing entries, 68
statistical phase (IRIS), 622
statistical sampling, 657
statutory accounting practices, 10, 12–13
 and Annual Statement, 74
 conservatism of, 89–90
 distinction between admitted and nonadmitted assets, 143–148
 and expense recognition, 99
 GAAP-statutory hierarchy, 23, 24
 and net premium, 147
 prepaid expenses, 249
 ratio analysis, 616–620
 reserves vs. GAAP reserves, 269–270, 278–280
 statutory to GAAP reconciliation, 167–170
 use in financial statements vs. GAAP, 84
 See also Annual Statement.
statutory accounting principles. *See* statutory accounting practices.
statutory financial statement, 141
statutory ratios, 616–620
 capital and surplus, 617
 financial leverage, 617–618
 liquidity, 616–617
 profitability, 618–620
statutory reserves, 269–270, 282–283. *See also* policy reserves.
statutory return on assets (ROA), 619
statutory solvency, 73–74, 177
 vs. economic solvency, 142
statutory to GAAP reconciliation, 167–170
step method, 502–504
step-down allocation. *See* step method.
stock, 38, 126–129, 201–211
 accounting for purchase and sale of, 205–206
 on annual report statement of operations, 126–129
 cash dividends, 206
 common, 127–128
 dividends, 207–208
 income from, 399–401
 issuing of, 359
 outstanding, 126
 preferred, 127–128
 presentation on Annual Return (Can.), 208–211
 presentation on Annual Statement (U.S.), 208–211
 treasury, 129
stock dividend, 127, 366
stock outstanding. *See* outstanding stock.
stock split, 207, 367
stockholder, 201
stockholders' equity. *See* owners' equity.
straight-line depreciation method, 99
strategic planning, 473
subsidiary companies, 80
 in annual reports, 110
subsidiary ledgers, 62–63
 bond information, 191
 expenses, 419
 mortgage loan information, 214
 stock information, 205
Summary of Operations
 changes in dividend liabilities, 310
 expenses, 432
 policy loans, 241
 revenues, 381
summary of operations. *See* statement of operations.
sunk cost, 487
supplementary contracts, 332, 334–335
supplementary contract with life contingencies (WLC), 334
supplementary contract without life contingencies (WOLC), 334
supplementary information, 133
supporting budgets, 530–532
surplus, 41, 157–158, 348
 direct changes in, 163
 divisible, 153
 financial reporting of, 375–377
 sources of changes in, 163–166
 special, 371–372
 under statutory accounting, 348
 unassigned, 372–373
 See also capital and surplus.
surplus debentures. *See* surplus notes.
surplus notes, 157–158, 360
 issuing of, 359–361
 statutory vs. GAAP treatment of, 157
surplus ratios. *See* capital and surplus ratios.
surplus strain, 288–294
suspense accounts, 340, 390, 654–655
SVO Manual, 148
system of accounts. *See* chart of accounts.
systematic and rational allocation, 99–100
 depreciation, 99–100

T

T-account, 50–52, 59
 closing entries, 69
 examples of, 54–56
 ledger postings, 63
tabular reserves. *See* policy reserves.
tangible asset, 183–184
taxes, 45, 46
 federal income, 420–428
 guaranty-fund assessments, 430–431
 premium, 428–430
 reserves calculated for, 294–295
 retaliatory, 430
taxes, licenses and fees, 420–432
 due or accrued, 339
tax reporting, 420–428
 accounting principles used for, 10

Technical Bulletin, 21
technical solvency. *See* economic solvency.
technology risk, 442
temporary accounts, 68–69, 381
tentative LICTI, 426–427
terminal dividend. *See* terminal policy dividend.
terminal policy dividend, 313
third-party-administered (TPA) plan, 396
third-party administrator, 396
Tier 1 (core) capital, 628
Tier 2 (supplementary) capital, 628
time analysis, 498–499
  actual, 499
  estimated, 498–499
  standard, 499
time line. *See* line diagram.
time value of money, 437–463
  insurance operations and, 460–463
  See also future value, present value.
time-adjusted rate of return method. *See* internal rate of return (IRR) method.
time-period concept, 94–95
tolerable loss ratio (TLR), 629
top-down budgeting, 526–527
total adjusted capital (TAC), 626
total asset turnover, 607
TPA plan. *See* third-party-administered plan.
traceable cost. *See* direct cost.
trading on the equity. *See* leverage.
transaction register, 60. *See also* journal.
transaction processing, 34–35
transfer pricing, 587–588
  transfer price, 587
transpositions, 66
Treasury bills, 183, 241
treasury operations, 242
treasury stock, 368–369
  cost method of accounting for, 368
  as owners' equity account, 41
  par method of accounting for, 368
trend analysis, 595–598
trend percentages. *See* trend analysis.
trial balance, 65–67
  sources of errors in, 66–67
true interest rate. *See* effective interest rate.

U

unassigned funds (surplus), 158, 372–373
  as owners' equity account, 41
unauthorized company, 354–355
uncollected income, 385. *See also* due income.
uncollected premiums (premiums outstanding), 147
unearned income, 154–155, 385. *See also* unearned premium reserves.
unearned premium reserves, 155, 285, 392–394
unearned premiums. *See* unearned premiums.
unexpected cost, 513
Uniform Final Examination (UFE), 27, 29
unit cost, 489–490
unit costing, 508–509
unit-of-measurement concept. *See* measuring-unit concept.
unpaid policy claims, 39
unqualified opinion (standard audit), 107, 658
unrealized gain (loss), 130, 369–371
  on bonds, 192
unrecorded deposits, 244
usage variance, 567–568
use of funds, 122

V

valuation date, 450, 454
valuation methods
  and balance sheets, 143
Valuation of Securities manual, 184
value-added activity, 509
variable budget. *See* flexible budget.
variable cost, 488
variance analysis, 566–570, 635
  overemphasis on, 583
variances, 475, 490, 566
velocity (of trends), 593
vertical analysis, 593, 598–601
vesting provision, 413

W-X

waiver-of-premium benefit, 327–328, 330
warrants, 235
writing down, 114, 148, 187, 369–370
  real estate, 229
  on statement of operations, 201

Y

yearly renewable term (YRT) reinsurance, 355–356
YRT reinsurance. *See* yearly renewable term reinsurance.

Z

ZBB. *See* zero-based budgeting.
zero-based budgeting (ZBB), 527–528